Lecture Notes in Computer Science 16120

Founding Editors

Gerhard Goos
Juris Hartmanis

Editorial Board Members

Elisa Bertino, *Purdue University, West Lafayette, IN, USA*
Wen Gao, *Peking University, Beijing, China*
Bernhard Steffen, *TU Dortmund University, Dortmund, Germany*
Moti Yung, *Columbia University, New York, NY, USA*

The series Lecture Notes in Computer Science (LNCS), including its subseries Lecture Notes in Artificial Intelligence (LNAI) and Lecture Notes in Bioinformatics (LNBI), has established itself as a medium for the publication of new developments in computer science and information technology research, teaching, and education.

LNCS enjoys close cooperation with the computer science R & D community, the series counts many renowned academics among its volume editors and paper authors, and collaborates with prestigious societies. Its mission is to serve this international community by providing an invaluable service, mainly focused on the publication of conference and workshop proceedings and postproceedings. LNCS commenced publication in 1973.

Jose Meseguer · Carlos A. Varela ·
Nalini Venkatasubramanian
Editors

Concurrent Programming, Open Systems and Formal Methods

Essays Dedicated to Gul Agha
to Celebrate His Scientific Career

 Springer

Editors
Jose Meseguer
University of Illinois Urbana-Champaign
Urbana, IL, USA

Carlos A. Varela
Rensselaer Polytechnic Institute
Troy, NY, USA

Nalini Venkatasubramanian
University of California, Irvine
Irvine, CA, USA

ISSN 0302-9743 ISSN 1611-3349 (electronic)
Lecture Notes in Computer Science
ISBN 978-3-032-05290-2 ISBN 978-3-032-05291-9 (eBook)
https://doi.org/10.1007/978-3-032-05291-9

© The Editor(s) (if applicable) and The Author(s), under exclusive license to Springer Nature Switzerland AG 2026
Chapter "Decentralizing University Governance: A Coordination Challenge" is licensed under the terms of the Creative Commons Attribution 4.0 International License (http://creativecommons.org/licenses/by/4.0/). For further details see license information in the chapter.

This work is subject to copyright. All rights are solely and exclusively licensed by the Publisher, whether the whole or part of the material is concerned, specifically the rights of translation, reprinting, reuse of illustrations, recitation, broadcasting, reproduction on microfilms or in any other physical way, and transmission or information storage and retrieval, electronic adaptation, computer software, or by similar or dissimilar methodology now known or hereafter developed.
The use of general descriptive names, registered names, trademarks, service marks, etc. in this publication does not imply, even in the absence of a specific statement, that such names are exempt from the relevant protective laws and regulations and therefore free for general use.
The publisher, the authors and the editors are safe to assume that the advice and information in this book are believed to be true and accurate at the date of publication. Neither the publisher nor the authors or the editors give a warranty, expressed or implied, with respect to the material contained herein or for any errors or omissions that may have been made. The publisher remains neutral with regard to jurisdictional claims in published maps and institutional affiliations.

The cover image shows Ajrak fabric from Sindh, reproduced with permission from Gul Agha.

This Springer imprint is published by the registered company Springer Nature Switzerland AG
The registered company address is: Gewerbestrasse 11, 6330 Cham, Switzerland

If disposing of this product, please recycle the paper.

Preface

This Festschrift gathers contributions from a wide range of international researchers to honor the lifelong scientific and teaching accomplishments of Prof. Gul Agha, a leading computer science researcher and educator with worldwide recognition for his work on software engineering, formal methods, programming languages, concurrency theory, distributed systems, and cyber-physical systems. The papers were presented at a symposium held at the Chicago Campus of the Siebel School of Computing and Data Science of the University of Illinois, Urbana-Champaign on October 6–7, 2025. This volume and the symposium collectively provide a broad and in-depth understanding of the scientific impact of Prof. Agha's ideas, which have inspired the work of many other researchers worldwide.

Gul Agha obtained his undergraduate degree at Caltech in 1977. He obtained his A.M (1980), M.S. (1982) and Ph.D. (1985) degrees at the University of Michigan, Ann Arbor, with John Holland (University of Michigan) and Carl Hewitt (MIT) as co-advisors. Prior to starting as an assistant professor at the University of Illinois, Urbana-Champaign (UIUC) in 1989, Gul was a Research Scientist and Lecturer at the MIT Artificial Intelligence Laboratory, and subsequently in the Department of Computer Science, Yale University.

Prof. Agha created the Open Systems Laboratory at UIUC, where he developed many of his most important ideas and has trained several generations of young researchers who have disseminated and further expanded these ideas in academia and industry. His work is very highly cited worldwide and has been recognized through many prestigious awards and honors. He has made fundamental contributions to concurrency theory, concurrent programming languages, composition and reflective adaptation of concurrent systems, formal methods, probabilistic systems and their statistical and probabilistic model checking analysis, software testing, and cyber-physical systems.

Open systems have significantly revolutionized concurrent computation theories, since they must support the addition of new components, the replacement of existing components, and dynamic changes in component interconnections. All these properties were beyond the scope of prior concurrency models such as Petri Nets, Milner's Calculus of Communicating Systems (CCS), and Hoare's Communicating Sequential Processes (CSP). Prof. Agha's work on the Actor model of computation formalized open systems properties, and directly influenced the development of further concurrency theories such as Milner et al.'s Π calculus. In contrast to prior concurrency theories, the Π calculus incorporates process mobility, or dynamic reconfiguration of process interconnections. This mobility of processes was motivated by the actor model of computation, as Milner himself expressed in his 1993 Turing Award lecture. At the programming language level, the flexibility of message-passing communication together with the distributed object-oriented abstraction provided by actors with their own internal state has revolutionized the area of programming languages, where nowadays many of the most advanced languages support various variants of the Actor model.

Prof. Agha's MIT Press monograph, Actors: A Model of Concurrent Computation in Distributed Systems, is the main reference for the actor theory of concurrent computation, and has had wide impact, spanning concurrency theory, programming languages, software engineering, multi-agent systems, and distributed computing. That book alone has been cited over 4,900 times. In the Agha, Mason, Smith, and Talcott (AMST) article, A Foundation for Actor Computation, published in the Journal of Functional Programming, several fundamental contributions to the Actor model of computation are made: first, an actor language is defined as an extension to the λ calculus with primitives for actor creation, asynchronous communication, and dynamic actor behavior changes; second, a formal operational semantics is specified as a labeled transition relation between actor configurations; third, three observational expression equivalences are defined: testing (or convex or Plotkin or Egli-Milner), must (or upper or Smyth), and may (or lower or Hoare) equivalences; and, fourth, AMST develop equational laws and proof techniques that help them discover that under the assumption of fairness, testing and must equivalences collapse into one.

As important a contribution as the Actor model has been to concurrency theory in particular, and computing in general, Prof. Agha's work has not stopped there, it has been a source of inspiration for many abstractions and reflective system composition primitives beyond Actors, which attempt to model, understand, and formalize concurrency, distribution, mobility, composition, and adaptivity of computing systems. Needless to say, these abstraction and composition concepts help tackle the increasingly complex properties of today's distributed systems, including the Internet, the Web, the Cloud, social and sensor networks, the Internet of Things, and future cyberinfrastructure.

In Agha, Wegner, and Yonezawa's co-edited book, Research Directions in Concurrent Object-Oriented Programming, and Agha's Communications of the ACM article, Concurrent Object-Oriented Programming, Agha's vision for the need for higher-level abstractions for concurrency is laid out. This vision has fueled over two decades of several important research directions in concurrent programming theory and practice.

Examples of higher-level abstractions include:

- Frolund and Agha's synchronizers, to coordinate multiple actors and denote atomic operations, and local synchronization constraints for enforcing partial orders in message processing within a single actor;
- Agha, Frolund, Panwar, and Sturman's onion skin model of reflective meta-actor composition;
- Varela and Agha's casts or actor groups managed by directors to accomplish hierarchical coordination, and universal actors for Internet-based mobile and distributed computing;
- Jamali and Agha's cyber-organisms, to model shared and constrained resources;
- Ren and Agha's RT-synchronizers, to model real-time synchronization constraints;
- Callsen and Agha's actor spaces, to integrate actors with Linda tuple-space coordination; and
- Venkatasubramanian, Talcott, and Agha's Two-Level Actor Model (TLAM), for coordination, adaptation, and resource management in middleware.

Agha's work on semantics foundations and formal-methods-based analysis and verification has been very wide-ranging and goes much further than the initial formal foundations for the Actor Model already mentioned above. For example, to deal with very large distributed systems of a cyber-physical nature and with intrinsic probabilistic features, Agha and his collaborators have developed new formal models of probabilistic distributed systems, formal specification languages for such systems such as the PMaude language, and new scalable methods to verify such systems such as statistical model checking verification, where his work with Sen and Viswanathan is seminal, and also scalable probabilistic model checking methods that take advantage of regularities and symmetries in very large distributed systems such as sensor networks.

Agha's pioneering work on the actor model and concurrent programming languages for scalable distributed computing (e.g., Actor Foundry, SALSA) has influenced modern software frameworks such as Scala/Akka, Erlang, and Microsoft Orleans Actor Framework, which have been used to program Twitter, LinkedIn, Facebook Chat, the British National Health Service portal, and hundreds of commercial cloud applications. Gul's entrepreneurial efforts to transition his work on structural health monitoring systems began in 2019, when he assumed the role of CEO at Embedor Technologies; he currently serves as Chief Scientist and Co-founder at StructureIQ, an insuretech venture for smart infrastructure.

Prof. Agha is a Fellow of the IEEE and a Fellow of the ACM. Other honors include the IBM Faculty Award, the ONR Young Investigator Award, and the ACM Recognition of Service Award.

The Open Systems Lab at UIUC has been the training ground for many of Gul Agha's students and postdoctoral researchers, and he has been a constant role model to his students and postdoctoral researchers. He has supervised 13 postdoctoral and visiting scholars, trained 34 doctoral students, and served as the primary advisor for multiple Master's theses, and we are truly honored to have had this lineage and deeply indebted to have received his guidance and mentorship. Several of these researchers and students have continued in academic life and have themselves trained new generations of students, others have applied Prof. Agha's ideas in innovative and highly successful ways in industry. Below we list postdoctoral and visiting researchers and Ph.D. and Master's students whose dissertations were supervised by Gul.

Professor Agha has been a valued colleague, mentor, and friend not only because of his intellectual abilities and his breadth and depth of vision, but also because of his personality, friendly and humble demeanor, and empathy with all sentient beings on planet Earth. It is truly a treasure for all of us to have had Gul's positive influence on our lives.

For those of us who have had the privilege of being advised by Gul, we can state that his influence goes beyond his role as an academic father. It has provided us with broader perspectives on life, we note:

- "his philosophy of life, his unwavering quest for understanding and new knowledge, his appreciation for all sentient life on Earth, and his keen sense of humor" (Carlos Varela);
- "his actions that indicate that one can be both deeply intellectual and deeply compassionate" (Nalini Venkatasubramanian);

- "he has a remarkable ability to recognize his students' potential and empower them in ways that foster independence, resilience, and self-discovery" (Shangping Ren); and
- "being advised by Gul meant getting a multi-dimensional education: in everything concurrency, from how to think to what amounts to good 'taste'; in the highest academic traditions; and finally in how to be a more ethical and giving human being" (Nadeem Jamali)

All technical papers in the Festschrift volume were reviewed by at least two reviewers. We thank all reviewers for their important contribution to the editorial quality of these papers.

We are most grateful to Nancy Amato, Dean of the Siebel School of Computing and Data Science, for her enthusiastic support of the symposium and for the resources that the Siebel School provided for it. We also cordially thank Mahesh Viswanathan for his many contributions as Local Arrangements Chair of the symposium, and the staff of the Chicago Campus of the Siebel School for their important help with administrative matters.

July 2025

Jose Meseguer
Carlos A. Varela
Nalini Venkatasubramanian

Gul Agha's Students

Postdoctoral Researchers and Visiting Scholars

[The first position is indicated.]
- Takuo Watanabe, University of Tokyo
- Etsuya Shibayama, Tokyo Institute of Technology
- Masahiko Saito, NEC
- Brian Nielsen, University of Aalborg
- Yeichang Kim, Dongguk University
- Deok-Gil Jung, Dong-Eui University
- Wooyoung Kim, University of Illinois, Urbana-Champaign
- Prasanna Thati, University of Illinois, Urbana-Champaign
- Timo Latvala, Helsinki University of Technology
- Yong Wang, Beijing University of Technology
- Kirill Mechitov, University of Illinois, Urbana-Champaign
- Yun Mo, Harbin Institute of Technology
- Karl Palmskog, Royal Institute of Technology (KTH), Sweden

Ph.D. Theses Supervised

[In most cases, the current affiliations are noted.]
- Svend Frolund, Coordinating Distributed Objects: An Actor-Based Approach to Synchronization, 1994 (Software Architect, Gatehouse)
- Daniel Sturman, Modular Specification of Interaction in Distributed Computing, 1996 (Advisor, Board Member, Magma, Hidden Door, Exotanium)
- Rajendra Panwar, Modular Specifications of Partitioning and Distribution Strategies, 1996 (Patent Associate, Fenwick & West)
- Christian Callsen, Open Distributed Heterogeneous Computing, 1996, jointly supervised with Arne Skou at University of Aalborg (Partner, OptimumIT, Denmark)
- Shangping Ren, An Actor-Based Framework for Real-Time Coordination, 1997 (Chair, Computer Science, San Diego State University).
- Anna Patterson, The Logic of Constructible Duality, 1997, jointly supervised with Vaughn Pratt (Founder, Ceramic.ai; Founder and Managing Partner, Gradient Ventures)
- WooYoung Kim, THAL: An Actor System for Efficient and Scalable Concurrent Computing, 1997 (Senior Staff Engineer, Qualcomm)
- Mark Astley, Customization and Composition of Distributed Objects: Policy Management in Distributed Software Architectures, 1999 (Managing Director, Two Sigma Investments)

- Nalini Venkatasubramanian, Resource Management in Global Distributed Systems, 1998 (Professor, University of California, Irvine)
- Carlos Varela, Worldwide Computing with Universal Actors: Linguistic Abstractions for Naming, Migration, and Coordination, 2001 (Professor, RPI)
- Nadeem Jamali, CyberOrgs: A Model for Complex Resource-Bounded Mobile Agents, 2003 (Professor, University of Saskatchewan)
- Prasannaa Thati, A Theory of Testing for Asynchronous Concurrent Systems, 2003 (Head of Equity, Citadel)
- Mahmood Reza Ziaei, An Equational Logic and a Coordination Language for Distributed Objects, 2006 (Head of Storage and Compute, Apple AI/ML Data Infrastructure)
- Myeong-Wuk Jang, Efficient Communication and Coordination for Large-Scale Multi-agent Systems, 2004 (Principal Researcher, Samsung)
- Po-hao Chang, Customizing Web Applications Through Adaptable Components and Reconfigurable Distribution, 2006 (Research Scientist, Code Eight)
- Abhay Vardhan, Learning to Verify Systems, 2006 (Senior Software Engineer, Uber ATG)
- Sandeep Uttamchandani, Polus: A Declarative Self-Refining Approach for Dynamic System Management, 2006 (VP of Enterprise AI, Palo Alto Networks)
- Predrag Tosic, Modeling and Analysis of the Collective Dynamics of Large-Scale Multi-agent Systems, 2006 (Associate Professor, University of Idaho)
- Koushik Sen, Scalable Automated Methods for Dynamic Program Analysis, 2006 (Professor, Computer Science, University of California, Berkeley)
- Sameer Sundresh, Request-Based Mediated Execution, 2008 (Software Engineer, Twitter)
- Youngmin Kwon, Probabilistic Modeling and Verification of Large Scale Systems, 2006 (Research Associate Professor, Computer Science, SUNY Korea)
- Liping Chen, Conformance Preserving Data Dissemination for Large-Scale Peer to Peer Systems, 2009 (Microsoft)
- MyungJoo Ham, Market-Based Coordination and Auditing Mechanisms for Self-interested Multi-robot Systems, 2009 (Principal Engineer, Samsung Research)
- Kirill Mechitov, A Service-Oriented Architecture for Dynamic Macroprogramming of Sensor Networks, 2010 (CTO, Embedor Technologies)
- Vilas Jagannath, Improved Regression Testing of Multithreaded Programs, 2011 (Anthropic)
- Vijay Anand Reddy Korthikanti, Towards Energy-Performance Trade-off Analysis of Parallel Applications, 2011 (Principal Research Scientist, NVIDIA)
- Rajesh Kumar, Efficient Execution of Fine-Grained Actors on Multicore Processors, 2012 (CTO, Farmer's Fridge)
- Parya Moinzadeh, I-AdMiN: A Framework for Deriving Adaptive Service Configuration in Sensor Networks, 2013 (Amazon Cloud)
- Peter Dinges, Symcretic Testing of Programs, 2014 (Google)
- Reza Shiftehfar, A Flexible Fine-Grained Adaptive Framework for Parallel Mobile Hybrid Cloud Applications, 2015 (Uber)
- Minas Charalambides, Actor Programming with Static Guarantees, 2017 (Citadel)
- Sihan Li, Whole-System Testing and Analysis of Actor Programs, 2019

- Atul Sandur, An Adaptive Placement Framework for Efficient Near-Data Stream Processing over Data Source Edge-Cloud Systems, 2022 (AMD)
- Dan Plyukhin, Fault-Tolerant and Fault-Recovering Garbage Collection for the Actor Model: A Collage-Based Approach, 2024 (University of Southern Denmark)
- Dipayan Mukherjee

Master's Theses Supervised

- Shakuntala Miriyala, Visual Representation of Actors Using Predicate Transition Nets, 1991 (Mercadence)
- Nalini Venkatasubramaniam, Hierarchical Garbage Collection in Scalable Distributed Systems, 1992 (Professor, Computer Science, University of California, Irvine)
- Chris Houck, Run-Time System Support for Distributed Actor Programs, 1992 (Cofounder, Netscape)
- Daniel Sturman, Fault-Adaptation for Systems in Unpredictable Environments, 1993 (Advisor, Board Member, Magma, Hidden Door, Exotanium)
- Mark Astley, Online Event-Based Visualization for Distributed Systems, 1996 (Managing Director, Two Sigma Investments)
- Abhay Vardhan, Distributed Garbage Collection of Active Objects: A Transformation and Its Applications to Java Programming, 1998 (Senior Software Engineer, Uber)
- Sandeep Uttamchandani, MultiSec: A Multi-protocol Adaptive Security Architecture for Distributed Systems, 2001 (VP of Enterprise AI, Palo Alto Networks)
- Can Zheng, RAODV: A Real-Time Reservation On-Demand Protocol for Wireless Ad Hoc Networks, 2003
- Mehwesh Nagda, DiffGen: A Toolkit for Generating Distributed Protocols from Differential Equations, 2004
- Nirman Kumar, A Rewriting Based Model for Probabilistic and Nondeterministic Systems, 2004 (Assistant Professor, Computer Science, University of Memphis)
- Sudarshan Srinivasan, Fast Range Queries Using Pre-aggregated in-Network Storage, 2004 (Vice President, Marketing, Dome9)
- Abhilash Patel, A Swapping Mechanism for Dynamic Task Assignment in Multi-agent Systems, 2004 (Convoy)
- Tom Brown, Decentralized Coordination with Crash Failures, 2005 (Software Engineer, Google)
- Predrag Tosic, Distributed Coalition Formation for Collaborative Large-Scale Multi-agent Systems, 2006 (Assistant Professor, University of Idaho)
- William Wendling, Thal++: A Concurrent Language for the Thal Runtime System, 2008 (Software Engineer, Google)

- Po-Hao Chang, Customizing Web Applications Through Adaptable Components and Reconfigurable Distribution, 2008
- Shuheng Huang, Performance of the Hierarchical Distributed Garbage Collection Algorithm in ActorFoundry, 2015
- Meena Harshita, Training Machine Learning Algorithms Using Actor Framework in Multi-core OR Cluster System, 2019
- Rohan Kasiviswanathan, Consistency in Actor Based Server-Client Architecture Based Applications, 2020

Volume Organization

Additional Reviewers

Kyungmin Bae
Elias Castegren
Tung-Chun Chang
Andrew Chio
Wolfgang De Meuter
Travis Desell
Santiago Escobar
Marco Giunti
Colin S. Gordon
Philipp Haller
Nadeem Jamali
Eva Kuehn
Zhiding Liang

Narciso Martí-Oliet
Peter Ölveczky
Shangping Ren
Camilo Rocha
Rubén Rubio
Yasmin Sarita
Oshani Seneviratne
Avaljot Singh
Marjan Sirjani
Jonas Spenger
Carolyn Talcott
Xinghui Zhao

Local Arrangements Chair

Mahesh Viswanathan

Personal Notes

Gul Agha, A Natural Born Actor

Jean-Pierre Briot[1,2]

[1] Sorbonne University, CNRS, LIP6, Paris, France
Jean-Pierre.Briot@lip6.fr
[2] PUC-Rio, Rio de Janeiro, Brazil
https://webia.lip6.fr/~briot/

Abstract. This short text is a quick summary of the scientific impact of Gul Agha's contributions on my research, as well as some anecdotes about the wonderful human being that I am very happy to know.

Keywords: Gul Agha · homage · impact · anecdotes

1 Gul's Scientific Impact

In the early 80's, I started my journey into computer science during my PhD, working on the concepts of object-oriented programming. I also participated in applying them to the modeling and processing of musical processes, a research project headed by Pierre Cointe at IRCAM [4], the research institute about music, acoustic and computing in Paris. This was a great experience, because object-oriented programming was burgeoning a lot, and also thanks to the opportunity to meet scientists and musicians from all over the world. There, I met with Henry Lieberman and started discovering the concept of actors, and also met with Akinori Yonezawa, respectively, collaborator and past PhD student of Carl Hewitt, the great visionary about actors and other great ideas. As time and concurrency of events are fundamental in musical processes, I got much interested into actors. In 1985, soon after defending my PhD, I was welcomed by Akinori Yonezawa for a postdoc in his lab in Tokyo, while he was starting to work on the design and implementation of an actor-based language named ABCL [13]. This was another great scientific and human experience.

There, I discovered the thesis [1] and first articles by Gul Agha. I was really impressed with the concision and clarity of his specification of actors. Notably, his concept of behavior replacement was a key contribution to clarify and unify various issues:

– internal concurrency of the processing of incoming messages (as soon as the behavior replacement is defined),
– (as well as) their synchronization (until the behavior replacement is defined),
– (and furthermore) regaining pure functional properties.

This clean foundation of actor programming gave me the inspiration to implement and classify various models of actors and concurrent objects in the Smalltalk environment [2, 3]. It also served as a foundation for implementing agents [6], as multi-agent systems were now burgeoning. Further works by Gul and his team, e.g., about coordination languages [5], meta-level programming [11], dynamic adaptation [12], fault-tolerance [10], etc., were also very influential for my own projects, e.g., about fault-tolerant multi-agent systems [7, 8]. Gul and I met on various occasions, in USA, France and other locations. I had the chance to visit Gul's lab at UIUC for a few months. And it was a great resourcing experience.

2 Gul's Personality

Through our encounters, I discovered Gul's amazing personality. He is always calm, positive, opened, generous and has a nice and peculiar sense of humor. He is also very serious about veganism[1], while being a *bon vivant*. We also have some mutual interests in topics such as culture, music and spirituality.

Some nice experience was after the PhD defense of Salima Hassas, in Lyon University in 1992. Some of the members of the defense committee, Gul, Les Gasser, Peter de Jong and me, made some gastronomy/oenology short tour in the close Beaujolais region. We had the experience of a marvelous lunch (and wine:) at the famous and Michelin starred Auberge du Cep, in Fleurie (a village in the Beaujolais region, as well as likely the most elegant Beaujolais appellation). Coming back to Lyon though the little roads was also unforgettable, the roads were purple, as harvesting had just happened, the air full of grape perfumes, and the winery buildings filled with the delicate noise of the grape juice ongoing fermentation. Hopefully (for us), Peter de Jong did not drink alcohol and thus happily took the responsibility for driving!

An unexpected encounter was in Rio de Janeiro during the Middleware 2003 conference. I had a paper accepted with Frédéric Peschanski [9], who after a PhD with me was doing a post-doc in Tokyo in Akinori Yonezawa's lab. We both arrived in Rio de Janeiro, him from Tokyo, me from Paris. I tried to call him at his hotel. The lobby connected me to some room. I guess that I said something like "Salut Frédéric", expecting to have him on the phone. But the person who replied me was definitely not Frédéric. At the same time, I thought "I know this voice!". Moreover, I had the feeling that this person was also reflecting about my own voice. Until, after a few seconds of silence, both Gul and I simultaneously realized about us[2]!

When I asked how he was and when he arrived in Rio, Gul answered me that he was just coming back from a walk on Copacabana beach (where his hotel was located), and that his watch had just been stolen. He added that he just had bought a new watch from some informal seller on the beach, adding that it was likely that this watch had been recently stolen too! Anyway, this was the opportunity to have a great dinner in Rio for

---

[1] This was a shock to me when I discovered the existence of a Meat Science Laboratory at UIUC.
[2] It is worth mentioning that I had no a priori information about the venue of Gul to the conference (and I guess vice versa).

the three of us. And soon after, Gul welcomed Frédéric for a wonderful short research stay in his lab at UIUC.

3 Conclusion

It has been a great chance for me to know Gul's scientific work and also him as a person. Congratulations Gul! Thank you for all your contributions, openness and generosity! Thank you for inspiring so many colleagues and students! Thank you for these great shared moments! All my best wishes for you and your family! Jean-Pierre

References

1. Agha, G.: Actors – A Model of Concurrent Computation in Distributed Systems. Series in Artificial Intelligence. MIT Press (1986). ISBN.978-0-262-01092-4
2. Briot, J.P.: Actalk: a testbed for classifying and designing actor languages in the Smalltalk-80 environment. In: Cook, S. (ed.) European Conference on Object-Oriented Programming (ECOOP 1989), pp. 109–129. British Computer Society Workshop Series, Cambridge University Press, Nottingham, UK, July 1989. ISBN: 0-521-38232-7
3. Briot, J.P.: An experiment in classification and specialization of synchronization schemes. In: Futatsugi, K., Matsuoka, S. (eds.) ISOTAS 1996. LNCS, vol. 1049, pp. 227–249. Springer, Kanazawa (1996). https://doi.org/10.1007/3-540-60954-7_53
4. Cointe, P., Briot, J.P., Serpette, B.: The formes language: a musical application of object-oriented concurrent programming. In: Yonezawa, A., Tokoro, M. (eds.) Object-Oriented Concurrent Programming, pp. 221–258. Computer System Series, MIT Press (1987). ISBN: 0-262-24026-2
5. Frølund, S., Agha, G.: A language framework for multi-object coordination. In: Nierstrasz, O.M. (eds.) ECOOP 1993. LNCS, vol. 707, pp. 346–360. Springer, Heidelberg (1993). https://doi.org/10.1007/3-540-47910-4_18
6. Guessoum, Z., Briot, J.P.: From active objects to autonomous agents. Concurrency 7(3), 68–76 (1999). https://doi.org/10.1109/4434.788781. (Special Series on Actors and Agents, edited by Dennis Kafura and Jean-Pierre Briot)
7. Guessoum, Z., Briot, J.P., Faci, N., Marin, O.: Towards reliable multi-agent systems - an adaptive replication mechanism. Multi-agent Grid Syst. (MAGS) Int. J. 6(1), 1–24 (2010). https://doi.org/10.1145/1082983.1082977
8. Marin, O., Bertier, M., Sens, P., Guessoum, Z., Briot, JP.: DARX - a self-healing framework for agents. In: Kordon, F., Sztipanovits, J. (eds.) Reliable Systems on Unreliable Networked Platforms. Monterey Workshop 2005. LNCS, vol. 4322, pp. 88–105. Springer, Heidelberg (2007). https://doi.org/10.1007/978-3-540-71156-8_5

9. Peschanski, F., Briot, J.P., Yonezawa, A.: Fine-grained dynamic adaptation of distributed components. In: Middleware 2003, LNCS, vol. 2672, pp. 123–142. Springer, Heidelberg (2003). https://doi.org/10.1007/3-540-44892-6_7
10. Sturman, D.C., Agha, G.: A protocol description language for customizing failure semantics. In: Proceedings of the 13th International Symposium on Reliable Distributed Systems, pp. 148–157. IEEE, Dana Point (1994). https://doi.org/10.1109/RELDIS.1994.336900
11. Varela, C.A., Agha, G.: A hierarchical model for coordination of concurrent activities. In: Ciancarini, P., Wolf, A.L. (eds.) COORDINATION 1999. LNCS, vol. 1594, pp. 166–182. Springer, Heidelberg (1999). https://doi.org/10.1007/3-540-48919-3_13
12. Varela, C.A., Agha, G.: Programming dynamically reconfigurable open systems with Salsa. SIGPLAN Not. **36**(12), 20–34 (2001). https://doi.org/10.1145/583960.583964
13. Yonezawa, A., Briot, J.P., Shibayama, E.: Object-oriented concurrent programming in ABCL/1. In: Conference on Object-Oriented Programming Systems, Languages and Applications (OOPSLA 1986). SIGPLAN Not. **21**(11), 258–268 (1986). ISBN: 0-89791-204-7

Gul Agha's Influence on Me

K. Mani Chandy

Simon Ramo Professor
California Institute of Technology

Abstract. What Gul Agha did for me.

1 Gul Agha's Contributions

I've known Gul for most of my working life. Gul has done pioneering work in the three areas that I've worked in: queuing theory and performance modeling of information systems; concurrent computing; and systems that detect and respond to significant events. I've followed Gul's work ever since we met years ago.

The other articles in this compendium describe Gul's research contributions at length. Let me merely point to an over-arching aspect of Gul's research direction: simplicity. The actor model is a superb example of simplicity and elegance in action. Gul isn't satisfied with elegant theory as his work on smart cities shows. Moreover, Gul has produced excellent students including Nalini Venkatasubramanian who is working with Caltech researchers on monitoring earthquakes and systems that provide critical resources.

The combination of simplicity coupled with application is rare. Gul is an exemplar.

A Personal Tribute to Gul Agha's Research Work

Paolo Ciancarini

Dipartimento di Informatica: Scienza e Ingegneria, University of Bologna, Italy

1 Introduction and First Encounter

If I remember well, I first met Gul Agha in late 1995 or early 1996 at a Symposium on Programming Languages held in Boston, organized by Peter Wegner. The symposium was highly engaging, with outstanding participants presenting their ideas, and it resulted in a collection of papers published by *ACM Computing Surveys*.

I recall Gul's insightful talk at the symposium [2], and I also gave a talk [10]. During some free time, we walked around the city together. Knowing that I was relatively unfamiliar with the workings of American academia, he kindly explained various aspects of it to me—tenure, endowments, and other institutional nuances. At that event, I was almost a complete unknown, while Gul was already a brilliant star in the field.

I should mention that prior to Boston, I had organized a workshop at ECOOP in Bologna in 1994, where Gul presented a paper [16], though I am not sure we had a chance to meet in person on that occasion.

2 Gul Agha's Scientific Legacy

Gul Agha's pioneering work in distributed programming models has had a profound and lasting impact on the field, and on myself personally. Building on the foundational ideas introduced by Carl Hewitt, Gul extended the Actor Model into a practical and formal framework for reasoning about distributed systems. His PhD thesis [1] introduced several key concepts now foundational in distributed computing:

- **Asynchronous Message Passing**: Actors communicate exclusively through non-blocking messages, enabling decoupling and resilience.
- **Encapsulation**: Each actor maintains its own state and behavior, supporting modularity and fault isolation.
- **Dynamic Creation**: Actors can create other actors dynamically, supporting scalable and adaptive architectures.
- **Location Transparency**: Actor identities are abstracted from physical location, allowing mobility and fault tolerance.

Gul later explored connections between the Actor Model and other paradigms. Notable among these are his studies on the integration of actors with functional programming [5], and the role of coordination and middleware [6]. These works have greatly influenced my own research.

His contribution extended into formal verification, particularly through the definition of operational semantics for actor-based systems [18], enabling formal analysis of properties like liveness, safety, and consistency. He also advanced model-checking techniques for concurrent distributed systems, bridging theory with practical correctness.

Gul's ideas have had a tremendous practical influence: programming frameworks such as Akka [9] and Erlang [3] build directly on principles he formalized. His research has had broad application in domains like telecommunications, IoT, and cloud computing.

3 My Research Trajectory: Bridging Actors and Coordination

During my PhD years in Pisa, I studied concurrent logic programming languages, particularly E. Shapiro's Concurrent Prolog [20]. Collaborating with Antonio Brogi, we introduced Shared Prolog, inspired by Linda-style coordination [7]. This led me to Yale, where I delved into coordination models and languages, especially Linda and its extensions [17].

I worked on *multiple tuple spaces* [12], a model bearing conceptual similarities to ActorSpaces. I extended these ideas into logic programming [9] and developed a temporal logic for coordination [14]. These ideas culminated in using multiple tuple spaces to specify distributed software architectures and systems involving mobile agents [11].

Interestingly, Gul also explored combining actors and tuple spaces in his ActorSpaces model [4], and in later work with Carlos Varela on hierarchical coordination [21]. These overlaps reinforced a shared vision of dynamic, modular concurrency.

My research can be seen as bridging Gul Agha's Actor Model and David Gelernter's Linda-based coordination paradigm. During the 1990s, I worked on formalizing Linda-style models using logic and process calculi [13], focusing on structured, distributed tuple spaces for modular coordination in open systems.

Unlike actors, which encapsulate behavior and interact through direct message passing, coordination models abstract away from individual behavior and focus on shared interaction patterns. This separation of computation from coordination enabled expressive forms of decoupled communication. I became increasingly interested in agents, similar to actors, but I viewed their interactions as mediated by shared, semantically structured coordination spaces.

This perspective led to work on coordination as a middleware concern, applicable across heterogeneous components and platforms. My vision of cooperative, multiagent systems culminated in the PageSpace architecture [8], which brought together aspects of both generative coordination and actor-like autonomy.

4 From Abstract Coordination Models to Modern Software Architectures

Over the past decades, software systems have undergone a profound transformation, shaped by concurrency theory, distributed computing, and mobility. The Actor Model, with its decentralized execution and asynchronous messaging, has become a cornerstone for building scalable, resilient systems—foundational to modern microservices and cloud-native platforms.

As distributed systems became ubiquitous, new coordination mechanisms including shared repositories, event-driven designs, and publish/subscribe brokers, emerged to manage dynamic interaction among components. These paradigms, including the ones derived from Agha's and Gelernter's work, aligned with trends in object-oriented and component-based design.

With the rise of agile methodologies in the early 2000s, software engineering embraced principles of iterative development, continuous adaptation, and responsive design. This agile mindset extended to system architecture, emphasizing loose coupling, resilience, and user-centered evolution.

I found the agile philosophy deeply compatible with the ideas of decentralized, cooperative systems. These insights led me to formulate the concept of *cooperative thinking* in software engineering [15], where software is understood as a social artifact mediating interaction among developers and users.

Today, cloud-native platforms, DevOps practices, and AI-driven automation are converging with actor-based concurrency and coordination models to create adaptive and intelligent software systems. The influence of Gul Agha's work is clearly visible in this convergence.

Conclusion

Gul Agha's contributions have fundamentally shaped our understanding of distributed computation. From the Actor Model to coordination-aware middleware, his insights continue to inspire researchers and practitioners. His work has provided rigorous foundations and practical blueprints for building modern, adaptive, and robust software systems.

Personally, Gul's ideas, generosity, and intellectual depth have guided and inspired much of my research journey. His vision for decentralized, resilient software continues to influence the architecture of the systems we build today.

Many thanks, Gul!

References

1. Gul, A.: Actors: A Model of Concurrent Computation in Distributed Systems. MIT Press, Cambridge (1986)

2. Gul, A.: Linguistic paradigms for programming complex distributed systems. ACM Comput. Surv. **28**(2), 295–296 (1996)
3. Gul, A.: Actors programming for the mobile cloud. In: Proceedings of 13th International Symposium on Parallel and Distributed Computing, pp. 3–9. IEEE (2014)
4. Gul, A., Callsen, C.J.: ActorSpaces: an open distributed programming paradigm. In: Chen, M.C., Halstead, R. (eds.) Proceedings of the Fourth ACM SIGPLAN Symposium on Principles & Practice of Parallel Programming (PPOPP), San Diego, California, USA, 19–22 May 1993, pp. 23–32. ACM (1993)
5. Gul, A.A., Ian, A.M., Scott, F.S., Carolyn, L.T.: A foundation for actor computation. J. Fun. Progr. **7**(1), 1–72 (1997)
6. Astley, M., Sturman, D.C., Agha, G.A.: Customizable middleware for modular distributed software. Commun. ACM **44**(5), 99–107 (2001)
7. Brogi, A., Ciancarini, P.: The concurrent language Shared Prolog. ACM Trans. Program. Lang. Syst. (TOPLAS) **13**(1), 99–123 (1991)
8. Ciancarini, P., Tolksdorf, R., Vitali, F., Rossi, D., Knoche, A.: Coordinating multiagent applications on the WWW: a reference architecture. IEEE Trans. Softw. Eng. **24**(5), 362–375 (1998)
9. Ciancarini, P.: Parallel logic programming using the Linda model of computation. In: Banâtre, J.-P., Le Métayer, D. (eds.) HLPPP 1991. LNCS, vol. 574, pp. 110–125. Springer, Heidelberg (1991). https://doi.org/10.1007/3-540-55160-3_38
10. Ciancarini, P.: Coordination models and languages as software integrators. ACM Comput. Surv. **28**(2), 300–302 (1996)
11. Ciancarini, P., Franze, F., Mascolo, C.: Using a coordination language to specify and analyze systems containing mobile components. ACM Trans. Softw. Eng. Methodol. (TOSEM) **9**(2), 167–198 (2000)
12. Ciancarini, P., Gelernter, A.: Distributed programming environment based on multiple tuple spaces. In: Proceedings of International Conference on Fifth Generation Computer Systems, pp. 926–933. Institute for New Generation Computer Technology, Tokyo (1992)
13. Ciancarini, P., Jensen, K.K., Yankelevich, D.: On the operational semantics of a coordination language. In: Ciancarini, P., Nierstrasz, O., Yonezawa, A. (eds.) ECOOP 1994. LNCS, vol. 924, pp. 77–106. Springer, Heidelberg (1995). https://doi.org/10.1007/3-540-59450-7_6
14. Ciancarini, M.M., Pazzaglia, L.: A logic for a coordination model with multiple spaces. Sci. Comput. Programm. **31**(2/3), 231–262 (1998)
15. Ciancarini, P., Missiroli, M., Russo, D.: Cooperative thinking: analyzing a new framework for software engineering education. J. Syst. Softw. **157** (2019)
16. Frølund, S., Agha, G.: Abstracting interactions based on message sets. In: Ciancarini, P., Nierstrasz, O., Akinori Y. (eds.) ECOOP 1994. LNCS, vol. 924, pp. 107–124. Springer, Heidelberg (1994). https://doi.org/10.1007/3-540-59450-7_7
17. Gelernter, D.: Multiple tuple spaces in Linda. In: Odijk, E., Rem, M., Syre, J.C. (eds.) PARLE 1989. LNCS, vol. 366, pp. 20–27. Springer, Heidelberg (1989). https://doi.org/10.1007/3-540-51285-3_30
18. Nielsen, B., Agha, G.: Semantics for an actor-based real-time language. In: Proceedings of 4th International Workshop on Parallel and Distributed Real-Time Systems, pp. 223–228. IEEE (1996)

19. Roestenburg, R., Williams, R., Bakker, R.: Akka in action. Simon and Schuster (2016)
20. Shapiro, E.: The family of concurrent logic programming languages. ACM Comput. Surv. (CSUR) **21**(3), 413–510 (1989)
21. Varela, C., Agha, G.: A hierarchical model for coordination of concurrent activities. In: Ciancarini, P., Wolf, A.L. (eds.) COORDINATION 1999. LNCS, vol. 1594, pp. 166–182. Springer, Heidelberg (1999). https://doi.org/10.1007/3-540-48919-3_13

A Role Model and Mentor

Xudong He

Florida International University, Miami, FL 33199, USA
hex@cs.fiu.edu

1 The First Meeting

The first time I met Prof. Gul Agha was attending the annual International Conference on Petri Nets in Osaka, Japan 1996, where Gul also organized the 2nd International Workshop on Object-Oriented Programming and Models of Concurrency.

During that time, I was working on hierarchical high-level Petri nets that have super places and transitions to support system abstraction and modularity and thus to make Petri nets more applicable to software engineering in general [1]. A formal definition of hierarchical predicate transition nets (HPrTNs) was given that integrated the new syntactical entities with classic dynamic semantics [2]. Due to the emergence of object-oriented (OO) design and programming in the mid 90s, researchers in concurrency community tried to integrate the OO concepts into varies concurrency models including classic concurrency model Petri nets and new emerging concurrency model Actors [3]. As a result, I also tried to use HPrTNs to model various OO concepts including classes, objects, and various class relationships. The results [4] were presented at the workshop organized by Gul. I met Gul the first time during the workshop and we had several interesting discussions during and after the workshop. This workshop paper was revised multiple times and after a long delay the final version [5] was published in a Lecture Notes in Computer Science volume edited by Gul in 2001.

After the workshop, Gul and I spent a day in touring the historic sites in Osaka (Picture 1). As a young just tenured associate professor, I got a lot of inspirations and advice from Gul on research and academic career. We have maintained a close relationship since then. Gul has supported me throughout these years and written recommendation letters for me during my professor promotion and many other applications.

2 Research Influence

2.1 Modeling Agent Systems using Petri Nets

Actors are a concurrent model for distributed systems. Motivated from the Actor approach for modeling distributed systems, I started to apply Petri nets to model agent-oriented systems [6–10]. We have extended predicate transition nets with channel concepts and employed a nets-within-nets paradigm [11] for defining the architecture of multi-agent system (MAS). The upper-level Petri net is used to define the system view of MAS, including the essential mechanisms of interactions, communications, and cooperation among multiple agents. The lower-level Petri nets are used to model the behaviors of individual agents. The key idea is the channel concept, which supports the communication between an agent with its environment. A synchronized communication occurs when two fireable transitions at two different net levels have a matching pair of input and output channel expressions.

2.2 Atomicity Violation Prediction

Concurrency bugs are hard to find and reproduce due to the large number of interleavings. Most non-deadlock concurrency bugs are atomicity violation bugs due to the un-protected accesses of shared variables by multiple threads. Dynamic approaches for studying atomicity violations include monitor-based methods that require atomicity violations to manifest during monitored runs and predictive methods that explore atomicity violations in alternative interleavings extracted from some sample instrumented runs. Predictive methods use either (1) under-approximate models: the set of extracted interleavings with the exact same read-after-write relationships as in the instrumented runs, which are a subset of all feasible interleavings; or (2) over-approximate models: the set of all possible interleavings extracted from the instrumented runs, which may not be feasible in the original program due to data constraints and ad-hoc synchronization. Gul has done work on predictive method for under-approximate models [12], which provided some idea for our work [13] on a post-prediction analysis method for improving the precision of the prediction results obtained through over-approximation while achieving better overage than that obtained through under-approximation.

2.3 Modeling and Analyzing Cyber Physical Systems

In 2017, I served as the program chair of the International Conference on Software Engineering and Knowledge Engineering and invited Gul as the keynote speaker (Picture 2). His talk on cyber physical systems (CPS) provided me a lot of inspiration to work on CPS.

In subsequent years, I have worked on (1) general modeling and analysis approaches for CPS using Petri nets [14, 15], (2) special hybrid predicate transition nets for studying CPS [16], and (3) establishing relationships between high-level Petri nets and deep neural nets (DNNs) and then modeling and analyzing CPS with machine learning components [17, 18]. More recently, I have focused on the stability analysis of CPS controlled by DNNs [19, 20], which is critical for the trustworthiness of the widespread application of machine learning and artificial intelligence.

References

1. Reisig, W.: Petri nets in software engineering. In: Brauer, W., Reisig, W., Rozenberg, G. (eds.) ACPN 1986. LNCS, vol. 255, pp. 63–96. Springer, Heidelberg (1986). https://doi.org/10.1007/3-540-17906-2_22
2. He, X.: A formal definition of hierarchical predicate transition nets. In: Billington, J., Reisig, W. (eds.) ICATPN 1996. LNCS, vol. 1091, pp. 212–229. Springer, Heidelberg (1996). https://doi.org/10.1007/3-540-61363-3_12
3. Agha, G.: Actors: A Model of Concurrent Computation in Distributed Systems. MIT Press (1996)
4. He, X., Ding, Y.: Object-oriented specification using hierarchical predicate transition nets. In: Proceedings of 2nd International Workshop on Object-Oriented Programming and Models of Concurrency (OOMC 1996), Osaka, Japan (1996)
5. He, X., Ding, Y.: Object orientation in hierarchical predicate transition nets. In: Agha, G.A., De Cindio, F., Rozenberg, G. (eds.) Concurrent Object-Oriented Programming and Petri Nets. LNCS, vol. 2001, pp. 196–215. Springer, Heidelberg (2001). https://doi.org/10.1007/3-540-45397-0_6
6. Ding, J.D., Clarke, P., Xu, D., He, X., Deng, Y.: A formal model-based approach for developing an interoperable mobile agent system. Multi-agent Grid Syst. Int. J. **2**(4), 401–412 (2006)
7. Lian, J., Shatz, S., He, X.: Flexible coordinator design for modeling resource sharing in multi-agent systems. J. Syst. Softw. **82**(10), 1709–1729 (2009)
8. Chang, L., Shatz, S., He, X.: A methodology for modeling multi-agent systems using nested petri nets. Int. J. Softw. Eng. Knowl. Eng. - IJSEKE. **22**(7), 891–926 (2012)
9. Chang, L., He, X.: A methodology to analyze multi-agent systems modeled in high level petri nets. Int. J. Softw. Eng. Knowl. Eng. - IJSEKE. **25**(7), 1199–1235 (2015)
10. He, X.: A comprehensive survey of petri net modeling in software engineering. Int. J. Softw. Eng. Knowl. Eng. - IJSEKE. **23**(5), 589–626 (2013)
11. Kohler, M., Moldt, D., Rolke, H.: Modeling mobility and mobile agents using nets within nets. In: van der Aalst, W.M.P., Best, E. (eds.) ICATPN 2003. LNCS, vol. 2679, pp. 121–139. Springer, Heidelberg (2003). https://doi.org/10.1007/3-540-44919-1_11
12. Sen, K., Rosu, G., Agha, G.: Detecting errors in multithreaded programs by generalized predictive analysis of executions. In: Proceedings of the 7th IFIP International Conference on Formal Methods for Open Object-Based Distributed Systems (FMOODS 2005), pp. 211–226. Athens, Greece (2005)
13. Zeng, R., Sun, Z., Liu, S., He, X.: A Method for Improving the Precision and Coverage of Atomicity Violation Predictions. In: Baier, C., Tinelli, C. (eds.) TACAS 2015. LNCS, vol. 9035, pp. 116–130 Springer, Heidelberg (2015). https://doi.org/10.1007/978-3-662-46681-0_8

14. He, X., Dong, Z., Yin, H., Fu, Y.: A framework for developing cyber-physical systems. Int. J. Softw. Eng. Knowl. Eng. - IJSEKE. **27**(9), 1361–1386 (2017)
15. He, X.: Modeling and analyzing cyber physical systems using high level petri nets. In: Proceedings of the 2018 IEEE International Conference on Software Quality, Reliability & Security (QRS 2018), QRS Companion, Lisbon, Portugal, pp. 469–476 (2018)
16. He, X., Alam, D.: Hybrid predicate transition nets - a formal method for modeling and analyzing cyber-physical systems. In: Proceedings of the 2019 IEEE International Conference on Software Quality, Reliability & Security (QRS 2019), Sofia, Bulgaria, pp. 216–227 (2019)
17. He, X.: Modeling cyber physical systems with learning enabled components using hybrid predicate transition nets. In: Proceedings of 2021 IEEE 21st International Conference on Software Quality, Reliability and Security Companion (QRS-C), Hainan, China (2021)
18. He, X.: Analyzing cyber physical systems with learning enabled components using hybrid predicate transition nets. In: Proceedings of the 34th International Conference on Software Engineering and Knowledge Engineering, July 1–10 (Online) (2022)
19. He, X.: Building safe and stable deep neural net controllers through deep reinforcement learning and deep imitation learning. In: Proceedings of the IEEE 22nd International Conference on Software Quality, Reliability and Security, Guangzhou, China (2022)
20. He, X.: An approach to build and verify stable neural network controllers for cyber physical systems with non-linear dynamics. In: Proceedings of the IEEE 23rd International Conference on Software Quality, Reliability and Security, Chiang Mai, Thailand (2023)

Hakuna Matata and Beyond: Life Lessons from Gul Agha

Shangping Ren

Department of Computer Science, San Diego State University, CA, USA
sren@sdsu.edu

Abstract. The Festschrift Symposium honoring Gul Agha provides a perfect opportunity to reflect on the profound influence he has had on his students, colleagues, and the broader field of computer science. For me, the years spent as Gul's Ph.D. student from 1992 to 1997 were transformative. His guidance went beyond research. In this tribute, I would like to share a few unforgettable moments that have profoundly shaped my life.

From China to the Library: A Journey Toward Independence

Growing up during the Chinese Cultural Revolution time profoundly shaped my personality. As a child of intellectuals who were oppressed during that turbulent time, I grew up timid, shy, and deeply unsure of myself. The cultural environment emphasized conformity and obedience, leaving little room for independent thought or self-expression. In schools, professors steered every step, and students simply carried out the instructions. Life was about survival and duty—not choice.

When I joined Gul's research group in 1992, I carried these ingrained habits and insecurities with me. I was used to being told what to do, so when I nervously asked Gul, "What should I do?" I expected clear instructions. Instead, Gul replied, "What do you want to do?"

I was stunned and at a loss for words. "Whatever you want me to do," I mumbled. Gul smiled patiently and said, "Find whatever you want to do in the library." His words left me feeling overwhelmed. How could I possibly figure out what to do on my own? Yet, as I spent hours in the library, exploring papers and topics, I discovered something I had never experienced before: the freedom to think for myself. Slowly, curiosity replaced fear, and I began identifying research areas that genuinely excited me. Though the process was daunting, it was also deeply empowering.

This moment marked a profound cultural and personal shift. Gul's approach challenged me to break free from the constraints of my past and embrace the idea that I had choices. It wasn't just an academic lesson; it was a life-altering realization. For the first time, I felt that my own thoughts mattered and that I could chart my own path.

Protecting and Empowering: A Lesson in Confidence

In the early days of my Ph.D. study, I was still adjusting to a new environment and culture. I remained internally shy and insecure. As a non-native English speaker, I also worried about my communication skills and was hesitant to speak up in discussions.

One day, during a casual exchange, someone made a lighthearted joke about my accent. Though it was meant in good humor, I could not help but feel self-conscious. Gul responded with genuine warmth: "Do you realize how remarkable it is that Shangping is accomplishing all of this in a second language?" At that moment, he made me see my efforts in a new light.

That moment perfectly illustrated Gul's remarkable ability to uplift and empower his students. His thoughtful words instilled me a newfound confidence that I had not anticipated. Over time, this encouragement helped me find my voice, both within academic discussions and in broader contexts. Through his kindness, I learned to embrace my unique experiences as a source of strength.

Embracing Worry as a Strength

It is no secret that I am a worrier. Friends and colleagues often joke that if I had nothing to worry about, I would invent something. For years, I saw this trait as a weakness—a source of stress that held me back. But Gul had a different perspective. "Your worry is what makes you thorough," he once told me. "It is what ensures you are prepared." Those words were a revelation. Instead of dismissing my tendency to worry, Gul helped me see it as a strength. He showed me how to channel my anxiety into careful planning and diligent work, without letting it paralyze me.

Under his mentorship, I learned to strike a balance between preparation and action. I realized that while it is important to anticipate challenges, it is equally important to move forward despite uncertainties. Gul's perspective transformed the way I approach problems, allowing me to turn what I once saw as a flaw into one of my assets.

"Hakuna Matata": A Lesson in Perspective

Years after completing my Ph.D., life took me on a different path. I worked in industry for over five years and started a family, which included raising my son. When I finally got the chance to return to academia, I was thrilled but also overwhelmed. The prospect of balancing research, teaching, and family life while striving for tenure felt daunting. Seeking guidance, I turned to Gul once again.

"How do I navigate this?" I asked, hoping for a step-by-step plan. Instead, Gul smiled and said, "Hakuna matata." I blinked in confusion. The phrase was unfamiliar to me, and Gul, ever the teacher, suggested I ask my son. When I did, my son's face lit up. "It means 'no worries,'" he explained enthusiastically, referencing Disney's The Lion King. I could not help but laugh at the simplicity and profundity of Gul's advice. He was reminding me not to let stress overshadow the joy of pursuing my passion. As someone who tends to overthink and worry—often excessively—this message was exactly what I needed. Gul's lighthearted yet wise words encouraged me to focus on what truly mattered, rather than being consumed by anxiety. Since then, "Hakuna matata" has become a mantra that helps me face challenges with a calm and optimistic mindset.

Taking on New Challenges: Moving Forward with Confidence

Nearly 20 years after graduating, I found myself at another crossroads. I had the opportunity to move from the Illinois Institute of Technology in Chicago to San Diego State University to take on the role of department chair. The decision was not an easy one. The role came with significantly different responsibilities, and the move meant uprooting my comfortable life and stepping into unfamiliar territory.

As I weighed my options, I found myself reflecting on Gul's earlier mentorship. His lessons about independence, resilience, and optimism gave me the courage to embrace the challenge. I remembered how he had encouraged me to explore my own path back in the library and how his words—"Hakuna matata"—had carried me through many moments of uncertainty.

In the end, I decided to take the leap. Gul's influence continued to guide me, reminding me to focus on the possibilities rather than my fears. Even in the midst of adjusting to my new role and responsibilities, his advice allowed me to sleep more peacefully at night, knowing that I could handle whatever came my way.

Gratitude for a Lifelong Mentor

As I reflect on these moments, I am struck by the depth of Gul's mentorship. He has a unique ability to see his students' potential and guide them in ways that foster independence, resilience, and self-discovery. His influence extends far beyond the technical aspects of research; he has shaped the way I think, work, and live.

Gul's impact on the field of computer science is undeniable, but his greatest legacy may be the countless students whose lives he has touched. I am profoundly grateful to be one of them. The lessons I learned from him—to seek my own path, to embrace challenges with optimism, and to view my worries as strengths—continue to guide me every day. As we celebrate Gul's extraordinary career and contributions, I am honored to share these reflections and to express my heartfelt thanks for his mentorship and friendship.

Contents

Actors and Concurrent Programming

A Formal Specification For Half a Century of Actor Systems 3
    Joeri De Koster and Wolfgang De Meuter

The AMST Language: Formal Verification and Execution of Actor Systems ... 36
    Carlos A. Varela

Actor Capabilities for Message Ordering 60
    Colin S. Gordon

Failure-Transparent Actors 81
    Jonas Spenger, Paris Carbone, and Philipp Haller

On the Development of the Active Object Paradigm: A Personal Account 114
    Olaf Owe

The C++ Actor Framework: A Scalable Fundament for Research
and Applications 144
    Dominik Charousset, Raphael Hiesgen, and Thomas C. Schmidt

Decoupling Isolation and Concurrency: An Actor-Centric View
of Behaviour-Oriented Concurrency 165
    Luke Cheeseman, Elias Castegren, Sophia Drossopoulou,
    Tobias Wrigstad, Sylvan Clebsch, and Matthew Parkinson

Open Systems and Applications

Actors for Timing Analysis of Distributed Redundant Controllers 189
    Marjan Sirjani, Edward A. Lee, Zahra Moezkarimi,
    Bahman Pourvatan, Bjarne Johansson, Stefan Marksteiner,
    and Alessandro V. Papadopoulos

Actors and Blockchains, Together 215
    Xiaohong Chen and Grigore Rosu

Decentralizing University Governance: A Coordination Challenge 237
    Eva Maria Kuehn

Industry 4.0 and Digital Twins: The Route Towards Customizable
Self-describing Products 259
   Michael Papazoglou, Bernd J. Krämer, and Amal Elgammal

Experiences with Composability for Resilient IoT Systems 279
   Nalini Venkatasubramanian, Fangqi Liu, and Yusuf Sarwar

Hamiltonian Formulation of a Finite-State Automaton 307
   YoungMin Kwon and Gul Agha

Decentralized Machine Learning with Asynchronous Communication 328
   Tavonput Luangphasy and Xinghui Zhao

Learning with Hypothesis Formation and Curiosity: An Actors Approach 346
   Nadeem Jamali, Aditya Phadke, and Zhe Chen

Formal Methods

Logical Time in Actor Systems 371
   Edward A. Lee

Open CPS: A Symbolic Model 393
   Farhad Arbab and Carolyn Talcott

Type Congruence, Duality and Iso-Recursive Binary Session Types 418
   Marco Giunti and Nobuko Yoshida

Programming and Verifying Actor Systems in Rewriting Logic 446
   José Meseguer

PMaude Revisited Through Probabilistic Strategies 475
   Rubén Rubio, Adrián Riesco, and Narciso Martí-Oliet

Modeling and Analyzing Real-Time Systems in Rewriting Logic 494
   Kyungmin Bae, Carlos Olarte, and Peter Csaba Ölveczky

Author Index 537

Actors and Concurrent Programming

A Formal Specification For Half a Century of Actor Systems

Joeri De Koster[✉][iD] and Wolfgang De Meuter[iD]

Vrije Universiteit Brussel, Pleinlaan 2, 1050 Brussels, Belgium
{Joeri.De.Koster,Wolfgang.De.Meuter}@vub.be

Abstract. The Actor Model is a message passing concurrency model that was originally proposed by Hewitt et al. in 1973. Half a century later a plethora of variations on this model have been explored for various programming languages and systems. So much so that precise definition of actor-based programming languages is lost and that the term *actor* has become highly conflated. The goal of this paper is to disambiguate different actor models by classifying them into four families, namely: *Classic Actors, Active Objects, Processes, and Communicating Event Loops*. This paper identifies and defines the *Isolated Turn Principle* as the key and unifying principle among all actor models. In order to uniquely categorise the four actor families, this paper provides a precise formal definition of the core subset for each of the four families of actor models by means of an operational semantics.

Keywords: Actor Model · Formal Specification

1 Introduction

The Actor model of computation is a model for concurrent computation that treats *actors* as the universal primitives of concurrent computation. Actors are objects that encapsulate both state and behavior, and can communicate with each other asynchronously by sending and receiving messages. The Actor model was first proposed by Carl Hewitt in 1973 [22] as a way to understand and reason about the behavior of large, concurrent systems.

The invention of the Actor Model is rooted in the research on object-oriented programming languages. Motivated to discover novel modularisation techniques to develop complex systems, the early sixties was a hotbed for formative ideas around object-oriented programming. The first widely recognised object-oriented programming language was specified in that same era (Simula, in 1965). Only a few years later, the Planner language was developed as part of Carl Hewitt's doctoral research at MIT's Artificial Intelligence Lab [21]. Planner introduced the notion of procedural embedding of knowledge. Influenced by ideas from object-oriented programming and his work on Planner, Hewitt and his graduate students invented the actor model of computation in 1973 [22].

One of the key features of the Actor model is that each Actor is completely self-contained and has its **own private state**. This means that an Actor's internal state cannot be directly accessed or modified by other Actors, only **messages** can be sent to it. This makes it easy to reason about the behavior of an Actor, as its behavior is determined solely by the messages that it receives and the internal state that it maintains.

Another important aspect of the Actor model is that all communication between Actors is **asynchronous**. This means that when an Actor sends a message to another Actor, it does not wait for a response, but instead continues to process other messages. This allows for high parallelism and scalability, and reduces the likelihood of contention and deadlock, as Actors can continue to process messages even if other Actors are blocked or slow.

Because of the isolation of state and the asynchronicity of its communication mechanism, the Actor Model is guaranteed to be free of low-level data races and deadlocks. This is a key property that unifies all actor model implementations.

However, there are also some challenges in using the Actor model in practice. One is that it can be difficult to reason about the global behavior of a system, since it is often difficult to see the interactions between different actors. Another is that it can be difficult to debug and test systems built using the Actor model since it can be hard to reproduce the same sequence of messages and interactions that led to a particular error or bug.

Despite these challenges, the Actor model has proven to be a powerful and versatile tool for building concurrent and distributed systems. Over the past 50 years, a plethora of programming languages that implement their own variation on the actor model have been developed. Each of these variations on the actor model comes with their own terminology, programming language concepts and run-time semantics. So much so, that the term *actor* has become so conflated that some researchers refrain from using it in their papers [12].

There are many properties and features along which different actor programming languages can be classified. In this paper we focus solely on those that impact their programming model. This paper disambiguates different actor models by classifying them into four families, each with their own programming model, namely: *Classic Actors, Active Objects, Processes, and Communicating Event Loops*. Section 2 provides a brief overview of the early history of the actor model. From Sect. 3 to Sect. 6, we highlight the key differences between each of the four families and give a formal definition for each by means of an operational semantics. An executable version of each of these semantics in PLT Redex is also available.[1] The goal of this formalisation is not to prove specific properties for each actor family, but rather give a precise formal definition that can serve as the basis for classifying various actor systems. This paper extends the classification of actor models done in previous work [15].

---

[1] https://gitlab.soft.vub.ac.be/jdekoste/actormodelhistorypltredex.

2 Early History of the Actor Model

The actor model was first introduced in a 1973 paper authored by Carl Hewitt and two of his graduate students: Peter Bishop and Richard Steiger [22]. The original goal was to have a programming model for safely exploiting concurrency in distributed workstations. The problem domain was modelling parallel communication based problem solvers. The first implementation of the actor model was in a Planner-like programming language that was modeled on actors [18], originally called Planner-73, but later renamed to PLASMA.

In PLASMA, actors communicate with each other via message passing which consists of sending a request from one actor (called the messenger) to another actor (called the target). The request and a reference to the messenger are packaged as an envelope and put into the inbox of the target actor (request: message; reply-to: messenger). Given that envelope, the behaviour of the target actor then specifies how the computation continues with respect to the request. The messenger is typically used as the reply address to which a reply to the request should be sent. The simplest control structure that uses this request-reply pattern in most programming languages is the procedure call and return. A recursive implementation of *factorial* written in PLASMA is given in Listing 1.1.

```
(factorial ≡
  (≡> [=n]
    (rules n
      (≡> 1
           1)
      (≡> (> 1)
           (n * (factorial <= (n - 1))))))))
```

Listing 1.1. Factorial function written in PLASMA.

In this example factorial is defined to be an actor of which the behaviour matches the requests of incoming envelopes with one element which will be called n. The rules for n are, if it is 1, then we send back 1 to the messenger of the envelope. Note that this is done implicitly. If it is greater than 1, we send a message to the factorial actor to recursively compute the factorial of (n - 1).

In December 1975, in an attempt to understand the Actor Model described by Hewitt, Sussman and Steele [35] wrote a continuation-based interpreter for a Lisp-like language called Scheme. They came to the conclusion that Hewitt's "actors" were very similar to scheme lambda expressions and had their roots in the lambda calculus [14]. In effect, sending a message to an actor that is in an idle state is very similar to invoking a continuation.

Throughout the history of the actor model, a plethora of different variations of the actor model have been designed. This paper categorizes the various adaptations of the actor model into four distinct families: Classic Actors, Active

Objects, Processes, and Communicating Event Loops. The subsequent four sections present a historical overview of each family and establish an operational semantics for the fundamental language features characterizing each variation.

3 The Classic Actor Model

The Actor Model only became more widely regarded as a general-purpose concurrency model in 1986, when it was recast in terms of three simple primitives by one of Carl Hewitt's former PhD students, namely Gul Agha [3,4]. Agha redefined the Actor Model in terms of three basic actor primitives: *create*, *send* and *become*. His vision of the Actor Model laid the foundations for a host of different other actor systems and these three primitives can still be found in various modern actor languages and libraries today.

The main focus of his work was to produce a platform for distributed problem solving in networked workstations. In his model concurrent objects, i.e. actors, are self-contained, independent components that interact with each other by asynchronous message passing. In his work he presents three basic actor primitives:

- **create**: Creates an actor from a behaviour description. Returns the address of the newly created actor.
- **send**: Asynchronously sends a message from one actor to another by using the address of the receiver. Immediately returns and returns nothing.
- **become**: Replaces the behaviour of an actor. The next message that will be received by that actor is processed by the new behaviour.

The example in listing 1.2 is written in the Rosette actor language [36] which was based on this model.

```
(define Cell
  (mutable [content]
    [put [newcontent]
      (become Cell newcontent)]
    [get
      (return 'got-content content)]))

(define my-cell (create Cell 0))
(get my-cell)
```

Listing 1.2. An actor in Rosette.

The **mutable** form is used to create an *actor generator* that is bound to Cell. That generator can be used with the **create** form to create an instance of that actor. Each actor instance has its own mailbox and behaviour. Following the keyword **mutable** is a sequence of identifiers that specify the mutable fields of that actor. In our example, any `Cell` actor will have one mutable field, namely the content of that cell. Subsequently, a specification is provided detailing all messages that are understood by the actor. Each message is defined by a name, followed by a table of arguments. In this instance, the put message expects a value that represents the new content. Thereafter, the body outlines the manner in which each message should be processed. To modify the state of a mutable field, the `become` form may be utilized to replace the actor's behavior via the actor generator. Additionally, the `return` form serves to implicitly transmit the result of a computation back to the sender of the original message.

These three primitives are the basic building blocks for many actor systems today and have been very influential in the development of any actor language that follows this work. A modern implementation of the Actor Model based on Agha's work [4] is the Akka [1,19] actor library for Scala. However, there are many other library implementations of this model for different languages such as Smalltalk (Actalk [10]) and C++ (ACT++ [25], Broadway [34] and Thal [27]).

The sequential subset of an actor model is the subset of expressions out of which a behaviour can be composed. In the case of the Classic Actor Model this sequential subset is mostly functional. Any state changes are specified by replacing the behaviour of an actor. This has an important advantage over conventional assignment statements as this severely coarsens the granularity of side-effecting operations that need to be considered when analysing a system. On the one hand, an actor can only change its own behaviour, meaning that the state of each actor is fully isolated. On the other hand, changing the behaviour of an actor only comes into effect when processing the next message. This means that the processing of a single message can be regarded as a single isolated operation. Throughout the rest of this paper we refer to this principle as **the Isolated Turn Principle**. This mechanism allows state updates to be aggregated into a single become statement and significantly reduces the amount of control flow dependencies between statements.

3.1 The Isolated Turn Principle

The semantics of the Classic Actor Model enables a *macro-step semantics* [5]. With the macro-step semantics, the Actor Model provides an important property for formal reasoning about program semantics, which also provides additional guarantees to facilitate application development. The macro-step semantics says that in an Actor Model, the granularity of reasoning is at the level of a **turn**, i.e., an actor processing a single message from its mailbox. A turn starts when the actor retrieves the message from its mailbox and ends when that message is fully processed. A single turn can be regarded as being processed in a single isolated step. The Isolated Turn Principle leads to a convenient reduction of the overall state-space that has to be considered in the process of formal reasoning. Furthermore, this principle is directly beneficial to application programmers, because the amount of processing done within a single turn can be made as large or as small as necessary, which reduces the potential for problematic interactions.

In other words, this principle guarantees that, during a single turn, an actor has a consistent view about its state and its environment.

To satisfy this principle, an actor system must satisfy both safety and liveness properties:

Safety. To satisfy safety the state of an actor must be *fully isolated*. This property is mainly guaranteed by adopting a *no-shared-state* policy between actors. Any composite value that is transmitted across actor boundaries is either copied, proxied, transferred or immutable. This property ensures that the processing of a single message in the Actor Model is free of low-level data races. In addition, the processing of a message cannot be interleaved with the processing of other messages of the same actor unless the execution of those different messages is also fully isolated. For example, an actor for which the behaviour was modified can already act on other incoming messages before fully processing the current message. Or implementations of the actor model can enable parallel execution of read only messages [31] without impacting safety guarantees.

Liveness. To guarantee liveness, the processing of a message cannot contain any blocking operations. Any message is always entirely processed from start to finish. Because of this property, processing a single message is free of deadlocks.

From the two properties above follows that if an Actor Model satisfies the Isolated Turn Principle, it is free of low-level data races and deadlocks. However, unlike other concurrency models such as Futures [7], the actor model is not fully deterministic. The Isolated Turn Principle only applies for the processing of a single message, considering the processing of several messages, these properties no longer hold. On the one hand, as the actor model only guarantees isolation within a single turn, high-level race conditions can still occur with bad interleaving of different messages. The general consensus when programming in an actor system is that when an operation spans several messages the programmer must provide a custom synchronisation mechanism to prevent potential bad interleavings and ensure correct execution. On the other hand, high-level deadlocks can still occur when actors are waiting on each other to send a message before progress can be made. In this case, all actors involved in an interaction are stuck, each waiting for the other to initiate communication to advance the interaction. Additionally, livelock can also occur when actors are actively processing messages and changing state, but the system as a whole makes no meaningful progress toward completion.

3.2 Operational Semantics of the Classic Actor Model

In this section we present a minimal operational semantics for the Classic Actor Model. An executable implementation in PLT Redex of this operational semantics can be found online.[2] The goal of this operational semantics and the operational semantics presented in subsequent sections is to provide a precise formal

---

[2] https://gitlab.soft.vub.ac.be/jdekoste/actormodelhistorypltredex.

definition for each of the different actor families and to highlight their key differences. We borrow some terminology of object-oriented programming to remain consistent with our usage of terminology throughout this paper. More concretely, we use objects to represent the behaviour of an actor. An actor's behaviour is composed of its interface (i.e. the set of messages it understands) and its state. Both of these can be represented by an object, the interface of an actor's behaviour is represented by the class of the corresponding object and the state by that object's values for its fields.

Semantic Entities

$$k \in \textbf{Configuration} ::= A$$
$$a \in A \subseteq \textbf{Actor} ::= \mathcal{A}\langle \iota_a, \mu, e, o \rangle$$
$$\mu \in \textbf{Mailbox} ::= \overline{m}$$
$$m \in \textbf{Message} ::= \mathcal{M}\langle msg, \overline{v} \rangle$$
$$o \in \textbf{Object} ::= \mathcal{O}\langle cls, \overline{v} \rangle$$
$$v \in \textbf{Value} ::= r \mid \texttt{null}$$
$$r \in \textbf{Reference} ::= \iota_a$$

$$\iota_a \in \textbf{ActorId}$$

Fig. 1. Semantic entities of the Classic Actor Model

Figure 1 lists the semantic entities for the Classic Actor Model. Caligraphic letters like $\mathcal{A}$ and $\mathcal{M}$ are used as *constructors* to distinguish the different semantic entities syntactically instead of using bare cartesian products.

In the Classic Actor Model a **Configuration** K consists of a set of running actors A. A configuration represents the whole state of a program in a single step. Each **Actor** a is represented by an identifier ι_a, a mailbox μ, the expression it is currently evaluating e, and an object that represents its behaviour o. The object that represents an actor's behaviour represents both that actor's interface as well as its state. Classic Actors can change their behaviour using a become statement that replaces this object, thereby changing either their interface, their state, or both. A **Mailbox** μ is an ordered list of pending messages. A mailbox is ordered to guarantee per-sender message ordering. A **Message** m has a message name msg that acts as a selector to invoke the correct method of the behaviour of the receiving actor and an ordered list of values $\overline{v}$ that represent the arguments to the message. An **Object** o has a classname cls that defines the actor's interface and a set of fields $\overline{v}$ that represent the actor's state. For simplicity, we have restricted the set of possible values to either be a reference to an actor r or the null value null. A **Reference** is always represented by an Actor's Id ι_a.

Figure 2 lists the syntax, evaluation contexts and initial configuration for Classic Actor programs.

Syntax. A Classic Actor **Program** p is a set of class definitions C of which one class is the *Main* class that has to implement the *run* method. A **Class** has a classname cls, a list of instance variables or fields $\overline{x_f}$, and a set of methods M. Each **Method** has a methodname msg and an associated lambda $\lambda \overline{x_m}.e$ for which the body consists of a single expression e. The expressions of the Classic Actor Model features a minimal set of syntactical elements. Local variables can be introduced using a *let* expression. The pseudovariable *self* always refers to the enclosing actor. Expression sequences $e\,;\,e$ are only introduced for convenience and are syntactic sugar for nested *let* expressions. Finally, it has syntax for the three main primitives of the Classic Actor model, namely: create, send, and become. create creates a new actor from the behaviour defined by the class with classname cls and initialises it's fields, send is used to send a message to an actor, and become is used to replace the behaviour of an actor (i.e. its interface can be replaced with a different class and its state can be replaced with different values).

Syntax
$p \in \textbf{Program} ::= C$
$C \subseteq \textbf{Class} ::= \texttt{class}\ cls\ \{\overline{x_f}; M\}$
$M \subseteq \textbf{Method} ::= msg \to \lambda \overline{x_m}.e$
$e \in \textbf{Expression} ::= \texttt{self}\,|\,x\,|\,\texttt{null}\,|\,e;e\,|\,\texttt{let}\,x = e\,\texttt{in}\,e\,|$
$\qquad\qquad\qquad\quad \texttt{create}(cls, \overline{e})\,|\,\texttt{send}(e, msg, \overline{e})\,|\,\texttt{become}(cls, \overline{e})$

$x \in \textbf{VarName}, cls \in \textbf{ClassName}, msg \in \textbf{MessageName}$

Runtime Syntax
$e ::= \ldots\,|\,r$

Evaluation Contexts
$\mathcal{E} ::= \square\,|\,\texttt{let}\,x = \mathcal{E}\,\texttt{in}\,e\,|\,\texttt{create}(cls, \overline{v}, \mathcal{E}, \overline{e})\,|\,\texttt{send}(\mathcal{E}, msg, \overline{e})\,|$
$\qquad \texttt{send}(v, msg, \overline{v}, \mathcal{E}, \overline{e})\,|\,\texttt{become}(cls, \overline{v}, \mathcal{E}, \overline{e})$

Syntactic Sugar
$e\,;\,e' \stackrel{\text{def}}{=} \texttt{let}\,x = e\,\texttt{in}\,e'\quad x \notin \text{FV}(e')$

Initial Configuration
$K_{init} = \{\mathcal{A}\langle\iota_a, \emptyset, \texttt{send}(\iota_a, run, \emptyset), \mathcal{O}\langle Main, \emptyset\rangle\rangle\}$

Fig. 2. Syntax of the Classic Actor Model

Runtime Syntax. Our reduction rules operate on so-called run-time expressions; these are a superset of source-syntax phrases. The additional form represents references r that can be used as return values for the aforementioned primitives.

Evaluation Contexts. We use evaluation contexts [17] to indicate what subexpressions of an expression should be fully reduced before the compound expression itself can be further reduced. $\mathcal{E}$ denotes an expression with a "hole". Each appearance of $\mathcal{E}$ indicates a subexpression with a possible hole. The intent is for the hole to identify the next subexpression to reduce in a compound expression.

Initial Configuration. For any program p the set of class definitions C is constant. We therefore do not include it as part of the run-time configuration. The initial configuration is always a singleton set with the single main actor. The main actor is initialised with an empty mailbox, a single **send** expression to self-send the *run* method, and an object that is an instance of the *Main* class. That object represents the main actor's interface.

Reduction Rules

Notation. A configuration A is a set of actors. To lookup and extract values from a set we use the notation $A = A' \cup \{a\}$. This splits the set A into a singleton set containing the desired actor a and the disjoint set $A' = A \smallsetminus \{a\}$. The notation $\mu = \mu' \cdot m$ deconstructs a sequence μ into a subsequence μ' and the last element m. We denote both the empty set and the empty sequence using $\varnothing$. The notation $\mathcal{E}[e]$ indicates that the expression e is part of a compound expression $\mathcal{E}$, and should be reduced first before the compound expression can be reduced further. We use the notation $[v/x]e$ to denote a variable substitution where all occurrences of x in e are replaced by v. We don't have nested lambda's, thus avoiding the need for capture-avoiding substitution.

The reduction rules are split into two layers. The *actor-local reduction rules* ($\longrightarrow_a$) in Fig. 3 define the rules that reduce an actor's expression and that do not involve any additional actors (i.e. the expression can be reduced in isolation). The *actor-global reduction rules* ($\longrightarrow_k$) in Fig. 4 define rules that involve multiple actors.

Actor-Local Reductions. Actors operate by perpetually taking the first message that matches their interface from their mailbox and then evaluating (reducing) the associated expression to a value. Messages are matched from right to left. Classic Actors have out of order message processing, if a message does not currently match the actor's interface, it is simply skipped and remains in the actor's mailbox. Classic Actors also have a flexible interface (that can be changed using a **become** expression), this facilitates what is known as "conditional synchronisation" [11] (e.g. implementing a blocking bounded buffer, or other more complex forms of synchronisation).

If no reduction rule is applicable to further reduce an expression, i.e., when the reduction is *stuck*, this signifies an error in the program. The only valid state in which an actor cannot be further reduced is when its current expression is fully reduced to a value and no message in its mailbox matches its current interface.

$$\text{(LET)} \over \mathcal{A}\langle \iota_a, \mu, \mathcal{E}[\texttt{let }x = v\texttt{ in }e], o\rangle \longrightarrow_a \mathcal{A}\langle \iota_a, \mu, \mathcal{E}[[v/x]e], o\rangle$$

$$\text{(BECOME)} \quad {o' = \mathcal{O}\langle cls, \overline{v}\rangle \over \mathcal{A}\langle \iota_a, \mu, \mathcal{E}[\texttt{become}(cls, \overline{v})], o\rangle \longrightarrow_a \mathcal{A}\langle \iota_a, \mu, \mathcal{E}[\texttt{null}], o'\rangle}$$

$$\text{(SELF-SEND)} \over \mathcal{A}\langle \iota_a, \mu, \mathcal{E}[\texttt{send}(\iota_a, msg, \overline{v})], o\rangle \longrightarrow_a \mathcal{A}\langle \iota_a, \mu \cdot \mathcal{M}\langle msg, \overline{v}\rangle, \mathcal{E}[\texttt{null}], o\rangle$$

$$\text{(RECEIVE)} \quad {o = \mathcal{O}\langle cls, \overline{v_f}\rangle \quad \texttt{class } cls \; \{\overline{x_f}; M\} \in C \quad e, \mu' = \texttt{match}(M, \mu) \over \mathcal{A}\langle \iota_a, \mu, v, o\rangle \longrightarrow_a \mathcal{A}\langle \iota_a, \mu', [\iota_a/\texttt{self}][\overline{v_f}/\overline{x_f}]e, o\rangle}$$

Fig. 3. Local Reduction Rules for Classic Actor Model

A value cannot be further reduced and the actor sits idle until it receives a new message that does match its interface.

We now explain the actor-local reduction rules ($\longrightarrow_a$) found in Fig. 3:

- LET: Reducing a "let"-expression simply substitutes the value of x for v in e.
- BECOME: This rule describes how actors can change their behaviour using the **become** primitive. A new object is created and entirely replaces the original behaviour of that actor. The become expression itself reduces to `null`.
- SELF-SEND: An asynchronous message sent to the same actor simply appends a new message to the end of that actor's own mailbox. The message send itself immediately reduces to `null`.
- RECEIVE: This rule describes the processing of messages in the mailbox of an actor. A new message can be processed only if two conditions are satisfied: Firstly, one of the messages in the mailbox of the actor matches its interface, and secondly, the current expression of the actor cannot be reduced any further (the expression is a value v). To match a message from the actor's mailbox μ with that actor's interface M the auxiliary function `match` is used. This function returns the body expression e of the matched method and an updated mailbox μ where the matched message was removed.

Actor-Global Reductions. We now explain the actor-global reduction rules found in Fig. 4:

- SEND: An asynchronous message sent to a different actor appends that message to the front of the mailbox of the recipient actor (the actor with identifier $\iota_{a'}$). The send expression itself reduces to `null`.
- CREATE: Reducing a create expression adds a new actor to the set of actors of the configuration. The newly created actor is initialised with an empty mailbox, `null` as its expression (the actor will be in an idle state), and a newly created object as its behaviour. The create expression itself reduces to a reference to that newly created actor $\iota_{a'}$.

(SEND)
$$A \cup \{\mathcal{A}\langle\iota_a, \mu, \mathcal{E}[\texttt{send}(\iota_{a'}, msg, \overline{v})], o\rangle\} \cup \{\mathcal{A}\langle\iota_{a'}, \mu', e', o'\rangle\}$$
$$\rightarrow_k A \cup \{\mathcal{A}\langle\iota_a, \mu, \mathcal{E}[\texttt{null}], o\rangle\} \cup \{\mathcal{A}\langle\iota_{a'}, \mu' \cdot \mathcal{M}\langle msg, \overline{v}\rangle, e', o'\rangle\}$$

(CREATE)
$$\frac{\iota_{a'} \text{ fresh} \quad o' = \mathcal{O}\langle cls, \overline{v}\rangle}{A \cup \{\mathcal{A}\langle\iota_a, \mu, \mathcal{E}[\texttt{create}(cls, \overline{v})], o\rangle\} \rightarrow_k A \cup \{\mathcal{A}\langle\iota_a, \mu, \mathcal{E}[\iota_{a'}], o\rangle\} \cup \{\mathcal{A}\langle\iota_{a'}, \varnothing, \texttt{null}, o'\rangle\}}$$

(CONGRUENCE)
$$\frac{a \rightarrow_a a'}{A \cup \{a\} \rightarrow_k A \cup \{a'\}}$$

Fig. 4. Global Reduction Rules for Classic Actor Model

– CONGRUENCE: this rule connects the actor-local reduction rules to the global configuration reduction rules.

$$\text{match}(M, \mathcal{M}\langle msg, \overline{v}\rangle \cdot \mu) \stackrel{def}{=} [\overline{v}/\overline{x_m}]e, \mu \quad \text{if } msg \rightarrow \lambda\overline{x_m}.e \in M$$
$$\text{match}(M, m \cdot \mu) \stackrel{def}{=} e, m \cdot \mu' \quad \text{if } e, \mu' = \text{match}(M, \mu)$$

Fig. 5. Auxiliary Functions

Auxiliary Functions. The auxiliary function match finds the first message (going from left to right) in the mailbox μ that matches the selector msg. To find a match, the mailbox cannot be empty ($\mu \neq \varnothing$). It has two return values: the body expression of the associated lambda where all parameters $\overline{x_m}$ have been substituted by the arguments of the message $\overline{v}$, and an updated mailbox where the selected message has been removed (Fig. 5).

3.3 Conclusion

Similar to the uniform object model of SmallTalk, the Classic Actor Model implements a uniform actor model in which every entity is an actor. The sequential subset of the model is entirely functional, and any state transitions must be aggregated within a become statement. The core programming model of Classic Actors does not accommodate first-class mutable composite values. The subsequent section provides an overview of the Active Object Model, which features two layers of actors and their mutable objects as an integral part of the core programming model. These elements can also be incorporated into Classic Actors without violating the Isolated Turn Principle, provided that any mutable object is transferred between actors via deep copy or via ownership transfer. Another distinguishing characteristic of Classic Actors is their ability to modify their interface and process incoming messages out of sequence, thereby facilitating conditional synchronization.

4 The Active Object Model

Around the same time that Agha reformulated Hewitt's actors in terms of OOP, another PhD student of Carl Hewitt, Akinori Yonezawa, worked on an object-oriented concurrent programming language called ABCL/1 [40]. In this language, each object has its own thread of control and may have its own local mutable memory. In this model state changes are not specified in terms of behaviour updates (become) but rather by traditional assignment statements. To maintain actor isolation, the mutable state of each active object is only accessible and mutable by the object's own thread of control. This means that state updates are also isolated and because messages are processed entirely sequentially the Isolated Turn Principle also holds for active objects.

```
[object Cell
  (state [contents := nil])
  (script
    (=> [:put newContent]
      contents := newContent)
    (=> [:get] @ From
      From <= contents))]

Cell <= [:get]
```

Listing 1.3. An active object in ABCL/1.

While this paper considers ABCL/1 to be the first active object programming language, the term *active object* was only coined much later. Independently from Yonezawa's work, in the early 2000s a number of other actor programming languages within the family of active object languages have been proposed [8], namely ASP [13], Rebeca [32], ABS [24] and Encore [9]. The distinguishing feature of these programming languages is that they implement a double-layered programming model where actors are composed out of *active* and *passive* objects and all passive objects are owned by exactly one actor. Each actor has a single root object called the *active* object. Every other object that is encapsulated by that actor is called a *passive* object. Different actors do not share memory, the active objects' whole object graph is deep-copied into the actor. When actors send a message to another actor, any passive object that is transmitted (and the transitive closure of all objects referenced by that passive object) is also copied, thus maintaining a no-shared-state policy and therefore guaranteeing the Isolated Turn Principle. This double-layeredness of the active object model uniquely distinguishes it from other actor models. Other examples of actor languages based on the Active Object Model include SALSA [39] and Orleans [2].

4.1 Operational Semantics

In this section we provide a minimal operational semantics for the Active Object Model. An executable implementation in PLT Redex of this operational semantics can be found online.[3] Because the operational semantics for the Active Object Model shares some similarities with the one for the Classic Actor Model we will only highlight (in red) the differences between both formalisms.

$$
\begin{aligned}
k \in \textbf{Configuration} &::= A \\
a \in A \subseteq \textbf{Actor} &::= \mathcal{A}\langle \iota_a, \mu, e, O, o \rangle \\
\mu \in \textbf{Mailbox} &::= \overline{m} \\
m \in \textbf{Message} &::= \mathcal{M}\langle msg, \overline{v} \rangle \\
o \in O \subseteq \textbf{Object} &::= \mathcal{O}\langle \iota_o, cls, \overline{v} \rangle \\
v \in \textbf{Value} &::= r \mid \texttt{null} \\
r \in \textbf{Reference} &::= \iota_a \mid \iota_o
\end{aligned}
$$

$\iota_a \in \textbf{ActorId}, \iota_o \in \textbf{ObjectId}$

Fig. 6. Semantic entities of the Active Object Model

Figure 6 lists the semantic entities for the Active Object Model. In the Active Object Model, each **Actor** a is represented by an identifier ι_a, a mailbox μ, the expression it is currently evaluating e, a heap of passive objects O, and an active object that represents its interface o. Contrary to the Classic Actor Model, in this model there is no **become** primitive to change the behaviour of an actor. The Active Object Model is a double-layered actor model where the interface of an actor is defined by its active object (i.e. facade of the actor) o, and its state by a heap of passive objects O. The interface of an active object does not change throughout the lifetime of the actor (i.e. the interface is fixed). However, because passive objects are mutable, an actor can change its own state and can therefore change how it reacts to certain messages depending on that state. Any **Object** o in this model also has an identifier ι_o that uniquely identifies that object. Because objects are now also first-class entities, we extend **References** to also include object identifiers ι_o.

Figure 7 lists the syntax, evaluation contexts and initial configuration for Active Object programs.

Syntax. A **Program** p is a set of class definitions C of which one class is the *Main* class that has to implement the *run* method. The definition of **Classes** and **Methods** are identical to the ones for the Classic Actor Model. The expressions of the Active Object Model have been extended with new syntax to create and modify passive objects and the **become** primitive has been removed. The **new** primitive creates a new instance of a class with classname cls and initialises its

---

[3] https://gitlab.soft.vub.ac.be/jdekoste/actormodelhistorypltredex.

fields with the values for expressions $\bar{e}$. Referencing and modifying a field in an object is done through the $e.x$ and $e.x = e$ syntax respectively. The dot notation is also used for invoking a method on an object $e.msg(\bar{e})$.

Syntax
$p \in \textbf{Program} ::= C$
$C \subseteq \textbf{Class} ::= \texttt{class}\ cls\ \{\overline{x_f}; M\}$
$M \subseteq \textbf{Method} ::= msg \rightarrow \lambda \overline{x_m}.e$
$e \in \textbf{Expression} ::= \texttt{self} \mid x \mid \texttt{null} \mid e\ ;\ e \mid \texttt{let}\ x = e\ \texttt{in}\ e \mid \texttt{create}(cls, \bar{e}) \mid \texttt{send}(e, msg, \bar{e}) \mid$
$\qquad\qquad\qquad\quad \texttt{new}(cls, \bar{e}) \mid e.x \mid e.x = e \mid e.msg(\bar{e})$

$x \in \textbf{VarName}, cls \in \textbf{ClassName}, msg \in \textbf{MessageName}$

Runtime Syntax
$e ::= \ldots \mid r$

Evaluation Contexts
$\mathcal{E} ::= \square \mid \texttt{let}\ x = \mathcal{E}\ \texttt{in}\ e \mid \texttt{create}(cls, \bar{v}, \mathcal{E}, \bar{e}) \mid \texttt{send}(\mathcal{E}, msg, \bar{e}) \mid \texttt{send}(v, msg, \bar{v}, \mathcal{E}, \bar{e}) \mid$
$\qquad \texttt{new}(cls, \bar{v}, \mathcal{E}, \bar{e}) \mid \mathcal{E}.x \mid \mathcal{E}.x = e \mid v.x = \mathcal{E} \mid \mathcal{E}.msg(\bar{e}) \mid v.msg(\bar{v}, \mathcal{E}, \bar{e})$

Syntactic Sugar
$e\ ;\ e' \overset{\text{def}}{=} \texttt{let}\ x = e\ \texttt{in}\ e' \quad x \notin \text{FV}(e')$

Initial Configuration
$K_{init} = \{\mathcal{A}\langle\iota_a, \emptyset, \texttt{send}(\iota_a, run, \emptyset), \emptyset, \mathcal{O}\langle\iota_o, Main, \emptyset\rangle\rangle\}$

Fig. 7. Syntax of the Active Object Model

Evaluation Contexts. Evaluation contexts for the new syntax have been added to ensure the newly added compound expressions are also reduced from left to right.

Initial Configuration. The initial configuration is changed such that the single *Main* actor is now initialised with an empty heap of passive objects and a single active object with a unique identifier ι_o.

The reduction rules are split into two layers. The *actor-local reduction rules* ($\longrightarrow_a$) in Fig. 8 define the rules that reduce an actor's expression and that do not involve any additional actors (i.e. the expression can be reduced in isolation). The *actor-global reduction rules* ($\longrightarrow_k$) in Fig. 9 define rules that involve multiple actors.

Actor-Local Reductions. Actors operate by perpetually taking the first message from their mailbox and processing it. If the message matches the actor's interface, the associated expression is evaluated (reduced) to a value. When the expression is fully reduced, the next message is processed. Contrary to the Classic Actor Model, messages are always processed in FIFO order. If the first message in the mailbox of an actor does not match the interface of the active object, and if no actor-local reduction rule is applicable to further reduce an expression, i. e., when the reduction is *stuck*, this signifies an error in the program. The only valid state in which an actor cannot be further reduced is when its current expression is fully reduced to a value and its mailbox is empty. A value cannot be further reduced and the actor sits idle until it receives a new message.

$$\text{(LET)}$$
$$\mathcal{A}\langle \iota_a, \mu, \mathcal{E}[\texttt{let } x = v \texttt{ in } e], O, o\rangle$$
$$\longrightarrow_a \mathcal{A}\langle \iota_a, \mu, \mathcal{E}[[v/x]e], O, o\rangle$$

$$\text{(NEW)} \qquad\qquad \text{(INVOKE)}$$
$$\frac{\iota_o \text{ fresh} \quad o' = \mathcal{O}\langle \iota_o, cls, \overline{v}\rangle}{\mathcal{A}\langle \iota_a, \mu, \mathcal{E}[\texttt{new}(cls, \overline{v})], O, o\rangle \longrightarrow_a \mathcal{A}\langle \iota_a, \mu, \mathcal{E}[\iota_o], O \cup o', o\rangle} \qquad \frac{\mathcal{O}\langle \iota_o, cls, \overline{v_f}\rangle \in O \quad \texttt{class } cls\ \{\overline{x_f}; M\} \in C \quad msg \to \lambda \overline{x_m}.e \in M}{\mathcal{A}\langle \iota_a, \mu, \mathcal{E}[\iota_o.msg(\overline{v})], O, o\rangle \longrightarrow_a \mathcal{A}\langle \iota_a, \mu, \mathcal{E}[[\iota_a/\texttt{self}][\overline{v_f}/\overline{x_f}][\overline{v}/\overline{x_m}]e], O, o\rangle}$$

$$\text{(FIELD-ACCESS)} \qquad\qquad \text{(FIELD-UPDATE)}$$
$$\frac{o' = \mathcal{O}\langle \iota_o, cls, \overline{v_f}\rangle \quad o' \in O \quad v = \textsf{lookup}(o', x_f)}{\mathcal{A}\langle \iota_a, \mu, \mathcal{E}[\iota_o.x_f], O, o\rangle \longrightarrow_a \mathcal{A}\langle \iota_a, \mu, \mathcal{E}[v], O, o\rangle} \qquad \frac{o' = \mathcal{O}\langle \iota_o, cls, \overline{v_f}\rangle \quad o'' = \textsf{update-field}(o', x_f, v)}{\mathcal{A}\langle \iota_a, \mu, \mathcal{E}[\iota_o.x_f = v], O \cup o', o\rangle \longrightarrow_a \mathcal{A}\langle \iota_a, \mu, \mathcal{E}[v], O \cup o'', o\rangle}$$

$$\text{(SELF-SEND)}$$
$$\mathcal{A}\langle \iota_a, \mu, \mathcal{E}[\texttt{send}(\iota_a, msg, \overline{v})], O, o\rangle$$
$$\longrightarrow_a \mathcal{A}\langle \iota_a, \mu \cdot \mathcal{M}\langle msg, \overline{v}\rangle, \mathcal{E}[\texttt{null}], O, o\rangle$$

$$\text{(RECEIVE)}$$
$$\frac{o = \mathcal{O}\langle \iota_o, cls, \overline{v_f}\rangle \quad \texttt{class } cls\ \{\overline{x_f}; M\} \in C \quad msg \to \lambda \overline{x_m}.e \in M}{\mathcal{A}\langle \iota_a, \mathcal{M}\langle msg, \overline{v}\rangle \cdot \mu, v, O, o\rangle \longrightarrow_a \mathcal{A}\langle \iota_a, \mu, [\iota_a/\texttt{self}][\overline{v_f}/\overline{x_f}][\overline{v}/\overline{x_m}]e, O, o\rangle}$$

Fig. 8. Local Reduction Rules for the Active Object Model

We now explain the actor-local reduction rules ($\longrightarrow_a$) found in Fig. 8:

– LET: Reducing a "let"-expression simply substitutes the value of x for v in e.
– NEW: Newly created passive objects are always owned by the actor that creates them, i. e. the newly created object is added to the heap of the actor for which the **new** expression was reduced. A new object is created with a

fresh identifier ι_o, its classname cls, and the initial values for its field $\overline{v}$. That new object is added to the heap of the actor and the expression reduces to a reference to that object.
- INVOKE: Actors can only synchronously invoke methods on their own local passive objects, i.e. the object has to be part of the heap of that actor. The class of the object and the corresponding method are looked up in C and M respectively. Invoking a method reduces to the body expression of the corresponding method. In this expression, the method parameters $\overline{x_m}$ are substituted with their respective message arguments $\overline{v}$. The field variables $\overline{x_f}$ are substituted with the respective field values $\overline{v_f}$ of the passive object, and the pseudovariable `self` is substituted with the reference to the actor ι_a.
- FIELD-ACCESS: For accessing a field of a passive object that object has to be part of the actor's heap. The auxiliary function `lookup` is used to retrieve the value of the corresponding field and the expression reduces to that value.
- FIELD-UPDATE: For updating a field we first extract the corresponding passive object from the heap using $O \cup o'$ and then use the auxiliary function `update-field` to change the value of the corresponding field in the object. The modified object is added again to the heap of the actor using $O \cup o''$ and the expression reduces to the value that was assigned to the field v.
- SELF-SEND: An asynchronous message sent to the same actor simply appends a new message to the end of that actor's own mailbox. The message send itself immediately reduces to `null`.
- RECEIVE: For Active Object actors, a new message can only be processed only if the current expression of the actor cannot be reduced any further (the expression is a value v). Unlike the Classic Actor Model, messages are always processed from left to right. The interface of an active object is fixed; consequently, a message is either understood or not, and deferring its execution offers no benefit. The first message is extracted from the mailbox of the actor using $\mathcal{M}\langle msg, \overline{v}\rangle \cdot \mu$. The corresponding method is looked up in the interface of the active object o. If there is no match, the evaluation is *stuck* and this signifies an error in the program. Finally, the current expression of the actor is replaced with the body expression of the corresponding method.

Actor-Global Reductions. We now explain the actor-global reduction rules found in Fig. 9:

- CREATE: Reducing a create expression adds a new actor to the set of actors of the configuration. To preserve actor isolation, active objects adopt a strict no-shared-state policy. As such, any passive object that is referenced by the arguments of the create primitive must be deep copied. The auxiliary function `pass` is used to create a set of passive objects O' that contains copies for all the objects that are in the transitive closure of the objects referenced by the arguments $\overline{v}$. It also returns a list $\overline{v'}$ with all the fresh references to the copied objects in $\overline{v}$. The newly created actor is initialised with an empty mailbox `null` as its expression (i.e. the actor will be in an idle state), the

$$\text{(CREATE)}$$
$$\frac{\iota_{a'}, \iota_o \text{ fresh} \quad \overline{v'}, O' = \mathsf{pass}(\overline{v}, O) \quad o' = \mathcal{O}\langle \iota_o, cls, \overline{v'}\rangle}{A \cup \{\mathcal{A}\langle \iota_a, \mu, \mathcal{E}[\mathtt{create}(cls, \overline{v})], O, o\rangle\} \longrightarrow_k A \cup \{\mathcal{A}\langle \iota_a, \mu, \mathcal{E}[\iota_{a'}], O, o\rangle\} \cup \{\mathcal{A}\langle \iota_{a'}, \varnothing, \mathtt{null}, O', o'\rangle\}}$$

$$\text{(SEND)}$$
$$\frac{\overline{v'}, O' = \mathsf{pass}(\overline{v}, O)}{A \cup \{\mathcal{A}\langle \iota_a, \mu, \mathcal{E}[\mathtt{send}(\iota_{a'}, msg, \overline{v})], O, o\rangle\} \cup \{\mathcal{A}\langle \iota_{a'}, \mu', e', O'', o'\rangle\} \longrightarrow_k A \cup \{\mathcal{A}\langle \iota_a, \mu, \mathcal{E}[\mathtt{null}], O, o\rangle\} \cup \{\mathcal{A}\langle \iota_{a'}, \mu' \cdot \mathcal{M}\langle msg, \overline{v'}\rangle, e', O'' \cup O', o'\rangle\}}$$

$$\text{(CONGRUENCE)}$$
$$\frac{a \longrightarrow_a u'}{A \cup \{a\} \longrightarrow_k A \cup \{a'\}}$$

Fig. 9. Global Reduction Rules for the Active Object Model

set of copied passive objects O' as its heap, and a newly created object o' as its active object. The create expression itself reduces to a reference to that newly created actor $\iota_{a'}$.
- SEND: An asynchronous message sent to a different actor appends that message to the front of the mailbox of the recipient actor (the actor with identifier $\iota_{a'}$). Similar to create, the auxiliary function pass is used to create a set of passive objects O' that contains copies for all the objects that are in the transitive closure of the objects referenced by the message arguments. The set of copied objects is added to the heap of the recipient actor using $O'' \cup O'$. The copied objects are added to the receiving actor before the message is processed. Because all references in $\overline{v'}$ are fresh and references cannot be forged, these objects will only be accessible once the message is taken from the actor's mailbox and processed. The send expression itself reduces to null.
- CONGRUENCE: this rule connects the actor-local reduction rules to the global configuration reduction rules.

Auxiliary Functions. The auxiliary functions lookup and update-field simply lookup a field or modify a field of a given passive object respectively.

The auxiliary function reach constructs a set of objects that is the transitive closure of all objects referenced by $\overline{v}$. Matching objects are removed from the original heap one by one using $O \cup o$. Every time this is done, all references to passive objects by the fields of removed object $\overline{v_f}$, are added to the list of *reachable* object references. If a reference is no longer part of the set of passive objects because it was previously removed (e. g. because of a circular reference), the reference is simply ignored and removed from the list.

The auxiliary function pass constructs a new set of copied objects that is the transitive closure of all objects referenced by $\overline{v}$. It uses the auxiliary function reach to first construct the set of all reachable objects O' and then constructs a new set O'' by replacing each object in O' with a copy for which its identifier and fields are replaced by fresh object identifiers given by σ. σ is a function that maps object identifiers ι_o in the original heap to fresh object identifiers $\iota_{o'}$. All other values (i.e. actor identifiers ι_a) are left unchanged.

$$\text{lookup}(\mathcal{O}\langle\iota_o, cls, \overline{v_f}\rangle, x_f) \stackrel{def}{=} \text{lookup}(\overline{x_f}, \overline{v_f}, x_f) \qquad \text{if class } cls \{\overline{x_f}; M\} \in C$$
$$\text{lookup}(x_f \cdot \overline{x_f}, v_f \cdot \overline{v_f}, x_f) \stackrel{def}{=} v$$
$$\text{lookup}(x'_f \cdot \overline{x_f}, v_f \cdot \overline{v_f}, x_f) \stackrel{def}{=} \text{lookup}(\overline{x_f}, \overline{v_f}, x_f)$$

$$\text{update-field}(\mathcal{O}\langle\iota_o, cls, \overline{v_f}\rangle, x_f, v) \stackrel{def}{=} \mathcal{O}\langle\iota_o, cls, \text{update-field}(\overline{x_f}, \overline{v_f}, x_f, v)\rangle \qquad \text{if class } cls \{\overline{x_f}; M\} \in C$$
$$\text{update-field}(x_f \cdot \overline{x_f}, v_f \cdot \overline{v_f}, x_f, v) \stackrel{def}{=} v \cdot \overline{v_f}$$
$$\text{update-field}(x'_f \cdot \overline{x_f}, v_f \cdot \overline{v_f}, x_f, v) \stackrel{def}{=} v_f \cdot \text{update-field}(\overline{x_f}, \overline{v_f}, x_f, v)$$

$$\text{reach}(\emptyset, \overline{v}) \stackrel{def}{=} \emptyset$$
$$\text{reach}(O, \emptyset) \stackrel{def}{=} \emptyset$$
$$\text{reach}(O \cup o, \overline{v} \cdot \iota_o) \stackrel{def}{=} o \cup \text{reach}(O, \overline{v} \cdot \overline{v_f}) \qquad \text{if } o = \mathcal{O}\langle\iota_o, cls, \overline{v_f}\rangle$$
$$\text{reach}(O, \overline{v} \cdot v) \stackrel{def}{=} \text{reach}(O, \overline{v}) \qquad \text{otherwise}$$

$$\text{pass}(\overline{v}, O) \stackrel{def}{=} \overline{\sigma(v)}, O''$$
$$\text{where } O' = reach(O, \overline{v})$$
$$O'' = \{\mathcal{O}\langle\sigma(\iota_o), cls, \overline{\sigma(v_f)}\rangle \mid \mathcal{O}\langle\iota_o, cls, \overline{v_f}\rangle \in O'\}$$
$$\sigma' = \{\iota_o \mapsto \iota'_o \mid \mathcal{O}\langle\iota_o, cls, \overline{v_f}\rangle \in O', \iota'_o \text{ fresh }\}$$

$$\sigma(v) \begin{cases} \sigma'(v) & \text{if } v \in \textbf{ObjectId} \\ v & \text{otherwise} \end{cases}$$

Fig. 10. Auxiliary Functions

4.2 Conclusion

The Active Object Model is characterised by its two-layered programming model consisting of *active* and *passive* objects. The sequential subset of the model follows an imperative paradigm, and to ensure actor isolation, any mutable object is consistently transferred by deep copy between actors. This mechanism ensures that the Active Object Model adheres to the Isolated Turn Principle. Active objects possess a single entry point, which is defined by a fixed interface (i.e. the active object) (Fig. 10).

5 Processes

Independently from Gul Agha and Akinori Yonezawa, T. Hoare, was also inspired by Carl Hewitt's Actor Model of computation. This inspiration lead him, in 1978, to introduce the formal language communicating sequential processes [23] to study the interactions between concurrent processes. Almost a decade later, in 1986, Joe Armstrong developed the first version of the Erlang programming language [6] while working for Ericsson and Ellemtel Computer Science Laboratories. The sequential parts of Erlang are heavily inspired by Prolog. Erlang draws a lot of inspiration from CSP for its concurrency model. Although none of the early papers about Erlang directly reference the Actor Model, its influence on the concurrency model of Erlang is undeniable. We therefore consider Erlang to be the first industry-strength language to adopt the actor model as its model of concurrency. It was developed as a declarative language for programming large industrial telecommunications switching systems.

While the communication mechanism of Erlang's processes is very close to that of the Classic Actor Model, different mechanics are used to achieve similar effects. Most notably, an actor is not modelled as a named behaviour. Rather actors are modelled as processes that run from start till completion. Erlang actors can use the primitive `receive` to specify what messages the executing actor can receive when the execution of a process reaches that expression. When evaluating a `receive` expression the actor pauses until a message is received. If a message is received, the matching code is evaluated and execution continues until a new `receive` block is evaluated. One can use recursion to ensure that an actor continuously processes incoming messages. What types of messages an actor understands throughout its lifetime is determined by the dynamic extent of the expression it is reducing.

```
loop(Contents) ->
  receive
    {put, NewContent} ->
      loop(NewContent);
    {get, From} ->
      From ! Contents,
      loop(Contents)
  end.

MyCell = spawn(loop, [nil]).
MyCell ! {get, self()}.
```

Listing 1.4. An Erlang process.

This is illustrated by listing 1.4. The `spawn` primitive creates a new Erlang process. This will call the provided function, `loop`, in a new process and returns that process' id. The cell uses the primitive `receive` to match incoming get- and put-messages. Once the message body is processed the loop function calls itself recursively to process the next message, passing along the updated state.

The Scala Actor Library [20] is another well-known implementation of the Process model. Other examples include Kilim [33] and SALSA [38].

5.1 Operational Semantics

In this section we provide a minimal operational semantics for the Process Model. An executable implementation in PLT Redex of this operational semantics can be found online.[4] In red, we highlight the differences between this formal specification and the one for the Classic Actor Model.

Figure 11 lists the semantic entities for the Process Model. In the Process Model, each **Actor** a is represented by an identifier ι_a, a mailbox μ, and the expression it is currently evaluating e. Contrary to the Classic Actor Model, the behaviour (i.e. interface and state) is defined by the expression the actor is currently reducing. An actor can *change* its interface by using the primitive `receive` to specify what types of messages it understands. The state of an actor is modeled by the expression itself. the Process Model is not a double-layered actor model, so we do not model objects in this formalism.

$$k \in \textbf{Configuration} ::= A$$
$$a \in A \subseteq \textbf{Actor} ::= \mathcal{A}\langle \iota_a, \mu, e \rangle$$
$$\mu \in \textbf{Mailbox} ::= \overline{m}$$
$$m \in \textbf{Message} ::= \mathcal{M}\langle msg, \overline{v} \rangle$$
$$v \in \textbf{Value} ::= r \mid \texttt{null}$$
$$r \in \textbf{Reference} ::= \iota_a$$

$$\iota_a \in \textbf{ActorId}$$

Fig. 11. Semantic entities of the Process Model

Figure 12 lists the syntax, evaluation contexts and initial configuration for the Process Model.

Syntax. Contrary to the Classic Actor Model and the Active Object Model, a Process **Program** p is a set of functions M (here called **Methods**, for consistency with the other formalisms). This set remains constant throughout the lifetime of the program execution and must contain a single method named *run*. The syntax for expressions is extended with function application $msg(\overline{e})$ and a new `receive` primitive. A new actor is no longer created (i.e. initialised) from a class name, but rather from a method name. Creating a new actor simply executes the corresponding method using the provided arguments in a new process.

Evaluation Contexts. Evaluation contexts for function application have been added to ensure arguments are also deterministically reduced from left to right.

---

[4] https://gitlab.soft.vub.ac.be/jdekoste/actormodelhistorypltredex.

Syntax
$p \in$ **Program** ::= M
$M \subseteq$ **Method** ::= $msg \to \lambda \overline{x_m}.e$
$e \in$ **Expression** ::= $\texttt{self} \mid x \mid \texttt{null} \mid e\,;\,e \mid msg(\bar{e}) \mid \texttt{let}\,x = e\,\texttt{in}\,e \mid$
$\qquad\qquad\qquad \texttt{create}(msg, \bar{e}) \mid \texttt{send}(e, msg, \bar{e}) \mid \texttt{receive}(\overline{msg \to \lambda \overline{x_m}.e})$

$x \in$ **VarName**, $msg \in$ **MessageName**

Runtime Syntax
$e ::= \ldots \mid r$

Evaluation Contexts
$\mathcal{E} ::= \square \mid msg(\bar{v}, \mathcal{E}, \bar{e}) \mid \texttt{let}\,x = \mathcal{E}\,\texttt{in}\,e \mid \texttt{create}(msg, \bar{v}, \mathcal{E}, \bar{e}) \mid \texttt{send}(\mathcal{E}, msg, \bar{e}) \mid \texttt{send}(v, msg, \bar{v}, \mathcal{E}, \bar{e})$

Syntactic Sugar
$e\,;\,e' \stackrel{\text{def}}{=} \texttt{let}\,x = e\,\texttt{in}\,e' \quad x \notin \text{FV}(e')$

Initial Configuration
$K_{init} = \{\mathcal{A}\langle \iota_a, \varnothing, run()\rangle\}$

Fig. 12. Syntax of the Process Model

Initial Configuration. The initial configuration is changed such that the single main actor is now initialised with a single expression that simply calls the main *run* method.

The reduction rules are again split into two layers (i. e. *actor-local reduction rules* $\longrightarrow_a$ and *actor-global reduction rules* $\longrightarrow_k$.

Actor-Local Reductions. Actors in this model are processes that run from start till completion. With respect to the operational semantics, this means that an actor will keep reducing its expression until it is fully reduced to a value. For simplicity, we do not model the removal of such actors from the configuration. Rather, when that happens, the actor sits idle and will no longer be able to process any incoming messages. If no reduction rule is applicable to further reduce an expression, i. e., when the reduction is *stuck*, this signifies an error in the program. The only valid state in which an actor cannot be further reduced is when its current expression is fully reduced to a value or when the current evaluation context contains a $\texttt{receive}$ expression and none of the messages in its mailbox match with the interface of that expression. When that happens, the actor sits idle until it receives a new message that does match its interface.

We now explain the actor-local reduction rules ($\longrightarrow_a$) found in Fig. 13:

- LET: Reducing a "let"-expression simply substitutes the value of x for v in e.
- RECEIVE: This rule describes the processing of messages in the mailbox of an actor. A new message can be processed only if two conditions are satisfied: the current evaluation context contains a $\texttt{receive}$ expression and one of the messages in the mailbox of the actor matches that $\texttt{receive}$ expression's interface. To match a message from the actor's mailbox the auxiliary function $\texttt{match}$ is used. This function returns the body expression e of the matched method

$$\text{(LET)} \over A\langle \iota_a, \mu, \mathcal{E}[\texttt{let } x = v \texttt{ in } e]\rangle \longrightarrow_a A\langle \iota_a, \mu, \mathcal{E}[[v/x]e]\rangle$$

$$\text{(RECEIVE)} \quad {e, \mu' = \text{match}(\overline{msg \to \lambda \overline{x_m}.e}, \mu) \over A\langle \iota_a, \mu, \mathcal{E}[\texttt{receive}(\overline{msg \to \lambda \overline{x_m}.e})]\rangle \longrightarrow_a A\langle \iota_a, \mu', \mathcal{E}[e]\rangle}$$

$$\text{(CALL)} \quad {msg \to \lambda \overline{x_m}.e \in M \over A\langle \iota_a, \mu, \mathcal{E}[msg(\overline{v})]\rangle \longrightarrow_a A\langle \iota_a, \mu, \mathcal{E}[[\iota_a/\texttt{self}][\overline{v}/\overline{x_m}]e]\rangle}$$

$$\text{(SELF-SEND)} \over A\langle \iota_a, \mu, \mathcal{E}[\texttt{send}(\iota_a, msg, \overline{v})]\rangle \longrightarrow_a A\langle \iota_a, \mu \cdot M\langle msg, \overline{v}\rangle, \mathcal{E}[\texttt{null}]\rangle$$

Fig. 13. Local Reduction Rules for Process Model

and an updated mailbox μ where the matched message was removed. The receive expression reduces to the body expression of the associated method and the actor's mailbox is updated.
- CALL: When an actor calls a function, that function is looked up in the constant set of functions M. The call expression reduces to the body expression of the corresponding method where the parameters $\overline{x_m}$ are substituted with the arguments to the call $\overline{v}$ and the pseudovariable self is substituted with a reference to the current actor ι_a.
- SELF-SEND: An asynchronous message sent to the same actor simply appends a new message to the end of that actor's own mailbox. The message send itself immediately reduces to null.

$$\text{(CREATE)} \quad {\iota_{a'} \text{ fresh} \quad msg \to \lambda \overline{x_m}.e \in M \over A \cup \{A\langle \iota_a, \mu, \mathcal{E}[\texttt{create}(msg, \overline{v})]\rangle\} \longrightarrow_k A \cup \{A\langle \iota_a, \mu, \mathcal{E}[\iota_{a'}]\rangle\} \cup \{A\langle \iota_{a'}, \varnothing, [\iota_{a'}/\texttt{self}][\overline{v}/\overline{x_m}]e\rangle\}}$$

$$\text{(SEND)} \over A \cup \{A\langle \iota_a, \mu, \mathcal{E}[\texttt{send}(\iota_{a'}, msg, \overline{v})]\rangle\} \cup \{A\langle \iota_{a'}, \mu', e'\rangle\} \longrightarrow_k A \cup \{A\langle \iota_a, \mu, \mathcal{E}[\texttt{null}]\rangle\} \cup \{A\langle \iota_{a'}, \mu' \cdot M\langle msg, \overline{v}\rangle, e'\rangle\}$$

$$\text{(CONGRUENCE)} \quad {a \longrightarrow_a a' \over A \cup \{a\} \longrightarrow_k A \cup \{a'\}}$$

Fig. 14. Global Reduction Rules for Process Model

Actor-Global Reductions. We now explain the actor-global reduction rules found in Fig. 14:
- CREATE: Reducing a create expression adds a new actor to the set of actors of the configuration. The newly created actor is initialised with a fresh identifier $\iota_{a'}$ and an empty mailbox. The method named msg is looked up in the constant set of methods M. The create expression reduces to the body

expression of the corresponding method where the parameters $\overline{x_m}$ are substituted with the arguments to the create expression $\overline{v}$ and the pseudovariable self is substituted with a reference to the newly created actor $\iota_{a'}$. The create expression itself reduces to the same reference to the newly created actor $\iota_{a'}$.
- SEND: An asynchronous message sent to a different actor appends that message to the front of the mailbox of the recipient actor (the actor with identifier ι_a). The send expression itself reduces to null.
- CONGRUENCE: this rule connects the actor-local reduction rules to the global configuration reduction rules.

$$\text{match}(M, \mathcal{M}\langle msg, \overline{v}\rangle \cdot \mu) \stackrel{def}{=} [\overline{v}/\overline{x_m}]e, \mu \quad \text{if } msg \to \lambda\overline{x_m}.e \in M$$
$$\text{match}(M, m \cdot \mu) \stackrel{def}{=} e, m \cdot \mu' \quad \text{if } e, \mu' = \text{match}(M, \mu)$$

Fig. 15. Auxiliary Functions

Auxiliary Functions. The auxiliary function match is identical to the one for the Classic Actor Model. It finds the first message (going from left to right) in the mailbox μ that matches the selector msg. It has two return values: the body expression of the associated lambda where all parameters $\overline{x_m}$ have been substituted by the arguments of the message $\overline{v}$ and an updated mailbox where the selected message has been removed (Fig. 15).

5.2 Conclusion

In the Process Model, actors are represented as processes that operate from start to completion. The interface of an actor is flexible and is defined by the dynamic extent of the expression it is reducing. Consequently, it is not always feasible to determine statically what interface an actor will possess throughout its lifespan. Nonetheless, this flexible interface facilitates processes in expressing conditional synchronization. Similar to the Classic Actor Model, state changes are aggregated in a single receive statement. Therefore, the process model also adheres to the Isolated Turn Principle.

6 Communicating Event Loops

Vulcan [26] is a concurrent object-oriented logic programming language that was also inspired by Hewitt's actor model of computation. It was developed in 1986 as a preprocessor for Concurrent Prolog by Kahn et al. at Xerox PARC. Dean Tribble, an intern at Xerox PARC during the eighties, developed the distributed programming language Joule in 1994. Joule can be seen as the most direct and important ancestor of the E programming language [29] developed by Mark Miller. E was the first language to introduce *the Communicating Event-loop Actor Model*. Similar to the Active Object Model, the Communicating Event-loop Actor Model is a double-layered model where actors (called *vats* in E) and objects co-exist. However, it has an important difference when compared to the Active Object Model in that it does not make a distinction between passive and active objects. In this model, actors do not have a single active object that serves as the entry point to that actor. Actors are not even first-class entities in this model. Rather, actors can obtain direct references to objects in the heap of another actor. Within an actor, references to objects owned by that same actor are called *near references*. References to objects owned by other actors are called *far references*. The type of reference determines the access capabilities of that actor's thread of execution on the referenced object. While actors can obtain direct references to objects owned by a different actor (far reference), they are not allowed to make immediate calls on those references. Generally, actors are introduced to one another by exchanging addresses. In the Communicating Event Loop model such an address is always in the form of a far reference to a specific object. The referenced object then defines how another actor can interface with that actor. The main difference between Communicating Event Loops (CEL) and other actor models seen so far was that other actor models usually only provide a single entry point or address to an actor (in other words, at any point in time, an actor can have only a single interface). A CEL actor can define multiple objects that all share the same mailbox and thread of control and hand out different references to those objects, thus essentially allowing one to model an actor that has multiple interfaces at the same time. This helps support a PoLP (principle of least privilege) style of programming [30], by facilitating the creation of many small, object-level interfaces, rather than a single large actor-level interface. The example in listing 1.5 illustrates how to create an object in E and send it an asynchronous message get.

When an object in one actor sends an asynchronous message to an object in another actor the message is enqueued in the mailbox of the owner of the receiver object and immediately returns a *promise*. That promise will be resolved with the return value of the message once that message is processed. It is not allowed for an actor to use a promise as a near reference. If an actor wants to make an immediate call on the value represented by a promise, like printing it on the screen, that actor must set up an action to occur when the promise resolves. This is done by using the when primitive. Promises in E are based on Argus's promises [28]. With the main difference being that accessing a promise in Argus is a blocking operation while E adopts a purely asynchronous model (i. e. executing the when primitive is also an asynchronous operation). When the promise for the value of the get message becomes resolved, the body of the when primitive is executed. During that execution the promise is resolved and can be used as a local object.

```
def cell {
  var contents := null
  to put(newContents) {
    contents := newContents
  }
  to get() {
    return contents
  }
}

var promise := cell<-get()
when (promise) -> {
  println(promise)
}
```

Listing 1.5. An actor in E.

The Communicating Event Loop model was later adopted by AmbientTalk [37], a distributed object-oriented programming language that was designed for developing applications on mobile ad hoc networks. AmbientTalk was designed as an *ambient-oriented programming* (AmOP) language [16]. It adds to the Actor Model a number of new primitives to handle disconnecting and reconnecting nodes in a network where connections are volatile. The core concurrency model however remains faithful to the original Communicating Event Loops of E.

6.1 Operational Semantics

In this section we provide a minimal operational semantics for Communicating Event Loops. An executable implementation in PLT Redex of this operational semantics can be found online.[5] Because the operational semantics for Communicating Event Loops shares a lot of similarities with the one for the Active Object Model we will only highlight (in red) the differences between both formalisms.

$$
\begin{aligned}
k \in \textbf{Configuration} &::= A \\
a \in A \subseteq \textbf{Actor} &::= \mathcal{A}\langle \iota_a, \mu, e, O \rangle \\
\mu \in \textbf{Mailbox} &::= \overline{m} \\
m \in \textbf{Message} &::= \mathcal{M}\langle \iota_o, msg, \overline{v} \rangle \\
o \in O \subseteq \textbf{Object} &::= \mathcal{O}\langle \iota_o, cls, \overline{v} \rangle \\
v \in \textbf{Value} &::= r \mid \texttt{null} \\
r \in \textbf{Reference} &::= \iota_a.\iota_o
\end{aligned}
$$

$$\iota_a \in \textbf{ActorId}, \iota_o \in \textbf{ObjectId}$$

Fig. 16. Semantic entities of the Communicating Event Loops Model

---

[5] https://gitlab.soft.vub.ac.be/jdekoste/actormodelhistorypltredex.

Figure 16 lists the semantic entities for Communicating Event Loops. In Communicating Event Loops, each **Actor** a is represented by an identifier ι_a, a mailbox μ, the expression it is currently evaluating e, and a heap of objects O. Contrary to the Active Object Model, there is no single active object that serves as the entry point to an actor. Rather, actors can share far references to objects in their own heap with other actors. Far references are modeled as a double identifier $\iota_a.\iota_o$ that identifies the referenced object and the actor that owns that object. Each of these far references can be used by other actors to send asynchronous messages. Therefore, any such far reference can serve as an entry point to an actor. However, the interface of the referenced objects cannot change throughout the lifetime of the actor. That means, while a Communicating Event-loop actor can have many interfaces, they remain fixed. Because messages are sent to an object within the heap of an actor, a **Message** has an additional identifier ι_o that identifies the target object of the message that was received.

Figure 17 lists the syntax, evaluation contexts and initial configuration for Communicating Event-loop Actor programs.

Syntax. Identical to the Classic Actor Model and the Active Object Model, a **Program** p is a set of class definitions C of which one class is the *Main* class that has to implement the *run* method. The definition of **Classes** and **Methods** has been left unchanged. With respect to the Active Object Model, the set of expressions that are part of the syntax also remains identical.

Syntax
$p \in$ **Program** ::= C
$C \subseteq$ **Class** ::= class cls $\{\overline{x_f}; M\}$
$M \subseteq$ **Method** ::= $msg \to \lambda \overline{x_m}.e$
$e \in$ **Expression** ::= self $\mid x \mid$ null $\mid e; e \mid$ let $x = e$ in $e \mid$ create$(cls, \overline{e}) \mid$ send$(e, msg, \overline{e}) \mid$
new$(cls, \overline{e}) \mid e.x \mid e.x = e \mid e.msg(\overline{e})$

$x \in$ **VarName**, $cls \in$ **ClassName**, $msg \in$ **MessageName**

Runtime Syntax
$e ::= \ldots \mid r$

Evaluation Contexts
$\mathcal{E} ::= \square \mid$ let $x = \mathcal{E}$ in $e \mid$ create$(cls, \overline{v}, \mathcal{E}, \overline{e}) \mid$ send$(\mathcal{E}, msg, \overline{e}) \mid$ send$(v, msg, \overline{v}, \mathcal{E}, \overline{e}) \mid$
new$(cls, \overline{v}, \mathcal{E}, \overline{e}) \mid \mathcal{E}.x \mid \mathcal{E}.x = e \mid v.x = \mathcal{E} \mid \mathcal{E}.msg(\overline{e}) \mid v.msg(\overline{v}, \mathcal{E}, \overline{e})$

Syntactic Sugar
$e; e' \stackrel{\text{def}}{=}$ let $x = e$ in e' $x \notin \text{FV}(e')$

Initial Configuration
$K_{init} = \{\mathcal{A}\langle \iota_a, \emptyset, \iota_a.\iota_o.run(), \{\mathcal{O}\langle \iota_o, Main, \emptyset\rangle\}\rangle\}$

Fig. 17. Syntax of the Communicating Event Loops Model

Initial Configuration. The initial configuration is changed such that the single *Main* actor is now initialised with a singleton set containing an object that is an instance of the *Main* class. The actor's expression is initialised with $\iota_a.\iota_o.run()$, which will synchronously invoke the *run* method on that object.

Actor-Local Reductions. Actors operate by perpetually taking the first message from their mailbox and processing it. Any received message is simply forwarded to the recipient object by synchronously invoking the corresponding method on that object. When the invocation expression is fully reduced to a value, the next message can be processed. Contrary to the Classic Actor Model and the Process Model, messages are always processed in order. If the first message in the mailbox of an actor does not match the interface of the recipient object, or if no actor-local reduction rule is applicable to further reduce an expression, i.e., when the reduction is *stuck*, this signifies an error in the program. The only valid state in which an actor cannot be further reduced is when its current expression is fully reduced to a value and its mailbox is empty. A value cannot be further reduced and the actor sits idle until it receives a new message.

(LET)
$$\mathcal{A}\langle \iota_a, \mu, \mathcal{E}[\texttt{let } x = v \texttt{ in } e], O\rangle$$
$$\longrightarrow_a \mathcal{A}\langle \iota_a, \mu, \mathcal{E}[[v/x]e], O\rangle$$

(INVOKE)
$$\mathcal{O}\langle \iota_o, cls, \overline{v_f}\rangle \in O$$
$$\texttt{class } cls \{\overline{x_f}; M\} \in C$$
$$msg \rightarrow \lambda \overline{x_m}.e \in M$$

(NEW)
ι_o fresh $o = \mathcal{O}\langle \iota_o, cls, \overline{v}\rangle$
$$\mathcal{A}\langle \iota_a, \mu, \mathcal{E}[\texttt{new}(cls, \overline{v})], O\rangle$$
$$\longrightarrow_a \mathcal{A}\langle \iota_a, \mu, \mathcal{E}[\iota_a.\iota_o], O \cup o\rangle$$

$$\mathcal{A}\langle \iota_a, \mu, \mathcal{E}[\iota_a.\iota_o.msg(\overline{v})], O\rangle$$
$$\longrightarrow_a \mathcal{A}\langle \iota_a, \mu, \mathcal{E}[[\iota_a.\iota_o/\texttt{self}][\overline{v_f}/\overline{x_f}][\overline{v}/\overline{x_m}]e], O\rangle$$

(FIELD-ACCESS)
$o = \mathcal{O}\langle \iota_o, cls, \overline{v_f}\rangle$ $o \in O$
$v = \texttt{lookup}(o, x_f)$
$$\mathcal{A}\langle \iota_a, \mu, \mathcal{E}[\iota_a.\iota_o.x_f], O\rangle$$
$$\longrightarrow_a \mathcal{A}\langle \iota_a, \mu, \mathcal{E}[v], O\rangle$$

(FIELD-UPDATE)
$o = \mathcal{O}\langle \iota_o, cls, \overline{v_f}\rangle$
$o' = \texttt{update-field}(o, x_f, v)$
$$\mathcal{A}\langle \iota_a, \mu, \mathcal{E}[\iota_a.\iota_o.x_f = v], O \uplus o\rangle$$
$$\longrightarrow_a \mathcal{A}\langle \iota_a, \mu, \mathcal{E}[v], O \cup o'\rangle$$

(SELF-SEND)
$$\mathcal{A}\langle \iota_a, \mu, \mathcal{E}[\texttt{send}(\iota_a.\iota_o, msg, \overline{v})], O\rangle$$
$$\longrightarrow_a \mathcal{A}\langle \iota_a, \mu \cdot \mathcal{M}\langle \iota_o, msg, \overline{v}\rangle, \mathcal{E}[\texttt{null}], O\rangle$$

(RECEIVE)
$$\mathcal{A}\langle \iota_a, \mathcal{M}\langle \iota_o, msg, \overline{v}\rangle \cdot \mu, v, O\rangle$$
$$\longrightarrow_a \mathcal{A}\langle \iota_a, \mu, \iota_a.\iota_o.msg(\overline{v}), O\rangle$$

Fig. 18. Local Reduction Rules for Communicating Event Loops

We now explain the actor-local reduction rules ($\longrightarrow_a$) found in Fig. 18:

- LET: Reducing a "let"-expression simply substitutes the value v for x in e.
- NEW: Newly created objects are always owned by the actor that creates them, i.e. the newly created object is added to the heap of the actor for which the new expression was reduced. The new expression reduces to a reference to the newly created object. That reference is a double identifier that references the object ι_o and the actor that created (or owns) the object ι_a.
- INVOKE: Actors can only synchronously invoke methods on their own objects, i.e. the object has to be part of the heap of that actor and the actor part of the reference ι_a needs to be the same as the actor identifier. In the result expression, the pseudovariable self is substituted with the reference to the object on which the method was invoked $\iota_a.\iota_o$.
- FIELD-ACCESS: Field access works identical to the Active Object Model, except that field access only works on references to objects that are owned by the actor dereferencing them (i.e. the actor part of the reference ι_a needs to be the same as the actor identifier).
- FIELD-UPDATE: Similar to field access.
- SELF-SEND: An asynchronous message sent to the same actor simply appends a new message to the end of that actor's own mailbox. The object part of the reference ι_o is copied into the message to later identify the recipient object. The message send itself immediately reduces to null.
- RECEIVE: A message can only be processed if the current expression of the actor cannot be reduced any further (the expression is a value v). Processing a message simply forwards that message to the recipient object. This is achieved by replacing the value with a synchronous invocation expression that invokes the corresponding method on the object that was the target of the message.

(CREATE)
$$\frac{\iota_{a'}, \iota_o \text{ fresh}}{A \uplus \{\mathcal{A}\langle \iota_a, \mu, \mathcal{E}[\texttt{create}(cls, \overline{v})], O\rangle\} \longrightarrow_k A \uplus \{\mathcal{A}\langle \iota_a, \mu, \mathcal{E}[\iota_{a'}.\iota_o], O\rangle\} \cup \{\mathcal{A}\langle \iota_{a'}, \varnothing, \texttt{null}, \{\mathcal{O}\langle \iota_o, cls, \overline{v}\rangle\}\rangle\}}$$

(SEND)
$$A \uplus \{\mathcal{A}\langle \iota_a, \mu, \mathcal{E}[\texttt{send}(\iota_{a'}.\iota_o, msg, \overline{v})], O\rangle\} \uplus \{\mathcal{A}\langle \iota_{a'}, \mu', e', O'\rangle\} \longrightarrow_k A \uplus \{\mathcal{A}\langle \iota_a, \mu, \mathcal{E}[\texttt{null}], O\rangle\} \cup \{\mathcal{A}\langle \iota_{a'}, \mu' \cdot \mathcal{M}\langle \iota_o, msg, \overline{v}\rangle, e', O'\rangle\}$$

(CONGRUENCE)
$$\frac{a \longrightarrow_a a'}{A \uplus \{a\} \longrightarrow_k A \cup \{a'\}}$$

Fig. 19. Global Reduction Rules for Communicating Event Loops

Actor-Global Reductions. We now explain the actor-global reduction rules found in Fig. 19:

- CREATE: Reducing a create expression adds a new actor to the set of actors of the configuration. The newly created actor is initialised with an empty mailbox, null as its expression (the actor will be in an idle state), and an object heap with a single object. The create expression itself reduces to a reference to that object $\iota_{a'}.\iota_o$.
- SEND: An asynchronous message sent to a different actor appends that message to the front of the mailbox of the recipient actor (the actor with identifier $\iota_{a'}$). To preserve actor isolation, event-loop actors adopt a strict no-shared-state policy. Contrary to the Active Object Model, where passive objects are shared by copy, references to objects in an event-loop actor can be freely shared between actors because they are always *tagged* with a reference to the actor that owns the object. Only the actor that owns an object is allowed to synchronously reference, mutate, or invoke methods on that object.
- CONGRUENCE: this rule connects the actor-local reduction rules to the global configuration reduction rules.

Auxiliary Functions. The auxiliary functions lookup and update-field are identical to the ones for the Active Object Model. They simply lookup a field or modify a field of a given passive object respectively (Fig. 20).

$$\text{lookup}(\mathcal{O}\langle\iota_o, cls, \overline{v_f}\rangle, x_f) \stackrel{def}{=} \text{lookup}(\overline{x_f}, \overline{v_f}, x_f) \quad \text{if class } cls \{\overline{x_f}; M\} \in C$$
$$\text{lookup}(x_f \cdot \overline{x_f}, v_f \cdot \overline{v_f}, x_f) \stackrel{def}{=} v$$
$$\text{lookup}(x'_f \cdot \overline{x_f}, v_f \cdot \overline{v_f}, x_f) \stackrel{def}{=} \text{lookup}(\overline{x_f}, \overline{v_f}, x_f)$$

$$\text{update-field}(\mathcal{O}\langle\iota_o, cls, \overline{v_f}\rangle, x_f, v) \stackrel{def}{=} \mathcal{O}\langle\iota_o, cls, \text{update-field}(\overline{x_f}, \overline{v_f}, x_f, v)\rangle \text{ if class } cls \{\overline{x_f}; M\} \in C$$
$$\text{update-field}(x_f \cdot \overline{x_f}, v_f \cdot \overline{v_f}, x_f, v) \stackrel{def}{=} v \cdot \overline{v_f}$$
$$\text{update-field}(x'_f \cdot \overline{x_f}, v_f \cdot \overline{v_f}, x_f, v) \stackrel{def}{=} v_f \cdot \text{update-field}(\overline{x_f}, \overline{v_f}, x_f, v)$$

Fig. 20. Auxiliary Functions

6.2 Conclusion

The Communicating Event Loop (CEL) Model is distinguished by its two-layered programming model, which comprises actors and objects. In this paradigm, actors are not first-class entities. Instead, a CEL actor can define multiple objects that share the same mailbox and thread of control while distributing distinct references to these objects. This functionality effectively allows an actor to possess multiple interfaces simultaneously, thereby facilitating a Principle of Least Privilege (PoLP) approach to programming. However, although a CEL actor can maintain numerous interfaces, all of these interfaces are predetermined and fixed.

Within this model, a message delivered to the inbox of an actor always targets a specific object. If the targeted object does not understand the message, the actor becomes stuck, which signifies an error within the program. The sequential subset of the model is imperative, and to ensure actor isolation, any mutable object is invariably passed by far reference. This mechanism ensures that the CEL Model upholds the Isolated Turn Principle.

7 General Conclusion

At its core, the actor model of computation is a very simple programming model with one central concept: the actor. Actors are simply isolated processes that communicate asynchronously via message passing. The main benefit of this strict isolation and asynchronous communication is that the actor model is free of low-level data races and deadlocks. In this paper we define this as a key unifying principle among all actor systems and name it the Isolated Turn Principle. However, when looking at the broader picture, half a century of research has lead to a plethora of different variations on the actor model, each with their own widely different properties.

This paper focusses primarily on the overlying programming model and identifies and defines four broad families along which any actor system can be categorised. Namely: *Classic Actors, Active Objects, Processes, and Communicating Event Loops*. This paper provides a brief history of some of the key programming languages and libraries that implement each of these four broad families of actor models. These programming languages and libraries have influenced and will continue to influence the design and rationale of other actor systems today.

This paper provides a precise formal definition for a core subset of the four families of actor models through an operational semantics. An executable version of these operational semantics implemented in PLT Redex is available. The Isolated Turn Principle is a core principle that unifies all actor systems. However, there are many other properties along which an actor system can be classified. While those properties remain largely dependent on the specific implementation of an actor system, there are still some general conclusions to be drawn.

- The sequential subset of Classic Actors and Processes is typically functional, while the Active Object Model and Communicating Event Loops are typically imperative. However, as long as the Isolated Turn principle is upheld, the choice does not really impact the concurrency properties of that system.
- Classic Actors and Processes have a flexible interface which facilitates conditional synchronisation, while the Active Object Model and Communicating Event Loops have a fixed interface. Communicating Event Loops is the only actor model where actors can create many small interfaces which supports a PoLP (principle of least privilege) style of programming.
- Actor models where actors have a flexible interface typically support out-of-order processing of messages while actor models where actors have a fixed interface typically process messages in FIFO order.

- The paradigm of the sequential subset directly determines whether state changes at the level of an actor are aggregated (for functional languages) or on a per-variable basis (for imperative languages).

References

1. Akka, inc. akka platform. https://akka.io/. Accessed 17 June 2025
2. Microsoft. orleans framework. https://learn.microsoft.com/en-us/dotnet/orleans/overview. Accessed 15 Sept 2014
3. Agha, G.: Actors: A Model of Concurrent Computation in Distributed Systems. MIT Press, Cambridge (1986)
4. Agha, G.: Concurrent object-oriented programming. Commun. ACM **33**(9), 125–141 (1990). https://doi.org/10.1145/83880.84528
5. Agha, G.A., Mason, I.A., Smith, S.F., Talcott, C.L.: A foundation for actor computation. J. Funct. Program. **7**(1), 1–72 (1997). https://doi.org/10.1017/S095679689700261X
6. Armstrong, J., Virding, R., Wikström, C., Williams, M.: Concurrent Programming in ERLANG, 2nd edn. Prentice Hall International (UK) Ltd., Hertfordshire (1996)
7. Baker, H.C., Hewitt, C.: The incremental garbage collection of processes. SIGPLAN Not. **12**(8), 55–59 (1977). https://doi.org/10.1145/872734.806932
8. Boer, F.D., et al.: A survey of active object languages. ACM Comput. Surv. **50**(5) (2017). https://doi.org/10.1145/3122848
9. Brandauer, S., et al.: Parallel objects for multicores: a glimpse at the parallel language ENCORE. In: Bernardo, M., Johnsen, E.B. (eds.) SFM 2015. LNCS, vol. 9104, pp. 1–56. Springer, Cham (2015). https://doi.org/10.1007/978-3-319-18941-3_1
10. Briot, J.P.: Actalk: a testbed for classifying and designing actor languages in the smalltalk-80 environment, pp. 109–129. University Press (1989)
11. Briot, J.P., Guerraoui, R., Lohr, K.P.: Concurrency and distribution in object-oriented programming. ACM Comput. Surv. **30**(3), 291–329 (1998). https://doi.org/10.1145/292469.292470
12. Bykov, S.: The curse of the a-word (2021). https://temporal.io/blog/sergey-the-curse-of-the-a-word. Accessed 01 Jan 2023
13. Caromel, D., Henrio, L., Serpette, B.P.: Asynchronous and deterministic objects. SIGPLAN Not. **39**(1), 123–134 (2004). https://doi.org/10.1145/982962.964012
14. Church, A.: An unsolvable problem of elementary number theory. Am. J. Math. **58**(2), 345–363 (1936)
15. De Koster, J., Van Cutsem, T., De Meuter, W.: 43 years of actors: a taxonomy of actor models and their key properties. In: Proceedings of the 6th International Workshop on Programming Based on Actors, Agents, and Decentralized Control, AGERE 2016, pp. 31–40. Association for Computing Machinery, New York (2016). https://doi.org/10.1145/3001886.3001890
16. Dedecker, J., Van Cutsem, T., Mostinckx, S., D'Hondt, T., De Meuter, W.: Ambient-oriented programming in AmbientTalk. In: Thomas, D. (ed.) ECOOP 2006. LNCS, vol. 4067, pp. 230–254. Springer, Heidelberg (2006). https://doi.org/10.1007/11785477_16
17. Felleisen, M., Hieb, R.: The revised report on the syntactic theories of sequential control and state. Theor. Comput. Sci. **103**(2), 235–271 (1992). https://doi.org/10.1016/0304-3975(92)90014-7

18. Greif, I., Hewitt, C.: Actor semantics of planner-73. In: Proceedings of the 2nd ACM SIGACT-SIGPLAN Symposium on Principles of Programming Languages, POPL '75, pp. 67–77. Association for Computing Machinery, New York (1975). https://doi.org/10.1145/512976.512984
19. Haller, P.: On the integration of the actor model in mainstream technologies: the scala perspective. In: Agha, G.A., Bordini, R.H., Marron, A., Ricci, A. (eds.) Proceedings of the 2nd edition on Programming systems, languages and applications based on actors, agents, and decentralized control abstractions, AGERE! 2012, Tucson, Arizona, USA, 21–22 October 2012, pp. 1–6. ACM (2012). https://doi.org/10.1145/2414639.2414641
20. Haller, P., Odersky, M.: Scala actors: unifying thread-based and event-based programming. Theor. Comput. Sci. **410**(2–3), 202–220 (2009). https://doi.org/10.1016/J.TCS.2008.09.019
21. Hewitt, C.: Planner: a language for manipulating models and proving theorems in a robot (1970)
22. Hewitt, C., Bishop, P., Steiger, R.: A universal modular actor formalism for artificial intelligence. In: Proceedings of the 3rd International Joint Conference on Artificial Intelligence, IJCAI'73, pp. 235–245. Morgan Kaufmann Publishers Inc., San Francisco (1973)
23. Hoare, C.A.R.: Communicating sequential processes. Commun. ACM **21**(8), 666–677 (1978). https://doi.org/10.1145/359576.359585
24. Johnsen, E.B., Hähnle, R., Schäfer, J., Schlatte, R., Steffen, M.: ABS: a core language for abstract behavioral specification. In: Aichernig, B.K., de Boer, F.S., Bonsangue, M.M. (eds.) FMCO 2010. LNCS, vol. 6957, pp. 142–164. Springer, Heidelberg (2011). https://doi.org/10.1007/978-3-642-25271-6_8
25. Kafura, D.: Act++: Building a concurrent C++ with actors. J. Object Oriented Program. **3**(1), 25–37 (1990). http://dl.acm.org/citation.cfm?id=90482.90493
26. Kahn, K., Tribble, E.D., Miller, M., Bobrow, D.G.: Vulcan: Logical Concurrent Objects, pp. 75–112. MIT Press, Cambridge (1987)
27. Kim, W.: Thal: an actor system for efficient and scalable concurrent computing (1997)
28. Liskov, B., Shrira, L.: Promises: linguistic support for efficient asynchronous procedure calls in distributed systems. In: Proceedings of the ACM SIGPLAN 1988 Conference on Programming Language Design and Implementation, PLDI '88, pp. 260–267. ACM, New York (1988). https://doi.org/10.1145/53990.54016
29. Miller, M.S., Tribble, E.D., Shapiro, J.: Concurrency among strangers. In: De Nicola, R., Sangiorgi, D. (eds.) TGC 2005. LNCS, vol. 3705, pp. 195–229. Springer, Heidelberg (2005). https://doi.org/10.1007/11580850_12
30. Saltzer, J.H., Schroeder, M.D.: The protection of information in computer systems. Proc. IEEE **63**(9), 1278–1308 (1975)
31. Scholliers, C., Tanter, E., De Meuter, W.: Parallel actor monitors: disentangling task-level parallelism from data partitioning in the actor model. Sci. Comput. Program. 80, 52–64 (2014). https://doi.org/10.1016/j.scico.2013.03.011
32. Sirjani, M., Movaghar, A., Shali, A., De Boer, F.S.: Modeling and verification of reactive systems using rebeca. Fund. Inform. **63**(4), 385–410 (2004)
33. Srinivasan, S., Mycroft, A.: Kilim: isolation-typed actors for java. In: Vitek, J. (ed.) ECOOP 2008. LNCS, vol. 5142, pp. 104–128. Springer, Heidelberg (2008). https://doi.org/10.1007/978-3-540-70592-5_6
34. Sturman, D., Agha, G.: A protocol description language for customizing failure semantics. In: 13th Symposium on Reliable Distributed Systems, 1994. Proceedings, pp. 148–157 (1994). https://doi.org/10.1109/RELDIS.1994.336900

35. Sussman, G.J., Steele, G.L., Jr.: Scheme: a interpreter for extended lambda calculus. Higher-Order Symb. Comput. **11**(4), 405–439 (1998)
36. Tomlinson, C., Kim, W., Scheevel, M., Singh, V., Will, B., Agha, G.: Rosette: an object-oriented concurrent systems architecture. In: Proceedings of the 1988 ACM SIGPLAN Workshop on Object-based Concurrent Programming, OOPSLA/ECOOP '88, pp. 91–93. ACM, New York (1988). https://doi.org/10.1145/67386.67410
37. Van Cutsem, T., Mostinckx, S., Boix, E.G., Dedecker, J., De Meuter, W.: Ambienttalk: object-oriented event-driven programming in mobile ad hoc networks. In: Proceedings of the XXVI International Conference of the Chilean Society of Computer Science, SCCC '07, pp. 3–12. IEEE Computer Society, Washington, DC (2007). https://doi.org/10.1109/SCCC.2007.4
38. arela, C., Agha, G.: Programming dynamically reconfigurable open systems with SALSA. SIGPLAN Not. 36(12), 20–34 (2001). https://doi.org/10.1145/583960.583964
39. Varela, C.A.: Programming Distributed Computing Systems: A Foundational Approach. The MIT Press, Cambridge (2013)
40. Yonezawa, A., Briot, J.P., Shibayama, E.: Object-oriented concurrent programming ABCL/1. In: Conference Proceedings on Object-oriented Programming Systems, Languages and Applications, OOPLSA '86, pp. 258–268. ACM, New York (1986). https://doi.org/10.1145/28697.28722

The AMST Language: Formal Verification and Execution of Actor Systems

Carlos A. Varela[✉][iD]

Rensselaer Polytechnic Institute, Troy, NY 12180, USA
cvarela@cs.rpi.edu

Abstract. We formalize Agha, Mason, Smith, and Talcott's actor language (AMST) [2] using the Athena proof assistant [3]. Since Athena is a dual deduction and computation language, we can both rigorously prove formal properties of actor systems, as well as synthesize executable actor code from the theory.

Keywords: Actor model · AMST language · Formal verification

1 Introduction

The actor model [1] is an elegant, simple, and expressive concurrent computation model. Agha, Mason, Smith, and Talcott formalized the model using a simple actor language extending the lambda calculus with three actor primitives [2]. We introduce an executable version of their language and call it *AMST*. Agha *et al.*'s paper presented the language's syntax, operational semantics, and theory, and we largely follow the original presentation. The lambda calculus [4] is used to model sequential computation within each actor. This sequential computing calculus is another elegant and simple model, yet Turing-complete, with only three syntactic constructs and one main semantic rule: β-reduction.

Athena is a many-sorted first-order logic proof assistant [3] that contains *methods* and *procedures* to abstract over deductions and computations respectively. When methods succeed, they produce *theorems*, which are guaranteed to be sound by the language, *i.e.*, they logically follow from the axioms assumed during the method's execution.

In this paper, we formalize AMST in Athena, providing a formal basis for reasoning with machine-checked proofs, as well as a method to *execute* AMST actor programs by viewing the theory not only as a set of first-order logic sentences encoding universally quantified equations, but also by viewing these equations as a set of left-to-right rewriting rules.

The paper's outline is as follows: Sect. 2 introduces the AMST actor language by way of examples illustrating how to execute AMST programs in Athena. Section 3 specifies AMST's syntax and operational semantics. The section includes a full machine-checkable proof of AMST actor expressions' unique decomposition into a reduction context and a redex. It also specifies computation sequences, computation trees, and fairness. Finally, Sect. 4 discusses the paper's contributions and potential future work.

2 AMST Actor Language

The AMST actor language is an extension of the untyped call-by-value lambda calculus with the following actor primitives:

- **send** for sending messages,
- **letactor** for actor creation, and
- **become** for changing behavior.

2.1 Trivial Examples

A simple actor behavior that expects its message to be an actor name, sends the message 5 to that actor, and becomes the same behavior, may be expressed as follows:

```
define B5 := (App Y
                  (Lambda 'y
                    (Lambda 'x
                      (Seq (Send (Var 'x) Five)
                           (Become (Var 'y))))))

define B5Test := (LetActor 'z B5 (Send (Var 'z) (Var 'a)))
```

where Var, Lambda, and App are constructs for lambda calculus expressions; Seq is syntactic sugar for sequential composition, Y is the call-by-value fixed-point recursion combinator, Five is syntactic sugar for Church numeral 5; Send, LetActor, and Become are actor primitives; and 'x, 'y, 'z, and 'a are Athena identifiers, which we use for variable and actor names.

Using Athena's eval procedure, we can use the AMST actor theory to execute this example, as follows:

```
> (eval (execute B5Test))

Term:
(Actors.kfg
 # Actor map redacted
 (MSet.insert
  (Actors.msg 'a
              (Lambda 'f
                (Lambda 'x
                  (App (Var 'f)
                    (App (Var 'f)
                      (App (Var 'f)
                        (App (Var 'f)
                          (App (Var 'f)
                            (Var 'x))))))))))
  MSet.null:(MSet.MSet Actors.Message)))
```

where we can observe that the final actor configuration contains a message to actor 'a with value 5 in Church numeral form $\lambda f.\lambda x.(f \ (f \ (f \ (f \ (f \ x)))))$.

An equivalent expression of this behavior is:

```
define B5' := (App Y
                   (Lambda 'y
                     (Lambda 'x
                       (Seq (Become (Var 'y))
                            (Send (Var 'x) Five)))))
```

since the order of executing the **become** and the **send** cannot be observed.

The behavior of a *sink*, an actor that ignores its messages and becomes the same behavior, is defined by

```
define Sink:= (App Y
                (Lambda 'b
                  (Lambda 'm
                    (Become (Var 'b)))))

define SinkTest := (LetActor 'z Sink (Send (Var 'z) (Var 'a)))
```

In this example, execution shows the following final configuration:

```
> (eval (execute SinkTest))

Term:
(Actors.kfg
 (FMap.update
  (pair 'f0
        (Ready
         (Lambda 'y
                 (App (App (Lambda 'x
                                   (App (Lambda 'b
                                                (Lambda 'm
                                                        (Become (Var 'b))))
                                        (Lambda 'y
                                                (App (App (Var 'x)
                                                          (Var 'x))
                                                     (Var 'y)))))
                           (Lambda 'x
                                   (App (Lambda 'b
                                                (Lambda 'm
                                                        (Become (Var 'b))))
                                        (Lambda 'y
                                                (App (App (Var 'x)
                                                          (Var 'x))
                                                     (Var 'y))))))
                      (Var 'y)))))
  (FMap.update
   (pair 'f1
         (Lambda 'x
                 (Var 'x)))
   (FMap.update
    (pair 'main
          (Lambda 'x
                  (Var 'x)))
    FMap.empty-map:(FMap.Map Ide AExp))))
 MSet.null:(MSet.MSet Actors.Message))
```

where we can observe the final actor configuration including an actor map with actor 'f0 encoding the **Sink** behavior—after expansion of the **Y** combinator, the actors 'f1 and main with **Nil** behavior—represented as the identity combinator $\lambda x.x$, and an empty multiset (**null**) representing the fact that the message to the sink actor was effectively consumed. We can also trace the actor program to see the transition labels in the actor computation as a list:

```
> (eval (trace SinkTest))

Term: (:: (Actors.fun 'main)
          (:: (Actors.fun 'main)
              (:: (Actors.fun 'main)
                  (:: (Actors.new 'main 'f0)
                      (:: (Actors.snd 'main)
                          (:: (Actors.rcv 'f0
```

```
                              (Var 'a))
                (:: (Actors.fun 'f0)
                  (:: (Actors.bec 'f0 'f1)
                      nil:(List Actors.Label)))))))))
```

where we can observe in the initial 'main actor—produced by execute and trace—three functional transitions converting the Sink expression into a value (expanding the Y combinator), the creation of the Sink actor named 'f0, the sending of message containing 'a from 'main to 'f0, the reception of the message by 'f0, and function application becoming ready to receive new messages with the same Sink behavior, and letting the (empty) continuation be processed by anonymous actor 'f1.

(execute e) is used to start the computation in a configuration with a single 'main actor mapped to the initial program e, and an empty network (multiset of messages.) It is defined in Athena as follows:

```
declare execute : [AExp] -> AConfig

assert* execute-def :=
[(((execute e) = (reduce* (kfg (['main e] ++ empty-map)
                              empty-mset)
                          (gen-fresh 'f 30)))]
```

where we pass an initial list of 30 fresh names to choose from, which explains why the actor executing the Sink behavior is named 'f0 and the continuation of the Sink actor after Become is named 'f1[1].

2.2 Actor Cells

A *reference cell*—one of the simplest stateful concurrent programs—can be represented in the AMST actor language, as follows:

```
define Cell :=
(App Y
  (Lambda 'b
    (Lambda 'c
      (Lambda 'm
        (If (App Get? (Var 'm))
            (Seq (Become (App (Var 'b) (Var 'c)))
                 (Send (App Cust (Var 'm)) (Var 'c)))
            (If (App Set? (Var 'm))
                (Become (App (Var 'b) (App Contents (Var 'm))))
                (Become (App (Var 'b) (Var 'c))))))))))
define CellTest :=
(LetActor 'a
  (App Cell Zero)
  (Seq (Send (Var 'a) (App MkSet Three))
       (Seq (Send (Var 'a) (App MkSet Four))
            (Send (Var 'a) (App MkGet (Var 'c))))))
```

with auxiliary functions to create *get* and *set* message types, and access their contents as follows:

```
define MkGet    := (Lambda 'c (Pr True (Var 'c)))
define MkSet    := (Lambda 'c (Pr False (Var 'c)))
```

---

[1] In general, we want to pass a lazily generated infinite list of fresh names.

```
define Get?      := 1st
define Set?      := (App (App Compose Not) 1st)
define Cust      := 2nd
define Contents  := 2nd
```

Executing this code can result in customer actor `'c` receiving a message containing 0, 3, or 4, depending on the cell's message processing order. Following is an execution where the customer actor gets 0, and the cell contains value 3 at the end of the execution:

```
> (eval (execute CellTest))

Term:
(Actors.kfg
 (FMap.update
  (pair 'f0
        (Ready (Lambda 'm
               # context redacted here for readability
                        (Send (App (Lambda 'p
                                      (App (Var 'p)
                                           (Lambda 'x
                                               (Lambda 'y
                                                   (Var 'y)))))
                                   (Var 'm))
                              (Lambda 'f
                                 (Lambda 'x
                                    (App (Var 'f)
                                        (App (Var 'f)
                                            (App (Var 'f)
                                                (Var 'x))))))))))
      # context redacted here for readability
      # additional "garbage" actors redacted
      FMap.empty-map:(FMap.Map Ide AExp))
  (MSet.insert (Actors.msg 'c
                           (Lambda 'f
                               (Lambda 'x
                                   (Var 'x))))
               MSet.null:(MSet.MSet Actors.Message)))
```

where 0 is represented as the Church numeral $\lambda f.\lambda x.x$, and the cell on a subsequent get request will send to the customer ((Cust m)) the Church numeral 3: $\lambda f.\lambda x.(f\ (f\ (f\ x)))$. Notice that booleans are represented as $\lambda x.\lambda y.x$ for True, and $\lambda x.\lambda y.y$ for False, and pairs are represented as abstractions that take True to obtain the first element, and False to obtain the second, which is why (Cust m)—which uses (2nd m)—takes m as a pair and applies False to it, to obtain the customer.

2.3 Join Continuations

A prototypical recursive computation such as a binary tree product can be made concurrent using the AMST actor language as follows:

```
1  define TProd :=
2    (App Y
3      (Lambda 'b
4        (Lambda 'self
5          (Lambda 'm
6            (Seq
7              (Become (App (Var 'b) (Var 'self)))
8              (If (App IsNat (App Tree (Var 'm)))
```

The AMST Language: Formal Verification and Execution of Actor Systems

```
 9                      (Send (App Cust (Var 'm)) (App Tree (Var 'm)))
10                      (LetActor
11                         'nc
12                         (App JoinC (App Cust (Var 'm)))
13                         (Seq (Send (Var 'self)
14                                    (Pr (App Left (App Tree (Var 'm)))
15                                        (Var 'nc)))
16                               (Send (Var 'self)
17                                    (Pr (App Right (App Tree (Var 'm)))
18                                        (Var 'nc))))))))))))
19
20 define JoinC :=
21    (Lambda 'c
22       (Lambda 'n1
23          (Become (Lambda 'n2
24             (Send (Var 'c) (App (App Mult (Var 'n1)) (Var 'n2)))))))
```

where `TProd` denotes the behavior of the actor computing the tree product, and `JoinC` denotes the behavior of a *join continuation* actor that receives the products of the left and right sub-trees (computed concurrently) and sends their product to its customer.

A sample interaction follows:

```
define Tree1 := (Pr (Pr One Two) False)
define Tree2 := (Pr (Pr Tree1 Three) False)

define TProdTest2 :=
   (LetActor 't (App TProd (Var 't))
      (Send (Var 't) (Pr Tree2 (Var 'c))))
```

where leaf trees are encoded as Church numerals and non-leaf trees are encoded as `(Pr (Pr Left Right) False)`[2], resulting in the following output (redacted to include only the network component of the final configuration):

```
> (eval (execute TProdTest2))
#...
(MSet.insert
 (Actors.msg 'c
              (Lambda 'x
                 (App (Lambda 'f
                         (Lambda 'x
                            (App (Var 'f)
                               (App (Var 'f)
                                  (App (Var 'f)
                                     (Var 'x))))))
                      (App (Lambda 'x
                              (App (Lambda 'f
                                      (Lambda 'x
                                         (App (Var 'f)
                                            (App (Var 'f)
                                               (Var 'x)))))
                                   (App (Lambda 'f
                                           (Lambda 'x
                                              (App (Var 'f)
                                                 (Var 'x))))
                                        (Var 'x))))
                           (Var 'x)))))
   MSet.null:(MSet.MSet Actors.Message))
#...
```

---

[2] `isNat`—as used in the `TProd` behavior's line 8–is a lambda calculus function that returns `True` for Church numerals, and `2nd` for pairs: $\lambda e.((e\ \lambda x.\text{True})\ \text{True})$.

where we notice that the customer actor 'c receives a message encoding $3 \times 2 \times 1$ (Church numeral multiplication is function composition.)

3 A Simple Lambda-Based Actor Language

In this section, we give the syntax and operational semantics of the AMST actor language.

3.1 Syntax

The syntax for AMST actor language expressions is given in Fig. 1, where the first three syntactic forms encode the lambda calculus, the Br form permits branching in a call-by-value language, and the last four syntactic forms encode the three actor primitives, plus a Ready primitive that allows an actor to change state without creating an anonymous actor[3].

```
structure AExp := (Var Ide)
               |  (Lambda Ide AExp)
               |  (App AExp AExp)
               |  (Br AExp AExp AExp)
               |  (LetActor Ide AExp AExp)
               |  (Send AExp AExp)
               |  (Become AExp)
               |  (Ready AExp)
```

Fig. 1. AMST actor language syntax.

We use the lambda calculus to represent nil, booleans, numbers, and pairs as follows:

```
# Combinators:
define I := (Lambda 'x (Var 'x))
define Compose := (Lambda 'f
                    (Lambda 'g
                      (Lambda 'x
                        (App (Var 'f) (App (Var 'g) (Var 'x))))))
define Nil := I

# Booleans
define True  := (Lambda 'x (Lambda 'y (Var 'x)))
define False := (Lambda 'x (Lambda 'y (Var 'y)))
define Not   := (Lambda 'b (App (App (Var 'b) False) True))
```

---

[3] The (Ready b) expression is used to signal that an actor can receive new messages with behavior b, a lambda abstraction, and it is written (b) in [2] which is distinguished from [e] which denotes sequential computing within the actor. In [5], we use Ready instead of Become to reduce the number of actor creations, which is useful when we implement actors as active objects. In AMST, we keep both forms, and we could show that (Ready b) is equivalent to (Become b) with an empty continuation.

The AMST Language: Formal Verification and Execution of Actor Systems   43

```
# Church Numerals
define Zero := (Lambda 'f (Lambda 'x (Var 'x)))
define One  := (Lambda 'f (Lambda 'x (App (Var 'f) (Var 'x))))
define Two  := (Lambda 'f (Lambda 'x (App (Var 'f)
                                         (App (Var 'f) (Var 'x)))))
define Three := # ...
define Four  := # ...
define Five  := # ...
define Succ := (Lambda 'n
                  (Lambda 'f (Lambda 'x
                    (App (Var 'f)
                         (App (App (Var 'n) (Var 'f)) (Var 'x))))))
define Mult := Compose

# Pairs
define PrC  := (Lambda 'x
                 (Lambda 'y
                   (Lambda 'b
                     (App (App (Var 'b) (Var 'x)) (Var 'y)))))
define 1st := (Lambda 'p (App (Var 'p) True))
define 2nd := (Lambda 'p (App (Var 'p) False))

define Pr := lambda (x y)
               (App (App PrC x) y)
```

Notice that `Pr` is an Athena procedure, which uses its `lambda` syntactic form, that takes two AMST expressions x and y and produces the AMST expression (App (App PrC x) y).

We also use the lambda calculus to represent let, sequencing, conditionals, and recursion, as follows:

```
# sequencing combinator
define Let := lambda (x e1 e2)
                (App (Lambda x e2) e1)
define SeqC := (Lambda 'x
                 (Lambda 'y
                   (App (Lambda 'z (Var 'y)) (Var 'x))))

define Seq := lambda (e1 e2)
                (App (App SeqC e1) e2)

# conditional form using Br
define If := lambda (b t e)
               let {fresh := (gen-fresh-e 'if (App t e))}
                 (App (Br b (Lambda fresh t) (Lambda fresh e)) (Var 'ifoo))

# applicative order Y combinator
define Y :=
(Lambda 'f
  (App (Lambda 'x (App (Var 'f)
                       (Lambda 'y (App (App (Var 'x) (Var 'x)) (Var 'y)))))
       (Lambda 'x (App (Var 'f)
                       (Lambda 'y (App (App (Var 'x) (Var 'x)) (Var 'y)))))))
```

3.2 Reduction Semantics for Actor Configurations

The operational semantics for the AMST actor language is given by a labeled transition relation on configurations. Actor configurations contain an actor map and a multi-set of messages representing messages in-transit.

```
datatype Message := (msg Ide AExp)

datatype AConfig := (kfg (FMap.Map Ide AExp) (MSet.MSet Message))
```

where `Ide` denotes Athena identifiers, such as `'a` which we use for variable and actor names; and `AExp` denotes an actor expression, as specified in Sect. 3.1.

Notation. `(FMap.Map Ide AExp)` denotes a finite map from identifiers to actor states, represented as actor expressions. `(MSet.MSet Message)` denotes a multi-set of messages. We define and overload the following operators:

```
define ++   := FMap.++
overload ++ MSet.++

define at   := FMap.at
define dom  := FMap.dom

define -    := MSet.-
overload -  FMap.-

define in   := MSet.in
overload in Set.in
overload in List.in
```

so that we may use `[a e] ++ amap` to denote the extension of actor map `amap` to include a mapping from `a` to `e`; but also so that we may use `(msg a v) ++ n` to denote the addition of a message to actor `a` with content `v` to the network, represented as multiset `n`. Furthermore, we may use `amap at a` to obtain the actor state corresponding to `a` in the actor map `amap`; `dom amap` to obtain the domain of actor map `amap`; `n - (msg a v)` to remove one occurrence of message `(msg a v)` from the network `n`; `amap - a` to remove the actor `a` from the actor map `amap`; `(msg a v) in n` to check whether a message is in the network; and `a in dom amap` to check for membership of actor named `a` in actor map `amap`.

Actor Configurations. An actor configuration with actor map `amap` and network `n` is denoted as `(kfg amap n)`.

The set of possible computations of an actor configuration is defined in terms of the labeled transition relation `reduce`:

```
# operational semantics transition labels
datatype Label := (fun Ide)
              |  (new Ide Ide)
              |  (snd Ide)
              |  (rcv Ide AExp)
              |  (bec Ide Ide)

# given a config and a label produces the next config
declare reduce : [AConfig Label] -> AConfig
```

where the five label types denote how the actor `a`—*in focus*—makes progress as follows:

- `(fun a)`, to denote functional (lambda calculus β-reduction) progress,
- `(new a a')`, to denote creation of actor `a'` by `a`,
- `(snd a)`, to denote message sending by actor `a`,
- `(rcv a v)`, to denote message reception by actor `a` with message content `v`, and
- `(bec a a')` to denote becoming a new actor behavior, and letting an anonymous actor `a'` carry out the remaining computation.

Decomposition and Reduction. To describe actor transitions, we classify expressions into *value* and *non-value* expressions:

```
structure AVal   := (VarV Ide)
                 |  (LambdaV Ide AExp)

structure AE    := (Val AVal)
                 |  (AppE AE AE)
                 |  (BrE AE AE AE)
                 |  (LetActorE Ide AE AE)
                 |  (SendE AE AE)
                 |  (BecomeE AE)
                 |  (ReadyE AE)
```

with the idea to decompose non-value actor expressions (**AE**) uniquely into a reduction context filled with a redex. Reduction contexts identify the subexpression of an expression that is to be evaluated next, to correspond to a left-first, call-by-value evaluation strategy.

Following is the definition of actor redexes (**ARedex**) and actor reduction contexts (**ARC**):

```
structure ARedex := (AppR AVal AVal)
                 |  (BrR AVal AE AE)
                 |  (LetActorR Ide AVal AE)
                 |  (SendR AVal AVal)
                 |  (BecomeR AVal)
                 |  (ReadyR AVal)

structure ARC    := Hole
                 |  (AppCL AVal ARC)
                 |  (AppCR ARC AE)
                 |  (BrC ARC AE AE)
                 |  (LetActorC Ide ARC AE)
                 |  (SendCL AVal ARC)
                 |  (SendCR ARC AE)
                 |  (BecomeC ARC)
                 |  (ReadyC ARC)
```

An expression **e** (in **AExp**) is either a value or it can be decomposed uniquely into a reduction context filled with a redex. Thus, local actor computation is deterministic.

Lemma 1 (Unique decomposition). $\forall e.(e \in AVal \vee (\exists! R, r)(e = R[r]))$.

To formally prove this lemma in Athena, we will first introduce some notation. To determine whether an expression is a value, we introduce the isValue predicate:

```
declare isValue : [AExp] -> Boolean

assert* isValue-def :=
[(isValue    (Var v))
 (isValue    (Lambda v e))
 (~ isValue  (App e1 e2))
 (~ isValue  (Br e1 e2 e3))
 (~ isValue  (LetActor v e1 e2))
 (~ isValue  (Send e1 e2))
 (~ isValue  (Become e'))
 (~ isValue  (Ready e'))]
```

where only the variable name and lambda abstraction forms are considered value expressions.

We also introduce a function `fill-in` to represent $R[r]$, *i.e.*, reduction context R filled in with redex r, as follows:

```
# R[r] is denoted as (fill-in R r)
declare fill-in : [ARC AExp] -> AExp

assert* fill-in-def :=
  [((fill-in Hole e)                = e)
   ((fill-in (AppCL val R) e)       = (App (val->aexp val) (fill-in R e)))
   ((fill-in (AppCR R ae) e)        = (App (fill-in R e) (ae->aexp ae)))
   ((fill-in (BrC R ae ae') e)      =
                            (Br (fill-in R e) (ae->aexp ae) (ae->aexp ae')))
   ((fill-in (LetActorC v R ae) e)  = (LetActor v (fill-in R e) (ae->aexp ae)))
   ((fill-in (SendCL val R) e)      = (Send (val->aexp val) (fill-in R e)))
   ((fill-in (SendCR R ae) e)       = (Send (fill-in R e) (ae->aexp ae)))
   ((fill-in (BecomeC R) e)         = (Become (fill-in R e)))
   ((fill-in (ReadyC R) e)          = (Ready (fill-in R e)))]
```

where we use auxiliary functions to convert the operational semantics-internal data types AVal and AE back to the AMST actor expressions AExp.

Finally, we define a `next-redex` function to take an actor expression in AExp, and optionally decompose it into a reduction context R (in ARC) and a redex r (in ARedex). If the expression is a value, we produce NONE, as follows:

```
# next-redex takes an actor expression AExp and optionally produces a
# reduction context R and a redex r
declare next-redex : [AExp] -> (Option (Pr ARC ARedex))

assert* next-redex-def :=
 [((next-redex (Var v))          = NONE)
  ((next-redex (Lambda v e))     = NONE)
  ((next-redex (App e1 e2)       = (SOME (pr Hole (AppR (aexp->val e1)
                                                        (aexp->val e2)))))
                         <== (  (next-redex e1 = NONE)
                              & (next-redex e2 = NONE)))
  ((next-redex (App e1 e2)       = (SOME (pr (AppCL (aexp->val e1) R) r)))
                         <== (  (next-redex e1 = NONE)
                              & (next-redex e2 = (SOME (pr R r)))))
  ((next-redex (App e1 e2)       = (SOME (pr (AppCR R (aexp->ae e2)) r)))
                         <== (next-redex e1 = (SOME (pr R r))))
  ((next-redex (Br e1 e2 e3)     = (SOME (pr Hole (BrR (aexp->val e1)
                                                       (aexp->ae e2)
                                                       (aexp->ae e3)))))
                         <== (next-redex e1 = NONE))
  ((next-redex (Br e1 e2 e3)     = (SOME (pr (BrC R (aexp->ae e2)
                                                    (aexp->ae e3)) r)))
                         <== (next-redex e1 = (SOME (pr R r))))
  ((next-redex (LetActor v e1 e2) = (SOME (pr Hole (LetActorR v (aexp->val e1)
                                                                (aexp->ae e2)))))
                         <== (next-redex e1 = NONE))
  ((next-redex (LetActor v e1 e2) = (SOME (pr (LetActorC v R (aexp->ae e2)) r)))
                         <== (next-redex e1 = (SOME (pr R r))))
  ((next-redex (Send e1 e2)      = (SOME (pr Hole (SendR (aexp->val e1)
                                                         (aexp->val e2)))))
                         <== (  (next-redex e1 = NONE)
                              & (next-redex e2 = NONE)))
  ((next-redex (Send e1 e2)      = (SOME (pr SendCL (aexp->val e1) R) r)))
                         <== (  (next-redex e1 = NONE)
                              & (next-redex e2 = (SOME (pr R r)))))
  ((next-redex (Send e1 e2)      = (SOME (pr SendCR R (aexp->ae e2)) r)))
                         <== (next-redex e1 = (SOME (pr R r))))
  ((next-redex (Become e)        = (SOME (pr Hole (BecomeR (aexp->val e)))))
                         <== (next-redex e = NONE))
  ((next-redex (Become e)        = (SOME (pr (BecomeC R) r)))
```

The AMST Language: Formal Verification and Execution of Actor Systems 47

```
                                <== (next-redex e = (SOME (pr R r))))
  ((next-redex (Ready e)        = (SOME (pr Hole (ReadyR (aexp->val e)))))
                                <== (next-redex e = NONE))
  ((next-redex (Ready e)        = (SOME (pr (ReadyC R) r)))
                                <== (next-redex e = (SOME (pr R r))))
]
```

where we use auxiliary functions to convert AMST actor expressions `AExp` into the operational semantics-internal structures `AVal` and `AE`.

Now, we can express Lemma 1 on unique decomposition of expressions:

```
define unique-redex-lemma :=
  (forall e . ((isValue e) |
               (exists R r . ((next-redex e = SOME (pr R r)) &
                  (forall R' r' . ((next-redex e = SOME (pr R' r')) ==>
                     ((R = R') & (r = r')))))))))
```

The proof is by structural induction on actor expressions:

```
 1  let {premise := lambda (e)
 2                    ((isValue e) |
 3                     (exists R r . ((next-redex e = SOME (pr R r)) &
 4                        (forall R' r' . ((next-redex e = SOME (pr R' r')) ==>
 5                           ((R = R') & (r = r'))))))));
 6       eVal := method (e)
 7                 (!chain<- [   (premise e)
 8                           <== (isValue e)                     [prop-taut]
 9                           <== true                            [isValue-def]]);
10       uniqueM := method (e R r redex-e)
11                    pick-any R' r'
12                      assume (next-redex e = SOME (pr R' r'))
13                        (!chain<- [((R = R') & (r = r'))
14                                <== ((pr R r) = (pr R' r'))           [pr-dt-axioms]
15                                <== ((SOME (pr R r)) = (SOME (pr R' r')))
16                                                                      [opt-axioms]
17                                <== (redex-e & (next-redex e = SOME (pr R' r')))
18                                     [method (p)
19                                        (!combine-equations
20                                           (!sym (!left-and p))
21                                           (!sym (!right-and p)))]
22                                <== true                              [prop-taut]]);
23       e1-cases := method (e e1 R1 r1 R2 r2)
24         let {ih-e1 := (premise e1);
25              existsP := (exists R r . ((next-redex e = SOME (pr R r))) &
26                            (forall R' r' . ((next-redex e = SOME (pr R' r')) ==>
27                               ((R = R') & (r = r')))));
28              _ := conclude existsP
29                     (!cases ih-e1
30                        assume e1-val := (isValue e1)
31                          let {no-redex-e1 :=
32                                 (!chain<- [   (next-redex e1 = NONE)
33                                           <== e1-val [val-no-redex]]);
34  #          ((next-redex e = (SOME (pr R1 r1))) <== (next-redex e1 = NONE))
35                               redex-e := (!chain<- [
36                                    ((next-redex e) = (SOME (pr R1 r1)))
37                                <== no-redex-e1                  [next-redex-def]]);
38                               unique := (!uniqueM e R1 r1 redex-e);
39                               _ := (!both redex-e unique)
40                              }
41                              (!egen* existsP [R1 r1])
42                        assume e1-noval :=
43                          (exists R r . ((next-redex e1 = SOME (pr R r)) &
44                             (forall R' r' . ((next-redex e1 = SOME (pr R' r')) ==>
45                                ((R = R') & (r = r'))))))
46  #          ((next-redex e = (SOME (pr R2' r2')))
47  #             <== (next-redex e1 = (SOME (pr R-e1 r-e1))))
48                          pick-witnesses R-e1 r-e1 for e1-noval e1-redex-unique
```

```
                    let {sub-redex := (make-sub [[R R-e1] [r r-e1]]);
                         R2' := (sub-redex R2);
                         r2' := (sub-redex r2);
                         redex-e1 := conclude
                             (next-redex e1 = SOME (pr R-e1 r-e1))
                               (!left-and e1-redex-unique);
                         redex-e := (!chain<- [
                             (next-redex e = (SOME (pr R2' r2')))
                                <== redex-e1                    [next-redex-def]]);
                         unique := (!uniqueM e R2' r2' redex-e);
                         _ := (!both redex-e unique)
                        }
                     (!egen* existsP [R2' r2'])
                    )}
             (!chain<- [(premise e) <== existsP [prop-taut]]);
   e1-e2-cases := method (e e1 e2 R1 r1 R2 r2 R3 r3)
       let {ih-e1 := (premise e1);
            ih-e2 := (premise e2);
            existsP := (exists R r . ((next-redex e = SOME (pr R r))) &
                 (forall R' r' . ((next-redex e = SOME (pr R' r')) ==>
                                   ((R = R') & (r = r')))));
            _ := conclude existsP
              (!cases ih-e1
                assume e1-val := (isValue e1)
                 let {no-redex-e1 := (!chain<- [
                       (next-redex e1 = NONE) <== e1-val [val-no-redex]])}
                  (!cases ih-e2
                    assume e2-val := (isValue e2)
 #  ((next-redex e = (SOME (pr R1 r1)))
 #     <== ( (next-redex e1 = NONE) & (next-redex e2 = NONE)))
                      let {no-redex-e2 := (!chain<- [
                           (next-redex e2 = NONE) <== e2-val [val-no-redex]];
                           redex-e := (!chain<- [
                               ((next-redex e) = (SOME (pr R1 r1)))
                                 <== (no-redex-e1 & no-redex-e2) [next-redex-def]]);
                           unique := (!uniqueM e R1 r1 redex-e);
                           _ := (!both redex-e unique)
                          }
                        (!egen* existsP [R1 r1])
                    assume e2-noval :=
                     (exists R r . ((next-redex e2 = SOME (pr R r)) &
                        (forall R' r' . ((next-redex e2 = SOME (pr R' r')) ==>
                                          ((R = R') & (r = r'))))))
 # ((next-redex (App e1 e2) = (SOME (pr R2' r2')))
 #    <== ((next-redex e1 = NONE) & (next-redex e2 = (SOME (pr R r)))))
                      pick-witnesses R-e2 r-e2 for e2-noval e2-redex-unique
                       let {sub-redex := (make-sub [[R R-e2] [r r-e2]]);
                            R2' := (sub-redex R2);
                            r2' := (sub-redex r2);
                            redex-e2 := conclude
                                (next-redex e2 = SOME (pr R-e2 r-e2))
                                  (!left-and e2-redex-unique);
                            redex-e := (!chain<- [
                                (next-redex e = (SOME (pr R2' r2')))
                                   <== (no-redex-e1 & redex-e2)
                                                            [next-redex-def]]);
                            unique := (!uniqueM e R2' r2' redex-e);
                            _ := (!both redex-e unique)
                           }
                         (!egen* existsP [R2' r2'])
                   )
                assume e1-noval :=
                   (exists R r . ((next-redex e1 = SOME (pr R r)) &
                      (forall R' r' . ((next-redex e1 = SOME (pr R' r')) ==>
                                        ((R = R') & (r = r'))))))
 # ((next-redex e = (SOME (pr R3' r3')))
 #    <== (next-redex e1 = (SOME (pr R r))))
                    pick-witnesses R-e1 r-e1 for e1-noval e1-redex-unique
```

```
117                      let {sub-redex := (make-sub [[R R-e1] [r r-e1]]);
118                           R3' := (sub-redex R3);
119                           r3' := (sub-redex r3);
120                           redex-e1 := conclude
121                              (next-redex e1 = SOME (pr R-e1 r-e1))
122                                (!left-and e1-redex-unique);
123                           redex-e := (!chain<- [
124                              (next-redex e = (SOME (pr R3' r3')))
125                              <== redex-e1                    [next-redex-def]]);
126                           unique := (!uniqueM e R3' r3' redex-e);
127                           _ := (!both redex-e unique)
128                           }
129                           (!egen* existsP [R3' r3'])
130                   )}
131             (!chain<- [(premise e) <== existsP [prop-taut11])
132      }
133   by-induction unique-redex-lemma {
134      (e as (Var v))        => (!eVal e)
135    | (e as (Lambda v e'))  => (!eVal e)
136    | (e as (App e1 e2))    => (!e1-e2-cases e e1 e2
137                               Hole (AppR (aexp->val e1) (aexp->val e2))
138                                    (AppCL (aexp->val e1) R) r
139                                    (AppCR R (aexp->ae e2)) r)
140    | (e as (Br e1 e2 e3))  => (!e1-cases e e1
141                               Hole (BrR (aexp->val e1) (aexp->ae e2)
142                                                        (aexp->ae e3))
143                                    (BrC R (aexp->ae e2) (aexp->ae e3)) r)
144    | (e as (LetActor v e1 e2)) => (!e1-cases e e1
145                               Hole (LetActorR v (aexp->val e1) (aexp->ae e2))
146                                    (LetActorC v R (aexp->ae e2)) r)
147    | (e as (Send e1 e2))   => (!e1-e2-cases e e1 e2
148                               Hole (SendR (aexp->val e1) (aexp->val e2))
149                                    (SendCL (aexp->val e1) R) r
150                                    (SendCR R (aexp->ae e2)) r)
151    | (e as (Become e1))    => (!e1-cases e e1
152                               Hole (BecomeR (aexp->val e1))
153                                    (BecomeC R) r)
154    | (e as (Ready e1))     => (!e1-cases e e1
155                               Hole (ReadyR (aexp->val e1))
156                                    (ReadyC R) r)
157   }
```

Lines 133–157 consider actor expressions in all their possible syntactic forms, and use the following Athena methods—the equivalent of lambda abstractions for deduction—to conclude the premise:

- eVal, for value expressions,
- e1-cases, for expressions that can only contain the reduction context in one argument position, and
- e1-e2-cases, for expressions that can contain the reduction context in two possible argument positions.

The eVal method (lines 6–9), concludes the premise for value expressions by using a backward implication chain, where the two steps are justified by the isValue definition axioms, and propositional tautology—namely, $p \rightarrow (p \vee q)$. We use the premise Athena procedure, (lines 1–5) to produce the first-order logic sentence desired for each individual actor expression.[4]

---
[4] Notice that a *procedure* producing a first-order logic sentence, such as premise, does not check whether it follows from the axioms; in contrast, a *method*, such as eVal, only succeeds to produce a "theorem", when it can deduce the expression logically from known axioms.

The `e1-cases` method (lines 23–63) takes the actor expression e, its subexpression e1 for which we are going to assume by inductive hypothesis that the premise is true, and the pairs $(R1, r1)$ and $(R2, r2)$ to consider the two decompositions of e for the cases on whether e1 is a value (lines 30–41), or not (lines 42–61). If e1 is a value, we can deduce that (next-redex e1 = NONE) by the `val-no-redex` lemma (lines 31–33), and that allows us to deduce that $R1[r1]$ is a valid decomposition of e by the `next-redex` definition (lines 35–37). We also deduce that this decomposition is unique by using the `uniqueM` method (line 38). Finally, we combine the decomposition existence, and its uniqueness (line 39), and use existential generalization to conclude the premise (line 41). If e1 is not a value, we know `e1-noval`, the second disjunct of the inductive hypothesis (lines 42–45). We pick witnesses R-e1 and r-e1 for this existentially quantified sentence, as the unique reduction context and redex, respectively for e1. Following, we can take the context and redex given in arguments R2 and r2 and substitute our witnesses for R and r getting R2' and r2' (lines 49–51). Subsequently, we prove that e can be decomposed into $R2'[r2']$ by using `next-redex`'s definition (lines 52–57). We also deduce that this decomposition is unique by using the `uniqueM` method (line 58). Finally, we combine the decomposition existence, and its uniqueness (line 59), and use existential generalization to conclude the premise (line 61). By propositional tautology, we can finally deduce the premise for e from the second disjunct named `existsP` (line 63).

The `uniqueM` method (lines 10–22) shows that for any decomposition of e, $R'[r']$, it must be the case that $R' = R$ and $r' = r$, assuming that $e = R[r]$ (`redex-e`). This method's deduction is justified by transitivity of equality (`combine-equations` method in lines 17–21), and datatype axioms for pairs and options, particularly, their *no-confusion* axioms (lines 13–16).

The `e1-e2-cases` method (lines 64–131) considers three possible decompositions for actor expression e: $R1[r1]$, $R2[r2]$, and $R3[r3]$. The method also takes advantage of the inductive hypotheses for sub-expressions e1 and e2 (lines 65–66). The deduction follows the cases of e1 being a value (lines 72–109), or not (lines 110–130). Inside the case of e1 being a value, we consider for e2 being a value (lines 76–87), or not (lines 88–108). When both e1 and e2 are values, we can demonstrate that R1 and r1 are the context and redex satisfying the unique decomposition property, in a similar way to the `e1-cases` method's `e1-val` case. When e1 is a value, and e2 is not a value, we pick witnesses R-e2 and r-e2 for the existentially quantified inductive hypothesis for e2, and use them to prove the unique decomposition $R2'[r2']$. Finally, when e1 is not a value, we demonstrate the unique decomposition of e into $R3'[r3']$. In these last two cases, we substitute the witness reduction context and redex into the arguments given to the method to create the respective unique reduction context and redex for e.

The `val-no-redex` lemma—used in lines 31–33, 73–74, and 79–80—is proven by structural induction on actor expressions. The first two forms Var and Lambda are values, and by the `next-redex` definition return NONE. The remaining (non-value) forms, use the `isValue` definition and contradiction (`from-complements` method) to prove the consequent of the implication.

The AMST Language: Formal Verification and Execution of Actor Systems

```
define val-no-redex :=
  (forall e . ((isValue e) ==> (next-redex e = NONE)))

let { eVal := method (e)
                assume (isValue e)
                  (!chain<- [ (next-redex e = NONE)
                              <== true                      [next-redex-def]]);
      eNoVal := method (e)
                  assume (isValue e)
                    (!from-complements
                     (next-redex e = NONE)
                     (isValue e)
                     (!chain<- [(~ isValue e) <== true  [isValue-def]]))}
by-induction val-no-redex {
  (e as (Var v))            => (!eVal e)
| (e as (Lambda v e))       => (!eVal e)
| (e as (App e1 e2))        => (!eNoVal e)
| (e as (Br e1 e2 e3))      => (!eNoVal e)
| (e as (LetActor v e1 e2)) => (!eNoVal e)
| (e as (Send e1 e2))       => (!eNoVal e)
| (e as (Become e'))        => (!eNoVal e)
| (e as (Ready e'))         => (!eNoVal e)
}
```

Following are the theorems that Athena outputs corresponding to the `val-no-redex` and `unique-redex-lemma` deductions above:

```
Sentence Actors.val-no-redex defined.

Theorem:
(forall ?e:AExp
  (if (Actors.isValue ?e:AExp)
      (= (Actors.next-redex ?e:AExp)
         NONE:(Option (Pr Actors.ARC Actors.ARedex)))))

Sentence Actors.unique-redex-lemma defined.

Theorem:
(forall ?e:AExp
  (or (Actors.isValue ?e:AExp)
      (exists ?R:Actors.ARC
        (exists ?r:Actors.ARedex
          (and (= (Actors.next-redex ?e:AExp)
                  (SOME (pr ?R:Actors.ARC ?r:Actors.ARedex)))
               (forall ?R':Actors.ARC
                 (forall ?r':Actors.ARedex
                   (if (= (Actors.next-redex ?e:AExp)
                          (SOME (pr ?R':Actors.ARC ?r':Actors.ARedex)))
                       (and (= ?R:Actors.ARC ?R':Actors.ARC)
                            (= ?r:Actors.ARedex ?r':Actors.ARedex)))))))))))
```

We can now proceed to define the operational semantics of AMST as a reduction relation for actor configurations—see Fig. 2.

The first two rules labeled (**fun a**), consider functional progress within an actor a, when its redex is either an **AppR** or a **BrR**. They rely on an auxiliary **beta** function to perform β-reduction (the main operational semantics rule from the lambda calculus) extended with branching, as follows:

```
declare beta: [AExp] -> AExp

assert* beta-def :=
  [(beta (App (Lambda v e1) e2)  = (sub e1 e2 v))
   (beta (Br e e1 e2)            = e1             <== (e = True))
   (beta (Br e e1 e2)            = e2             <== (e = False))]
```

```
# given a config and a label produces the next config
declare reduce : [AConfig Label] -> AConfig

assert* reduce-def :=
  [((reduce (kfg amap n) (fun a)) =
     (kfg ([a (fill-in R
                      (beta (App (val->aexp val)
                                 (val->aexp val'))))] ++
           (amap - a))
          n)
     <== (next-redex (option-val (amap at a)) =
                     (SOME pr R (AppR val val'))))
   ((reduce (kfg amap n) (fun a)) =
     (kfg ([a (fill-in R
                      (beta (Br (val->aexp val)
                                (ae->aexp ae) (ae->aexp ae'))))] ++
           (amap - a))
          n)
     <== (next-redex (option-val (amap at a)) =
                     (SOME pr R (BrR val ae ae'))))
   ((reduce (kfg amap n) (new a af)) =   # af fresh
     (kfg ([af (Ready (sub (val->aexp bv) (Var af) a'))] ++
           [a (fill-in R (sub (ae->aexp ae) (Var af) a'))] ++
           (amap - a))
          n)
     <== ((next-redex (option-val (amap at a)) =
                      (SOME pr R (LetActorR a' bv ae))) &
          (~ af in (dom amap))))
   ((reduce (kfg amap n) (snd a)) =
     (kfg ([a (fill-in R Nil)] ++ (amap - a))
          ((msg a' (val->aexp cv)) ++ n))
     <== ((next-redex (option-val (amap at a)) =
                      (SOME pr R (SendR (VarV a') cv)))))
   ((reduce (kfg amap n) (rcv a e')) =
     (kfg ([a (App (val->aexp bv) e')] ++ (amap - a))
          (n - (msg a e')))
     <== (((msg a e') in n) &
          (next-redex (option-val (amap at a)) =
                      (SOME pr R (ReadyR bv)))))
   ((reduce (kfg amap n) (bec a a')) =   # a' fresh
     (kfg ([a (Ready (val->aexp bv))] ++
           [a' (fill-in R Nil)] ++
           (amap - a))
          n)
     <== ((next-redex (option-val (amap at a)) =
                      (SOME pr R (BecomeR bv))) &
          (~ a' in (dom amap))))
  ]
```

Fig. 2. AMST actor language operational semantics.

which itself relies on alpha-equivalence of expressions—to compare e to True and False, and the substitution function:

```
# (sub e1 e2 v) denotes e1{e2/v}
declare sub: [AExp AExp Ide] -> AExp

assert* sub-def :=
  [((sub (Var v) e v)        = e)
   ((sub (Var v) e v2)       = (Var v) <== v =/= v2)
   ((sub (Lambda v e) e2 v)  = (Lambda v e))
   ((sub (Lambda v e) e2 v2) = (Lambda v (sub e e2 v2)) <== v =/= v2)
   ((sub (App e1 e2) e v)    = (App (sub e1 e v) (sub e2 e v)))
```

The AMST Language: Formal Verification and Execution of Actor Systems

```
((sub (Br e1 e2 e3) e v)      = (Br (sub e1 e v) (sub e2 e v) (sub e3 e v)))
((sub (LetActor v e1 e2) e v) = (LetActor v e1 e2))
((sub (LetActor v e1 e2) e v2) = (LetActor v (sub e1 e v2) (sub e2 e v2))
                                 <== v =/= v2)
((sub (Send e1 e2) e v)       = (Send (sub e1 e v) (sub e2 e v)))
((sub (Become e1) e v)        = (Become (sub e1 e v)))
((sub (Ready e1) e v)         = (Ready (sub e1 e v)))
]
```

The next four actor redexes are as follows:

The `LetActorR` redex reduction rule creates an actor with fresh name `af`, ready to process messages with behavior `bv` and lets the parent actor fill in the `LetActor` reduction context with expression `ae`. We substitute the fresh actor name `af` for `a'` in both the new actor's behavior and the continuation `ae`, so that both the actor and its parent know about this new actor name. This rule only is enabled if the fresh actor name in the label (`new a af`) is actually fresh, i.e., af $\notin$ (dom amap).

The `SendR` redex reduction rule adds a new message directed to actor `a'` to the network, and lets the sending actor `a` continue immediately with its continuation—i.e., its reduction context filled in with `Nil`.

The `ReadyR` redex reduction rule is enabled when there is a message directed to `a` in the network with content `e'`. Actor `a` applies its behavior (a lambda abstraction) to the incoming message's content, and one occurrence of the message is removed from the network (using multiset difference). Notice that the reduction context `R` is not used.

The `BecomeR` redex reduction rule makes the actor in focus `a`, `Ready` to receive subsequent messages with behavior `bv`, while creating an anonymous actor (with fresh and unknown name `a'`), to carry out its continuation. This rule only is enabled if the fresh actor name in the label (`bec a a'`) is actually fresh, i.e., $a' \notin$ (dom amap).

Definition 1 ((enabled k l)). *A transition* l *is* enabled *in the configuration* k, *written* (enabled k l), *iff there is a configuration* k' *such that* k' = (reduce k l). *Otherwise, the transition is disabled.*

We define an `enabled` function, using a `redexes` function that computes all the enabled transitions in a given configuration:

```
# given a config and a list of possible fresh names, produce multi-set
# of enabled transitions
declare redexes: [AConfig (List Ide)] -> (MSet.MSet Label)

assert* redexes-def :=
[((redexes (kfg amap n) fvars) = (redexes_dm (kfg amap n) (dom amap) fvars))]

declare enabled : [AConfig (List Ide) Label] -> Boolean

assert* enabled-def :=
[((enabled k fvars l) <==> l in (redexes k fvars))]
```

where the auxiliary `redexes_dm` function ensures that fresh names in labels do not conflict with existing actor names:

```
# given a config, a set of actor names, and a list of possible fresh
# names, produce multi-set of enabled transitions
declare redexes_dm: [AConfig (Set.Set Ide) (List Ide)] -> (MSet.MSet Label)

assert* redexes_dm-def :=
[((redexes_dm (kfg empty-map n) dm fvars) = empty-mset)
 ((redexes_dm (kfg ([a e] ++ amap) n) dm fvars) = (redexes_dm (kfg amap n) dm fvars)
        <== ((next-redex e) = NONE))
 ((redexes_dm (kfg ([a e] ++ amap) n) dm fvars) =
        ((fun a) ++ (redexes_dm (kfg amap n) dm fvars))
        <== ((next-redex e) = (SOME pr R (AppR val1 val2))))
 ((redexes_dm (kfg ([a e] ++ amap) n) dm fvars) =
        ((fun a) ++ (redexes_dm (kfg amap n) dm fvars))
        <== ((next-redex e) = (SOME pr R (BrR val ae ae'))))
 ((redexes_dm (kfg ([a e] ++ amap) n) dm (af :: fvars)) =
        ((new a af) ++ (redexes_dm (kfg amap n) dm fvars))
        <== (((next-redex e) = (SOME pr R (LetActorR a' val ae'))) &
             (~ af in dm)))
 ((redexes_dm (kfg ([a e] ++ amap) n) dm (af :: fvars)) =
        (redexes_dm (kfg ([a e] ++ amap) n) dm fvars)
        <== (((next-redex e) = (SOME pr R (LetActorR a' val ae'))) &
             (af in dm)))
 ((redexes_dm (kfg ([a e] ++ amap) n) dm fvars) =
        ((snd a) ++ (redexes_dm (kfg amap n) dm fvars))
        <== ((next-redex e) = (SOME pr R (SendR val1 val2))))
 ((redexes_dm (kfg ([a e] ++ amap) n) dm (a' :: fvars)) =
        ((bec a a')
        ++ (redexes_dm (kfg amap n) dm fvars))
        <== (((next-redex e) = (SOME pr R (BecomeR val))) &
             (~ a' in dm)))
 ((redexes_dm (kfg ([a e] ++ amap) n) dm (a' :: fvars)) =
        (redexes_dm (kfg ([a e] ++ amap) n) dm fvars)
        <== (((next-redex e) = (SOME pr R (BecomeR val))) &
             (a' in dm)))
 ((redexes_dm (kfg ([a e] ++ amap) n) dm fvars) =
        ((msgs n a) MSet.\/ (redexes_dm (kfg amap n) dm fvars))
        <== ((next-redex e) = (SOME pr R (ReadyR val))))
]
```

which itself depends on a `msgs` function to compute all labels corresponding to incoming messages for an actor a:

```
# for each message in network, create a label
declare msgs: [(MSet.MSet Message) Ide] -> (MSet.MSet Label)

assert* msgs-def :=
[((msgs empty-mset a) = empty-mset)
 ((msgs ((msg a e') ++ n) a) = ((rcv a e') ++ (msgs n a)))
 ((msgs ((msg a' e') ++ n) a) = (msgs n a) <== (a =/= a'))]
```

Computation Sequences and Paths

Definition 2 (Computation trees). *If* k *is a configuration, then we define the* computation tree *for* k, (ctree k), *to be the set of all finite sequences of labeled transitions of the form* $[l_i \mid k_{i+1} = (reduce\ k_i\ l_i) \wedge i < n]$ *for some* $n \in \mathbb{N}$, *with* $k = k_0$. *We call such sequences* computation sequences.

```
# computation sequence as a list of labels
define-sort CSequence := (List Label)
# computation tree as a set of computation sequences
define-sort CTree := (Set.Set CSequence)

# shortcut for variable names in different domains
```

```
define [cs rcs l rl] :=
       [?cs:CSequence ?rcs:CTree ?l:Label ?rl:(MSet.MSet Label)]

# +++ takes a Label l and a Computation Tree and prepends the label l
# to all the sequences in the set.
declare +++ : [Label CTree] -> CTree

assert* +++-def :=
[ (l +++ empty-set = (l :: nil) ++ empty-set)
  (l +++ (cs ++ rcs) = ((l :: cs) ++ (l +++ rcs)))
]

# computation tree as a set of computation sequences
declare ctree : [AConfig (List Ide)] -> CTree

# computation tree given a multiset of valid next labels
declare ctreel : [AConfig (MSet.MSet Label) (List Ide)] -> CTree

assert* ctree-def :=
[(((ctree k fvars) = (ctreel k (redexes k fvars) fvars))]

assert* ctreel-def :=
[(((ctreel k empty-mset fvars) = empty-set)
 ((ctreel k (l ++ rl) fvars) = ((l +++ (ctree (reduce k l) fvars))
                                Set.\/ (ctreel k rl fvars)))
]
```

Lemma 2 (Anonymity). *If* k' = (reduce k (bec a a')) *and* cs *is any computation sequence in the computation tree* (ctree k'), *then* cs *contains no transitions with label of the form* (rcv a' e).

```
define anonymity-lemma :=
  (forall k a a' cs fvars .
    ((cs in (ctree (reduce k (bec a a')) fvars)) ==>
       (forall e . (~ ((rcv a' e) in cs)))))
```

Definition 3 (Computation paths). *The sequences of a computation tree are partially ordered by the initial segment relation. A* computation path *from* k *is a maximal linearly ordered set of computation sequences in the computation tree* (ctree k). *It can be* infinite *or* finite.

```
# +++p takes a Label l and a Computation Path Tree and prepends the
# label l to all the sequences in the set.
declare +++p : [Label CTree] -> CTree

assert* +++p-def :=
[ (l +++p empty-set = empty-set)
  (l +++p (cs ++ rcs) = ((l :: cs) ++ (l +++p rcs)))
]

# computation paths as a set of maximal computation sequences
declare cpaths : [AConfig (List Ide)] -> CTree

# computation paths given a multiset of valid next labels
declare cpathsl : [AConfig (MSet.MSet Label) (List Ide)] -> CTree

assert* cpaths-def :=
[(((cpaths k fvars) = (cpathsl k (redexes k fvars) fvars))]

assert* cpathsl-def :=
[(((cpathsl k empty-mset fvars) = nil ++ empty-set)
```

```
((cpathsl k (1 ++ empty-mset) fvars) = (1 +++p (cpaths (reduce k 1) fvars)))
((cpathsl k (1 ++ rl) fvars) = ((1 +++p (cpaths (reduce k 1) fvars))
                                  Set.\/ (cpathsl k rl fvars))
                               <== (rl =/= empty-mset))]
```

The following example illustrates the difference between computation sequences and computation paths:

```
> (eval (ctree (kfg (['a (App I I)] ++ ['b (App I I)] ++ empty-map) empty-mset)
               (gen-fresh 'f 30)))

Term:
(Set.insert (:: (Actors.fun 'a)
                (:: (Actors.fun 'b)
                    nil:(List Actors.Label)))
  (Set.insert (:: (Actors.fun 'a)
                  nil:(List Actors.Label))
    (Set.insert (:: (Actors.fun 'b)
                    (:: (Actors.fun 'a)
                        nil:(List Actors.Label)))
      (Set.insert (:: (Actors.fun 'b)
                      nil:(List Actors.Label))
        Set.null:(Set.Set (List Actors.Label))))))

> (eval (cpaths (kfg (['a (App I I)] ++ ['b (App I I)] ++ empty-map) empty-mset)
                (gen-fresh 'f 30)))

Term:
(Set.insert (:: (Actors.fun 'a)
                (:: (Actors.fun 'b)
                    nil:(List Actors.Label)))
  (Set.insert (:: (Actors.fun 'b)
                  (:: (Actors.fun 'a)
                      nil:(List Actors.Label)))
    Set.null:(Set.Set (List Actors.Label))))
```

where we notice that the computation tree includes non-maximal sequences, whereas the computation paths only include the two maximal sequences where both transitions in actors a and b have occurred, albeit in different orders.

Since the result of a transition is uniquely determined by the starting configuration and the transition label, computation sequences and paths can be equally represented by their initial configuration and the sequence of transition labels. The sequence of configurations can be computed by induction on the index of occurrence.

Definition 4 (Cfig). *Let* k *be a configuration and let* $L = [l_i | i < \infty]$ *be a sequence of labels corresponding to a computation from* k. *The ith configuration of the computation from* k *determined by* L, Cfig(k,L,i) *is defined by induction on* i *as follows:*

1. *Cfig*$(k, L, 0) = k$
2. *Cfig*$(k, L * [l_i], i + 1) = k'$ *where* $K' =$ (reduce *Cfig*(k, L, i) l_i). *Thus, the path* π *determined by* k,L *is the sequence*

$$[Cfig(k, L, i) \mid i < \infty]$$

The AMST Language: Formal Verification and Execution of Actor Systems

(cfig k L) computes the configuration resulting after executing a finite list of labeled transitions L starting from k:

```
# executes a finite computation sequence following list of labels
declare cfig : [AConfig (List Label)] -> AConfig

assert* cfig-def :=
  [((cfig k nil) = k)
   ((cfig k (l :: rest)) = (cfig (reduce k l) rest))]
```

Notice that the cfig function computes Cfig(k,L) = Cfig(k,L,Len(L)).

Fairness. Not all paths are admissible. We rule out those computations that are unfair, *i.e.*, those in which there is some transition that should eventually happen but does not. A path π in the computation tree (ctree k), is *fair*, written (fair π) if each enabled transition eventually happens or becomes permanently disabled.

Definition 5 ((fair π)).
$(fair\ \pi) \iff (\forall i < \infty)(\exists l)(enabled\ k_i\ l) \implies$
$(((\exists j \geq i)(reduce\ k_j\ l) = k_{j+1}) \lor (\exists j > i)(\forall j' > j)(\neg(enabled\ k_{j'}\ l)))$

```
declare fair : [AConfig CSequence] -> Boolean

assert* fair-def :=
[(((fair k cs) <==>
   (cs in (ctree k fvars)) &
   (forall i .
     (exists l . (enabled (reduceN k (take cs i)) fvars l))
     ==> l in (drop cs i) |
         (exists j .
           i < j &
           forall j' . j < j' ==>
             (~ (enabled (reduceN k (take cs j')) fvars l)))))]
```

Definition 6 (Fair computation trees). *For a configuration k, we defined its fair computation tree* (ftree k) *to be the subset of its computation tree that contains fair paths.*

$$(ftree\ k) = \{\pi \in (ctree\ k)\ |\ (fair\ \pi)\}$$

```
declare ftree: [AConfig (List Ide)] -> CTree
assert* ftree-def :=
  [(cs in (ftree k fvars) <==> (cs in (ctree k fvars) & (fair k cs)))]
```

Lemma 3 (Fair finite paths). *A finite path is fair.*

Proof. If (Len π) = M, then by maximality we must have that $\forall l.\neg$(enabled Cfig(k, π) l). Consequently the path is fair, since all enabled transitions have either occurred or become disabled.

4 Discussion

We have presented an executable operational semantics for the Agha, Mason, Smith, and Talcott (AMST) simple lambda-based actor language introduced in [2][5] The theory has been written in the Athena dual computation and deduction language [3] which enables us to not only evaluate expressions in the language but also formally prove properties about it.

The theory is presented as sets of equations that serve two purposes: first, each set of equations is syntactic sugar for a set of universally quantified first-order logic sentences, which are construed as axioms for the theory. We have illustrated the proof of the unique expression decomposition lemma (Lemma 1 in [2]) by structural induction. Second, the set of equations can be viewed as rewrite rules from left to right, and used to convert ground terms into normal forms by Athena's `eval` function. We use this capability to *execute* actor expressions as illustrated by several examples in the paper.

Future work includes fully encoding the actor theory in [2], including compositional aspects (*i.e.*, modeling receptionists and external actors for configurations), equivalence of expressions (may, must, and test equivalences, and the partial collapse to two equivalences under fairness), equivalence of configurations, laws of expression equivalence, and proof methods for verification of actor systems. Athena also can be used to generate code for the theory (using its `fun` form to introduce equation sets) which can be explored to generate executable actor code in different actor languages.

In Honor of Gul Agha

Gul has been a great influence in my academic and non-academic life. When reading his book on Actors [1], I was immediately captivated by the elegance, simplicity, and expressive power of this concurrent computation model. Agha, Mason, Smith, and Talcott presented a simple actor language, its operational semantics, and theory [2]. I have used that language, called here AMST, to introduce concurrency to thousands of students at RPI for over 20 years. In all this time, it would have been great to be able to *execute* programs written in this language. As an honor to Gul and his legacy on the concurrent programming and concurrency theory communities, I decided to make AMST an executable language while keeping the original spirit of developing a theory of actors with laws of expression equivalence. The Athena dual computation and deduction language [3] was a timely choice for developing the executable AMST theory.

Gul Agha has never stopped to be an *academic father* to me. I was extremely lucky to have him as my Ph.D. advisor at UIUC, and over the years, I have grown to increasingly appreciate his philosophy of life, his unwavering quest for understanding and new knowledge, his appreciation for all sentient life on Earth, and his keen sense of humor while diplomatically but firmly pointing out injustices and nonsensical politics at all levels of society. I am truly honored to be his academic descendant.

---

[5] The AMST theory is available open-source at https://wcl.cs.rpi.edu/amst/.

References

1. Agha, G.: Actors: A Model of Concurrent Computation in Distributed Systems. MIT Press, Cambridge (1986)
2. Agha, G., Mason, I.A., Smith, S.F., Talcott, C.L.: A foundation for actor computation. J. Funct. Program. **7**, 1–72 (1997)
3. Arkoudas, K., Musser, D.: Fundamental Proof Methods in Computer Science. MIT Press, Cambridge (2017)
4. Church, A.: The Calculi of Lambda Conversion. Princeton University Press, Princeton (1941)
5. Varela, C.A.: Programming Distributed Computing Systems: A Foundational Approach. MIT Press, Cambridge (2013). http://wcl.cs.rpi.edu/pdcs

Actor Capabilities for Message Ordering

Colin S. Gordon

Drexel University, Philadelphia, PA 19104, USA
csgordon@drexel.edu

Abstract. Actor systems are a flexible model of concurrent and distributed programming, which are efficiently implementable, and avoid many classic concurrency bugs by construction. However they must still deal with the challenge of messages arriving in unexpected orders.

We describe an approach to restricting the orders in which actors send messages to each other, by equipping actor references—the handle used to address another actor—with a protocol restricting which message types can be sent to another actor and in which order using that particular actor reference. This endows the actor references with the properties of (flow-sensitive) static capabilities, which we call actor capabilities.

By sending other actors only restricted actor references, actors may control which messages are sent in which orders by other actors. Rules for duplicating (splitting) actor references ensure that these restrictions apply even in the presence of delegation. The capabilities themselves restrict message send ordering, which may form the foundation for stronger forms of reasoning. We demonstrate this by layering an effect system over the base type system, where the relationships enforced between the actor capabilities and the effects of an actor's behaviour ensure that an actor's behaviour is always prepared to handle any message that may arrive.

Keywords: Actor systems · Capability systems · Type-and-effect systems

1 Introduction

Actor systems have long been of interest since Hewitt's original conception of the idea [40], both for anthropomorphic, intuitive appeal similar to that which boosted early interest in object-oriented programming (leading to work on active objects [5,58])—and because the programming model enjoys many natural benefits that make it particularly well-suited to structuring concurrent and distributed programs. Compared to popular shared-memory concurrency models like POSIX threads, the actor model inverts control so that all actions in the system occur in response to asynchronous messages. This avoids classic issues with data races[1] and deadlocks. Instead actor systems suffer from difficulties

---

[1] Though actor implementations embedded in imperative programming languages may need additional techniques [14,35,51,66] to share data that was once or may again be mutable.

ensuring that messages are sent or received in expected orders [4,38,67], including the possibility that a message arrives before or after an actor is using a behaviour ready to process that particular message.

Static checking of message ordering in message passing systems is a classic problem, studied in many settings. Nielson, Nielson, and Amtoft [2,57] examined this problem for Concurrent ML (CML) in the 1990s, proposing what we now recognize as sequential [65] (a.k.a., flow-sensitive) type-and-effect systems for ensuring sends and receives in that synchronous message passing environment were in agreement between different threads. Work on session types began around the same time [43,44], initially for pairs of processes, and later for arbitrary numbers of processes. (And as it turns out, those can be formulated as effect systems as well [59].) Each of these has a language for describing *all* communication behaviour of a process, yielding possibly-complex specifications. (We discuss this further in Sect. 5.)

Effect systems are closely related to static *capability systems*, which typically trade off some expressivity and precision for dramatic increases in brevity of specifications [30]. Rather than allowing a program to do whatever it pleases and attempting to analyze that after the fact with effects, these systems require a specific capability for the program to perform any operation of interest. Dynamic capability systems do this via the dynamic semantics of the language: the operation literally cannot execute without the availability of a capability value [49,54]. Actor systems are already a form of dynamic capability system—an actor X can only send messages to another actor Y if it possesses the actor reference for Y, and provides it to the send operation. Static capability systems instead use static checking—usually a type(-and-effect) system—to restrict what a region of code can do by restricting which (static) capabilities are accessible to that code. In this way, the set of input capabilities can give an upper bound on the effect of a program fragment [15,30].

A less widely-acknowledged aspect of static capability systems is that by restricting the creation or duplication of capabilities, it becomes possible to enforce *global* invariants with *local* checks [30], which has been employed throughout decades of work on what are now collectively known as *reference capabilities*, where the capability restrictions are attached to each reference to an object. This encompasses many ownership (and universe) type systems [6,7,22], read-only reference systems [28,35,68,70,71], and rely-guarantee reasoning applied between references [33,34,52,53], to name just a few variants.

In this paper we explore this idea adapted to *actor references* rather than heap references, in a version of these ideas we call *actor capabilities*. Each actor reference carries a restriction, given as a formal language over message types, restricting the order in which messages may be sent using that particular reference; different references to the same actor may carry different capabilities/restrictions, allowing highly *localized* checks for message ordering. We also make an unusual choice compared to most capability systems: rather than assuming each actor is created with a specific fixed language, we allow each actor to dynamically create *new* capabilities for itself—tracked with an effect system. The result is a type system which combines flow-sensitive capabilities with flow-sensitive (sequential [65]) effects in a highly-integrated way.

2 An Intuitive Explanation of Actor Capabilities

Current actor system implementations come in two varieties: those which allow actors to send any message type to any actor at any time, and those which attach a type parameter to actor references (handles used to address another actor) which restrict the types of messages that can be sent. The former category includes early versions of Akka and modern versions of Akka.NET, as well as all dynamically-typed actor languages and libraries (Erlang, Elixir, etc.). The latter category includes modern Akka, which we focus on because it is closest to what we propose. *All* actor systems in either category effectively handle messages by case analysis of the message's dynamic type. Akka (now) uses the Scala type ActorRef[T] to represent a handle to send a particular actor messages of type T. This is both a dynamic capability and a static capability:

- It is impossible to send an actor a message without obtaining an ActorRef[T] referring to it. These actor references cannot be forged by a program. Thus an actor reference is effectively a form of dynamic object capability [54].[2]
- To send an actor a message of type U, code must use an ActorRef[T] where U <: T (U is a subtype of T). To send some other message of type B, the code would still need an ActorRef[B]—even if a developer knew (correctly!) that the recipient would *always* accept a B, the corresponding actor reference would be required by the type system. Multiple actor references to the same actor with different (incomparable!) message type bounds can exist. Thus this already has much in common with reference capability systems.

Akka also ensures that if an ActorRef[T] exists for a specific actor, then that actor will *always* accept messages of type T. With the capability properties above, this invariant ensures that all messages that can be sent will be handled. The code of Fig. 1 offers a useful starting point to dig into this a bit more, to call out the specific aspects of this situation we must generalize to deal with the set of valid messages changing over time.

The ExampleActor is an object which when invoked (i.e., by ExampleActor() implicitly calling the apply method) creates a new behaviour, defined in the presence of an Akka-selected ActorContext for the newly-created actor; for our purposes, this is effectively a container for the new actor's self reference context.self of type ActorRef[MessageBase] (though of course Akka uses it for much more). The new actor is created by Behaviors.setup. beh is a recursively defined Behavior[MessageBase], indicating that this is a behavior which accepts messages of type MessageBase (not shown). Akka's functional API (the

---

[2] We are intentionally side-stepping discussions of capability-safety and ambient authority raised by the ability to look up an actor reference by the actor's name.

```
import akka.actor.typed.*
import akka.actor.typed.scaladsl.*
object ExampleActor {
  def apply(): Behavior[MessageBase] =
    Behaviors.setup((context: ActorContext[MessageBase]) => {
      val beh : Behavior[MessageBase] = // Recursively-defined behaviour
        Behaviors.receiveMessage((msg: MessageBase) => {
          msg match { // Inspect the message type
            case Heartbeat(sender) => // if it is a heartbeat...
              val returnAddress : ActorRef[Heartbeat] = context.self
              sender ! HeartbeatResponse(returnAddress) // reply
              beh // Return next behaviour from this case
            ... // other message cases omitted
          } })
      beh // Make beh the initial behaviour
    }))
}
```

Fig. 1. A simple Scala program using the Typed Akka API.

one used in this example[3]) requires each behaviour to return a new behavior to handle the next message, which this code does in each branch of the `match` statement, returning itself (so after handling one message, the behavior explicitly signals that it will be used to handle the next message as well).

The one shown case of the behavior responds to the `Heartbeat` subclass of `MessageBase` by first extracting a new reference for the sender to directly message this actor in the future (the message may have been routed indirectly through other actors). The type of the "return address" reference is specialized to its intended use: `ActorRef[Heartbeat]`. `ActorRef[MessageBase]` is a subtype of `ActorRef[Heartbeat]`—`ActorRef` is contravariant in its type parameter. So via subtyping the `context.self` reference, which can be used to send any subtype of `MessageBase`, can be coerced to a more restrictive type, which can only be used to send further `Heartbeat` messages. This more restrictive reference is then sent back to the sender.

2.1 A Capability View of Safety Guarantees

Notice that we derive important safety guarantees from the type system: the original requestor can never use the `ActorRef` sent back with the response to send the `ExampleActor` a message type it does not handle, and the actor is statically known to handle all messages it receives.[4] We obtain this from the (sometimes implicit) three-way agreement across:

- The `ActorRef[MessageBase]` (from `context.self`) specifies the expected type of messages sent to the actor. In particular, all other actor references to this actor are derived from `context.self` or the spawn operation (which yields an `ActorRef` of the same type), and by contravariance specify only

---

[3] Akka also has an object-oriented API, and both are heavily used, but the functional API is quite close to both classic actor calculi [1] and our formal development.
[4] We are using handle in a loose sense here; the behaviour might simply ignore some subtypes of `MessageBase` (intentionally or due to a developer's mistake).

subtypes of `ActorRef[MessageBase]`—for any `ActorRef[T]` referring to this actor, `T <: MessageBase`.
- The `Behavior[MessageBase]` specifies the expected message (super)type for incoming messages, and `context.self`'s type parameter to `ActorRef` will always match the behaviour's type parameter.
- The send operation (`!` operator) at the recipient of the response (`sender`) only allows messages of type `Heartbeat` to be sent via an `ActorRef[Heartbeat]`

`ActorRef[T]` can be seen as a family of static capabilities. Owning one for a particular `T` *only* permits sending values of (subtypes of) type `T`, even if the destination actor can accept additional message types. The fact that each new capability to a certain actor is created with *at most* the permissions of the capability it was copied from means that creation of new capabilities/actor references collectively preserve a global invariant that no part of the program possesses a capability to send anything but a `MessageBase` in this example. This property of creating new `ActorRef` s from old is similar to a cross-cutting theme in much of the static capability literature, though only some work makes this fully explicit [10, 33, 34, 52, 53] (as we will need to do later). As all actor references are either returned from the actor creation (not shown) or derived from the actor's self-reference (`context.self`), both of which have an `ActorRef` parameter matching the `Behavior` parameter, this collectively maintains the global property [30] that no actor reference can be used to send a message that will not be handled by the installed behaviour. While each behaviour returns a possibly-different behaviour for handling future incoming messages, the type system ensures the new behaviour's message type matches the current behaviour, so previously-shared references to the actor never become invalid (i.e., never permit sending messages unexpected by some future behaviour of the same target actor).

This is a valuable property, and the reason that newer versions of Akka switched *to* this typed API, rather than using a general `ActorRef` type without a type parameter (called the "classic" API), which could be sent messages of any type. However, it does come at a cost. It is common for actors to move through multiple lifecycle phases, where some messages are (temporarily or permanently) irrelevant, yet a correct program must still explicitly include code to handle those unexpected messages. The older untyped Akka API allowed code to simply switch to a new behaviour which might not handle *any* of the message types it previously received! This was convenient for code that was correct, but nothing statically prevented bugs where one actor would send another a message of a type it either expected to never see again or to not see yet. Technically, the same can still happen with the typed API if `MessageBase` is actually `Object`, it is simply less pronounced because developers are encouraged to use smaller type hierarchies. It would be desirable to preserve the kinds of safety guarantees targeted by this implicitly capability-based API, while extending them to *fully* resolve the question of certain message types arriving at unexpected times.

2.2 Extending the Capability View for Message Ordering

This capability-based view of how Akka (and similar actor systems) ensure all messages are handled can be extended to deal with the case where actors' set of accepted messages change arbitrarily over time.

The key idea we will employ is to replace the single type parameter of Akka's `ActorRef` with a formal language over types—thus specifying a set of allowable *sequences* of messages that may be sent to that actor. This allows the specification of actor references that permit sending just a single message, a fixed number of messages, sending a certain message type just once and others an unbounded number of times, alternating message types in a particular way, or other interesting restrictions—the notion of a formal language is quite general.

On top of this, we must preserve and extend the three-way agreement described above. When an actor reference is duplicated, we cannot (in general) allow the reference to be duplicated at the same type. Otherwise an `ActorRef` that permitted sending exactly one message of type T could first be copied, then used to send a T, then the copy could be used to send a T, circumventing the intended restriction of the original capability. So we must adapt machinery for carefully tracking splitting of capabilities [9, 10, 33, 34, 52, 53] to ensure the number and relative ordering of message sends are preserved when actor references are duplicated—including handling the subtleties from the new copies being usable in any (possibly-interleaved) order. Fortunately there are existing tools in formal language theory we can use to guide the design here.

The other pieces of preserving and extending this three-way correspondence are the send operation, and agreement between actor references and behaviour typing. The send operation clearly must be typed in a flow-sensitive manner, to track when a send "uses up" one allowed message type. The more complex piece is maintaining agreement between these consumable actor reference capabilities and a more flexible behaviour typing that allows actors to start and stop accepting messages of various types. The challenge is to ensure that previously-shared capabilities continue to remain valid when an actor changes behaviours.

If we treat Akka's existing `ActorRef[T]` as a capability to send a sequence of messages of types in $\{\tau \mid \tau <: T\}^*$, then ensuring every future handler for the actor must handle the same types is sufficient to ensure old capabilities remain valid, because the message types are fixed permanently (invariant), so ensuring that the initial actor references and initial behaviour agree on T at actor creation time is a sufficient check. But if both the permissions of remaining capabilities, and the future behaviours' domains change over time, we will need additional machinery to synchronize those changes. We will use an effect system for this, where duplicating/splitting a capability for the current actor will create obligations for future message handling tracked in effects.

3 An Actor Capability Language

Figure 2 gives the syntax, and dynamic semantics of a simple actor language (abbreviated to omit entirely standard aspects). As in the most classic versions

$$\begin{array}{rl}
\text{Expressions} & e ::= n \mid b \mid \langle e,e \rangle \mid e \oplus e \mid \neg e \mid \text{if } e\, e\, e \mid (\lambda_f x.\, e) \mid \rho \mid \text{beh}_L(\overline{\tau \rightsquigarrow e}) \mid \text{spawn}(e) \\
\text{Operators} & \oplus \in + \mid - \mid \times \mid \div \mid \vee \mid \wedge \\
\text{Actor Stores} & \sigma \in \text{Location} \rightharpoonup \text{beh}_L(\overline{\tau \rightsquigarrow e}) \\
\text{Message Queues} & \mu \in \text{list}(\text{Value} \times \text{Type} \times \text{Location}) \\
\text{Global Message Queues} & \gamma \in \text{Location} \times \text{Location} \rightharpoonup \text{list}(\text{Value} \times \text{Type})
\end{array}$$

$\boxed{\mu; \sigma; e \xrightarrow{L}_\ell \mu'; \sigma'; e'}$ Booleans, natural numbers, pairs, and (recursive) functions omitted

$$\text{E-Self} \frac{}{\mu; \sigma; \text{self}_L \xrightarrow{\{L\}}_\ell \mu; \sigma; \ell} \qquad \text{E-Spawn} \frac{\text{IsBehaviour}(v) \quad \text{fresh } \ell'}{\mu; \sigma; \text{spawn}(v) \xrightarrow{\{\epsilon\}}_\ell \mu; \sigma \uplus \ell \mapsto v; \ell'}$$

$$\text{E-Send} \frac{l \Downarrow_\ell \ell_{\text{dst}}; \mu; \sigma \qquad e \Downarrow_\ell v; \mu'; \sigma'}{\mu; \sigma; \text{send}_\tau(\ell_{\text{dst}}, v) \xrightarrow{\{\epsilon\}}_\ell \mu + (v, \tau, \ell_{\text{dst}}); \sigma; ()}$$

$\boxed{\sigma; \gamma \Rightarrow \sigma'; \gamma'}$ E-MsgHandled
$$\frac{\tau \in \overline{\tau} \qquad \emptyset; \emptyset; e_\tau[\text{msg} \mapsto v] \xrightarrow{L}{}^*_\ell \mu'; \sigma'; v'}{\sigma[\ell \mapsto \text{beh}(\overline{\tau \rightsquigarrow e})]; \gamma[\ell, \text{sender} \mapsto (v, \tau) :: \overline{vs}] \Rightarrow \sigma[\ell \mapsto v'] \uplus \sigma'; \text{enqueue}(\ell, \gamma, \mu)}$$

where $\text{enqueue}(\ell, \gamma, \mu)$ extends each $\gamma(\ell_{\text{destination}}, \ell)$ with $\mu(\ell)$ by appending, thus preserving message ordering between endpoints, without committing to delivery order across actors.

Fig. 2. An actor language, partial operational semantics

of semantics for the actor model [1], an actor is a reactive program, executing only in response to an incoming message. The actor's message handling is defined by a *behaviour*, which we model as a partial function from types to handling expressions for each accepted incoming message type. In response to a message, the message handler may create other actors and/or send messages to existing (or newly-allocated) actors. $\mu; \sigma; e \xrightarrow{L}_\ell \mu'; \sigma'; e'$ says that with initial outgoing message queue μ and locally-spawned actors σ, expression e running as actor ℓ steps to e', resulting in message queue μ' (which always extends μ) and locally-spawned actors σ' (which always extends σ). The L indicates the cumulative self-capabilities generated by the reduction, which is the empty string except when reducing an annotated self expression. Iterated single stepping shuffles these formal languages together—an operation discussed in detail with the type system. The language L is purely an instrumentation and does not influence execution. Local actor reduction is deterministic in this calculus.

The full program steps by reducing an individual actor's reaction to any message ready for delivery: $\sigma; \gamma \Rightarrow \sigma'; \gamma'$ has one rule, delivering an available message to an actor *which is able to handle it* in the sense of running a matching handler to completion (i.e., termination). The handler body is expected to reduce to another behaviour, which may be the same behaviour or a new behaviour. (Note that this is also how many modern actor frameworks, such as Akka, work as well.) Message delivery is tracked per send-receive pair and is in-order between any pair of actors in a single direction, but incoming messages from different actors may be interleaved arbitrarily. Configurations where all actors either diverge[5] for any of the next incoming messages or do not handle them are stuck. Configurations where at least one actor may continue executing are *not* stuck.

Failures. In typical actor implementations, if an actor does not support a particular message type, either the message is dropped (the runtime simply doesn't deliver the message at all), explicitly ignored/passes through a generic handler which matches on message type, or an exception is delivered to the receiving actor. Regardless of typical handling in implementations, sending a message to an actor that does not expect that message type is typically an error we would like to statically prevent. We abstract the three possibilities above as a stuck transition in our formalization.

Actor State and Recursive Behaviours. In our calculus, there is no mutable state, so changes to the state of an actor between messages must be encoded by returning a new behaviour which somehow captures the updated state. Because our functions are always recursively defined, we can for example encode a count of messages received as

$$(\lambda_f state.\ \mathsf{beh}(\mathbf{0} \rightsquigarrow f\ (state + 1)))\ 0 \qquad (1)$$

That is, *state* binds the current count, and in response to receiving a unit message, the new behaviour is defined by recursively calling the function with the count incremented by one. The issues involved in direct mutable state are discussed in Sect. 5.

Note that 1 above also highlights the construction of a recursive behaviour *indirectly* through the use of a recursive function. Real actor framework implementations frequently include direct self-references in their behaviours (e.g., if a behaviour is modeled as an object, the standard `this` refers to the behaviour) or have ways to implicitly repeat a behaviour if a change in behaviour is not explicitly requested. Both of these can be encoded in our calculus.

Actor Self-Reference and Recursive Behaviours. Actors may retrieve their own address using the self operator. Note that in our calculus, self is an *operator*, not a variable bound to the current actor's reference. While self could be modeled as a variable, our type system treats self somewhat differently from variables, for reasons explained in Sect. 4.2.

4 Actor Capabilities for Guaranteed Message Handling

The language in the previous section permits actors to send messages to other actors that they are not prepared to handle—messages of types that may not be

---

[5] Non-terminating message handlers are always a bug in actor programs, as they prevent the actor from handling any messages in the future. Another static analysis could be used to ensure termination.

$$\begin{array}{rl} \text{Types} & \tau ::= \mathbb{B} \mid \mathbb{N} \mid \mathbf{1} \mid \tau \times \tau \mid \tau \xrightarrow{\chi} \tau \mid \mathsf{ActorRef}(L) \mid \mathsf{Beh}(L) \\ \text{Effects} & \chi \in \mathcal{L}(\tau) \\ \text{(Formal) Languages} & L \in \mathcal{L}(\tau) \\ \text{Paths} & p ::= x \mid p.1 \mid p.2 \end{array}$$

$\boxed{\Gamma \vdash e : \tau \dashv \Gamma' \mid \chi}$ Rules for booleans, conditionals, numbers, and pairs omitted

T-App
$$\dfrac{\Gamma \vdash e_1 : \tau \xrightarrow{\chi} \tau' \dashv \Gamma' \mid \chi_1 \quad \Gamma' \vdash e_2 : \tau \dashv \Gamma'' \mid \chi_2}{\Gamma \vdash e_1\ e_2 : \tau' \dashv \Gamma'' \mid \chi_1 \sqcup \chi_2 \sqcup \chi}$$

T-Lam
$$\dfrac{\Gamma \vdash \Gamma \prec \Gamma * \Gamma \quad \Gamma, f : \tau \xrightarrow{\chi} \tau', x : \tau \vdash e : \tau' \dashv \Gamma \mid \chi}{\Gamma \vdash (\lambda_f x.e) : \tau \xrightarrow{\chi} \tau' \dashv \Gamma \mid \{\epsilon\}}$$

T-Contract
$$\dfrac{\Gamma \vdash \tau \prec \tau' * \tau'' \quad \Gamma, x : \tau', x : \tau'', \Gamma' \vdash e : \tau \dashv \Gamma' \mid \chi}{\Gamma, x : \tau, \Gamma' \vdash e : \tau \dashv \Gamma' \mid \chi}$$

T-Weaken
$$\dfrac{\Gamma, \Gamma' \vdash e : \tau \dashv \Gamma'' \mid \chi}{\Gamma, x : \tau, \Gamma' \vdash e : \tau \dashv \Gamma'' \mid \chi}$$

T-Var $\dfrac{}{\Gamma, x : \tau \vdash x : \tau \dashv \Gamma \mid \{\epsilon\}}$ T-Self $\dfrac{}{\Gamma \vdash \mathsf{self}_L : \mathsf{ActorRef}(L) \dashv \Gamma \mid L}$

T-Send $\dfrac{\Gamma \vdash e : \tau \dashv \Gamma' \mid \chi \quad \Gamma' \vdash_{\mathsf{path}} p : \mathsf{ActorRef}(L) \rightsquigarrow \mathsf{ActorRef}(\tau^{-1}L) \vdash \Gamma'' \quad \tau^{-1}L \neq \emptyset}{\Gamma \vdash \mathsf{send}_\tau(p, e) : \mathbf{0} \dashv \Gamma'' \mid \chi}$

T-Spawn
$$\dfrac{\Gamma \vdash e : \mathsf{Beh}(L) \dashv \Gamma' \mid \chi \quad L' \subseteq L}{\Gamma \vdash \mathsf{spawn}(e) : \mathsf{ActorRef}(L') \dashv \Gamma' \mid \chi}$$

T-If
$$\dfrac{\Gamma \vdash e_c : \mathbb{B} \dashv \Gamma' \mid L_c \quad \forall b \in \{t, f\}.\, \Gamma' \vdash e_b : \tau \dashv \Gamma_b \mid L_b}{\Gamma \vdash \mathsf{if}\ e_c\ e_t\ e_f : \tau \dashv \Gamma_t \cap \Gamma_f \mid L_c \sqcup (L_t \cup L_f)}$$

T-Beh
$$\dfrac{\forall i \in 1..n.\ \Gamma, \mathsf{msg} : \tau_i \vdash e_i : \mathsf{Beh}\left((\tau_i^{-1}L) \sqcup L'_i\right) \dashv \Gamma'_i \mid L'_i \quad \mathsf{disjoint}(\overline{\tau})}{\Gamma \vdash \mathsf{beh}_L(\overline{\tau \rightsquigarrow e^n}) : \mathsf{Beh}(L) \dashv \epsilon \mid \{\epsilon\}}$$

$\boxed{\Gamma \vdash \tau \prec \tau * \tau}$ S-ActorRef $\dfrac{L' \sqcup L'' \subseteq L}{\Gamma \vdash \mathsf{ActorRef}(L) \prec \mathsf{ActorRef}(L') * \mathsf{ActorRef}(L'')}$

S-SelfSplit $\dfrac{\tau \in \{\mathbb{B}, \mathbb{N}, \mathbf{1}\} \vee \tau = \tau' \xrightarrow{\chi} \tau'}{\Gamma \vdash \tau \prec \tau * \tau}$ S-Pair $\dfrac{\Gamma \vdash \tau \prec \tau * \tau \quad \Gamma \vdash \sigma \prec \sigma * \sigma}{\Gamma \vdash \tau \times \sigma \prec \tau \times \sigma * \tau \times \sigma}$

Fig. 3. A capability type-and-effect system for our actor language. A standard exchange rule is omitted. Behaviour types are *not* splittable.

dealt with by the target actor's behaviour at the time of message delivery. This section develops a type-and-effect system to ensure such errors are detected statically by the type checker. Conceptually, there are two aspects. The first aspect, which gives rise to the name of our technique, is to equip actor references with a capability structure that restricts how they are used. Section 4.1 explains that structure and how the use is enforced. Section 4.2 then explains how the system ensures consistency between an actor capability sent to another actor and the subsequent behaviours of a given actor.

Capabilities and effects are both formal languages over the set of types.

4.1 Substructural Actor Capabilities and Splitting

Actor capabilities in our type system are equipped with a *formal language* L drawn from Type*, and thus describe the sequence of message types that may be sent via that actor reference.[6] Because the language describes both a restriction on the use of the value and a guarantee to the possessor that uses within that restriction should be valid, we call these actor references capabilities. An invariant we maintain is that the combined use of any and all actor capabilities (references) to some actor, in any interleaved order, should be allowed and handled by the actor they refer to—after all, if each capability is held by a different actor, they could potentially be used in any order! Such interleaving can be represented by the shuffle ($\sqcup\!\sqcup$) operator. The shuffle of two words $x = x_1 \ldots x_k$ and $y = y_1 \ldots y_k$ (with x_i and y_i being possibly-empty subwords, not necessarily characters) is defined as

$$x_1 \ldots x_k \sqcup\!\sqcup y_1 \ldots y_k = x_1 y_1 \ldots x_k y_k$$

which is lifted to languages as

$$L_1 \sqcup\!\sqcup L_2 = \{x \sqcup\!\sqcup y \mid x \in L_2, y \in L_2\}$$

That is, the shuffle of two languages consists of all possible interleavings of words from each language.

This gives us a way to control duplication of capabilities, to share actor references without increasing the permissions available to some code. Consider the case of an actor reference with type ActorRef(nop* · act · nop*) (momentarily assuming our languages are described by regular expressions, which is not a requirement of the formal development). This reference can be used to send as many nop messages as desired or necessary, but may only be used to send an act message once—exactly once. Simply duplicating that reference at the same type results in *two* actor references which could *each* be used to send an act message, and repeated duplication would then permit sending unlimited such messages. Instead, we borrow an idea from the reference capability literature, of *splitting* types with such restrictions [9,10,33,34,52,53]. We borrow Gordon's notation [33,34] in Fig. 3: $\Gamma \vdash \tau \prec \tau' \divideontimes \tau''$ justifies splitting a variable of type τ into two copies, one of type τ' and the other of type τ''. This is used by the contraction rule (T-CONTRACT). We call primitive types and closures *reflexively splittable* because they may be split without change (truly copied). Pairs split element-wise (S-PAIR). Actor references split using language shuffle (S-ACTORREF). Thus we could split our example actor reference into one of type ActorRef(act) and one of type ActorRef(nop*), because the shuffle of those two

---

[6] Technically the set of all types forms an infinite alphabet (one may have, at a minimum, n-ary tuples of unit for each $n \in \mathbf{N}$), but in the absence of polymorphic recursion, any given program only mentions a finite number of types (those used in behaviour case labels), and we assume Type denotes that set, avoiding subtleties of infinite alphabets.

protocol languages is contained in the original:

$$\frac{\mathsf{act} \sqcup \mathsf{nop}^* \subseteq \mathsf{nop}^* \cdot \mathsf{act} \cdot \mathsf{nop}^*}{\Gamma \vdash \mathsf{ActorRef}(\mathsf{nop}^* \cdot \mathsf{act} \cdot \mathsf{nop}^*) \prec \mathsf{ActorRef}(\mathsf{act}) \divideontimes \mathsf{ActorRef}(\mathsf{nop}^*)} \text{ S-ActorRef}$$

Note that behaviours are *not* splittable—they are linear, and the absence of a rule for splitting behaviours is by design. This allows a behaviour to capture a non-reflexively-splittable variable and use it. *Recursive* behaviours are encoded via recursive lambda expressions which return behaviours, and lambdas may only capture reflexively-splittable values—so any substructural values used in such behaviours are freshly created each time the recursive function is invoked.

Consumption. The point of use for an actor reference is via sending a message (T-Send). This rule types the message to send, and uses an *updating* typing judgment on paths to both retrieve the type of the path prior to use (a variable, or "field chasing" from a variable bound to a tuple), and update that type (either updating the type of the variable directly, or updating the type of appropriate—possibly nested—tuple components) to reflect sending a message of type τ. The judgment returns the updated type environment. This structure is chosen because our type system uses contraction deliberately, and may have multiple bindings for the same variable; separately typing the path and updating the output type environment would introduce difficulties ensuring the binding used for the pure typing was the same variable updated after the send, and it is simpler to do both at once.

$\tau^{-1}L$ is the derivative operator on formal languages, which includes all possible *completions* of words in L that start with the chosen element of the alphabet:

$$\alpha^{-1}L = \{w \mid \alpha \cdot w \in L\}$$

Of course the purpose of our actor reference type is two-fold: to enforce a usage discipline on code that holds an actor reference (addressed above), and to guarantee that uses according to that discipline are valid. The second purpose is partly addressed by splitting (which ensures an actor cannot increase the set of message sequences it can send to another actor) and partly addressed by effects (which allow relating the capabilities that exist for an actor to its intended behaviours).

Program Typing. If actors only run in response to messages, how does the system begin? A program is given by the behaviour e for an initial actor, which must accept (at least) the unit type as a message. The initial configuration for a system has actor pool $\{\ell_0 \mapsto e\}$ and global message queue $\{\ell_0, \ell_0 \mapsto ((), \mathbf{0}) :: \mathbf{nil}\}$, from which point the only available reduction (which *is* available) is to deliver the unit message to the initial actor. So top-level programs are typed by

$$\text{T-Program } \frac{\emptyset \vdash e : \mathsf{Beh}(\overline{\tau}) \quad \mathbf{0} \in \overline{\tau}}{\vdash e \text{ prog}}$$

4.2 Consistency of Actor Capabilities, Behaviours and Effects

To discuss consistency between behaviours and capabilities, we must discuss the typing of behaviours. The type $\mathsf{Beh}(L)$ characterizes a behaviour which will accept message sequences in L, though this does not fully characterize the future behaviour of the actor using this behaviour. L is intuitively an over-approximation of how all *existing* capabilities to send to that behaviour could collectively be used—all capabilities that existed *prior* to that behaviour handling a message. Note that this does *not* require knowing the exact history of the program: it is limited to the actor using the behaviour, and refers only to the *unused* capabilities, not past usage of capabilities. This information is necessary for typing behaviours because they represent *unresolved promises* for future message acceptance. At the same time, an actor with such a behaviour installed may end up accepting more than L in the future, because when the behaviour handles a message, it may create additional obligations for its actor to handle in the future, which we track using a static effect system.

The Effect of Capability Creation. The starting point for all effects is T-SELF, which captures the creation of a new self-reference capability that is usable according to some particular language. Other rules simply accumulate an over-approximation of created capabilities. Subexpressions that run together in order (such as a function, argument, and latent function effect in an application expression per T-APP) have their effects shuffled together with $⧢$, as collectively all created capabilities could be used in an interleaved fashion. Expressions that may run alternatively are combined with union—the rule for conditionals combines the conditional effect L_c with the true- and false-branch effects L_t and L_f as $L_c ⧢ (L_t \cup L_f)$, capturing that the condition always runs before either branch, but it is statically unknown which branch will execute.

Note that $⧢$ distributes over $\cup$ on both sides, so with $\{\epsilon\}$ as the unit for $⧢$, these effects form a total commutative effect quantale [31]. It follows both from that framework's soundness results (and from our later proofs) that the effect of an expression over-approximates the shuffle-interleaving of all self-capabilities created during a local expression's reduction.

Note that the system tracks the *creation* of new capabilities for the current actor, *not* which capabilities are *actually sent* to other actors! This is both simpler than distinguishing between sending a self-reference or another actor's reference, and also reflects the fact that an actor can send itself messages, in which case those would need to be handled by later behaviours.[7]

Typing Behaviours. T-BEH in Fig. 3 is subtle, but captures the relationship between past promises, locally-created capabilities, and future message acceptance. Unsurprisingly, the rule requires typing each branch of the behaviour's body, with the expectation that the result is a new behaviour (which will be

---

[7] It is of course also conservative: an actor may create a self-reference that it then discards, but the discarded capability will still be captured in the effect and become a new (un-dischargeable) obligation for the actor.

used to handle future messages). Those messages the actor handles in the future may come from one of two sources, each reflected in an argument to the shuffle ($\shuffle$) operator. The left argument $\tau_i^{-1}L$ models the fact that each branch of the behaviour handles a different incoming message type (which must have been justified by a previously-existing capability accounted for by L), but any remaining capabilities that existed before might still exist and be usable to send further messages. So the left argument captures that the obligation to accept an initial τ has been discharged. The right argument L_i corresponds to new capabilities to the current actor which this message-handler may have created, which are then *additional* obligations for the future which did not previously exist, so are not reflected in the original L. L_i is guaranteed to include all new obligations because it is also the *effect* of the message handler. So requiring the behaviour returned after handling τ_i to have type $\mathsf{Beh}\left((\tau_i^{-1}L) \shuffle L_i'\right)$ ensures that both previously-existing obligations and newly-created obligations will be supported by the next handler.

For example, in the nop/act example of the previous section, if the actor has only given out that one capability discussed previously, L would be nop*·act·nop*. In typing the handler for act, the derivative of that history assumption by act would be nop*, reflecting that the one promised handling of act was settled, and if that was the only such capability distributed, then no future behaviour would necessarily be forced by that old capability (which was now partly consumed) to handle additional act messages. The derivative handles this. However, if in response to the act message the handler created a new capability for the actor which granted permission to send another act message, then the future behaviour would need to reflect that, hence the requirement that the next behaviour also handle the languages of all newly-created capabilities—incorporated via $\shuffle$.

Spawning New Actors, and Initial Capabilities. The one remaining matter to attend to is creating an actor with a specific behaviour—the rules discussed so far ensure that *if the history assumptions are accurate they remain accurate*, and T-SPAWN establishes the initial accuracy. T-SPAWN requires that the assumed protocol L' for the initial external capability is a subset of the language L that the spawned behaviour assumes exists prior to its execution.

4.3 Soundness

Due to space constraints we omit details of the type soundness proof, and give only a brief overview here; see the associated technical report [32] for more detail. We use the syntactic approach to type safety. Soundness of effect tracking follows typical form for syntactic proofs of sequential (flow-sensitive) effect systems [31], but in this case integrated with tracking of a flow-sensitive runtime actor capability map mirroring Γ's usage, to track each actor's unused capabilities to send messages to other actors. There is both a local (per-actor) and global version of each of preservation and progress.

The essence of ensuring that outstanding capabilities match the expectations of their respective target actors is that locally, the shuffle of all capabilities an actor possess to another actor ℓ before handling a message ($\Sigma(\ell)$) is related to the remaining capabilities after handling it ($\Sigma'(\ell)$) by a derivative of messages sent. If the handler sent messages $\overline{v}$ of types $\overline{\tau}$ to ℓ, then $\Sigma'(\ell) \sqcup \mathsf{caps}(\ell, \overline{(v, \tau)}) = \overline{\tau}^{-1}\Sigma(\ell)$, where $\mathsf{caps}(\ell, \overline{(v, \tau)})$ is the shuffle of all capabilities as passed through outgoing messages (though the formal proof deals with them as an additional level of existentials, not as something computed from the values and message types). The right side of that equality reflects what is left of the original capabilities after using some to send values, and the left side reflects what is remaining to type the reduced expression, plus the capabilities that were transferred out via messages. Thus if a capability with protocol $\tau_1 \cdot \tau_2 \cdot \tau_3$ were used once to send a τ_1 and the remainder (now a capability for $\tau_2 \cdot \tau_3$) were then sent in an outgoing message, the send of τ_1 would be reflected in the derivative on the right, and the message-bound remainder would be accounted for in the caps (if the leftover capability were retained rather than transferred, it would instead be accounted for in $\Sigma'(\ell)$).

5 Related Work

Our system draws on many areas of prior work, including substructural type systems and reference capabilities, but those were discussed earlier. We focus this section not on an exhaustive explanation of the many sources of inspiration for this work (largely covered by related work discussions of the previously-cited papers), but instead on comparing our work against other approaches to ensuring that actors (or active objects) and processes handle specific message sequences and send compatible message sequences to others.

A classic point of reference for this is Nierstrasz's work [58] on *regular types*, assigning finite-state-based specifications of object behaviour, as the sequence of messages accepted and the resultant responses. His exposition explores the structure of these specifications and informally how they might apply to objects, but provides no application of these types to a concrete programming language, and focuses on composing applications by way of one object using another as its sole client. This focus on the behaviour of the active object itself over time is also nearly dual to ours: regular types for active objects describe the process behaviour summatively, while in our (source-level) type system, no summative language-oriented description of an actor's accepted messages exists! Instead static knowledge of an actor's accepted language can only be assembled from various capabilities. Active objects, as nicely captured in de Koster et al.'s taxonomy of actor language variants [19], do not permit changing the set of accepted messages over time. Support for such changes is an explicit goal of this work.

Our calculus is pure, but many popular actor frameworks are in languages with mutable state, and permit sharing references across actors on the same machine [11,36]. The introduction of direct mutable heaps raises classic issues of balancing safety and efficiency of sending messages. Deep copying of state is always sound, but highly inefficient, especially when the data being sent is either immutable or the sender discards its own access to the mutable data after sending. This has motivated a great deal of work on various flavors of uniqueness and mutation control, including a great deal of work applying the reference capability notions discussed in the introduction to track forms of unique ownership transfer or object immutability [9,10,14,28,34,35,60]. Some of this work [14,35] has specifically been applied to actor systems.[8] However, incorporating two orthogonal flavors of capabilities—the actor capabilities proposed here, along with the reference capabilities from existing work—would distract from the main technical development of capabilities for controlling message ordering in actor systems.

An alternative approach to managing state sharing and exchange between actors is the introduction of specially-shared capsules. De Koster et al. [18,20] introduce *domains*, which are shared-memory constructs which actors asynchronously request access to (akin to asynchronous mutex acquisition). Similarly, Cheeseman et al.'s *cowns* [12] (named for *concurrent ownership*) are shared resources accessed by asynchronously-spawned computations that run only when all required cowns are available at once. Some of the most closely related work to ours also falls into this group: Caldwell et al. [8] describe a specialized data exchange environment called a *dataspace*, as well as an effect system describing behaviour over time for actors and data—effectively dual to our approach of restricting actor behaviours with capabilities. Similar to Skalka et al. [63,64], their effects give abstract summaries of actor behaviour, which can then be used to model-check properties of the program—the effect types for both Skalka et al.'s work and Caldwell et al.'s work give a model that is verified to soundly abstract the program code. Establishing a formal relationship between our capabilities and behavioural effects like Caldwell et al.'s, akin to Craig et al.'s formal relationship between flow-insensitive capabilities and flow-insensitive effects [15] would be intriguing future work.

Session types [44,48], choreographic programming [16,27,62], and multitier programming [69] solve the issue of agreement between the messages accepted by a given process and message sent to it by others in the inverse way of what we describe here. Instead of analyzing correctness of processes in isolation, these approaches start with a single program describing all global behaviour, and a compiler generates code (or in the case of session types, synchronization skeletons) for individual processes via a projection process. These approaches are generally applied to *synchronous* message passing, though Harvey et al. [37] and Neykova et al. [56] have adapted session types to actors (though still using a global description of the full orchestration which is then projected for each of a fixed set of roles). By contrast, our lack of a global type is a trade-off. On one hand, there is no complete closed description of behaviour separate from the code itself, which can be useful for understanding the system as a whole. On the other hand, actors in our approach can be specified and checked in isolation (e.g., as library components), without needing to know a priori how they fit into a larger system, because any messages accepted by the actor beyond those described in the initial capability returned from **spawn** are chosen by the actor itself. Like

---

[8] Now that the relevant NDAs are long-expired, we can finally say in writing that the context for [35] was the Midori [23] derivative of Singularity [24,45], where processes were essentially actors.

Caldwell et al.'s work [8], the type of a process in these approaches describes *all* of the process's future behaviour, rather than only the promises it has made to its environment about its behaviour (as in our work).

Originating around the same time as classic binary session types [43], Nielson and Nielson [57] described one of the earliest flow-sensitive effect systems, for ensuring Concurrent ML (CML) processes sent and received *synchronous* messages in an expected order. This early similarity turned out to be quite relevant, as session types can be recast as an effect system (and vice versa) [59]. Thus the idea of applying effect systems—or an equivalent formalism—to ensure correct message request ordering is itself far from new. And the idea of using capabilities to restrict effects is also not new, going back past recent formal connections [15] to many earlier expositions of effects [39,50] in an implicit form.

Two aspects of our approach distinguish it from this established body of work. First, this is to the best of our knowledge the first use of flow sensitive *capabilities* (a form of coeffect [13]) to achieve safe ordering. While the relationship to a putative effect system achieving the same ends has not been formally pursued, and this likely carries some of the downside of capabilities (vs. effects) outlined in our prior work [30] (which applied only to flow-insensitive effect systems), it also carries a unique advantage in system design not discussed in that paper. While effect systems may obtain greater precision in reasoning about side effects [30], they do so at the cost of needing to "reconstruct" behaviour and check compatibility after the fact. In contrast, our capability formulation of the problem inverts this checking, and places each actor (and its original allocation site) in firm control of how other actors interact with it—the protocols of the self-capabilities an actor sends to others directly constrain those others' interactions a priori, localizing checks to a far greater extent than in CML or session types—no direct global accounting of behaviour is required to exist.

Second—and a complementary factor in not requiring a global behavioural description to exist—is our use of an effect system to track capability *creation*. This differs from most static capability work, which typically assumes all possible capabilities for something exist upon its creation, and must be passed through the program. Instead we treat actors' retrieval of a new self-reference as a *dynamic* capability creation—via effects. While it has long been recognized that both coeffects (e.g., capabilities) and effects are required to reason about various combinations of independently-interesting static analyses and language semantics [17,26], ours is one of very few examples of mixing coeffects and effects *as part of a single static analysis*.

Another body of work with a more nuanced relationship to the work reported here is the concept of *mailbox types*, as originally proposed by de'Liguoro and Padovani [21] and later implemented for an actor language with explicit mailboxes by Fowler et al. [25]. The core idea there is to drastically restrict aliasing of mailbox references, and use the near-linearity to reason about the contents of the *current actor's* mailbox, using commutative regular expressions. Beyond their implementation of their system, and experience applying it to some benchmark programs, there are three key differences between this idea and actor capabilities.

First is that the behaviour tracking is almost inverted: rather than restricting senders to only send what the recipient expects, the recipient is instead restricted to only *request* things from the mailbox which are known to have been sent to it. Mailbox types are predicated on the *selective receive* operation present in some actor frameworks, which retrieves a message of specified type. Thus mailbox types prevent an actor from issuing a selective receive which would fail. Second is that only message multiplicity is tracked, because of the commutative regular expressions; the use of selective receive makes this the appropriate modeling choice, though most actor frameworks include both normal and selective receive, making integration of our ideas and theirs interesting future work. Third, they use a combination of second-class values and a mild relaxation of linearity to deal with aliasing of mailboxes and strong updates to mailbox types. By contrast, we permit many aliases to each actor whose usage restrictions we track, by ensuring that each alias is independently usable (via $\sqcup$); again, their choice is a reasonable one for their setting, as each mailbox is expected to be consumed by only one actor.

Program logics have also been used for reasoning about correctness of actor messages. Gordon [29] proposed modal assertions of the form $@_l(P)$ inspired by hybrid logic [3], indicating that P was true of the state of the actor at l. Thus assertions true at the sending actor could be packaged in this way, and communicated as part of message invariants; a rely-guarantee-style relation constraining state evolution worked together with a restriction to only send assertions stable with respect to that relation ensured the assertions about other actors were never invalidated, but limited what could be proved to assertions over monotonically-evolving portions of state (though CRDTs have shown this can be made more flexible than it initially appears [61]). More recently some program logics (instantiations of IRIS [46]) have tied together ideas from session types and verification for simple actor languages [41,42]. This work handles protocols similar to binary (for Actris) or multiparty (for Multris) session types, but each message has not only a value but a set of assertions that the recipient may assume upon receipt of the corresponding value. This is much more powerful and flexible than Gordon's approach, at the cost of complexity. Gordon's system was prototyped as a library for the automated verification tool Dafny, while the modern approaches rely on IRIS embedded in an interactive proof assistant. The key point of comparison to the present work is that Actris and Multris do ensure the absence of unhandled messages, but the specifications for doing so are essentially traditional session types. Compatibility when delegating use of a channel to another process is checked via an ad hoc simulation search procedure akin to Militão et al.'s [52]. In contrast, our use of shuffle uncovers a clean algebraic structure underlying common uses of sharing and resharing the addresses of other processes, though it is less general than Actris and Multris, where the correct continuation of a protocol may depend on the specific value sent.

Acknowledgments. Thanks to Gul Agha for his influential work on the actor model, which forms the basis for much of my research career (via the work I am most known for [35] and some of the work I am most fond of [29]); as well as some of what I most enjoy teaching (using actors when teaching distributed computing). Agha's work [1, 47] has been the source for a significant amount of my own learning to think about concurrent programs and their implementation, and by chance he has had a direct influence on individual people who have influenced me during time in industry and academia [55]. Thanks also to Ivan Beschastnikh, for asking me in 2012 how I could apply reference capabilities to distributed systems. It took 13 years, but I think I've finally articulated a good answer, even if handling faults remains future work. Audience members at IWACO 2024 provided useful feedback on a more abstract version of the ideas presented here. Thanks to Jonathan Schuster for bringing mailbox types to my attention, and to Lindsey Kuper for bringing my preprint to Jonathan's attention. This work was supported by NSF Award #CCF-2007582.

References

1. Agha, G.: Actors: A Model of Concurrent Computation in Distributed Systems. MIT Press (1986)
2. Amtoft, T., Nielson, F., Nielson, H.R.: Type and Effect Systems: Behaviours for Concurrency. Imperial College Press, London (1999)
3. Areces, C., ten Cate, B.: Hybrid logics. In: Studies in Logic and Practical Reasoning, vol. 3, pp. 821–868. Elsevier (2007)
4. Bagherzadeh, M., Fireman, N., Shawesh, A., Khatchadourian, R.: Actor concurrency bugs: a comprehensive study on symptoms, root causes, API usages, and differences. Proc. ACM Program. Lang. 4(OOPSLA), 1–32 (2020)
5. Boer, F.D., et al.: A survey of active object languages. ACM Comput. Surv. (CSUR) **50**(5), 1–39 (2017)
6. Boyapati, C., Lee, R., Rinard, M.: Ownership types for safe programming: preventing data races and deadlocks. In: OOPSLA (2002)
7. Boyapati, C., Rinard, M.: A parameterized type system for race-free java programs. In: OOPSLA (2001)
8. Caldwell, S., Garnock-Jones, T., Felleisen, M.: Programming and reasoning about actors that share state. J. Funct. Program. **34** (2024). https://doi.org/10.1017/S0956796824000091
9. Castegren, E., Wrigstad, T.: Reference capabilities for concurrency control. In: 30th European Conference on Object-Oriented Programming, ECOOP 2016 (2016)
10. Castegren, E., Wrigstad, T.: Relaxed linear references for lock-free programming. In: 31st European Conference on Object-Oriented Programming, ECOOP 2017 (2017)
11. Charousset, D., Hiesgen, R., Schmidt, T.C.: CAF-the C++ actor framework for scalable and resource-efficient applications. In: Proceedings of the 4th International Workshop on Programming based on Actors Agents & Decentralized Control, pp. 15–28 (2014)
12. Cheeseman, L., et al.: When concurrency matters: behaviour-oriented concurrency. Proc. ACM Program. Lang. **7**(OOPSLA2), 1531–1560 (2023)
13. Choudhury, V., Krishnaswami, N.: Recovering purity with comonads and capabilities. Proc. ACM Program. Lang. 4(ICFP), 1–28 (2020)
14. Clebsch, S., Drossopoulou, S., Blessing, S., McNeil, A.: Deny capabilities for safe, fast actors. In: Proceedings of the 5th International Workshop on Programming Based on Actors, Agents, and Decentralized Control, pp. 1–12. ACM (2015)

15. Craig, A., Potanin, A., Groves, L., Aldrich, J.: Capabilities: effects for free. In: International Conference on Formal Engineering Methods (ICFEM) (2018)
16. Cruz-Filipe, L., Montesi, F., Peressotti, M.: A formal theory of choreographic programming. J. Autom. Reason. **67**(2), 21 (2023)
17. Dal Lago, U., Gavazzo, F.: A relational theory of effects and coeffects. Proc. ACM Program. Lang. **6**(POPL), 1–28 (2022)
18. De Koster, J., Marr, S., D'Hondt, T., Van Cutsem, T.: Domains: safe sharing among actors. Sci. Comput. Program. **98**, 140–158 (2015)
19. De Koster, J., Van Cutsem, T., De Meuter, W.: 43 years of actors: a taxonomy of actor models and their key properties. In: Proceedings of the 6th International Workshop on Programming Based on Actors, Agents, and Decentralized Control, pp. 31–40 (2016)
20. De Koster, J., Van Cutsem, T., D'Hondt, T.: Domains: safe sharing among actors. In: Proceedings of the 2nd Edition on Programming Systems, Languages and Applications Based on Actors, Agents, and Decentralized Control Abstractions, pp. 11–22 (2012)
21. de'Liguoro, U., Padovani, L.: Mailbox types for unordered interactions. In: 32nd European Conference on Object-Oriented Programming (ECOOP 2018), pp. 15–1. Schloss Dagstuhl–Leibniz-Zentrum für Informatik (2018)
22. Dietl, W., Drossopoulou, S., Müller, P.: Generic universe types. In: ECOOP (2007)
23. Duffy, J.: (2015). https://joeduffyblog.com/2015/11/03/blogging-about-midori/
24. Fähndrich, M., et al.: Language support for fast and reliable message-based communication in singularity OS. In: Proceedings of the 1st ACM SIGOPS/EuroSys European Conference on Computer Systems 2006, EuroSys 2006, pp. 177–190. ACM (2006). https://doi.org/10.1145/1217935.1217953
25. Fowler, S., Attard, D.P., Sowul, F., Gay, S.J., Trinder, P.: Special delivery: programming with mailbox types. Proc. ACM Program. Lang. **7**(ICFP), 78–107 (2023)
26. Gaboardi, M., Katsumata, S.Y., Orchard, D., Breuvart, F., Uustalu, T.: Combining effects and coeffects via grading. In: Proceedings of the 21st ACM SIGPLAN International Conference on Functional Programming, pp. 476–489 (2016)
27. Giallorenzo, S., Montesi, F., Peressotti, M.: Choral: object-oriented choreographic programming. ACM Trans. Program. Lang. Syst. **46**(1), 1–59 (2024)
28. Giannini, P., Servetto, M., Zucca, E., Cone, J.: Flexible recovery of uniqueness and immutability. Theoret. Comput. Sci. **764**, 145–172 (2019)
29. Gordon, C.S.: Modal assertions for actor correctness. In: Proceedings of the 9th ACM SIGPLAN International Workshop on Programming Based on Actors, Agents, and Decentralized Control, pp. 11–20 (2019)
30. Gordon, C.S.: Designing with static capabilities and effects: use, mention, and invariants (pearl). In: 34th European Conference on Object-Oriented Programming (ECOOP 2020). Schloss Dagstuhl-Leibniz-Zentrum für Informatik (2020)
31. Gordon, C.S.: Polymorphic iterable sequential effect systems. ACM Trans. Program. Lang. Syst. (TOPLAS) **43**(1), 1–79 (2021)
32. Gordon, C.S.: Actor capabilities for message ordering (extended version). Technical report (2025). https://arxiv.org/abs/2502.07958
33. Gordon, C.S., Ernst, M.D., Grossman, D.: Rely-guarantee references for refinement types over aliased mutable data. In: Proceedings of the 34th ACM SIGPLAN Conference on Programming Language Design and Implementation, pp. 73–84 (2013)
34. Gordon, C.S., Ernst, M.D., Grossman, D., Parkinson, M.J.: Verifying invariants of lock-free data structures with rely-guarantee and refinement types. ACM Trans. Program. Lang. Syst. (TOPLAS) **39**(3), 1–54 (2017)

35. Gordon, C.S., Parkinson, M.J., Parsons, J., Bromfield, A., Duffy, J.: Uniqueness and reference immutability for safe parallelism. In: Proceedings of the ACM International Conference on Object Oriented Programming Systems Languages and Applications, pp. 21–40 (2012)
36. Haller, P.: On the integration of the actor model in mainstream technologies: the Scala perspective. In: Proceedings of the 2nd Edition on Programming Systems, Languages and Applications Based on Actors, Agents, and Decentralized Control Abstractions, pp. 1–6 (2012)
37. Harvey, P., Fowler, S., Dardha, O., Gay, S.J.: Multiparty session types for safe runtime adaptation in an actor language. In: 35th European Conference on Object-Oriented Programming (ECOOP 2021). Schloss Dagstuhl-Leibniz-Zentrum für Informatik (2021)
38. Hedden, B., Zhao, X.: A comprehensive study on bugs in actor systems. In: Proceedings of the 47th International Conference on Parallel Processing, pp. 1–9 (2018)
39. Henglein, F., Makholm, H., Niss, H.: Effect types and region-based memory management. In: Pierce, B.C. (ed.) Advanced Topics in Types and Programming Languages, chap. 3, pp. 87–136. MIT Press (2005)
40. Hewitt, C., Bishop, P., Steiger, R.: A universal modular actor formalism for artificial intelligence. In: Proceedings of the 3rd International Joint Conference on Artificial Intelligence, pp. 235–245 (1973)
41. Hinrichsen, J.K., Bengtson, J., Krebbers, R.: Actris: session-type based reasoning in separation logic. Proc. ACM Program. Lang. 4(POPL), 1–30 (2019)
42. Hinrichsen, J.K., Jacobs, J., Krebbers, R.: Multris: functional verification of multiparty message passing in separation logic. Proc. ACM Program. Lang. 8(OOPSLA2), 1446–1474 (2024)
43. Honda, K., Vasconcelos, V.T., Kubo, M.: Language primitives and type discipline for structured communication-based programming. In: Hankin, C. (ed.) ESOP 1998. LNCS, vol. 1381, pp. 122–138. Springer, Heidelberg (1998). https://doi.org/10.1007/BFb0053567
44. Honda, K., Yoshida, N., Carbone, M.: Multiparty asynchronous session types. In: Proceedings of the 35th Annual ACM SIGPLAN-SIGACT Symposium on Principles of Programming Languages. POPL 2008 (2008). https://doi.org/10.1145/1328438.1328472
45. Hunt, G.C., Larus, J.R.: Singularity: rethinking the software stack. SIGOPS Oper. Syst. Rev. **41**(2), 37–49 (2007). https://doi.org/10.1145/1243418.1243424
46. Jung, R., Krebbers, R., Jourdan, J.H., Bizjak, A., Birkedal, L., Dreyer, D.: Iris from the ground up: a modular foundation for higher-order concurrent separation logic. J. Funct. Program. **28**, e20 (2018)
47. Karmani, R.K., Shali, A., Agha, G.: Actor frameworks for the JVM platform: a comparative analysis. In: Proceedings of the 7th International Conference on Principles and Practice of Programming in Java, pp. 11–20 (2009)
48. Lagaillardie, N., Neykova, R., Yoshida, N.: Implementing multiparty session types in rust. In: International Conference on Coordination Languages and Models, pp. 127–136. Springer (2020)
49. Levy, H.M.: Capability-Based Computer Systems. Digital Press (1984)
50. Marino, D., Millstein, T.: A generic type-and-effect system. In: TLDI (2009)
51. Milano, M., Turcotti, J., Myers, A.C.: A flexible type system for fearless concurrency. In: Proceedings of the 43rd ACM SIGPLAN International Conference on Programming Language Design and Implementation, pp. 458–473 (2022)

52. Militão, F., Aldrich, J., Caires, L.: Composing interfering abstract protocols. In: 30th European Conference on Object-Oriented Programming, ECOOP 2016 (2016). https://doi.org/10.4230/LIPIcs.ECOOP.2016.16
53. Militão, F., Aldrich, J., Caires, L.: Rely-guarantee protocols. In: Jones, R. (ed.) ECOOP 2014. LNCS, vol. 8586, pp. 334–359. Springer, Heidelberg (2014). https://doi.org/10.1007/978-3-662-44202-9_14
54. Miller, M.: Robust composition: towards a unified approach to access control and concurrency control. Johns Hopkins University (2006)
55. Miller, M.S., Tribble, E.D., Shapiro, J.: Concurrency among strangers: programming in e as plan coordination. In: Trustworthy Global Computing: International Symposium, TGC 2005, Edinburgh, UK, 7–9 April 2005. Revised Selected Papers, pp. 195–229. Springer (2005)
56. Neykova, R., Yoshida, N.: Multiparty session actors. Logical Methods Comput. Sci. **13** (2017)
57. Nielson, F., Nielson, H.R.: From CML to process algebras. In: CONCUR (1993)
58. Nierstrasz, O.: Regular types for active objects. In: Proceedings of the Eighth Annual Conference on Object-Oriented Programming Systems, Languages, and Applications, OOPSLA 1993, pp. 1–15. Association for Computing Machinery, New York (1993). https://doi.org/10.1145/165854.167976
59. Orchard, D., Yoshida, N.: Effects as sessions, sessions as effects. In: Proceedings of the 43rd Annual ACM SIGPLAN-SIGACT Symposium on Principles of Programming Languages, pp. 568–581 (2016)
60. Servetto, M., Pearce, D.J., Groves, L., Potanin, A.: Balloon types for safe parallelisation over arbitrary object graphs. In: Workshop on Determinism and Correctness in Parallel Programming (WoDet) (2013)
61. Shapiro, M., Preguiça, N., Baquero, C., Zawirski, M.: Conflict-free replicated data types. In: Stabilization, Safety, and Security of Distributed Systems: 13th International Symposium, SSS 2011, Grenoble, France, 10–12 October 2011. Proceedings 13, pp. 386–400. Springer (2011)
62. Shen, G., Kashiwa, S., Kuper, L.: Haschor: functional choreographic programming for all (functional pearl). Proc. ACM Program. Lang. **7**(ICFP), 541–565 (2023)
63. Skalka, C.: Types and trace effects for object orientation. High.-Order Symbolic Comput. **21**(3) (2008)
64. Skalka, C., Smith, S., Van Horn, D.: Types and trace effects of higher order programs. J. Funct. Program. **18**(2) (2008)
65. Tate, R.: The sequential semantics of producer effect systems. In: POPL (2013)
66. Team, S.L.: Data Race Safety. https://www.swift.org/migration/documentation/swift-6-concurrency-migration-guide/dataracesafety/
67. Torres Lopez, C., Marr, S., Gonzalez Boix, E., Mössenböck, H.: A study of concurrency bugs and advanced development support for actor-based programs, pp. 155–185. Springer (2018)
68. Tschantz, M.S., Ernst, M.D.: Javari: adding reference immutability to java. In: OOPSLA (2005). https://doi.org/10.1145/1094811.1094828
69. Weisenburger, P., Wirth, J., Salvaneschi, G.: A survey of multitier programming. ACM Comput. Surv. (CSUR) **53**(4), 1–35 (2020)
70. Zibin, Y., Potanin, A., Ali, M., Artzi, S., Kiezun, A., Ernst, M.D.: Object and reference immutability using java generics. In: ESEC-FSE (2007). https://doi.org/10.1145/1287624.1287637
71. Zibin, Y., Potanin, A., Li, P., Ali, M., Ernst, M.D.: Ownership and immutability in generic java. In: OOPSLA (2010). https://doi.org/10.1145/1869459.1869509

Failure-Transparent Actors

Jonas Spenger[1(✉)], Paris Carbone[1,2], and Philipp Haller[1]

[1] EECS and Digital Futures, KTH Royal Institute of Technology, Stockholm, Sweden
{jspenger,parisc,phaller}@kth.se
[2] Digital Systems, RISE Research Institutes of Sweden, Stockholm, Sweden

Abstract. Failures in a distributed system are not only possible but expected and notoriously difficult to handle. For this reason, it is imperative to provide system-level means for building failure-transparent services, i.e., services which transparently recover from failures, effectively masking them. Towards this, this paper presents a syntax and semantics for compositionally failure-transparent actors. It is structured around three kinds of failure-transparent compositions: composition within a system; between systems; and application-level composition. For the former two, we prove that the semantics is failure transparent by simulation using prophecy variables. For the latter, we discuss its implementation; additionally, we discuss the necessity for leaking system-level failures to the application-level. The presented material provides low-level building blocks for failure-transparent services, thus greatly simplifying their construction.

Keywords: Actor model · Failure transparency · Service composition · Operational semantics

1 Introduction

Building distributed systems is hard, as the programmer's adage goes. Indeed, failures are notoriously difficult to handle in a distributed system. Moreover, they are not only possible but *expected* in a long-running distributed system [17]. As a result, distributed systems and services must gracefully deal with failures. One such way is for the system to provide system-level means for *failure transparency* [22,34,37,56,57], *i.e.*, effectively masking failures from the application-level, thus allowing applications to be failure agnostic.

Towards this, a recent kind of system termed *durable execution systems* [16, 43,44,51] provide system-level failure-transparency within the system itself; and tools for failure-transparent composition on the application-level, a necessary aspect for real applications [26,46,50,55]. The programming models of these systems are *actor-like* [48], *i.e.*, they provide entities akin to actors [5,28] which communicate by message passing, but typically lack the ability to dynamically spawn new actors. For this reason, we also refer to them in this paper as *failure-transparent actor-like* systems, sometimes also omitting the suffix *like*.

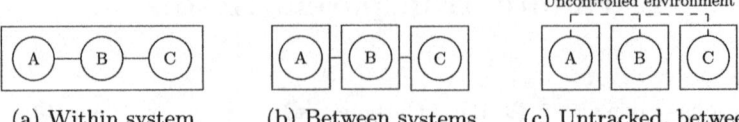

Fig. 1. Kinds of compositions of failure-transparent actor systems.

Whereas failure-transparent actor-like systems [16,43,44,51] are actively developed by a growing community, their formal guarantees have not been extensively studied. Particularly, there has been no formal study of failure-transparent actors, nor the failure-transparent composition of actor systems. However, failure transparency itself has been extensively studied in other contexts [22,34,37,56,57]. Application-level failure-transparent compositions, on the other hand, follow the contrary perspective that certain system-level failures are better handled by the application [26,46]. This was also noted by recent work on reliable actors [50], stating that the goal of the programming model should be to "facilitate authoring fault recovery code", rather than achieving failure transparency. Yet, it remains open how the different principles for failure transparent compositions are related and can be combined.

This paper aims to fill this gap by considering three kinds of composition of failure-transparent actors (Fig. 1, circles are actors, rectangles are systems):

(a) Composition within a (failure-transparent actor) system.
(b) Composition between separate systems.
(c) Untracked application-level composition between systems.

For the former two, we provide a syntax and semantics, and prove that the semantics is failure transparent [56] by simulation using prophecy variables [1,33]. For the latter, we discuss how to implement failure-transparency on the application-level for compositions of services using actor supervision and timeout/retry limits. Furthermore, we discuss by example the contrary perspective of *leaking* system-level failures to the application-level and its necessity [26,46,50,55] in the context of failure-transparent actor systems. Our goal is to simplify the construction of reliable distributed services using the building blocks presented in this paper.

Contributions

- We present a syntax and semantics for *failure-transparent actors* (Sect. 3).
- We provide extensions to the syntax and semantics for the *composition of actor systems*, in which external actions/side-effects are immediately enqueued but their observation deferred (Sect. 4).
- We prove that the semantics is *failure transparent* [56] by simulation using prophecy variables (Theorem 1, Theorem 2).
- We discuss *application-level failure transparency* and *leaking system-level failures* by means of actor supervision and timeout/retry limits (Sect. 5).

Listing 1. Counting actor.

```
1  def behavior = ( count ⇒ sndr ⇒
2    send sndr count;
3    behavior(count+1) );
4  def log = ( msg ⇒
5    print(msg);
6    log );
7  ...
```

```
6   ...
7   val a = ( spawn behavior(0) );
8   val b = ( spawn ( msg ⇒
9     send a unit;
10    send a unit;
11    log ) );
12  send b unit
```

2 End-to-End Reliable Services

End-to-end reliable services are distributed compositions of services which are reliable from one *end* to another, or, in other words, the whole *composition* is reliable. *Reliability*, as used in this paper, refers to *failure transparency* [56]: a safety property which informally states that a failure-transparent composition should exhibit an observed behavior as though no failures occurred. The kinds of failures which may occur include node failures, message loss, and network partitions, and can be difficult to handle depending on context. *End-to-end exactly-once processing* is related to compositional failure transparency; however, its meaning may differ depending on context, thus we refrain from using it further.

2.1 Actors and Tools for Reliability

Actor systems [5,9,25,28] have long been used for creating reliable services [7]. The actor model provides what is termed the *isolated turn principle* [31]. That is, actors process one message at a time without blocking, sharing no state with other actors, thus avoiding issues associated with shared mutable state. Further, actor systems typically provide low-level tools for reliability, such as *hierarchical actor supervision* [8], in which the supervisor is notified of the failure of the supervised actor, such that the supervisor can handle the failure on the *application-level*, *i.e.*, as part of the user code. However, even with these tools, it remains difficult to build reliable distributed services.

The counting actor example [29] shown in Listing 1 helps illustrate some of the challenges of building reliable distributed services. The example listings use the following style. We write named definitions as **def** name = body binding the name to the body; value bindings as **val** name = value; statements sequenced by semicolons; actor behaviors as anonymous functions in curried form that receive one message and execute the body returning the next behavior as msg ⇒ body ; spawning new actors as **spawn** behavior returning its reference; asynchronously sending a message to actor a by **send** a message. The example in Listing 1 consists of two actors, a and b. Actor a maintains a count of the number of messages it has received, and increments this count for each message that it receives, replying with the previous count. Actor b sends two messages to actor a, and then switches to a behavior which logs every message that it receives. To start the computation, actors a and b are spawned, and one unit message is sent to actor b.

We would expect that the program prints the numbers 0 followed by 1 on the console for a local execution in a standard actor system.

Instead, consider running the program distributed with actor a running on one node, and b on another, in which each node locally restarts in case of a failure. Under these circumstances, the program may exhibit *surprising* behaviors. For example, it may never print anything, if the messages sent to actor a are lost due to the a's node failing just after receiving the message but before processing it. Or, perhaps actor b crashes after sending the first message, then recovers and sends two more messages. In this case, the numbers 0, 1, and 2 are printed. These behaviors are surprising to the programmer as they are an artifact of system-level failures and recoveries, in which messages may be processed zero, one, or multiple times.

2.2 Reliable Actors

In this paper, we explore the idea of using failure-transparent actors as low-level building blocks for reliable services. That is, contrasting to standard actor systems, a failure-transparent actor system should exhibit failure transparency, and provide tools for end-to-end failure transparency. Thus, failure-transparent actors aim to greatly reduce the complexity of building reliable distributed services.

For example, in a failure-transparent actor system, the counting actor example from Listing 1 would execute as expected, printing the numbers 0 and 1, even in the presence of failures. The canonical use case of failure transparent actor systems [16,43,44,51] is reliably orchestrating complex workflows. This includes business workflows such as a checkout workflow that involves reserving an item, interacting with an external payment service, sending the order confirmation, and subsequently tracking the order as it is shipped [16,44,51], as well as the development of AI agents [16,44,51]. These use cases are made possible by the underlying failure transparency guarantees, making it possible to write complex distributed interactions, whilst minimizing the failure-handling code.

In the following sections, we present three kinds of composition of failure-transparent actors, all of which can be used to build reliable distributed services. For the first two, system-level failures are masked from the application-level; for the third, system-level failures are handled on the application-level, which may be preferred in some cases.

3 Failure-Transparent Actors

This section presents a syntax and semantics for failure-transparent actors. Furthermore, we prove a theorem that states that the semantics is failure transparent [56] by simulation using prophecy variables [1,33]. As prophecy variables are not commonly used, we start by providing a brief introduction to them.

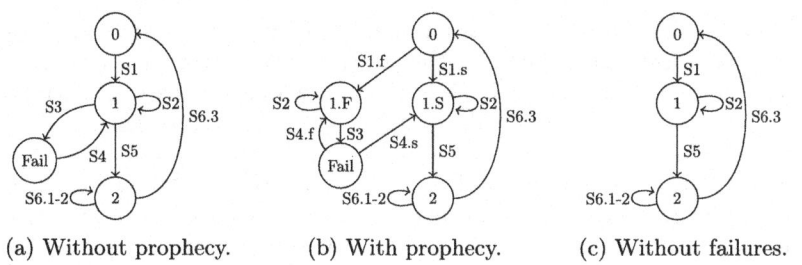

Fig. 2. Actor state machine corresponding to the syntax and semantics at different levels of abstraction.

3.1 Prophecy Variables

Prophecy variables [1,33] are a type of *auxiliary variables* [1], or *ghost variables* [38]. They are added to a formal model for the purpose of showing that one model implements another. In this paper, they are added to the syntax and semantics, for the purpose of constructing the simulation relation in the simulation proof, *i.e.*, showing that one execution behavior simulates another.

A prophecy variable accurately predicts the outcome of a future event, in our case, whether the processing of a message will succeed or fail. And so, by using this information, the simulation relation can decide to not simulate the evaluation steps of a message which is predicted to fail.

Although there are general constructive principles for using prophecy variables without altering the semantics [33], we use them in a direct way to later simplify the construction of the simulation relation. In our use, prophecy variables are always randomly reassigned before their next use.

3.2 Actors as State Machines

Figure 2 represents the later presented actor syntax and semantics as a state machine. By considering different compositions of the derivation rules, we identify three different levels of abstraction: the semantics with failures but without prophecy variables (Fig. 2a); the semantics with failures and prophecy variables (Fig. 2b); and the semantics without failures (Fig. 2c).

The implementation is modeled by Fig. 2a. An actor starts in the initial state 0. A message is scheduled for processing by transitioning by the derivation rule $S1$ to state 1. The actor proceeds by evaluating the processing of the message by derivation rule $S2$. The actor may fail nondeterministically, by transitioning to the state *Fail* by derivation rule $S3$. It may then recover from the failure by transitioning back to state 1 by derivation rule $S4$. The actor is finished processing when it has evaluated the term to a value, in which case it may have produced a set of side-effecting actions such as sending messages and spawning actors. Once finished, it may transition to state 2 by derivation rule $S5$, at which point it applies the actions using rules $S6.1$-2 remaining in state 2, and transitions back to state 0 by derivation rule $S6.3$.

Even though the implementation model is failure transparent with respect to the semantics without failures, it is not trivial to show so. For example, it is unclear for an actor in state 1 whether or not it will fail or succeed. Therefore, it is difficult to know whether nondeterministic message-processing evaluations by rule $S2$ should correspond to evaluations in the failure-free semantics, if it will later fail. Instead, prophecy variables are used to distinguish between these.

Figure 2b represents the state machine with prophecy variables. Here, the transitions are labeled by a suffix s or f to indicate whether the execution is predicted to succeed or fail, respectively. Similarly, the states are labeled with suffix S or F to indicate whether the prophecy is to succeed or fail, respectively. This way, an execution in state $1.F$ is known to eventually fail, whereas an execution in state $1.S$ is known to eventually succeed.

This knowledge is used to construct a mapping from the states of the execution with prophecies (Fig. 2b) to the execution without failures (Fig. 2c), and we use the same mapping of states to construct the simulation relation later in the proof (Theorem 1, Theorem 2). In particular, states $1.F$ and Fail are mapped to state 0, that is, the states of an expected failed execution are mapped to the initial state. The other states are mapped to their corresponding states, *i.e.*, 0 to 0, $1.S$ to 1, and 2 to 2.

3.3 Syntax and Semantics

The presented syntax and semantics formalize the failure-transparent actor model corresponding to the state machine representation in Fig. 2. In this section, we first present the syntax and semantics for the evaluation of actor terms, and then for the full configurations of a failure-transparent actor system. The syntax and semantics were inspired by a presentation of a non-failure-transparent actor system by Fowler et al. [21] which we found appropriate for our purposes. Throughout we use $\bot$ to represent an undefined value.

An actor term (Fig. 3) consists of the usual terms of untyped lambda calculus, and three actor-specific terms: *send t u* for sending a message, *spawn t* for spawning a new actor, and *self* for obtaining a reference to the actor itself. When evaluating a term, an actor may produce actions as side effects. This includes the *Send* action, and the *Spawn* action. The evaluation order is defined by the evaluation contexts. Evaluating a term such as *send a v* produces the *unit* value and the action $\{Send\ a\ v\ i_{fresh}\}$, where i_{fresh} is a fresh identifier.

The state of the execution is represented by a configuration (Fig. 4), consisting of the prophecy p, the actor's identifier/reference a, and a tuple representing its stable storage $\langle M, \sigma, l \rangle$, as well as a tuple representing its volatile storage $\langle t, X \rangle$. The stable storage contains the actor's mailbox M, behavior/state σ, and lock l. The lock may be in one of three states, each corresponding to a different state in the actor state machine (Fig. 2): $\bot$ corresponds to state 0, $\langle 1, m \rangle$ to state 1, and $\langle 2, X \rangle$ to state 2. The lock may contain additional information which is necessary for the recovery, such as the message m which is currently being processed, as the message is removed from the mailbox the first time the processing starts. Actions and messages are all unique. This is ensured by the

Syntax					
t, u ::=		terms:	X ::= $\emptyset \mid X \cup X$		actions:
	x, y, z	variable	$\{Send\ a\ v\ i\}$		send
	a, b, c	actor ref	$\{Spawn\ a\ \lambda x.t\}$		spawn
	$\lambda x.t$	abstraction			
	$unit$	unit	$E[\circ]$ ::= $[\circ] \mid E[\circ]\ t \mid \lambda x.t\ E[\circ]$		contexts:
	$t\ u$	application	send $E[\circ]\ t$		send-1
	$send\ t\ u$	send	send $a\ E[\circ]$		send-2
	$spawn\ t$	spawn	spawn $E[\circ]$		spawn
	$self$	self ref			
			Semantics	$F[t] \to^a E[t'] \| X$	
v, w ::=		values:	$E[(\lambda x.t)\ v] \to$	$E[t[v/x]]$	
	x, y, z	variable	$E[send\ a\ v] \to$	$E[unit] \mid \{Send\ a\ v\ i_{fresh}\}$	
	a, b, c	actor ref	$E[spawn\ \lambda x.t] \to$	$E[a] \mid \{Spawn\ a_{fresh}\ \lambda x.t\}$	
	$\lambda x.t$	abstraction	$E[self] \to^a$	$E[a]$	
	$unit$	unit			

Fig. 3. Actor syntax and semantics.

Syntax			
C, D, E ::= $p\ \langle a, \langle M, \sigma, l \rangle, \langle t, X \rangle \rangle \mid C \parallel D \mid \epsilon$			configurations
p	::= $\bot \mid succ \mid fail$	prophecy	*Structural Congruence*
M	::= $\emptyset \mid M \cup X$	mailbox	$C \parallel D \equiv D \parallel C$
σ	::= $\bot \mid \lambda x.t$	behavior	$C \parallel (D \parallel E) \equiv (C \parallel D) \parallel E$
l	::= $\bot \mid \langle 1, v \rangle \mid \langle 2, X \rangle$	lock	$C \parallel \epsilon \equiv C$

Fig. 4. Configuration syntax and structural congruence rules.

use of fresh values upon their creation (Fig. 3). The prophecy p is always $\bot$ in states 0 and 2, and either *succ* or *fail* in state 1. This way it is mapped to states 1.S and 1.F respectively. To simplify the semantics, configurations may be reorganized according to the structural congruence rules (Fig. 4).

The semantics consist of nine derivation rules (Fig. 5) of the form $C \to C'$ representing a transition of the state machine (Fig. 2). The rules are straightforward interpretations of the state machine. Important is to note the transitions of the prophecy variable, in some rules such as ($S1$, $S6$), it is required to be undefined, *i.e.*, $\bot$, in the current state. In some rules, the prophecy is either *succ* or *fail* and is left unchanged ($S2$). We represent the nondeterministic assignment of a fresh prophecy variable as p', in which case p' is either *succ* or *fail*.

The apply rules are different as they involve interaction between configurations. Apply send ($S6.1$) applies a send action, taking a message from the sending actor's stable set of actions, and adding it to the receiving actor's mailbox. We have omitted a rule for the case when the sending and receiving actor are the same, although it is straightforward to add [21]. Apply spawn ($S6.2$) creates a fresh actor with actor reference b and an empty mailbox.

$$\boxed{C \to C'}$$

Semantics

(S1) Schedule actor
$\bot \langle a, \langle M \uplus m, \sigma, \bot \rangle, \langle \bot, \bot \rangle \rangle \to p' \langle a, \langle M, \sigma, \langle 1, m \rangle \rangle, \langle \sigma w, \emptyset \rangle \rangle$, if $m = \{Send\ a\ w\ i\}$, $p' \in \{succ, fail\}$

(S2) Evaluate actor
$p \langle a, \langle M, \sigma, \langle 1, m \rangle \rangle, \langle t, X \rangle \rangle \to p \langle a, \langle M, \sigma, \langle 1, m \rangle \rangle, \langle t', X \cup X' \rangle \rangle$, if $t \to^a t' \mid X'$, $p \in \{succ, fail\}$, $X' = \{Send\ b\ w\ i\}$ or $X' = \{Spawn\ b\ \lambda x.w\}$ or $X' = \emptyset$

(S3) Fail actor
$fail \langle a, \langle M, \sigma, \langle 1, m \rangle \rangle, \langle t, X \rangle \rangle \to fail \langle a, \langle M, \sigma, \langle 1, m \rangle \rangle, \langle \bot, \bot \rangle \rangle$

(S4) Recover actor
$fail \langle a, \langle M, \sigma, \langle 1, m \rangle \rangle, \langle \bot, \bot \rangle \rangle \to p' \langle a, \langle M, \sigma, \langle 1, m \rangle \rangle, \langle \sigma w, \emptyset \rangle \rangle$, if $m = \{Send\ a\ w\ i\}, p' \in \{succ, fail\}$

(S5) Finish actor evaluation
$succ \langle a, \langle M, \sigma, \langle 1, m \rangle \rangle, \langle v, X \rangle \rangle \to \bot \langle a, \langle M, v, \langle 2, X \rangle \rangle, \langle \bot, \bot \rangle \rangle$

(S6.1) Apply send
$\bot \langle a, \langle M, \sigma, \langle 2, X \uplus \{Send\ b\ w\ i\} \rangle \rangle, \langle \bot, \bot \rangle \rangle \parallel p_b \langle b, \langle M_b, \sigma_b, l_b \rangle, \langle t_b, X_b \rangle \rangle$
$\to \bot \langle a, \langle M, \sigma, \langle 2, X \rangle \rangle, \langle \bot, \bot \rangle \rangle \parallel p_b \langle b, \langle M_b \uplus \{Send\ b\ w\ i\}, \sigma_b, l_b \rangle, \langle t_b, X_b \rangle \rangle$

(S6.2) Apply spawn
$\bot \langle a, \langle M, \sigma, \langle 2, X \uplus \{Spawn\ b\ \lambda x.w\} \rangle \rangle, \langle \bot, \bot \rangle \rangle \to \bot \langle a, \langle M, \sigma, \langle 2, X \rangle \rangle, \langle \bot, \bot \rangle \rangle \parallel \bot \langle b, \langle \emptyset, \lambda x.w, \bot \rangle, \langle \bot, \bot \rangle \rangle$

(S6.3) Apply empty
$\bot \langle a, \langle M, \sigma, \langle 2, \emptyset \rangle \rangle, \langle \bot, \bot \rangle \rangle \to \bot \langle a, \langle M, \sigma, \bot \rangle, \langle \bot, \bot \rangle \rangle$

(S0)
$C \parallel D \to C' \parallel D$, if $C \to C'$

Fig. 5. Configuration semantics.

The semantics models an execution in which actors may fail and recover. The notion of stable and volatile state corresponds to an implementation in which the stable state is stored durably, and the volatile state is stored in memory on some processing node. Moreover, rule $S5$ corresponds to an implementation in which it is possible to durably store the actor's behavior, lock, and produced actions in a single atomic step.

3.4 Transparent Failure Recovery

We prove a theorem which states that the presented syntax and semantics is failure transparent according to the definition by Veresov et al. [56]. Failure transparency, informally, states that a system is failure transparent if it is observed to behave as though no failures have occurred. A formal definition of the used failure transparency$_2$ notion is given in Sect. D.

Theorem 1. *The presented semantics for composition within a failure-transparent actor system is failure transparent.*

Proof. The full proof is available in the appendix (Sect. B). The proof is done by the *simulation proof strategy* (Definition 8), thus implying by Theorem 3 that the semantics is *failure transparent*$_2$ (Definition 14). The main proof idea is to use the prophecy variables to construct a simulation relation R between the full semantics and the failure-free semantics, which corresponds to the mapping of the state machines as described in Sect. 3.2, such that the observed values of any pair of configurations in the relation R are the same for some defined observation function. □

4 Composition of Systems

Whereas the previous section presented a failure-transparent actor system, this section considers the failure-transparent composition of actor systems. We present an extension to the syntax and semantics for expressing compositions of actor systems; messaging between these actor systems; and a failure recovery mechanism. Similarly to the last section, we show that this semantics is failure transparent.

4.1 Extensions to the Syntax and Semantics

The syntax and semantics extend the previous semantics in order to model the communication between two separate actor systems (Fig. 6). We keep our modifications minimal. Rather than explicitly modeling separate actor systems, we introduce a new operation, *atomicSend*, to represent the transmission of a message between actors which might belong to different actor systems.

Unlike the standard *send* operation, *atomicSend* immediately enqueues the *AtomicSend* action into the receiving actor's mailbox upon evaluation (*S*2.1). Consequently, its effects are not stored to stable storage prior to delivery. This models the lack of control on side-effecting actions when communicating with an external system. In such cases, the actions are immediate and may stem from evaluations which later fail. Processing such actions could lead to a non-failure-transparent execution. The mechanism for ensuring failure transparency is described below.

The first rule (*S*1.1) schedules an *AtomicSend* message m for processing if the message is part of the observable state of the actor's mailbox. This is defined as the operation $observe_2(M) = \{AtomicSend\ b\ w\ i \in M \mid AtomicCommit\ b\ i \in M\}$, i.e., the set of *AtomicSend* messages in the mailbox for which there is a corresponding *AtomicCommit* message with the same identifier i in the mailbox. By restricting the scheduling to only such messages, the actor avoids scheduling an *AtomicCommit* message which was sent during a failed execution. This is because a failed execution would never send the corresponding *AtomicCommit* message. The second rule (*S*2.1) evaluates a term which produces an *AtomicSend*

```
Actor Syntax...
t, u ::= ...                      terms:         E[∘] ::= ...                              contexts:
    atomicSend t t            atomic send         atomicSend E[∘] u      atomic send-2
                                                  atomicSend a E[∘]      atomic send-3
X ::= ...                        actions:
    {AtomicSend a w i}         a-send         Actor Semantics...        $E[t] \to^a E[t']|X$
    {AtomicCommit a i}         a-commit       E[atomicSend a w] →
                                                  E[unit] | {AtomicSend a w $i_{fresh}$}
```

Semantics... $C \to C'$

(S1.1) Schedule actor
$\bot \ \langle a, \ \langle M \uplus m, \sigma, \bot \rangle, \ \langle \bot, \bot \rangle \rangle \ \to \ p' \ \langle a, \ \langle M, \sigma, \langle 1, m \rangle \rangle, \ \langle \sigma w, \emptyset \rangle \rangle$, if
$m = \{AtomicSend\ a\ w\ i\}, m \in observe_2(M), p' \in \{succ, fail\}$

(S2.1) Evaluate actor
$p \ \langle a, \ \langle M, \sigma, \langle 1, m \rangle \rangle, \ \langle t, X \rangle \rangle \ \| \ p_b \ \langle b, \ \langle M_b, \sigma_b, l_b \rangle, \ \langle t_b, X_b \rangle \rangle \ \to$
$p \ \langle a, \ \langle M, \sigma, \langle 1, m \rangle \rangle, \ \langle t', X \uplus \{AtomicCommit\ b\ i\} \rangle \rangle \ \| \ p_b \ \langle b, \ \langle M_b \uplus$
$\{AtomicSend\ b\ w\ i\}, \sigma_b, l_b \rangle, \ \langle t_b, X_b \rangle \rangle$, if $t \to^a t' \ | \ \{AtomicSend\ b\ w\ i\}$,
$p \in \{succ, fail\}$

(S4.1) Recover actor
$fail \ \langle a, \ \langle M, \sigma, \langle 1, m \rangle \rangle, \ \langle \bot, \bot \rangle \rangle \ \to \ p' \ \langle a, \ \langle M, \sigma, \langle 1, m \rangle \rangle, \ \langle \sigma w, \emptyset \rangle \rangle$, if
$m = \{AtomicSend\ a\ w\ i\}, p' \in \{succ, fail\}$

(S6.4) Apply atomic commit
$\bot \ \langle a, \ \langle M, \sigma, \langle 2, X \uplus \{AtomicCommit\ b\ i\} \rangle \rangle, \ \langle \bot, \bot \rangle \rangle \ \| \ p_b \ \langle b, \ \langle M_b, \sigma_b, l_b \rangle, \ \langle t_b, X_b \rangle \rangle \to$
$\bot \ \langle a, \ \langle M, \sigma, \langle 2, X \rangle \rangle, \ \langle \bot, \bot \rangle \rangle \ \| \ p_b \ \langle b, \ \langle M_b \uplus \{AtomicCommit\ b\ i\}, \sigma_b, l_b \rangle, \ \langle t_b, X_b \rangle \rangle$

Fig. 6. Extensions to the configuration syntax and semantics.

action, and immediately enqueues it in the receiving actor b's mailbox. Additionally, the sending actor stores the *AtomicCommit* action to its volatile state. The recovery rule ($S4.1$) recovers the execution of a failed actor scheduled to process an *AtomicSend* message. The apply rule ($S6.4$) applies the *AtomicCommit* action, by adding the *AtomicCommit* action to the receiving actor's mailbox, such that the corresponding *AtomicSend* message from thereon is visible by the $observe_2$ operation and can thus be scheduled.

Consider an example of two actor systems with actors a and b from the respective systems, starting in a configuration in which actor a is scheduled to process an *AtomicSend a unit i* action with the behavior $\lambda x.\ atomicSend\ b\ x$. In a successful execution, actor a first evaluates the message by rule ($S2.1$), thereby enqueuing *AtomicSend b unit i'* in actor b's mailbox. Then, after finishing the evaluation ($S5$) and applying the action ($S6.4$), it enqueues *AtomicCommit b i'* in actor b's mailbox. Now, as both the *AtomicCommit b i'* and *AtomicSend b unit i'* actions are in actor b's mailbox, the $observe_2$ operation will make the message schedulable for processing by actor b according to rule ($S1.1$). By contrast, consider a failed execution in which actor a fails by rule

(S3) immediately after enqueuing the message in actor b's mailbox. Actor a's volatile state is lost due to the recovery, including the action $AtomicCommit\ b\ i'$. As the action is lost, it will never be enqueued in actor b's mailbox, thus the message $AtomicSend\ b\ unit\ i'$ will never become schedulable for processing by actor b. Consequently, any $AtomicSend$ message sent during a failed execution will never be scheduled by the receiver due to the missing $AtomicCommit$ action.

4.2 Transparent Failure Recovery for Compositions

Similar to Sect. 3.4, we prove a theorem that states that the presented semantics is failure transparent. Due to the potential for $AtomicSend$ actions from failed executions being delivered immediately to the receiving actor's mailbox, we need to additionally use the $observe_2$ function to filter and keep only the $AtomicSend$ messages with a corresponding $AtomicCommit$, as is done in rule (S1.1). Thus, we alter the observation function used in Sect. 3.4 to additionally filter each actor's mailbox by discarding $AtomicSend$ actions with missing $AtomicCommit$ actions.

Theorem 2. *The presented semantics for composition between failure-transparent actor systems is failure transparent.*

Proof. The full proof is available in the appendix (Sect. C). The proof is done similarly to the proof of Theorem 1, by simulation using prophecy variables and the new observation function. □

Thus, we have shown that the presented failure-transparent actor system is failure transparent for compositions both within (Theorem 1) and between systems (Theorem 2). Next, we discuss application-level composition.

5 Application-Level Failure Transparency

Building on the system-level techniques presented in previous sections, this section explores application-level means for the failure-transparent composition of failure-transparent actor systems by presenting an extension to the syntax and semantics with actor supervision and timeout/retry limits. The composition is on the *application-level*, as either the user code or some library implements the mechanism for ensuring end-to-end failure transparency, rather than the system itself as was the case in the previous section. The drawback of this approach, however, is that we cannot provide any system-level failure-transparency guarantees for the composition as the application-level code may be incorrect, therefore we do not prove that the semantics is failure transparent.

Failure transparency on the application-level provides two benefits. First, it is applicable to compositions of systems that do not have system-level support for composition. For example, it is common practice to implement a connector to an external storage system as a library. Second, in some cases, application-level failure handling is preferred over system-level failure handling [26,46]. As we will explore, if another system is not responding, it may be better to time out the operation, return a failure, and let the application code decide how to handle the failure, rather than waiting indefinitely and blocking the caller.

5.1 Actor Supervision, Timeout/Retry Limits

In order to deal with system-level failures on the application-level, we extend the presented actor semantics with actor supervision and timeout/retry limits. We can also use durable futures and promises to a similar effect. In essence, both approaches extend the system with the ability to stop the execution of a repeatedly failing computation, and leak the failure to the application, so that the application can handle the failure.

The syntax and semantics are extended by two additional operations. The full syntax and semantics are available in the appendix (Sect. A). First, the *watch* operation is used for building an actor supervision hierarchy [7,8]. It enables an actor to *watch* another actor. An actor persistently fails by either exceeding a predefined timeout/retry limit for the processing of a message, or by choosing to fail. Second, the *spawn* operation also specifies a timeout/retry limit set to a finite or infinite value, *i.e.*, $R(n)$ where $n \in \mathbb{N} \cup \{inf\}$. Thus, a failure-transparent behavior as in Sect. 3 is emulated by an infinite timeout/retry limit. The *watching* actor receives a *Fail* message when the *watched* actor persistently fails, and can subsequently handle the failure. We will see how these primitives are used next for expressing end-to-end reliable services.

5.2 Example Patterns

Listing 2 implements the same mechanism as in Sect. 4 but on the application-level by means of infinitely retrying executions. The example defines a transfer behavior, which performs an atomic transfer of a message msg to an actor at address addr. It repeatedly creates a fresh transaction identifier and sends an *ASend* message to the receiving actor. It also spawns a new actor which infinitely retries to send an *AComm* message to the receiving actor for the corresponding transaction identifier. Both spawned actors end in a stopped behavior, where stopped is defined as: **def stopped** = (msg ⇒ **stopped**) . Importantly, the example code may send several *ASend* messages for different transaction identifiers; however, we know that it will only ever send *AComm* messages for one and the same transaction identifier corresponding to the last successful execution of the outer block. This way, the receiver can use the same function $observe_2$ as in Sect. 4 to filter out the corresponding messages, thus implementing compositional failure transparency by emulating the method in Sect. 4.

Listing 2. Atomic message transfer.

```
1  def transfer = ( (msg, addr) ⇒
2    val txid = ( fresh );
3    req.post(
4      addr,
5      ASend(msg, txid));
6    send spawn R(inf) ( x ⇒
7      req.post(
8        addr,
9        AComm(txid));
10     stopped
11   ) unit;
12   stopped );
13
14 val a = ( spawn R(inf) transfer );
15 send a (msg, addr)
```

Listing 3. Idempotent booking.

```
1  def book = ( (admin, user, item) ⇒
2    val replyTo = ( self );
3    val txid = ( fresh );
4    watch send spawn R(5) (
5      service.book(item, txid);
6      send replyTo Resp(...);
7      stopped
8    ) unit;
9    res ⇒ res match
10     case Resp(...) ⇒ send user ...
11     case Fail(...) ⇒ send admin ...
12     stopped );
13
14 val a = ( spawn R(inf) book );
15 send a (admin, user, item)
```

In contrast to the previous example, it may be necessary to *not* mask failures by infinitely retrying [26,50,55]. Listing 3 shows a code example for booking an item in an idempotent service [26]. The defined book behavior creates a fresh transaction identifier and spawns and watches a new actor which attempts to book an item for that transaction identifier up to five retries. If the booking succeeds, then the spawned actor sends back a response to the caller. If the service is down, or the booking repeatedly fails, then a *Fail* message is sent to the watching actor. The booking behavior continues by handling either case. In case of a failure, a message is sent internally to some administrator for further handling.

It is necessary to leak such a failure, as the service booking may otherwise be retried indefinitely, blocking the caller. For example, the user may want to cancel the booking if it is not successful after some time; this would not be possible if it was retried indefinitely. However, leaking failures has a downside. It may be the case that the booking succeeded, even though the actor failed. In such a case, the error needs to be handled manually by external means [26,55]. These ideas have been previously discussed in related work [26,46,50,55].

6 Related Work

The actor model was first introduced by Carl Hewitt at MIT in the early 1970s as a formalism for reasoning agents [27,28]. The seminal contributions of Gul Agha include the development of the actor model as a basis for concurrent object-oriented programming [3,5] as well as the model's formal foundations in the context of open distributed systems [4]. Open distributed systems allow "the addition of new components, the replacement of existing components, and changes in interconnections between components, largely without disturbing the functioning of the system." [4] Agha et al. have shown the suitability and the power of the actor model as a basis for a theory of open distributed computation.

The actor model has since seen wide adoption in the software industry [31]. Widely used implementations include the Erlang programming language [7,9,19], Scala Actors [23,25], Akka [36], and Elixir [53] to name a few. They provide light-weight processes where fault tolerance is achieved through actor supervision hierarchies. Our work retains the light-weight nature and isolation of actors, with the difference however that crashed actors are automatically and transparently recovered by the system. Other actor-based languages such as AmbientTalk [18] focus on mobile peer-to-peer applications, the E programming language [39] emphasizes capability-based security, and the actor languages Pony [54], Encore [11], and LaCasa [24] ensure data-race freedom of shared memory by using reference capabilities. These are orthogonal concerns to our main focus on failure transparency. Actor garbage collection [15,41,42] is an important aspect of actor applications, which also applies to failure-transparent actors as presented here.

The syntax and semantics presented in this paper were influenced by work by Fowler et al. [21]. The *failure-aware actor model* (FAM) presented in [40] models actor failures as transitions between a *failed* and *available* state, in which the stable storage persists across failures, but lacks a notion of volatile storage as found in our work. Furthermore, the FAM model provides additional fairness assumptions which can be used for liveness properties, something which is not considered in our work. The *transactors* model presented in [20] extends the actor model with constructs for transactional processing, thus enabling reliable fault-tolerant programs. The introduced constructs include *checkpoint*, *rollback*, and *stabilize*, *i.e.*, making itself temporarily immutable, for orchestrating transactional processing across multiple actors. The semantics is proven to simulate a failure-free subset of the semantics, similar to our work; additionally, the liveness of a proposed checkpointing protocol is proven.

Recent years have seen a growing interest in distributed actor-like programming models [45] with various degrees of failure transparency [48]. The *Virtual Actor Model* [10,13] was introduced by Microsoft Research in the Orleans system. Virtual actors are logical entities, for which physical instances are reached by addressing them to an explicit key. However, virtual actors do not have the ability to spawn new actors [48]. Many other systems have since adopted similar ideas to encapsulate state and functions as objects [12,35,47,50,52], some of which are failure-transparent [12,35,47,52], and others not [10,13,50]

Failure transparency [34,57] is a desirable property of otherwise unwieldy distributed systems [12,30,37,56]. This paper uses a specific failure-transparency definition [56], which resembles *implementation* with *refinement mapping* [1,2], and simulation with *observable equivalence* [12]. The used definition is a safety property, thus it is not concerned with liveness [6,32] or fairness unlike other definitions [22,37]. The observation that a fully failure-transparent system is not necessarily a desirable property as the application-level may be better at handling failures is an observation which has been made in previous work [26, 46,55], notably so in the context of reliable actor systems [50].

Systems related to this work may be referred to as *durable execution systems* [16,43,44,51], *stateful serverless* [12,52], and others [47–50]. Similar to our work, durable execution systems focus on failure-transparent composition of services which may span multiple systems, with internal failure-transparency, and application-level failure-transparency for compositions. Other notable failure-transparent computing systems include MapReduce [17], Apache Spark [58], and Apache Flink [14], however, these are restricted to acyclic communication topologies. To the best of our knowledge, there is no failure-transparent actor system which has a *spawn* operation [48].

7 Conclusions and Future Work

This paper presents a syntax and semantics for failure-transparent actors. It is structured around three kinds of failure-transparent compositions: within the system, between systems, and on the application-level. The semantics is shown to be failure transparent. Two examples for application-level composition are discussed to highlight their effectiveness and necessity for dealing with system-level failures on the application-level. The presented work serves as an overview on failure-transparent actors as low-level building blocks for the construction of reliable distributed services.

In future work, we plan to mechanize the proofs. Furthermore, we plan to apply the proof technique involving simulation and prophecy variables to other related works on failure transparency.

Acknowledgments. The authors would like to thank the anonymous reviewers for their helpful comments. This study was partially funded by Digital Futures under a Research Pairs Consolidator grant (PORTALS).

Disclosure of Interests. The authors have no competing interests to declare that are relevant to the content of this article.

A Extensions for Application-Level Failure Transparency

This section provides the syntax and semantics extensions for the application-level failure transparency presented in Sect. 5. In particular, it introduces the *watch* operation, and introduces a retry limit for the *spawn* operation.

The syntax extensions are shown in Fig. 7. The *watch t* operation registers the actor to watch another actor with reference t. The *spawn $R(n)$ t* operation spawns a new actor with a retry limit $R(n)$, such that the new actor is retried up to n times for each message it processes. The corresponding actions, evaluation contexts, as well as actor semantics are added. Specifically, an entry $R(n)$ is added to the actor configuration, denoting the configured retry limit. The retry limit of a scheduled message is kept in the lock $\langle 1, v, R(n) \rangle$, which is decremented by one for each retry, such that the actor fails if the retry limit reaches zero.

Figure 7 shows the semantics extensions. In particular, it shows the rules with interesting modifications with respect to the new extensions, omitting the rules from previous sections for which it suffices to thread through the retry limit $R(n)$. Rule $(S1.2)$ schedules an actor for a *Fail* message if the actor watched

```
Actor Syntax...
t, u ::= ...                    terms...      E[o] ::= ...                       contexts...
        R(n ∈ ℕ ∪ {inf})        retry           spawn E[o] t                     spawn-1
        spawn t t               spawn           spawn R(n) E[o]                  spawn-2
        watch t                 watch           watch E[o]                       watch
X ::= ...                       actions...    Actor Semantics...        │ E[t] →ᵃ E[t']∥X │
        {Spawn R(n) a λx.t}     spawn         E[spawn R(n) λx.t] →
        {Watch a}               watch           E[unit] | {Spawn R(n) a_fresh λx.t}
        {Fail a}                fail          E[watch a] → E[unit] | {Watch a}

Configuration Syntax...
C, D, E ::= ... | p ⟨a, R(n), ⟨M, σ, l⟩, ⟨t, X⟩⟩                    l = ... | ⟨1, v, R(n)⟩
```

Semantics... │ C → C' │

(S1.2) Schedule actor
⊥ ⟨a, R(n), ⟨M ⊎ m, σ, ⊥⟩, ⟨⊥, ⊥⟩⟩ → p' ⟨a, R(n), ⟨M, σ, ⟨1, m, R(n)⟩⟩, ⟨σw, ∅⟩⟩,
if m = {Watch b}, {Fail b} ⊆ M, p' ∈ {succ, fail}

(S2.2) Evaluate actor
p ⟨a, R(n), ⟨M, σ, ⟨1, m, R(n')⟩⟩, ⟨t, X⟩⟩ → p ⟨a, R(n), ⟨M, σ, ⟨1, m, R(n')⟩⟩, ⟨t', X ∪ X'⟩⟩, if t →ᵃ t' | X', p ∈ {succ, fail}, X' = {Watch a} or X' = {Spawn R(n'') a_fresh λx.t}

S4.2 Recover actor
fail ⟨a, R(n), ⟨M, σ, ⟨1, m, R(n')⟩⟩, ⟨⊥, ⊥⟩⟩ → p' ⟨a, R(n) ⟨M, σ, ⟨1, m, R(n'')⟩⟩, ⟨⊥, ⊥⟩⟩, if n' = inf or n' > 0, n'' = n' − 1, p' ∈ {succ, fail}

(S5.2) Fail-stop actor
fail ⟨a, R(n) ⟨M, σ, ⟨1, m, R(0)⟩⟩, ⟨⊥, ⊥⟩⟩ → ⊥ ⟨a, R(n), ⟨M, σ, ⟨2, {Fail a}⟩⟩, ⟨⊥, ⊥⟩⟩

(S6.5) Apply fail-stop
⊥ ⟨a, R(n), ⟨M, σ, ⟨2, {Fail a}⟩⟩, ⟨⊥, ⊥⟩⟩ ∥ p_b ⟨b, R(n_b), ⟨M_b, σ_b, l_b⟩, ⟨t_b, X_b⟩⟩ →
⊥ ⟨a, R(n), ⟨M, σ, ⟨2, {Fail a}⟩⟩, ⟨⊥, ⊥⟩⟩ ∥ p_b ⟨b, R(n_b), ⟨M_b ⊎ {Fail a}, σ_b, l_b⟩, ⟨t_b, X_b⟩⟩

Fig. 7. Extensions for application-level failure transparency.

a failed actor and the watched actor has failed. Rule ($S2.2$) evaluates an actor which produces either a *Watch* or a *Spawn* action. A failed actor may recover by rule ($S4.2$), which decrements its retry limit; in the case of an infinite retry limit, decrementing it will still yield an infinite retry limit. A failed actor is persistently failed by rule ($S5.2$) once its retry limit reaches zero. Once failed, the actor is stuck in rule ($S6.5$), in which it may apply its fail action by sending a *Fail* message to other actors. Any actor may receive the *Fail* message by rule ($S6.5$), although only actors which have watched the failed actor may also schedule the *Fail* message by rule ($S1.2$).

B   Proof of Theorem 1

The proof structure in Theorem 1 and Theorem 2 follows the *simulation proof strategy* (Definition 8) which implies *failure transparency*$_2$ (Definition 14) by Theorem 3. It entails the following steps.

1. Define a semantics consisting of a set of semantic rules S.
2. Define a subset of these rules as the failure-related rules $F \subseteq S$.
3. Define the set of initial configurations K.
4. Define the observability function O which returns the observed value of configurations.

Now, what remains is to show that the semantics is failure transparent$_2$ by the simulation proof strategy.

5. Pick a relation R over the configurations of the semantics S.
6. Let $I = \{(C, C) \mid C \in K\}$.
7. Prove: $I \subseteq R \wedge S \sim_R (S \setminus F) \wedge (\forall (C, C') \in R.\ O(C) = O(C'))$.

We proceed by proving Theorem 1. The proof for Theorem 2 is found in Sect. C.

Proof. The set of derivation rules are divided into the set of all semantic rules ($\{$ S0, S1 $succ$, S1 $fail$, S2 $succ$, S2 $fail$, S3, S4 $succ$, S4 $fail$, S5, S6.1, S6.2, S6.3$\}$), and the set of failure-free rules ($\{$S0, S1 $succ$, S2 $succ$, S5, S6.1, S6.2, S6.3$\}$). Here, we distinguish between a rule in which a prophecy is set to $succ$ or $fail$, such that the failure-free rules never set the prophecy to $fail$.

To differentiate between the two sets of rules, we denote a derivation in the full set of rules by $C_F \to_F C'_F$, and in the failure-free set of rules by $C \to C'$.

The observation function *observe* is defined as the function which only observes stable events of the stable storage of a configuration.

Definition 1 (*observe*).

$$observe(p\ \langle a, \langle M, \sigma, l \rangle, \langle t, X \rangle \rangle) = \langle a, M \uplus M', \sigma \rangle$$

where $M' = \{m\}$ if $l = \langle 1, m \rangle$, else $M' = \emptyset$. The function is defined for the parallel composition of configurations as expected.

The set of initial configurations K is defined as the set of all configurations in which all actors are in their initial state, *i.e.*, their prophecy and lock are $\bot$.

The relation R is defined so that it corresponds to the mapping of state machines as presented in Sect. 3.2.

Definition 2 (*R*). $C_F R C$ iff

– *Case 1: prophecy* $p = \bot$
  - $C_F = \bot\ \langle a, \langle M, \sigma, l \rangle, \langle t, X \rangle \rangle$
  - $C = C_F$

- Case 2: prophecy $p = succ$
    - $C_F = succ \ \langle a, \langle M, \sigma, l \rangle, \langle t, X \rangle \rangle$
    - $C = C_F$
- Case 3: prophecy $p = fail$
    - $C_F = fail \ \langle a, \langle M, \sigma, \langle 1, m \rangle \rangle, \langle t, X \rangle \rangle$
    - $C = \bot \ \langle a, \langle M \uplus m, \sigma, \bot \rangle, \langle \bot, \bot \rangle \rangle$
- Case 4: empty
    - $C_F = \epsilon$
    - $C = \epsilon$
- Case 5: recursive
    - $C_F = C_{F1} \parallel C_{F2}$
    - $C = C_1 \parallel C_2$
    - $C_{F1} R C_1$
    - $C_{F2} R C_2$

What remains is to prove the three conditions for the chosen definitions as outlined in the seventh and final step.

The first condition, i.e., $\{(C, C) \mid C \in K\} \subseteq R$, follows from the definition of R and K, as it can be seen that for any pair of initial configurations (C, C) that it will match Case 1 of R by the prophecy being $\bot$ and by $C = C$.

The third condition, i.e., $(\forall (C_F, C) \in R. \ observe(C_F) = observe(C))$, follows from the definitions of R and $observe$, as it can be seen that for all configurations C_F and C with $C_F R C$, that $observe(C_F) = observe(C)$.

What remains is to show that $S \sim_R (S \setminus F)$ as follows (Definition 7). Given a pair of configurations C_F and C, where $C_F R C$, and $C_F \to_F C'_F$, we must show that there exists some C' such that $C \to^* C'$ and $C'_F R C'$. We do so by case analysis on the last derivation step used for $C_F \to_F C'_F$. To simplify the proof, we start by considering two general cases, which are later used for the other cases.

- General Case G1
    - Given C_F, C'_F, s.t.
        * $C_F = p \ \langle a, \langle M, \sigma, l \rangle, \langle t, X \rangle \rangle$, where the prophecy $p \in \{true, \bot\}$
        * $C'_F = p' \ \langle a, \langle M', \sigma', l' \rangle, \langle t', X' \rangle \rangle$, where the prophecy $p' \in \{true, \bot\}$
        * $C_F \to_F C'_F$
    - Given C s.t. $C_F R C$
    - Prove: exists C' s.t. $C'_F R C'$ and $C \to^* C'$
        * $C = C_F$, by definition of R
        * Choose $C' = C'_F$.
        * $C'_F R C'$, follows from $C'_F = C'$, and R Case 1 or 3
        * $C \to C'$, follows from $C_F \to_F C'_F$, and $C = C_F$, $C' = C'_F$, and $p \neq fail$ □
- General Case G2
    - Given C_F, C'_F, s.t.
        * $C_F = fail \ \langle a, \langle M, \sigma, \langle 1, m \rangle \rangle, \langle t, X \rangle \rangle$, i.e., the prophecy $p = fail$
        * $C'_F = fail \ \langle a, \langle M, \sigma, \langle 1, m \rangle \rangle, \langle t', X' \rangle \rangle$

- Case S1
  - Subcase S1 with $p' = succ$. Follows directly from General Case 1.
  - Subcase S1 with $p' = fail$
    * Given C_F, C'_F s.t.
      · $C_F = \bot \; \langle a, \; \langle M \uplus \{m\}, \sigma, \bot \rangle, \; \langle \bot, \bot \rangle \rangle$
      · $C'_F = fail \; \langle a, \; \langle M, \sigma, \langle 1, m \rangle \rangle, \; \langle \bot, \bot \rangle \rangle$
      · $C_F \to_F C'_F$
    * Given C s.t. $C_F R C$
    * Prove: exists C' s.t. $C'_F R C'$, and $C \to^* C'$
      · Choose $C' = C$
      · $C = \bot \; \langle a, \; \langle M \uplus \{m\}, \sigma, \bot \rangle, \; \langle \bot, \bot \rangle \rangle$, follows from $C_F R C$
      · $C'_F R C'$, follows from R Case 3
      · $C \to^0 C'$, follows from $C = C'$ □

- Case S2
  - Subcase S2 with $p = succ$. Follows directly from General Case 1.   □
  - Subcase S2 with $p = fail$. Follows directly from General Case 2.   □
- Case S3. Follows directly from General Case 3.   □
- Case S4
  - Subcase S4 with $p' = fail$. follows directly from General Case 3.
  - Subcase S4 with $p' = succ$
    * Given C_F, C'_F s.t.
      · $C_F = fail \; \langle a, , \; \langle M, \sigma, \langle 1, m \rangle \rangle, \; \langle \bot, \bot \rangle \rangle$
      · $C'_F = succ \; \langle a, , \; \langle M, \sigma, \langle 1, m \rangle \rangle, \; \langle \sigma \; m, \emptyset \rangle \rangle$
      · $C_F \to_F C'_F$
    * Given C s.t. $C_F R C$.
    * Prove: exists C' s.t. $C'_F R C'$ and $C \to^* C'$.
      · Choose $C' = C'_F$
      · $C = \bot \; \langle a, \; \langle M \uplus \{m\}, \sigma, \bot \rangle, \; \langle \bot, \bot \rangle \rangle$, follows from $C_F R C$
      · $C'_F R C'$, follows from R Case 2
      · $C \to C'$, follows by application of S1   □

- Case S5. Follows directly from General Case 1.   □
- Case S6.1 Apply send.
  - Given C_{F1}, C_{F2}, C'_{F1}, C'_{F2} s.t. $(C_{F1} \parallel C_{F2}) \to_F (C'_{F1} \parallel C'_{F2})$ by S6.1 Apply send
  - Given C_1, C_2 s.t. $(C_{F1} \parallel C_{F2}) R (C_1 \parallel C_2)$
  - Note $C_{F1} R C_1$, $C_{F2} R C_2$ by R Case 5
  - Note $C_1 = C_{F1}$ by $C_{F1} R C_1$ and R Case 1

- Prove: exists C'_1, C'_2 s.t. $(C_1 \parallel C_2) \to^* (C'_1 \parallel C'_2)$ and $(C'_{F1} \parallel C'_{F2})R(C'_1 \parallel C'_2)$
  * Choose $C'_1 = C'_{F1}$
  * $C'_{F1}RC'_1$, follows from R Case 1
  * Subsubcase $p_b \in \{succ, \bot\}$
    · Note $C_2 = C_{F2}$, follows from $C_{F2}RC_2$ and R Case 1 or Case 3
    · Choose $C'_2 = C'_{F2}$
    · $C'_{F2}RC'_2$, follows from R Case 1 or 2
    · $(C'_{F1} \parallel C'_{F2})R(C'_1 \parallel C'_2)$, follows from R Case 5 and the above
    · $C_1 \parallel C_2 \to C'_1 \parallel C'_2$, follows from $C_1 = C_{F1}$, $C_2 = C_{F2}$, $C'_1 = C'_{F1}$, $C'_2 = C'_{F2}$, and $C_{F1} \parallel C_{F2} \to C'_{F1} \parallel C'_{F2}$ by S6.1 Apply send □
  * Subsubcase $p_b = fail$
    · Note $C_{F2} = fail\ \langle b, \langle M_b, \sigma_b, \langle 1, m \rangle \rangle, \langle t_b, X_b \rangle \rangle$
    · Choose $C_2 = \bot\ \langle b, \langle M_b \uplus \{m\}, \sigma_b, \bot \rangle, \langle \bot, \bot \rangle \rangle$
    · $C_{F2}RC_2$ by R Case 3
    · Note $C'_{F2} = fail\ \langle b, \langle M_b \uplus \{w\}, \sigma_b, \langle 1, m \rangle \rangle, \langle \bot, \bot \rangle \rangle$.
    · Choose $C'_2 = \bot\ \langle b, \langle M_b \uplus \{w\} \uplus \{m\}, \sigma_b, \bot \rangle, \langle \bot, \bot \rangle \rangle$.
    · $C'_{F2}RC'_2$ by R Case 3
    · $(C'_{F1} \parallel C'_{F2})R(C'_1 \parallel C'_2)$, follows from R Case 5 and the above
    · $C_1 \parallel C_2 \to C'_1 \parallel C'_2$, follows from S6.1 Apply send for the chosen configurations □

- Case S6.2 Apply spawn
  - Given C_{F1}, C'_{F1}, C'_{F2} s.t. $C_{F1} \to_F C'_{F1} \parallel C'_{F2}$ by S6.2 Apply spawn
  - Given C_1 s.t. $C_{F1}RC_1$
  - Note $C_1 = C_{F1}$ by $C_{F1}RC_1$ and R Case 1
  - Prove: exists C'_1, C'_2 s.t. $C_1 \to^* C'_1 \parallel C'_2$ and $(C'_{F1} \parallel C'_{F2})R(C'_1 \parallel C'_2)$
    * Choose $C'_1 = C'_{F1}$
    * $C'_{F1}RC'_1$, follows from R Case 1
    * Choose $C'_2 = C'_{F2}$
    * $C'_{F2}RC'_2$, follows from R Case 1
    * $(C'_{F1} \parallel C'_{F2})R(C'_1 \parallel C'_2)$, follows from R Case 5 and the above
    * $C_1 \to C'_1 \parallel C'_2$, follows from $C_1 = C_{F1}$, $C'_1 = C'_{F1}$, $C'_2 = C'_{F2}$, and $C_{F1} \to C'_{F1} \parallel C'_{F2}$ by S6.2 Apply spawn □
- Subcase S6.3 Apply empty. Follows directly from General Case 1. □

This concludes the proof of Theorem 1. □

C   Proof of Theorem 2

Proof. The proof of Theorem 2 follows a similar structure to the proof of Theorem 1 from Sect. B, with the addition of showing some inductive properties.

The set of derivation rules from Sect. B are extended by adding the following rules to the full set of rules $\{S1.1\ succ, S1.1\ fail, S2.1\ succ, S2.1\ fail,$

S4.1 succ, S4.1 fail, S6.4}, and the following to the set of failure-free rules { S1.1 succ, S2.1 succ, S6.4}. The set of initial configurations is defined similarly to Sect. B, with the difference that mailboxes do not contain any *AtomicSend* or *AtomicCommit* messages.

The observation function $observe_2$ is defined similarly to Sect. B, with the difference that it filters out *AtomicSend* actions for which there is no corresponding *AtomicCommit* action with the same identifier in the mailbox.

Definition 3 ($observe_2$).

- $observe_2(p\ \langle a, \langle M, \sigma, l\rangle,\ \langle t, X\rangle\rangle) =$
  - $\langle a,\ M' \cup M'' \cup M''',\ \sigma\rangle$

Where
- $M' = \{m\}\ if\ l = \langle 1, m\rangle,\ else\ M' = \emptyset$
- $M'' = \{m \in M\ |\ m = \{Send\ a\ w\ i\}\}$
- $M''' = \{m \in M\ |\ m = \{AtomicSend\ a\ w\ i\} \wedge \{AtomicCommit\ a\ i\} \in M\}$

For the construction of the simulation relation, we additionally tag each *AtomicSend* and *AtomicCommit* message with the prophecy variable p that was active during the action's creation. That is, $\{p\ AtomicSend\ a\ w\ i\}$ and $\{p\ AtomicCommit\ a\ i\}$ are tagged with p where p is either *succ* or *fail*. For example, rule $(S2.1)$ is modified such that the created actions are tagged with the prophecy variable p, thus capturing the prophecy variable. By tagging the actions with prophecy variables, we can reason about which actions may eventually be observed, thus simplifying the construction of the simulation relation. Note, however, that the observation function $observe_2$ does not use prophecy variables, thus the observation function can be used to observe a real execution of a system in which the prophecy variables are nonexistent.

We define a function *Clean* which cleans the configurations and mailboxes by removing all actions which are tagged with the prophecy variable $p = fail$.

Definition 4 (*Clean*).

- $Clean(M) =$
  - $\{m \in M\ |\ m \notin \{(fail\ AtomicSend\ a\ w\ i), (fail\ AtomicCommit\ a\ i)\}\}$
- $Clean(p\ \langle a, \langle M, \sigma, l\rangle,\ \langle t, X\rangle\rangle) =$
  - $p\ \langle a, \langle Clean(M), \sigma, l\rangle,\ \langle t, X\rangle\rangle$
- $Clean(C_1\ \|\ C_2) =$
  - $Clean(C_1)\ \|\ Clean(C_2)$

The simulation relation R_2 is defined as a combination of the simulation relation R presented in previous section and the *Clean* function.

Definition 5 (R_2). $C_F R_2 C$ iff $Clean(C_F) R C$

What remains is to show that the three conditions hold as outlined in the proof structure in Sect. B.

The first condition, i.e., $\{(C,C) \mid C \in K\} \subseteq R_2$, follows by a similar reasoning to Sect. B, as the initial configurations contain no *AtomicSend* or *AtomicCommit* messages, thus the cleaned configurations are equal to the original configurations.

The third condition, i.e., $(\forall (C_F, C) \in R_2. \; observe_2(C_F) = observe_2(C))$, follows from the following reasoning. For all cases in R_2, the actor reference a and behavior σ are the same, thus it suffices to show that the observed mailboxes are the same. From R_2 we know that the observed mailboxes M_F and M from configurations C_F and C, respectively, contain the same set of *Send* messages. Further, by inductive reasoning, we can show that M_F and M contain the same set of *AtomicSend* messages with corresponding *AtomicCommit* messages. Thus, the observed mailboxes are the same, and so $observe_2(C_F) = observe_2(C)$.

Before proceeding with the simulation proof, we show a lemma which is later used in its proof.

Lemma 1. $p \; \langle a, \langle M, \sigma, \langle 1, m \rangle \rangle, \langle t, X \rangle \rangle \implies m \in observe_2(M \uplus m)$

Proof. To reach the configuration $p \; \langle a, \langle M, \sigma, \langle 1, m \rangle \rangle, \langle t, X \rangle \rangle$, the message m must have been scheduled by the rule $(S1.1)$. By rule $(S1.1)$, the message m can only be scheduled if it is in the $observe_2$ set of $M \uplus m$, thus $m \in observe_2(M \uplus m)$.

What remains is to show that $S \sim_{R_2} (S \setminus F)$ similarly to Sect. B. To simplify the proof, we will focus on the new extensions. The rules treated in Theorem 1 do not add or remove any *AtomicSend* or *AtomicCommit* messages to the mailboxes, thus it is straightforward to apply a similar case analysis as done in Theorem 1. We proceed by case analysis on the last derivation step used for $C_F \to_F C'_F$ for the new extensions.

- Case S1.1. Subcase $p' = succ$.
  - Given C_F, C'_F s.t.
    * $C_F = \bot \; \langle a, \; \langle M \uplus \{m\}, \sigma, \bot \rangle, \langle \bot, \bot \rangle \rangle$
    * $C'_F = succ \; \langle a, \; \langle M, \sigma, \langle 1, m \rangle \rangle, \langle \sigma w, \emptyset \rangle \rangle$, where $m = \{AtomicSend \; a \; w \; i\}$
    * $C_F \to_F C'_F$
  - Given C s.t. $C_F R_2 C$.
  - Prove: exists C' s.t. $C'_F R_2 C'$ and $C \to^* C'$.
    * Note: $C = \bot \; \langle a, \; \langle M' \uplus \{m\}, \sigma, \bot \rangle, \langle \bot, \bot \rangle \rangle$, where $Clean(M \uplus \{m\}) = M' \uplus \{m\}$, follows from $C_F R_2 C$
    * Note: $Clean(M) = M'$, follows from $Clean(M \uplus \{m\}) = M' \uplus \{m\}$ and the definition of $Clean$
    * Choose $C' = succ \; \langle a, \; \langle M', \sigma, \langle 1, m \rangle \rangle, \langle \sigma w, \emptyset \rangle \rangle$
    * $C'_F R_2 C'$, follows from R_2 with $Clean(M) = M'$ and R Case 2
    * $C \to C'$, follows by application of S1.1 □
- Case S1.1. Subcase $p' = fail$.
  - Given C_F, C'_F s.t.

Failure-Transparent Actors   103

* $C_F = \bot \ \langle a, \ \langle M \uplus \{m\}, \sigma, \bot \rangle, \ \langle \bot, \bot \rangle \rangle$
* $C'_F = \textit{fail} \ \langle a, \ \langle M, \sigma, \langle 1, m \rangle \rangle, \ \langle \sigma w, \emptyset \rangle \rangle$, where $m = \{AtomicSend \ a \ w \ i\}$
* $C_F \rightarrow_F C'_F$
- Given C s.t. $C_F R_2 C$.
- Prove: exists C' s.t. $C'_F R_2 C'$ and $C \rightarrow^* C'$.
  * Note: $C = \bot \ \langle a, \ \langle M' \uplus \{m\}, \sigma, \bot \rangle, \ \langle \bot, \bot \rangle \rangle$, where $\textit{Clean}(M \uplus \{m\}) = M' \uplus \{m\}$, follows from $C_F R_2 C$
  * Choose $C' = C$
  * $C'_F R_2 C'$, follows from R_2 with $\textit{Clean}(M \uplus \{m\}) = M' \uplus \{m\}$ and R Case 3
  * $C \rightarrow^0 C'$, follows by $C' = C$ □
- Case S.2.1. Subcase $p = \textit{succ}$.
  - Given C_{F1}, C_{F2}, C'_{F1}, C'_{F2} s.t. $(C_{F1} \ \| \ C_{F2}) \rightarrow_F (C'_{F1} \ \| \ C'_{F2})$ by S2.1 Evaluate actor
  - Given C_1, C_2 s.t. $(C_{F1} \ \| \ C_{F2}) R_2 (C_1 \ \| \ C_2)$
  - Prove: exists C'_1, C'_2 s.t. $(C_1 \ \| \ C_2) \rightarrow^* (C'_1 \ \| \ C'_2)$ and $(C'_{F1} \ \| \ C'_{F2}) R_2 (C'_1 \ \| \ C'_2)$
    * Choose C'_1 and C'_2 such that $(C_1 \ \| \ C_2) \rightarrow (C'_1 \ \| \ C'_2)$ by step S2.1, exists by $(C_{F1} \ \| \ C_{F2}) R_2 (C_1 \ \| \ C_2)$
    * Choose M_1, M_2, M'_1, M'_2, M_{F1}, M_{F2}, M'_{F1}, M'_{F2} from the corresponding configurations
    * $M_{F1} = M'_{F1}$, $M_1 = M'_1$, by S.2.1
    * $\textit{Clean}(M'_{F1}) = M'_1$, follows by $C_{F1} R_2 C_1$, and $M_{F1} = M'_{F1}$, $M_1 = M'_1$
    * $C'_{F1} R_2 C'_1$, follows by R_2 with $\textit{Clean}(M'_{F1}) = M'_1$ and R Case 2
    * $M_{F2} \uplus \{AtomicSend \ b \ w \ i\} = M'_{F2}$, $M_2 \uplus \{AtomicSend \ b \ w \ i\} = M'_2$, follows by S.2.1
    * $\textit{Clean}(M_{F2}) = M_2$, follows by $C_{F2} R_2 C_2$
    * $\textit{Clean}(M'_{F2}) = M'_2$, follows by $\textit{Clean}(M_{F2}) = M_2$, and $M_{F2} \uplus \{AtomicSend \ b \ w \ i\} = M'_{F2}$, $M_2 \uplus \{AtomicSend \ b \ w \ i\} = M'_2$
    * $C'_{F2} R_2 C'_2$ by R_2 with $\textit{Clean}(M'_{F2}) = M'_2$ and R Case 2
    * $(C'_{F1} \ \| \ C'_{F2}) R_2 (C'_1 \ \| \ C'_2)$, follows from R_2 with R Case 5 and the above   □
- Case S.2.1. Subcase $p = \textit{fail}$.
  - Given C_{F1}, C_{F2}, C'_{F1}, C'_{F2} s.t. $(C_{F1} \ \| \ C_{F2}) \rightarrow_F (C'_{F1} \ \| \ C'_{F2})$ by S2.1 Evaluate actor
  - Given C_1, C_2 s.t. $(C_{F1} \ \| \ C_{F2}) R_2 (C_1 \ \| \ C_2)$
  - Prove: exists C'_1, C'_2 s.t. $(C_1 \ \| \ C_2) \rightarrow^* (C'_1 \ \| \ C'_2)$ and $(C'_{F1} \ \| \ C'_{F2}) R_2 (C'_1 \ \| \ C'_2)$
    * Choose $C'_1 = C_1$, $C'_2 = C_2$
    * Choose M_1, M_2, M'_1, M'_2, M_{F1}, M_{F2}, M'_{F1}, M'_{F2} from the corresponding configurations
    * $C_{F1} R_2 C_1$, $C_{F2} R_2 C_2$, by $(C_{F1} \ \| \ C_{F2}) R_2 (C_1 \ \| \ C_2)$
    * $C'_{F1} R_2 C'_1$, by $C_{F1} = C'_{F1}$, $C_{F1} R_2 C_1$, $M_{F1} = M'_{F1}$, $M_1 = M'_1$
    * $\textit{Clean}(M_{F2}) = \textit{Clean}(M'_{F2})$, by definition of $\textit{Clean}$ and $p = \textit{fail}$
    * $C'_{F2} R_2 C'_2$, by $\textit{Clean}(M_{F2}) = \textit{Clean}(M'_{F2}) = M_2 = M'_2$, $C_{F2} R_2 C_2$

* $(C'_{F1} \parallel C'_{F2}) R_2 (C'_1 \parallel C'_2)$, follows from R_2 with R Case 5 and the above
* $(C_1 \parallel C_2) \to (C'_1 \parallel C'_2)$, follows by $C'_1 = C_1$, $C'_2 = C_2$ □
- Case S.4.1. Subcase $p' = fail$. Follows from analogous treatment to Theorem 1 as the mailbox M does not change. □
- Case S.4.1. Subcase $p' = succ$. Follows from analogous treatment to Theorem 1 and Lemma 1. □
- Case S.6.4.
  • Given C_{F1}, C_{F2}, C'_{F1}, C'_{F2} s.t. $(C_{F1} \parallel C_{F2}) \to_F (C'_{F1} \parallel C'_{F2})$ by S6.4
  • Given C_1, C_2 s.t. $(C_{F1} \parallel C_{F2}) R_2 (C_1 \parallel C_2)$
  • Prove: exists C'_1, C'_2 s.t. $(C_1 \parallel C_2) \to^* (C'_1 \parallel C'_2)$ and $(C'_{F1} \parallel C'_{F2}) R_2 (C'_1 \parallel C'_2)$
    * Choose C'_1 and C'_2 such that $(C_1 \parallel C_2) \to (C'_1 \parallel C'_2)$ by step S6.4, exists by $(C_{F1} \parallel C_{F2}) R_2 (C_1 \parallel C_2)$
    * Choose M_1, M_2, M'_1, M'_2, M_{F1}, M_{F2}, M'_{F1}, M'_{F2} from the corresponding configurations
    * $M_{F1} = M'_{F1}$, $M_1 = M'_1$, by S6.4
    * $Clean(M'_{F1}) = M'_1$, follows by $C_{F1} R_2 C_1$, and $M_{F1} = M'_{F1}$, $M_1 = M'_1$
    * $C'_{F1} R_2 C'_1$ by R_2 with $Clean(M'_{F1}) = M'_1$ and R Case 3
    * $M_{F2} \uplus \{AtomicCommit\ b\ i\} = M'_{F2}$, $M_2 \uplus \{AtomicCommit\ b\ i\} = M'_2$, by S6.4
    * $Clean(M_{F2}) = M_2$, follows by $C_{F2} R_2 C_2$
    * $Clean(M'_{F2}) = M'_2$, follows by $Clean M_{F2} = M_2$, and $M_{F2} \uplus \{AtomicCommit\ b\ i\} = M'_{F2}$, $M_2 \uplus \{AtomicCommit\ b\ i\} = M'_2$
    * $C'_{F2} R_2 C'_2$ by R_2 with $Clean(M'_{F2}) = M'_2$ and the above
    * $(C'_{F1} \parallel C'_{F2}) R_2 (C'_1 \parallel C'_2)$, follows from R_2 with R Case 5 and the above
    * $(C_1 \parallel C_2) \to (C'_1 \parallel C'_2)$, follows by the chosen C'_1, C'_2 above □

This concludes the proof of Theorem 2. □

D Proof of Theorem 3

Theorem 3 states, informally, that the *simulation proof strategy* used in Theorem 1 and Theorem 2 is a sufficient condition for proving *failure transparency$_2$*. In fact, it proves a more general result, namely that the simulation proof strategy is a sufficient condition for *monotonic observational explainability$_2$*. As failure transparency is defined as a special case of observational explainability, it suffices to prove the more general result and show that the parameters are chosen according to its definition.

To proceed with the proof, we first need to define the terms used in the theorem. It should be noted that we use adapted definitions to the ones from the original definition of *failure transparency* from the paper [56]. But we do so for good reason. First, the used *observability functions* in this paper are not monotonic, thus we could not directly use the definition from [56] which requires this. Second, we present the definitions in a notational style consistent with the rest of this paper.

To differentiate between the original definitions and our new definitions, we denote the new adapted definitions as *monotonic observational explainability$_2$* and *failure transparency$_2$*.

D.1 Simulation

Definition 6 (Relation). *A relation R is a set of pairs of configurations. We may write $C_1 R C_2$ as a shorthand for $(C_1, C_2) \in R$.*

The used simulation relation between two semantics or systems is defined as follows. S_1 and S_2 denote two separate semantics consisting of a set of semantic rules. We use $C_1 \to_{S_1} C_1'$ to denote that $C_1 \to C_1'$ is derivable in S_1, that is, an execution step of the form $C_1 \to C_1'$ is derivable in the semantic rules of S_1. The definition states that S_1 R-simulates S_2 if for every pair of configurations C_1 and C_2 in the relation R, if there exists an execution step from C_1 to C_1' in S_1, then there exists a corresponding sequence of execution steps in the second semantics from C_2 to some configuration C_2' s.t. $C_1' R C_2'$.

Definition 7 (Simulation). *S_1 R-simulates S_2, denoted as $S_1 \sim_R S_2$, iff:*

$$\forall C_1, C_2 : C_1 R C_2 \implies \forall C_1' : C_1 \to_{S_1} C_1' \implies \exists C_2' : C_2 \to_{S_2}^* C_2' \land C_1' R C_2'$$

A simulation proof is a proof about one semantics S simulating another semantics S'. The specific form of the *simulation proof strategy* used in this paper is of the following form. In contrast to what is common, it additionally requires that any pair of configurations in the relation R is observably equivalent for the provided *observability functions* [56] O and O'. Here, I is the set of pairs of initial configurations of the two semantics S and S'.

Definition 8 (Simulation Proof Strategy).

$$\exists R.\ I \subseteq R\ \land\ S \sim_R S'\ \land\ (\forall (C, C') \in R.\ O(C) = O'(C'))$$

D.2 Observational Explainability [56] and Failure Transparency [56]

The verbatim definitions of *failure transparency* and *observational explainability* taken from [56] are as follows. Note that the notational conventions may be confusing due to differences to this paper.

Definition 9 (Observational Explanation (From [56])). *A sequence of configurations C of length n is explained by a sequence of configurations C' of length n' with respect to observability functions O and O', denoted as $C \overset{O}{\rightleftharpoons}^{O'} C'$, if:*

$$\forall m < n.\ \exists m' < n'.\ O(C_m) = O'(C'_{m'})$$

Definition 10 (Observational Explainability (From [56])). *The set of rules R is observationally explainable by R' with respect to their observability functions O and O' and the translation relation T, denoted as $R \underset{}{\overset{T}{\rightleftharpoons}}{}^{O'}_{O} R'$, if:*

$$\forall c' \in \text{dom}(T). \ \forall c. \ c'Tc \implies \forall C \in \mathbb{E}^R_c. \ \exists C' \in \mathbb{E}^{R'}_{c'}. \ C \underset{}{\overset{O}{\rightleftharpoons}}{}^{O'} C'$$

Definition 11 (Failure Transparency (From [56])). *A set of rules R is failure-transparent with respect to failure rules $F \subseteq R$ for a monotonic observability function O and a set of initial configurations K, this is denoted as $R \backslash\!\backslash^O_K F$, iff:*

$$R \underset{}{\overset{\{(c,c) \ | \ c \in K\}}{\rightleftharpoons}}{}^{O}_{O} (R \setminus F)$$

Monotonic observational explainability is not explicitly defined within a definition environment, but rather as part of a lemma in [56]. This is its definition from the paper in expanded form. In particular, what differs to Definition 10, is the explicit requirement that the mapping h of configurations is monotonically increasing, as this definition does not explicitly require the observability functions to be monotonic.

Definition 12 (Monotonic Observational Explainability (From [56])).

$$\forall c' \in \text{dom}(T). \ \forall c. \ c'Tc \implies \forall C \in \mathbb{E}^R_c. \ \exists C' \in \mathbb{E}^{R'}_{c'}.$$
$$\exists [h_k]^n_k. \ (\forall k < n. \ \forall k' \leq k. \ h_{k'} \leq h_k)$$
$$\wedge \ (\forall m < n. \ \exists m' = h_m < n'. \ O(C_m) = O'(C'_{m'}))$$

D.3 Monotonic Observational Explainability$_2$

We have adapted Definition 12 in the following way. First, its notation is adapted to be consistent with the rest of this paper, and it is fully expanded for simplicity. Second, we have added an additional requirement that the initial states are observably equivalent. We believe that this is a useful requirement. Lastly, note that the observability functions are not required to be monotonic, in contrast to Definition 10.

Definition 13 (Monotonic Observational Explainability$_2$). *S is monotonically observationally explainable by S' with respect to observability functions O and O', and the set of pairs of initial states I, denoted as $S \underset{2}{\overset{I}{\rightleftharpoons}}{}^{O'}_{O} S'$, iff:*

$$\forall C_0, C'_0 : (C_0, C'_0) \in I \implies (O(C_0) = O'(C'_0)) \ \wedge$$
$$\forall \overline{C} : |\overline{C}| = n \ \wedge \ C_0 \rightarrow_S C_1 \rightarrow_S \ldots \rightarrow_S C_{n-1} :$$
$$\exists \overline{C'} : |\overline{C'}| = n' \ \wedge \ C'_0 \rightarrow_{S'} C'_1 \rightarrow_{S'} \ldots \rightarrow_{S'} C'_{n'-1} :$$
$$\exists \overline{h} : |\overline{h}| = n \ \wedge \ (\forall k < n : \ \forall k' \leq k : \ h_{k'} \leq h_k)$$
$$\wedge \ (\forall m < n : \ h_m < n'. \ O(C_m) = O'(C'_{h_m}))$$

D.4 Failure Transparency$_2$

We define *failure transparency$_2$* in a similar way to Definition 11, with the difference that we instead use monotonic observational explainability$_2$, and thus the observability function is not required to be monotonic. Further, to keep conistent with the notation of the rest of this paper, we will adapt it similarly to Definition 13.

Definition 14 (Failure Transparency$_2$). *S is* failure transparent *with respect to failure-related semantic rules $F \subseteq S$ for an observability function O and a set of initial configurations K, iff:*

$$S \; O \xrightleftharpoons[2]{\{(C,C) \mid C \in K\}} O \; (S \setminus F)$$

D.5 Theorem and Proof

We are now ready to present the theorem and its proof. The *simulation proof strategy* as used in Theorem 1 and Theorem 2 is a sufficient condition for *monotonic observational explainability$_2$*.

Theorem 3.

$$(\exists R. \; I \subseteq R \; \wedge \; S \sim_R S' \; \wedge \; (\forall (C, C') \in R. \; O(C) = O'(C')))$$
$$\implies$$
$$(S \; O \xrightleftharpoons[2]{I} O' \; S')$$

Proof. The proof is done as follows. Given an arbitrary sequence of configurations $\overline{C}$ of an execution in S, the proof inductively constructs a sequence of configurations $\overline{C'}$ and a mapping of configurations $\overline{h}$ s.t. the conditions of Definition 13 are satisfied. The assumed simulation relation R is used to construct the sequence of configurations; the mapping is constructed such that it follows the simulation relation, that is, when an execution step to some configuration C_i is taken, then there exists by R an execution step to some configuration C'_j; and h is constructed such that it maps C_i to C'_j by $h_i = j$. As a consequence of this construction of C' and h, we know that $\overline{C'}$ is an execution of S', and that h is a monotonically increasing mapping of configurations. Last, by the assumption that $\forall (C, C') \in R. \; O(C) = O'(C')$, we can show that the mapped configurations are observably equivalent as each mapped pair is in R by construction.

- Assumption: R s.t. $I \subseteq R \wedge S \sim_R S' \wedge (\forall (C, C') \in R \implies O(C) = O'(C'))$
- Prove: $S \; O \xrightleftharpoons[2]{I} O' \; S'$
- Given: $C_0, C'_0 : (C_0, C'_0) \in I$.

- Given: $\overline{C}: |\overline{C}| = n \wedge C_0 \to_S C_1 \to_S \ldots \to_S C_{n-1}$.
- Choose $\overline{C'}, \overline{h}$, by inductive construction s.t. :
  - IA1: $\wedge |\overline{C'}| = n' \wedge C'_0 \to_{S'} C'_1 \to_{S'} \ldots \to_{S'} C'_{n'-1}$
    * i.e., $\overline{C'}$ is an execution of S'.
  - IA2: $\wedge |\overline{h}| = n \wedge (\forall k < n: \forall k' \leq k: h_{k'} \leq h_k)$
    * i.e., h is a monotonically increasing mapping of configurations.
  - IA3: $\wedge (\forall m < n: h_m < n' \wedge C_m R C'_{h_m})$
    * i.e., the execution/mapping is in the simulation relation.
  - IA4: $\wedge (\forall m < n: h_m < n' \wedge O(C_m) = O'(C'_{h_m}))$
    * i.e., the mapped configurations are observably equivalent.
  - Base case:
    * Given C_0, C'_0 s.t. $(C_0, C'_0) \in I$
    * Given $\overline{C} = C_0$.
    * Choose: $\overline{C'} = C'_0$ and $\overline{h} = h_0$ where $h_0 = 0$.
    * IA1: $\overline{C'}$ is an execution of S'.
    * IA2: $\overline{h}$ is monotonic.
    * IA3: $C_0 R C'_0$
      · Proof: by assumption $I \subseteq R$.
    * IA4: $O(C_0) = O'(C'_0)$
      · Proof: by assumption $\forall (C, C') \in R. O(C) = O'(C')$.

  - Inductive step: Given some m s.t. $(m-1) < n$ and the induction assumption holds for the prefix $\overline{C_p}$ of $\overline{C}$ of length m, the prefix h_p of h of length m, and the prefix $\overline{C'_p}$ of $\overline{C'}$ of length m'. To show is that the induction assumptions hold for: $\overline{C_p} \circ C_m$; $\overline{C'_p} \circ \ldots \circ C'_{h_m}$; and $\overline{h_p} \circ h_m$.
    * Choose: C_m from $\overline{C}$ for which $C_{m-1} \to_S C_m$
    * Note: $C_{m-1} R C'_{h_{m-1}}$ by the induction assumption
    * Choose: $D, \overline{D}$ s.t. $C'_{h_{m-1}} \to_{S'} \overline{D}_0 \to_{S'} \ldots \to_{S'} \overline{D}_{|\overline{D}|-1}$ s.t. $C_m R D$.
      In the case that $\overline{D}$ is non-empty, then $D = \overline{D}_{|\overline{D}|-1}$, else $D = C'_{h_{m-1}}$.
      · Proof: such a $D, \overline{D}$ exists by the simulation relation $S \sim_R S'$. Since $C_{m-1} R C'_{h_{m-1}}$ and $C_{m-1} \to_S C_m$, therefore by simulation there exists some configuration D s.t. $C'_{h_m} \to^*_{S'} D$ and $C_m R D$ where $\overline{D}$ is the sequence of configurations leading to D.
    * Choose the next prefix $\overline{C'_p} \circ \overline{D}$, where $D_{|D|-1} = C'_{h_m}$.
    * Choose the next prefix $\overline{h_p} \circ h_m$, where $h_m = h_{m-1} + |\overline{D}|$.
    * IA1: $\overline{C'_p} \circ \overline{D}$ is an execution of S'.
      · Proof: by construction, $\overline{D}$ is a valid execution of S' starting from the last configuration of $\overline{C_p}$, and $\overline{C_p}$ is an execution of S' by the induction assumption.
    * IA2: $\overline{h_p} \circ h_m$ is monotonic.
      · Proof: by construction, $h_{m-1} \leq h_{m-1} + |\overline{D}| = h_m$, and the inductive assumption.
    * IA3: $C_m R C'_{h_m}$.

- Proof: by construction C'_{h_m} is chosen above such that $C_m R C'_{h_m}$, as $C'_{h_m} = D$ and $C_m R D$.
* IA4: $O(C_m) = O'(C'_{h_m})$.
  - Proof: this follows as a consequence of IA3 and the assumption $\forall (C, C') \in R.\ O(C) = O'(C')$.

□

This concludes the proof of Theorem 3.   □

References

1. Abadi, M., Lamport, L.: The existence of refinement mappings. Theor. Comput. Sci. **82**(2), 253–284 (1991). https://doi.org/10.1016/0304-3975(91)90224-P
2. Abadi, M., Lamport, L.: Conjoining specifications. ACM Trans. Program. Lang. Syst. **17**(3), 507–534 (1995). https://doi.org/10.1145/203095.201069
3. Agha, G.: Concurrent object-oriented programming. Commun. ACM **33**(9), 125–141 (1990). https://doi.org/10.1145/83880.84528
4. Agha, G., Mason, I.A., Smith, S.F., Talcott, C.L.: A foundation for actor computation. J. Funct. Program. **7**(1), 1–72 (1997). https://doi.org/10.1017/S095679689700261X
5. Agha, G.A.: ACTORS - a model of concurrent computation in distributed systems. MIT Press Series in Artificial Intelligence, MIT Press (1986). https://doi.org/10.7551/mitpress/1086.001.0001
6. Alpern, B., Schneider, F.B.: Defining liveness. Inf. Process. Lett. **21**(4), 181–185 (1985). https://doi.org/10.1016/0020-0190(85)90056-0
7. Armstrong, J.: Erlang–a survey of the language and its industrial applications. In: Proceedings of INAP, vol. 96, pp. 16–18 (1996)
8. Armstrong, J.: Making reliable distributed systems in the presence of software errors. Ph.D. thesis, KTH Royal Institute of Technology, Stockholm, Sweden (2003). https://nbn-resolving.org/urn:nbn:se:kth:diva-3658
9. Armstrong, J., Virding, R., Williams, M.: Concurrent programming in ERLANG. Prentice Hall (1993)
10. Bernstein, P., Bykov, S., Geller, A., Kliot, G., Thelin, J.: Orleans: distributed virtual actors for programmability and scalability. Technical report MSR-TR-2014-41 (2014). https://www.microsoft.com/en-us/research/publication/orleans-distributed-virtual-actors-for-programmability-and-scalability/
11. Brandauer, S., et al.: Parallel objects for multicores: a glimpse at the parallel language Encore. In: Bernardo, M., Johnsen, E.B. (eds.) Formal Methods for Multicore Programming - 15th International School on Formal Methods for the Design of Computer, Communication, and Software Systems, SFM 2015, Bertinoro, Italy, 15–19 June 2015, Advanced Lectures. Lecture Notes in Computer Science, vol. 9104, pp. 1–56. Springer (2015). https://doi.org/10.1007/978-3-319-18941-3_1
12. Burckhardt, S., Gillum, C., Justo, D., Kallas, K., McMahon, C., Meiklejohn, C.S.: Durable functions: semantics for stateful serverless. Proc. ACM Program. Lang. **5**(OOPSLA), 133:1–133:27 (2021). https://doi.org/10.1145/3485510

13. Bykov, S., Geller, A., Kliot, G., Larus, J.R., Pandya, R., Thelin, J.: Orleans: cloud computing for everyone. In: Chase, J.S., Abbadi, A.E. (eds.) ACM Symposium on Cloud Computing in conjunction with SOSP 2011, SOCC 2011, Cascais, Portugal, 26–28 October 2011, pp. 16:1–16:14. ACM (2011). https://doi.org/10.1145/2038916.2038932
14. Carbone, P., Katsifodimos, A., Ewen, S., Markl, V., Haridi, S., Tzoumas, K.: Apache Flink^{TM}: stream and batch processing in a single engine. IEEE Data Eng. Bull. **38**(4), 28–38 (2015). http://sites.computer.org/debull/A15dec/p28.pdf
15. Clebsch, S., Franco, J., Drossopoulou, S., Yang, A.M., Wrigstad, T., Vitek, J.: Orca: GC and type system co-design for actor languages. Proc. ACM Program. Lang. **1**(OOPSLA), 72:1–72:28 (2017). https://doi.org/10.1145/3133896
16. DBOS, Inc.: DBOS (2025). https://www.dbos.dev/. Accessed 31 Jan 2025
17. Dean, J., Ghemawat, S.: MapReduce: simplified data processing on large clusters. In: Brewer, E.A., Chen, P. (eds.) 6th Symposium on Operating System Design and Implementation (OSDI 2004), San Francisco, California, USA, 6–8 December 2004, pp. 137–150. USENIX Association (2004). http://www.usenix.org/events/osdi04/tech/dean.html
18. Dedecker, J., Van Cutsem, T., Mostinckx, S., D'Hondt, T., De Meuter, W.: Ambient-oriented programming in AmbientTalk. In: Thomas, D. (ed.) ECOOP 2006 - Object-Oriented Programming, 20th European Conference, Nantes, France, 3–7 July 2006, Proceedings. Lecture Notes in Computer Science, vol. 4067, pp. 230–254. Springer (2006). https://doi.org/10.1007/11785477_16
19. Ericsson AB: Erlang (2025). https://www.erlang.org/. Accessed 30 May 2025
20. Field, J., Varela, C.A.: Transactors: a programming model for maintaining globally consistent distributed state in unreliable environments. In: Palsberg, J., Abadi, M. (eds.) Proceedings of the 32nd ACM SIGPLAN-SIGACT Symposium on Principles of Programming Languages, POPL 2005, Long Beach, California, USA, 12–14 January 2005, pp. 195–208. ACM (2005). https://doi.org/10.1145/1040305.1040322
21. Fowler, S., Lindley, S., Wadler, P.: Mixing metaphors: actors as channels and channels as actors. In: Müller, P. (ed.) 31st European Conference on Object-Oriented Programming, ECOOP 2017, 19–23 June 2017, Barcelona, Spain. LIPIcs, vol. 74, pp. 11:1–11:28. Schloss Dagstuhl - Leibniz-Zentrum für Informatik (2017). https://doi.org/10.4230/LIPICS.ECOOP.2017.11
22. Gärtner, F.C.: Fundamentals of fault-tolerant distributed computing in asynchronous environments. ACM Comput. Surv. **31**(1), 1–26 (1999). https://doi.org/10.1145/311531.311532
23. Haller, P.: On the integration of the actor model in mainstream technologies: the Scala perspective. In: Agha, G.A., Bordini, R.H., Marron, A., Ricci, A. (eds.) Proceedings of the 2nd Edition on Programming Systems, Languages and Applications Based on Actors, Agents, and Decentralized Control Abstractions, AGERE! 2012, 21–22 October 2012, Tucson, Arizona, USA, pp. 1–6. ACM (2012). https://doi.org/10.1145/2414639.2414641
24. Haller, P., Loiko, A.: LaCasa: lightweight affinity and object capabilities in Scala. In: Visser, E., Smaragdakis, Y. (eds.) Proceedings of the 2016 ACM SIGPLAN International Conference on Object-Oriented Programming, Systems, Languages, and Applications, OOPSLA 2016, part of SPLASH 2016, Amsterdam, The Netherlands, 30 October–4 November 2016, pp. 272–291. ACM (2016). https://doi.org/10.1145/2983990.2984042
25. Haller, P., Odersky, M.: Scala Actors: unifying thread-based and event-based programming. Theor. Comput. Sci. **410**(2–3), 202–220 (2009). https://doi.org/10.1016/j.tcs.2008.09.019

26. Helland, P., Campbell, D.: Building on quicksand. In: Fourth Biennial Conference on Innovative Data Systems Research, CIDR 2009, Asilomar, CA, USA, 4–7 January 2009, Online Proceedings (2009). https://www.cidrdb.org/. http://www-db.cs.wisc.edu/cidr/cidr2009/Paper_133.pdf
27. Hewitt, C., Baker, H.G.: Laws for communicating parallel processes. In: Gilchrist, B. (ed.) Information Processing, Proceedings of the 7th IFIP Congress 1977, Toronto, Canada, 8–12 August 1977, pp. 987–992. North-Holland (1977)
28. Hewitt, C., Bishop, P.B., Steiger, R.: A universal modular ACTOR formalism for artificial intelligence. In: Nilsson, N.J. (ed.) Proceedings of the 3rd International Joint Conference on Artificial Intelligence, Stanford, CA, USA, 20–23 August 1973, pp. 235–245. William Kaufmann (1973). http://ijcai.org/Proceedings/73/Papers/027B.pdf
29. Imam, S.M., Sarkar, V.: Savina - An actor benchmark suite: enabling empirical evaluation of actor libraries. In: Boix, E.G., Haller, P., Ricci, A., Varela, C.A. (eds.) Proceedings of the 4th International Workshop on Programming based on Actors Agents & Decentralized Control, AGERE! 2014, Portland, OR, USA, 20 October 2014, pp. 67–80. ACM (2014). https://doi.org/10.1145/2687357.2687368
30. Kallas, K., Zhang, H., Alur, R., Angel, S., Liu, V.: Executing microservice applications on serverless, correctly. Proc. ACM Program. Lang. **7**(POPL), 367–395 (2023). https://doi.org/10.1145/3571206
31. De Koster, J., Van Cutsem, T., De Meuter, W.: 43 years of actors: a taxonomy of actor models and their key properties. In: Clebsch, S., Desell, T., Haller, P., Ricci, A. (eds.) Proceedings of the 6th International Workshop on Programming Based on Actors, Agents, and Decentralized Control, AGERE 2016, Amsterdam, The Netherlands, 30 October 2016, pp. 31–40. ACM (2016). https://doi.org/10.1145/3001886.3001890
32. Lamport, L.: Proving the correctness of multiprocess programs. IEEE Trans. Software Eng. **3**(2), 125–143 (1977). https://doi.org/10.1109/TSE.1977.229904
33. Lamport, L., Merz, S.: Prophecy made simple. ACM Trans. Program. Lang. Syst. **44**(2), 6:1–6:27 (2022). https://doi.org/10.1145/3492545
34. Lee, P.A., Anderson, T.: Fault tolerance, pp. 51–77. Springer Vienna, Vienna (1990). https://doi.org/10.1007/978-3-7091-8990-0_3
35. Li, T., Chandramouli, B., Burckhardt, S., Madden, S.: DARQ matter binds everything: performant and composable cloud programming via resilient steps. Proc. ACM Manag. Data **1**(2), 117:1–117:27 (2023). https://doi.org/10.1145/3589262
36. Lightbend, Inc.: Akka (2022). https://akka.io/. Accessed 07 July 2022
37. Lowell, D.E.: Theory and practice of failure transparency. Ph.D. thesis, University of Michigan, USA (1999). https://hdl.handle.net/2027.42/132190
38. Marcus, M., Pnueli, A.: Using ghost variables to prove refinement. In: Wirsing, M., Nivat, M. (eds.) Algebraic Methodology and Software Technology, 5th International Conference, AMAST 1996, Munich, Germany, 1–5 July 1996, Proceedings. Lecture Notes in Computer Science, vol. 1101, pp. 226–240. Springer (1996). https://doi.org/10.1007/BFB0014319
39. Miller, M.S., Tribble, E.D., Shapiro, J.S.: Concurrency among strangers. In: De Nicola, R., Sangiorgi, D. (eds.) Trustworthy Global Computing, International Symposium, TGC 2005, Edinburgh, UK, 7–9 April 2005, Revised Selected Papers. Lecture Notes in Computer Science, vol. 3705, pp. 195–229. Springer (2005). https://doi.org/10.1007/11580850_12
40. Paul, S., Agha, G., Patterson, S., Varela, C.A.: Eventual consensus in Synod: verification using a failure-aware actor model. Innov. Syst. Softw. Eng. **19**(4), 395–410 (2023). https://doi.org/10.1007/S11334-022-00463-5

41. Plyukhin, D., Agha, G.: A scalable algorithm for decentralized actor termination detection. Log. Methods Comput. Sci. **18**(1) (2022). https://doi.org/10.46298/LMCS-18(1:39)2022
42. Plyukhin, D., Agha, G., Montesi, F.: CRGC: fault-recovering actor garbage collection in Pekko. Proc. ACM Program. Lang. **9**(PLDI), 945–969 (2025). https://doi.org/10.1145/3729288
43. Resonate HQ, Inc.: Resonate (2025). https://www.resonatehq.io/. Accessed 31 Jan 2025
44. Restate: Restate (2024). https://restate.dev/. Accessed 31 Jan 2025
45. Ricci, A., Haller, P. (eds.): Programming with Actors - State-of-the-Art and Research Perspectives, Lecture Notes in Computer Science, vol. 10789. Springer (2018). https://doi.org/10.1007/978-3-030-00302-9
46. Saltzer, J.H., Reed, D.P., Clark, D.D.: End-to-end arguments in system design. ACM Trans. Comput. Syst. **2**(4), 277–288 (1984). https://doi.org/10.1145/357401.357402
47. Spenger, J., Carbone, P., Haller, P.: Portals: an extension of dataflow streaming for stateful serverless. In: Scholliers, C., Singer, J. (eds.) Proceedings of the 2022 ACM SIGPLAN International Symposium on New Ideas, New Paradigms, and Reflections on Programming and Software, Onward! 2022, Auckland, New Zealand, 8–10 December 2022, pp. 153–171. ACM (2022). https://doi.org/10.1145/3563835.3567664
48. Spenger, J., Carbone, P., Haller, P.: A survey of actor-like programming models for serverless computing. In: de Boer, F.S., Damiani, F., Hähnle, R., Johnsen, E.B., Kamburjan, E. (eds.) Active Object Languages: Current Research Trends, Lecture Notes in Computer Science, vol. 14360, pp. 123–146. Springer (2024). https://doi.org/10.1007/978-3-031-51060-1_5
49. Spenger, J., Huang, C., Haller, P., Carbone, P.: Portals: a showcase of multi-dataflow stateful serverless. Proc. VLDB Endow. **16**(12), 4054–4057 (2023). https://doi.org/10.14778/3611540.3611619. https://www.vldb.org/pvldb/vol16/p4054-spenger.pdf
50. Tardieu, O., Grove, D., Bercea, G., Castro, P., Cwiklik, J., Epstein, E.A.: Reliable actors with retry orchestration. Proc. ACM Program. Lang. **7**(PLDI), 1293–1316 (2023). https://doi.org/10.1145/3591273
51. Temporal Technologies: Temporal (2025). https://temporal.io/. Accessed 31 Jan 2025
52. The Apache Software Foundation: Apache Flink Stateful Functions (2023). https://nightlies.apache.org/flink/flink-statefun-docs-stable/. Accessed 18 May 2023
53. The Elixir Team: Elixir (2025). https://elixir-lang.org/. Accessed 30 May 2025
54. The Pony Developers: Pony (2025). https://www.ponylang.io/. Accessed 30 May 2025
55. Tornow, D.: Handling failures from first principles (2022). https://dominik-tornow.medium.com/handling-failures-from-first-principles-1ed976b1b869. Accessed 31 Jan 2025
56. Veresov, A., Spenger, J., Carbone, P., Haller, P.: Failure transparency in stateful dataflow systems. In: Aldrich, J., Salvaneschi, G. (eds.) 38th European Conference on Object-Oriented Programming, ECOOP 2024, 16–20 September 2024, Vienna, Austria. LIPIcs, vol. 313, pp. 42:1–42:31. Schloss Dagstuhl - Leibniz-Zentrum für Informatik (2024). https://doi.org/10.4230/LIPICS.ECOOP.2024.42
57. Wensley, J.H.: SIFT: Software implemented fault tolerance. In: American Federation of Information Processing Societies: Proceedings of the AFIPS '72 Fall

Joint Computer Conference, 5–7 December 1972, Anaheim, California, USA - Part I. AFIPS Conference Proceedings, vol. 41, pp. 243–253. AFIPS/ACM/Thomson Book Company, Washington D.C. (1972). https://doi.org/10.1145/1479992.1480025
58. Zaharia, M., et al.: Resilient distributed datasets: a fault-tolerant abstraction for in-memory cluster computing. In: Gribble, S.D., Katabi, D. (eds.) Proceedings of the 9th USENIX Symposium on Networked Systems Design and Implementation, NSDI 2012, San Jose, CA, USA, 25–27 April 2012, pp. 15–28. USENIX Association (2012). https://www.usenix.org/conference/nsdi12/technical-sessions/presentation/zaharia

On the Development of the Active Object Paradigm: A Personal Account

Olaf Owe

Department of Informatics, University of Oslo, Oslo, Norway
olaf@ifi.uio.no

Abstract. This paper gives a personal account of research activity performed over decades by the author and his collaborators towards developing expressive and efficient object-oriented language paradigms for distributed systems. The goal is to enable expressive and efficient programs with a mathematically simple semantics, so that programming and verification are as simple as possible. Starting from traditional object-oriented principles, the paper suggests ways to deal with major challenges related to concurrency, communication, inheritance, flexibility of code reuse, and openness. The resulting language can be classified as an active object language, which can be seen as a modernization of object orientation for concurrent systems. The language integrates several aspects of the Actor Model in an object-oriented, imperative setting.

The focus of the paper is simplicity of modeling, specification, and reasoning. Behavioral subtyping is replaced by the more liberal concept of *interface behavioral subtyping*, and a renewed notion of subclass inheritance allows unrestricted reuse of code and specifications, supported by reasoning control. These benefits are shown useful for subclassing as well as for program evolution. A notion of hierarchy independence limits reverification in the case of multiple inheritance, so that only changed classes and subclasses inheriting from them need to be reverified.

1 Introduction

This paper gives a personal account of the story of going from object-oriented languages to modern active object languages. It gives a summary of research activity over several decades, mainly driven by the author and his collaborators. The story starts with the cooperation with Ole-Johan Dahl and continues with the research development going from more classical object-oriented concepts to an active object language paradigm. The derived active object paradigm is similar to the Actor Model in many aspects, in particular with respect to the concurrency model and asynchronous message passing, but is somewhat different due to the embracement of object-oriented principles, such as the two-way interaction style inherent in the method concept. Active objects are concurrent (like actors) and cooperate by methods call, implemented by asynchronous message passing, while actors communicate solely by asynchronous message passing, see the survey [13]. Neither paradigm allows sharing through remote data access.

For distributed systems, the choice of what should be the unit of concurrency and the interaction and cooperation mechanisms, is essential. The Actor Model [1] is appealing because it has a compositional semantics, unifying interaction and cooperation mechanisms through message passing. It is clearly simpler than the shared variable setting and the general thread-based model where a thread may execute code on several objects, and where non-trivial interference complicates the semantics. For object-oriented systems, the natural unit of interaction is the object [17]. Concurrent objects interacting by remote method calls correspond to actors, allowing two-way interaction by means of remote method calls rather than one-way interaction by messages as in actors.

A problem with interaction by remote methods calls is that it traditionally relies on active waiting for the calling object. Efficient two-way interaction is possible when adding a *suspension* mechanism allowing a caller to handle other processes and method calls while passively waiting for a certain response. This can be realized by an *internal process queue* of uncompleted method activations for each object, combined with cooperative scheduling. Future-free (two-way) interaction simplifies programming and reasoning (see Sect. 4).

The class and interfaces of an object are traditionally statically defined, in contrast to actors, which are not confined by static class descriptions. Dynamic reconfigurability is essential in the Actor Model [4]. The requirement that each object permanently belongs to a class, imposes constraints on the behavior of an object [2]. It is shown below how to compensate for that by means of a *dynamic class construct*, allowing class updates and changes at runtime. Furthermore, dynamic features include a notion of dynamic subsystem with internal concurrency allowing objects to join and leave dynamically, and a notion of dynamic service discovery, allowing dynamic detection of objects in an environment.

It is well known that behavioral subtyping severely limits the flexibility of subclassing by requiring subclasses to maintain all properties of their superclasses, referred to as the *inheritance dilemma*. The limitations in reusability caused by behavioral subtyping, have made object-oriented subclassing less attractive in applicative and declarative languages, including actors [5] and rewriting logic [64,72]. In order to overcome the inheritance dilemma, each object variable is typed by an interface (rather than a class), called *interface abstraction*, and a renewed notion of inheritance is developed, supporting *interface behavioral subtyping* where a subclass may freely reuse superclass code, and may even violate superclass behavior, as long as the subclass interface is respected. The programmer has full control of what superclass behavior should be inherited and what should not be inherited. Class-wise reasoning is supported (see Sect. 5). The approach also applies to (a disciplined version of) multiple inheritance, which is crucial in the setting of class updates and program evolution.

This paper summarizes earlier work around active object languages, mainly by the author and his collaborators, presenting a language fragment with the following advantages and features: blocking and non-blocking method interaction, (single and multiple) inheritance, flexible reuse of code and specifications, dynamic update of class code, object and service discovery, subsystem abstraction, history-based specification and reasoning, class-wise and compositional reasoning, and compliance checking of consent-based privacy aspects. These features are relevant for object-oriented languages as well as active object languages.

In order to accommodate the mentioned features, certain language constructs are added for increased efficiency and expressiveness, including *suspension, cointerfaces, superclass qualification, service discovery, superobjects* and *class updates*; and a certain programming discipline is required, such as *interface abstraction, history-based invariants*, and maintenance of class invariants upon suspension.

The guiding principle in this work has been ease of verification. The presentation is (mostly) high level, while technical details can be found in the underlying papers. Some simplifications are made here, including the treatment of events. The paper focuses on interaction and inheritance mechanisms, and does not discuss aspects related to self-calls and exception handling. The presentation avoids the use of futures since they complicate reasoning.

Paper Outline. To provide a historical basis for the object-oriented philosophy, Sect. 2 gives an account of main ideas from the initial work on object-oriented languages by Ole-Johan Dahl and Kristen Nygaard. Their work was an inspiration for object-oriented and active object languages. The next sections present the language setting (Sect. 3), class-wise and compositional history-based reasoning (Sect. 4), a renewed notion of subclassing and reasoning support (Sect. 5), constructs for reconfigurability (Sect. 6), security and privacy (Sect. 7), and a conclusion (Sect. 8). An appendix shows notational conventions.

2 The Legacy of Ole-Johan Dahl and Kristen Nygaard

Ole-Johan Dahl and Kristen Nygaard received the Turing Award in 2001 for ideas fundamental to the emergence of object-oriented programming, through their design of the programming languages Simula I and Simula 67. Simula 67 contained classes, inheritance by subclasses, dynamic generation of objects, late (and static) binding, as well as a notion of static objects. Their motivation was system description and the need for a language to model real-world concepts, considering how to reflect real-world scenarios such as service-oriented systems and customers. Simula I was completed in 1964 and Simula 67 in 1967 [18,19]. Early versions of Simula (Simula I) used examples such as airport systems with passengers and clerks as "activities" [50]. According to the original ideas of Simula, an object would in general have its own activity, as well as data and operations. Objects with activity, called *active objects*, were reflecting "independent processes", and objects without activity (but still with data and procedures) were called *passive* [50]. In Simula 67 these ideas were realized by allowing objects to be co-routines, the natural way at that time to imitate concurrent processes. In today's world, a natural adaptation would be to let objects be concurrent, and one would obtain a distributed system by a set of objects running in parallel and interacting solely by remote method calls. This is the approach taken in Dahl's later works [17,21]. Active objects were a key idea of Simula [12], and Simula was an inspiration for the concurrency model of actors although Simula only supports co-routines and not true concurrency [48].

Simula was an extension of Algol 60, adding object-orientation. As Algol 60 did not have user-defined types, neither did Simula. This was seen as a weakness by Dahl and Nygaard, as well as the lack of protection of local class invariants [17]. Ole-Johan Dahl wrote: "At the Common Base Conference Kristen Nygaard and I proposed to enrich the language with class-like types. The proposal was turned down by the participants responsible for implementations. Today it would seem a better idea to build a programming language around a good general type concept, and subsequently add type-like classes" [15]. Dahl later worked with the author on algebraically defined types and how these can be integrated in an object-oriented setting [16,20,21,23,53].

As a main principle in his work, Dahl would take ease of verification as a measure of the quality of a program, and take simplicity of the verification system as a measure of the quality of a programming language. The book *Verifiable Programming* [16] elaborates on this. Clearly, verifiability does not give an absolute measure of quality since it depends not only on the programming language, but also on the specification principles and the reasoning system, and a more expressive language would in general be more difficult to handle than a simpler one. However, it may be used as a relative measure: If adding or changing a language construct increases verifiability, one may favor that change as long as expressiveness and efficiency are not sacrificed. *Ease of verification* is adopted as a guiding principle for the language discussions of this paper.

In joint work with Dahl [22], a methodology for class specification, implementation, and verification is suggested to remedy shortcomings in the RM-ODP standardization. The suggested language uses active objects for concurrent, mutable units that change over time, communicating by method calls and returns, while an algebraic, applicative sublanguage captures immutable data and abstract data types. A class definition has two parts, the *class specification* and the imperative *class implementation*. This has the advantage that interfaces and classes have the same name space, but gives somewhat less flexibility than separate interfaces. Class specifications (interfaces) are given by identifying the signature of the methods (called operations) which an object o of the class can handle, as well as any assumptions on a caller (if any), and the guarantees of the object, both expressed by predicates over the history of events. An assumption on a caller object c is expressed by the history of events to o initiated by c, and a guarantee is expressed by an invariant expressed over the history of events observed by the object, i.e., the events received by o plus the events initiated by o. Method implementations may be guarded by guards enforcing user requirements and/or enforcing the invariant of the enclosing class. When not satisfied, the former kind of guards leads to errors and the latter kind leads to delayed execution. The latter kind of guard could also be given in the middle of a method, delaying the remaining part of the method execution, meaning that each section of the method can be seen as a critical region, each maintaining the class invariant, and that an object could have a queue of delayed method executions.

A verification system is formalized, including class-wise verification (ensuring that the class implementation maintains the class invariant, and that the class invariant implies the class specification invariant). Compositional assumption/guarantee-style reasoning is formalized and demonstrated. Composition reduces to conjunction of guarantees, using a style of history-based inductive reasoning. The built-in notion of critical regions allows simple sequential-style class reasoning. Inheritance and so-called "heritage anomalies" were addressed.

The language (called OUN for *Oslo University Notation*) was further developed in [58,59], adding dynamic class updates, allowing classes to be modified at runtime, something we felt was essential for long-lived systems. The assumption/guarantee-style reasoning was formalized further in [35,58,59]. OUN was the basis for the *Creol* language [36–38], with a number of later extensions, including inheritance semantics [35]. A high level summary is given in [33]. Creol was is in turn the basis for the *ABS* language [34], adding object groups and software product lines, but without support for object-oriented inheritance.

Below a core language developed from Creol is outlined, and a program example similar to that in [22] is given in Sect. 3.2. The example illustrates unrestricted reuse of code and behavior.

3 Language Setting and a Program Example

A core language is used to present and demonstrate main ideas, as well as examples. The active object paradigm presented here is imperative and supports standard object-oriented principles such as inheritance, encapsulation, and dynamic generation of objects. However, the objects are concurrent, long-lived, and can be used in ways beyond that of the standard object-oriented setting, supporting suspension, runtime discovery of objects and services, subsystem abstraction, and program evolution. Method invocations and returns are realized by message passing between the caller and callee in an asynchronous manner. Suspension allows an object to handle a number of processes, being incoming calls, continuations of calls, or self-calls representing self-activity. Non-terminating self-activity can be realized by loops or recursive cycles using suspension or non-blocking self-calls to allow periods with reactive behavior. A class may have an initial method, starting self-activity. This results in a language paradigm which follows the imperative, object-oriented programming paradigm more closely than the actor languages, while embracing the concurrency model of the Actor Model.

The language considered is strongly typed with declaration of interfaces and classes with unique names. An underlying (side-effect-free) applicative data type language allows definition of inductive data types, subtypes, and functions, including lists, sets, and finite mappings. Apart from standard statements such as assignment, different kinds of suspension and call statements are introduced.

Each object variable is typed by an interface stating the externally visible operations on the object and their behavior (*interface abstraction*), as suggested in [22,36,52,59], and also in the Actor Model [3]. This implies that remote access to fields is not possible, since interfaces do not have fields. Thereby sharing as well as race conditions are avoided. We say that an object *supports* F if the runtime class of the object implements F or a subinterface of F. The type system guarantees that at runtime the object referred to by a variable of declared interface F will support F; this is called the *interface substitution principle* [55].

Simple semantics is desirable, and even more, reasoning simplicity. In this setting, partial correctness is useful to express axiomatic semantics and to detect reasoning difficulties. As each method is typically small, method termination is often easy to detect. It suffices that each infinite loop or internal call-chain (ignoring one-way calls) has a suspension point. Blocking remote calls may cause deadlock, but deadlock is avoided when any chain of two-way remote calls has at least one suspension point [61].

3.1 Major Language Elements

An *interface* is defined by a number of superinterfaces (describing inheritance at the interface level), a number of method declarations (without body), and an interface invariant expressing visible, abstract object states. Due to interface abstraction, it is not meaningful to specify the state of an object through fields. (Another reason is that an interface may have several class implementations, possibly with different fields.) Furthermore, pre/post-conditions of a method may not be useful for a remote caller since fields used in the condition are not in the name space of the caller. However, pre/post-conditions are useful in order to deal with self-calls and reasoning inside a class, especially for inherited code.

Therefore, the *communication history* of an object represents the state of the object, and an interface invariant is expressed by means of this history. The communication history in a given state of an object o is the sequence of the events reflecting messages sent by o or messages received by o. These events define the *alphabet of the object*, denoted αo, and the history is called the *local history* of o. An interface F is described by an invariant over the communication history of the *self* object, excluding events reflecting self-calls, using the syntax **inv** $I_F(h)$ where h denotes the history of *self* where method completions by *self* are restricted to methods of F. For instance, an invariant of a bank account could say that the account balance is never negative, say **inv** $bal(h) \geq 0$ where the function bal may be defined by induction over the history h. Different interfaces of an object may then describe different usage of the object, for instance a *car* object may have an internet interface and a separate driver interface.

Cointerfaces enable type control of the caller object and enable type-correct call-backs. The method prefix **with** J specifies that the method's caller object must support the interface J, letting *caller* be an implicit parameter of type J. The method may do call-backs to *caller* using methods of J. This gives protection of the usage of the method, since only J objects may call it, and at the same time enables type-correct call-backs. The type system guarantees absence of method-not-understood errors at runtime [40,43]. In the example 3.2, interface Database and class DATABASE require that callers of the interface methods support interface User. Class DATABASE makes use of this cointerface to build its data structure.

A *class C* consists of fields (including class parameters) and a number of method definitions, plus a class invariant. Method definitions have local variables, and a body, given by a statement list ending with a return statement in each path. Formal parameters are read-only, due to reasoning considerations. A class invariant $I_C(h,w)$ is expressed by using the fields w and the local history (h) over the alphabet of the class C, as given by the methods defined in the class, including self-calls. Interfaces of the class are declared by the keyword **implements**, and direct superclasses are declared in a list (using **extends**). Flexible sublassing, not limited by behavioral subtyping, is introduced in Sect. 5.

We consider objects with their own virtual processor; thus at most one process in an object can be active at a given time. However, method activations may be *suspended* (by **await** statements) to allow other processes to continue, and thereby avoid active waiting. This allows sequential reasoning inside a class, and suspension control is programmed within each method. Thus, neither notification nor signaling from other objects or processes is needed, which simplifies reasoning. The suspension mechanism requires a *process queue* for each object.

Upon suspension, the remaining part of a method invocation is suspended and placed in the process queue, while the object may continue with another (enabled) process or incoming call instead, while passively waiting for the suspended process to be enabled. Enabledness is controlled by guards, either a boolean condition b on the object state (fields) or the presence of a return value of a call made by the object. Scheduling is non-deterministic (but fair). The conditional suspension **await** b suspends while waiting for b to become true. The suspending call **await** $x := o.m(a)$ initiates the call to m and suspends while passively waiting for the callee o to complete the call. Here a is the parameter list.

Suspension can be used at the beginning of a method to ensure availability of some resources, or in the middle of a method, for instance to wait for the reply of a method call. As an example, a method *openRead* to provide read access to a database could start with **await** $writers = 0$; $readers := readers + 1$, and a method *openWrite* to provide write access could start with **await** $writers = 0 \land readers = 0$; $writers := writers + 1$, assuming that *readers* and *writers* are fields, and that the class invariant is $writers = 1 \land readers = 0 \lor writers = 0$. Readers and writers may use these operations to get access to the database using passive waiting, assuming that a database user calls *write* after *openWrite* and before *closeWrite*, and calls *read* after *openRead* or *openWrite* and before the corresponding closing operation. The protection can be enforced by using cointerfaces to keep track of the permitted objects, rather than using counters.

3.2 Example: Shared Database with Read/Write Protection

A class DATABASE to control read and write access to a database is sketched below, extending a class BASICDATABASE without protection. A cointerface is used to check that write operations of a user object are enclosed by openWrite and `closeWrite` calls of the user; and similarly, that read-only access of a user is enclosed by `openRead` and `closeRead` calls, for protection against active writers. The variable wr identifies the current writer, if any, and variable rs identifies the current set of readers. Hence, `openWrite` requires `wr=null` and `rs=∅`. A similar example is treated in [22], including versions with reader and writer priority.

Interfaces are given in Fig. 1 and classes in Fig. 2. We assume the types:

```
type Data = ...  // data, using no() to represent no data
type Fail = fail()  // to indicate a failure
type Data? = Data | Fail  // data or a failure
```

where | denotes (disjoint) union of types, such that T is a subtype of $T|T'$.

An invariant is expressed by a predicate referring to the (predefined) history h of type $Hist$, and by functions defined after the keyword **where**. Inductive function definitions consist of several equations, typically one for each generator case, using **other** to match cases not yet dealt with. Generators for lists are nil and append. The specifications in this example use only one kind of event, namely reply events. The event $self.m(y;v)!c$ reflects that the current object sends a reply message to the caller c, where y are the formal parameters and v is the returned value. This can be abbreviated to $m(y;v)!c$ in local specifications, and to $m(y;v)!$ if c is not needed, and to $m(y)!$ if v is not needed.

The infix syntax $\_;\_$ is used for sequence append/concatenation, $\_+\_$ is used to add an element to a set, $\_-\_$ is used to remove an element from a set, $\_\&\_$ denotes conjunction, and $\_|\_$ denotes disjunction. Type $Void$ has only one possible value, $void()$. A mapping M is here a set of pairs, where $M+(k,d)$ adds the pair (k,d), overwriting any earlier pairs with key k. The lookup function $M[k]$ gives the data value bound to k, if any, otherwise $no()$.

For simplicity, each declaration is preceded by a keyword, such as **var** (for fields, method-local variables, and mathematical variables), **op** (for methods), and **func** (for functions). Keywords are written in boldface, while // is used for comments. An **if** statement has a closing **fi**, but not an **if** expression. Variables and method names start with a lower-case letter, interface and type names are capitalized, and class names are written in upper case. For simplicity function definitions use variables as typed in formal parameters, possibly primed, and variables declared after **where**. In interface `Database` and class `DATABASE`, the **with** clause applies to all methods. Note that only the current writer may succeed with `closeWrite` and `write`, which is guaranteed by the use of cointerfaces!

The statement **return** e returns the value of e and terminates the process. It may be omitted for a $Void$ method. The statement **return** $o.m(a)$ abbreviates

$x := o.m(a);$ **return** x (where x is a type-correct local variable);

and the statement **return await** $o.m(a)$ is semantically the same as

await $x := o.m(a);$ **return** x

```
 1  interface BasicDatabase{
 2    op Data read(k:Key)  // the returned value is val(h,k)
 3    op Void write(k:Key,d:Data)
 4    inv ok(h) where
 5    func ok : Hist -> Bool
 6      ok(nil)                 = true
 7      ok(h;read(k;d)!)        = d=val(h,k)
 8      ok(h;write(k,d)!)       = ok(h)
 9    func val : Hist * Key -> Data
10      val(nil,k)              = no()
11      val((h;read(k;d)!),k')  = val(h,k')
12      val((h;write(k,d)!),k')= if k=k' then d else val(h,k')
13    }
14
15  interface Database{
16    with User {
17      op Void openRead()
18      op Void openWrite()
19      op Void closeRead()
20      op Void closeWrite()
21      op Bool write(k:Key,x:Data)
22      op Data? read(k:Key)
23    }
24    inv ok(h) where var b : Bool
25    func val : Hist * Key -> Data
26      val(nil,k)              = no()
27      val(h;write(k,d;b)!,k') = if b & k=k' then d else val(h,k')
28      val(h;other,k)          = val(h,k)
29    func ok : Hist -> Bool
30      ok(nil)                 = true
31      ok(h;write(k,d;b)!c)    = ok(h) & b=(c=writer(h))
32      ok(h;read(k;d)!c)       = ok(h) & d=
33        if c=writer(h) | c in readers(h) then val(h,k) else fail()
34      ok(h;openWrite()!)      = ok(h) & writer(h)=null & readers(h)=∅
35      ok(h;openRead()!)       = ok(h) & writer(h)=null
36      ok(h;other)             = ok(h)
37    func writer : Hist -> User
38      writer(nil)             = null
39      writer(h;openWrite()!c) = c
40      writer(h;closeWrite()!c)= if c=writer(h) then null
41                                else writer(h)
42      writer(h;other)         = writer(h)
43    func readers : Hist -> Set[User]
44      readers(nil)            = ∅
45      readers(h;openRead()!c ) = readers(h) + c
46      readers(h;closeRead()!c) = readers(h) - c
47      readers(h;other)        = readers(h)
48  }
```

Fig. 1. Types and Interfaces of the Database Example.

```
class BASICDATABASE implements BasicDatabase {
// shared database with unprotected read and write operations
  var db: Map[Key, Data]; // the database db is a mapping
  op Data read(k:Key) {return db[k]} // lookup, possibly no()
  op Void write(k:Key,d:Data) {db:=db+(k,d)} // overwriting
  inv BasicDatabase:inv & forall k. db[k]=val(h,k)
}

class DATABASE implements Database extends BASICDATABASE {
  var rs: Set[User] := ∅; // rs denotes set of current readers
  var wr: User := null; // wr denotes current writer
  inv (rs=∅ | wr=null) & forall k. db[k]=val(h,k)
      & rs=readers(h) & wr=writer(h)
  with User {
    op Void openRead() {await wr=null;
    rs:=rs+caller}
    op Void openWrite() {await wr=null & rs=∅;
    wr := caller}
    op Void closeRead() {rs := rs-caller}
    op Void closeWrite(){if caller=wr then wr:=null fi}
    op Data? read(k:Key){if caller=wr | caller in rs
      then return BASICDATABASE:read(k) else return fail() fi}
    op Bool write(k:Key,x:Data){if caller=wr
      then return BASICDATABASE:write(k,x) else return false fi}
  }
}
```

Fig. 2. Classes of the Database Example.

except that the process is terminated after initiating the call to m, delegating to o to return the value directly to caller [52].

A method name may be qualified by a superclass name to identify the superclass method. We allow both static and late binding of self-calls, using colon for the former, as in BASICDATABASE:read(k). Function names may also be qualified (by a syperclass or superinterface), allowing distinction between Database:ok(h) and BasicDatabase:ok(h). Similarly, A:inv refers to the invariant of A, letting the syntax $A :$ **inv** denote $I_A(h/\alpha A, w')$, where w' are the fields of class A. In the example, interface BasicDatabase could have used a postcondition for read (in line 2) specifying that the returned value is $val(h,k)$. Then the invariant and the ok function could have been omitted.

The flexibility of our notion of subclassing (see Sect. 5) is illustrated in three ways: i) by unrestricted method redefinitions in subclass DATABASE (where *read* breaks contravariance, and *write* has an unrelated return type), ii) by overriding the superclass invariant, and iii) by overriding the declared interface of the superclass. The overriding is needed since the invariants of BASICDATABASE and BasicDatabase are not correct in the subclass. Redefined methods may call superclass methods as long as these calls are type-correct, as done in lines 22 and 24. Interface Database does not extend BasicDatabase since it does not satisfy the invariant of BasicDatabase. Reuse of code is increased by allowing unrestricted method redefinitions. A database is created by **var** d : Database := **new** DATABASE(), using the interface for typing.

3.3 Method Calls with and Without Suspension

Consider a remote method call, using the syntax $x := o.m(a)$, where the callee o is an external object supporting a (type-correct) method m, a is the parameter list, and x is the variable receiving the return value. This reflects two-way interaction. In the setting of concurrent objects, the default way of performing such a method call is that the calling object blocks while the callee object (o) is executing the method when free to do so [21]. If the return value is not needed, one may use the syntax $o!m(a)$ to reflect one-way interaction and avoid waiting, called an *asynchronous call*. We distinguish between $o!m(a)$ and $o.m(a)$, where the latter call blocks until the call is completed, but without making use of the return value, whereas the first will continue without blocking (similar to message passing). The asynchronous call mechanism may be generalized to multicast and broadcast, messaging all objects of a given set or interface, respectively [33].

For two-way interaction, one may reduce the waiting time and improve efficiency by adding a list of statements s (a *tail*) allowing the caller to do something *while waiting*, using the syntax $x := o.m(a)$ **do** s **od** where the caller blocks after performing s if the return value has not arrived. A similar efficiency can be achieved with the use of futures [44].

These cases of blocking can be avoided with a suspending call

await $x := o.m(a)$ **do** s **od**

The caller makes the call to o, does s, and suspends if the return value of the call has not arrived. When a return value v arrives, the suspended process becomes enabled and performs $x := v$ when scheduled. The tail is optional and can be used to ensure that an invariant state is reached before suspending. An object making suspending calls is alive and able to respond to incoming calls and to finish suspended processes. For instance, a user of a Database d for storing mutual relationships between user objects could say.

await $d.openWrite(); d.write(self, caller); d.write(caller, self); d!closeWrite()$

The process suspends while waiting for write-access, and the asynchronous call $d!closeWrite$ gives no waiting.

Note that the **do-od** construct allows a process to wait for replies from several outstanding calls to objects in the environment. For instance, the code **await** $x := o.m(a)$ **do await** $x' := o'.m'(a')$ **od**; $rest$ generates two calls before suspending, and when both return messages have arrived, the object continues with executing the rest of the process (captured by $rest$). Similarly, the code $x := o.m(a)$ **do** $x' := o'.m'(a')$ **od**; $rest$ generates two calls before waiting for both results. As shown in [44], the expressiveness of this style of future-free programming is superior to that of programming with explicit futures (i.e., declared future variables). A detailed comparison of different interaction paradigms with and without futures, their expressiveness and their operational and axiomatic semantics is given in [44]. Further improvements in efficiency can be obtained by allowing statements of the form $\{s_1||s_2||...\}$ where the statement lists s_i are executed in any order, but such that when one statement list suspends, another may continue [37]. (Statement lists may run in parallel when there are no read/write conflicts on fields.) Further discussions on drawbacks and benefits of the future mechanism, as well as possible improvements, are given in [30,31].

A modeling framework for different kinds of communication media is given in [39], including wireless networks and radio communication, as well as loosely and tightly connected (FIFO) objects. As considered in Sect. 6.3, one may communicate in an unknown environment, using the syntax $x :=$ **acquire** F to find an object supporting interface F.

4 Class-Wise and Compositional Reasoning with Histories

Section 4.2 describes compositional reasoning of (sub)systems, building on a simplified notion of events, given in Sect. 4.1.

In order to express partial correctness, we use Hoare-style triples of the form $\{P\} \, s \, \{Q\}$ where s denotes a statement(list), and P and Q are state assertions, with the meaning that if s terminates normally and the pre-state of s satisfies the precondition P, the postcondition Q must hold in the post-state of s. In particular, since there is no remote field access, assignment satisfies the classical partial correctness axiom of sequential languages, i.e., $\{Q_e^x\} \, x := e \, \{Q\}$, expressing that a precondition is derived from the postcondition by replacing each occurrence of the variable x by the expression e (renaming bound variables if needed).

For the example, maintenance of $rs = \emptyset \vee wr = null$ for openRead requires

$$\{rs = \emptyset \vee wr = null\} \, \textbf{await} \, \, wr = null; rs := rs + caller \, \{rs = \emptyset \vee wr = null\}$$

which reduces to

$$\{(rs = \emptyset \vee wr = null) \wedge wr = null\} \, rs := rs + caller \, \{rs = \emptyset \vee wr = null\}$$

by the following Hoare-style axiom for reasoning about conditional suspension:

$$\{I_C(h, w)\} \, \textbf{await} \, b \, \{I_C(h, w) \wedge b\}$$

This gives the verification condition $wr = null \Rightarrow wr = null$, which is trivial. Both method openRead and openWrite maintain $rs = \emptyset \vee wr = null$, but not without the await statements.

4.1 Events, Histories, and Local Reasoning

For the setting of two-way method interaction implemented by message passing, one may in general consider four kinds of communication events. For a method call $o.m(a)$ made by c with parameter list a, these events would be i) the initiation of the call made by c, ii) the reception of the call by o, iii) the reply of the call made by o, and iv) the reception of the reply by c.

However, for specification purposes, the reply events are in general more interesting than the call events [22]. For a call $o.m(a)$ made by an object c, we therefore consider the following two kinds of events in our histories:

- $o.m(a;v)!c$, reflecting that o sends to c the reply to the call $o.m(a)$

- $o.m(a;v)?c$, reflecting that c receives from o the reply to the call $o.m(a)$

The former is in the alphabet of o (the callee) and the latter in the alphabet of c (the caller). This means that distinct objects have disjoint alphabets, which makes compositional reasoning possible. The alphabet of a class or interface contains events of the form $self.m(a;v)!c$ and $o.m(a;v)?self$, which may be abbreviated to $m(a;v)!c$ and $o.m(a;v)?$, respectively. Wellformedness of the global history of a system ensures that every occurrence of $o.m(a;v)?c$ must be preceded by an occurrence of $o.m(a;v)!c$. This states that a message must be sent before it can be received, and that values received are those that are sent.

Moreover, each of these events can be connected to the code: $m(y;v)!caller$ can be seen as a side-effect of the return statement of m where y is the list of formal parameters; and $o.m(a;v)?$ can be seen as a side-effect of the completion of a call $o.m(a)$ where v is the returned value. More specifically, for partial correctness reasoning, the statement **return** e can be understood as the assignment

$$h := (h; self.m(y;e)!caller)$$

where y is the list of formal parameters. Furthermore, a remote blocking call $x := o.m(a)$ **do** s **od** can be understood as the statement sequence

$$s;\ x' := some;\ h := (h; self.m(a;x')?o);\ x := x'$$

where $some$ represents an underspecified value, used here for reasoning purposes. This value is then determined by means of compositional reasoning considering a subsystem containing both the caller and callee object. Wellformedness ensures that the received value in the reply event of the caller, must be equal to the returned value of the corresponding return event of the callee. The auxiliary variable x' is needed to avoid binding any occurrences of x in a.

By means of a non-executable **assume** statement used for the purpose of partial correctness, conditional suspension **await** b can be understood as

$$w := some;\ h := (h; some);\ \textbf{assume}\ I_C(h,w) \wedge b$$

where **assume** has the axiom $\{P\}$ **assume** $b\,\{P \wedge b\}$. The assumption ensures that the invariant and b hold after suspension. A suspending call with a tail, **await** $x := o.m(a)$ **do** s **od**, can be understood as the sequence

$s;\ w := some;\ x' := some;\ h := (h; some; o.m(a; x')?);\ x := x';$ **assume** $I_C(h, w)$

Thus, the new values of w, x, h satisfy the invariant.

From this understanding, one may derive reasoning rules for each of the constructs, including the simple rule for conditional suspension above and the following rule for return statements

$$\{I_C(h; m(y; e)!caller, w)\}\ \textbf{return}\ e\,\{I_C(h, w)\}$$

where y is the list of formal parameters and e is the expression returned.

For a blocking remote call, say $x := o.m(a)$, one can derive the reasoning rule

$$\{\forall x'. Q^{x,\ h}_{x'\ h; o.m(a;x')?}\}\ x := o.m(a)\ \{Q\}$$

Here the quantifier reflects that x is locally unknown, and x' is needed to avoid binding occurrences of x in e. In the precondition, x and x' refer to the value of x before and after the call, respectively. For a suspending call, the rule is

$$\{I_C(h, w) \wedge \forall w, x', h'.\ Q^{x,\ h,}_{x'\ h; h'; o.m(a;x')?}\}\ \textbf{await}\ x := o.m(a)\,\{I_C(h, w) \wedge Q\}$$

Here the quantification of w and h' reflects that fields may have changed and that the history has grown, but such that the receive event is the last after the call, see [52] for further details.

Reasoning about calls, return, and suspension can therefore be done by sequential-style Hoare logic, including the side-effects on the history, and using universal quantification in the precondition of statements modeled with use of *some*. Blocking self-calls are implemented as for sequential programs (by means of a runtime stack) and do not contribute to events recorded in the history. This makes reasoning about blocking self-calls different from that of blocking remote calls. The reasoning rule for blocking self-calls is omitted. Section 5 will discuss reasoning about inherited code.

Note that two identical calls by the same caller may return different results since the calls could be scheduled at different times when the callee has different states, and this may differ with different executions. Reasoning with simplified events as in our approach, entails that one does not see which reply belongs to which call. This corresponds to the non-determinism inherent in asynchronous communication. In contrast, explicit futures allow identification of results with calls, but different executions may result in different results, so one may control the identification but not the resulting values. Thus, explicit futures are not helpful in reasoning, and also complicate history-based specifications in that more variables are needed. Explicit futures introduce an extra level of complexity in compositional reasoning since one would need to match call-events with return events by means of future identities, and these identities are unknown at reasoning time, giving rise to additional quantification [25,26]. Global reasoning is simpler with future-free events as in our approach than with explicit futures.

4.2 Compositional Reasoning About Systems

Compositional reasoning about concurrent objects is difficult with pre/postconditions since the caller and callee have different name spaces. For remote calls, fields used in the conditions of a callee are not in the name space of the caller, even the histories have different alphabets, and the histories may have grown before the call is executed. At the interface level, one should not talk about fields since different class implementations of the interface may use different fields.

Reasoning by history invariants does not have these problems. Compositional reasoning about concurrent systems can be derived from the principle of Neelam Soundarajan [63], which uses a *compatibility predicate* relating the global and local histories. This can be exploited in our setting as follows: At the beginning of the execution of a method, and after suspension, one may assume that the class invariant holds. In return one must verify that it is reestablished at method end and upon suspension. When interacting with another object, one may assume that the object will satisfy its interface invariant. This gives rise a reasoning principle for systems and subsystems of concurrent objects, deriving an invariant for a (sub)system S, say $I_S(h)$ where h is the history of S, i.e., the history of all objects in S. The local history of an object o in S will then be $h/\alpha o$. This use of disjoint alphabets simplifies the notion of compatibility of [63].

We may derive an invariant for S from the invariants of the objects in S: The invariant for the (sub)system is the conjunction of the interface invariants for each object in the (sub)system, applied to the local history of the object, together with a clause $wf(h)$ stating that the total history is wellformed:

$$I_S(h) = wf(h) \wedge \bigwedge_{(o:F) \in S} I_{o:F}(h/\alpha o)$$

where $I_{o:F}(h)$ is the invariant of interface F where all explicit and implicit occurrences of *self* are replaced by o. Note that projection by the relevant alphabet captures the connection between the history of S and the histories of the individual objects. Wellformedness expresses that a message can only be received after it is sent, and that values received are as sent.

From $I_S(h)$ one can obtain an external specification of S (for the communication with its environment) by considering the external history of S. The external history of S, $external_S(h)$, is defined inductively by ignoring internal events inside S and replacing internal objects by S. The external invariant of S is then $I_S(external_S(h))$. A user-defined external invariant for S, say $J_S(h)$, is proved if it follows from I_S, i.e., $I_S(external_S(h)) \Rightarrow J_S(h)$. Section 6.3 will look at a notion of dynamic subsystems where the set of internal objects and their interfaces can be derived from the history.

The compositional reasoning rule can be generalized to the assumption/guarantee reasoning style, which allows each interface invariant to rely on assumptions on the environment. Assumptions typically restrict input events. The assumptions can be discharged by induction of the history, showing that each output event of an object satisfies the assumptions of the receiver object in addition to its own guarantee, assuming that earlier events satisfy all assumptions and guarantees. Contract specifications for subsystems can then be handled. This style of reasoning has been explored in [22,35,58,59].

The compositional reasoning rule can also be generalized to synchronous events, allowing objects to have overlapping alphabets. For instance, the event reflecting an **acquire** statement could be a synchronous event between the caller and the chosen object. Synchronous events of two or more objects, would appear in their local histories and also in the composed history. Their correspondence is captured by the projection operator letting all objects agree on the synchronous events. This could be used to capture generation of objects and superobjects, and also for explicit synchronization statements, say of multi-object movements.

A more high level and abstract way of providing synchronization is by means of restrictions on the system history. These restrictions must then be enforced by the runtime system and need not be verified. With respect to the compositional reasoning rule, such implicit synchronization restrictions may be embedded in the wellformedness predicate. These techniques are similar to reasoning techniques of the actor framework [6,70], and their support for coordination [3].

5 Reasoning in Presence of Unrestricted Sublassing

The traditional way of reasoning about classes is based on the use of classes for type control. An object variable typed by a class C may at runtime refer to an object of a subclass of C. The natural way of reasoning is then to ensure that all subclasses of C satisfy the behavior of C [47], as done in Java reasoning [46]. Thus, all future subclasses of C must respect the specifications given in C, something which puts behavioral restrictions on all subclasses of C, unless the specifications given in C are weak. Neither is desirable, especially in an open-ended class hierarchy where the purpose of future subclasses is not known a priori.

In contrast, our setting builds on the *interface substitution principle*: An object variable typed by an interface F may at runtime refer to an object supporting F, and classes may not be used for typing. The natural way of reasoning is then to ensure that all subinterfaces of F satisfy the behavior of F. One may even let classes redefine behavior. In this setting there are no restrictions on code and specification reuse! Each class is verified separately, ensuring that each object of that class satisfies its interfaces. No requirements are imposed on subclasses. Subclasses may or may not reuse behavior.

In order to verify a class C, one must verify that all specifications given in C are satisfied, that inherited methods (exported by an interface) also satisfy the invariant of C, and that the use of inherited code agrees with the invariant of C. For instance, reasoning about suspension in inherited code must use the invariant of C. The advantage is that late binding can be resolved at verification time, and that the class specification of C can be strong since it only applies to C objects, and need not be satisfied for subclasses [55].

Independence of code reuse from reuse of specification gives flexible reuse. But since a class C may violate behavior in a superclass, reasoning results from a superclass cannot in general be reused in C. Thus, reasoning results from the superclass must in general be redone or re-validated in the context of C. This means that we should be more specific about the context of a reasoning result. The verification of a class does not depend on subclasses, but it will depend on superclasses from which it inherits code or behavioral specifications.

5.1 Unrestricted Reuse of Code and Behavior

In order to combine behavioral subtyping with unrestricted reuse of code and behavior, a non-standard notion of sublassing is used. Methods may be overridden as usual, and also *superclass behavior may be overridden*: Class invariants may be overridden simply by stating a new invariant, possibly reusing the invariant of a superclass as a conjunct. If no invariant is given, those of the superclasses are inherited. Likewise, interfaces of superclasses may be overridden simply by stating a new **implements** list; and if no new list is given, those of the superclasses are inherited. Inheritance of pre/post-conditions of methods is handled similarly. In this way the programmer has full control of what superclass behavior should be inherited and what should not be inherited. A class may therefore violate the class invariant of a superclass it extends, and a method may violate the specification given in a superclass. This approach, called *behavioral interface subtyping* [55], supports the *interface substitution principle*, and is more liberal than lazy behavioral subtyping [27,28]. The need for this is demonstrated in the example in Fig. 2 where class DATABASE violates the interface invariant of its superclass.

A redefinition of a method from an interface must obey contravariance, but a redefinition of a method from a superclass need not! For instance, the redefinition of *read* in DATABASE has a smaller input type (due to the with-clause) and larger result type, and the redefinition of *write* has a different return type than in BASICDATABASE.

A class must satisfy its invariant initially and at suspension and at method end (and similarly for pre/post-conditions of methods), and must satisfy the invariants of interfaces it implements. Further details can be found in [51,52].

An interface invariant is satisfied by C if it implies the interface invariant for the class history when restricted to the alphabet of the interface, i.e.,

$$I_C(h,w) \Rightarrow I_F(h/\alpha F)$$

where $\_/\_$ is the projection operator, reducing a history by a set of events, giving the subsequence where events outside the set are ignored.

5.2 Multiple Inheritance and Healthiness

Multiple inheritance is useful during evolution, allowing an old class to be updated by adding a new superclass and a new interface. However, the combination of multiple inheritance and late binding may cause confusion when several classes define the same methods. To avoid confusion, we insist on a *healthy binding* strategy. The late binding of a self-call occurring in a method of class B should bind to a class that is strongly related to B, otherwise it may bind to a class that is not intended as a subclass of B and cause an unexpected binding. Two classes A and B are said to be *strongly related*, denoted $A \lesseqgtr B$, if $A \leq B$ or $B \leq A$, where $A \leq B$ is the transitive and reflexive subclass relationship. Thus, two classes are strongly related if they are the same or if one is a direct or indirect superclass of the other. A late bound call must not bind to a superclass of the actual class that is not a subclass of the class of the call.

The healthy binding strategy suggested in [55] is considering the class of the executing object (the actual class), the superclass where a given self-call occurs (the class of the call), and the class defining the called method detected at runtime (the class of the method). Healthy binding requires that the class of the method is strongly related to the actual class and to the class of the call.

We allow static and late bound self-calls, and use superclass names to qualify a method name when needed, letting the syntax $A\!:\!m$ denote static binding of the m defined or inherited in A, and letting $A.m$ denote late binding of the m defined or inherited in A. (Thus, dot-notation is used both for remote calls, $o.m$, and for qualified self-calls, $A.m$.) In class A, the syntax $A\!:\!m$ and $A.m$ may be abbreviated to $:m$ and $.m$, respectively. Fields may be qualified as in $C\!:\!x$. For late binding, it is required that $A.m$ is bound to a class that is strongly related to both A, the class of the call, and the actual class (not a subclass of the actual class). This principle is called *healthy binding*.

In case of multiple inheritance, binding can be based on the order given in the superclass list, using the first superclass if that gives a type-correct binding, similar to how mixins work [32]. During evolution, new superclasses are added at the end of the superclass list. This way, old bindings of $A.m$ are not affected by new superclasses of A. For both static and late binding, it is required that the static typing detects at least one candidate for the call. This guarantees that binding will succeed at runtime.

The binding of static self-calls can be resolved statically, $A\!:\!m$ is bound to the first class found with a type-correct method definition, searching through the superclasses of A, denoted $bind(A, m)$. The binding of late bound calls cannot in general be resolved statically, since the same method call may be bound differently depending on the actual class. However, in the setting of interface abstraction, it suffices to verify each class C implementing an interface F, letting the verification of C be done under the assumption that C is the actual class at runtime. This means that we know the runtime class at verification time. Thus, late binding can be resolved at verification time, for each choice of actual class.

However, this requires reverification of inherited code when earlier verification results have a different actual class. In particular, the treatment of suspension and self-calls in inherited code depends on the actual class C, as detailed below.

5.3 Reasoning About Inherited Code

In order to reason about inherited code in a class C, we will therefore use reasoning statements of the form

$$\vdash_{C,B} \{P\}\, s\, \{Q\}$$

expressing that $\{P\}\, s\, \{Q\}$ is satisfied in the context of the actual class C with B as the class enclosing s. Binding of late bound self-calls in s is then done by:

- $bind(C, B, A.m) = D$ if $C \leq D \wedge D \lneq A \wedge D \lneq B$, taking the first such D with a *suitable* definition of m, searching from C.

A definition is "suitable" if it is a contravariant redefinition of the method defined/inherited in B. In contrast, remote calls $o.m$ are late bound and typed against the definition of the method in the interface of o.

For instance, the axiom for conditional suspension in Sect. 4 is now reformulated as $\vdash_{C,B} \{I_C(h, w)\}$ **await** $b\, \{I_C(h, w) \wedge b\}$, using the invariant of C, and not the one of B. For non-inherited code in C, we use $\vdash_{C,C} \{P\}\, s\, \{Q\}$. Verification of a pre/post-condition pair (P, Q) for a method m inherited by C from class B is done by

$$\vdash_{C,B} \{P\}\, body_{B,m}\, \{Q\}$$

where $body_{B,m}$ denotes the body of m in class B. For self-calls $A{:}n$ and $A.n$ in this body, verification of a pre/post condition pair (P, Q) is then handled by

$$\vdash_{C,D} \{P\}\, body_{D,n}\, \{Q\}$$

where D is $bind(A, n)$ or $bind(C, B, A.n)$, respectively. If the method is exported through an interface of C, we must verify

$$\vdash_{C,B} \{I_C(h, w)\}\, body_{B,n}\, \{I_C(h, w)\}$$

and in particular, for methods m defined in C itself and exported by an interface

$$\vdash_{C,C} \{I_C(h, w)\}\, body_{C,m}\, \{I_C(h, w)\}$$

In addition, we must verify any pre/post-conditions imported or explicitly stated in C, and these may then be used in the proofs of maintenance of the invariant. Often $\vdash_{B,B} \{P\}\, s\, \{Q\}$ implies $\vdash_{C,B} \{P\}\, s\, \{Q\}$, for instance when s does not contain suspension nor local calls, and then reverification of s is not needed in the context of C. In this case, one may conclude $\vdash_{C,B} \{P \wedge L\}\, s\, \{Q \wedge L\}$ where L refers to fields of C that are not fields of B. For the example in Sect. 3.2, this is the case when C is DATABASE and B is BASICDATABASE. It follows that the redefined *read* and *write* methods maintain the invariant of DATABASE.

Finally, one must prove that class C satisfies the interface invariant of each implemented interface, either directly from the invariant (as explained in Sect. 3.1) or indirectly by reconsidering each method implementation. For a method m implemented by s; **return** e, where e is an expression, and an interface invariant $ok(h)$ with the equation $ok(h; m(y; x)!c) = ok(h) \land R(h, y, x, c)$, one must prove (in context C):

$\{I_C(h, w)\} \, s \, \{I_C(h; m(y; e)!caller, w)\}$ and $\{I_C(h, w)\} \, s \, \{R(h, y, e, caller)\}$.
For openWrite the latter reduces to $\{I_{\text{DATABASE}}(h, db, rs, wr) \land wr = null \land rs = \emptyset\} \, wr := caller \, \{writer(h) = null \land readers(h) = \emptyset\}$, which is trivial using the DATABASE invariant and $ok(h; openWrite()!)$. Proving the interface specification for the other methods is also straight forward since the example is simple.

6 Constructs Supporting Reconfigurability

This section discusses three ways of supporting reconfigurability and openness (in addition to dynamic generation of objects): Program evolution, dynamic reconfigurability, and a notion of dynamic subsystems and service discovery.

6.1 Program Evolution

Programs need to be maintained for several reasons, for instance to extend the services of a class or subsystem, to accommodate new user requirements, to restructure the class hierarchy, to fix bugs, privacy, or security weaknesses in the code, or to improve specifications and provide better guarantees. This will involve changes in code or specifications, often both. One should be able to change a class in the middle of a class hierarchy, not only at the end. This means that classes below a changed class can be affected if they reuse code that is changed. This is useful for refactoring, by reordering the inheritance hierarchy.

Flexibility is desirable and essential in this respect, in the sense that one should be able to make changes to the code of a system as needed, without any restrictions. One should also be able to make changes to specifications; and there should be reasoning support such that reverification is simple.

We sketch an approach [55] that supports full flexibility, in the sense that one may change a class in whatever way desired (not violating type correctness). The approach supports *hierarchy independence* and *modification independence*, meaning that changes in one class C will only affect the class itself and subclasses. This means that superclasses of C need not be reverified, and that reverification of subclasses can be done in a cycle-free manner. Moreover, if C needs to be changed, this can be done independently of the changes of subclasses.

However, program evolution requires reverification, each modified class and each subclass must be reverified. Making a new version of a class C can be compared to making a subclass of C and then replacing C by that subclass. Our notion of subclassing and inheritance allows flexibility with respect to reuse of code and behavior. Reverification of C is then similar to what has been explained above for inheritance. In order to make indirect superclass dependencies more direct, the use of $B:m$ and $B.m$ should require that B itself defines method m.

The support for flexibility is described below: Program evolution can be done by adding new classes, subclasses, interfaces, and subinterfaces, and by changing old classes. In particular, one may provide more functionality, and old functionality may be reduced. The functionality of a class may be extended by adding methods and making them visible to the environment by adding support for new interfaces. Methods may be added by defining new method definitions in a class, or in a superclass, or by adding a superclass that provides new methods. The only restriction is that one may not modify interfaces. However, an interface F may be removed when all occurrences of F are replaced by an updated version of the interface, provided implements clauses are reverified.

Variables, methods, interfaces, and classes may be removed as long as type correctness is maintained. One may remove an interface F from the implements clause of a class C provided the typing of generated objects of class C remains correct. And one may upgrade a class C by adding a new interface F and adding a new superclass C', letting C' implement the new methods in F. As mentioned, a redefined method need not respect the typing of superclass definitions, but any given class may only define one method with the same name. This flexibility allows superclasses to be added later without checking the typing of subclasses.

In this setting, multiple inheritance can be useful assuming a healthy binding strategy to avoid confusion and unexpected bindings of late bound self-calls when several classes define the called methods. The proof of hierarchy independence in [55] builds on healthiness.

6.2 Dynamic Reconfigurability

In the setting of long-lived systems, there is a need to renew or update the software at runtime. An approach to do this is by means of a dynamic class upgrade mechanism, allowing one or more classes to be changed at runtime and allowing addition of new classes and interfaces [42,58,59]. The runtime system defined in [42] allows such upgrades by special messages. After updating a class the existing objects of the class can be updated independently and at different times, for instance when they are idle. The approach entails that one does not need to stop the system, instead the updates are done gradually, and one does not need to stop an object that is being updated. The objects may even run some processes with an old version of the code and some with the new. The runtime system uses a simple version control system to make the objects aware of which version they are running and when they need to update. Safe type checking can be adapted to this setting [71]. The dynamic class update mechanism is somewhat similar to program evolution except that the updates are done gradually at runtime. Much of the same verification techniques can be used; however, the presence of new and old code in the process queue is a complication, which can be overcome when old and new invariants are maintained. Otherwise, an object must be upgraded when the process queue is empty, and after establishing the new invariant. A similar notion of runtime upgrades was independently developed for the Erlang language [7,66], and new versions of code may coexist with old versions. Moreover, Erlang supports major ideas of the active object paradigm, but in a functional language setting. Thus, invariant-based verification as developed here is not supported.

6.3 A Notion of Dynamic Subsystems

Following [14,40], we allow dynamic generation of "superobjects". A *superobject* is a subsystem that can be referenced, and can be seen as a normal object from the outside, but is implemented by a set of concurrent objects on the inside, in contrast to the notion of object groups (cogs) in the *ABS* language [34]. The set of objects inside a superobject can change dynamically. Objects may dynamically join and leave a superobject, possibly changing the interfaces of the superobject.

A generated superobject is initially empty, but objects may join or leave the superobject, and at the same time enrich the interface of the superobject. Let O be a superobject, then the statement **join** O **as** F can be made by an object o supporting F to join O and make interface F available from outside the superobject. From the outside one may then use O as a normal F object, say by making calls to it, and such a call is handled by one of the objects inside the superobject exporting F (or a subinterface of F). If there are several such objects, one of them is chosen non-deterministically to receive the call request (letting an idle F object, if any, take the call). Furthermore, an object in O may leave O, or withdraw some of its services to the environment by the statement **leave** O **as** F. Typing implications for the environment are avoided when other objects in O still support F. Join and leave events are recorded in the history.

In this dynamic setting, there is a need to discover objects and services, and we add a construct for service discovery. The statement $x :=$ **acquire** F **in** O detects some object o in O that supports F and assigns it to x. The choice of o is non-deterministic, but idle objects are preferred. Discovery of services outside a group may also be very useful, using the syntax $x :=$ **acquire** F. In addition, one may use broadcast to reach all objects of a given interface, by an asynchronous call to the interface, say $Waiter!fire()$ **in** *restaurant*, using the example below.

As an example, a *restaurant* may be defined as a superobject with a number of internal *Waiter* objects, and an internal superobject *kitchen*, with personnel working in the kitchen. The virtual *kitchen* object exports a method $makeDish$ with *Waiter* as cointerface. A customer coming from the outside could acquire a *Waiter* object ($myWaiter :=$ **acquire** $Waiter$ **in** $restaurant$), and then order dishes from that waiter, say **await** $myWaiter.makeOrder(...)$ (or $myWaiter!makeOrder(...)$ if the result is not needed), which in turn makes a call to the kitchen, say **await** $kitchen.makeDish(...)$. This means that the waiter is not blocked and gets notified when the dish is ready, while the person in the kitchen taking the order will be busy making the dish.

7 Other Aspects and Considerations

Security. Security aspects for active objects include information flow analysis through a secrecy-type system to capture inter-object communication [57,62], defining local and global non-interference for active objects in a non-deterministic runtime environment. Static analysis through a secrecy-type system and a trace analysis system capture inter-object and network communication, respectively. Successful static analysis guarantees *interaction non-interference* [62].

Static detection of call flooding is reported in [56], which can be exploited for static detection of distributed denial of service (DDoS) attacks [29]. The detection is hard to do dynamically without access to the system program code.

A notion of *security wrappers* prevents leakage of secure information from concurrent objects. A service provider may use security wrappers to protect its services in an insecure environment. The run-time system automatically adds wrappers to insecure components [45]. Security and safety wrappers can be used in several settings [60], but are here used for communicating by means of futures since the origin of a future is implicit, which causes security challenges. Cointerfaces facilitate improvements of both security and privacy aspects [62,69].

Privacy. For active object languages language-based approaches to privacy have been studied in several ways, focusing on consent-based privacy inspired by GDPR. Language extensions are made to be able to talk about concepts such as data subjects, entities, purposes, and access rights. Privacy policies are then formulated by means of these concepts, and a notion of *privacy compliance* is defined. Certain privacy violations can be found by static checking, while runtime checking is required for full compliance, and for runtime changes in the policies.

In particular, [69] defines a static system that guarantees a static notion of privacy compliance, while [68] defines a runtime system ensuring compliance, where the compliance checks are made in the kernel of the operating system, which means that it could be used for other languages. At runtime, data subjects can make consent changes and request to see all personal data stored about them. An approach where personal data may refer to several data subjects is given in [9], guaranteeing compliance by means of a runtime system. In [8] the runtime checks are generated through static analysis and transformed to checks at the start of a method activation. This means that activations not satisfying the checks will stay on the process queue until they are satisfied. This has the advantages of avoiding program executions that "get stuck" due to runtime errors resulting from privacy checks. The approach also avoids redoing the same checks.

Privacy compliance essentially checks each data access involving personal information, ensuring that the data subject has given consent to the responsible entity to exercise the access in question for the given purpose. However, in both static and runtime analysis there are challenging questions, such as: how to detect the purpose, how to detect the data subject, and how to detect who is responsible for the processing, and how responsibility is transferred to data processors. The above approaches differ in these respects, using a static or dynamic way of solving a question, either automatically or by explicit help from the programmer.

Smart Contracts. As smart contracts cannot be changed, support for modeling, specification, and reasoning is essential. An active object language specialized for smart contracts, developed in [54], gives protection against tampering and gives added trust. It provides mechanisms for safety, security, and privacy, with class-wise verification. It is shown that history-based specification and reasoning are useful for smart contracts. The history is part of the executable language (read-only) and abstracts information normally found on blockchain. The approach is more high level than Solidity and offers less need for roll-backs.

Implementations and Tool Support. There exist operational semantics for the different versions of the language paradigm, and executable interpreters built from the operational semantics using the Maude modeling language [67,72]. This includes versions with time [11,41] and probabilities [10]. The basic active object model can be supported on top of Java by means of a Java package [49].

There exists maintained support, including compilers and a number of tools, for the ABS language [65], which has the same core concurrency model with suspension, but without support for cointerfaces and object-oriented inheritance. However, ABS supports many other features, including exception handling, futures, real-time, software product lines, digital twins, and cloud programming. This paper does not convey the contributions of the ABS language. The present language fragment has a simpler reasoning system than ABS and its notion of delta-oriented specifications, see for instance [24] using symbolic assumptions.

Possible Impact. The benefits of simple class-wise reasoning as above could be adopted in a real programming language with active objects, by allowing user-defined data types and functions, cointerfaces, and suspension, while insisting on interface abstraction and history-based invariants for classes and interfaces. Support for flexible inheritance and reasoning requires free reuse/redefinition of superclass invariants and declared interfaces, requiring healthy binding of methods in the case of multiple inheritance. Subsystem abstraction and privacy compliance checking can then be added. Popular object-oriented languages such as Java, JML, and Ruby do not enforce interface abstraction.

8 Conclusion

The paper looks at how imperative, object-oriented languages can be devised to support distributed systems by means of active objects running in parallel, combining active and reactive behavior, and exchanging information by method interaction, implemented by asynchronous message passing. The focus is on simplicity of modeling, specification, and reasoning. For this reason, the kernel language is future-free and without remote field access. The paper gives a personal account based on contributions of the author.

Efficient two-way method interaction is met by allowing suspension, and in particular, the combination of method calls with suspension enables passive waiting for method replies. The caller then has the freedom to choose the most suitable interaction style, choosing passive or active waiting, regardless of the method definition. The *cointerface mechanism* is useful for security and privacy, in addition to improved typing control, even for call-backs.

The considered programming language fragment has a compositional semantics, allowing compositional reasoning based on event histories and invariants over these, exploiting that the objects have disjoint alphabets for asynchronous events. Class-wise verification is done by sequential style partial correctness reasoning, incorporating the effects on the local event history. Compositional reasoning is done by conjunction of the local invariants of composed objects, with the addition of a requirement expressing wellformedness of the composed history.

Based on *interface abstraction*, a flexible form of inheritance supports unrestricted reuse of code and specifications. Interfaces and invariants of a superclass can be overridden as needed. Program evolution based on this notion offers full flexibility and reasoning control, in the sense that code and behavior may be changed as desired, and reverification is supported, limiting the verification conditions to changed classes and subclasses inheriting from these. *Healthy binding* is required for multiple inheritance. The flexibility and reasoning control of inheritance and program evolution extend state-of-the-art.

An approach to *subsystem abstraction* allows an object to represent a subsystem consisting of concurrent objects. This is useful in system design to reduce the complexity of large systems, and provides openness by allowing the subsystem to be dynamic, both with respect to the interfaces offered by the subsystem and with respect to its internal object structure. Service discovery is supported.

In order to deal with dynamic reconfiguration, dynamic class upgrades allow a class to be revised, changed, or upgraded during runtime. This mechanism is supported by an operational semantics that allows the updates to be implemented object-wise so that different objects of the same class are updated independently and at different times, with an underlying notion of version control.

The language fragment outlined here is in many ways inspired by the Actor Model and has a similar concurrency model, using active objects in a traditional, imperative setting with Hoare-style verification support and history-based object invariants. Rather than using futures and replacements as in the Actor model, suspension is used to avoid undesired blocking.

Acknowledgments. I am indebted to Ole-Johan Dahl for decades of close collaboration, and to Kristen Nygaard, Neelam Soundararajan, José Meseguer, Carl Hewitt, and Gul Agha for inspiration. I thank previous PhD students, colleagues, and coauthors for cooperation; and I thank Peter Ölveczky for valuable comments and encouragement!

A Notational Conventions for Meta-Variables

Upper-Case Letters		Lower-Case Letters	
A, B, C, D	class	a	actual parameter list
F, J	interface	b	boolean condition
I	invariant	c	(caller) object
L	local assertion	e	expression
O	superobject	h	history
P, Q, R	state predicate	m, n	method
S	(sub)system	o	object
T	type	s	statement (list)
		v	value
		x	variable
		y	list of formal parameters
		w	list of fields

References

1. Agha, G.: ACTORS: A Model of Concurrent Computations in Distributed Systems. The MIT Press, Cambridge (1986)
2. Agha, G.: An overview of actor languages. SIGPLAN Not. **21**(10), 58–67 (1986)
3. Agha, G.: Concurrent object-oriented programming. Commun. ACM **33**(9), 125–141 (1990)
4. Agha, G., Hewitt, C.: Concurrent programming using actors: exploiting large-scale parallelism. In: Maheshwari, S.N. (ed.) FSTTCS 1985. LNCS, vol. 206, pp. 19–41. Springer, Heidelberg (1985). https://doi.org/10.1007/3-540-16042-6_2
5. Agha, G., Thati, P.: An algebraic theory of actors and its application to a simple object-based language. In: Owe, O., Krogdahl, S., Lyche, T. (eds.) From Object-Orientation to Formal Methods. LNCS, vol. 2635, pp. 26–57. Springer, Heidelberg (2004). https://doi.org/10.1007/978-3-540-39993-3_4
6. Agha, G.A.: Abstracting interaction patterns: a programming paradigm for open distributed systems. In: Najm, E., Stefani, J.-B. (eds.) Formal Methods for Open Object-based Distributed Systems. IAICT, pp. 135–153. Springer, Boston (1997). https://doi.org/10.1007/978-0-387-35082-0_10
7. Armstrong, J.: Making reliable distributed systems in the presence of software errors. Ph.D. thesis, Royal Institute of Technology, Stockholm, Sweden (2003)
8. Baramashetru, C.P., Giannini, P., Tarifa, S.L.T., Owe, O.: A type system for data privacy compliance in active object languages. Art Sci. Eng. Program. (2025)
9. Baramashetru, C.P., Tarifa, S.L.T., Owe, O.: Integrating data privacy compliance in active object languages. In: de Boer, F.S., Damiani, F., Hähnle, R., Johnsen, E.B., Kamburjan, E. (eds.) Active Object Languages: Current Research Trends. LNCS, vol. 14360, pp. 263–288. Springer, Cham (2024). https://doi.org/10.1007/978-3-031-51060-1_10
10. Bentea, L., Owe, O.: A probabilistic framework for object-oriented modeling and analysis of distributed systems. In: Beckert, B., Damiani, F., Gurov, D. (eds.) FoVeOOS 2011. LNCS, vol. 7421, pp. 105–122. Springer, Heidelberg (2012). https://doi.org/10.1007/978-3-642-31762-0_8
11. Bjørk, J., Johnsen, E.B., Owe, O., Schlatte, R.: Lightweight time modeling in timed Creol. In: Ölveczky, P.C. (ed.) Proceedings First International Workshop on Rewriting Techniques for Real-Time Systems. EPTCS, vol. 36, pp. 67–81 (2010)

12. Black, A.P.: Object-oriented programming: Some history, and challenges for the next fifty years. Inf. Comput. **231**, 3–20 (2013)
13. Boer, F.D., et al.: A survey of active object languages. ACM Comput. Surv. **50**(5) (2017)
14. Clarke, D., Johnsen, E.B., Owe, O.: Concurrent objects à la carte. In: Dams, D., Hannemann, U., Steffen, M. (eds.) Concurrency, Compositionality, and Correctness. LNCS, vol. 5930, pp. 185–206. Springer, Heidelberg (2010). https://doi.org/10.1007/978-3-642-11512-7_12
15. Dahl, O.-J.: Value types and object classes. ASU Newslett. **20**(1), 8–20 (1992). https://www.mn.uio.no/ifi/english/about/ole-johan-dahl/bibliography/value-types-and-object-classes.pdf
16. Dahl, O.-J.: Verifiable programming. In: Prentice Hall International Series in Computer Science. Prentice Hall (1992)
17. Dahl, O.-J.: The birth of object orientation: the Simula languages. In: Owe, O., Krogdahl, S., Lyche, T. (eds.) From Object-Orientation to Formal Methods. LNCS, vol. 2635, pp. 15–25. Springer, Heidelberg (2004). https://doi.org/10.1007/978-3-540-39993-3_3
18. Dahl, O.-J., Myhrhaug, B., Nygaard, K.: SIMULA 67 Common Base Language. Norwegian Computing Center Report S-2, 1968 (1968). (Revised version: Norwegian Computing Center Report 743, 1984)
19. Dahl, O.-J., Nygaard, K.: SIMULA - an ALGOL-based simulation language. Commun. ACM **9**(9), 671–678 (1966)
20. Dahl, O.-J., Owe, O.: A presentation of the specification and verification project ABEL. ACM SIGSOFT Softw. Eng. Notes **10**(4), 28–32 (1985)
21. Dahl, O.-J., Owe, O.: Formal development with ABEL. In: Prehn, S., Toetenel, H. (eds.) VDM 1991. LNCS, vol. 552, pp. 320–362. Springer, Heidelberg (1991). https://doi.org/10.1007/BFb0019999
22. Dahl, O.-J., Owe, O.: Formal methods and the RM-ODP. Technical Report 261, University of Oslo, Dept. of Informatics (1998). https://www.nb.no/items/URN:NBN:no-nb_digibok_2009042000005?page=19
23. Dahl, O.-J., Owe, O., Bastiansen, T.J.: Subtyping and constructive specification. Nord. J. Comput. **5**(1), 19–49 (1998)
24. Damiani, F., Owe, O., Dovland, J., Schaefer, I., Johnsen, E.B., Yu, I.C.: A transformational proof system for delta-oriented programming. In: de Almeida, E.S., Schwanninger, C., Benavides, D. (eds.) 16th International Software Product Line Conference, SPLC '12, Volume 2, pp. 53–60. ACM (2012)
25. Din, C.C., Owe, O.: A sound and complete reasoning system for asynchronous communication with shared futures. J. Log. Algebraic Methods Program. **83**(5–6), 360–383 (2014)
26. Din, C.C., Owe, O.: Compositional reasoning about active objects with shared futures. Formal Aspects Comput. **27**(3), 551–572 (2015)
27. Dovland, J., Johnsen, E.B., Owe, O., Steffen, M.: Incremental reasoning with lazy behavioral subtyping for multiple inheritance. Sci. Comput. Program. **76**(10), 915–941 (2011)
28. Dovland, J., Johnsen, E.B., Owe, O., Yu, I.C.: A proof system for adaptable class hierarchies. J. Log. Algeb. Meth. Program. **84**(1), 37–53 (2015)
29. Fazeldehkordi, E., Owe, O., Ramezanifarkhani, T.: A language-based approach to prevent DDoS attacks in distributed financial agent systems. In: Fournaris, A.P., et al. (eds.) IOSEC/MSTEC/FINSEC -2019. LNCS, vol. 11981, pp. 258–277. Springer, Cham (2020). https://doi.org/10.1007/978-3-030-42051-2_18

30. Fernandez-Reyes, K., Clarke, D., Castegren, E., Vo, H.: Forward to a promising future. In: Serugendo, G.D.M., Loreti, M. (eds.) COORDINATION 2018. LNCS, vol. 10852, pp. 162–180. Springer, Cham (2018). https://doi.org/10.1007/978-3-319-92408-3_7
31. Fernandez-Reyes, K., Clarke, D., Henrio, L., Johnsen, E.B., Wrigstad, T.: Godot: all the benefits of implicit and explicit futures. In: Donaldson, A.F. (ed.) 33rd European Conference on Object-Oriented Programming (ECOOP 2019). Leibniz International Proceedings in Informatics (LIPIcs), vol. 134, pp. 2:1–2:28. Dagstuhl, Germany (2019). Schloss Dagstuhl – Leibniz-Zentrum für Informatik
32. Flatt, M., Krishnamurthi, S., Felleisen, M.: Classes and mixins. In: Proceedings of the 25th ACM SIGPLAN-SIGACT Symposium on Principles of Programming Languages, POPL '98, New York, NY, USA, pp. 171–183. ACM (1998)
33. Johnsen, E.B., Blanchette, J.C., Kyas, M., Owe, O.: Intra-object versus inter-object: concurrency and reasoning in Creol. In: Zhao, J., Stolz, V. (eds.) Proceedings of the 2nd International Workshop on Harnessing Theories for Tool Support in Software. Electronic Notes in Theoretical Computer Science, vol. 243, pp. 89–103. Elsevier (2008)
34. Johnsen, E.B., Hähnle, R., Schäfer, J., Schlatte, R., Steffen, M.: ABS: a core language for abstract behavioral specification. In: Aichernig, B.K., de Boer, F.S., Bonsangue, M.M. (eds.) FMCO 2010. LNCS, vol. 6957, pp. 142–164. Springer, Heidelberg (2011). https://doi.org/10.1007/978-3-642-25271-6_8
35. Johnsen, E.B., Owe, O.: Object-oriented specification and open distributed systems. In: Owe, O., Krogdahl, S., Lyche, T. (eds.) From Object-Orientation to Formal Methods. LNCS, vol. 2635, pp. 137–164. Springer, Heidelberg (2004). https://doi.org/10.1007/978-3-540-39993-3_9
36. Johnsen, E.B., Owe, O.: An asynchronous communication model for distributed concurrent objects. Softw. Syst. Model. **6**(1), 39–58 (2007)
37. Johnsen, E.B., Owe, O., Arnestad, M.: Combining active and reactive behavior in concurrent objects. In: Proceedings of Norsk Informatikkonferanse (NIK'03). Tapir (2003)
38. Johnsen, E.B., Owe, O., Axelsen, E.W.: A run-time environment for concurrent objects with asynchronous method calls. Electron. Notes Theoret. Comput. Sci., **117**, 375–392 (2005). Proceedings of the Fifth International Workshop on Rewriting Logic and Its Applications (WRLA 2004)
39. Johnsen, E.B., Owe, O., Bjørk, J., Kyas, M.: An object-oriented component model for heterogeneous nets. In: de Boer, F.S., Bonsangue, M.M., Graf, S., de Roever, W.-P. (eds.) FMCO 2007. LNCS, vol. 5382, pp. 257–279. Springer, Heidelberg (2008). https://doi.org/10.1007/978-3-540-92188-2_11
40. Johnsen, E.B., Owe, O., Clarke, D., Bjørk, J.: A formal model of service-oriented dynamic object groups. Sci. Comput. Program. **115–116**, 3–22 (2016)
41. Broch Johnsen, E., Owe, O., Schlatte, R., Tapia Tarifa, S.L.: Validating timed models of deployment components with parametric concurrency. In: Beckert, B., Marché, C. (eds.) FoVeOOS 2010. LNCS, vol. 6528, pp. 46–60. Springer, Heidelberg (2011). https://doi.org/10.1007/978-3-642-18070-5_4
42. Johnsen, E.B., Owe, O., Simplot-Ryl, I.: A dynamic class construct for asynchronous concurrent objects. In: Steffen, M., Zavattaro, G. (eds.) FMOODS 2005. LNCS, vol. 3535, pp. 15–30. Springer, Heidelberg (2005). https://doi.org/10.1007/11494881_2
43. Johnsen, E.B., Owe, O., Creol, I.C.Y.: A type-safe object-oriented model for distributed concurrent systems. Theor. Comput. Sci. **365**(1–2), 23–66 (2006)

44. Karami, F., Owe, O., Ramezanifarkhani, T.: An evaluation of interaction paradigms for active objects. J. Log. Algebraic Methods Program. **103**, 154–183 (2019)
45. Karami, F., Owe, O., Schneider, G.: Information-flow control by means of security wrappers for active object languages with futures. In: Asplund, M., Nadjm-Tehrani, S. (eds.) NordSec 2020. LNCS, vol. 12556, pp. 74–91. Springer, Cham (2021). https://doi.org/10.1007/978-3-030-70852-8_5
46. Leavens, G.T., Naumann, D.A.: Behavioral subtyping, specification inheritance, and modular reasoning. ACM Trans. Program. Lang. Syst. **37**(4), 13:1-13:88 (2015)
47. Liskov, B.H., Wing, J.M.: A behavioral notion of subtyping. ACM Trans. Program. Lang. Syst. **16**(6), 1811–1841 (1994)
48. Madsen, O.L.: Building safe concurrency abstractions. In: Agha, G., et al. (eds.) Concurrent Objects and Beyond. LNCS, vol. 8665, pp. 66–104. Springer, Heidelberg (2014). https://doi.org/10.1007/978-3-662-44471-9_4
49. McDowell, C., Owe, O.: Towards a light-weight approach for concurrent active objects in Java. Technical report, University of California, Santa Cruz (UCSC) (2015). https://users.soe.ucsc.edu/~charlie/pubs/creolJava2C.pdf
50. Nygaard, K., Dahl, O.-J.: The development of the SIMULA languages. ACM SIGPLAN Notices **13**(8), 245–272 (1978)
51. Owe, O.: Reasoning about inheritance and unrestricted reuse in object-oriented concurrent systems. In: Ábrahám, E., Huisman, M. (eds.) IFM 2016. LNCS, vol. 9681, pp. 210–225. Springer, Cham (2016). https://doi.org/10.1007/978-3-319-33693-0_14
52. Owe, O.: Verifiable programming of object-oriented and distributed systems. In: Petre, L., Sekerinski, E. (eds.) From Action Systems to Distributed Systems - The Refinement Approach, pp. 61–79. Chapman and Hall/CRC (2016)
53. Owe, O., Dahl, O.-J.: Generator induction in order sorted algebras. Formal Aspects Comput. **3**(1), 2–20 (1991)
54. Owe, O., Fazeldehkordi, E.: A lightweight approach to smart contracts supporting safety, security, and privacy. J. Log. Algebraic Methods Program. **127**, 100772 (2022)
55. Owe, O., Fazeldehkordi, E., Lin, J.-C.: A framework for flexible program evolution and verification of distributed systems. In: Hammoudi, S., Pires, L.F., Selić, B. (eds.) MODELSWARD 2019. CCIS, vol. 1161, pp. 320–349. Springer, Cham (2020). https://doi.org/10.1007/978-3-030-37873-8_14
56. Owe, O., McDowell, C.: On detecting over-eager concurrency in asynchronously communicating concurrent object systems. J. Log. Algebraic Methods Program. **90**, 158–175 (2017)
57. Owe, O., Ramezanifarkhani, T.: Confidentiality of interactions in concurrent object-oriented systems. In: Garcia-Alfaro, J., Navarro-Arribas, G., Hartenstein, H., Herrera-Joancomartí, J. (eds.) ESORICS/DPM/CBT -2017. LNCS, vol. 10436, pp. 19–34. Springer, Cham (2017). https://doi.org/10.1007/978-3-319-67816-0_2
58. Owe, O., Ryl, I.: OUN: a formalism for open, object-oriented, distributed systems. In: Victor, B., Yi, W. (eds.) NWPT'99: The 11th Nordic Workshop on Programming Theory (1999). Full version: https://www.mn.uio.no/ifi/english/people/emeriti/olaf/papers/oun-aug99.pdf
59. Owe, O., Ryl, I.: On combining reasoning control with distribution and openness in object oriented systems. In: Haveraaen, M., Owe (eds.) NWPT'00: The 12th Nordic Workshop on Programming Theory (2000). Full version: https://www.mn.uio.no/ifi/english/people/emeriti/olaf/papers/ounrr278.pdf

60. Owe, O., Schneider, G.: Wrap your objects safely. Electron. Notes Theoret. Comput. Sci. **253**(1), 127–143 (2009). Proceedings of the Sixth International Workshop on Formal Engineering approches to Software Components and Architectures (FESCA 2009)
61. Owe, O., Yu, I.C.: Deadlock detection of active objects with synchronous and asynchronous method calls. In: Proceedings of 27th Norsk Informatikkonferanse, NIK 2014. Bibsys Open Journal Systems, Norway (2014)
62. Ramezanifarkhani, T., Owe, O., Tokas, S.: A secrecy-preserving language for distributed and object-oriented systems. J. Log. Algebraic Methods Program. **99**, 1–25 (2018)
63. Soundararajan, N.: Axiomatic semantics of communicating sequential processes. ACM Trans. Program. Lang. Syst. (TOPLAS) **6**(4), 647–662 (1984)
64. Stehr, M.-O., Meseguer, J.: Pure type systems in rewriting logic: specifying typed higher-order languages in a first-order logical framework. In: Owe, O., Krogdahl, S., Lyche, T. (eds.) From Object-Orientation to Formal Methods. LNCS, vol. 2635, pp. 334–375. Springer, Heidelberg (2004). https://doi.org/10.1007/978-3-540-39993-3_16
65. The ABS Home Page. The ABS language. https://abs-models.org/
66. The Erlang Home Page. The Erlang language. https://www.erlang.org/
67. The Maude Home Page. The Maude system. https://maude.cs.illinois.edu/wiki/The_Maude_System
68. Tokas, S., Owe, O.: A formal framework for consent management. In: Gotsman, A., Sokolova, A. (eds.) FORTE 2020. LNCS, vol. 12136, pp. 169–186. Springer, Cham (2020). https://doi.org/10.1007/978-3-030-50086-3_10
69. Tokas, S., Owe, O., Ramezanifarkhani, T.: Static checking of GDPR-related privacy compliance for object-oriented distributed systems. J. Log. Algebraic Methods Program. **125**, 100733 (2022)
70. Yonezawa, A., Hewitt, C.: Modelling distributed systems. In: Reddy, R. (ed.) Proceedings of the 5th International Joint Conference on Artificial Intelligence, pp. 370–376. William Kaufmann (1977)
71. Yu, I.C., Johnsen, E.B., Owe, O.: Type-safe runtime class upgrades in Creol. In: Gorrieri, R., Wehrheim, H. (eds.) FMOODS 2006. LNCS, vol. 4037, pp. 202–217. Springer, Heidelberg (2006). https://doi.org/10.1007/11768869_16
72. Ölveczky, P.C.: Designing Reliable Distributed Systems: A Formal Methods Approach Based on Executable Modeling in Maude. UTCS, Springer, London (2017). https://doi.org/10.1007/978-1-4471-6687-0

The C++ Actor Framework: A Scalable Fundament for Research and Applications

Dominik Charousset[1](✉), Raphael Hiesgen[2], and Thomas C. Schmidt[2]

[1] Interance, Hamburg, Germany
d.charousset@interance.io
[2] HAW Hamburg, Hamburg, Germany
{raphael.hiesgen,t.schmidt}@haw-hamburg.de

Abstract. The C++ Actor Framework (CAF) has evolved from an experimental research project to a mature, production-ready domain specific language in C++. CAF supports type safety and flexible networking, implements the concepts of actor composition and message flows, and serves as a highly efficient fundament for concurrent and distributed applications. It is continuously deployed in research and commercial systems. In this paper, we first present a high-level overview of the framework and then focus on selected applications in security research and performance-critical commercial systems, all of which rely on specific characteristics of CAF.

Keywords: Actor model · C++ · security · scalability · measurement

1 Introduction

Parallel hardware is ubiquitous. Smartphones, laptops, desktops, and servers all have long moved to multicore processors. Systems as a whole span across hosts and build distributed systems, such as closely coupled compute clusters, distributed cloud services, and many traditional client-server applications. Software in general and especially portable core components need to be scalable to adjust to the different environments and requirements. To ease the approachability of these systems and to make their capabilities available to everyone, frameworks that get used by many developers should offer APIs that do not require domain specific knowledge to avoid the many pitfalls and achieve scalability. The actor model [19] offers an approach to meet these challenges. Hewitt et al. [19] proposed the actor model in 1973 as part of their work on artificial intelligence. Later, Agha formalized the model in his dissertation [2] and introduced mailboxes for processing actor messages. He created the foundation of an open, external communication [3].

Initially created under the name libcppa [13,14], the C++ actor framework, short CAF [12], has taken a decade-long journey from a Master's thesis to an established open-source project that is used in industry. The goal was an implementation of the actor model in C++ that offers a high-level API to developers to make efficient use of parallel and distributed systems. C++ has a reputation for efficient and performance-critical applications. To achieve these qualities CAF was benchmarked frequently during development to evaluate the current implementations and find the right path forward. Many of these decisions were anchored in research and presented in workshops and at conferences [11,12,21,38].

As an implementation of the actor model, its core concepts found their way into CAF, interpreted for C++. Error handling follows the concept of monitors [19] but takes inspiration from the refined failure propagation in Erlang [6]. Message passing is naturally network-transparent and efficient, optimized with copy-on write types. However, CAF also provides type-safe message passing interfaces based on the C++ type system, which allows developers to avoid certain errors with little overhead. To address the requirements of modern distributed applications, which often go beyond purely TCP-based communication between actors, CAF integrated a newly designed network stack that focuses on extendability and configurability [21,30].

CAF managed to find success beyond research. It supports all major platforms (Linux, Windows, macOS, and BSD), which means continuously supporting major compilers and ensuring that core components perform well with the respective OS APIs. Although its APIs evolved over time, changes were done with care and aimed to achieve a cohesive and modern API that allows the runtime to perform well. In rare cases, features were removed that turned out not to be viable, *e.g.,* due to large overhead or inconsistencies with the rest of the framework. Attracting and caring for a community is constant work for opensource projects. Offering an approachable documentation, clean code, and easy channels to interact help CAF foster interaction the community and contributions.

We present the status of CAF and briefly introduce notable features in Sect. 2 focusing on the *core module* that implements local actors and the *net module* for writing distributed actor applications and network APIs. Next, we present an application of CAF in research for building a scalable and robust measurement system in Sect. 3. In Sect. 4, we present three applications from industry that are built on CAF. Each making use of different aspects of CAF: parallel computations, responsive message passing, and distributed computations. Finally, we conclude this work in Sect. 5.

2 CAF – The C++ Actor Framework

Since its inception in 2011, CAF [12] has grown from a research prototype into a mature software platform. After releasing a total of 19 alpha and beta versions that incrementally moved CAF from a proof-of-concept phase to a production-ready state, the development team behind CAF released the 1.0 milestone in mid 2024. While this was an important milestone for the project, CAF has been used for industrial applications long before that. Since 2022, Interance[1] offers commercial support for CAF and funds its continuous development.

---

[1] https://www.interance.io/.

CAF was developed to bring a framework for high-level parallel and distributed programming to native C++. Traditionally, applications use handcrafted code for both tasks. Writing code to scale with available resources and efficiently handle network operations requires domain-specific knowledge and careful consideration. CAF not only implements an efficient and scalable runtime but offers a domain-specific language (DSL) to write actors in a readable and convenient way. The implementation faced four core challenges: (*i*) Pattern matching is not natively offered by C++ but essential to the expressive DSL of CAF. (*ii*) An efficient message passing implementation that provides fast and lean actor messaging. (*iii*) A scalable scheduler that handles hundreds, thousands, or even millions of actors and utilizes the available resources efficiently. (*iv*) An efficient network layer with easy serialization for actor messages.

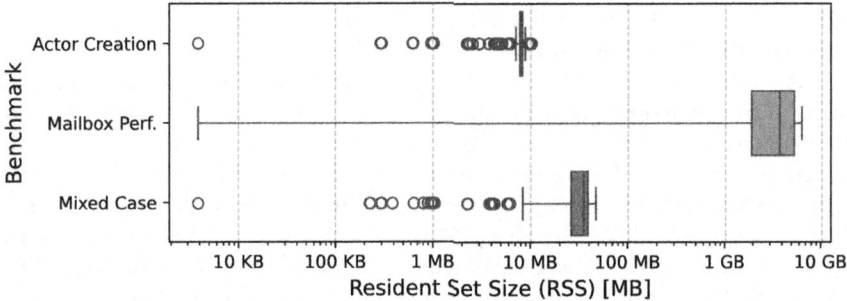

Fig. 1. Memory consumption in three CAF benchmarks. *Actor Creation*: Recursively create actors to compute 2^{20}. *Mailbox Perf.*: 100 actors each sent 1 000 000 messages in a N:1 communication scenario. *Mixed Case*: Rings of actors repeatedly pass a token around.

Figure 1 shows the memory consumption of CAF in three benchmarks [12]. The *actor creation* creates many actors with litte other overhead. It primarily shows that CAF efficiently handles resources to manage large amounts of actors. In the second benchmark, *mailbox performance*, CAF shows that it can concurrently create and send messages, thus quickly consuming memory. The only bottleneck is the parallel access to the mailbox of the receiver. *Mixed case* represents a scenario that has many actors, 100 rings of 100 actors, that repeatedly pass a token along the ring. Here, the resource use is once again low and predictable. Overall, the benchmarks show the strength of the native runtime and its lean actor implementation.

The core challenges were already solved in early versions of CAF. On the way to its 1.0 release, the implementations in CAF evolved, some features going through multiple iterations to optimize performance and expressiveness. The stable feature set now enables a wide range of applications. A modular approach allows developers to only include the modules they need for their application. CAF is separated into five modules: *core*, *I/O*, *net*, *OpenSSL*, and *test*.

2.1 The Actor Core

The *core module* is the centerpiece of CAF and required to write CAF-based applications. As the foundational module, it has the largest feature set.

Actors. CAF offers dynamically and statically typed, garbage-collected (reference counted) actors. Communication between actors is network agnostic and transparent at the API level. Developers have the choice to provide additional interface information to enable type-checks for messages (static typing). Otherwise, CAF falls back to type-checks at runtime (dynamic typing). This is not a binary choice, and applications can use both APIs simultaneously. Dynamically typed actors are often used for helper actors only visible in a single translation unit. In contrast, public interfaces benefit from the additional safety of statically typed actors.

To provide deterministic cleanup of actors and their resources, CAF built its garbage collection on top of reference counting. Since C++ does not deploy a garbage collector, there are no "GC cycles" that could delay memory reclamation. This allows CAF to release and re-use memory as soon as an actor reaches a reference count of zero, which is particularly beneficial for high-performance applications that spawn many short-lived actors. In distributed actor systems, CAF currently maintains a reference at the network layer for actors exposed to remote nodes to enable deserialization of actor addresses. This reference is automatically dropped once the actor terminates. While this approach works well for applications that explicitly manage actor lifecycles, it means that actors exposed to the network will have a reference count of at least one until they terminate. This creates a subtle but important difference in behavior between local and distributed actors: applications that rely solely on reference counting for actor lifecycle management may behave differently when actors communicate across process boundaries. We discuss ongoing work to address this limitation in Sect. 5.

Flow Processing. CAF provides a high-level API for building processing pipelines in a data-oriented way. They complement the message-based actor communication with a declarative approach to expressing complex processing pipelines. Data flows can span multiple actors and may connect actors to other, non-actor components such as a WebSocket connection. The flow API in CAF closely follows the ReactiveX specification [33], but extends it with a seamless interface between flows and regular actor messages.

Figure 2 shows a simple example of a declarative flow. The actor `src` is declared as the source for a sequence of numbers from 1 to 5. First, `make_observable()` (line 3) prepares it be observable later, turning it into a factory. The two following functions augment the factory by declaring which data the actor will provide: the first five values (`take(5)`) of a sequence of integers starting with 1 (`iota(1)`). With `observe_on(snk)` (line 6) the actor `src` is created as an observable that is connected to the actor `snk`. The function also

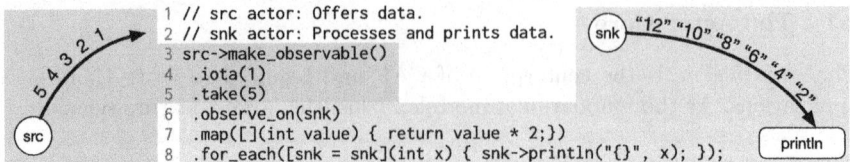

```
1 // src actor: Offers data.
2 // snk actor: Processes and prints data.
3 src->make_observable()
4   .iota(1)
5   .take(5)
6   .observe_on(snk)
7   .map([](int value) { return value * 2;})
8   .for_each([snk = snk](int x) { snk->println("{}", x); });
```

Fig. 2. CAF flow is a declarative API to express processing pipelines on top of actors. The code describes a flow between a source and a sink in a single statement. The source produces a series of 5 integers that are doubled and printed by the sink.

allows describing the behavior on snk in the same statement. map applies a given function to each element in a sequence, doubling its value in this case. Similarly, for_each applies a function to each element but cannot mutate them, which we use to print the values.

Software Metrics. Deploying large-scale applications requires constant monitoring, especially when deploying to the cloud. Software metrics are numerical values that aggregate health and performance characteristics such as current memory usage, CPU utilization, message throughput into time series. A monitoring system such as Prometheus enables deployment teams to understand system behaviors and alerts on critical events. CAF collects important metrics by default and provides an API for developers to instrument their code. These metrics can be collected programmatically and exported via HTTP to Prometheus (when using the I/O or net module).

Type Inspection and Serialization. CAF must be able to serialize and deserialize messages at runtime to enable network agnostic messaging between actors. Since C++ has no built-in facilities to rely on in the current language versions, CAF includes an API for developers to enable CAF to serialize and deserialize custom types. Due to the close relationship to core features of CAF, this functionality is part of the core module. Developers that never intend to make use of the type inspection can explicitly disable it.

Scheduling. CAF includes two flavors of actors: blocking and cooperatively scheduled, with the latter being the (recommended) default. When implementing scheduled actors, each actor requires only a few hundred bytes overhead, allowing applications to dynamically scale up to several thousand actors on a single node. By default, CAF uses a work-stealing scheduler that can efficiently run a large set of actors concurrently on many cores [11]. CAF also includes a work-sharing implementation that can perform better for some workloads on nodes with only a few cores. As the name suggests, blocking actors are meant for operations that block the execution thread. To avoid blocking threads from the cooperative scheduler–and in the worst case, the whole actor system–these actors run in their own execution context and can transparently interact with other actors.

2.2 Networking API and Distribution

The *I/O module* enables distributing actors across the network. It provides an API for connecting to remote actors, observing lifetimes of other nodes in the network, and to start actors remotely. By default, communication between CAF nodes uses TCP, is unencrypted, and assumes a private network. The optional OpenSSL module enables encrypted communication between CAF nodes.

Environment-specific protocols, *e.g.,* CoAP [35] or DCTCP [8], and the advent of new transport protocols, *e.g.,* QUIC [26], demand a flexible network stack. The next iteration of the networking module (*net module* for short) [30] focuses on extendability and configurability. It extends CAF with a construction kit for interfacing with various network protocols while also including ready-to-use APIs for common protocols. Notable features of this module include:

Layered Protocol Stack API Design. Layering plays an important role in the design of the net module. A protocol layer is a class that implements a single processing step in a communication pipeline. Multiple layers are organized in a protocol stack. Each layer may only communicate with its direct predecessor or successor in the stack. At the bottom of the protocol stack is usually a transport layer. For example, a TCP octet stream layer that manages a stream socket and provides access to input and output buffers to the upper layer. Each layer then adds one protocol layer. For example, an application could combine a TCP transport with a WebSocket layer and a user-defined application layer protocol on top.

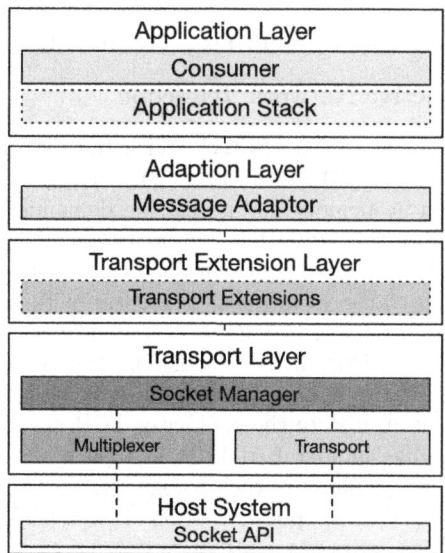

Fig. 3. CAF *net* offers an extensible network layer.

Figure 3 visualizes the approach of the new network layer. It was built with reusable layers in mind that can add to the functionality of lower layers. The multiplexer runs an event loop based on the async I/O facilities of the OS (poll, epoll, or kqueue). The socket Manager above abstracts over the socket API to read and write data and manage connections for specific transport protocols. The optional transport extension layer adds additional functionality to transport protocols, *e.g.,* ordering to UDP. The adoption layer ensures a unified interface into the application stack, independent of the communication semantics of a lower layer. Type-safe interfaces ensure that layers that can be composed, *i.e.,* can be compiled, work together.

HTTP Client and Server APIs. Especially in service-oriented deployment models, HTTP interfaces are common. Both for retrieving data from other services and to make data available to others. Hence, CAF includes APIs to bridge between internal actor communication and external message exchange over HTTP.

WebSocket Client and Server APIs. The WebSocket protocol enables applications to exchange a stream of messages with external systems, which naturally fits the flow API in CAF. Actors can consume and produce a flow of WebSocket frames to transfer text or binary data between an external system and the actor.

For HTTP and WebSocket, CAF offers a declarative, high-level API that hides the setup steps for the protocol layer stack. In both APIs, encryption can be enabled declaratively to have CAF use TLS at the transport layer.

3 CAF Application in Security Research

3.1 Spoki: A Reactive Network Telescope

Scanners are ever-present on the Internet. With the rise of stateless-scanning, popularized by ZMap (2013) [18] and Mirai (2016) [5], Internet-wide scans have become cheap enough in memory and processing demands to enable scan campaigns on mass. During this time the share of irregular TCP SYN packets—a trait of many stateless scanners—rose sharply. The Transmission Control Protocol (TCP), a dominant transport protocol on the Internet, marks the first packets sent by each participant with a SYN flag. Subsequent packets that acknowledge receipt set the ACK flag. During the year 2020, we observed shares of roughly 75% irregular SYNs at three vantage points around the globe—at a network telescope, an IXP, and an ISP. In the context of TCP, stateless scanning probes for open ports by sending handcrafted TCP SYN packets, which avoids state in the local network state. Replies are then recognized via SYN cookies embedded in the packets and reflected in replies (TCP SYN ACK packets). While stateless scanning is not harmful on its own—although it could cause DDoS attack when focused—malicious actors use scanning to identify potential targets. In a second phase, they return to attack previously responsive hosts.

Spoki [23] is a new kind of network telescope that interacts with scanners generically on the transport layer. It can trigger the second scanning phase, learn more about scanner intentions, and collect their payloads. It is built on top of the C++ Actor Framework (CAF) to meet the scaling demands of modern Internet traffic. CAF provides efficient message passing, scalability, and building blocks for distributed deployments to Spoki.

Design Goals. *Responsiveness.* Spoki interacts with scanners in real time. Prompt responses are necessary to interact with the tools and network stacks of scanners without running into timeouts. Spoki does not delay responses.

Scalability. Network telescope deployments differ drastically. The largest telescopes span millions of IP prefixes whereas a few hundred addresses are enough for small network telescopes. Spoki addresses both deployments and only consumes the necessary resources, *i.e.,* it scales from commodity hardware to large multicore servers.

Stability. Network telescopes are long-running measurement tools. Security phenomena are unknown in advance and collected data might even offer insight into incidents that only become known later. As such, they should be always operative with little downtime and run stable for years.

Distribution. Larger deployments often strictly limit network access of hosts. In those cases, the permissions of users are usually limited and controlled, as well. As an example, compute nodes that run the processing logic might not have unrestricted access to craft the response packets Spoki sends. We want Spoki to be suitable for such scenarios by distributing its components. The prober might run on an edge node with increased permissions while the remaining tasks of Spoki can be located on a compute node, running in user space.

Advantage of the Actor Model for Spoki. We decided to build Spoki using CAF to address our design requirements. The native implementation in C++ grants an efficient and predictable memory management that does not interfere with our runtime. Actors can easily run concurrently if there is enough work. They encourage specialized components that work independently and perform their tasks in isolation. Distributing functionality over many actors allows Spoki to fully exploit the available resources. Resources still need to match the expected load, *i.e.,* large network telescopes require mode resources than small ones.

Spoki is a highly parallel application. Traditionally, such code is prone to race conditions and deadlocks. These can be mostly avoided by actors, leaving room to focus on other challenges. Additionally, the actor model encourages small components that are easy to reason about. Finally, the network transparency of message passing allows us to distribute components with little effort.

Design. Spoki is separated into four basic components as visualized in Fig. 4:

Ingestion Reads packets using libtrace [4] and routes them to core actors.
Core Makes decisions, *e.g.*, requests probes and forwards payloads for logging.
Logging Collects packets and payloads, buffers data, writes logs to disk.
Prober Sends probes to accept (TCP SYN-ACK) and reset (RST) connections.

Each component is built from one or more actor types. The ingestion is an exception. It uses traditional threads started by libtrace that read packets from a network interface and hands them to a custom callback. Here, Spoki filters unwanted traffic before routing packets to actors from the core component for processing Routing is based on source addresses to allow core actors to keep state, *e.g.*, to implement rate limiting or keep state for crypto operations.

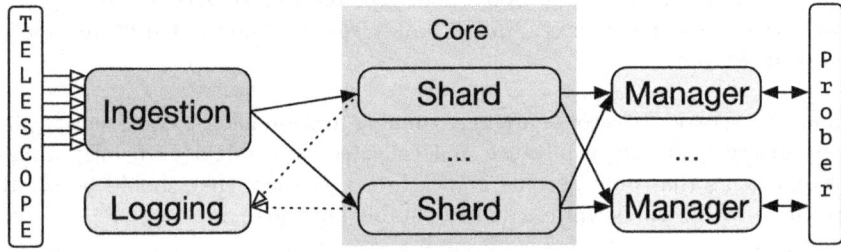

Fig. 4. The architecture of Spoki.

The prober component is built from a manager and the prober itself. The manager keeps state to track probes in progress and log probe results to disk. Spoki originally used scamper [28] for probing. However, newer versions alternatively come with a prober implementation that is more specialized to handle the requirements of Spoki. It sacrifices flexibility for higher probe rates.

Evaluation. We evaluated Spoki with the packet volumes observed at large network telescopes, which reached 800k packets per second (PPS) in 2020. To leave room for future developments, we probed Spoki with up to 1 million PPS in steps of 250k PPS and noted how many parallel components were necessary to handle the respective packet load. The test hardware was a large server with 128 cores and 512 GB RAM running Linux. Figure 5 visualizes the necessary replication, using Scamper as a prober. While Scamper is limited to a probing rate of 20k, running many instances in parallel allowed Spoki to meet the demand. This was one of our motivations for implementing a new prober.

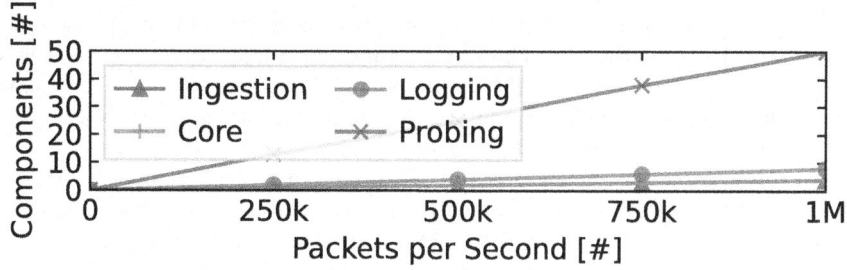

Fig. 5. Performance analysis of Spoki.

Deployment. Spoki has been running continuously on four /24 IPv4 network prefixes since 2020 and on two /48 IPv6 network prefixes since 2023. One vantage point is located in the US and the other three are located in the EU. Given the small size network prefixes—at least compared to the high target during evaluation—each instance only uses few resources and can easily run on a VM (4 cores, 32 GB RAM) while keeping resources mostly idle for further processing. Downtimes were not caused by errors in Spoki but results of environment issues, *e.g.,* disk space.

3.2 Observing Two-Phase Scanners

Using data collected by the continuous monitoring of Spoki, we examined Internet-wide scanners in two measurement studies.

Turning our network telescope responsive tempted stateless scanners to return in a second phase. Both phases can be distinguished through characteristics of the initial SYN. The first phase uses irregular TCP SYNs that have a high TTL, no TCP options, or a well-known IP ID value. However, in the following second phase, TCP SYNs match those expected from common operating systems. Spoki revealed that roughly a third of the observed sources returned in a second phase during the three-month observation period in 2020.

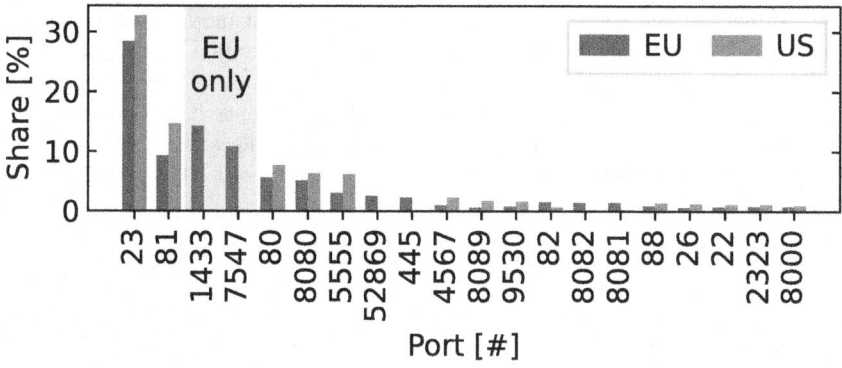

Fig. 6. Top 20 ports targeted by two-phase scanners.

Figure 6 shows a distribution of the top 20 ports targeted by two-phase scanners in the EU and the US. The most-scanned port (23, telnet) is frequently targeted by the Mirai botnet [5]. A first phase to find hosts that likely have telnet running is followed by attempts to log in and infect the system. Mirai also targets port 2323 to a lesser extent, here on place 19.

We observe clearly geographically localized scans focused on the EU for two ports. Port 1433 for the Tabular Data Stream (TDS) protocol is used by Microsoft SQL and likely related to a bug in SIMATIC, an automation system by Siemens AG. Scans targeting port 7547, which fits TR-069, likely relates to a bug in home routers that are predominantly deployed in Europe. At our EU vantage point, we further observed topologically localized scans. Here, some scans focused on targets within the same /16 IPv4 address block, a bias previously observed in worms [10].

The collected payloads further highlight the maliciousness of these scans. Among payloads, we found exploits targeting IoT devices, Android vulnerabilities, and others. Using a threat intelligence company to access the maliciousness of source address showed that the share of malicious sources is higher among those scanners that engage in two-phase scanning (55% to 70%) than among all scanners (≈35%).

3.3 Dissecting the Log4Shell Incident

The Log4Shell remote code execution (RCE) vulnerability was disclosed on December 10, 2021 [24,25]. It received the most severe rating and follows other vulnerabilities that made headlines in the community and beyond, such as Heartbleed [17,36] and Spectre [27]. Log4Shell can be exploited through vulnerable deployments of the Log4j library, a widely used logging framework for Java applications. The exploit uses a string evaluation feature of Log4j that can be tricked into initiating a connection to a remote system to download and run code using JNDI, which eventually lets attackers run arbitrary code.

We observed the first scans on the day of the disclosure. While Cloudflare [29] and Cisco [15] already reported isolated scans before public disclosure, we only observed scans thereafter. Aggressive scanning reached its peak about a week later. While we saw signs of benign scans from threat-intelligence companies during the first 14 days, malicious actors showed continued activity, albeit at reduced scan volumes. During the initial wave of scans, a few heavy hitters had a large impact and caused significant spikes in events. One source heavily focused on the US only, indicating geographical targeted scanning behavior. The US vantage point generally observed more scans than each EU vantage point.

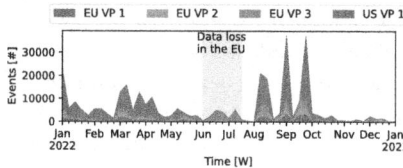
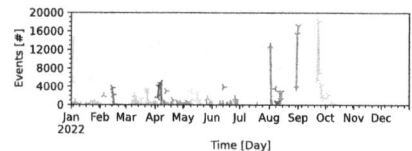

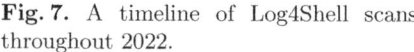

Fig. 7. A timeline of Log4Shell scans throughout 2022.

Fig. 8. Each color signifies a different IP of a large log4Shell scanner.

2022 saw peaks of scanning in March and April as well as in August and September (Fig. 7). Using the source addresses and remote-server information from the payloads allows us to cluster events. This reveals a large cluster spanning multiple countries that sent about 60% of all events we recorded. The source addresses of scans rotated regularly (Fig. 8) while the server addresses in the payload rarely changed. Scanning addresses are frequently reported, easily end up on blocklists and thus require frequent changes. In contrast, the backend servers only become known through analysis of the payloads.

Log4Shell is not associated with a specific port or service, as it targets an implementation detail common across various applications: the use of the Log4j library. The attack can be detected by scanning payloads for URLs that cause the vulnerable library to contact remote servers and potentially download an exploit. These URLs–prefixed with "`jndi:`" to instruct Log4j to perform a query via the Java Naming and Directory Interface (JNDI)–can reveal information about attackers and their infrastructure.

The URL *scheme* determines the type of external service Log4j contacts via JNDI. Our measurements showed that LDAP is by far the most commonly used service. Only a few payloads included URLs using DNS or RMI schemes. Contact information for the external *hosts* revealed that most services used during the exploit are located in hosting networks (Europe: 70%, US: 80%). These hosts are attractive to attackers because they offer reliable connectivity and uptime, while typically not performing proactive scans, making them less likely to appear on blocklists. While LDAP was the most common protocol, over 90% of the URLs used *port* 1389 instead of the default LDAP port (389). Finally, with one exception, the *paths* in the URLs were not conformant with the RFC. Two frequently observed path patterns stood out: `/Exploit` and a group of paths containing the segment `Base64`. The latter group also included a segment with a base64-encoded string that decodes to shell code designed to download and execute malware from an HTTP server.

By correlating the scheme, port, and path information, we identified an open-source project named `JNDIExploit`, which provides an easy-to-set-up server that listens on port 1389 and responds to a wide range of queries matching the `Base64` payloads we collected. Each response includes a Java object that executes the shell code encoded in the request. This server predates the Log4Shell vulnerability, as the underlying JNDI exploit had been known earlier. Log4Shell repurposed it into a remotely exploitable vulnerability. Although the original project was no longer available, we found multiple forks still in circulation.

Like most severe vulnerabilities, Log4Shell appeared suddenly and had a large impact. Since scans started quickly, it is infeasible to design, implement, and deploy measurement systems in reaction. This highlights the importance to write robust measurement systems that are "always on".

4 A Scalable Foundation for Performance-Oriented Industrial Applications

One of the main reasons the actor model has drawn attention from academics and practitioners alike is its applicability to many problem domains. Enabling a wide range of applications has thus always been a central desire in the evolution of CAF.

Combining a low memory footprint per actor with an efficient scheduling infrastructure enables actor-based applications to scale vertically, which makes the model attractive for single-process applications that target multicore machines. Further, the message-based program flow makes it easy for developers to reason about the system behavior and data races are avoided by design as there is no sharing of state between actors.

Since actors inherently communicate via messages, they only require a network-transparent messaging layer with a middleware layer to dispatch messages across the network to enable vertical scaling. A distributed system of actors dynamically grows and shrinks with user demand.

Finally, many applications need to interface with external systems and services by using some form of standardized messaging interface such as HTTP/REST. This naturally fits the message-based programming paradigm of the actor model, which in turn reduces the mental load on developers since they can reason about the system in terms of input and output messages, regardless of whether they are considering internal or external components.

For the remainder of this section, we have selected three applications from different software companies as case examples, each highlighting a different set of requirements.

4.1 xSTUDIO: Scalability Through Fine-Grained Actor Composition

xSTUDIO [1] is a feature-rich, open-source playback and review application designed to meet the diverse needs of filmmakers throughout the production process developed by DNEG, an award-winning visual effects and animation studio. The software is tuned to the workflows in visual effects (VFX) and animation where teams need to handle large numbers of clips and dynamically build playlists and edits, so artists can review their work collaboratively.

Projects easily contain hundreds of media files. These need to be read, decoded into frames, and cached for playback and reviewing. Figure 9 shows a high-level view of the media data model and playback engine of xSTUDIO. The media data management model visualizes the relationship between playlists and the media they contain, which is in turn built from media source, *e.g.*, files on disk, which contain media streams. The playback engine is responsible for synchronizing the media loaded in the player and outputting it via the viewport and audio device. Playheads run independently of the UI, except for frame synchronization. Sub-playheads stream individual media items, such as a media source or timeline. A central playback controller has the timing loop to ensure media is kept in sync and output at the correct frame rate. The application also supports plugins that can be written in Python. Neither of these tasks should interrupt user interaction or current playback. Instead, the UI should be quickly populated with loaded data and remain responsive under load. Four technical goals were formulated to meet these requirements: (*i*) separation of UI and backend, (*ii*) scalability to take advantage of available resources, (*iii*) non-blocking interfaces and loose coupling between components, and (*iv*) a clean API for internal and external use.

Conceptually, xSTUDIO is entirely composed of actors, from menu items and UI elements to components of the playback engine. This helps meet the first three design goals as it introduces a clean separation between UI and the backend based on message passing. Actors also offer a good foundation to build scalable applications. Building fine-grained components instead of large monolithic actors further supports this goal. Message passing enables loose coupling between components and is naturally asynchronous and non-blocking. An actor interface that connects Python via message passing eases the development of extensions while keeping the application core efficient and scalable. Extensions run in a separate thread to avoid interferences with the scheduler and the global interpreter lock (GIL) of Python.

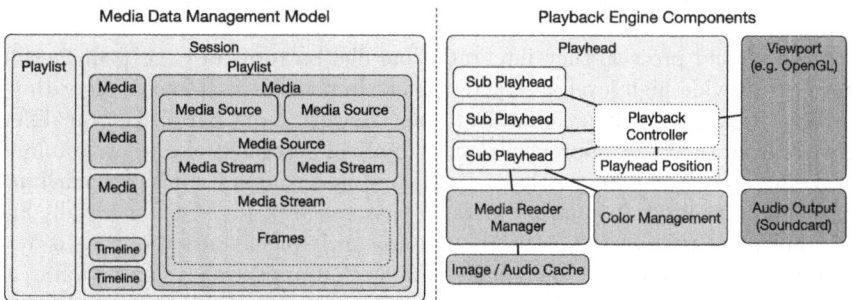

Fig. 9. A high-level overview of the media data model and the playback engine components in xSTUDIO. Following a message passing approach every class is an actor.

xSTUDIO is an example for an application that uses CAF for concurrency. The main benefits here being the high level of abstraction provided by the actor model when implementing applications with many concurrent components and dynamic workloads that need to be orchestrated.

4.2 0LF: A Low-Latency Trading Platform

0LF is proprietary software developed by ATS (advanced technology solutions[2]), an Italian company that develops solutions for financial markets. The software provides a trading platform and an order execution management system that allows modular incorporation of third-party modules.

Since 0LF is operating at the Euronext markets, maintaining a low latency is crucial. Order traversal times must consistently stay in the one-digit millisecond range. At the same time, the system must be able to keep up with high throughput and operates as an extensible platform that requires modularity and interfacing with external systems. In cooperation with the University of Pisa, ATS worked on improving the message passing latency in CAF [37]. In its default configuration, the CAF scheduler sleeps when idle. While this reduces power consumption and CPU usage, it also negatively affects latency in low and medium message rates. A motivating measurement showed that latencies at 10 msg/s can be 60× higher than at 10 000 msg/s. Tuning the scheduler to an aggressive configuration that avoids sleeping massively reduces the difference to a factor below 2× at the cost of high CPU utilization. The paper proposes a new scheduler configuration alongside a light-weight event signaling implementation. Signaling is based on standard synchronization primitives (`std::mutex` and `std::condition_variable`) and thus remains portable across operating systems. An extensive evaluation shows that the proposed implementation shows optimal latency and power consumption for lower and high message rates but slightly increases CPU utilization compared to the default scheduler configuration.

In a second project, they integrated parallel patterns in CAF [34]. Parallel patterns provide high level abstractions that implement well-known algorithms, such as `Map`, `Map-Reduce`, and `Flat Map`. However, the parallelization differs greatly from the actor approach. Each individual actor is typically programmed as a single threaded entity. By orchestrating many actors, multicore machines can be fully utilized. In contrast, parallel patterns are parallelized internally and a complement to actors. The paper presents an implementation of `Map`, a well-known function from functional programming that applies a given function to all elements in a collection. Given a function that has no side effects and independent elements, `Map` can be run in parallel on each element. Their implementation orchestrates a pool of actors that perform the calculations with a single actor as the entry point. To avoid interference between the parallel pattern and the actor system scheduler, they introduce thread-pinning to the CAF runtime, which

---

[2] https://www.atscom.it.

allows assigning OS threads to CPU cores. An evaluation shows the scalability of the implementation, highlighting the improvement of the thread-pinning approach, which also leads to lower and more predictable latency.

CAF allows the developers to reason about the entire software in a single, coherent set of abstractions. The efficient runtime environment of CAF enables actors to shine in such performance-critical applications while keeping the flexibility of an open system, in which actors can be added and new software components can be integrated continuously without changing existing actors. Some OLF instances count nearly 1M actors to parallelize tasks and maximize throughput of the system. Bridging with third-party applications that communicate over well-established technologies such as WebSocket is also straightforward due to the networking module in CAF.

4.3 Tenzir: Composable Pipelines for Security Data

Tenzir, maintained by the company of the same name, emerged from VAST [39]. VAST laid the grounds for efficiently querying large data corpuses that Tenzir extends to a data pipeline engine for security teams.

Cyber-attacks are becoming increasingly more sophisticated and professionalized. Even cautious institutions and companies cannot always prevent intruders from gaining access to their systems, especially if intruders exploit zero-day vulnerabilities or gain access to phished credentials. Security teams not only try to minimize the attack surface but also invest in infrastructure to detect breaches as early as possible and to perform forensic analyses. Log files collected from security-relevant applications and network traffic monitoring [31] provide insight into relevant events. All this data needs to be analyzed, either automatically as part of an ongoing surveillance, or manually as part of an investigation targeting a breach or specific incident. Tenzir allows security teams to combine data from various sources and run complex queries on the entirety of the dataset either as part of a manual analysis or to ingest the resulting data into other alert systems.

Users write queries as pipelines of data processing steps. Tenzir parses these pipelines into a directed acyclic graph (DAG) of independent processing steps, see Fig. 10. For each step, Tenzir spawns an "exec node actor" that receives data from its predecessor (or from a data source) and sends enriched or filtered data to its successor (or to a sink). Together, these actors form a concurrent processing pipeline. These actors can also be distributed across the network.

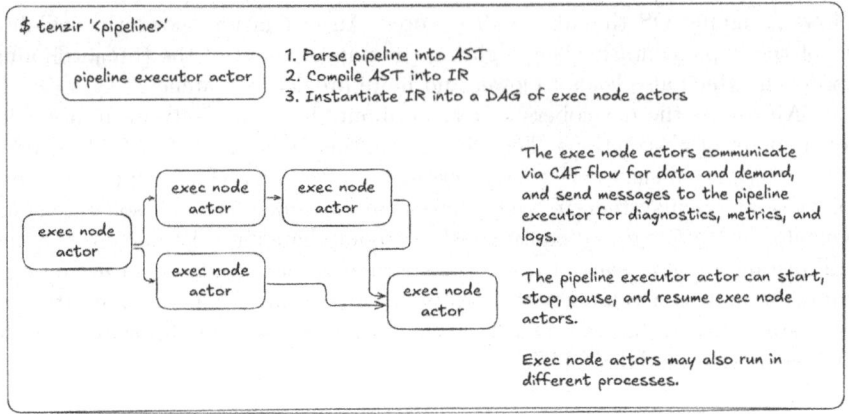

Fig. 10. Tenzir constructs graphs of actors from user queries. The *abstract syntax tree* (AST) of the pipeline description is compiled in an *intermediate representation* (IR) and instantiated as a *directed acyclic graph* (DAG) of actors.

Transforming the query description into a network of actors allows the independent processing steps to run in parallel. The processing graph is built with the flow API of CAF, which brings flow control and allows Tenzir to ensure that fast producers cannot overwhelm downstream consumers. Each stage in the pipeline signals demand to its predecessor. Since data may only be sent downstream if demand is available, this automatically throttles data flow to a sustainable rate. Tenzir also spawns a pipeline executor actor that supervises the actors that execute a query. This actor can stop, pause, or resume individual actors in the pipeline at runtime, *e.g.*, to cancel a computation a user is no longer interested in.

Large datasets are organized through "tenzir-nodes". Each tenzir-node consists of a set of actors for data ingestion and for supervising pipeline executions. Multiple tenzir-node instances may run at a site to collect data or to run ongoing queries. This allows Tenzir to run continuous queries that attach to a live data source and continuously produce results. When running queries, Tenzir can instantiate pipelines on available tenzir-node instances to access stored data and to distribute workloads.

Tenzir is a poster child of a data-focused application that makes heavy use of the flow API in CAF. The actor paradigm not only allows for efficient local processing in parallel pipeline steps, but also lay the foundation for distributed processing, in this case to extend the processing capabilities of Tenzir across multiple nodes.

5 Conclusion and Outlook

CAF has demonstrated that a resource-efficient, native runtime environment sets the stage for a wide range of applications of the actor model. With only a few hundred bytes overhead per actor, largely scaling applications can reasonably spawn hundreds of thousands of actors per node. The C++ runtime utilizes reference counting to automatically detect and free unreachable memory regions. Thus, the native runtime reclaims memory of messages and actors as early as possible—in contrast to garbage collectors of virtualized environments, such as on the Java virtual machine (JVM). Efficient reclamation combined with a low memory footprint reduce the overall memory load significantly [12], which in turn allows developers to decompose their application into many actors while still using available compute and memory resources efficiently.

While CAF's reference counting approach works well for managing memory in local actor hierarchies, distributed actor systems present additional challenges. In particular, network-layer references to remote actors can prevent the timely reclamation of unreachable actors. Extending this implementation across process boundaries echoes foundational work by Birrell et al. [9] on distributed reference counting for network objects, where the key idea is to track remote references and safely reclaim distributed components without global coordination. Recent research adapts these ideas to actor systems, such as Orca, a co-designed garbage collector and type system in the Pony language [16], or the fully decentralized algorithm to detect actor termination proposed by Plyukhin and Agha, which does not rely on causal message delivery [32]. Adapting such techniques to CAF could enable safe and efficient automatic reclamation in distributed deployments while preserving deterministic cleanup and high-performance characteristics.

The available scheduler in CAF has demonstrated its scalability in practice, efficiently dispatching close to a million actors in 0LF with low latency. However, the current default implementation based on work-stealing [11] does not consider memory locality or cache proximity. Optimizing memory access would allow CAF to make more efficient use of modern multicore architectures. While preliminary research exists for (i) utilizing techniques such as thread pinning [34] to optimize memory access or for (ii) implementing a NUMA-aware scheduler [40] in CAF, these approaches have not yet advanced to readily available tools or APIs for CAF developers. In the latter case, we have identified significant upsides for some workloads when using a NUMA-aware scheduling infrastructure but at the same time identified workloads that notably underperform. Further research is required to better understand the tradeoffs between these approaches and whether we can offset worst case scenarios or, alternatively, give CAF users tools and recommendations to opt into alternative scheduler implementations for applications that benefit most from them.

On the other end of the spectrum, CAF has still much untapped potential to bring actor programming to resource-constrained devices with single core architectures that are optimized for energy consumption instead of raw performance. On these systems, multi-threading is generally very limited due to the overhead of context switching or simply not available. To target such platforms, CAF would need to provide a scaled-down runtime that minimizes memory allocations, works entirely event-loop based, and supports suitable protocols [20,22]—first experiments have been promising on RIOT [7]. Due to the modular architecture in CAF, implementing a scheduler tailored for embedded systems seems rather straightforward. Further, we have recently added (internal) APIs in CAF that also make the mailbox implementation exchangeable. This recent change allows us to provide a specialized mailbox implementation that turns actor messaging into events that we can enqueue to the global event queue. We wish to make CAF a feasible option wherever C++ is available.

Last but not least, emerging Internet protocols, such as QUIC [26] and the related HTTP/3, have not found their way into CAF yet. While the need for exchangeable protocol layers has driven the development of the new networking stack (Sect. 2.2, [30]), implementing alternative transports and measuring their impact on actor applications is still on our roadmap.

References

1. Academy Software Foundation: xStudio. GitHub. https://www.dneg.com/xstudio/. code at https://github.com/AcademySoftwareFoundation/xstudio
2. Agha, G.: Actors: A Model of Concurrent Computation In Distributed Systems. MIT Press, Cambridge (1986)
3. Agha, G., Mason, I.A., Smith, S., Talcott, C.: Towards a theory of actor computation. In: Cleaveland, W.R. (ed.) CONCUR 1992. LNCS, vol. 630, pp. 565–579. Springer, Heidelberg (1992). https://doi.org/10.1007/BFb0084816
4. Alcock, S., WAND: libtrace. GitHub. https://github.com/LibtraceTeam/libtrace
5. Antonakakis, M., et al.: Understanding the mirai botnet. In: 26th USENIX Security Symposium (USENIX Security 17), pp. 1093–1110. USENIX Association, Vancouver (2017)
6. Armstrong, J.: Making reliable distributed systems in the presence of software errors. Ph.D. thesis, Department of Microelectronics and Information Technology, KTH, Sweden (2003)
7. Baccelli, E., et al.: RIOT: an open source operating system for low-end embedded devices in the IoT. IEEE Internet Things J. **5**(6), 4428–4440 (2018). https://doi.org/10.1109/JIOT.2018.2815038
8. Bensley, S., Thaler, D., Balasubramanian, P., Eggert, L., Judd, G.: Data Center TCP (DCTCP): TCP Congestion Control for Data Centers. RFC 8257, IETF (2017). https://doi.org/10.17487/RFC8257
9. Birrell, A., Evers, D., Nelson, G., Owicki, S., Wobber, T.: Distributed Garbage Collection for Network Objects. Technical report, Systems Research Center (1993). http://birrell.org/andrew/papers/116-NetObjGC.pdf
10. Casado, M., Garfinkel, T., Cui, W., Paxson, V., Savage, S.: Opportunistic measurement: extracting insight from spurious traffic. In: Proceedings of the Fourth Workshop on Hot Topics in Networks (HotNets-IV) (2005)
11. Charousset, D., Hiesgen, R., Schmidt, T.C.: CAF - The C++ actor framework for scalable and resource-efficient applications. In: Proceedings of the 5th ACM SIGPLAN Conference on Systems, Programming, and Applications (SPLASH '14), Workshop AGERE!, pp. 15–28. ACM, New York (2014)
12. Charousset, D., Hiesgen, R., Schmidt, T.C.: Revisiting actor programming in C++. Comput. Lang. Syst. Struct. **45**, 105–131 (2016). https://doi.org/10.1016/j.cl.2016.01.002
13. Charousset, D., Schmidt, T.C.: libcppa - designing an actor semantic for C++11. In: Proceedings of C++Now (2013). http://arxiv.org/abs/1301.0748

14. Charousset, D., Schmidt, T.C., Hiesgen, R., Wählisch, M.: Native actors – a scalable software platform for distributed, heterogeneous environments. In: Proceedings of the 4rd ACM SIGPLAN Conference on Systems, Programming, and Applications (SPLASH '13), Workshop AGERE!, pp. 87–96. ACM, New York (2013)
15. Cisco Talos: Threat Advisory: Critical Apache Log4j vulnerability being exploited in the wild (2022). https://blog.talosintelligence.com/2021/12/apache-log4j-rce-vulnerability.html
16. Clebsch, S., Franco, J., Drossopoulou, S., Yang, A.M., Wrigstad, T., Vitek, J.: Orca: GC and type system co-design for actor languages. Proc. of the ACM on Program. Lang. **1**(OOPSLA), 1–28 (2017). https://doi.org/10.1145/3133896
17. Durumeric, Z., et al.: The matter of heartbleed. In: Proceedings of ACM IMC, pp. 475–488. ACM, New York (2014)
18. Durumeric, Z., Wustrow, E., Halderman, J.: ZMap: fast internet-wide scanning and its security applications. In: In Proceedings of the 22nd USENIX Security Symposium, pp. 605–620 (08 2013)
19. Hewitt, C., Bishop, P., Steiger, R.: A universal modular ACTOR formalism for artificial intelligence. In: Proceedings of the 3rd IJCAI, pp. 235–245. Morgan Kaufmann Publishers Inc., San Francisco (1973)
20. Hiesgen, R., Charousset, D., Schmidt, T.C.: Embedded actors – towards distributed programming in the IoT. In: Proceedings of the 4th IEEE International Conference on Consumer Electronics - Berlin, ICCE-Berlin'14, , pp. 371–375. IEEE Press, Piscataway (2014)
21. Hiesgen, R., Charousset, D., Schmidt, T.C.: A configurable transport layer for CAF. In: Proceedings of the 9th ACM SIGPLAN Conference on Systems, Programming, and Applications (SPLASH '18), Workshop AGERE!, pp. 1–12. ACM, New York (2018). https://doi.org/10.1145/3281366.3281369
22. Hiesgen, R., Charousset, D., Schmidt, T.C., Wählisch, M.: Programming actors for the internet of things. Ercim News **101**, 25–26 (2015). http://ercim-news.ercim.eu/en101/special/programming-actors-for-the-internet-of-things
23. Hiesgen, R., Nawrocki, M., King, A., Dainotti, A., Schmidt, T.C., Wählisch, M.: Spoki: unveiling a new wave of scanners through a reactive network telescope. In: Proceedings of 31st USENIX Security Symposium, pp. 431–448. USENIX Association, Berkeley (2022). https://www.usenix.org/system/files/sec22-hiesgen.pdf
24. Hiesgen, R., Nawrocki, M., Schmidt, T.C., Wählisch, M.: The race to the vulnerable: measuring the log4j shell incident. In: Proceedings of Network Traffic Measurement and Analysis Conference (TMA), pp. 1–9. IFIP, Laxenburg (2022). https://tma.ifip.org/2022/wp-content/uploads/sites/11/2022/06/tma2022-paper40.pdf
25. Hiesgen, R., Nawrocki, M., Schmidt, T.C., Wählisch, M.: The Log4j incident: a comprehensive measurement study of a critical vulnerability. IEEE Trans. Netw. Serv. Manag. (TNSM) **21**(6), 5921–5934 (2024). https://doi.org/10.1109/TNSM.2024.3440188
26. Iyengar, J., Thomson, M.: QUIC: A UDP-Based Multiplexed and Secure Transport. RFC 9000, IETF (2021). https://doi.org/10.17487/RFC9000. https://doi.org/10.17487/RFC9000
27. Kocher, P., et al.: Spectre attacks: exploiting speculative execution. Commun. ACM **63**(7), 93–101 (2020)
28. Luckie, M.: Scamper. website. https://www.caida.org/catalog/software/scamper/
29. Matthew Prince (Cloudflare): (2022). https://twitter.com/eastdakota/status/1469800951351427073

30. Otto, J., Hiesgen, R., Charousset, D., Schmidt, T.C.: Revisiting the network stack in CAF. In: Proceedings of the 11th ACM SIGPLAN Conference on Systems, Programming, and Applications (SPLASH '20), Workshop AGERE!, pp. 1–9. ACM, New York (2020). https://doi.org/10.1145/3427760.3428340
31. Paxson, V.: Bro: a system for detecting network intruders in real-time. Comput. Netw. **31**(23–24), 2435–2463 (1999)
32. Plyukhin, D., Agha, G.: A scalable algorithm for decentralized actor termination detection. Log. Methods Comput. Sci. **18**(1) (2022). https://doi.org/10.46298/lmcs-18(1:39)2022
33. ReactiveX: An API for asynchronous programming with observable streams. website. https://reactivex.io
34. Rinaldi, L., Torquati, M., Mencagli, G., Danelutto, M., Menga, T.: Accelerating actor-based applications with parallel patterns. In: 27th Euromicro International Conference on Parallel, Distributed and Network-Based Processing, pp. 140–147 (2019)
35. Shelby, Z., Hartke, K., Bormann, C.: The Constrained Application Protocol (CoAP). RFC 7252, IETF (2014). https://doi.org/10.17487/RFC7252. https://doi.org/10.17487/RFC7252
36. The MITRE Corporation: CVE-2014-0160 (2022). https://cve.mitre.org/cgi-bin/cvename.cgi?name=cve-2014-0160
37. Torquati, M., Menga, T., Matteis, T.D., Sensi, D.D., Mencagli, G.: Reducing message latency and CPU utilization in the CAF actor framework. In: 26th Euromicro International Conference on Parallel, Distributed and Network-Based Processing, PDP 2018, pp. 145–153. IEEE Computer Society, Washington (2018)
38. Triebe, M., Charousset, D., Hiesgen, R., Schmidt, T.C.: Das C++ Actor Framework im Leistungsvergleich. In: Report 302, 8. GI/ITG Workshop Leistungs-, Zuverlässigkeits- und Verlässlichkeitsbewertung von Kommunikationsnetzen und verteilten Systemen (MMBnet15), pp. 83–89. Universität Hamburg, Dept. Informatik, Hamburg (2015)
39. Vallentin, M., Paxson, V., Sommer, R.: VAST: a unified platform for interactive network forensics. In: Proceedings of the USENIX Symposium on Networked Systems Design and Implementation (NSDI) (2016)
40. Wölke, S., Hiesgen, R., Charousset, D., Schmidt, T.C.: Locality-guided scheduling in CAF. In: Proceedings of the 8th ACM SIGPLAN Conference on Systems, Programming, and Applications (SPLASH '17), Workshop AGERE!, pp. 11–20. ACM, New York (2017)

Decoupling Isolation and Concurrency: An Actor-Centric View of Behaviour-Oriented Concurrency

Luke Cheeseman[1](✉), Elias Castegren[1], Sophia Drossopoulou[2], Tobias Wrigstad[1], Sylvan Clebsch[3], and Matthew Parkinson[4]

[1] Uppsala University, Uppsala, Sweden
{luke.cheeseman,elias.castegren,tobias.wrigstad}@it.uu.se
[2] Imperial College, London, UK
s.drossopoulou@imperial.ac.uk
[3] Azure Research, Austin, USA
sylvan.clebsch@microsoft.com
[4] Azure Research, Cambridge, UK
mattpark@microsoft.com

Abstract. The actor model is an elegant concurrency model with the actor as the central concept. An actor encapsulates a thread of control and isolated state, communicating with other actors exclusively via message passing. This makes reasoning about the behaviour of a single actor simple, but, due to the coupled units of isolation and concurrency, performing atomic operations involving multiple actors becomes harder. Recent work on behaviour-oriented concurrency mitigates this by explicitly decoupling isolation and concurrency.

In this paper we explore the connections between the actor model and behaviour-oriented concurrency and the effects of (de)coupling the units of isolation and concurrency. We derive the semantics of behaviour-oriented concurrency by starting from a semantics of the actor model and gradually decoupling isolation and concurrency. We show that behaviour-oriented concurrency generalises the actor model by proving a simulation theorem: a program in the actor model has a corresponding program using behaviour-oriented concurrency.

1 Introduction

The actor paradigm was introduced in 1973 by Carl Hewitt et al. [16], formalised by Irene Greif [13] in 1975, and again by Gul Agha [1] in 1986 as a computational model for handling concurrency in distributed systems. It has also been used as an elegant model for single-node concurrency. The actor is the fundamental unit of computation in the paradigm; an actor encapsulates a single-threaded control loop, isolated state, and an interface through which other actors can communicate via asynchronous message passing. The goal of the paradigm is to simplify the many complexities of concurrent programming into one concept: sending messages to actors. This simplification provides structure to concurrent code, improving the programmer's ability to understand and reason about their program.

We can view the actor paradigm as marrying together an object with concurrency in object-oriented programming [2]. Typically in object-oriented programming, message-passing (or "calling a method"), is handled synchronously in the calling thread. If we were to introduce multiple threads calling methods on an object, then we must expect, and prevent, data-races. Instead, in the actor paradigm, the actor uses its own thread to process the messages one at a time, thus freeing the programmer the concerns of synchronisation, data-races, *etc.*.

This design intentionally creates a tight coupling between the *unit of isolation* and the *unit of concurrency*. In the actor context the unit of isolation is the fragment of the program state reachable only by a single actor, and the unit of concurrency is the single-thread control loop of an actor. This design entails that an actor's thread can only access that actor's state and conversely that an actor's state can only be accessed by that actor's thread. This is the key to the elegance and simplicity of the model: computation internal to an actor permits sequential reasoning.

Recent work on *behaviour-oriented concurrency* (BoC) demonstrates how tightly coupling isolation and concurrency can create tensions between atomicity and a program's inherent concurrency [9]. It introduces an alternative concurrency paradigm to address these challenges in a non-distributed setting. BoC draws inspiration from the actor model, but differentiates itself by decoupling the units of isolation and concurrency, relieving some of the tensions in program design. In this paper we demonstrate this inspiration by reimagining the actor model paradigm, decoupling isolation and concurrency, to arrive at BoC.

We make the following contributions:

- We highlight the inherent tensions of the actor model that comes from coupling concurrency and isolation (Sect. 2),
- We show how these tensions can be relieved by behaviour-oriented concurrency (Sect. 3),
- We derive the formal semantics of behaviour-oriented concurrency by starting from a formal actor semantics and modifying it until we arrive at behaviour-oriented concurrency (Sect. 4),
- We prove that the semantics for behaviour-oriented concurrency can simulate the actor semantics we started from (Sect. 5).

After the main contributions we discuss our results in Sect. 6 and conclude in Sect. 7.

2 Actors and the Tensions of Coupling Concurrency and Isolation

Coupling the units of concurrency and isolation leads to tension between the ability to reason atomically about updates to state, and the degree of concurrency inherent in a program.

We can illustrate this tension in designing a solution to the classic bank transfer example. Take two bank accounts from which we can withdraw money, and to which we can deposit money. We want to be able to *atomically* transfer

```
1   actor Account
2     var balance: U64
3     var frozen: Bool = false
4
5     new open(balance': U64) =>
6       balance = balance'
7
8     be withdraw(amount: U64) =>
9       if ((not frozen) and (balance >= amount)) then
10        balance = (balance - amount)
11      end
12
13    be deposit(amount: U64) =>
14      if (not frozen) then
15        balance = (balance + amount)
16      end
```

Listing 2.1. A naive implementation of accounts using actors.

money from one account to another account. This means it should be not be possible for another operation involving either account to take place during the transfer, nor should we be able to lose money in the system.

Listing 2.1 shows a naive implementation (written in Pony [19]) where each bank account is modelled as an actor. Two actors can concurrently operate on their accounts, but we are unable to express atomic transfer of money between accounts in a straightforward manner. Note that both withdraw and deposit can fail, either due to accounts being frozen or due to there not being enough funds for a withdrawal. If we instead modelled a bank as an actor encapsulating all of its accounts, we get atomic transfer of money straightforwardly, but operations on unrelated accounts will be serialised.

If we pursue the goal of highly concurrent programs, modelling each account as an actor, then we will need to build a protocol to ensure transfers can complete atomically. Two-phase commit is an often relied upon protocol to achieve atomic transfer between two actors; this involves a third actor to coordinate the transfer. Figure 1 shows two-phase commit with a coordinator c synchronising accounts s and r (acks may be omitted when message failure cannot occur).

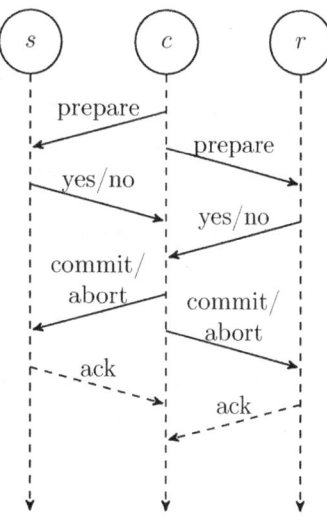

Fig. 1. Two-phase commit

```pony
 1  actor Coordinator
 2    var from: Account
 3    var to: Account
 4    var amt: U64
 5    var aborted: Bool = false
 6    var from_ok: Bool = false
 7    var to_ok: Bool = false
 8
 9    new create(from': Account,
10                to': Account,
11                amt': U64) =>
12      from = from'
13      to = to'
14      amt = amt'
15      from.prep_withdraw(amt, this)
16      to.prep_deposit(this)
17
18    be confirm_withdraw() =>
19      if aborted then
20        from.abort_transaction()
21        return
22      end
23      from_ok = true
24      if to_ok then
25        from.commit_withdraw(amt)
26        to.commit_deposit(amt)
27      end
28
29    // deposit logic analogous
30
31    be abort() =>
32      aborted = true
33      if to_ok then
34        to.abort_transaction()
35      elseif from_ok then
36        from.abort_transaction()
37      end
38
39    ...
40
41  fun transfer(s: Account, r: Account, amt: U64) =>
42    Coordinator(s, r, amt)

43  actor Account
44    var balance: U64
45    var frozen: Bool = false
46    var in_transaction: Bool = false
47
48    new open(balance': U64) =>
49      balance = balance'
50
51    be abort_transaction() =>
52      in_transaction = false
53
54    be prep_withdraw(amt: U64,
55                      c: Coordinator) =>
56      if (not in_transaction) and
57         (not frozen) and
58         (balance >= amt) then
59        in_transaction = true
60        c.confirm_withdraw()
61      else
62        c.abort()
63      end
64
65    be commit_withdraw(amt: U64) =>
66      balance = (balance - amt)
67      in_transaction = false
68
69    be prep_deposit(c: Coordinator) =>
70      if (not in_transaction) and
71         (not frozen) then
72        in_transaction = true
73        c.confirm_deposit()
74      else
75        c.abort()
76      end
77
78    be commit_deposit(amt: U64) =>
79      balance = (balance + amt)
80      in_transaction = false
```

Listing 2.2. Two-phase commit for actors. Logic related to the problem at hand (rather than synchronisation) highlighted in blue.

Listing 2.2 shows a Pony program implementing atomic transfers between accounts using two-phase commit. Code that is *not* related to synchronisation (the same as in Listing 2.1) is highlighted in blue. For a transfer scenario involving a Coordinator c, coordinating the transfer of the amount a, from Account s to Account r the two-phase commit proceeds as follows:

1. c receives a request to transfer a funds from s to r (constructor on Line 9).
2. c tells s and r to reserve/accept a funds (Line 15). If they confirm, s and r will ignore further messages (Lines 59 and 72) until released by c.
3. s and r either confirms the transfer to c (Lines 60 and 73) or reports back that they cannot fulfill the request.
4. If both s and r confirms, c sends a commit message to s and r causing them to perform their operations (Line 25). If one confirms and the other aborts, c sends the confirming actor a message to abort (Lines 20 and 31).
5. After receiving confirm messages s and r can both continue to process messages (Lines 67 and 80).

Compare this with the bank-as-actor implementation:

1. The bank c receives a request to transfer a funds from s to r. The bank verifies that both accounts exist and can withdraw and deposit a funds and performs the corresponding withdrawal and deposit actions.

The coupling of the unit of isolation and concurrency brings a complexity to both the programmer and the program when building these atomic operations.

In conclusion: when problem decomposition perfectly fits the actor model, actor solutions are simple and elegant. However, when the fit is imperfect, the coupling of unit of concurrency to unit of isolation that permits sequential reasoning causes problems: fine-grained actors require bespoke complex protocol implementations to reason about state spread across several actors; coarse-grained actors unnecessarily serialise unrelated computation.

3   Behaviour-Oriented Concurrency

Behaviour-oriented concurrency has the same goal as actors: to simplify the complexities of concurrent programming. However, instead of abstracting concurrency to sending messages to actors, BoC abstracts concurrency into spawning tasks that operate over explicitly declared state. BoC, like actors, brings structure to concurrency.

To achieve this goal, BoC reimagines the actor paradigm. We take a step back from actors and coupling the units of isolation and concurrency into an actor, and intentionally decouple them into two distinct concepts. The unit of isolation is the concurrent owner, or *cown* (pronounced 'cone'), a single entry point into an isolated fragment of the program state. The unit of concurrency is the *behaviour*, an asynchronous unit of work that explicitly lists its required cowns. Behaviours execute asynchronously with exclusive access to their required cowns [9].

In this section we will use the C++ BoC runtime API to discuss the concepts of BoC [25]. A cown restricts access to an isolated part of shared state. In Listing 3.1, we define an Account struct, Lines 1 to 4, and construct an Account protected by a newly created cown, Line 8. The account is inaccessible through the cown until the cown is acquired by a behaviour. This means that the attempted access to the balance on Line 11 is a program error.

```
struct Account {
  uint64_t balance = 0;
  bool frozen = false;
};

int main() {
  cown<Account> acc =
    make_cown<Account>();

  // invalid direct access
  acc.balance += 10;
}
```

Listing 3.1. Creating cowns to protect data

The only way to gain access to the contents of the account, and indeed any cown, is to *spawn* a behaviour that requires it. Spawning a behaviour is achieved using the **when** construct which takes the cowns to acquire, between regular braces (...), and a lambda function to apply when the cowns are available. The behaviour will run in the future, asynchronously, when the cowns are not in use by any other behaviour. Behaviours cannot acquire more cowns or release access to cowns throughout their execution and cowns are implicitly released at the end of a behaviour's execution.

In Listing 3.2 we define a function transfer which takes two Account wrapped in cown and an amount to transfer between the accounts. We first spawn a behaviour, Lines 4 to 6, which requires the source account s. [=] instructs C++ to capture amount by value. The arguments of the lambda must match up with the arguments of the **when**, *i.e.*, each cown<T> must be matched with an acquired<T>. When the cown is

```
void transfer(cown<Account> s,
  cown<Account> r, uint64_t amount) {

  when(s)<<[=](acquired<Account> s){
    s.balance -= amount
  };

  when(r)<<[=](acquired<Account> r){
    r.balance += amount
  };
}
```

Listing 3.2. Spawning behaviours

available the behaviour may run and will reduce the balance of the account. Similarly, we spawn a second behaviour, Lines 8 to 10, which increases the balance of the destination account r. Note that behaviours run asynchronously: the transfer function will complete directly, regardless of when the behaviours run.

A defining feature of BoC, with respect to actors, is that behaviours can require and use multiple cowns. Such behaviours will only run when none of the required cowns are in use by other behaviours. When such a behaviour does run, it will have access to the contents of *all* cowns, allowing us to construct more complicated behaviours that depend on and affect the state of multiple cowns. Listing 3.3 demonstrates this key feature of BoC in the context of the bank transfer. We define a behaviour that requires both cowns s and r, the behaviour checks if both accounts are able to perform the transaction and if so completes it. This transfer is an atomic operation by construction of the BoC paradigm.

BoC allows us to create ad-hoc atomic operations that operate over the state of multiple cowns. The type of the data which the cown protects does not have to provide an interface which guarantees a certain degree of atomicity (as per behaviours in actors). Moreover, if one of the cowns is currently in use elsewhere the running of the behaviour is simply delayed without having to resort to protocols like two-phase commit with retries.

3.1 Deadlock Freedom and Causality

It is important to note that spawning is a synchronous action performed by transfer, but starting and running the behaviours are asynchronous actions performed by the runtime. Thus, assuming the two accounts do not alias, the increase and decrease behaviours in Listing 3.2 can execute in parallel, or in either order. To further stress the importance of this point, in Listing 3.4 the nested behaviour which increases the balance of r, Lines 2 to 4, does *not* have access to the account s.

```
1  when(s)<<[=](acquired<Account> s){
2    when(r)<<[=](acquired<Account> r){
3      r.balance += amount
4    };
5    s.balance -= amount
6  }
7
8  when(r)<<[=](acquired<Account> r){
9    when(s)<<[=](acquired<Account> s){
10     s.balance += amount
11   };
12   r.balance -= amount
13 };
```

Listing 3.4. Deadlock-free behaviours

The outer behaviour spawns the inner behaviour synchronously and continues executing the rest of its behaviour. This means that the operation which reduces the balance of s, Line 5, and the operation which increases the balance of r, Line 3, may be executing in parallel. Moreover, by construction, BoC is *deadlock-free*. In Listing 3.4 we construct two pairs of behaviours, where the cowns required for the inner and outer behaviours are swapped. If **when** is (erroneously) viewed as a synchronous lock-guard, then one could reasonably expect a potential deadlock, however a deadlock is not possible here.

```
1  void transfer(cown<Account> s, cown<Account> r, uint64_t amount) {
2    when(s, r)<<[=](acquired<Account> s, acquired<Account> r) {
3      if (s.balance >= amount && !s.frozen && !r.frozen) {
4        s.balance -= amount
5        r.balance += amount
6      }
7    };
8  }
```

Listing 3.3. Behaviours with multiple cowns

Finally, BoC guarantees causal ordering between behaviours, which we refer to as a *happens before* order. A behaviour b happens before another behaviour b' iff b and b' require overlapping sets of cowns, and b is spawned before b' in program order. In Listing 3.5, b1 and b2 do not require the same cowns and thus can execute in parallel, whereas both b1 and b2 overlap with the cowns required by b3 and thus b3 will only execute after both b1 and b2. By similar reasoning, b4 can only execute after b3 (and thus also after b1). The causal ordering offered by BoC lets programmers reason about orderings also of nested behaviours. There are interesting design patterns that have been explored in other literature on BoC [8,9]. We do not explore causal ordering further in this paper.

3.2 Behaviour-Oriented Concurrency is Concurrent Procedural Programming

Just as actor programs can be viewed as marrying objects with concurrency in object-oriented programming, BoC can be viewed as marrying procedures with concurrency. A BoC program is constructed as a collection of behaviours which define the cowns they require and the operations that they will perform on these cowns; the programmer only needs to define these operations and does not have to consider the complexities of synchronisation, deadlocks and so on.

Finally, BoC can also be used to simulate actor programs. Actor programs can be translated into BoC programs by using one cown per actor and creating behaviours which operate over this isolated actor state. The program sketched in Listings 3.1 and 3.2 behaves exactly like the actor program in Listing 2.1. In the next two sections we show that this simulation relation also holds formally.

4 From Actors to Behaviour-Oriented Concurrency

In this section we explain behaviour-oriented concurrency formally in terms of actors. We do so by starting from a high-level actor semantics, gradually changing it until we have a formal semantics of BoC that is equivalent to previous work [9]. In Sect. 5 we prove that for each change the updated semantics simulates the previous semantics, with the corollary that BoC can simulate the actor model.

The changes made to the actor semantics do not reflect how BoC was actually developed, but each change represents an important insight into its design. Our goal is to highlight the similarities and differences between the actor model and BoC and show how BoC generalises the actor model.

```
1  when(s)<<[=](acquired<Account> s){ /* b1 */ };
2  when(r)<<[=](acquired<Account> r){ /* b2 */ };
3  when(s, r)<<[=](acquired<Account> s, acquired<Account> r){/* b3 */};
4  when(s)<<[=](acquired<Account> s){ /* b4 */ };
```

Listing 3.5. Partially-ordered behaviours

The rest of this section is structured as follows. Section 4.1 presents the semantics of traditional actors. Section 4.2 moves all messages into a single global data structure, making scheduling a centralised concern instead of a concern spread across all actors. Section 4.3 makes actors ephemeral, releasing the resources of an actor whenever it is idle. Section 4.4 introduces the ability for messages to have multiple receivers, producing a semantics that is equivalent to BoC. Finally, Sect. 4.5 discusses how to formalise isolated actor states.

4.1 Traditional Actors, Formally

The focus in our formal development is on actors and BoC as *concurrency models* that go on top of some otherwise sequential language. We are not interested in the details of the underlying language, so we keep it abstract. The underlying language is the same for all the actor semantics and will only change slightly for BoC (cf. Section 4.4).

We use E as the state of a sequential process, which could be as simple as an expression or more complex such as a stack with local variables and other state. We use h as a global heap that the underlying language operates over. We assume the existence of a relation $\iota \vdash E, h \hookrightarrow E', h'$ representing a small-step evaluation of some sequential process E (to E'), operating on the heap h (resulting in h'). The relation also includes the identifier ι of the running actor, for example to allow the semantics of the underlying language to restrict which data in the heap h can be accessed by the process, as exemplified in Sect. 4.5.

In order to interact with the concurrency model, the underlying language can also take two kinds of effect-producing steps. The relation $\iota \vdash E, h \hookrightarrow_{\text{create } \iota'} E', h'$ represents the effect of creating an actor with identifier ι'. The step $\iota \vdash E, h \hookrightarrow_{\text{send } \iota' \ E''} E', h'$ represents sending a message containing E'' to an actor with identifier ι'.

Figure 2 shows the syntax and semantics of the actor model. An actor a consists of its identifier ι, the state of its currently executing behaviour e, and its message queue q. The e can be a sequential process E, or ϵ if the actor is idle. Each message in the message queue q is represented by another E. A configuration of the actor model consists of its set of actors A and the global heap h. Each rule selects a single actor from A, using ⊎ to mean that there is no other actor with the same identifier in A:

Definition 1. *Disjoint union by address.*

$$A \uplus (\iota, e, q) \triangleq \begin{cases} A \cup (\iota, e, q) & \text{if } \iota \notin \{\iota' \mid (\iota', e', q') \in A\} \\ \textit{undefined} & \textit{otherwise} \end{cases}$$

There are five rules that can step an actor. In rule STEP, an actor ι executes a single step without producing any effect (other than the updated heap). In rule END, an actor turns idle when its current behaviour is *finished*, a predicate that holds when no further sequential steps are possible. In rule RECV, an idle actor proceeds by processing the next message in its queue. In rule CREATE, an actor produces the create effect, which results in a new idle actor with an empty queue being added to the set of actors (note that the definition of ⊎ ensures that the identifier ι' is not in A). Finally, in rule SEND, an actor produces the send effect, which results in the specified message being added to the queue of the receiver (the message is appended through a slight abuse of notation). The second premise of the rule is there to handle self sends: if $\iota = \iota'$ then $A = A'$ and the message is added to the message queue of ι, otherwise ι is one of the actors in A'.

We argue that this semantics captures the essence of actors as a concurrency model, with just enough detail about the underlying language to allow interaction (through the create and send effects). The isolated state of an actor is represented by its identifier ι, and this state is coupled with the actor as a unit of concurrency: an actor with identifier ι will only ever take steps $\iota \vdash E, h \hookrightarrow E', h'$, and sending a message to this actor is the only way to make such a step happen. Some features of actor systems, such as selective receives and messages being delivered out-of-order, are not captured explicitly by our semantics but can be modelled in the underlying language by adding information in the local state E or global state h.

$$a ::= (\iota, e, q) \quad q ::= E :: q \mid \epsilon$$
$$e ::= E \mid \epsilon \quad A \in \mathcal{P}(a)$$

$$\frac{\iota \vdash E, h \hookrightarrow E', h'}{A \uplus (\iota, E, q), h \rightsquigarrow_a A \uplus (\iota, E', q), h'} \text{ STEP} \quad \frac{\textit{finished}(E)}{A \uplus (\iota, E, q), h \rightsquigarrow_a A \uplus (\iota, \epsilon, q), h} \text{ END}$$

$$\frac{}{A \uplus (\iota, \epsilon, E :: q), h \rightsquigarrow_a A \uplus (\iota, E, q), h} \text{ RECV}$$

$$\frac{\iota \vdash E, h \hookrightarrow_{\text{create } \iota'} E', h'}{A \uplus (\iota, E, q), h \rightsquigarrow_a A \uplus (\iota, E', q) \uplus (\iota', \epsilon, \epsilon), h'} \text{ CREATE}$$

$$\frac{\iota \vdash E, h \hookrightarrow_{\text{send } \iota' E''} E', h' \quad A \uplus (\iota, E', q) = A' \uplus (\iota', e, q')}{A \uplus (\iota, E, q), h \rightsquigarrow_a A' \uplus (\iota', e, q' :: E''), h'} \text{ SEND}$$

Fig. 2. Syntax and high-level semantics of traditional actors

4.2 Processes with a Shared Message Queue

Our main motivation for BoC is decoupling the units of isolation and concurrency. In order to synchronise multiple concurrent entities, we need to have a centralised view of all pending work in the system. This is hard when each actor has their own message queue. The first change we make to our actor semantics is therefore to merge all queues into a single global one. Since we will be deviating

$$a^M ::= (\iota, e) \qquad M ::= (\iota, E) :: M \mid \epsilon$$
$$e ::= E \mid \epsilon \qquad A^M \in \mathcal{P}(a^M)$$

$$\dfrac{\iota \vdash E, h \hookrightarrow E', h'}{A \uplus (\iota, E), M, h \leadsto_m A \uplus (\iota, E'), M, h'} \text{ STEP} \qquad \dfrac{\textit{finished}(E)}{A \uplus (\iota, E), M, h \leadsto_m A \uplus (\iota, \epsilon), M, h} \text{ END}$$

$$\dfrac{(\iota, \_) \notin M_1}{A \uplus (\iota, \epsilon), M_1 :: (\iota, E) :: M_2, h \leadsto_m A \uplus (\iota, E), M_1 :: M_2, h} \text{ RECV}$$

$$\dfrac{\iota \vdash E, h \hookrightarrow_{\text{create } \iota'} E', h'}{A \uplus (\iota, E), M, h \leadsto_m A \uplus (\iota, E') \uplus (\iota', \epsilon), M, h'} \text{ CREATE}$$

$$\dfrac{\iota \vdash E, h \hookrightarrow_{\text{send } \iota' \ E''} E', h'}{A \uplus (\iota, E), M, h \leadsto_m A \uplus (\iota, E'), M :: (\iota', E''), h'} \text{ SEND}$$

Fig. 3. The syntax and semantics of actors with a centralised message queue. The actor set A^M is written as A to reduce clutter.

from the previous definition of an actor, we will be using the term *process* in place of actor going forward. Note that we are using processes to implement an actor system in Sects. 4.2 and 4.3.

Figure 3 shows the syntax and semantics after this modification. Processes, written as A^M to distinguish them from actors in the previous semantics, now only contain an identifier and a currently running expression. The configuration is extended to contain a list M of messages in flight, each message containing the identifier of the receiving process and a sequential process E as before.

The rules STEP, END, and CREATE are the same as before as they do not concern sending or receiving messages. In rule RECV an idle process starts processing *its own* next message in the global queue (we slightly abuse notation to concatenate M_1 and M_2). In rule SEND a process produces the send effect, which results in a message addressed to specified process being appended to the global message queue.

4.3 Ephemeral Processes

Looking at the processes in Fig. 3, there is no persistent state in a process after it has finished its running behaviour[1]. This is in line with our end goal of decoupling the units of isolation and concurrency: once a behaviour over some isolated state is done we want to allow other behaviours to run over that same and possibly other pieces of isolated state. Thus we want to "release" isolated state when it is not being accessed. We model this in our semantics by making processes

---

[1] A process may have persistent state in h, but this is not stored in the process itself.

$$\frac{\iota \vdash E, h \hookrightarrow E', h'}{A \uplus (\iota, E), M, h \leadsto_e A \uplus (\iota, E'), M, h'} \text{ Step} \quad \frac{\textit{finished}(E)}{A \uplus (\iota, E), M, h \leadsto_e A, M, h} \text{ End}$$

$$\frac{(\iota, \_) \notin A \cup M_1}{A, M_1 :: (\iota, E) :: M_2, h \leadsto_e A \uplus (\iota, E), M_1 :: M_2, h} \text{ Start}$$

$$\frac{\iota \vdash E, h \hookrightarrow_{\text{create } \iota'} E', h'}{A \uplus (\iota, E), M, h \leadsto_e A \uplus (\iota, E'), M, h'} \text{ Create}$$

$$\frac{\iota \vdash E, h \hookrightarrow_{\text{send } \iota' \ E''} E', h'}{A \uplus (\iota, E), M, h \leadsto_e A \uplus (\iota, E'), M :: (\iota', E''), h'} \text{ Send}$$

Fig. 4. Semantics of ephemeral processes

ephemeral. This means that processes are removed as soon as they finish a behaviour and are started up again whenever a new message needs processing.

Figure 4 shows the semantics of ephemeral processes (the syntax is the same as in the previous section). Rules STEP and SEND are identical to the previous semantics. In rule END a process is removed when its behaviour is *finished* (instead of making it idle as previously). In rule START, which corresponds the previous rule RECV, a message is selected with a recipient that is not running in A and that does not have another message earlier in the queue. A process is started up to run that message. Finally, we ponder what it means to create a process when processes are ephemeral. Since we start processes when needed and remove them as soon as they are done, creating a process is no longer meaningful. In rule CREATE, the create effect is simply ignored.

4.4 Behaviour-Oriented Concurrency, Formally

We are now ready to define the semantics of behaviour-oriented concurrency. The main difference to the previous semantics is that messages can now have multiple receivers. This means that we need to start by changing our underlying language so that we can spawn behaviours with more than one recipient. While we are at it, we will also remove the create effect since the last semantics made it a no-op.

We use E^b as the state of a sequential process of our new underlying language and assume that it operates over some global heap h^b. We assume the existence of two stepping relations, one that touches the heap $\bar{\iota} \vdash E^b, h^b \hookrightarrow E_2^b, h_2^b$ (we use $\bar{\iota}$ for a set of zero or more identifiers) and one that produces an effect spawning a behaviour with multiple receivers $\bar{\iota} \vdash E^b, h^b \hookrightarrow_{\text{spawn } \bar{\iota'} \ E_3^b} E_2^b, h_2^b$. We use the same kind of identifiers ι as for the actor semantics to highlight their connection, even though there is no longer a concept of an actor. Here we think of ι as the identifier of some isolated resource.

$$b ::= (\bar{\iota}, E^b)$$
$$P ::= b :: P \mid \epsilon$$
$$R \in \mathcal{P}(b)$$

$$\frac{\bar{\iota} \vdash E, h \hookrightarrow E', h'}{R \uplus (\bar{\iota}, E), P, h \rightsquigarrow_b R \uplus (\bar{\iota}, E'), P, h'} \text{ STEP} \qquad \frac{\textit{finished}(E)}{R \uplus (\bar{\iota}, E), P, h \rightsquigarrow_b R, P, h} \text{ END}$$

$$\frac{\{\iota \mid (\iota, \_) \in R \cup P_1\} \cap \bar{\iota} = \emptyset}{R, P_1 :: (\bar{\iota}, E) :: P_2, h \rightsquigarrow_b R \uplus (\bar{\iota}, E), P_1 :: P_2, h} \text{ START}$$

$$\frac{\bar{\iota} \vdash E, h \hookrightarrow_{\text{spawn } \bar{\iota}', E''} E', h'}{R \uplus (\bar{\iota}, E), P, h \rightsquigarrow_b R \uplus (\bar{\iota}, E'), P :: (\bar{\iota}', E''), h'} \text{ SPAWN}$$

Fig. 5. Syntax and semantics of behaviour-oriented concurrency. We write E and h instead of E^b and h^b to avoid clutter.

Figure 5 shows the syntax and semantics of behaviour-oriented concurrency. Behaviours b consist of a set of resource identifiers $\bar{\iota}$ and a currently running sequential process E^b. There is a global list of pending behaviours P as well as a set of currently running behaviours R. We use a similar version of the disjoint union from before, but extended to handle multiple identifiers:

Definition 2. *Disjoint union by held resources.*

$$R \uplus (\bar{\iota}, E) \triangleq \begin{cases} R \cup (\bar{\iota}, E) & \text{if } \bar{\iota} \cap \{\iota \mid \iota \in \bar{\iota} \wedge (\bar{\iota}, E) \in R\} = \emptyset \\ \text{undefined} & \text{otherwise} \end{cases}$$

The rules are very similar to the ephemeral processes except that each running behaviour is associated with multiple identifiers $\bar{\iota}$. In the rule START a pending behaviour starts running, assuming none of its required resources are either currently running (in R) or have been scheduled earlier (in P_1). Note that this is analogous to a message receive in the ephemeral process model, but with multiple receivers. In the rule SPAWN a new behaviour is spawned and added to the list of pending behaviours. Note again that this is analogous to a message send in the ephemeral process model, but with multiple receivers.

Because each behaviour can now synchronise over any number of resources, this concurrency model can express concurrent dependencies that are not easily expressible in the actor model. However, if we limit ourselves to always requiring exactly one resource we get a concurrency model that simulates the actor model: each actor is represented by a singleton resource and each message is represented by a behaviour on that resource. We formalise this intuition in Sect. 5.

4.5 Formalising Isolated State

In all our semantics, the underlying language is kept abstract. This means that the concept of isolation is also kept abstract. While many actor systems achieve data-race freedom through isolation, it is not required for reasoning about actors as a concurrency model. In this section we give an example of how the underlying language of the actor semantics in Fig. 2 could be defined so that each actor operates on its own local heap. For simplicity, we still keep all other details about the underlying language abstract.

The actor semantics works on a global heap h. We instantiate this heap as $h \triangleq \overline{\iota \times H}$, a set of tuples containing an actor identifier ι and a *heaplet* H, which could for example map names to values. The intuition is that the tuple (ι, H) contains the isolated state of actor ι in the heaplet H. We assume the existence of a relation $E, H \hookrightarrow E', H'$ representing a small-step evaluation of a sequential process E in heaplet H. We use this relation to instantiate the previously assumed small-step evaluation used in the STEP rule (using $\uplus$ in a similar manner as before):

$$\frac{E, H \hookrightarrow E', H'}{\iota \vdash E, h \uplus (\iota, H) \hookrightarrow E', h \uplus (\iota, H')} \text{ EVAL}$$

This rule uses the ι to select the right heaplet H from the global heap h and evaluates only under that heaplet in a frame-rule-like fashion. The rule with the create effect $\iota \vdash E, h \hookrightarrow_{\text{create } \iota'} E', h'$ would extend h with a new empty heaplet associated with the new actor ι', meaning an actor would always be created together with its heaplet. The rule for sending messages does not need to be aware of heaplets.

Again, we note that our actor semantics does not *require* actors operating on isolated state, but it supports it as exemplified here. Section 6.2 brings up some existing actor systems that enforce isolated state.

5 Meta-theory: Simulation Theorems

In this section we prove a number of simulation theorems about the semantics in Sect. 4 with the final corollary that the semantics of behaviour-oriented concurrency in Fig. 5 simulates the actor semantics in Fig. 2.

5.1 Shared-Queue Processes

The actor semantics in Fig. 3 is equivalent to the semantics of shared-queue processes in Fig. 2. We could prove a bisimulation, but since our end goal is showing that BoC can simulate actors we will be stop at proving a simulation here as well. We define a similarity relation $\mathcal{R}_1$ which relates actors from A with processes in A^M and their global message queue M:

Definition 3. *Similarity of traditional actors and shared-queue processes.* A set of traditional actors A is similar to a set of processes A^M with a shared message queue M, written $\mathcal{R}_1(A, A^M, M)$, iff:

1. A has an actor (ι, e, q) for some q iff A^M has a process (ι, e),
2. for each message (ι, E) in M, there is some process (ι, e) in A^M,
3. for each actor (ι, e, q), filtering only the messages for ι from M yields q.

The first property states that dropping the local queues from the actors in A result in the same queue-less processes as in A^M. The second property states that every message in M has a valid address (the identifier of an existing process). The third property states that the local queue of each actor ι can be recreated by filtering only the messages addressed to ι in M.

We show that each step with the traditional actors corresponds to a step from a similar configuration in the semantics with the centralised queue and that the resulting configurations are also similar:

Theorem 1 (Processes with a shared queue simulate traditional actors).
If $\mathcal{R}_1(A, A^M, M)$ and $A, h \leadsto_a A_2, h_2$, then there exists A_2^M and M_2 such that $A^M, M, h \leadsto_m A_2^M, M_2, h_2$ and $\mathcal{R}_1(A_2, A_2^M, M_2)$.

The proof is by cases on the rule used to step A. The cases for STEP and END are trivial after using the first property of $\mathcal{R}_1$ to find the corresponding process in A^M. In the case for CREATE, in order to satisfy the third property of $\mathcal{R}_1$, we make use of the second property of $\mathcal{R}_1$ to ensure that there are no spurious messages for the newly created process already in M. In the case for RECV we use third property of $\mathcal{R}_1$ to get that the first message in the local message queue is also the first message addressed to that process in M. Removing that message from both queues preserves similarity. Finally, in the case for SEND we note that similarity is preserved when adding a message to the end of the global queue M and adding a message to the corresponding actor's local queue in A.

5.2 Ephemeral Processes

Because process creation is ignored, the ephemeral processes in Fig. 4 are not equivalent to the persistent processes in Fig. 3: creating the same process twice is not allowed with persistent processes. We can however prove that ephemeral processes simulate persistent processes by setting up a similarity relation $\mathcal{R}_2$ which relates processes in A^M with ephemeral processes (written as A^e):

Definition 4. *Similarity of shared-queue processes and ephemeral processes.*
A set of processes A^M with a shared queue is similar to a set of ephemeral processes A^e, written $\mathcal{R}_2(A^M, A^e)$, iff:

1. for all processes (ι, E) in A^M we have (ι, E) in A^e,
2. for all idle processes (ι, ϵ) in A^M we have no process with identifier ι in A^e.

The first property ensures that each running persistent process corresponds to a running ephemeral process. The second property ensures that any idle persistent process does not have an ephemeral process running another behaviour.

We show that when starting from similar configurations, each step in A^M has a corresponding step in A^e that preserves similarity.

Theorem 2 (Ephemeral processes simulate processes with a shared queue).
If $\mathcal{R}_2(A^M, A^e)$ and $A^M, M, h \leadsto_m A_2^M, M_2, h_2$, then there exists A_2^e such that $A^e, M, h \leadsto_e A_2^e, M_2, h_2$ and $\mathcal{R}_2(A_2^M, A_2^e)$.

The proof is by cases on which rule was used to step A^M. The cases for STEP and SEND are trivial. In the case for END the process turns idle which preserves similarity when its ephemeral counterpart is removed. Similarly, in the case for RECV we know that there is no ephemeral process in A^e corresponding to the idle process in A^M, so the premise of the START rule is satisfied and the use of $\uplus$ is well defined. In the case for CREATE, an idle process is created, which preserves similarity with the unextended A^e due to the second property of $\mathcal{R}_2$.

5.3 Behaviour-Oriented Concurrency

The similarity relation between ephemeral processes (Fig. 4) and behaviour-oriented concurrency (Fig. 5) is slightly more involved since we have different underlying languages. We start by assuming a similarity relation between the underlying languages. This can be thought of as the properties of an imagined compilation of E processes into E^b processes.

Parameter 1 *Similarity of underlying languages.* We assume the existence of a similarity relation between the two underlying languages, written $\mathcal{R}_{ul}(E, E^b)$, as well as a similarity relation between their respective heaps, written $\mathcal{R}_h(h, h^b)$. The similarity relations are assumed to have the following properties:

1. If $\mathcal{R}_{ul}(E, E^b)$, $\mathcal{R}_h(h, h^b)$ and $\iota \vdash E, h \hookrightarrow E', h'$ for some ι, then there exists E_2^b and h_2^b such that $\{\iota\} \vdash E^b, h^b \hookrightarrow E_2^b, h_2^b$, $\mathcal{R}_{ul}(E', E_2^b)$ and $\mathcal{R}_h(h', h_2^b)$,
2. If $\mathcal{R}_{ul}(E, E^b)$, $\mathcal{R}_h(h, h^b)$ and $\iota \vdash E, h \hookrightarrow_{\text{create } \iota'} E', h'$ for some ι', then there exists E_2^b and h_2^b such that $\{\iota\} \vdash E^b, h^b \hookrightarrow E_2^b, h_2^b$, $\mathcal{R}_{ul}(E', E_2^b)$ and $\mathcal{R}_h(h', h_2^b)$,
3. If $\mathcal{R}_{ul}(E, E^b)$, $\mathcal{R}_h(h, h^b)$ and $\iota \vdash E, h \hookrightarrow_{\text{send } \iota', E''} E', h'$ for some ι' and E'', then there exists E_2^b, E_3^b and h_2^b such that $\{\iota\} \vdash E^b, h^b \hookrightarrow_{\text{spawn } \{\iota'\}, E_3^b} E_2^b, h_2^b$, $\mathcal{R}_{ul}(E', E_2^b)$, $\mathcal{R}_h(h', h_2^b)$ and $\mathcal{R}_{ul}(E'', E_3^b)$,
4. If $\mathcal{R}_{ul}(E, E^b)$ and *finished*(E), then *finished*(E^b).

The first property states that evaluation in the context of an process ι corresponds to evaluation in the context of a singleton resource $\{\iota\}$. The second property states that producing a create effect corresponds to some non-effectful computation. The third property states that producing a send effect corresponds to producing a spawn effect with a singleton resource and a similar behaviour. The fourth property states that a sequential process is *finished* when its similar counterpart is.

The simulation relation between BoC and ephemeral processes can now be formulated as follows.

Definition 5. *Similarity of ephemeral processes and behaviour-oriented concurrency.* A set of ephemeral processes A^e with a shared queue M is similar to a set of running behaviours R and pending behaviours P, written $\mathcal{R}_3(A^e, M, R, P)$, iff:

1. for all processes (ι, E) in A^e we have $(\{\iota\}, E^b)$ in R, such that $\mathcal{R}_{ul}(E, E^b)$,
2. the number of processes in A^e is the same as the number of running behaviours in R,
3. for each message (ι, E) in M there is a pending behaviour $(\{\iota\}, E^b)$ at the corresponding index of P such that $\mathcal{R}_{ul}(E, E^b)$,
4. the number of pending messages in M is the same as the number of pending behaviours in P.

The first two properties state that there is a one-to-one correspondence between running processes and running behaviours. The second two properties state that there is a one-to-one correspondence between pending messages and pending behaviours. With this similarity relation we can now show a simulation between BoC and ephemeral processes.

Theorem 3 (Behaviour-oriented concurrency simulates ephemeral processes).
If $\mathcal{R}_3(A^e, M, R, P)$, $\mathcal{R}_h(h, h^b)$ and $A^e, M, h \leadsto_e A_2^e, M_2, h_2$, then there exists R_2, P_2 and h_2^b such that $R, P, h^b \leadsto_b R_2, P_2, h_2^b$ and $\mathcal{R}_3(A_2^e, M_2, R_2, P_2)$ and $\mathcal{R}_h(h_2, h_2^b)$.

The proof is by cases on which rule was used to step A^e. In each case we use the first two properties of $\mathcal{R}_3$ to ensure that each process has a corresponding behaviour. By the first property of Parameter 1 this behaviour can take a similarity-preserving step. In the case for STEP this is enough to show preservation of similarity. In the case for CREATE we additionally use the second property of Parameter 1 to get that we can take a corresponding step. In the case for END we use the fourth property of Parameter 1 to get that the corresponding behaviour is also finished.

In the case for START we use the second two properties of $\mathcal{R}_3$ to get that there is a corresponding pending behaviour. Because all behaviours have a singleton resource the premise is transferable to the set-disjointness formulation in BoC. Finally, in the case for SEND we use the third property of Parameter 1 to get that the send effect corresponds to a spawn effect of a similar behaviour with a singleton resource.

We can now formulate our final corollary which states that BoC simulates actors when restricted to singleton resource sets.

Theorem 4 (Behaviour-oriented concurrency simulates traditional actors).
If $\mathcal{R}_{ul}(E, E^b)$, $\mathcal{R}_h(h, h^b)$ and $\{(\iota, E, \epsilon)\}, h \leadsto_a^* A', h'$, then there exists R', P' and h_2^b such that $\{(\{\iota\}, E^b)\}, \emptyset, h^b \leadsto_b^* R', P', h_2^b$ and $\mathcal{R}_h(h', h_2^b)$.

Proof is by induction over the $\leadsto_a^*$ relation (the reflexive and transitive closure of $\leadsto_a$). With a single actor and an empty message queue it is trivial to show that we can use $\mathcal{R}_3$, $\mathcal{R}_2$ and $\mathcal{R}_1$ to connect the two semantics. Through the simulation theorems we have shown that similarity is preserved by each step, so each step in the traditional actor semantics has a corresponding step in BoC.

6 Discussion

Comparing the actor semantics in Fig. 2 and the semantics of behaviour-oriented concurrency in Fig. 5, the flexibility that comes with decoupling the units of isolation and concurrency is visible in how each behaviour in BoC can run with an arbitrary number of resources $\bar{\iota}$ in rule STEP instead of just the one. Any set of running behaviours can be thought of as a set of temporary actors whose local state consists of the union of the held resources. When a behaviour finishes in rule END, these resources are freed up to be used by in other configurations by other behaviours. This reconfigurability is a key difference between actors and BoC.

From a programming point of view, even though we have shown that behaviour-oriented concurrency can simulate actors, there is a philosophical difference in how an actor is a persistent entity with a stable identity. In behaviour-oriented concurrency, a behaviour is anonymous and has no memory after it finishes, except for what may be encoded into the resources it handles. This difference is analogous to the difference between the strong encapsulation of objects in object-oriented programming and the handling of dynamic data in procedural programming.

Going back to the bank transfer example from Sect. 2 we can reinforce the differences between the actor and BoC models by comparing their executions. We do so using two diagrams in Fig. 6: Fig. 6a for actors and Fig. 6b for BoC. These diagrams focus on the order of events rather than mirroring the syntactic representation in the semantics. However, the syntactic representations allow the orders presented in the diagrams.

Figure 6a demonstrates the execution of three actors, the sender s, receiver r, and coordinator c. The actors coordinate the transfer of money from s to r using two-phase commit. As per Fig. 2, each of the messages of an actor are totally ordered (with respect to each other) based on the order in which they were received. Once received, a message can be processed at some arbitrary time in the future, but not before earlier received messages,[2] nor whilst an actor is processing another message. Message sends are instantaneous. Note that there are several

---

[2] Recall that these semantics do not consider selective receives.

different possible executions but two-phase commit ensures the outcome is always the same.

Figure 6b demonstrates the execution of a BoC program with three cowns: the sender s, receiver r, and coordinator c. The program transfers money from s to r, with c initiating the transfer. As per Fig. 5, all behaviours are totally ordered by a spawn order (but partially ordered when we consider the behaviours' required resources). We represent a behaviour having access to multiple resources by presenting the times in which a cown is available or in use by a running behaviour (which implicitly acquires and releases the cowns at the start and end of its execution).

The two figures demonstrate that the actor behaviour executes using only the actors' states whilst BoC behaviours can access multiple states. Actor messages have a partial order whilst BoC programs have a total spawn order, and – in this example – that the actor program requires more messages to achieve the same outcome as the BoC program.

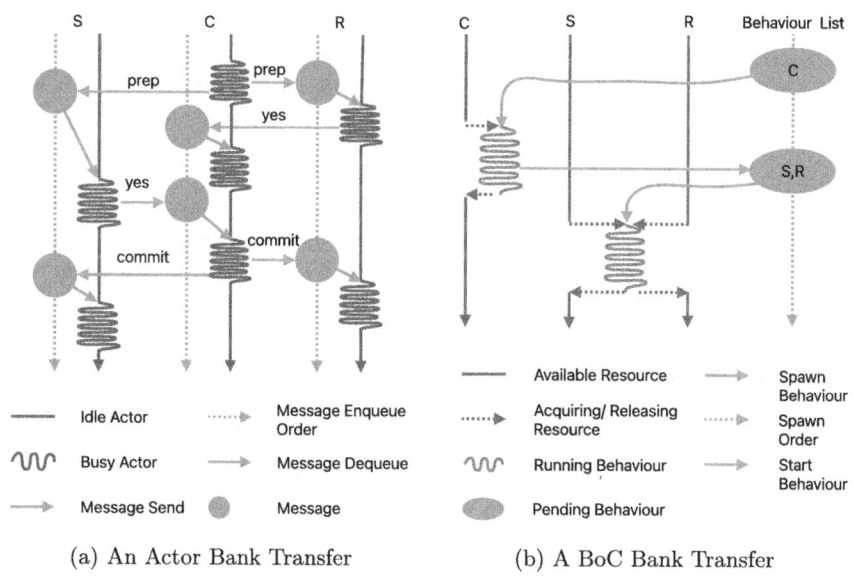

(a) An Actor Bank Transfer (b) A BoC Bank Transfer

Fig. 6. Comparing bank transfer executions

6.1 Working Around the Actor Model

Many actor systems have features that sidestep the pure actor model. Erlang ensures isolation by copying all data passed in messages but also features the Erlang Term Storage (ETS), a mutable map data type that can be shared between actors [3]. With the ETS, actors can communicate without using message passing. Operations on the ETS are synchronised, meaning that they are subject to race conditions but not data races. The same properties are inherited by languages building on the Erlang runtime, such as Elixir [12].

A survey on actor programs in Scala shows that programmers frequently mix the actor model with other concurrency constructs such as futures and threads, either due to limitations of the actor libraries used or limitations of the actor model itself [24]. There are extensions of actors in Scala to support transactional memory [15] and fork/join parallelism [17]. The Chocola language, an extension of Clojure, also allows mixing actors with futures and transactions [23]. The C++ Actor Framework (CAF) complements message passing with streams that can be used to send data between actors [5].

An approach to avoiding the performance problem of coarse-grained actors is permitting actors to encapsulate several threads of control. This either compromises simplicity by relying on means other than isolation to ensure that behaviours do not interfere, or compromises correctness if no such means is added. This complexity may spill into the implementation. Examples of actor systems to go down this route include Joelle [18] which relied on an effect system to reason about what behaviours were permitted to execute in parallel in a single actor and Encore [7]. The latter introduced the notion of a "hot object" whose behaviours were implemented using lock-free algorithms [6] and turned message sends into synchronous method calls under the hood. The latter controversial design stemmed from Encore's runtime system being based on Pony's, which scheduled actors rather than individual messages (which would be a more reasonable design when actors are parallel). Encore notably also needed to invent a separate memory management scheme [26] to handle concurrent accesses inside an actor. These examples are anecdotal evidence that trying to address performance issues in actor systems by making actors parallel comes with significant complexity costs.

6.2 Isolation in Practice

Ensuring isolation (or similar concepts) has been the focus of a number of research and engineering efforts. Here we explore a few of these efforts to convince the reader that the required isolation we have claimed thus far is a realistic expectation.

Behaviour-oriented concurrency was co-designed with a static type system called Reggio which guarantees that the heap is a forest of regions, each region with a single external entry point [4]. This type system enforces strong guarantees on the references that may exist in a program, and how data can be moved around the program. In the semantics in Fig. 5, each ι could represent the unique entry point to the root of a region tree. A dynamic application of this type system is also being pursued in Python [20].

Erlang and Elixir ensure that there is no shared data by passing all data by value [3,12]. Another approach is taken by Pony and Encore which both feature a shared heap, but whose type systems ensure that data passed by reference in messages is either immutable or is passed together with its ownership so that at most one actor at a time can access the data [7,10,22]. Other actor systems that support ownership transfer of data between actors include Joelle [18], Kilim [21] and LaCasa [14].

Rust has been introducing [11] many programmers to ownership and borrowing. In Rust, data must have at most one owner, providing a single unique entry point to that data, but mutable and immutable references can be borrowed by those that need it (with the guarantee that the reference cannot escape).

7 Conclusion

In this paper we have examined behaviour-oriented concurrency through the lens of the actor model. We have shown that the key difference between the two comes from the decoupling of the unit of isolation from the unit of concurrency. Using Actors, programmers have to decide on the granularity of isolation at the point of construction of an actor. In BoC on the other hand, this decision can be delayed until the point of construction of the behaviour. This frees the programmer from the need for implementing complicated synchronisation protocols.

The actor model can be thought of as a natural extension of object-oriented programming to a concurrent setting; an actor encapsulates its state just as an object does, but synchronises concurrent messages by running them with its own thread of control, thereby avoiding data races. In the same way, BoC can be thought of as an extension of procedural programming to a concurrent setting. A behaviour is a concurrent one-off procedure which temporarily encapsulates its required resources. In order to synchronise behaviours and avoid data races, the runtime tracks the dependencies of the required resources of each behaviour and schedules them based on these dependencies.

An important feature of the actor model is that it scales from single-node concurrent programs to distributed programs. There is currently no story for distribution in BoC, and the reconfigurability of isolated state and the need for a centralised view of the available work makes this non-trivial. It remains a venue of future work to investigate an adaptation of BoC that works for distributed computing.

References

1. Agha, G.: Actors: a model of concurrent computation in distributed systems. MIT Press (1986)
2. Agha, G.: Concurrent object-oriented programming. Commun. ACM **33**(9), 125–141 (1990)
3. Armstrong, J.: A history of Erlang. In: HOPL III, pp. 6–1–6–26. ACM (2007)
4. Arvidsson, E., et al.: Reference capabilities for flexible memory management. Proc. ACM Program. Lang. **7**(OOPSLA2) (2023)
5. The C++ actor framework. https://www.actor-framework.org/. Accessed Feb 2025
6. Castegren, E., Wrigstad, T.: Relaxed linear references for lock-free data structures. In: üller, P.M. (ed.) 31st European Conference on Object-Oriented Programming, ECOOP 2017, June 19-23, 2017, Barcelona, Spain, volume 74 of LIPIcs, pp. 6:1–6:32. Schloss Dagstuhl - Leibniz-Zentrum für Informatik (2017)

7. Castegren, E., Wrigstad, T.: Encore: Coda. In: de Boer, F.S., Damiani, F., Hähnle, R., Johnsen, E.B., Kamburjan, E. (eds.) Active Object Languages: Current Research Trends, volume 14360 of Lecture Notes in Computer Science, pp. 59–91. Springer (2024)
8. Cheeseman, L.: Behaviour-Oriented Concurrency. PhD thesis, Imperial College London (2024)
9. Cheeseman, L., et al.: When concurrency matters: Behaviour-oriented concurrency. Proc. ACM Program. Lang. 7(OOPSLA2) (2023)
10. Clebsch, S.: Pony: Co-designing a Type System and a Runtime. PhD thesis, Imperial College London (2017)
11. Crichton, W., Gray, G., Krishnamurthi, S.: A grounded conceptual model for ownership types in Rust. Proc. ACM Program. Lang. 7(OOPSLA2) (2023)
12. The Elixir programming language. https://elixir-lang.org. Accessed Feb 2025
13. Greif, I.: Semantics of Communicating Parallel Processes. PhD thesis, Massachusetts Institute of Technology (1975)
14. Haller, P., Loiko, A.: LaCasa: lightweight affinity and object capabilities in scala. In: Proceedings of the 2016 ACM SIGPLAN International Conference on Object-Oriented Programming, Systems, Languages, and Applications, pp. 272–291. ACM (2016)
15. Hayduk, Y., Sobe, A., Harmanci, D., Marlier, P., Felber, P.: Speculative concurrent processing with transactional memory in the actor model. In: Baldoni, R., Nisse, N., van Steen, M. (eds.) OPODIS 2013. LNCS, vol. 8304, pp. 160–175. Springer, Cham (2013). https://doi.org/10.1007/978-3-319-03850-6_12
16. Hewitt, P.B., Steiger, R.: A universal modular actor formalism for artificial intelligence. In: Proceedings of the 3rd International Joint Conference on Artificial Intelligence, IJCAI'73, pp. 235–245, San Francisco, CA, USA (1973). Morgan Kaufmann Publishers Inc
17. Imam, S., Sarkar, V.: Habanero-Scala: Async-finish programming in Scala. In: The Third Scala Workshop (Scala Days 2012) (2012)
18. Östlund, J.: Language Constructs for Safe Parallel Programming on Multi-cores. PhD thesis, Department of Information Technology, Uppsala University (2016)
19. Pony tutorial. https://tutorial.ponylang.io/. Accessed June 2025
20. Explorations into a programming model for BoC in the Python runtime. https://github.com/matajoh/pyrona. Accessed Feb 2025
21. Srinivasan, S., Mycroft, A.: Kilim: Isolation-typed actors for Java. In: ECOOP, volume 8, pp. 104–128. Springer (2008)
22. Steed, G., Drossopoulou, S.: A principled design of capabilities in pony. https://www.ponylang.io/media/papers/a_prinicipled_design_of_capabilities_in_pony.pdf (2016)
23. Swalens, J., De Koster, J., De Meuter, W.: Chocola: composable concurrency language. ACM Trans. Program. Lang. Syst. 42(4) (2021)
24. Tasharofi, S., Dinges, P., Johnson, R.E.: Why do Scala developers mix the actor model with other concurrency models? In: Castagna, G. (ed.) ECOOP 2013. LNCS, vol. 7920, pp. 302–326. Springer, Heidelberg (2013). https://doi.org/10.1007/978-3-642-39038-8_13
25. Research programming language for concurrent ownership. https://github.com/microsoft/verona. Accessed Feb 2025
26. Yang, A.M., Wrigstad, T.: Type-assisted automatic garbage collection for lock-free data structures. In: Proceedings of the 2017 ACM SIGPLAN International Symposium on Memory Management. ACM (2017)

Open Systems and Applications

Actors for Timing Analysis of Distributed Redundant Controllers

Marjan Sirjani[1(✉)], Edward A. Lee[2], Zahra Moezkarimi[1],
Bahman Pourvatan[1], Bjarne Johansson[1,3], Stefan Marksteiner[1,4],
and Alessandro V. Papadopoulos[1]

[1] Mälardalen University, Västerås, Sweden
{marjan.sirjani,zahra.moezkarimi,bahman.pourvatan,stefan.marksteiner,
alessandro.papadopoulos}@mdu.se
[2] University of California at Berkeley, Berkeley, USA
eal@berkeley.edu
[3] ABB AB, Västerås, Sweden
bjarne.johansson@se.abb.com
[4] AVL List GmbH, Graz, Austria
stefan.marksteiner@avl.com

Abstract. We use two actor-based languages, Timed Rebeca and Lingua Franca, to show modeling, model checking, implementation, and timing analysis of an industry-suggested algorithm for role selection in distributed control systems with redundancy. The algorithm prioritizes consistency over availability in trade-off situations. We show scenarios that simulate the environment and possible faults and use the Timed Rebeca model checking tool to investigate whether they may cause a failure. We also show the maximum latency that can be tolerated without causing inconsistency. We then use the coordination language Lingua Franca to implement the model. It can also simulate network switches, allowing you to set up test scenarios that include network degradation, such as switch failures, packet losses, and excessive latency. This can be set up as a hardware-in-the-loop simulation, where the actual node implementations interact with simulated switches and the network.

Prologue

To honor the profound impact of Gul Agha's visionary contributions to concurrent computation and the actor model, we dedicate this work to him with deep admiration. On a personal note, the first author expresses heartfelt gratitude for Gul's deep wisdom, vast knowledge, peaceful manner, and warm, unwavering support—qualities that have left a lasting impression both intellectually and personally.

1 Introduction

The actor model is among the pioneering ones in addressing concurrent and distributed applications. The model was originally introduced by Hewitt in the

70s as a formalism for artificial intelligence and an agent-based language for programming distributed systems [5,7,8]. The actor model is then promoted as a model of concurrent computation in distributed systems in Gul Agha's PhD thesis in 1985 [3] and as a conceptual foundation for concurrent object-oriented programming [1,2]. The actor model has been used both as a framework for theoretical understanding of concurrency and as the basis for several practical implementations of concurrent and distributed systems.

Rebeca is introduced as an actor-based language with model checking support in 2001 by Sirjani et al. [29,30], and the timed version is introduced in 2007 [14,25,26]. The language design follows the principle to keep the core language as simple as possible and suitable for analysis [24]. Rebeca is imperative rather than functional, and actors are units of concurrency, meaning there is no intra-actor concurrency. Lingua Franca is an actor-based language introduced in 2019 [18,19] based on the reactors coordination model first presented by Lohstroh et al. [20]. The reactor model combines several ideas to enable determinism while preserving much of the style of actors. The reactor model uses timestamps to make programs deterministic by default and uses a logical model of time that can be associated with physical time to provide control over timing during execution. Timed Rebeca is extended to support priorities in execution of actors and handlers of actors to adopt the Lingua Franca's deterministic order of execution when there is more than one reaction enabled at the same logical time [15,27,28].

The timestamps introduced in Timed Rebeca and in Lingua Franca introduce some significant differences compared to Hewitt-Agha actors. The programs become more deterministic, particularly with the use of priorities in Timed Rebeca, but they also introduce the possibility of unfairness. In particular, it is possible to create programs that exhibit Zeno conditions, meaning that there will be an infinite number of events with timestamps below some finite threshold. Such programs may be unfair because events with timestamps larger than the finite threshold will never be processed. Also, although dynamic communication topologies are supported by both Timed Rebeca and Lingua Franca, we do not consider it here. It is not needed for the applications we consider. Dynamic actor creation is possible in LF, but again, not needed here. It is not supported by Timed Rebeca because it makes formal verification considerably more difficult.

In this paper, we use an industry-suggested algorithm for redundancy role selection in distributed control systems with redundancy to demonstrate how we use Timed Rebeca and Lingua Franca for timing analysis for a distributed and concurrent system where timing is crucial and can change the outcome. The Network Reference Point Failure Detection (NRP FD) algorithm is designed to detect failures between redundant controllers [11]. The algorithm prioritizes consistency over availability in tradeoff situations but minimizes the possibility of lack of availability. We model-checked the NRP FD algorithm in [10], checked the situations that cause dual primaries, and generated test cases. Here, we show the time analysis to find the minimum time between failures that can cause double primaries.

In distributed applications, Brewer's CAP theorem tells us that when networks become partitioned (P), one must give up either consistency (C) or availability (A). Consistency is agreement on the values of shared variables; availability is the ability to respond to reads and writes, accessing those shared variables [6]. Lee et al. [17] explain that in real-time systems, the time it takes for a software subsystem to respond through an actuator to a stimulus from a sensor is a critical property of the system. They, therefore, generalize the notion of availability to include this time, not just the system's response time to human users. A software subsystem where sensor-to-actuator response time is large is less available than one for which it is small. They argue that availability, a real-time property of a system, and consistency, a logical property, relate numerically to clock synchronization and latencies introduced by networks and computation. They replace the P in CAP with L, representing latencies that include execution times, network delays, and clock synchronization errors. The CAP theorem becomes the CAL theorem, which gives an algebraic relationship between the three quantities: consistency, availability, and latency.

In the following, we will briefly overview Timed Rebeca and Lingua Franca languages and explain the NRP FD algorithm. Then we show how NRP FD is modeled in Timed Rebeca and how model checking the Timed Rebeca model can help for time analysis of the algorithm. Using model checking, we can find the combinations of timing configurations of the controllers and switches (including heartbeat and ping periods and network delays) and the time between fault occurrences that can cause inconsistencies. We then use Lingua Franca to implement and simulate these situations.

2 Actor-Based Languages, Timed Rebeca and Lingua Franca

Rebeca (Reactive Object Language) [23,29] is an actor-based language designed to model and formally verify reactive concurrent and distributed systems. In Rebeca models, reactive objects known as rebecs resemble actors with no shared variables, asynchronous message passing, and unbounded message buffers. Each rebec has a single thread of execution. Communication with other rebecs is achieved by sending messages, and periodic behavior is executed by sending messages to itself. Rebeca has no explicit receive statement, and its send statements are non-blocking. Each rebec has variables, methods (message servers), and a dedicated message queue for received messages. How a rebec reacts to a message is specified in message servers. The rebec processes messages by de-queuing from the top and executing the corresponding message server non-preemptively. The state of a rebec can change during the execution of its message servers through assignment statements.

Rebeca is an imperative language with syntax similar to Java. A Rebeca model consists of several reactive classes and a main section. Each reactive class describes the type of a certain number of rebecs. Rebecs (actors) are instantiated in the main block. While message queues in the semantics of Rebeca are inherently unbounded, a user-specified upper bound for the queue size is necessary to ensure a finite state space during model checking. Reactive classes include constructors, which share the same name as the class. These constructors are responsible for initializing the actor's state variables and placing initially required messages in the actor's message buffer.

In this work, we use Timed Rebeca (the timed extension of Rebeca) [14,26] with a global logical time. Timed Rebeca considers synchronized local clocks for all actors throughout the model. Instead of a message queue, Timed Rebeca uses a message bag in which messages carry their respective time tags. The sender tags its local time to a message when sending. Timed Rebeca introduces three timing primitives: "delay," "after," and "deadline." A delay statement represents the passage of time for an actor while executing a message server, i.e., it is used to model computation times. All other statements are assumed to execute instantaneously. The keywords "after" and "deadline" are augmented to a message send statement. The term "after(n)" means it takes n units of time for a message to reach its receiver. Using the after construct, we can model network delay and periodic events. We can use a nondeterministic assignment to n and model nondeterministic arrival times for a message (event). The term "deadline(n)" conveys that if the message is not retrieved within n units of time, there will be a timeout. An abstract syntax of Timed Rebeca is provided in Appendix A. Timed Rebeca is extended with priorities [28]. Priorities are assigned to rebecs and message handlers to control the order of their execution and hence enhance the determinism of the system's behavior [15]. If more than one actor or event is enabled at the same logical time, the model checker builds all the possible execution traces. Using priorities, you can cut some of the branches or even completely control the order in which events are handled at that logical time.

Lingua Franca (LF) [18,20] is a coordination language designed for embedded real-time systems. Software components are called "reactors." The messages exchanged between reactors have logical timetags drawn from a discrete, totally ordered model of time. Every reactor will react to incoming messages in timetag order. The Lingua Franca compiler ensures that all logically simultaneous messages are processed in precedence order, making the computation deterministic even with parallel execution.

The Lingua Franca code consists of a set of reactors and a main reactor. Reactors contain state variables, input and output ports, and physical actions and reactions. The body of reactions can be written in the target language supported by LF, including C, C++, and TypeScript. In each case, the LF compiler generates a standalone executable in the target language. A reactor may also react to a "physical action," typically triggered by some external event such as a sensor. The physical action will be assigned a timetag based on the current physical clock on the machine hosting the reactor.

Lingua Franca includes a notion of a deadline, a relation between logical time and physical time, as measured on a particular platform. Specifically, a program may specify that the invocation of a reaction must occur within some physical time interval of the logical timestamp of the message. This, together with physical actions, can be used to ensure some measure of alignment between logical time and some measurement of physical time.

3 Industrial Controller Redundancy and NRP FD Algorithm

Industrial controllers are robust and specialized computers designed to execute control applications in a deterministic and reliable manner. These controllers form the foundation of automation solutions across diverse domains, such as propulsion and energy generation automation on ships and ventilation automation in traffic tunnels. They are also crucial in domains like offshore oil extraction platforms, where downtime is highly undesirable due to safety and economic considerations [10]. To enhance reliability in such systems, single points of failure in the automation infrastructure, including controllers, are mitigated through redundancy. Controller redundancy typically implies a standby redundancy scheme, where one controller functions as the active primary while a secondary remains on standby [22]. These controllers, or Distributed Controller Nodes (DCNs), manage processes via Field Communication Interfaces (FCIs) connected to input/output (I/O) devices interfacing with the physical environment. The controllers monitor the state of the physical process by sampling values from the I/O devices through the FCI. Based on these readings, they compute appropriate output values to drive the process toward a desired state. The standby controller requires regular updates on the state from the primary and heartbeat signals; consequently, effective communication between the controllers is essential.

In case of communication failure between the redundant controllers, two strategies are available: (i) disabling redundancy when only one communication path remains or (ii) continuing in redundant mode. These strategies align with the CAP theorem. Disabling redundancy maintains consistency but sacrifices availability, while continuing in redundant mode risks consistency if the failure of the final link is indistinguishable from the failure of the active controller. The NRP FD algorithm is designed to detect failures between a redundant controller pair while preserving consistency and minimizing the availability tradeoff. In a typical standby redundancy setup, one controller acts as the active primary and the other as the standby backup. Only the primary controller provides output to the FCI and connected I/O devices to maintain consistency. Upon detecting a primary controller failure, the backup assumes the primary role. For this synchronization and role determination, communication between the controllers, typically over a switched network, is vital [4,16]. The controllers are often connected via dual, independent network paths, forming a redundant network (see Fig. 1). NRP FD is a push-based failure detection algorithm. The primary controller sends heartbeat messages at fixed intervals to the backup over the redundant network [11]. Using a Network Reference Point (NRP) distinguishes NRP FD from other heartbeat-based algorithms. The NRP serves as a reference on the network, typically a switch, and must meet two criteria: (i) it should not share any common cause failure with the DCNs, and (ii) it should be accessible by at most one DCN in the event of network partitioning. Each DCN maintains a list of NRP candidates for additional robustness. If the designated NRP fails while communication paths remain functional between the redundant pair, the primary can propose an alternative NRP candidate to the backup.

In Fig. 1, the upper network comprises switches SwitchA1, and SwitchA2, SwitchA3. The primary controller's NRP candidates are SwitchA1 and SwitchB1, and the backup's are SwitchA3 and SwitchB3, with the current NRP set to SwitchA1.

The operational behavior of NRP FD can be summarized as follows: the primary controller selects an NRP from its candidates and communicates this choice in the heartbeat messages. It continually monitors its ability to reach the NRP. If the NRP becomes unreachable, the primary proposes a new NRP to the backup. The primary forfeits the primary role if the backup does not acknowledge the proposed change within a predefined timeframe. Meanwhile, the backup monitors heartbeats from the primary. If no heartbeat is received within a set interval, the backup verifies its ability to reach the NRP. If it can reach the NRP, the backup assumes the primary role.

4 Modeling of NRP FD Using Timed Rebeca

For modeling and verification of the NRP FD, we use the Timed Rebeca and its integrated model checker tool, Afra. For modeling, we have followed the protocol specifications for NRP FD in [11] and refined the model based on discussions with industrial partners to ensure accuracy and relevance. This version enhances the previous model provided in [9] by making overall improvements, removing unnecessary conditions, and modifying the message handling flow. These changes

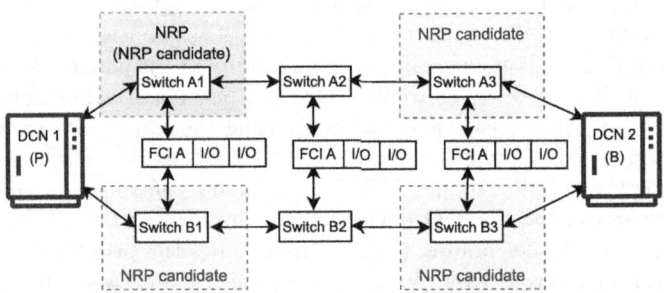

Fig. 1. A redundant network with the NRP and NRP candidates highlighted.

result in a model that more accurately reflects real-world behavior. The complete updated model can be found in Appendix B and also on the Rebeca GitHub page[1].

In the Timed Rebeca model, each node and switch is modeled as an actor. They communicate by message passing. A Rebeca model consists of reactive class definitions that dictate the behavior of rebecs (actors) in the system. Their responses to messages (and timed events) are handled by message servers. Figure 2 illustrates selected parts of the Timed Rebeca model for NRP FD. The model is extensible, allowing an increase in the number of switches and nodes.

The NRP-FD model has two main element types: Nodes and Switches. Each of these element types is defined as a reactive class, with Node (Fig. 2, line 9) and Switch (Fig. 2, line 40). Each reactive class has a constructor, which is a unique method that runs when an object (rebec) is instantiated. This constructor initializes the variables. In the main section (Fig. 2, lines 60-70), we instantiate two nodes (DCN1 and DCN2 with ids 100 and 101) and six switches (switchA1-switchA3 and switchB1-switchB3). A node can be either a primary node or a backup node. A switch can be either terminal (connected to a DCN) or non-terminal (not directly connected to a DCN). A switch can also serve as an NRP candidate, an NRP, or none of these roles. For each network, each node has an NRP candidate switch. For DCN1, the candidates are switchA1 (id 1) and switchB1 (id 4). For DCN2, the candidates are switchA3 (id 3) and switchB3 (id 6) (Fig. 2, lines 68-69). The parameters used when instantiating these objects are used to define their roles and pass important information to the constructor.

At the start of the algorithm, DCN1 (id 100) is set as the primary node in the instantiation (second parameter in lines 68-69 of Fig. 2). In the Node reactive class, there are two known rebecs, meaning the node can send messages to them. The constructor of Node calls the runMe message server (Fig. 2, line 21). In runMe (Fig. 2, line 28), the DCN checks its current state using the mode variable and executes the corresponding behavior (Fig. 2, lines 30-34). At the end of runMe (Fig. 2, line 35), the method calls itself using "runMe() after(heartbeat_period);", making it a periodic event. This ensures that runMe runs at every heartbeat interval, as defined by heartbeat_period in the code (Fig. 2, line 1). The heartbeat period must be significantly larger than other timing parameters to process all events within a single heartbeat cycle. The choice of timing parameters is carefully considered to make the model as realistic as possible. More details on timing will be discussed in the following.

In NRP FD, DCNs operate in four modes, including WAITING, BACKUP, PRIMARY, and FAILED, as shown in Fig. 3. The behavior of the nodes based on their roles are defined in the message server runMe. Figure 4 presents key parts of the message server runMe. From this point forward, both Fig. 3 and the Fig. 4 can be followed together for a better understanding.

In the Rebeca model, each DCN starts in the WAITING mode, which is set in the Node constructor (Fig. 2, line 18). The primary id (Myprimary) is passed to both nodes in the instantiation, and when a node is in WAITING mode, it

---

[1] https://rebeca-lang.org/allprojects/DistributedControllers.

```
1   env int heartbeat_period = 20;
2   env int max_missed_heartbeats = 2;
3   env int ping_timeout =10;
4   env int nrp_timeout = 10;
5   env byte NumberOfNetworks = 2;
6   env int switchA1failtime = 0;
7   ...
8   env int networkDelay = 1;
9   reactiveclass Node (20){
10      knownrebecs {Switch out1, out2;}
11      statevars {...}
12      Node (int Myid, int Myprimary, int NRPCan1_id, int NRPCan2_id, int myFailTime) {
13          id = Myid;
14          NRPCandidates[0] =NRPCan1_id;
15          NRPCandidates[1] =NRPCan2_id;
16          NRP_network = -1;
17          primary = Myprimary;
18          mode = WAITING;
19          ...
20          if(myFailTime!=0) nodeFail() after(myFailTime);
21          runMe();
22      }
23      msgsrv new_NRP_request_timed_out(){...}
24      msgsrv ping_timed_out() {...}
25      msgsrv pingNRP_response(int mid){...}
26      msgsrv new_NRP(int mid,int prim, int mNRP_network, int mNRP_switch_id) {...}
27      msgsrv request_new_NRP(int origin) {...}
28      msgsrv runMe(){
29          if(?(true,false)) nodeFail();
30          switch(mode){
31              case 0: //WAITING : ...
32              case 1: //PRIMARY : ...
33              case 2: //BACKUP : ...
34              case 3: //FAILED : ...
35          self.runMe() after(heartbeat_period);
36      }
37      msgsrv heartBeat(byte networkId, int senderid) {...}
38      msgsrv nodeFail(){...}
39  }
40  reactiveclass Switch(10){
41      knownrebecs {...}
42      statevars {...}
43      Switch (int myid, byte networkId, boolean term, Switch s1, Switch s2, int myFailTime, Node n1) {
44          mynetworkId = networkId;
45          id = myid;
46          terminal=term;
47          amINRP = false;
48          failed = false;
49          switchTarget1 = s1;
50          switchTarget2 = s2;
51          ...
52      }
53      msgsrv switchFail(){ failed = true; amINRP=false;}
54      msgsrv pingNRP_response(int senderNode){...}
55      msgsrv request_new_NRP(int senderNode) {...}
56      msgsrv pingNRP(int switchNode, int senderNode, int NRP) {...}
57      msgsrv new_NRP(int senderNode, int mNRP_network, int mNRP_switch_id) {...}
58      msgsrv heartBeat(byte networkId, int senderNode) {...}
59  }
60  main {
61      @Priority(1) Switch switchA1():(1, 0, true , switchA2 , switchA2 , switchA1failtime, DCN1);
62      @Priority(1) Switch switchA2():(2 ,0, false , switchA1 , switchA3 , switchA2failtime, null);
63      @Priority(1) Switch switchA3():(3, 0, true , switchA2 , switchA2 , switchA3failtime, DCN2);
64      @Priority(1) Switch switchB1():(4, 1, true , switchB2 , switchB2 , switchB1failtime, DCN1);
65      @Priority(1) Switch switchB2():(5, 1, false , switchB1 , switchB3 , switchB2failtime, null);
66      @Priority(1) Switch switchB3():(6, 1, true , switchB2 , switchB2 , switchB3failtime, DCN2);

68      @Priority(2) Node DCN1(switchA1, switchB1):(100, 100, 1, 4, node1failtime);
69      @Priority(2) Node DCN2(switchA3, switchB3):(101, 100, 3, 6, node2failtime);
70  }
```

Fig. 2. An abstracted version of the Timed Rebeca model of NRP FD (The full version is in Appendix B).

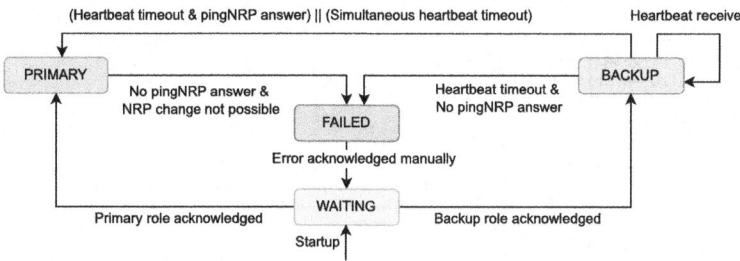

Fig. 3. Different modes of a DCN in NRP FD in the Rebeca model. The initial mode is WAITING, from which the node transitions to either PRIMARY or BACKUP, depending on the value passed to its constructor. From PRIMARY, the node moves to FAILED if, after sending a pingNRP, it does not receive a response from the NRP within the deadline and is unable to switch to another NRP. In the BACKUP mode, the node transitions to PRIMARY if the heartbeat times out and pingNRP detects a reachable NRP, or if the heartbeat timeout occurs simultaneously on both networks. In the latter case, the BACKUP node assumes that the PRIMARY node has failed, as simultaneous failures in both networks are unlikely. The node remains in BACKUP mode as long as it continues receiving heartbeats. If heartbeats stop and there is no response to the ping of the NRP, it transitions to FAILED and remains in that mode until it is manually restored.

determines its role based on this id. If it is the designated primary, it transitions accordingly, and an NRP is announced (Fig. 4, lines 4-11); otherwise, it transits to the BACKUP mode (Fig. 4, line 12).

In PRIMARY mode, the primary DCN checks if the NRP is reachable by sending a pingNRP message. The pingNRP message is sent based on the network where the NRP is located. This message is handled by the pingNRP message server (Fig. 2, line 56). In a real system, pingNRP could be implemented using an Internet Control Message Protocol (ICMP) echo request (ping) or another suitable protocol based on the NRP's capabilities. If the NRP does not respond, the primary attempts to announce a new NRP, provided there are available alternatives, using the new_NRP message server (Fig. 2, line 57). Once a valid NRP is confirmed, the primary DCN starts sending heartbeats on both networks. If no NRP is available, the primary transitions to the FAILED mode (implemented in the ping_timed_out, Fig. 2, line 24).

In the BACKUP mode, the DCN monitors heartbeats from the primary. To minimize false positives caused by temporary network disturbances, the heartbeat period and tolerance limits (i.e., the number of missed heartbeats allowed before declaring a timeout) must be carefully set. Since DCN redundancy typically relies on two independent network paths, the backup expects to receive a heartbeat on each path within every period. If heartbeats are missed on both paths simultaneously, it likely indicates a primary failure rather than a network issue. To optimize failover, NRP FD allows the backup to transition directly to PRIMARY mode when it detects simultaneous heartbeat timeouts, skipping the pingNRP exchange (Fig. 4, line 29-32). However, this optimization slightly increases the

```
 1  msgsrv runMe() {
 2   switch(mode) {
 3    case 0: //WAITING :
 4     if (id == primary) {
 5      mode = PRIMARY;
 6      NRP_network++;
 7      if (NRP_network < NumberOfNetworks) {
 8       NRP_switch_id = NRPCandidates[NRP_network];
 9       if (NRP_network == 0) out1.new_NRP(id, NRP_network, NRP_switch_id);
10       else out2.new_NRP(id, NRP_network, NRP_switch_id);
11      } else NRP_network = NumberOfNetworks;
12     } else mode = BACKUP;
13     break;
14    case 1: //PRIMARY :
15     if (NRP_network == 0) {
16      ping_pending = true;
17      out1.pingNRP(id, NRP_switch_id) after(networkDelay);
18      ping_timed_out() after(ping_timeout);
19     } else {
20      ping_pending = true;
21      out2.pingNRP(id, NRP_switch_id) after(networkDelay);
22      ping_timed_out() after(ping_timeout);
23     }
24     NRP_pending = true;
25     break;
26    case 2: //BACKUP :
27     heartbeats_missed_1++;
28     heartbeats_missed_2++;
29     if (heartbeats_missed_1 > max_missed_heartbeats && heartbeats_missed_2 >
             max_missed_heartbeats) {
30      if (heartbeats_missed_1==heartbeats_missed_2) {
31       mode = PRIMARY;
32       primary = id;
33      } else {
34       become_primary_on_ping_response = true;
35       ping_pending = true;
36       if (NRP_network == 0){
37        out1.pingNRP(id, NRP_switch_id) after(networkDelay);
38       } else {
39        out2.pingNRP(id, NRP_switch_id) after(networkDelay);
40       }
41       ping_timed_out() after(ping_timeout);
42      }
43     } else if (heartbeats_missed_1 > max_missed_heartbeats  heartbeats_missed_2 >
             max_missed_heartbeats) {
44      if (NRP_network==0 && heartbeats_missed_1 > max_missed_heartbeats) {
45       ping_pending = true;
46       out1.pingNRP(id, NRP_switch_id) after(networkDelay);
47       ping_timed_out() after(ping_timeout);
48      } else if (NRP_network ==1 && heartbeats_missed_2 > max_missed_heartbeats) {
49       ping_pending = true;
50       out2.pingNRP(id, NRP_switch_id) after(networkDelay);
51       ping_timed_out() after(ping_timeout);
52      }
53      heartbeats_missed_1 = (heartbeats_missed_1>max_missed_heartbeats+1)?
             max_missed_heartbeats+1:heartbeats_missed_1;
54      heartbeats_missed_2 = (heartbeats_missed_2>max_missed_heartbeats+1)?
             max_missed_heartbeats+1:heartbeats_missed_2;
55     }
56     break;
57    case 3: //FAILED :
58     break;
59   }
60   self.runMe() after(heartbeat_period);
61  }
```

Fig. 4. Different modes of a DCN and their corresponding behavior in the message server runMe.

risk of dual primaries, which can be caught by model checking. We set the max_missed_heartbeat to 2 (Fig. 2, line 2). The variables heartbeats_missed_1 and heartbeats_missed_2 act as counters for tracking missed heartbeats on the two networks. These counters increase at each period and reset when a heartbeat is successfully received (in message server heartBeat, Fig. 2, line 37).

The backup DCN continuously monitors the count of missed heartbeats for each network. If both counters exceed the limit defined by max_missed_heartbeat (Fig. 4, line 29), the backup assumes a failure has occurred. We set the variable become_primary_on_ping_response to true, which will be checked later in message server pingNRP_response. The backup then sends a pingNRP message to the NRP to check its reachability (Fig. 4, line 34-43). If the NRP responds, confirming its accessibility, the DCN transitions from BACKUP to PRIMARY mode (pingNRP_response in (Fig. 2, line 25). Otherwise, if one of the counters exceeds, it will check the NRP reachability based on the network on which it is located. Finally, the heartbeats_missed1 and heartbeats_missed2 are bound accordingly.

In the FAILED mode, NRP FD remains inactive until it receives a manual acknowledgment confirming that the underlying issues causing the failure have been resolved.

In the previous work [10], we performed model checking and removed the transition from backup mode to the primary in simultaneous network failures, as it could lead to dual primaries. Here, while consistency remains the priority, we also strive to maintain availability by keeping the model aligned with the specification. Therefore, we retain this improvement in this paper and analyze the minimum possible time interval between failures that can still be considered non-simultaneous. We will discuss the timing analysis in the following sections.

Accuracy of the Model. Our model closely reflects real-world conditions by accurately representing the network topology and DCN interactions. The decision to tolerate up to two lost heartbeats is based on the low bit error rate of Gigabit Ethernet and the fact that a heartbeat message can fit within a standard 1500-byte Ethernet frame. This indicates a low probability of losing heartbeat messages, particularly across two separate networks, thereby reducing the chance of false positives caused by regular disruptions. The reaction time, which is the time from a primary failure to when the backup takes over the primary role, is determined by the heartbeat_period and max_missed_heartbeats.

In [10], we use a rationale to set the timing parameters. In this paper, we changed the numbers to reduce the size of the state space during model checking while keeping the numbers proportional to real-world settings. Here, we define the heartbeat_period as 20 time units and set the ping_timeout and nrp_timeout to 10 time units. The networkDelay is considered as 1 unit of time. When DCNs ping NRP, we use the keyword after and set it to networkDelay. These values are chosen to be proportional to real-world values while preserving the sequence of message exchanges. Although they may vary slightly, our model should handle all timing events within one period of 20 time units. We use the after construct, where the execution order needs to be respected.

5 Time Analysis of NRP FD: Consistency, Availability, Latency

For the structure in Fig. 1, we claim that the code in the previous section will not lead to dual primaries unless we get "simultaneous" failures in the two networks. In the code in Fig. 4 on line 30, we see the comparison between the number of missed heartbeats in the two networks. If the number of missed heartbeats is the same for both networks then the backup takes over and becomes the primary. The reasoning is that the "simultaneous" failure of both networks is very unlikely, so the algorithm assumes that the primary is down in this situation. This relaxes the requirement for consistency by allowing dual primaries in rare cases, thereby improving availability, meaning that the backup can successfully take over. Dual primaries can only occur when network failures are "simultaneous," something that can be made arbitrarily unlikely.

Here, we quantify "simultaneous" and show how to construct a Rebeca program that nondeterministically allows all possible non-simultaneous switch failures. We then perform model checking on the resulting program and verify that dual primaries cannot happen when the time between switch failures is sufficiently long.

Let H be the heartbeat period. The primary node will send the nth heartbeat at time $nH + P$, where P is the ping timeout. The addition of P is so that the primary verifies that it still has access to the NRP before sending a heartbeat. The program is designed to use P as a fixed offset. It pings the NRP at time nH and then waits for P time units. If it receives a response to the ping within this time period, then it will send a heartbeat at time $nH + P$.

Assume that the delay on each network hop is N time units. In Fig. 1, there are three switches and, therefore, four network hops from the primary to the backup node. The backup will receive the heartbeat if the first switch does not fail before $nH + P + N$, the second switch does not fail before $nH + P + 2N$, and the third switch does not fail before $nH + P + 3N$.

Let t_A be the time at which network A fails for the first time, and t_B the time at which network B fails for the first time. We define the network failures to be "simultaneous" if t_A and t_B satisfy the following inequalities for some natural number n:

$$(n-1)H + P + iN < t_A \leq nH + P + iN \\ (n-1)H + P + jN < t_B \leq nH + P + jN \quad (1)$$

where $i, j \in \{1, 2, 3\}$ denotes which switch failed (first, second, or third along the path from the primary to the backup).

Assume without loss of generality that $t_A \leq t_B$. For such a simultaneous failure, the earliest possible t_A occurs if the first switch fails ($i = 1$) and

$$t_A = (n-1)H + P + N + 1 \quad (2)$$

The $+1$ accounts for strict inequality (time is quantized here).

In such a simultaneous failure, the latest possible time t_B for network B to fail is

$$t_B = nH + P + 3N \tag{3}$$

where we have chosen $j = 3$. Hence, the largest possible time difference between failures for them to be considered "simultaneous" is

$$t_B - t_A = H + 2N - 1. \tag{4}$$

Hence, our claim is that our controllers will not yield dual primaries as long as

$$|t_B - t_A| \geq H + 2N. \tag{5}$$

To verify this using model checking, we augment the Rebeca program with a `FailureController` reactive class, shown in Fig. 5 This code assumes a heartbeat period of $H = 20$ and a network latency $N = 1$. The constructor, on line 12, ensures that the first failure does not occur in the first two heartbeat periods. After two heartbeat periods, the handler `chooseFailureTime` is invoked. It nondeterministically chooses a possible failure time between zero and 19 and then invokes `maybeFail` after that time (Fig. 5, line 18). The `maybeFail` handler first decides nondeterministically whether a failure will occur at this time, and, if so, nondeterministically selects one of the six switches to fail. If no failure occurs, then (on line 37) it repeats `maybeFail` one time unit later. If a failure does occur, then (on line 35), it ensures that `min_interval` elapses before the next possible failure. We set `min_interval` to 23 (Fig. 5, line 4), based on the inequality (5), considering that the heartbeat is 20 and the N is 1 unit of time, and +1 for strict inequality (to be sure that we will not have a simultaneous failure).

We implemented the algorithm in Rebeca and provided an assertion that inequality (5) holds. On our first attempt, the assertion failed. Afra's counterexample revealed a corner case in our code in which the behavior did not match the assumptions stated above. Specifically, the Primary sends a ping to the NRP and waits for a timeout period. If it receives the response to the ping within that timeout period, then it sends a heartbeat. If not, it sends a message to acquire a new NRP. In this latter event, our first implementation did not send a heartbeat message in this cycle. The next heartbeat message was sent one full cycle later.

We now face a choice. We can either refine the assumptions in the derivation above and derive a new inequality,

$$|t_B - t_A| \geq 2H + 2N, \tag{6}$$

or we can modify the code to match the original assumption. Either strategy works. The model checker verifies that our first implementation satisfies (6) and that a slightly modified implementation satisfies (5). This shows how the details of the implementation can affect the timings in a way that is hard to notice by analytical approaches.

```
env int heartbeat_period = 20;
env int networkDelay = 1;
...
env int min_interval = 23;
...
reactiveclass FailureController(10) {
    knownrebecs {
        Switch switchA1, switchA2, switchA3, switchB1, switchB2, switchB3;
    }
    statevars {}
    FailureController () {
        self.chooseFailureTime() after(2*heartbeat_period); // Let startup phase pass
    }
    msgsrv chooseFailureTime() {
        int failure_time = ? (0, 1, 2, 3, 4, 5, 6, 7, 8, 9, 10, 11, 12, 13, 14, 15, 16,
            17, 18, 19);
        self.maybeFail() after (failure_time);
    }
    msgsrv maybeFail() {
        boolean failure = ? (false, true);
        byte s = ? (1, 2, 3, 4, 5, 6);
        if (failure) {
            if (s == 1) {
                switchA1.switchFail();
            } else if (s == 2) {
                switchA2.switchFail();
            } else if (s == 3) {
                switchA3.switchFail();
            } else if (s == 4) {
                switchB1.switchFail();
            } else if (s == 5) {
                switchB2.switchFail();
            } else if (s == 6) {
                switchB3.switchFail();
            }
            maybeFail() after (min_interval);
        } else {
            maybeFail() after (1);
        }
    }
}
...
main {
    @Priority(1) FailureController failureC(switchA1, switchA2, switchA3, switchB1,
        switchB2, switchB3):();

    @Priority(1) Switch switchA1():(1, 0, true , switchA2 , switchA2 , switchA1failtime,
        DCN1);
    ...
}
```

Fig. 5. FailureController reactive class.

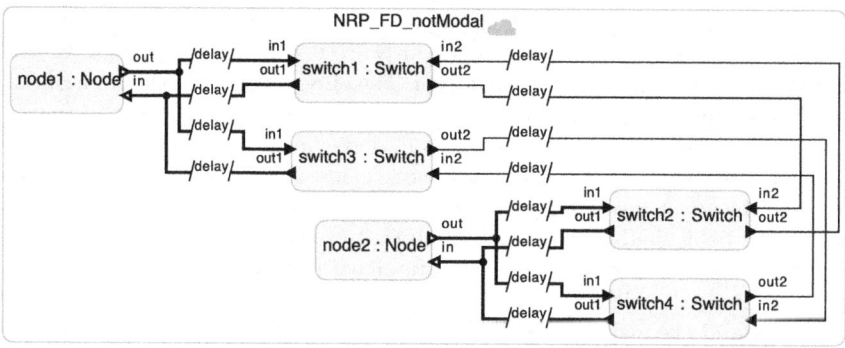

Fig. 6. Diagram of a Lingua Franca realization of a two-node/two-network example (closed).

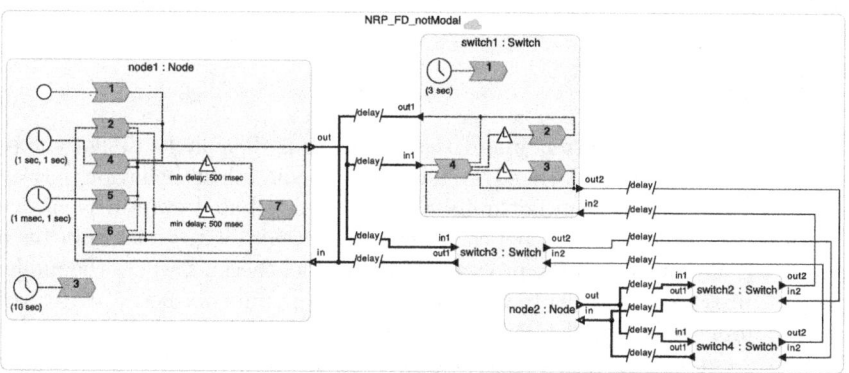

Fig. 7. Diagram of a Lingua Franca realization of a two-node/two-network example where node 1 and switch1 are expanded.

6 Implementation and Simulation of NRP FD Using Lingua Franca

Lingua Franca bridges the modeling in Timed Rebeca to the implementation, most importantly by aligning the logical and physical time. An (automatically generated) diagram of an LF realization of a two-node/two-network version of the NRP system is shown in Fig. 6. One of the two nodes is expanded in Fig. 7, showing some implementation details. The realization has the form of a modal model [21], where a finite-state machine (represented by bubbles and arcs in the diagram) governs the switching between modes of operation, and each mode defines reactions (represented by grey chevrons in the diagram). The reactions encapsulate C code that reacts to timestamped input events.

The LF tools translate the node into a C program that can be installed in a deployed system, and, therefore, the code used for modeling and simulation is the same as the code used in deployment. Moreover, the generated C code for the nodes can be run on the same hardware it will be deployed on, thereby enabling hardware-in-the-loop simulation. The only difference is that in modeling and simulation, the simulated network switches determine the timestamps of messages that arrive at a node, whereas in deployment, a local clock measuring physical time will determine the timestamps. Consequently, the simulation model can reproduce test cases that may be seen in the field, and when those cases are seen in the field, the behavior will match that of the simulation.

The figure shows a test case that simulates particular network delays and specified times at which components fail. For example, the connections between the nodes and the switches are decorated with *after* delays, notated /delay/, where delay is a parameter specifying a time value. These delay annotations determine the timestamps at which the nodes receive messages in the simulation, whereas in a deployed system, these timestamps will be determined by a physical clock.

7 Discussion

The interaction of concurrency and timing makes it difficult to design correct algorithms for distributed timed systems and predict their behavior entirely. Using timed actors, we can faithfully model the distributed event-driven algorithms and programs, and model checking helps reveal the possible problems or bugs in the algorithm and the program. Using model checking where the models are more abstract comparing to what presented here would not necessarily reveal how the implementation details affect the behavior. We showed the method in this paper and our experiment demonstrated the possible complications of interaction of concurrency and timing.

The method is general and can be applied to other event-driven reactive systems. For example, the same approach can be used in autonomous driving (AD) or communication protocols. In both cases, components can be modeled as actors interacting with each other. The behavior, along with the fault injection patterns, can be easily applied at different detail levels. For instance, in an AD system, the detail could be coarse by describing the behavior of interacting driving functions or more fine by modeling the actual communication traffic running between two (or more) electronic control units implementing these functions.

Timed Rebeca is used for timing analysis in different applications, including analysis of timing properties in interoperable medical systems by Zarneshan et al. [31], and analyzing real-time wireless sensor and actuator networks by Khamespanah et al. [13] where Gul Agha is a co-author. In [12], Khamespanah et al. compared analytical methods and model checking using Afra for schedulability analysis of WSAN applications. This paper is different in its approach; here we model failures and implementation details, and reveal how these details can change the timing features of the system.

A Rebeca Syntax

The abstract syntax of Timed Rebeca from [24] is shown in Fig. 8.

$$Model ::= Class^*\ Main$$
$$Main ::= \textbf{main}\ \{\ InstanceDcl^*\ \}$$
$$InstanceDcl ::= className\ rebecName(\langle rebecName\rangle^*) : (\langle literal\rangle^*);$$
$$Class ::= \textbf{reactiveclass}\ className\ \{\ KnownRebecs\ Vars\ MsgSrv^*\ \}$$
$$KnownRebecs ::= \textbf{knownrebecs}\ \{\ VarDcl^*\ \}$$
$$Vars ::= \textbf{statevars}\ \{\ VarDcl^*\ \}$$
$$VarDcl ::= type\ \langle v\rangle^+;$$
$$MsgSrv ::= \textbf{msgsrv}\ methodName(\langle type\ v\rangle^*)\ \{\ Stmt^*\ \}$$
$$Stmt ::= v = e;\ |\ v =?(e, \langle e\rangle^+);\ |\ Call;\ |\ \textbf{delay}(t);\ |\ if\ (e)\ \{\ Stmt^*\ \}[else\ \{\ Stmt^*\ \}]$$
$$Call ::= rebecName.methodName(\langle e\rangle^*)\ [\textbf{after}(t)]\ [\textbf{deadline}(t)]$$

Fig. 8. An abstract syntax for Timed Rebeca. The identifiers, className, rebecName, methodName, literal, and type, are self-explanatory. The identifier v denotes a variable. The symbol e denotes an expression, which can be either arithmetic, boolean, or a non-deterministic choice. Angular brackets ⟨...⟩ serve as meta-parenthesis, with superscript + denoting at least one repetition and superscript ∗ denoting zero or more repetitions. Meanwhile, using ⟨...⟩ with repetition indicates a comma-separated list. Square brackets [...] indicate that the enclosed text is optional [24].

B Timed Rebeca Model of the NRP FD

```
 1 // Timed Rebeca model for NRP FD.
 2 // This program models a redundant fault tolerant system where a primary node, if and
       when it fails,
 3 // is replaced by a backup node. This version models network switch failures that are
       spaced
 4 // sufficiently far apart in time that dual primaries do not emerge. To manage the
       state-space
 5 // size, the heartbeat period and other time values are reduced.
 6 //
 7 // The protocol is described in this paper:
 8 // Bjarne Johansson; Mats Råberger; Alessandro V. Papadopoulos; Thomas Nolte,
       "Consistency Before
 9 // Availability: Network Reference Point based Failure Detection for Controller
       Redundancy," paper
10 // draft 8/15/23.
11 //
12 // The key idea in this protocol is that when a backup fails to detect the heartbeats of
       a primary
13 // node, it becomes primary only if it has access to Network Reference Point (NRP),
       which is a point
14 // in the network.
15 //
16 // The Primary sends heartbeats on two networks,
17 // if the Backup receives the heartbeats from both networks then all is fine.
18 // If it receives the heartbeat only from one network the Backup pings the NRP, if NRP
       replies all is fine,
```

```
19  // if not
20  // If Backup misses heartbeats on both networks then it assumes that the Primary failed
        and pings NRP,
21  // if NRP replies, Backup becomes the Primary
22  // if not ...
23  //
24  // The Rebeca code is adopted from the LF code by Edward Lee and Marjan Sirjani, and
        refined by Bahman Pourvatan

26  // Timing configuration
27  env int heartbeat_period = 20;
28  env int max_missed_heartbeats = 2;
29  env int ping_timeout = 10;
30  env int nrp_timeout = 10;  // Timeout for requesting a new NRP
31  // Node Modes
32  env byte WAITING = 0;
33  env byte PRIMARY = 1;
34  env byte BACKUP = 2;
35  env byte FAILED = 3;
36  env byte NumberOfNetworks = 2;
37  // for testing
38  env int fails_at_time = 0;  //zero for no failure
39  env int switchA1failtime = 0;
40  env int switchA2failtime = 0;
41  env int switchA3failtime = 0;
42  env int switchB1failtime = 0;
43  env int switchB2failtime = 0;
44  env int switchB3failtime = 0;
45  env int node1failtime = 0;
46  env int node2failtime = 0;
47  env int networkDelay = 1;

49  // Minimum time between switch failures is H + 2N + 1, where H is the heartbeat_period
        and N is the networkDelay.
50  // The +1 is needed because of the nondeterministic ordering of message handlers.
51  // If a switch receives a switchFail() message at some time t, it nondeterministically
        may forward
52  // a heartbeat message that happens to arrive at the same time.
53  // The +1 ensures that the failure occurs after the message has been forwarded.
54  env int min_interval = 23;

56  // Generate switchFailure messages to switches that are nondeterministically chosen.
57  // This class ensures a minimum interval of min_interval between any two switch failures.
58  reactiveclass FailureController(10) {
59      knownrebecs {
60          Switch switchA1, switchA2, switchA3, switchB1, switchB2, switchB3;
61      }
62      statevars {}
63      FailureController () {
64          self.chooseFailureTime() after(2*heartbeat_period);  // Let startup phase pass.
65      }
66      msgsrv chooseFailureTime() {
67          int failure_time = ? (0, 1, 2, 3, 4, 5, 6, 7, 8, 9, 10, 11, 12, 13, 14, 15, 16,
                17, 18, 19);
68          self.maybeFail() after (failure_time);
69      }
70      msgsrv maybeFail() {
71          boolean failure = ? (false, true);
72          byte s = ? (1, 2, 3, 4, 5, 6);
73          if (failure) {
74              if (s == 1) {
75                  switchA1.switchFail();
76              } else if (s == 2) {
77                  switchA2.switchFail();
78              } else if (s == 3) {
79                  switchA3.switchFail();
80              } else if (s == 4) {
81                  switchB1.switchFail();
```

```
            } else if (s == 5) {
                switchB2.switchFail();
            } else if (s == 6) {
                switchB3.switchFail();
            }
            maybeFail() after (min_interval);
        } else {
            maybeFail() after (1);
        }
    }
}

reactiveclass Node (20){
    knownrebecs {
        Switch out1, out2;
    }
    statevars {
        byte mode;
        int id;
        int [2] NRPCandidates;
        int heartbeats_missed_1;
        int heartbeats_missed_2;
        int NRP_network;
        int NRP_switch_id;
        boolean NRP_pending;
        boolean become_primary_on_ping_response;
        int primary;
        boolean ping_pending;
    }
    Node (int Myid, int Myprimary, int NRPCan1_id, int NRPCan2_id, int myFailTime) {
        id = Myid;
        NRPCandidates[0] = NRPCan1_id;
        NRPCandidates[1] = NRPCan2_id;
        heartbeats_missed_1 = 0;
        heartbeats_missed_2 = 0;
        NRP_network = -1;
        NRP_switch_id = -1;
        NRP_pending = true;
        become_primary_on_ping_response = false;
        primary = Myprimary;
        ping_pending = false;
        mode = WAITING;
        if(myFailTime!=0) nodeFail() after(myFailTime);
        runMe();
    }
    // Check whether a response was received to request_new_NRP() and fail if not.
    msgsrv new_NRP_request_timed_out() {
        if (mode == BACKUP) {
            if (NRP_pending) {
                NRP_pending = false;
                mode = FAILED;
            }
        }
    }
    // logical action ping_timed_out(ping_timeout)
    msgsrv ping_timed_out() {
        if (mode == BACKUP) {
            if (ping_pending) {
                // Backup node did not get a response to the ping of the NRP.
                ping_pending = false;
                NRP_network++;
                // Request a new NRP, unless it pinged the NRP because both networks had
                        missed heartbeats.
                if (become_primary_on_ping_response) {
                    become_primary_on_ping_response = false;
                    mode = FAILED;
                } else if (NRP_network < NumberOfNetworks) {
                    // Request a new NRP should be possible.
```

```
149                    NRP_pending = true;
150                    NRP_switch_id = NRPCandidates[NRP_network];
151                    if (NRP_network == 0) out1.request_new_NRP(id) after(networkDelay);
152                    else out2.request_new_NRP(id) after(networkDelay);
153                    self.new_NRP_request_timed_out() after(nrp_timeout);
154                } else {
155                    NRP_network = NumberOfNetworks;
156                    mode = FAILED; // Operator intervention required.
157                }
158            }
159        } else if (mode == PRIMARY) {
160            if (ping_pending) {
161                // NRP did not respond to ping. Try to find a new NRP, if possible, and
                       fail otherwise.
162                NRP_pending = true;
163                NRP_network++;
164                if (NRP_network < NumberOfNetworks) {
165                    // Select the NRP candidate on the new network and ping it.
166                    NRP_switch_id = NRPCandidates[NRP_network];
167                    if (NRP_network == 0) out1.new_NRP(id, NRP_network,NRP_switch_id)
                            after(networkDelay);
168                    else out2.new_NRP(id, NRP_network,NRP_switch_id) after(networkDelay);
169                } else {
170                    NRP_network = NumberOfNetworks;
171                    mode = FAILED; // Operator intervention required.
172                }
173            } else {
174               out1.heartBeat(0, id) after(networkDelay);
175               out2.heartBeat(1, id) after(networkDelay);
176            }
177        }
178    }
179    msgsrv pingNRP_response(int mid) {
180        if (mode == BACKUP) {
181            ping_pending = false;
182            if (become_primary_on_ping_response) {
183                // Confirmed that NRP is accessible even though heartbeats are missing on
                       both networks.
184                become_primary_on_ping_response = false;
185                mode = PRIMARY;
186                primary = id;
187            }
188        } else if (mode == PRIMARY) {
189            ping_pending = false;
190            if (NRP_pending) {
191                NRP_pending = false; // NRP is confirmed.
192            }
193        }
194    }
195    msgsrv new_NRP(int mid, int mNRP_network, int mNRP_switch_id) {
196        NRP_network = mNRP_network;
197        NRP_switch_id = mNRP_switch_id;
198        if (NRP_network == 0) heartbeats_missed_1 = 0;
199        else heartbeats_missed_2 = 0;

201        NRP_pending = false;
202    }
203    msgsrv request_new_NRP(int origin) {
204        NRP_network++;
205        if (NRP_network < NumberOfNetworks) {
206            NRP_switch_id = NRPCandidates[NRP_network];
207            if (NRP_network == 0) out1.new_NRP(id, NRP_network, NRP_switch_id);
208            else out2.new_NRP(id, NRP_network, NRP_switch_id);
209        }
210    }
211    msgsrv runMe() {
212        switch(mode) {
213            case 0: //WAITING :
```

```
                    if (id == primary) {
                        mode = PRIMARY;
                        NRP_network++;
                        if (NRP_network < NumberOfNetworks) {
                            NRP_switch_id = NRPCandidates[NRP_network];
                            if (NRP_network == 0) out1.new_NRP(id, NRP_network, NRP_switch_id);
                            else out2.new_NRP(id, NRP_network, NRP_switch_id);
                        } else NRP_network = NumberOfNetworks;
                    } else mode = BACKUP;
                    break;
                case 1: //PRIMARY :
                    if (NRP_network == 0) {
                        ping_pending = true;
                        out1.pingNRP(id, NRP_switch_id) after(networkDelay);
                        ping_timed_out() after(ping_timeout);
                    } else {
                        ping_pending = true;
                        out2.pingNRP(id, NRP_switch_id) after(networkDelay);
                        ping_timed_out() after(ping_timeout);
                    }
                    NRP_pending = true;
                    break;
                case 2: //BACKUP :
                    heartbeats_missed_1++;
                    heartbeats_missed_2++;
                    if (heartbeats_missed_1 > max_missed_heartbeats && heartbeats_missed_2 >
                            max_missed_heartbeats) {
                        if (heartbeats_missed_1==heartbeats_missed_2) { // Simultaneous
                                heartbeat misses.
                            mode = PRIMARY;
                            primary = id;
                        } else {
                            become_primary_on_ping_response = true;
                            ping_pending = true;
                            if (NRP_network == 0){
                                out1.pingNRP(id, NRP_switch_id) after(networkDelay);
                            } else {
                                out2.pingNRP(id, NRP_switch_id) after(networkDelay);
                            }
                            ping_timed_out() after(ping_timeout);
                        }
                    } else if (heartbeats_missed_1 > max_missed_heartbeats &
                            heartbeats_missed_2 > max_missed_heartbeats) {
                        // Heartbeat missed on one network but not yet on the other.
                        // Ping the NRP to make sure we retain access to it so that we can be
                            an effective backup.
                        if (NRP_network==0 && heartbeats_missed_1 > max_missed_heartbeats) {
                            ping_pending = true;
                            out1.pingNRP(id, NRP_switch_id) after(networkDelay);
                            ping_timed_out() after(ping_timeout);
                        } else if (NRP_network ==1 && heartbeats_missed_2 >
                                max_missed_heartbeats) {
                            ping_pending = true;
                            out2.pingNRP(id, NRP_switch_id) after(networkDelay);
                            ping_timed_out() after(ping_timeout);
                        }
                        heartbeats_missed_1 = (heartbeats_missed_1>max_missed_heartbeats+1)?
                                max_missed_heartbeats+1:heartbeats_missed_1;
                        heartbeats_missed_2 = (heartbeats_missed_2>max_missed_heartbeats+1)?
                                max_missed_heartbeats+1:heartbeats_missed_2;
                    }
                    break;
                case 3: //FAILED :
                    break;
            }
            self.runMe() after(heartbeat_period);
        }
        msgsrv heartBeat(byte networkId, int senderid) {
```

```
275            if (mode==BACKUP) {
276                if (networkId == 0) heartbeats_missed_1 = 0;
277                else heartbeats_missed_2 = 0;
278            }
279        }
280        msgsrv nodeFail() {
281            primary=-1;
282            mode = FAILED;
283            NRP_network=-1;
284            NRP_switch_id=-1;
285            heartbeats_missed_1 = 0;
286            heartbeats_missed_2 = 0;
287            NRP_pending = true;
288            become_primary_on_ping_response = false;
289            ping_pending = false;
290        }
291    }

293    reactiveclass Switch(10) {
294        knownrebecs {
295        }
296        statevars {
297            byte mynetworkId;
298            int id;
299            boolean failed;
300            boolean amINRP;
301            boolean terminal;
302            Node nodeTarget1;
303            Switch switchTarget2;
304            Switch switchTarget1;
305        }
306        Switch (int myid, byte networkId, boolean term, Switch s1, Switch s2, int
                  myFailTime, Node n1) {
307            mynetworkId = networkId;
308            id = myid;
309            amINRP = false;
310            failed = false;
311            switchTarget1 = s1;
312            switchTarget2 = s2;
313            terminal=term;
314            nodeTarget1=n1;
315            if (myFailTime!=0) switchFail() after(myFailTime);
316        }
317        msgsrv switchFail() {
318            failed = true;
319            amINRP=false;
320        }
321        msgsrv pingNRP_response(int senderNode) {
322            if (!failed) {
323                if (terminal && senderNode <= 100) {
324                    nodeTarget1.pingNRP_response(id) after(networkDelay); //Pass back
325                } else if (senderNode>id) {
326                    switchTarget1.pingNRP_response(id) after(networkDelay);
327                } else {
328                    switchTarget2.pingNRP_response(id) after(networkDelay);
329                }
330            }
331        }
332        msgsrv request_new_NRP(int senderNode) {
333            if (!failed) {
334                if (terminal && senderNode < 100) nodeTarget1.request_new_NRP(id)
                      after(networkDelay);
335                else if (senderNode > id) switchTarget1.request_new_NRP(id)
                      after(networkDelay);
336                else switchTarget2.request_new_NRP(id) after(networkDelay);
337            }
338        }
339        msgsrv pingNRP(int senderNode, int NRP) {
```

```
340            if (!failed) {
341                if (NRP == id) {
342                    if (senderNode < 100) switchTarget2.pingNRP_response(id)
                               after(networkDelay); //Response
343                    else nodeTarget1.pingNRP_response(id) after(networkDelay);
344                } else {
345                    if(senderNode < 100) {
346                        if(senderNode>id) switchTarget1.pingNRP(id, NRP) after(networkDelay);
347                        else switchTarget2.pingNRP(id, NRP) after(networkDelay);
348                    } else {
349                        switchTarget2.pingNRP(id, NRP) after(networkDelay);
350                    }
351                }
352            }
353        }
354        msgsrv new_NRP(int senderNode, int mNRP_network, int mNRP_switch_id) {
355            if (!failed) {
356                if (id == mNRP_switch_id) amINRP=true;
357                else amINRP=false;

359                if (terminal && senderNode < 100) nodeTarget1.new_NRP(id, mNRP_network,
                           mNRP_switch_id); //Pass back
360                else if(senderNode>id) switchTarget1.new_NRP(id, mNRP_network,
                           mNRP_switch_id);
361                else switchTarget2.new_NRP(id, mNRP_network, mNRP_switch_id);
362            }
363        }
364        msgsrv heartBeat(byte networkId, int senderNode) {
365            if (!failed) {
366                if (terminal && senderNode < 100) nodeTarget1.heartBeat(networkId,id)
                           after(networkDelay);
367                else if (senderNode > id) switchTarget1.heartBeat(networkId,id)
                           after(networkDelay);
368                else switchTarget2.heartBeat(networkId,id) after(networkDelay);
369            }
370        }
371 }
372 main {
373     @Priority(1) FailureController failureC(switchA1, switchA2, switchA3, switchB1,
               switchB2, switchB3):();

375     @Priority(1) Switch switchA1():(1, 0, true , switchA2 , switchA2 , switchA1failtime,
               DCN1);
376     @Priority(1) Switch switchA2():(2 ,0, false , switchA1 , switchA3 ,
               switchA2failtime, null);
377     @Priority(1) Switch switchA3():(3, 0, true , switchA2 , switchA2 , switchA3failtime,
               DCN2);
378     @Priority(1) Switch switchB1():(4, 1, true , switchB2 , switchB2 , switchB1failtime,
               DCN1);
379     @Priority(1) Switch switchB2():(5, 1, false , switchB1 , switchB3 ,
               switchB2failtime, null);
380     @Priority(1) Switch switchB3():(6, 1, true , switchB2 , switchB2 , switchB3failtime,
               DCN2);

382     @Priority(2) Node DCN1(switchA1, switchB1):(100, 100, 1, 4, node1failtime);
383     @Priority(2) Node DCN2(switchA3, switchB3):(101, 100, 3, 6, node2failtime);
384 }
```

References

1. Agha, G.: An overview of actor languages. In: Wegner, P., Shriver, B.D. (eds.) Proceedings of the 1986 SIGPLAN Workshop on Object-Oriented Programming, OOPWORK 1986, Yorktown Heights, New York, USA, June 9-13, 1986, pp. 58–67. ACM (1986). https://doi.org/10.1145/323779.323743

2. Agha, G., Hewitt, C.: Actors: A conceptual foundation for concurrent object-oriented programming. In: Shriver, B.D., Wegner, P. (eds.) Research Directions in Object-Oriented Programming, pp. 49–74. MIT Press (1987)
3. Agha, G.A.: Actors: a Model of Concurrent Computation in Distributed Systems (Parallel Processing, Semantics, Open, Programming Languages, Artificial Intelligence). Ph.D. thesis, University of Michigan, USA (1985). http://hdl.handle.net/2027.42/160629
4. Åkerberg, J., Furunäs Åkesson, J., Gade, J., Vahabi, M., Björkman, M., Lavassani, M., Nandkumar Gore, R., Lindh, T., Jiang, X.: Future industrial networks in process automation: Goals, challenges, and future directions. Appl. Sci. **11**(8), 3345 (2021)
5. Atkinson, R.R., Hewitt, C.: Parallelism and synchronization in actor systems. In: Graham, R.M., Harrison, M.A., Sethi, R. (eds.) Conference Record of the Fourth ACM Symposium on Principles of Programming Languages, Los Angeles, California, USA, January 1977, pp. 267–280. ACM (1977). https://doi.org/10.1145/512950.512975
6. Brewer, E.A.: Towards robust distributed systems (abstract). In: Neiger, G. (ed.) Proceedings of the Nineteenth Annual ACM Symposium on Principles of Distributed Computing, July 16-19, 2000, Portland, Oregon, USA, p. 7. ACM (2000). https://doi.org/10.1145/343477.343502
7. Hewitt, C., Bishop, P., Steiger, R.: A universal modular actor formalism for artificial intelligence. In: Proceedings of the 3rd International Joint Conference on Artificial Intelligence, pp. 235–245. Morgan Kaufmann Publishers Inc. (1973). http://ijcai.org/Proceedings/73/Papers/027B.pdf
8. Hewitt, C., Bishop, P.B., Greif, I., Smith, B.C., Matson, T., Steiger, R.: Actor induction and meta-evaluation. In: Fischer, P.C., Ullman, J.D. (eds.) Conference Record of the ACM Symposium on Principles of Programming Languages, Boston, Massachusetts, USA, October 1973, pp. 153–168. ACM Press (1973). https://doi.org/10.1145/512927.512942
9. Johansson, B., et al.: Systematic test case generation for distributed redundant controllers using model checking (extended abstract) (2024)
10. Johansson, B., Pourvatan, B., Moezkarimi, Z., Papadopoulos, A., Sirjani, M.: Formal verification of consistency for systems with redundant controllers. Electron. Proc. Theoret. Comput. Sci. **399**, 169–191 (2024)
11. Johansson, B., Rågberger, M., Papadopoulos, A., Nolte, T.: Consistency before availability: Network reference point based failure detection for controller redundancy. In: ETFA, pp. 1–8 (2023)
12. Khamespanah, E., Mohaqeqi, M., Ashjaei, M., Sirjani, M.: Schedulability analysis of WSAN applications: Outperformance of a model checking approach. In: 27th IEEE International Conference on Emerging Technologies and Factory Automation, ETFA 2022, Stuttgart, Germany, September 6-9, 2022, pp. 1–8. IEEE (2022). https://doi.org/10.1109/ETFA52439.2022.9921644
13. Khamespanah, E., Sirjani, M., Mechitov, K., Agha, G.: Modeling and analyzing real-time wireless sensor and actuator networks using actors and model checking. Int. J. Softw. Tools Technol. Transf. **20**(5), 547–561 (2018) https://doi.org/10.1007/S10009-017-0480-3
14. Khamespanah, E., Sirjani, M., Sabahi-Kaviani, Z., Khosravi, R., Izadi, M.: Timed rebeca schedulability and deadlock freedom analysis using bounded floating time transition system. Sci. Comput. Program. **98**, 184–204 (2015). https://doi.org/10.1016/j.scico.2014.07.005

15. Khosravi, R., Khamespanah, E., Ghassemi, F., Sirjani, M.: Actors upgraded for variability, adaptability, and determinism. In: Workshop on State-of-the-Art of Active Objects, pp. 226–260 (2024). https://doi.org/10.1007/978-3-031-51060-1_9
16. Leander, B., Johansson, B., Lindström, T., Holmgren, O., Nolte, T., Papadopoulos, A.V.: Dependability and security aspects of network-centric control. In: 2023 IEEE 28th International Conference on Emerging Technologies and Factory Automation (ETFA), pp. 1–8. IEEE (2023). https://doi.org/10.1109/ETFA54631.2023.10275344
17. Lee, E.A., Akella, R., Bateni, S., Lin, S., Lohstroh, M., Menard, C.: Consistency vs. availability in distributed cyber-physical systems. ACM Trans. Embed. Comput. Syst. **22**(5s), 138:1–138:24 (2023). https://doi.org/10.1145/3609119
18. Lohstroh, M., Lee, E.A.: Deterministic actors. In: Forum on Specification and Design Languages (FDL), (September 2-4 2019)
19. Lohstroh, M., Menard, C., Bateni, S., Lee, E.A.: Toward a lingua franca for deterministic concurrent systems. ACM Trans. Embedded Comput. Syst. (TECS) **20**(4), Article 36 (2021)
20. Lohstroh, M., Schoeberl, M., Goens, A., Wasicek, A., Gill, C.D., Sirjani, M., Lee, E.A.: Actors revisited for time-critical systems. In: Proceedings of the 56th Annual Design Automation Conference 2019, DAC 2019, Las Vegas, NV, USA, June 02-06, 2019, p. 152. ACM (2019). https://doi.org/10.1145/3316781.3323469
21. Schulz-Rosengarten, A., Hanxleden, R.v., Lohstroh, M., Lee, E.A., Bateni, S.: Polyglot modal models through lingua franca. In: Cyber-Physical Systems and Internet of Things Week (CPS-IoT), pp. 337–242 (2023)
22. Simion, A., Bira, C.: A review of redundancy in plc-based systems. Advanced Topics in Optoelectronics, Microelectronics, and Nanotechnologies XI **12493**, 269–276 (2023). https://doi.org/10.1117/12.2644462
23. Sirjani, M.: Rebeca: Theory, applications, and tools. In: de Boer, F.S., Bonsangue, M.M., Graf, S., de Roever, W.P. (eds.) Formal Methods for Components and Objects, 5th International Symposium, FMCO 2006, Amsterdam, The Netherlands, November 7-10, 2006, Revised Lectures. Lecture Notes in Computer Science, vol. 4709, pp. 102–126. Springer (2006). https://doi.org/10.1007/978-3-540-74792-5_5
24. Sirjani, M.: Power is overrated, go for friendliness! expressiveness, faithfulness, and usability in modeling: the actor experience. In: Lohstroh, M., Derler, P., Sirjani, M. (eds.) Principles of Modeling - Essays Dedicated to Edward A. Lee on the Occasion of His 60th Birthday. LNCS, vol. 10760, pp. 423–448. Springer (2018). https://doi.org/10.1007/978-3-319-95246-8_25
25. Sirjani, M., de Boer, F.S., Jaghoori, M.M.: Task scheduling in rebeca. In: NWPT 2007, pp. 16–18 (2007)
26. Sirjani, M., Khamespanah, E.: On time actors. In: Ábrahám, E., Bonsangue, M.M., Johnsen, E.B. (eds.) Theory and Practice of Formal Methods. LNCS, vol. 9660, pp. 373–392. Springer (2016)
27. Sirjani, M., Lee, E.A., Khamespanah, E.: Model checking software in cyberphysical systems. In: COMPSAC 2020, pp. 1017–1026. IEEE (2020)
28. Sirjani, M., Lee, E.A., Khamespanah, E.: Verification of cyberphysical systems. Mathematics **8**(7) (2020). https://doi.org/10.3390/math8071068
29. Sirjani, M., Movaghar, A., Mousavi, M.: Compositional verification of an object-based model for reactive systems. In: AVoCS 2001 (2001). https://rebeca-lang.org/assets/papers/2001/CompositionalVerificationOfAnObjectBasedModelForReactiveSystems.pdf

30. Sirjani, M., Movaghar, A., Shali, A., de Boer, F.S.: Modeling and verification of reactive systems using rebeca. Fundam. Informaticae **63**(4), 385–410 (2004)
31. Zarneshan, M., Ghassemi, F., Khamespanah, E., Sirjani, M., Hatcliff, J.: Specification and verification of timing properties in interoperable medical systems. Log. Methods Comput. Sci. **18**(2) (2022). https://doi.org/10.46298/LMCS-18(2:13)2022

Actors and Blockchains, Together

Xiaohong Chen[1] and Grigore Rosu[1,2(✉)]

[1] Pi Squared Inc., Champaign, IL 61822, USA
xiaohong.chen@pi2.network
[2] University of Illinois, Urbana, IL 61801, USA
grosu@illinois.edu

Abstract. FastSet is a distributed protocol for decentralized finance and settlement, which is inspired from both actors and blockchains. Account holders cooperate by making claims, which can include payments, holding and transferring assets, accessing and updating shared data, medical records, digital identity, and mathematical theorems, among others. The claims are signed by their owners and are broadcast to a decentralized network of validators, which validate and settle them. Validators replicate the global state of the accounts and need not communicate with each other. In sharp contrast to blockchains, strong consistency is purposely given up as a requirement. Yet, many if not most of the blockchain benefits are preserved, while capitalizing on actor's massive parallelism.

Keywords: Blockchain · Distributed system · Concurrency · Actor model

1 Introduction

Blockchains are strongly consistent distributed systems in which account holders cooperate by making transactions. Transactions are intents of actions, which need to be given a state to execute in order to materialize. Transactions are signed by their owners and broadcast to a decentralized network of nodes, sometimes called miners or validators. The nodes play dice in order to identify a proposer for the next block (or sequence) of transactions. Nodes replicate the global state and follow a consensus protocol by which the proposed block is processed by all the nodes, thus materializing all the transactions in the block and each node updating its state accordingly. In the end, the transactions submitted to the blockchain are totally ordered, and thus so are the states in between.

Strongly consistent distributed systems [6,8,9,12] "behave like one computer", which is the desirable property for blockchains, but are notorious for higher latency and lower performance and scalability—they require coordination and

---

This paper is dedicated to Gul Agha, leader of the actor model of concurrency, who has taught generations of students that concurrent programming is hard only if you do not have the right model.

communication between nodes to maintain consistency. At the other extreme stands the actor model [1,7], aiming at highly parallel computing and massive concurrency. Actors are the basic building blocks of concurrent computation and communicate only through messages. In response to a message it receives, an actor can modify its own private state, create more actors together with code governing their behavior, and send messages to other actors.

There is no doubt that blockchains play an important role in modern finance. Also, blockchains have demonstrated, in our view irreversibly, that decentralization is not only possible in the world of digital assets, but also very much desirable. Not only decentralization addresses the single point of failure, corruption, and censorship vulnerabilities, but equally importantly, through blockchains, it has lead to the Web3 philosophy and movement: users own their digital assets, from money to diplomas and medical records to pictures and messages, and they and only they can transfer them and decide who has access to what. However, a major overhaul is needed in order to scale blockchains and achieve the level of high performance and low cost required by recent applications. For example, few blockchains can consistently perform more than 1,000 transactions per second (TPS) and it takes seconds, sometimes minutes, to settle a transaction. Metaphorically, because of the total order on transactions that they enforce by their nature, blockchains require the entire universe to squeeze through a narrow pipe. Completely unrelated transactions are required to stay in line and wait to be sequenced in some order that the blockchain must globally choose when forming its next block. This is clearly not scalable, even if all transactions are initiated by humans. The situation is in fact much worse, because AI and AI agents doing transactions on humans' behalf are already here to stay and they require a payment system able to perform millions of TPS, most of which micro-transactions whose cost is expected to be negligible, in the order of fractions of a cent. Blockchains cannot do this. A massively parallel decentralized infrastructure for payments in particular and computing in general is required.

A series of papers before 2008 culminating with Bitcoin [11], have incrementally built a belief that a total order on transactions ought to be required in any distributed/decentralized payment system in order to avoid the infamous double spending attack: an account sending two concurrent transactions attempting to spend the same coin with two different recipients. A total ordering enforced on transaction settlement indeed solves the double spending problem, but is it really necessary? Recent works starting around 2019 [2,4,5] propose a radically different way to approach the problem, a truly concurrent approach where payments can be generated and settled in different orders by different nodes without breaking the semantics of payments. The key insight of these works is that the order in which an account receives payments is irrelevant, and so is the order in which different accounts send payments—provided each account stays valid: no double spending and sufficient balance. That is, as far as the nodes/validators are in agreement on the *set* of locally valid transactions that took place in the system, consensus on a total order is unnecessary. We believe that this apparently simple and innocent observation marks a crucial breakthrough moment in decentralized finance. A moment where the tyranny of sequentiality is abolished and the door is open to innovations that will lead to the next generation of decentralized, yet truly concurrent, safe and scalable infrastructure for digital assets.

Inspired by this recent work on weaker variants of consensus in the context of cryptocurrencies [2,4,5], as well as by the unbounded concurrent computing promise of the actor model [1,7], in this paper we discuss at a high-level FastSet, a general-purpose distributed computing protocol that generalizes the payment system protocol FastPay [2]—we encourage the reader to consult [3] for a detailed presentation of FastSet. FastSet performs nearly embarrassingly parallel settlement of arbitrary verifiable claims, including verifiable computations in arbitrary programming languages. Specifically, FastSet allows a set of *clients* to settle verifiable *claims* consistently, using a set of *validators*. Clients broadcast their claims to all validators. Validators validate the received claims and replicate the system state based on the order in which they receive the claims. Importantly, similarly to FastPay but in sharp contrast to blockchains, the FastSet validators do not need to communicate with each other, nor directly achieve consensus on any values or orders or blocks or computations.

What makes the problem difficult is that claims can have side effects on the validators' states. However, if claims issued by different clients are *weakly independent*, a notion that generalizes the property of commutativity on payments [2,4,5] discussed above to arbitrary state-effectful computations, then the validators' states will remain (strongly eventually) consistent in spite of the different orders in which they receive and process the claims.

Like in blockchains, FastSet accounts have a state (e.g., a balance) and are required to sign any claims they issue. We present the protocol in Sect. 2, requiring only abstract notions of state, claim, and claim validity and effect. How claims are generated, e.g., randomly by users or programmatically by contracts, is irrelevant for the core protocol and its correctness (Theorem 1). However, to make it practical, implementations of FastSet have to offer specific types of claims and specific ways to generate them. In Sect. 3 we propose an actor-inspired language for generating claims, which we call the FastSet Language, abbreviate SETL[1], and pronounce "settle". Some accounts are controlled by users, others by SETL programs (or scripts, or contracts). The difference is that the user-controlled accounts are free to issue any claims, including ones that create new accounts and interact with them, while the contract-based accounts can only issue claims as prescribed by their SETL program/script/contract.

Like in the actor model, accounts are regarded as actors that communicate only with the actors they know about, and can create new accounts/actors and then communicate with them. Since validators maintain replicas of the global system state, all the actors/accounts are also replicated on all validators. This should not be regarded as a deviation from the underlying thesis of the actor model, where each actor is meant to be a separate process interacting concur-

---

[1] Not to be confused with the SET Language https://en.wikipedia.org/wiki/SETL invented in late 1960s, based on the mathematical theory of sets.

rently with the other actors, but rather as a high-availability high-resilience decentralized implementation of an actor system. Moreover, the actor model is particularly suitable for a language like SETL for two additional reasons: (1) each validator can itself be a high-performance concurrent system, which receives and processes potentially millions of claims per second, so SETL must be a high-performance concurrent programming language; and (2) since each validator receives the claims in different orders, yet all of them (strongly eventually consistently) are expected to replicate the same state, SETL concurrent programs must be easy to reason about, in particular to prove their determinism.

2 The FastSet Protocol

In this section we describe the FastSet protocol, depicted in Fig. 1.

2.1 Participants

FastSet involves two types of participants:

Clients. These are account/address holders, who can make *claims*. They can be users, apps (contracts, web2, games), L1s, L2s, micro-chains, AI agents, service providers, execution engines/layers, provers (mathematical, ZK), TEEs, oracles, VRFs, AI compute/inferencers, indexers, history query providers, verifiers (execution, semantics and/or ZK proof based), fact claimers (KYC providers, digital identity providers, academic or medical records, etc.), token issuers (stablecoins, ERCs, NFTs, RWAs, etc.), etc.

Validators. These process claims made by the clients, while at the same time maintaining consistency in the global knowledge about the overall system: balances of all tokens and additional data/state of all clients, global state of the entire protocol, like the set of all the claims that were settled, etc.

All participants possess a key pair consisting of a private signature key and the corresponding public verification key. If msg is a message and p is a participant, then $\langle msg \rangle_p$ denotes the message signed by p, whose authenticity can be publicly checked. Like in blockchains, in FastSet the public key of a client a serves as the public account number, or the address of a. Additional layers of privacy can be added if desired, but that is out of the scope of this paper.

2.2 Claims and Weak Independence

We define FastSet parametrically, on top of two important abstractions, *claims* and their *weak independence*, which we discuss next.

A *claim* is any statement that is independently *verifiable*. To help the verifiers, the claim provider may associate additional evidence to the claim, such as a proof or a witness or even an authoritative signature; how claims provide evidence and how verifiers verify a claim is orthogonal to FastSet and is not our concern in this paper. Here are some examples of claims: "I am Joe Smith" (a fact where the signer is important); "Pythagoras theorem" (a fact where the signer is less important); "the price of gold is 100 USD" (an oracle); "the next random number is 17" (a VRF); "I want to buy a ticket to this concert" (an intent); "the result to your query is 42" (an AI service provided); "Python program `fibonacci` on input 10 evaluates to 55" (verifiers may re-execute, or require a math or ZK proof based on Python formal semantics); "my Angry Birds score is 739" (requires 3rd party or ZK proof); "my next move in this chess game with Alice is Nf3" (modifying a shared storage location sequentially); "I vote YES for that petition" (modifying a shared storage location non-sequentially); "I, Grigore, pay Alice 10 USD" (a payment, modifying two storage locations).

For simplicity and generality, we only assume a global state in FastSet, which will be replicated in each validator. In practice, each client will have their own reserved state space, but that stronger assumption is not needed to prove the correctness of FastSet; all we need is that claims issued by different clients are weakly independent, to be discussed shortly. What is important is that a claim may or may not be valid in a given state (e.g., a payment is invalid when the sender's balance is not enough), and that the processing of a claim can and usually does change the state (e.g., even an otherwise side-effect-free claim may be counted, at a minimum). We write $c \downarrow_s$ whenever a claim c is valid in a state s, and in that case $[\![c]\!]s$ denotes the state obtained after processing c in s. We extend these notations to sequences of claims $c_1 \, c_2 \ldots c_k$ as expected: $c_1 \, c_2 \ldots c_k \downarrow_s$ means that each claim in the sequence is valid in the state obtained after processing the previous ones, and $[\![c_1 \, c_2 \ldots c_k]\!]s$ is the state obtained after processing the entire sequence. The root of difficulty in FastSet, as well as in concurrent and distributed systems in general, is the fact that claim sequences issued by different interacting clients may arrive to validators interleaved in different ways, which may make their states diverge inconsistently.

Drawing inspiration from concurrency theory (e.g., Mazurkiewicz traces [10]), where two events are independent iff they can be processed in any order with the same result, we say that two claims c and c' are *weakly independent*, written $c \parallel c'$, iff once each of them is independently valid, they can be processed in any order and the final result is the same: $c \parallel c'$ iff for any state s, if $c \downarrow_s$ and $c' \downarrow_s$ then $c \, c' \downarrow_s$, $c' \, c \downarrow_s$, and $[\![c \, c']\!]s = [\![c' \, c]\!]s$. Therefore, we weaken the classic notion of independence by requiring it to hold only in those states in which both claims are already valid. This assumption is critical for FastSet because it allows to handle payments and asset transfers as particular claims, and thus generalize FastPay [2]. Here are some examples of weakly independent claims:

- Totally (not weakly) independent claims whose validity has nothing to do with each other, such as: facts which are independently verifiable/true; state queries which are pure, that is, return results but have no side effects; state accesses, including writes/updates, but of disjoint storage locations.
- Commutative operations on a shared location: writing the same value, like in setting a one-way flag to "true"; adding numbers, positive only like in voting or both positive and negative like in reputation systems (e.g., the karma system of Reddit); multiplying numbers, like in aggregating signatures;

adding elements to a set, like in signing petitions, bidding in an auction, or submitting (an intent to make) a transaction; adding elements to a canonical data-structure, like to a sorted list (which is re-sorted after each addition).
- Updates of CRDTs, abbreviating Commutative [13,14] or Conflict-free [15] Replicated Data Types, which are data-types used in the context of distributed systems with the property that concurrent updates on them commute. CRDTs were used mainly in concurrent text editing, but the concept is general and includes many interesting examples, such as integer vectors, sets, maps, and even graphs (with some reasonable restrictions).
- Payments and, more generally, asset transfers from different clients.

Payments are, in particular, a very important use case of FastSet. As critically observed by the authors of FastPay [2], payments have the key property of commutativity on the recipient. Specifically, if Charlie receives payments from both Alice and Bob, then Charlie will end up with the same balance/state no matter in what order the two payments from Alice and Bob are received. And so will Alice and Bob. It can be easily seen that any two payments made by distinct clients are weakly independent. But they are *not* necessarily independent with the standard notion of independence [10]. For example, the claims "Alice pays Bob 1 USD" and "Bob pays Charlie 1 USD" are (weakly independent but) not independent: indeed, consider a state in which Alice has 1 USD and Bob has 0 USD. The same state also demonstrates that two payments made by the same client are not necessarily weakly independent, e.g., "Alice pays Bob 1 USD" and "Alice pays Charlie 1 USD". The weak independence of payments by different clients says that the overall state of the system will be the same independently of the order in which they are processed, provided that the initial state of the system allows for each payment to be independently made.

Non-examples of weak independence include claims acquiring the same mutex, or arbitrary accesses of a shared location where at least one is a write. In particular, and this might look surprising at first sight, an exact balance claim is *not* weakly independent with payment claims to that account. For example, Alice's claim "I have 20 USD" is not weakly independent with payment claims made by others to Alice. On the other hand, monotonic balance claims of the form "I have at least 20 USD" are weakly independent with payments made by others. A challenge for FastSet implementations is to determine what constitutes claims on their network and how they want to enforce weak independence.

2.3 Assumptions

In its most basic form, FastSet's clients and validators form a bipartite graph, where each client is connected to each validator but the clients and, respectively, the validators, are not connected to each other. Specifically, the only communication required by the basic protocol is for each client and each validator to be able to send signed messages to each other. In practice, however, some clients will likely communicate with each other outside of the protocol in order to orchestrate and optimize their individual communication with the validators.

For example, a user's AI agent may require an approval from the user before buying a ticket; instead of communicating exclusively through claims and waiting for each of them to be settled by FastSet before proceeding to the next step, the user and the agent can both send their claims in parallel and settle the transaction faster and cheaper. Similarly, in practice validators will likely have mechanisms to communicate with each other in order to synchronize their states faster than waiting for clients to send them the missing certificates. However, such side communication mechanisms are outside the scope of this paper.

At a high-level, FastSet works as follows. At any given moment, any client can broadcast to validators an ordered block of claims in a signed message. Each validator checks the validity of each block of claims received from each client, and if everything checks the validator approves the block by signing the client's message and sending it back to the client without updating its state yet. The client collects approvals from validators and once it reaches quorum it broadcasts a confirmation message to all validators. Once a validator receives the confirmation it proceeds to updating its state. Special care must be paid by the validator to order the state updates to avoid inconsistencies. Eventually, all validators will consistently settle all the valid claims made by all the clients.

The validators do not question, nor check the intent behind or the client-specific semantics of the client's claims. The validators only check the claims' validity and settle them if valid, operations which are expected to be very efficient; indeed, in practice these operations involve no computations other than updating client balances and storage locations with given values. In other words, from validators' perspective the client claims are just simple commands that they must comply with after a few sanity checks. Any computations using programs or smart contracts in various programming languages and VMs happen within the clients, using their resources and not validators'. It is not validators' concern whether client's computations are adequate or correct according to client's intended semantics or specs or terms and conditions or whatever promises they may have made to their clients. All the validators need to know is the block of claims that the client issues as a result of those potentially complex computations. As an analogy, the validators play the role of an operating system (OS) in a computer, whose job is to ensure consistency across the various programs being executed; the programs are the clients of the OS and all they do from OS's perspective is to issue ordered blocks of commands (the claims).

FastSet therefore gives clients ultimate freedom in what claims they can issue. Without any additional verification, it is quite possible that some clients may make mistakes, some of them even maliciously. For example, the client may hold user assets, such as in the case of a bank, or a centralized exchange, or a blockchain. That is, users may send their assets to the client in expectation of some services. Without any additional verification, there is nothing to prevent the client from stealing users' assets. Even without any evil intent, a client's account may be operated by a complex program which may have subtle errors (such as unintended non-determinism) and thus sometimes produce an incorrect sequence of claims. Even without any program at all, a user client like Alice may mistype 11 instead of 1 when sending a payment to Bob, in which case additional verification, like a multi-sig, would have helped.

There is no silver-bullet solution to cover all types of claim verification that clients or applications need or will ever need. To continue to give clients maximum flexibility, yet to allow the honest clients to verifiably prove themselves to their users, FastSet provides the capability for clients to set up verifiers and a quorum among those in order for its claims to be considered valid by the FastSet validators. Verifiers are themselves clients on the network, whose role is to provide specialized verification services. For example, a verifier can be specialized in verifying program executions in EVM (or Python, or Java, etc.) and clients, e.g., blockchains (or AI agents, or exchanges, etc.), can use it. Such a verifier may re-execute the EVM program to check the result, or may verify a proof produced by an external compute, such as a ZK proof or a TEE proof or even just a signature by some trusted authority (e.g., a centralized exchange which offers services to its KYC-ed clients). It is the client's full responsibility to decide what verifiers to include in their set and what quorum is sufficient.

Implementations of FastSet may optionally provide a simple hardwired programming or scripting language to generate sequences of claims. Programs, or smart contracts, or scripts in this language would be executed by the validators on behalf of clients. That is, instead of providing a block of claims to each validator, a client would provide a script that instructs validators how to generate the block of claims on their behalf, possibly using a client-provided input, at the cost of paying some gas fees to the validators. In this case, clients must pay special care to ensure that each validator deterministically generates the same claims in the same order. Section 3 presents a candidate scripting language.

To simplify the presentation of FastSet and to uniformly capture more use cases, we assume the existence of a proxy that facilitates the interaction between a client, its verifiers, and the validators. The proxy is just a helper which only affects the liveness, but not the safety of the protocol. All it does is to forward or broadcast messages signed by the various participants, and to blindly aggregate signatures ($\#\{sig_1, sig_2, ...\}$). Should the proxy fail to do its job for whatever reason, anybody can replace it and redo the tasks that were missed, including the client. Proxy can be a client (the sender of the original message containing the claim sequence, or a different client such as a beneficiary or a verifier or a service provider), or a validator, or any combination of these for all or for any of the two services it provides, namely broadcasting client messages and aggregating validator signatures. That is, there could be zero, one, or more proxies for each client or application deployed on FastSet. If zero, then the client initiating the claims can do the job of the proxy, or any of the validators.

An honest validator always follows the FastSet protocol, while a faulty (or Byzantine) validator may deviate arbitrarily. Assume $3f + 1$ validators, with a fixed unknown subset of at most f Byzantine validators. A *quorum* is defined as any subset of $2f + 1$ validators. A protocol message signed by a quorum of validators is *certified* and called a *certificate*.

2.4 FastSet

The validator's goal is to consistently replicate the global state, while at the same time offer services through an API. Each validator v is assumed to maintain the following data at a minimum, and to offer it through its API at request:

- A state $v.state$, which is its version of the global state that is replicated in each validator. In implementations of FastSet the state may be partitioned in objects and storage locations owned by or associated to different clients, as well as shared objects and locations, but this distinction is not necessary in the presentation of the core protocol, because the weak independence abstraction between claims by different clients suffices. Each validator may have a different state at any given moment due to message delays and to the massive parallelism allowed by FastSet. Yet, we will show that the various state replicas are consistent and they eventually converge.
- Sets $v.settled$ and $v.presettled$ of client submitted messages, which collectively capture all the knowledge that v has about the claims that have achieved validator quorum in the network. The claims in (the messages in) $v.settled$ have already been processed by v, meaning that their effect on $v.state$ has already been applied and v is ready to process the next block of claims by the same client. The claims in (the messages in) $v.presettled$ have not been processed yet by v, but will be processed as v is ready for them. We will show that all messages in $v.presettled$ will be eventually processed and thus moved to $v.settled$.
- For each client/account/address a some data $v(a)$ including: $v(a).nonce$, a sequence number counting the claim settlement requests by a; $v(a).pending$, a temporary placeholder containing at most one (latest valid) message received from a. FastSet implementations may hold more client-specific data. Immediate candidates can be $v(a).verifiers$, a set of verifiers that a uses to verify its claim blocks, especially when it uses the same verifiers for all messages, and related, $v(a).quorum$, a number of verifiers that a considers sufficient in order for its claim blocks to be considered verified.

Figure 1 shows how FastSet works. It is a seven-step protocol.

① Client a broadcasts a block of claims $c_1 c_2 \ldots c_k$, paired with its local nonce n, in a message $\langle c_1 c_2 \ldots c_k, n \rangle_a$ that it signs, say m. The nonce helps the validators synchronize with the client, making sure that they execute the client's claims in the intended order. An honest client should never submit two different claim blocks with the same nonce, because that is the FastSet equivalent of a double spending attempt. Regardless, the protocol will ensure that the client will only be able to obtain validator quorum on at most one claim block per nonce. A client submitting multiple claim blocks with the same nonce risks to get stuck in a pending status with the validators and never achieve quorum to make progress. We do not treat this situation here, but implementations of FastSet may choose to allow clients to clear their pending status for a fee, to give them an exit situation in case their programs have errors but at the same time to discourage them from attempting to break or slow down the protocol.

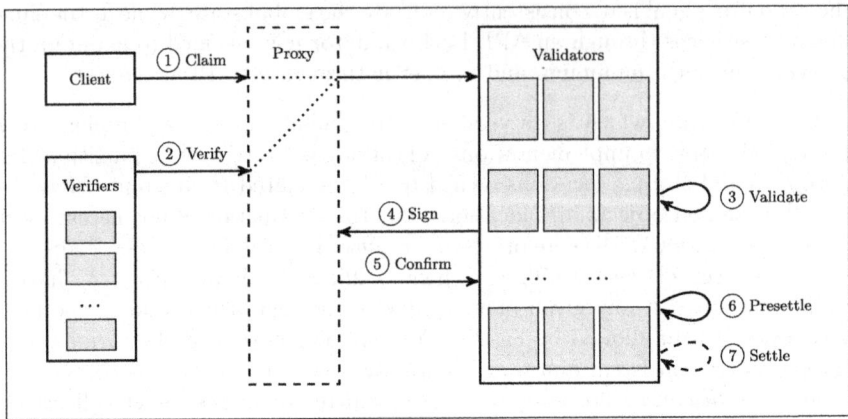

Proxy is a helper and only affects liveness, not safety. It can be a client (the sender of the original message containing the claim sequence, or a different client such as a beneficiary or a verifier or a service provider), a validator, or any combination of these for all or for any of the two services it provides: broadcasting messages to validators and signature aggregation ($\#\{sig_1, sig_2, ...\}$).

① ② Client a claims $c_1 c_2 ... c_k$ by signing message $m := \langle c_1 c_2 ... c_k, n \rangle_a$, where n is its local nonce (incremented after each message). An appropriate set of verifiers $T := \{t_1, t_2, ..., t_l\}$ approve m by signing it: $\langle m \rangle_{t_1}, \langle m \rangle_{t_2}, ..., \langle m \rangle_{t_l}$. Proxy aggregates the verifiers' signatures and broadcasts $\langle m \rangle_{\#T}$ to all validators.

③ Upon receiving $\langle m \rangle_{\#T}$ with $m = \langle c_1 c_2 ... c_k, n \rangle_a$, validator v validates m by checking: signature of a is valid; $v(a).nonce = n$; $v(a).pending \subseteq \{m\}$; the verifiers' aggregated signature $\#T$ is valid and reaches the client-specified quorum; and finally, $c_1 c_2 ... c_k \downarrow_{v.state}$.

④ Validator v signs m, sends $\langle m \rangle_v$ to proxy, and sets $v(a).pending := \{m\}$.

⑤ Once a validator quorum is reached on message m, proxy creates certificate $\langle m \rangle_\#$ and broadcasts it to all validators.

⑥ Upon receiving $\langle m \rangle_\#$, each validator v: checks the quorum $\#$; checks $m \notin v.presettled \cup v.settled$; adds m to $v.presettled$. Note that this m in Step 6 can be different from the m in Step 4, even for the same client a.

⑦ Settle any message in $v.presettle$ that can be settled: if $m = \langle c_1 c_2 ... c_k, n \rangle_a$ in $v.presettled$ with $v(a).nonce = n$ and $c_1 c_2 ... c_k \downarrow_{v.state}$ then $v.state := [\![c_1 c_2 ... c_k]\!] v.state$, increment $v(a).nonce$, reset $v(a).pending := \emptyset$, move m to $v.settled$. This step 7 can and should be executed continuously.

Fig. 1. FastSet protocol.

② Validators will not attempt to validate any received claim block before it accumulates an appropriate number of verifiers which approve it. This information being public, verifiers and clients have multiple ways to synchronize to get this task done. The simplest, but also the least efficient and riskiest for the client, is for the client to just submit its message and assume that its verifiers listen to some validator and will thus get informed when the client message was settled, then verify it, sign it and send it to the proxy which then aggregates all their signatures and sends them to the validators. A more efficient approach is for the client to inform its verifiers as soon as it sends the original message, so they can start their verification process immediately. An even more efficient approach in some applications could be for the client to send its verifiers its intent to execute a program, also known to the verifiers, so that they can start their verification while the client is still working on generating its claim block, allowing program execution and its verification to take place in parallel.

③ Once the validator v has been informed that a client's claim block $c_1 c_2 \ldots c_k$ accumulated the quorum of verifiers, it can proceed to validating it. The obvious and cheap checks are the signatures, the nonce, and the verifier quorum. We have deliberately left open the decision on where the verifiers and the verifier quorum are stored: some implementations of FastSet may store them in the validator, e.g., $v(a).verifiers$ and $v(a).quorum$, in which case the check becomes $|T \cap v(a).verifiers| \geq v(a).quorum$; others may store them as additional items in the message, besides the claim block and nonce; others may include a special claim in the block, say at the end, claiming the verifiers and quorum. In all cases, however, the verifiers and their quorum are part of the contract that the application makes with its users, so it is important that the validators enforce them. The validator also checks that there is no different message sent by the same client with the same nonce that is pending, that is, it checks $v(a).pending \subseteq \{m\}$. In other words, if there is any message pending then it must be the exact same message m. This ensures that the client does not, intentionally or not, attempt to initiate double-spending attacks or non-deterministic computations. Note that messages from validators can be delayed or lost, so the client or its proxy may attempt to submit m multiple times until they receive validator confirmation, which is why $v(a).pending$ is allowed to already contain m. Finally, validator v is ready to check the validity of the actual claim block $c_1 c_2 \ldots c_k$ in its state $v.state$, that is, $c_1 c_2 \ldots c_k \downarrow_{v.state}$. Note that the validator does not update its state at this stage. Indeed, the block has not achieved validator (not verifier) quorum yet, which means that the client may still possibly achieve quorum on a different block with other validators.

④ Validator v now approves the claim block by signing the original client's message and sending it back. The validator also sets $v(a).pending$ to $\{m\}$, so from here on it will accept no other messages from a until m is settled. If the validator received the same message m from a that it approved already, it sends its approval again to account for previous messages having been potentially lost.

⑤ When the proxy accumulates validator quorum on message m, it creates a certificate $\langle m \rangle_{\#}$ by aggregating all the received validator confirmations and broadcasts it back to all validators. This certificate is proof that quorum has been achieved and at this moment the state updates in all the validators are imminent, i.e., cannot be stopped anymore once they receive the certificate.

⑥ When a validator v receives such a valid certificate $\langle m \rangle_\#$, it knows with certainty that a quorum of validators have already validated m, so it is safe to process and settle m. But that needs to be done only once, to avoid applying the same updates twice or more, so v first checks that m is not already settled, or considered to be settled, i.e., presettled. If that is the case, then v should settle m. However, v may not be ready to settle m, in the sense that the nonce or the claim block of m may not be valid for v. In fact, there is no guarantee that v even participated in the quorum of $\langle m \rangle_\#$, or that v is even aware of the existence of the client that originally sent m, because that particular client and v could have been disconnected by now. Taking into account all these situations, v only adds m to $v.presettle$ for now.

⑦ The liveness result, 4 in Theorem 1, says that if other validators settled more claims than v, then v should also be able to make progress and settle more claims. That is, if v continuously scans $v.presettle$ it will eventually find messages which are valid and thus can be settled, because FastSet assumes that all messages are eventually delivered. Implementations of FastSet will likely include mechanisms for validators to request updates of missing settled claims from other validators and populate their presettled set with them in order to make faster progress. Note that right before m is settled in this step 7 of the protocol, $v(a).pending$ can be either empty or $\{m\}$. The former happens when v did not get a chance to participate in the quorum on m, so v never checked $c_1 \, c_2 \ldots c_k \downarrow_{v.state}$ (e.g., if a had enough balance to make a payment); however, since $v(a).nonce = n$, v is ready to settle m as soon as $c_1 \, c_2 \ldots c_k \downarrow_{v.state}$, and it does exactly that. The latter happens when v has already signed m and was waiting for a quorum including other validators as well to be formed. The monotonicity result, 3 in Theorem 1, says that it is safe to settle m as is, that is, checking $c_1 \, c_2 \ldots c_k \downarrow_{v.state}$ is theoretically unnecessary. However, we choose to keep this definedness check. As seen in [3], implementations of FastSet may choose to allow applications to disobey the weak independence requirement. Keeping the definedness check will guarantee that the validator's state stays well-defined, the damage being contained to possibly locking the non-conforming accounts.

Theorem 1. *[3] Under the assumptions in Sect. 2.3, FastSet is correct, i.e.:*

1. Security *All certificates generated at Step 5 are consistent, that is, only one per client per nonce. Therefore, FastSet prevents double-spending.*
2. Determinism *The order in which a validator receives the messages is irrelevant.*
3. Monotonicity *Once a client can settle a message, it will continue to be able to settle it regardless of what other clients do.*
4. Liveness *Validators do not get stuck: if one makes progress, then all do.*

3 Examples and Applications

FastSet was defined parametrically in Sect. 2, on top of abstract notions of claim and state. However, to implement FastSet and build applications, we need a claim language and concrete states. Such a candidate language inspired from actors is proposed in [3], called SETL, together with a collection of typical Web3 programs: multi-sigs, voting, escrow, verifiable computing, custom assets and payments, auctions, app-chains and blockchains. SETL programs are called *scripts* because they are expected to be small, although some scripts can be non-trivial—due to the massively parallel nature of FastSet and the fact that validators may have different states at the same time. Here we only discuss three such programs at a high level, voting, digital assets and auctions, to illustrate the practicality of FastSet and its relationship to the actor model.

We remind the reader that the most common blockchain functionality, that of a payment system over a native token (e.g., Bitcoin), is supported by default as explained in Sect. 2.2. SETL provides a primitive transfer(to,value) for this; e.g., if alice wants to transfer 3 native tokens to bob, then she submits and settles the claim $\langle\texttt{transfer(bob,3)}\rangle_{\texttt{alice}}$. We will explain SETL on the fly, on a by-need basis in order to understand the three examples.

3.1 Voting

Voting is common on blockchains, yet it is an inherently parallel activity in which the order of votes is irrelevant, making FastSet ideal for it. An authority needs to set up and create a vote poll and then allow voters who are verified to vote. Finally, the authority should announce the results.

Let us consider a simple voting scenario, where the authority, say gov, who is also responsible for verifying the voters, wants to accumulate MIN valid votes to pass some MOTION. Then gov can create a contract using the SETL script:

```
BASIC_VOTE[MIN]:
    voted : Set;  // users who voted
    constructor {
        voted := empty;
    }
    instance constructor {
        not(instance.owner in voted); // guard: must be true
        verify(contract.owner, 1);    // authority verifies voter
        voted.add(instance.owner);
    }
    passed() { size(voted) >= MIN; }
```

The script above is a code template parametric on MIN. It has a contract field voted, which is a set that accumulates all the users that voted. The contract constructor block initializes voted to empty. The contract can generate two more types of blocks, one which is an instance constructor and the other, passed(), which is reserved to the contract owner. These are discussed below.

To create a contract, gov has to sign a message effectively claiming a contract with the code template above instantiated with some value, say 1000. Let MOTION be the unique identifier (i.e., a hash or number) associated to this claim, that is:

$$\text{MOTION} = \langle \texttt{contract(BASIC\_VOTE[1000])} \rangle_{\texttt{gov}}$$

All a voter has to do in order to vote is create an instance of this contract:

$$\langle \texttt{instance(MOTION)} \rangle_{\texttt{alice}}$$
$$\langle \texttt{instance(MOTION)} \rangle_{\texttt{bob}}$$
$$\langle \texttt{instance(MOTION)} \rangle_{\texttt{charlie}}$$

As the code shows, when an instance is created, the `instance.owner` is verified by gov and added to the set of `voters`. In SETL, `verify` takes a set of verifiers (first argument) and a quorum (second argument) to sign the block as part of Step 2 of the FastSet protocol (Fig. 1). The guard in the instance constructor ensures that no other instance of the same contract can be created by the same voter, that is, each voter can only vote once. Indeed, the semantics of guards in SETL is "ignore if true, invalidate the block if false".

The contract owner can announce the result whenever MIN is reached:

$$\langle \texttt{MOTION.passed()} \rangle_{\texttt{gov}}$$

The toy voting script above was overly simplified on purpose, to highlight the concurrent programming capability of FastSet and SETL, and their relationship to the actor model. In practice, voting contracts will likely separate vote registration from voting itself, allow for several voting options, have weighted votes, a deadline, etc. A contract creation by `contract.owner` effectively creates an actor, whose state is the set `voted` initialized to empty. By the semantics of SETL, only the contract owner can send `passed()` messages to the contract actor. Indeed, in SETL, `instance` fields form the state of the contract instance actors, and these instance actors can only initiate `instance` blocks according to the contract. The fields which do not have an `instance` modifier form the state of the contract actor, and the blocks which do not have an `instance` modifier can only be generated by the contract owner. In SETL, anybody can create instances of the contract. In our case here the instances have no state, because there are no instance fields, but they all execute the instance constructor at creation. Effectively, each instance is an actor controlled by the `instance.owner`. Instance actors communicate with the contract actor by means of the `voted` contract field—its monotonic updates can and should be regarded as messages sent by the instances to the contract. Faithfully to the actor model, actors only communicate with actors they have knowledge about.

A clarification is needed with regard to the fact that owners of contracts and of instances, respectively, can sign on their behalf. In Sect. 2, FastSet stipulates that each account a can only submit claim blocks which are signed by a. In SETL, on the other hand, each contract creation and each instance of it becomes an actor, which has its own state and address. However, it would be rather inconvenient and likely insecure and unmanageable by users to allow each actor to own its own private key to sign all its claim blocks. Instead, SETL allows the contract-based actors to only be controlled by their owners, technically just other accounts that have a private key and thus can sign messages. That is, the unique owner of the created contract, or the unique owner of some instance of it, is the only entity that can sign blocks on behalf of the address corresponding to the associated contract or instance actor. This is not a modification of the FastSet protocol, but rather a particular implementation of it. Indeed, a single private key can be used to generate infinitely many public keys through various methods, like hierarchical deterministic (HD) wallets or different cryptographic algorithms. These different public keys are deterministically derived from the same private key and are used as contract-based actor addresses in SETL, although there is only one initial pairing between a private key and its primary public key.

We would like to take the opportunity to further discuss this simple voting contract below, because it touches upon a few important aspects of FastSet that make it different from blockchains.

First, unless gov maintains a list of voters they verified off-set, it is impossible to precisely know the number of votes. Indeed, even if alice reaches validator quorum on $\langle\texttt{instance(MOTION)}\rangle_{\texttt{alice}}$, she or her proxy may have delayed sending the certificate back to validators, so she might have never been added to the set of voters on some validators. Even if that certificate has been sent, some validators may be delayed in their execution of the Step 7 of FastSet and have not updated their state yet. The crucial guarantee, however, is that no validator will settle $\langle\texttt{instance(MOTION)}\rangle_{\texttt{alice}}$ twice. If voters need to prove that they indeed voted, the contract can be modified by adding a new block

```
instance voted() { instance.owner in voted; }
```

and now alice can settle $\langle\texttt{motion\_alice.voted()}\rangle_{\texttt{alice}}$ and use its certificate as proof—here motion_alice is the instance $\langle\texttt{instance(MOTION)}\rangle_{\texttt{alice}}$.

Similarly and for the same reasons, it is impossible for alice to know with certainty whether her vote was actually counted, that is, that it contributed to claim $\langle\texttt{MOTION.passed()}\rangle_{\texttt{gov}}$ being settled. This is the case even if alice settled a claim $\langle\texttt{motion\_alice.voted()}\rangle_{\texttt{alice}}$ like discussed above chronologically before $\langle\texttt{MOTION.passed()}\rangle_{\texttt{gov}}$ on some validator(s) that she uses to observe the voting process. Since chronological order is useful in cases like above, and for other reasons, [3] extends FastSet and SETL with claim timestamping: claim issuers timestamp each claim block, and validators check and approve the timestamp.

Finally, it is insightful to note that although it may appear that a (malicious or not) voter can attempt to create two different instances and submit them concurrently to the validators in the hope that they both get settled, that is not possible thanks to the fact that each account has a nonce and at most one message is allowed in a validator's pending for any given account (steps 3 and 4 in Fig. 1). A voter attempting to create two concurrent (same nonce) instances would therefore risk to get its account stuck. There is nothing to prevent voters from attempting to create two instances in sequence, each issued with a different nonce, but in that case they are processed in order and the second one will fail on all validators as soon as they processed the first one, as intended.

3.2 Non-native Tokens and Digital Assets

Below is a simple contract template that mints a token only at contract creation time and the total supply is assigned to the contract owner. We expect token contracts to be more involved, with flexible minting and verifiers for it (e.g., gov, bank, etc.), possibly with approvals and transfer-from capabilities like in Ethereum ERC20 tokens. Our goal here is to keep it simple in order to demonstrate that tokens can be very efficiently supported by FastSet.

```
TOKEN[NAME,SUPPLY]:
    name    : String;
    balance : Address -> Int;
    constructor {
        name := NAME;
        balance[contract.owner] := SUPPLY;
    }
    instance transfer_token(to,v) {
        v > 0;  // guard: must be true
        balance[instance.owner] >= v;
        balance[instance.owner] -= v;
        balance[to] += v;
    }
```

Here, we name the non-native token transfer function `transfer_token`, so that it is not confused with the native transaction function `transfer`.

One can now create a TOKEN contract and make a first transfer as follows:

$$USDC = \langle contract(TOKEN["USDC",1000000]) \rangle_{circle}$$
$$circle\_wallet = \langle instance(USDC) \rangle_{circle}$$
$$alice\_USDC = \langle instance(USDC) \rangle_{alice}$$
$$\langle circle\_wallet.transfer\_token(alice,1000) \rangle_{circle}$$

Note that the contract owner, `circle`, also needed to create an instance of the contract in order to gain access to claim blocks reserved for instances. The recipient of the transfer, `alice`, also happened to create an instance wallet, although that was not needed in order to receive transfers. Indeed, even if `bob` does not have an instance of USDC, the following is still possible:

$$\langle alice\_USDC.transfer\_token(bob,100) \rangle_{alice}$$

All the non-native tokens and assets are stored in the contract, in its `balance` field. Whenever `bob` wants to get access to the 100 tokens that `alice` transferred to him, he can simply create an instance:

$$\text{bob\_USDC} = \langle \text{instance(USDC)} \rangle_{\text{bob}}$$

and see the 100 tokens in his balance.

A successful token can result in many transfers made by many users in parallel, especially if used for payments. For example, VISA averages 20,000 transactions per second. With the advancement of AI and AI agents, it is expected that the demand for higher rates for payments and micro-payments will significantly grow, perhaps to the order of millions of transfers per second. FastSet is ready for the challenge. It can settle a theoretically unlimited number of claims per second, including transfer claims like above. Indeed, there is nothing to prevent two transfers made by different accounts to proceed concurrently—we assume that location updates are atomic, which can be ensured using conventional synchronization mechanisms (e.g., software locks or hardware transactions).

But is the result deterministic, regardless of how the transfers are interleaved and settled by each of the validators? Theorem 1 ensures the correctness of the protocol, including its validator determinism, whenever the weak independence property holds. Because digital asset transfers in general and payments in particular represent an important use case for FastSet, below we prove the weak independence property of the TOKEN contract above. Suppose that two different accounts, a1 and a2, can issue claim blocks

$$\langle \text{transfer\_token(b1,v1)} \rangle_{\text{a1}}$$
$$\langle \text{transfer\_token(b2,v2)} \rangle_{\text{a2}}$$

That implies v1 > 0 and balance[a1] >= v1, and respectively, v2 > 0 and balance[a2] >= v2. We have to prove that the balances of a1, a2, b1, and b2 are, respectively, the same no matter in which order the two transfer claims are processed. We analyze several cases, depending on whether b1 and b2 are equal or not, or if any of them or both are equal to any of a1 or a2. The most common case is that b1 and b2 are distinct and also distinct from a1 and a2. Then in both cases the balances are clearly the same: a1-v1, a2-v2, b1+v1, b2+v2. If b1==b2==b and are different from a1 and a2, then the balances are also the same: a1-v1, a2-v2, and b+v1+v2. If b1==a2 and b2 is distinct, then the balances are also the same: a1-v1, a2-v2+v1, and b2+v2. If b1==a2 and b2==a1, then the balances are the same, too: a1-v1+v2, a2-v2+v1. Finally, if b1==b2==a2 then the balances are: a1-v1, a2+v1. The remaining cases are similar. Consequently, the TOKEN contract satisfies the weak independence requirement that guarantees its determinism no matter how the transfer claim blocks by different accounts are permuted. Because the (atomic) addition and subtraction operations on integers are commutative, an even stronger property holds: the individual claims in different blocks can also be further interleaved. This gives validators the freedom to maximize the parallelism and thus the throughput of token transfers.

3.3 Auctions

Auctions tend to be complex contracts, where a set of bidders submit their bids for an item. The auctioneer keeps the highest bid and the highest bidder receives the item, while the other bidders redeem their funds that were outbidden. There are many variations of auction contracts, which, to our knowledge, fall in two broad categories when it gets to how the bidders redeem their funds: either they do it themselves, usually by calling a withdraw function when permitted, or the auctioneer sends each of them their bids back when the auction ends. None of these approaches is possible within SETL, due to its deliberately restricted nature. Indeed, there is no way for an account to withdraw any funds from another account, at least not with the current implementations of the native `transfer` and the contract `transfer_token` block in Sect. 3.2: the other account has to send the funds explicitly. Also, SETL currently has no mechanism to iterate through all the keys of a map (this might be needed, eventually).

We here present a different type of auction contract, which takes full advantage of the parallel nature of FastSet. The key insight is that the highest bidder pays the previously highest bidder back, and sends the difference to the contract. This way, the contract only locks the auctioneer's item and the highest bid, so there is no need to send any funds back to the outbidden participants.

```
AUCTION[ITEM,BIDDING_TIME]:
    stopBiddingTime : Int;
    highestBidder : Address;
    highestBid : Int;

    constructor {
        ITEM.transfer_token(contract, 1);
        stopBiddingTime := time + BIDDING_TIME;
        highestBidder := contract.owner;
        highestBid := 0;
    }
    instance bid(amount) {
        time <= stopBiddingTime;
        if (amount > highestBid) {
            transfer(highestBidder, highestBid);
            transfer(contract, amount - highestBid);
            highestBidder := instance;
            highestBid := amount;
        }
    }
    instance withdraw(amount) {
        transfer(instance.owner, amount);
    }
    end() {
        time > stopBiddingTime;
```

```
        ITEM.transfer_token(highestBidder.owner,1);
        transfer(contract.owner, highestBid);
}
```

The auctioneer creates the contract above, at the same time sending it the `ITEM` for bidding, as well as a `BIDDING_TIME` for how long bidding is allowed, e.g., $\text{AliceTicket} = \langle \text{contract}(\text{AUCTION}[\text{ticket\_item},1000])\rangle_\text{alice}$. The SETL time construct is instantiated by the client with its current timestamp, and is verified by validators that it is within adequate network delays [3]. For simplicity we assume only one item, which is a token as in Sect. 3.2. This item is locked in the contract until the auction ends. The contract initializes the `highestBidder` as the contract owner, `alice` in our case, so the contract owner can redeem the item in case nobody bids on it during the specified period.

Note the use of the conditional statement in the `instance bid(amount)` block. Unlike guards, which are invalid when false, conditional statements control the execution flow but are always valid. However, if the executing branch of the conditional encounters an invalid claim, then the entire block is invalid; this would be the case, for example, if the instance bids a larger `amount` than what it holds. Bidders create instances of the contract, send funds to their instances in order to bid them, initiate `bid` blocks through their instances, and finally withdraw from their instances whatever funds were not used for bidding, e.g.,

$\text{auction3} = \langle \text{instance}(\text{AliceTicket})\rangle_\text{bob}$
$\langle \text{transfer}(\text{auction3},100)\rangle_\text{bob}$ — bob sends 100 to its instance
$\langle \text{auction3.bid}(25)\rangle_\text{bob}$ — bob sends 25 to AliceTicket (not alice)
$\text{tk\_alice} = \langle \text{instance}(\text{AliceTicket})\rangle_\text{charlie}$
$\langle \text{transfer}(\text{tk\_alice},50)\rangle_\text{charlie}$ — charlie sends 50 to its instance
$\langle \text{tk\_alice.bid}(30)\rangle_\text{charlie}$ — sends 25 to auction3 and 5 to AliceTicket
$\langle \text{auction3.bid}(40)\rangle_\text{bob}$ — sends 30 to tk_alice and 10 to AliceTicket

Bidding stops after the allowed time, and then the auctioneer (the contract owner) issues an `end()` block which sends the item to the highest bidder and the paid amount from the contract to the contract owner. For example,

$\langle \text{AliceTicket.end}()\rangle_\text{alice}$ — sends 40 to alice and ticket to bob

At any moment during or after the auction ends, the bidders can withdraw any available funds from their instances, e.g.,

$\langle \text{tk\_alice.withdraw}(50)\rangle_\text{charlie}$ — charlie withdraws its funds
$\langle \text{auction3.withdraw}(60)\rangle_\text{bob}$ — bob withdraws everything left

The weak independence assumption that guarantees the correctness of Fast-Set is still obeyed by the contract above, but it is less obvious than in the previous examples. Before we show that weak independence holds, let us first illustrate the power, but also the complexity of concurrency, in order to appreciate the critical role that weak independence plays. The potential problem is that the shared field `highestBid` can be both written and read by different instances.

Consequently, multiple bidders may bid concurrently and, although their individual bids get quorum, they may potentially not be able to settle. For example, in the scenario above suppose that both bob and charlie send their first bids at the same time and the validators receive their bid claims at the same time. Both claims are valid in Step 3 of the FastSet protocol (Fig. 1) regardless of which is processed first, because at that step the validator states are not modified. All validators therefore sign both claims and quorum is achieved for both.

Suppose now that half of the validators receive/process the two bids in one sequence in their Step 7, say bob first and charlie second, while the other half in the other sequence, charlie first and bob second. In both cases the contract will hold 30 tokens, charlie will be the highest bidder, bob's instance balance of 100 tokens is unaffected, and charlie's instance balance is 20 tokens. However, in the second case, bob's bid never took place, in the sense that the body of the conditional statement was not executed. But, importantly, bob's bid block was still valid, so in the end all validators are in the same state and with the same claims settled. Since bob's instance balance was not affected on any of the validators, his next $\langle$auction3.bid(40)$\rangle_{\text{bob}}$ correctly outbids charlie on all validators. We leave it as an exercise to the curious reader to notice that weak independence would be violated if we replaced the conditional statement with a guard that invalidated the block when the amount was not higher than the highest bid. In [3] we discuss this case in more depth and propose an extension of FastSet that would work with such examples, where weak independence is allowed to be temporarily broken. We also leave it as an exercise to the reader to notice that the weak independence assumption would also be violated if the previously highest bid would be returned directly to the owner of the instance, instead of to the instance itself. We discuss this case in more depth in [3] as well.

Let us now prove that the AUCTION contract obeys weak independence. The interesting case is when two independently highest bids are submitted at the same time. Regardless of the order in which they are processed in a given state, once both are processed the state is the same: the currently highest bidder's instance is paid back, the winner of the two bids becomes the highest bidder, and the state of the loser of the two bids stays unchanged.

4 Conclusion

This paper discussed FastSet, an actor-inspired replica-based distributed protocol for embarrassingly parallel settlement of claims. A *claim* is any statement that comes with a proof, such as a payment or more generally a digital asset transfer, a realized blockchain transaction or more transactions that form a block, an execution of a program in a programming language or virtual machine, an AI model inference or fine tuning, a TEE execution, a vote, an auction bid, among many others. A *proof* is anything that is verifiable and is accepted by the application or user/account that uses the claim: a signature (simple, aggregated, TEE, etc.), a cryptographic/ZK proof, a mathematical proof, a formal semantics derivation, a program (re)execution, and so on. The verification of all proofs which are not signatures is deferred to special service providers, called *verifiers* which are account holders like any other applications/users. The replicas, called *validators*, only validate signatures, regarded as the simplest and fastest way to check proofs, and settle the claims. Each claim can be verified, validated, and *settled optimally*: independently and in parallel with any other claim. The validators need not communicate with each other, so there is no consensus in the strict sense of the word as used in blockchains. Specifically, FastSet is not strongly consistent [8], but it is strongly eventually consistent [15].

FastSet should not be regarded as the foundation for the next blockchain. It should be regarded as the Web3 infrastructure on which the next wave of blockchains and decentralized and verifiable computing applications will be built.

References

1. Agha, G.A.: Actors: A Model of Concurrent Computation in Distributed Systems. MIT Press, Cambridge (1986)
2. Baudet, M., Danezis, G., Sonnino, A.: FastPay: High-performance byzantine fault tolerant settlement. In: AFT '20: 2nd ACM Conference on Advances in Financial Technologies, New York, NY, USA, October 21-23, 2020, pp. 163–177. ACM (2020)
3. Chen, X., Rosu, G.: Fastset: Parallel claim settlement (2025)
4. Guerraoui, R., Kuznetsov, P., Monti, M., Pavlovic, M., Seredinschi, D.-A.: The consensus number of a cryptocurrency (extended version) (2019)
5. Guerraoui, R., Kuznetsov, P., Monti, M., Pavlovic, M., Seredinschi, D.-A.: The consensus number of a cryptocurrency. Distrib. Comput. **35**(1), 1–15 (2022)
6. Herlihy, M., Wing, J.M.: Linearizability: a correctness condition for concurrent objects. ACM Trans. Program. Lang. Syst. **12**(3), 463–492 (1990)
7. Hewitt, C., Bishop, P.B., Steiger, R.: A universal modular ACTOR formalism for artificial intelligence. In: Proceedings of the 3rd International Joint Conference on Artificial Intelligence. Standford, CA, USA, August 20-23, 1973, pp. 235–245. William Kaufmann (1973)
8. Lamport, L.: Time, clocks, and the ordering of events in a distributed system. Commun. ACM **21**(7), 558–565 (1978)
9. Lamport, L.: The part-time parliament. ACM Trans. Comput. Syst. **16**(2), 133–169 (1998)
10. Mazurkiewicz, A.: Trace theory. In: Brauer, W., Reisig, W., Rozenberg, G. (eds.) Advances in Petri Nets 1986, Part II: Proceedings of an Advanced Course, Bad Honnef, 8.–19. September 1986, vol. 255. LNCS, pp. 279–324. Springer (1987)
11. Nakamoto, S.: Bitcoin: A peer-to-peer electronic cash system, November 2008. Accessed: 2025-06-15
12. Ongaro, D., Ousterhout, J.K.: In search of an understandable consensus algorithm. In: Proceedings of the 2014 USENIX Annual Technical Conference, USENIX ATC 2014, Philadelphia, PA, USA, June 19-20, 2014, pp. 305–320, Philadelphia, PA, June 2014. USENIX Association
13. Preguiça, N., Shapiro, M., Legatheaux Martins, J.: Designing a commutative replicated data type for cooperative editing systems. Research Report TR-02-2008 DI-FCT-UNL, Universidade Nova de Lisboa, Dep. Informática, FCT (2008)

14. Shapiro, M., Preguiça, N.: Designing a commutative replicated data type. Research Report RR-6320, Institut National de Recherche en Informatique et en Automatique (INRIA), October 2007
15. Shapiro, M., Preguiça, N., Baquero, C., Zawirski, M.: Conflict-free replicated data types. In: Défago, X., Petit, F., Villain, V. (eds.) SSS 2011. LNCS, vol. 6976, pp. 386–400. Springer, Heidelberg (2011). https://doi.org/10.1007/978-3-642-24550-3_29

Decentralizing University Governance: A Coordination Challenge

Eva Maria Kuehn(✉)

Faculty of Informatics, TU Wien, Vienna, Austria
eva.kuehn@tuwien.ac.at
http://www.complang.tuwien.ac.at/eva

Abstract. The current academic landscape is often shaped by political and financial influences, restricting access to education and compromising research independence. To address these challenges, we introduce "FreeUniversity.dao", a university model grounded in the principles of a Decentralized Autonomous Organization (DAO). FreeUniversity.dao emphasizes academic freedom, openness, and equitable access to education, leveraging blockchain and DeFi technologies to establish a transparent and sustainable framework for global learning and research. It envisions a politically neutral and corruption-free governance model that prioritizes transparency, fairness, and accessibility. Decision-making processes are designed to be participatory, democratic, rewarding merits and contributions, and involving the community in all major decisions, including rule changes and further developments. For traditional university institutions FreeUniversity.dao offers a migration path to DAO-based structures.

While this paper does not present a fully realized DAO design, it outlines the core concepts, coordination challenges, and foundational elements required to build such a system. It aims to be a starting point for further exploration and discussion about the future of academic governance. An example workflow illustrates how the DAO could work in practice and motivates how current processes can be improved to reduce interventions that could jeopardize the integrity of scientific research.

Keywords: DAO · Academic Governance · Coordination · Free University

1 Introduction

The current academic landscape is increasingly influenced by political, financial, personal or other power interests, This is a threat to fair educational and research opportunities and the allocation of resources and positions. To counter these challenges, we propose *FreeUniversity.dao*, a decentralized university grounded in the principles of Decentralized Autonomous Organizations (DAOs). Numerous surveys and case studies [2,11,16,17,23,26,27] provide detailed definitions, classifications, and taxonomies of DAOs, particularly focusing on governance structures. Leveraging blockchain technology and decentralized finance (DeFi), FreeUniversity.dao aims to establish a sustainable, inclusive, and transparent framework for education and research whose goal is to put the benefit of society first. Our approach emphasizes clear boundaries between science and politics and attempts to mitigate personal and power interests. It envisions a future where research treats actual topics most important to society, where everyone has equal opportunities and access to education and can contribute, and where actors are fairly rewarded for their merits and contributions through royalties and tokens. The crucial question is: Can decentralization transform the governance of education and science for global equity and innovation? Naturally, this paper cannot cover all facets and issues of a DAO-based university that follows the principles of decentralized science [30]. The contribution is intended to start a discussion, outline key points of a vision and mission, and present many open questions that need to be explored further with a broader community.

FreeUniversity.dao's vision is to establish a new type of academic institution that reimagines education and research through innovative and decentralized approaches. We aspire to create a global platform where access to *education is free*, independent of financial status, origin, or social background. This institution will uphold the principles of *academic freedom*, fostering research and teaching that remain untouched by political, commercial or other inappropriate influences to ensure scientific integrity and creativity. Through *collaboration*, it will connect students, educators, and industry partners to co-create practical and socially impactful solutions. Using the advantages of blockchain and distributed ledger technologies [20], we aim to *decentralize* financial and administrative processes, ensuring transparency, independence, and self-determination. Ultimately, our vision is to set new *global standards* for sustainable and inclusive education, and to win universities worldwide to participate in this model.

FreeUniversity.dao's mission is to make education universally accessible by eliminating tuition fees and instead relying on innovative financing and funding mechanisms such as token-based systems and subsidies. Accreditation processes will be transparent and participatory, with academic credits and titles awarded through decentralized governance systems. Academic freedom shall be preserved, allowing research to be conducted without external pressures and guided by scientific merit and participatory decision-making. All governance decisions will be decentralized, democratic and transparent, so that everyone has a voice and can help shape the university. Academic processes shall adhere to the highest standards of integrity, ethics, and quality assurance. Diversity, inclusion, and equity will be at the center of every activity, with proactive measures to ensure fairness and combat discrimination. Sustainability and innovation will underpin both institutional operations and the content of education and research, promoting advancements in technology and society.

The paper is structures as follows: Sect. 2 outlines the fundamental elements for a DAO-driven university. Section 3 summarizes related work and motivates the need for a new concept. Section 4 sketches the steps to bootstrap FreeUniversity.dao technically and organizationally. Section 5 shows as a coordination example the appointment process as it is today, and how its workflow could be realized in FreeUniversity.dao. Section 6 evaluates risks in the traditional and the DAO-driven workflow. Section 7 summarizes the presented ideas.

2 Fundamentals of a Decentralized University

The idea behind FreeUniversity.dao is rooted in academia, but with the potential for broader applicability. It aims to enhance traditional university structures, using the Austrian university law as a reference point. Important processes in this model include the recruitment of staff, the allocation of research grants and the awarding of academic credits.

A DAO consists of predefined rules that allow all processes (workflows) within the organization to run automatically, without a central coordinator managing or influencing them. This rule set can be compared to the constitution of a state or the corporate bylaws of a company. A specific requirement, in addition to modeling correct workflows, is the definition of "meta-rules", which allow changes to this constitution while adhering to the same principles. To use a metaphor, a DAO is like a ship that is sent off on its own and must manage itself after launch, with the ship being so well-designed and verified that it always better fulfills the defined goals and never violates the established mission.

2.1 Structure

FreeUniversity.dao shall be a governance model that can exist in digital, physical, or hybrid forms. The concept begins with the creation of a global, universal DAO framework that can later incorporate and coordinate traditional universities. These institutions can gradually integrate DAO processes into their operations, starting with governance functions like appointment processes. For example, when a university announces a vacancy and funding, the DAO triggers the appointment process, with community participation in decision-making.

This approach is similar to the concept of a digital twin, as discussed in [22], where a physical object is mirrored by a corresponding digital structure. In this sense, a traditional university can evolve into a hybrid entity, with part or all of its governance decentralized and managed digitally. The interaction between digital DAO structures and physical universities leads to a "phygital" system, where both teaching and research occur on-line and at physical locations, while governance remains decentralized. National adaptations are possible, but must align with the DAO's governance framework, i.e., universities can require country-specific customizations, but any changes must be voted on and align with the DAO's core principles.

The concept of a phygital university can also be established by starting with the pure digital DAO as explained above, but creating the physical twin that did not yet exist. This introduces an added complexity, as local campuses or physical locations need to be integrated into the governance structure, with decisions about acquiring and managing physical resources such as buildings, infrastructure, and equipment. I.e., additional layers of coordination are required. Just like the governance processes for the digital aspects of the university, the physical aspects will need to be coordinated by the DAO. In this way, new spaces can become part of the global network and benefit from the same governance mechanisms that the digital DAO offers.

2.2 Actors

The decentralized structure of FreeUniversity.dao foresees that all its actors are treated equally [32], can participate in governance and decision-making, and have a role in shaping the academic institution's future. A *DAO actor* is any individual, organization or partner who is registered and whose profile is verified on the DAO by its community. They differ in terms of their roles, interests, contributions, and reward expectations. The *DAO community* comprises all DAO actors. Every actor participates in the proposal and evaluation of actual topics, decision about resources, and in the determination of the governance structure of the DAO, receiving rewards for qualified contributions.

Students seek unrestricted access to high-quality education on an equal basis, along with fair assessment and internationally recognized credits and degrees. They expect education to consistently incorporate the latest technological advancements, provide strong career prospects, and cover the current topics. They desire quality coaching from qualified DAO actors, and to acquire scholarships. Outstanding students should also have the opportunity to contribute to curriculum development, with their evaluations of instructors and course content duly considered. Moreover, in the process of filling academic positions, students – as is usual at universities – should be granted a voice and be allowed to participate in voting, particularly regarding teaching appointments.

Professors either have already earned their title at a traditional university (which must be controlled by the DAO community) or were hired through DAO processes, whether at the virtual DAO or at a physical university. They are motivated to receive rewards for their merits, which include contributions to teaching, research output, peer reviewing, student mentoring, contributions to the community and the DAO, creation of intellectual property rights, start-up formation, grant acquisition, international collaborations, event organization, project implementations and partnerships with industry.

Researchers and lecturers are scientists who participate in research projects or contribute to teaching, but have not yet obtained a professorial title. They have basically the similar motivations, as well as contribution and reward possibilities in the DAO, as professors.

Administrative staff are individuals who contribute their expertise in controlling processes, participating in committees, handling legal matters, and other administrative functions.

Universities outsource workflows for a fee to the DAO to save time and resources and to make the processes less error prone for influences from outside or scientific misconduct. Basically, this is without risk, because if DAO-processes are not working, the university can either improve them with the consent of the community or switch back to purely physical processes. Its advantages are to save resources and therefore money: DAO processes are more efficient, not error-prone, compliant with all legal requirements, and free from interference by misbehaving actors pursuing their own interests instead of serving the common good. Such a university receives certificates for all the processes it hands over to FreeUniversity.dao, which will improve the university's image and attract scientists and students to the university. Students and researchers prefer to go to universities that offer transparent and fair governance structures and seamless international cooperations, as the many trends of DAOs in this direction already prove. Also, coorperations in teaching and research bring benefits.

Partners. This group includes: sponsors, donors, and investors. Companies commission research, book expert courses and acquire intellectual property rights (IPRs). The government and funding organizations provide grants and subsidies for research and education, commission think tank tasks etc. Venture capitalists contribute entrepreneurial know-how, invest in spin-offs and receive tokens.

2.3 Coordination

A decentralized educational institution must coordinate the complex network of the diverse actors, each with its own interests. The core challenge is ensuring secure governance in a decentralized environment. Two selected DAO examples that illustrate these difficulties are:

In the MakerDAO [31] at first, decision-making was highly centralized, leading to conflicts and a lack of transparency. As the organization moved towards a more decentralized structure, it became clear that the existing rules were not sufficiently precise. The absence of clearly defined responsibilities and decision-making processes made it difficult to reach consensus. The solution came with the introduction of Maker Improvement Proposals (MIPs) and the Core Unit Framework, which established clear governance structures and decentralized task distribution. These frameworks improved decision-making efficiency and transparency, but challenges such as conflicts of interest and the balance between centralization and decentralization remain ongoing concerns.

Proof of Humanity (PoH) DAO [10] is a decentralized identity verification system that uses a social vouching mechanism to create a sybil-resistant registry of real humans, enabling applications such as Universal Basic Income (UBI). PoH faced a major crisis due to power imbalances in its token-based voting system, where large token holders (whales) gained disproportionate influence over decision-making. Disputes arose over the management of the treasury, UBI token inflation, and the overall direction of the project, leading to internal conflicts and, ultimately, a hard fork. The crisis highlighted the risk of centralization in token-based voting, the necessity of well-defined decision-making processes, and the need for conflict resolution mechanisms.

The lesson we learn from MakerDAO, PoH DAO and from the literature [11,19,28] is that effective, robust and complete coordination rules are essential, that there is no one best solution and that research is still needed. Key coordination tasks within FreeUniversity.dao include: *Decentralized Decision-Making and Voting:* Voting and governance tokens facilitate decentralized governance, where actors e.g., vote proportionally to their stake, or have one vote per actor, or use quadratic voting etc. [16]. This shall ensure that decisions reflect the collective interests of the DAO actors. *Resource Management:* Transparent and verifiable allocation of resources make it possible to align research and educational offerings with the community's needs and priorities. *Creating Synergies:* Collaboration among all actors is promoted in order to contribute meaningfully to the shared goal. *Innovation and Evolution:* A rapid and continuous improvement and adaptation to new challenges and opportunities is an advantage of DAOs. As an example, there must be rules to change the DAO, rules for rapid investment in new start-ups including IPR regulations etc. *Supporting Participation:* A DAO relies on active participation from all actors to achieve consensus. If such engagement is lacking, the DAO must incorporate mechanisms to ensure that no processes become stalled. *Avoiding Accumulation of Power:* To avoid monopolization of power and rights [24,25] introduce "True Autonomous Organizations (TAOs)" to overcome the limitations of token-based decision-making in traditional DAOs. By shifting from token-weighted voting to contribution-based and on-demand resource allocation, TAOs ensure equitable distribution of power and resources, prioritizing fairness and active participation over wealth concentration.

3 Related Work

Related approaches include DAOs, which deal with university, education, research, IPR management, publication of scientific work, or promotion of research. We highlight the DAOs that are of particular interest to our work in bold and italics, and only provide links to their websites. The following portals that list DAOs were examined: DeepDAO[1] the "leading discovery and analytics engine for the DAO ecosystem", TALLY[2], Alchemy[3], and DAO Central[4]. The results of each search are listed in alphabetical order.

At DeepDAO, 27 entries were found in the category of "Decentralized Science", of which the following are interesting: *AntidoteDAO* sets to leverage web3 to fund cancer research and promote open science. *AthenaDAO* is a decentralized community of researchers, funders, and advocates working to advance women's health research, education, and funding. *bio.xyz* is a biotech DAO accelerator and DeSci meta-governance layer. *Cannabis Genome DAO* is a marketplace & seed bank for open-access cannabis research. *Data Lake* is creating a global Medical Data Donation system based on blockchain technology. *Beaker DAO* is a collective set to support the expansion of decentralized science through research funding and Intellectual Property management. *CureDAO*'s mission is to accelerate clinical discovery by creating a community-owned digital health platform to

---

[1] deepdao.io.
[2] www.tally.xyz/explore.
[3] www.alchemy.com/top/daos.
[4] daocentral.com.

discover how millions of factors like foods, drugs, and supplements affect human health. *DeSci Exchange* builds a free data marketplace to accelerate scientific discovery, with prime initial focus on Health. *Foresight Institute* is a research organization and non-profit that supports the beneficial development of high-impact technologies. **FrontierDAO**[5] supports research related with space und fusion technologies using Web3. It also provides FrontierRegistry, an on-chain publishing platform for scientists, engineers, academics, researchers and citizen scientists to publish their research and Intellectual Property (using NFTs), immutably on the blockchain. *GenomesDAO* is a biotech DAO focused on the safe, private, and auditable monetization of genomic data. *LabDAO* is a collective of scientists and web3 builders set to accelerate progress in the life sciences. *MedDAO* creates new incentives and systems for a global, distributed medical knowledge network. *MoonDAO* aims to decentralize access to outer-space exploration and research. *NeuraDAO* is creating a democratized, circular funding ecosystem to accelerate neurotech R&D. *PsyDAO* is a collective of researchers, therapists and artists funding research. **ResearchHub Foundation**[6] offers a community-driven approach to ranking and prioritizing scientific work by using crowd-sourced upvotes and reputation scores to filter and highlight valuable research to be funded and carried out [4]. It supports an own crypto currency (ResearchCoin). *TalentDAO* aims to build a decentralized community-reviewed publication protocol for the social sciences. *The Science DAO* is a venture fund and think tank, incubator engine, and accelerator platform. *VitaDAO* supports projects researching diseases of aging and repairing age-related damage.

The TALLY networks were searched for "uni", "edu", "desci", and "research". Three DAOs were found, but only *EduDAO* has a website (but no DAO) saying it is an alternative funding platform for education and nonprofits.

Alchemy has listed 47 DAOs covering the categories "Creator", "Gaming" and "Venture", but none of these categories fit into our search scheme.

At DAO Central, the categories "Education DAOs" and "DeSci DAOs" are interesting. The found and still existing DAOs are: *Bankless DAO* educates the world on how to adopt decentralized and permissionless money systems. *Developer DAO* accelerates the education and impact of a new wave of Web3 builders. *Molecule* is a funding and tokenization platform for biopharma intellectual property. *Odyssey DAO* provides free guides to onboard 1 million to Web3. *Vita DAO* funds cutting-edge aging research to extend healthy human lifespan, and democratizes ownership of Intellectual Property.

Finally, ChatGPT[7] was prompted to name DAOs in this context. Beyond EduDAO, ResearchHub, TalentDAO, and VitaDAO that were already mentioned above, it found the following DAOs: *BitDAO* supports builders of the decentralized economy. **College DAO**[8] is a digital infrastructure designed to facilitate decentralized education, leveraging the physical infrastructure of universi-

---

[5] frontierdao.xyz, linktr.ee/frontierdao, opensea.io/FrontierDAO.
[6] www.researchhub.foundation.
[7] chatgpt.com.
[8] collegedao.io.

ties worldwide. This framework aims to establish and empower learning hubs, where students can engage with frontier technologies by coordinating research, technical development, and learning experiences on campus in a self-organized, self-governed, and self-sustaining way. It integrates currently 100 universities worldwide and is highly active in organizing events. *Ed3 DAO* empowers educators on emerging technologies through on-line courses. *Education DAO* seems to provide accessible, community-driven education about blockchain and decentralization, but no documentation nor clear mission statement could be found. *EDU-DAO* is a platform for blockchain training and education institutions, but only a website and no DAO was found. *GitcoinDAO* provides the tools, expertise, and services that empower ecosystems to launch and scale impactful grants programs without the administrative burden, but only a website and no DAO was found. *LearnWeb3DAO* proves free, full stack, high quality education to become a Web3 expert. *MolochDAO*'s members contribute capital with the sole intention of giving it all away to fund Ethereum infrastructure as an essential digital public good. *Open Source University (OSSU)* is a community of students of all levels, completing a comprehensive, project based, open-source computer science curriculum, helping each other and sharing their experiences and code through github and community forums; but only a website and no DAO was found. *UniversityDAO* proposes a tokenized university that aims to end student debt. Students get crypto tokens for their tuition fees, these are locked in a wallet and only after graduation students may sell them. Provided there is a market for these coins, the students may get their tuition fees back. But beyond a whitepaper, of which the authors say it has flaws and is incomplete, no further information exists.

In summary, the most important objectives of the analyzed DAOs, which are intended to benefit the community, comprise: *) Joint examination of papers and proposals, *) Funding of education and research, *) Evaluation of scientific work through voting, *) Management of intellectual property rights (e.g. IPR-NFTs, licensing of IPRs to industry), *) Supporting of democratic decision finding by giving equal chances to all stakeholders (e.g., based on contributions and achievements), *) Support of free and distributed education (e.g. learning centers, open access to education), and *) Publication with open access to research.

These visions are also pursuited by FreeUniversity.dao and can be taken as a guide to learn from. There are many possible ways how to achieve these goals. Cooperations with DAOs that were already successful in their respective goals, should be aimed for. In particular, cooperation with the following pioneering and/or successful DAOs would be desirable in order to achieve a FreeUniversity.dao that combines all of the above objectives in a virtual, decentralized organization: with FrontierDAO for publishing IPRs, with ResearchHub Foundation for evaluating and ranking proposed research topics, and with CollegeDAO for self-* decentralized learning and international networking with universities.

The differentiating features of FreeUniversity.dao are: (1) to combine all the above objectives in one virtual DAO with an initial focus on Computer Science related topics, as this is particularly well suited to on-line mode, and (2) not only be a virtual organization, but also to gradually and step by step integrate existing universities into the concept of a "free university" and thus achieve an integration into real education and research systems. Physical universities is where research and teaching is carried out today, experience lies, reputable people work, and money is invested by governments. FreeUniversity.dao wants to break up and improve the governance structures of the existing universities and show a migration path towards decentralization. However, we have to consider that complete virtualization is only conceivable in certain subject areas and even there the physical exchange and collaboration of students and faculty members on a campus cannot be replaced (see the successful example of CollegeDAO).

4 Bootstrapping FreeUniversity.dao

The core idea is to establish a single global DAO that acts as an overarching governance framework (see Sect. 2.1). It can start and operate entirely in a digital format, enabling research and education to take place exclusively on-line. In a next step, it shall incorporate physical universities that wish to join and delegate some or all of their governance processes to the DAO.

Phase 1: White Paper. A founding team must first present the concept of the DAO in a concise white paper based on the ideas of this paper. This will aim to convince potential supporters and contributors. The white paper should outline vision, mission, structure, coordination principles required for different governance processes, funding model, roadmap, and benefits of the DAO, laying the groundwork for subsequent discussions and feedback.

Phase 2: Constitutional (Meta-)Rules. The research community is invited to participate in the creation of the global governance structure. This requires to define and verify the constitutional rules and meta-rules that will serve as the core framework for the fully digital DAO, as well as for all associated physical universities. These rules can be seen as automatized workflows that ensure the secure operation and continued development of the DAO. For example, meta-rules are needed to define how a new rule is introduced or how an existing rule is changed by voting, e.g. by qualified majority, which means that the community is always involved in the verification and adaptation process. They must also include the development of a transparent on-boarding process for physical universities, requiring them to present their governance documents and demonstrate that they are aligning their internal structures with the DAO guidelines. We propose using formal methods, e.g., coordination models like the Actor Model [1] or the Peer Model [21], to model and verify all rules and their realization as smart contracts. Also in this phase, albeit off-chain, decisions will be carried out in a democratic and decentralized way (cf. Ethereum's EIPs [7]). "A DAO is typically governed through a process of developing and advancing proposals that implement changes to the DAO." [16].

Phase 3: Implementation. A development team, that is also rewarded for its contribution, will take care for the implementation and testing of the DAO.

It must be an open and scalable software architecture that offers global interoperability, i.e. exchange of resources, knowledge and research between the universities as well as cooperation in workflows. Its further development shall be possible. The phase includes a pilot operation with selected first real actors, limited to a specific region or university network.

Phase 4: FreeUniversity.dao. Next phase is the launch and operation of the DAO, starting with an ICO (Initial Coin Offering) and the first processes like verification of actors' profiles (the first ones will be verified by the group of founders so that the community can start growing), recruiting the first professors, admission students, and accept sponsors and industry partners.

Phase 5: Phygital FreeUniversity.dao. FreeUniversity.dao is now in full operation and can start with the continuous on-boarding of physical universities. The adaptation and further development of the DAO will take place according to its constitution.

5 Example Workflow

The selection process for academic positions is an example of a complex coordination task. It is an essential process, as the outcome has a significant impact on the careers of academics and the future of the university. It is also a delicate process where, on the one hand, the visibility of candidates and documents is extremely sensitive: Applicants do not want their application to be published, especially if they did not win; and assessments, discussions and votes cannot be published because conclusions can be drawn about the applicants. On the other hand, maximum transparency and fairness should be guaranteed. The opinions of various experts must be harmonized to produce an objective outcome that takes all perspectives into account while ensuring the integrity of the scientific process. This process is structured around a committee that integrates a peer review mechanism with external peers. For the topic of peer reviewing alone, it has already been recognized that current problems can be improved by measures proposed by the FreeUniversity.dao such as standardization, transparency, reward systems, credits, autonomy and self-administration [13] as well as decentralization and using blockchain mechanisms [3,5,6,9,12,14,15,18,29].

University processes are generally well-regulated, particularly in the context of state-funded positions, and also non-discrimination and the promotion of gender equality [8], particularly when mandated by law, must be adhered to. Nevertheless, vulnerabilities can still emerge that undermine their integrity. One concrete example is when members of the selection committee have already favored a particular candidate ("preferred candidate") for the position before the process begins. These committee members may act with bias, engage in collusion, fail to assess other candidates fairly, or disregard the merits of alternative applicants. In such cases, the selection process may be skewed, with arguments being made solely in favor of the favored candidate, leading to an unjust decision. This presents a significant risk to the credibility and fairness of academic hiring, particularly when the process is not thoroughly transparent or when checks and balances are not effectively implemented. If the university management also acts impartially, then it is usually very difficult to counteract this problem.

5.1 Appointment Procedure as it is Today

Figure 1 depicts how this workflow typically proceeds today and is based on knowledge of the Austrian University Act; however, the process will likely look similar in other countries. We assume that the university already has a multi-year development plan in place, which outlines the staffing plan.

Step "approval of resources": Once resources are available, the rector releases funds for a new position, and the appointment process begins.

Step "selection of AC": The dean or rector nominates faculty members to the appointment committee (AC), whereby possible biases should be taken into account. The equal opportunities committee also nominates a committee (EOC), which is part of the AC, but has no voting rights.

Step "job announcement": The AC drafts the job posting including the required criteria, which is then published by the rector.

Step "application": Candidates apply.

Step "enough applications?": If there are not enough applications, the AC may still invite candidates and prolong the application phase.

Step "exclusion of candidates": Unsuitable candidates who do not meet the formal requirements are excluded from the process in this early stage.

Step "selection of RC": External reviewers are appointed by the AC to evaluate the candidates. The members of the reviewing committee (RC) shall not know each other and do not meet. Possible reviewer biases should be identified.

Step "reviews": Each reviewer prepares its comparative reviewing reports for all candidates and sends them to the AC.

Step "selection of candidates": The next step is the selection of candidates by the AC for the hearings.

Step "hearings": The hearings are open to the entire faculty, except for the interviews that take place with the individual candidates after the hearings. Only the AC, dean, and possibly members of the rectorate can participate in these private hearings.

Step "decision": Finally, the AC convenes to decide about the ranking of the top three candidates, which is submitted to the rectorate. Candidates may also be ranked ex-aequo, or fewer than three candidates may be proposed, though this is uncommon. The decision is made by voting, which in well-justified cases might be anonymous upon request. The entire process should be well-documented. So far, all documents of the AC are only accessible to the dean and the rectorate.

Step "arbitration": If there are objections by the EOC, an arbitration process must be started and its outcome must be taken into account by the rector. The escalation stages are: internal clarification, proceedings before the arbitration commission of the university, and court proceedings. If there is no objection, the rector can select any candidate of the list. The choice must be approved by the EOC, otherwise an arbitration process must be started (see above).

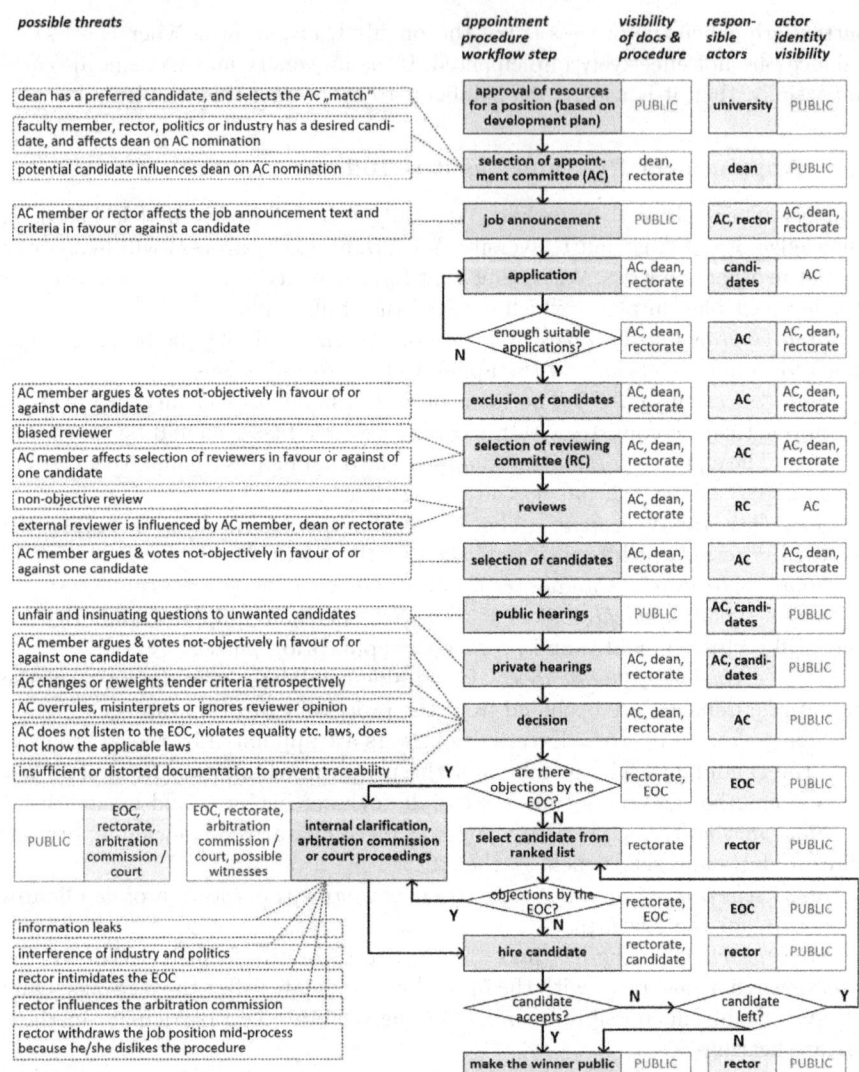

Fig. 1. Appointment process without DAO.

Step "hire candidate": Finally, the rector hires the resulting candidate.

Step "make the winner public": If the candidate accepts, the process terminates by publicizing the winner. Otherwise, the process continues with the next candidate on the list. All process documents are kept secret.

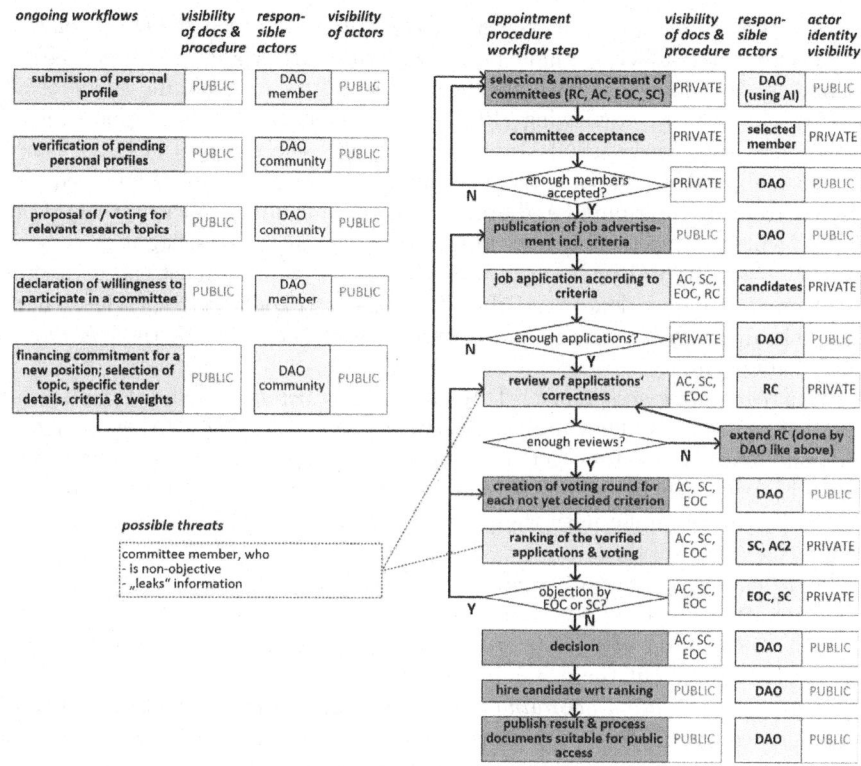

Fig. 2. Appointment process with DAO.

5.2 Appointment Procedure in FreeUniversity.dao

Figure 2 illustrates a possible workflow for an appointment process in FreeUniversity.dao. Dark gray boxes are steps that are automatically executed by the DAO. Unlike a centralized university with a predefined research plan, any DAO actor can propose research topics at any time, so that a collection of current and community-driven research topics is created. Using voting, the community can rank the topics similar to research proposals in FrontierDAO (see Sect. 3). Also, everyone can submit (and update) an own personal profile, which must be certified by (at least) one already certified DAO actor. This includes checking the correctness of the profile data, and the correct association between e.g., email and wallet. Certified profiles are published as NFTs. For possibly needed discussions off-chain social media and chat channels can be used, using nick names in order to maintain anonymity of the actors, and not being allowed to reveal the identity; and for the sharing of documents distributed file systems like IPFS shall be used to minimize on-chain storage. Everything must be secured with blockchain's cryptographic mechanisms.

Step "selection and announcement of committees": When the DAO community decides that sufficient funds for a new position are available and has agreed on tender conditions that have also been reviewed by an EOC, members for all needed committees – reviewing (RC), appointment (AC), equal opportunities (EOC) and supervisory (SC) – are automatically selected by the DAO, based on personal profiles and using AI. The committees are made up of qualified representatives, are distributed and are anonymous (including to each other). E.g., the AC will be composed of the respective curia: professors, assistant professors, and students; the RC must contain experts in the topic; the SC needs people with controlling experience; and the EOC includes experts with gender experience. The event that a new committee was created is emitted by the DAO via a blockchain event.

Step "committee acceptance": DAO actors must listen to the blockchain event via their application. They use their certified account to check if they belong to the committee. If so, they get a voting key, encrypted with their public key. Note that the committee members and their votes remain anonymous to each other and to the public until the process is decided. Qualified contributions to committees earn tokens.

Step "enough members accepted?": If not enough members have accepted, the committee selection is extended.

Step "publication of job advertisement with criteria": Next the DAO emits the information about the new job position.

Step "job application according to criteria": Interested candidates apply and fill in the required criteria catalogue with their data. The advantage of everyone answering all the criteria themselves is that no merits are missed or can be ignored by reviewers or AC members.

Step "enough applications?": If there are not enough applications, the job advertisement is repeated.

Step "review of applications' correctness": Each reviewer must accept a bias declaration and check for one or more candidates, whether the completed self-assessment along the criteria corresponds to the truth, and prepare a review report. If not all reviewers submit their reports, the DAO must extend the RC. All candidate information remain confidential to the reviewers and AC at this stage (how this can be implemented on the blockchain is sketched for the voting step of the AC below).

Step "creation of voting round for each not yet decided criterion": The DAO creates a voting round for each criterion that is not yet finally decided.

Step "ranking of the verified applications & voting": If all applications are verified by the RC, the AC trusts the information provided by the candidates. For anonymous voting, each AC member must conceal its identity, by creating and using a second wallet, of which nobody knows who owns it. The entire communication is encrypted with the AC member's voting key. With the anonymous wallet the AC member pulls a ballot and a bias declaration from the DAO, generates a vote for who best, second best a.s.o. fulfills the respective criterion and sends the vote to the blockchain, which implicitly also implies acceptance of the bias declaration. The vote must be accompanied by a justification of how the AC member has assessed and quantified it. Simple issues are e.g. higher number of publications, and better quality of publications. But for more complex points such as industry experience, for example, you can say that founding a start-up is more important than being employed by a company. Voting takes place in first come first serve mode: there are more committee members invited than needed, so if there are enough votes, the voting round is closed. Note that the reviewers are not known to the AC; and the AC members do not know each other.

Step *"objection by EOC or SC?"*: After the voting rounds are completed, the EOC and the SC must control the process, after having accepted their bias declaration. Their incentive is to get rewards for participation, especially if they find demonstrable errors. The EOC checks if laws with regard to diversity, equality, discrimination, women's advancement etc. were considered in discussions, decisions and justifications. The SC checks the process with regard to completeness, inconsistencies, factuality, contradictions etc. E.g., if the AC members used inconsistent quantification arguments, the workflow is rolled back and a new voting round is opened on that criterion.

Step *"decision"*: FreeUniversity.dao automatically calculates the decision based on criteria weights and voting results.

Step *"hire candidate wrt to ranking"*: The candidates are asked in the order of the list. A candidate can accept or decline.

Step *"publish result & process documents suitable for public access, and pay out rewards"*: Eventually, information necessary for the public to assess the process is disclosed like the identities of the committee members, but not what each single person voted. The candidate names and applications are not made public, only the winner. The quantification of merits for each criterion are published (in anonymized form) etc. This ensures transparency, while maintaining the necessary confidentiality (see columns termed "visibility" in Fig. 2). After this step, there is no rollback any more, because otherwise endless disputes could occur, but sanctions such as the exclusion or blacklisting of actors etc. can be carried out by the DAO community. Finally, all rewards for contributing to the process are calculated and paid out.

5.3 Adaptations for a Phygital University

Let us assume that a traditional university wants to outsource its application processes to FreeUniversity.dao. In a first step, the rector must tell the DAO that there is money allocated for a position. Optionally the university may select the topic for the new position or may leave it to the DAO as described above. In the first case, the university will also determine the specific tender details, criteria and weights. Apart from that, the process runs as described for the digital DAO (see Fig. 2), only the hiring of a candidate is done by the rector.

6 Evaluation

Let us classify potential risks of a breach of scientific integrity as follows:

Indiscretion refers to information leaks to unauthorized or external parties, despite the confidential nature of the process. E.g.: Information might be disclosed to the media to create political or public pressure on the actors.

Influence refers to internal or external influence of or compulsion on involved actors, because of supervisor relationships, personal benefits, subsidiary agreements, hidden deals etc. E.g.: The rector is influenced by external parties like politics or industry, and in turn influences AC members. Students or assistants serving on the AC are pressured to align with their adviser's preferences, especially if the adviser also belongs to the AC, to maintain favor for academic or career reasons. There exist hidden quid pro quo agreements, like mutual support for applicants in next recruitment processes.

Arbitrariness refers to non-compliance with the law – whether due to ignorance or intent. E.g.: disregarding the EOC's arguments, wrong or no justification of decisions, unequal treatment of candidates' merits, modifying or re-weighting of the tender and evaluation criteria mid-process, ignoring the requirement to promote women, ignoring gender equality mandates, discrimination, and not documenting the process sufficiently or in a distorted way.

Non-objectivity refers to biased, non-factual, subjective evaluation. E.g.: non-objective biased expert opinion, contradictory review including not-logical conclusions, lack of care in the evaluation, stating false facts, influenced commissioned opinion, and non-objective composition of committees.

6.1 Analysis of Potential Threats in the Traditional Workflow

Specific, selected risks of this type associated with the various steps of the appointment process are shown in Fig. 1 on the left in dashed boxes and are explained below:[9]

Step "selection of AC": The dean or rector may favor a certain candidate, or be influenced by politics or industry, and form the AC strategically by selecting

---

[9] These issues are taken from an actual and publicly fought out court case, carried out by the Austrian supreme administrative court. There was a massive influence from politics and industry on the university concerned. Selected misconducts comprise: (a) A candidate's merits were ignored. (b) A student admitted to voting based on their professor's preference rather than their own opinion. (c) The justification for the top-ranked candidate was incorrect, because he never held the assumed director position. (d) A professor admitted ignorance of the women's promotion act. (e) Lacking factual arguments, the AC altered criteria in their final meeting to favor a preferred candidate; this was even documented. (f) The judge ruled the documentation inadequate due to missing justification for the ranking. (g) A witness testified that an AC member said, "If the woman were a man, she would get the job," but this was omitted from the records. (h) A press leak fostered bias toward the preferred candidate and pressured the EOC. (i) After the EOC took the appeal to court, the rector dismissed its chair from their university position without clear justification. (j) During the proceedings, the rector appointed the chair of the arbitration commission as vice-rector. (k) Seeing he would lose, the rector unlawfully canceled the position, rendering the appeal meaningless.

members likely to support this candidate. Faculty members with a preferred candidate might attempt to sway the dean's decisions on AC nominations to include members who would favor their choice. A candidate may try to directly influence the dean during the nomination process to ensure favorable AC composition.

Step *"job announcement"*: An AC member with a secret preference for a specific candidate might manipulate the job posting to include criteria that only his/her preferred candidate can meet, thereby reducing competition.

Step *"exclusion of candidates"*: AC members might dismiss certain candidates on unjustifiable grounds to limit competition for their preferred choice.

Step *"selection of RC"*: Biasedness of a reviewer is not recognized or ignored by the AC; or the reviewer does not declare it properly and does not refuse therefore the reviewing. AC members might influence the selection of reviewers to include those favorably disposed toward their preferred candidate while excluding those who may provide unbiased or unfavorable evaluations.

Step *"reviews"*: A reviewer might be non-objective, non-factual, careless, biased etc. An actor might attempt to contact external reviewers privately to sway their evaluations.

Step *"selection of candidates"*: AC members may argue and vote for or against a candidate to be invited for the hearings based on biased, subjective, non-objective preferences rather than logical or evidence-based reasoning.

Step *"hearings"*: AC members, dean, or members from the rectorate might ask unfair and insinuating questions to unwanted candidates, whereas preferred candidates are treated in a very friendly manner.

Step *"decision"*: AC members may argue and vote non-objectively (see footnote $9^{(a)}$) in favor of or against one candidate due subjective preferences or influences (see footnote $9^{(b)}$), not applying logical or evidence-based reasoning. (see footnote $9^{(c)}$) Although discussions may steer in a specific direction, individual votes may not align with these discussions. AC members may vote without having carefully analyzed all documents or being aware of their duties according to the applicable law. (see footnote $9^{(d)}$) Especially in this step, the above mentioned risk that AC members change or re-weight tender criteria retrospectively is high. (see footnote $9^{(e)}$) Without sufficient or distorted documentation (see footnote $9^{(f)}$) of the entire process including discussions and decisions, transparency and accountability are compromised, particularly in cases where voting outcomes conflict with prior discussions or if the argumentation was non-objective or violates the law. (see footnote $9^{(g)}$) The AC might overrule, misinterpret or ignore reviewer opinions.

Step *"arbitration"*: Especially in this step the risks of information leaks are high. (see footnote $9^{(h)}$) There might be an unauthorized interference of industry and politics, trying to influence actors. (see footnote $9^{(h)}$) The rector might intimidate members of the EOC. (see footnote $9^{(i)}$) The rector might exert influence on the arbitration commission (see footnote $9^{(j)}$), which like the EOC is also part of the university. Finally, the rector might withdraw the job position mid-process. (see footnote $9^{(k)}$)

6.2 Analysis of Potential Threats in the DAO Workflow

In FreeUniversity.dao there are only two threats regarding scientific misconduct: 1) a committee member acting non-objectively and 2) an information leak caused by an actor. These issues cannot be fully prevented but can be mitigated, detected, and sanctioned. Ad 1) Unlike conventional appointment processes, an AC member in the DAO workflow cannot be externally influenced, as their identity remains unknown during the process.[10] If an AC member acts unethically or makes unsound decisions, it is solely due to their individual choices. Ad 2) Passing on information to achieve a specific goal is rather pointless.

In addition, the correctness of the process and its implementation must be verified. There must not be a standstill if there is not enough participation despite incentive mechanisms. If, for example, there are not enough active members in commissions, the reviewers do not deliver on time, or there are repeated objections, then as we have learned in Sect. 2.3 further coordination mechanisms and fallbacks must be introduced, which are still missing in the workflow shown.

6.3 Supplements for a Phygital University

If the DAO process was performed for a university, two further risks are: 3) If the university specified the tender, it could have been tailored for a preferred candidate. In this case, in the DAO process in step "*objection by EOC and SC*," the respective committees must carefully check if that applies to the outcome. 4) The rector could withdraw the position mid-process. It could help if the university deposited the funds for the position in the DAO in advance.

6.4 Summary and Discussion

Many of the risks in traditional processes (see above) can be mitigated by FreeUniversity.dao through automation and a good design of the process rules: External influence is nearly impossible because actors remain anonymous during parts of the process and only they can view relevant data. Not even committee members know each other. This also reduces indiscretion and leaks, as actors gain little from sharing information. The processes are automatically controlled by the DAO, preventing arbitrariness. Everything is documented, as discussions are in writing and the smart contract requires complete information (e.g., each criterion answer must be justified per candidate per tender criteria). SC and EOC oversee the process. Transparency allows monitoring at any time: At the end, key information verifying process integrity is made public. For appointments, reasoning for each criterion is disclosed without candidate names. Committee member identities are published, but not individual votes. The result, including vote count, is also published. Decentralization is crucial. A major flaw in university structures is that the EOC and arbitration commission belong to the same

---

[10] It's unlikely that a DAO actor discovers committee members, especially with enough participants from diverse universities or countries, though not impossible.

university, making them subordinate to the rector, who can exert pressure. A decentralized DAO with many participants reduces the risk of actors meeting and colluding in the real world. The risk of individual unethical behavior cannot be entirely eliminated. However, the community can identify misconduct patterns, e.g., if an actor frequently opposes majority consensus or behaves inconsistently with discussions. The DAO can use AI-based algorithms to detect such behavior. Governance mechanisms may sanction actors, e.g., by restricting them from serving as reviewers or committee members. Such measures gradually remove untrustworthy actors, preserving system integrity.

Please note that a list of criteria could be viewed critically, as it should not be used to prevent innovation. One solution would be to make the criteria more open and require applicants to have particular merits that cannot be foreseen in advance. However, it must then be objectively argued why, for example, the invention of a patent is more important than two years of work in industry, etc. and this argumentation must then also be adhered to in other workflows.

Other workflows – such as designing curricula, awarding grades, accrediting DAO degrees through universities, distributing utility tokens for contributions, selecting research topics, voting on research topics, granting funding, allocating resources, forming partnerships, verifying profiles, managing intellectual property rights (IPRs), etc. – must be developed analogously. This can take place either during Phase 3 or continuously in Phase 5 (see Sect. 4). It must always be evaluated why decentralized governance is, first, accurate and, second, superior to the centralized process.

7 Conclusion

This paper presented a vision for an autonomous, decentralized university and developed a corresponding mission statement. The primary aim is to ensure independence from external and potentially distorting influences such as politics, government, and industry-forces that often serve to preserve power rather than promote the common good. Another goal is to increase efficiency in traditional universities by allowing them to outsource selected governance processes to the DAO, to make education free for all, and to be able to transform research into products more quickly. At its current stage, FreeUniversity.dao remains a conceptual framework and a collection of open research questions to be explored and refined within the academic and educational community. An example workflow was presented to illustrate how DAO-based coordination can offer clear advantages over traditional processes.

For a functioning university DAO, coordination is the key to success. Only when all actors collaborate effectively and their resources and expertise are meaningfully combined can the vision of a transparent, independent, and inclusive educational institution be realized. Coordination is essential not only for daily operations but also for ensuring long-term sustainability and innovation. To ensure that the constitutional rules of FreeUniversity.dao are both consistent and enforceable, formal methods are proposed for their specification and verification. Roles, permissions, and coordination constraints can be described using temporal logics or rule-based specification languages such as TLA+ or Alloy, or through executable coordination frameworks like Reo. Distributed governance structures – such as dynamic committee formation, reconfigurable workflows, or adaptive voting rules – can be modeled using the Actors Model or the Peer Model. These tools enable simulation and formal analysis of system properties like deadlock-freedom, liveness, and consistency in voting and authority hierarchies. E.g., a rule "any amendment to the core mission requires a two-thirds majority" can be formally encoded and verified to prevent procedural bypasses.

To encourage participation from existing universities, FreeUniversity.dao introduces a governance-as-a-service model. This allows institutions to delegate specific governance tasks (e.g., hiring, accreditation) to the DAO while preserving their national identity and autonomy. Incentives for universities to join could include cost reduction through automation, increased legitimacy through transparent processes, and new funding mechanisms via tokenization and community engagement. While the long-term vision is a globally coordinated DAO, a pragmatic path may begin with a few universities acting as pilot institutions gradually delegating selected governance processes – such as faculty selection or course accreditation – to FreeUniversity.dao, using it as a testbed for iterative development.

At a time when research and education is increasingly influenced by centralized, often political or financial interests, coordination in a DAO represents an opportunity to break through this system, challenge the traditional governance structures, and establishing a new, fairer form of research and knowledge transfer. Given the inherent complexity of decentralized coordination, the realization of FreeUniversity.dao and how it can evolve independently while ensuring adherence to its mission statement, represents a significant technical challenge. To address this, we propose to initiate a call to the coordination research community: Which coordination models, languages, or verification tools could best contribute to this endeavor, and at what stages of the system would they be most effective? This paper aims to lay a conceptual foundation and open this discussion. We look forward to engaging with the community at the symposium to jointly explore how the ideas and tools from coordination research can help bring this vision to life.

References

1. Agha, G.A.: ACTORS: A Model of Concurrent Computation in Distributed Systems. MIT Press (1990)
2. Alawadi, A., Kakabadse, N., Kakabadse, A., Zuckerbraun, S.: Decentralized autonomous organizations (DAOs): stewardship talks but agency walks. J. Bus. Res. **178** (2024). https://doi.org/10.1016/j.jbusres.2024.114672
3. Alipour, S., Elahimanesh, S., Jahanzad, S., et al.: Improving grading fairness and transparency with decentralized collaborative peer assessment. Proc. ACM Hum.-Comput. Interact. **8**(CSCW1) (2024). https://doi.org/10.1145/3637350
4. Armstrong, B.: Ideas on how to improve scientific research. Medium (2019). https://barmstrong.medium.com/ideas-on-how-to-improve-scientific-research-9e2e56474132

5. Avital, M.: Digital transformation of academic publishing: a call for the decentralization and democratization of academic journals. J. Assoc. Inf. Syst. **25**(1), 172–181 (2024). https://doi.org/10.17705/1jais.00873
6. Barbuta, D.E., Alexandrescu, A.: A decentralized paper dissemination system employing blockchain technology, peer review and expert badges. In: 27th International Conference on System Theory, Control and Computing (ICSTCC), pp. 321–326 (2023). https://doi.org/10.1109/ICSTCC59206.2023.10308453
7. Becze, M., Jameson, H., et al.: EIP-1: EIP Purpose and Guidelines. Ethereum Improvement Proposals (2015). https://eips.ethereum.org/EIPS/eip-1
8. van den Brink, M., Benschop, Y.: Gender practices in the construction of academic excellence: sheep with five legs. Organization **19**(4), 507–524 (2012). https://doi.org/10.1177/1350508411414293
9. Choi, D.H., Seo, T.S.: Development of an open peer review system using blockchain and reviewer recommendation technologies. Sci. Ed. **8**(1), 104–111 (2021). https://doi.org/10.6087/kcse.237
10. Cossar, S., Merk, T., Kamalova, J., De Filippi, P.: Proof of Humanity: Ethnographic Research of a "Democratic" DAO. Research project report, European University Institute (EUI) (2024). https://hal.science/hal-04855850
11. Ding, Q., Liebau, D., Wang, Z., Xu, W.: A survey on decentralized autonomous organizations (DAOs) and their governance. World Sci. Ann. Rev. Fintech **01** (2023). https://doi.org/10.1142/S281100482350001X
12. Duh, E.S., Duh, A., Droftina, U., et al.: Publish-and-Flourish: decentralized co-creation and curation of scholarly content. arXiv (2018). https://doi.org/10.48550/arXiv.1810.10263
13. Ferreira, C., Bastille-Rousseau, G., Bennett, A.M., Ellington, E.H., et al.: The evolution of peer review as a basis for scientific publication: directional selection towards a robust discipline? Biol. Rev. Camb. Philos. Soc. **91**(3), 597–610 (2016). https://doi.org/10.1111/brv.12185
14. Finke, A., Hensel, T.: Decentralized peer review in open science: a mechanism proposal. arXiv (2024). https://doi.org/10.48550/arXiv.2404.18148
15. Gruendler, J., Melnyk, D., Pourdamghani, A., Schmid, S.: DecentPeeR: a self-incentivised & inclusive decentralized peer review system. In: 2024 IEEE International Conference on Blockchain and Cryptocurrency (ICBC), pp. 394–396. IEEE (2024). https://doi.org/10.1109/icbc59979.2024.10634376
16. Han, J., Lee, J., Li, T.: A review of DAO governance: recent literature and emerging trends. J. Corp. Financ. **91**, 102734 (2025). https://doi.org/10.1016/j.jcorpfin.2025.102734
17. Hassan, S., Filippi, P.D.: Decentralized autonomous organization. Internet Policy Rev. **10**(2) (2021). https://doi.org/10.14763/2021.2.1556
18. Janze, C.: Design of a decentralized peer-to-peer reviewing and publishing market. In: 25th European Conference on Information Systems (ECIS) (2017). https://aisel.aisnet.org/ecis2017_rp/110
19. Kharman, A.M., Smyth, B.: Perils of current DAO governance. arXiv (2024). https://doi.org/10.48550/arXiv.2406.08605
20. Kuehn, E.M.: A distributed ledger technology based on shared write-once objects. In: Boreale, M., Corradini, F., Loreti, M., Pugliese, R. (eds.) Models, Languages, and Tools for Concurrent and Distributed Programming. LNCS, vol. 11665, pp. 136–151. Springer, Cham (2019). https://doi.org/10.1007/978-3-030-21485-2_9
21. Kuehn, E.: The peer model tool-chain. Sci. Comput. Program. **223** (2022). https://doi.org/10.1016/j.scico.2022.102876

22. Kuehn, E.M.: A new business model in the fine arts realm based on NFT certificates and pearl codes. Digital Business **4**(2) (2024). https://doi.org/10.1016/j.digbus.2024.100079
23. Kumar, S., Upadhyay, P., Rani, N.: Towards blockchain decentralized autonomous organizations (DAO) design. Inf. Syst. Front. (2024). https://doi.org/10.1007/s10796-023-10455-w
24. Li, J., Liang, X., Qin, R., Wang, F.Y.: From DAO to TAO: finding the essence of decentralization. In: IEEE Int. Conf. on Systems, Man, and Cybernetics (SMC), pp. 4283–4288 (2023). https://doi.org/10.1109/SMC53992.2023.10394591
25. Li, J., Wang, F.Y.: The TAO of blockchain intelligence for intelligent Web 3.0. IEEE/CAA J. Automatica Sinica **10**(12), 2183–2186 (2023). https://doi.org/10.1109/JAS.2023.124056
26. Llyr, B., Slavin, A.: DAOs for Impact. World Economic Forum (2023). https://www.weforum.org/publications/daos-for-impact/, white Paper
27. Sims, A.: DAOs (Decentralised Autonomous Organisations) v DINOs (DAO in Name Only or Decentralised in Name Only). SSRN (2024). http://dx.doi.org/10.2139/ssrn.4716559
28. Sonmez, F.O., Mulligan, C., Knottenbelt, W., Jungnickel, M.: DAO Governance: Voting Power, Participation, and Controversy – a Review and an Empirical Analysis. SSRN (2024). http://dx.doi.org/10.2139/ssrn.5008958
29. Tenorio-Fornes, A., Tirador, E.P., Sánchez-Ruiz, A.A., Hassan, S.: Decentralizing science: towards an interoperable open peer review ecosystem using blockchain. Inf. Process. Manage. **58**(6) (2021). https://doi.org/10.1016/j.ipm.2021.102724
30. Wang, F.Y., Ding, W., Wang, X., et al.: The DAO to DeSci: AI for free, fair, and responsibility sensitive sciences. IEEE Intell. Syst. **37**(2), 16–22 (2022). https://doi.org/10.1109/MIS.2022.3167070
31. Wong Ellinger, E., Mini, T., Gregory, R.W., Dietz, A.: Decentralized autonomous organization (DAO): the case of MakerDAO. J. Inf. Technol. Teach. Cases **14**(2), 265–272 (2024). https://doi.org/10.1177/20438869231181151
32. Woods, D.R., Benschop, Y., van den Brink, M.: What is intersectional equality? A definition and goal of equality for organizations. Gend. Work Org. **29**(1), 92–109 (2022). https://doi.org/10.1111/gwao.12760

Open Access This chapter is licensed under the terms of the Creative Commons Attribution 4.0 International License (http://creativecommons.org/licenses/by/4.0/), which permits use, sharing, adaptation, distribution and reproduction in any medium or format, as long as you give appropriate credit to the original author(s) and the source, provide a link to the Creative Commons license and indicate if changes were made.

The images or other third party material in this chapter are included in the chapter's Creative Commons license, unless indicated otherwise in a credit line to the material. If material is not included in the chapter's Creative Commons license and your intended use is not permitted by statutory regulation or exceeds the permitted use, you will need to obtain permission directly from the copyright holder.

Industry 4.0 and Digital Twins: The Route Towards Customizable Self-describing Products

Michael Papazoglou[1], Bernd J. Krämer[1(✉)], and Amal Elgammal[1,2,3]

[1] Scientific Academy for Service Technology, Behlertstr. 3A, 14467 Potsdam, Germany
kraemer@servtech.info
[2] Faculty of Computers and Artificial Intelligence, Cairo University, Cairo 12613, Egypt
[3] Egypt University of Informatics, New Administrative Capital, Cairo 19519, Egypt

Abstract. Industry 4.0 fundamentally transforms traditional manufacturing by ushering in a new era of data- and knowledge-driven digital production systems. This paper introduces *Manufacturing Blueprints*, a proven knowledge-based framework that bridges the gap between physical and digital manufacturing. At its core, Manufacturing Blueprints comprises an innovative manufacturing knowledge model and a robust programming environment that enables the representation, storage, retrieval, cross-correlation, and processing of critical digital manufacturing knowledge. This includes product design, production processes, service quality, operational parameters, timing, and control mechanisms. As a comprehensive digital twin solution, Manufacturing Blueprints addresses the entire lifecycle of intelligent products, encompassing product development, production optimization, and performance management. By fully digitizing physical assets and processes, the framework seamlessly integrates factory sites, plants, and self-regulating machines, enabling customized output and dynamic resource allocation. This approach not only aligns with the vision of Industry 4.0 but also facilitates a seamless transition between the physical and digital realms of product design and production. Manufacturing Blueprints represents a transformative step toward realizing the full potential of smart, interconnected, and adaptive manufacturing ecosystems.

Keywords: Industry 4.0 · digital twin · manufacturing knowledge · manufacturing blueprints · product customization · product ideation and design

1 Introduction

Industry 4.0 represents a transformative shift in manufacturing, laying the foundation for fully connected factories characterized by the digitization and interconnection of supply chains, production equipment, and production lines. By leveraging advanced digital information technologies, Industry 4.0 integrates connected machines, process automation, and manufacturing units to create an integrated, automated, and optimized production flow. This enables the production of highly customized products while improving efficiency, agility, and innovation across manufacturing environments.

The manufacturing lifecycle under Industry 4.0 begins with product ideation and extends through digital design, physical development, delivery, and ongoing maintenance. This holistic approach fosters flexible and agile manufacturing ecosystems where production units and plants collaborate seamlessly, optimizing performance and efficiency. Central to this paradigm is the convergence of processes, systems, machines, devices, sensors, actuators, and communication technologies, all interacting digitally and physically to create a "smart" factory of the future.

At the heart of this transformation is the concept of the digital twin—a virtual representation of physical assets and processes that enables real-time monitoring, simulation, and optimization [1]. Digital twins bridge the gap between the digital and physical worlds, allowing manufacturers to overlay virtual models onto physical products at any stage of production. This capability empowers designers and engineers to make informed decisions about materials, processes, and production sequences using advanced visualization tools such as 3D CAD/CAM systems. By simulating and analyzing product behavior in the virtual realm, manufacturers can ensure that physical products perform as intended in real-world conditions.

Digital twins can be categorized into three types, each serving a distinct purpose in the manufacturing lifecycle:

1. **Product Digital Twins**: Create a digital-physical connection to enable efficient design and validation of new products. This allows manufacturers to analyze product behavior under various conditions and make design adjustments in the virtual world to ensure optimal performance in the field.
2. **Production Digital Twins**: Simulating manufacturing processes on the shop floor facilitates improved production planning. Using product digital twins and digital threads, manufacturers can optimize production under diverse conditions and what-if scenarios before physical production begins.
3. **Performance Digital Twins**: Capture and analyze vast amounts of data from smart products and plants to provide actionable insights for decision-making, enhancing quality and operational performance.

The true value of the digital twins in manufacturing is the ability to simulate, validate, and optimize entire production systems. They enable manufacturers to test how products—including their primary parts and sub-assemblies—will be built using specific manufacturing processes and production lines. Additionally, digital twins allow for the projection of alternative production sequences, providing visibility into the operation of production systems and enabling continuous optimization.

However, achieving this level of customization and integration requires overcoming significant challenges. Current manufacturing systems often lack the flexibility to adapt to changing parameters, and the implementation of digital twins demands the integration of innovative, disruptive technologies. These include smarter, more reliable, and secure plug-and-play systems that seamlessly connect digital and physical components. To address these challenges, new modeling and processing languages are needed to represent, share, and process product and manufacturing knowledge, facilitating the transition from digital designs to physical products.

This paper aligns with the Industry 4.0 vision of transitioning from linear, sequential supply chain operations to interconnected digital supply networks. It presents a comprehensive framework for enabling customizable product manufacturing through the integration of the three types of digital twins. Specifically, the paper introduces:

- **A Manufacturing Knowledge Model**: This model, known as the *Manufacturing Blueprint Knowledge Model* [2], explicitly represents digital product design by collecting, storing, and processing actionable data from every stage of the product lifecycle. It harmonizes supplier perspectives and provides an end-to-end, holistic view of the production chain, with generic properties applicable to diverse smart manufacturing applications.
- **A Manufacturing Blueprint Meta-Programming Language**: This language translates generic product representations into composable production-level activities and processes, which are then transformed into product artifacts. As a next-generation code-generating program, it allows developers to define custom behaviors for basic language operations using advanced abstraction mechanisms, enabling the creation of highly customizable digital products.

Finally, the paper demonstrates the practical application of the meta-programming model and language in producing customizable digital products for industrial-strength aerospace applications. By bridging the gap between digital and physical manufacturing, this approach paves the way for realizing the full potential of Industry 4.0.

2 Related Work

The ability to collect, integrate, and process heterogeneous manufacturing knowledge and data is central to supporting the key tenets of Industry 4.0 addressed in this article: digital twins, customizable products, and Meta-Programming Languages (MPLs) for manufacturing environments. These topics are discussed in the following sub-sections, with an emphasis on recent advancements, gaps in the literature, and how the proposed approach addresses these gaps.

2.1 Digital Twin

The concept of Digital Twins (DTs) was first introduced by Grieves in 2003 [1], but its practical implementation has only gained momentum in recent years due to advancements in enabling technologies such as simulation, data acquisition, sensors, cloud computing, and big data analytics [2]. These technologies have transformed DTs from a conceptual framework to a practical tool with applications across various domains, including product design, production planning, and monitoring [3]. A recent state-of-the-art review of 50 papers and eight patents [3] highlights that 18% of DT applications focus on product design, 35% on production processes (primarily execution phases), and 47% on monitoring processes (mostly prognostic health monitoring). However, the integration of DTs into production planning remains underexplored, particularly in terms of formal knowledge models and IT implementations.

Compared to the earlier work presented in [2], this paper significantly advances the blueprinting concept by formalizing a multi-layered meta-programming environment. It also integrates these with digital twin types, providing a full lifecycle perspective and enabling seamless co-design, customization, and production planning. This article introduces programmatic operators and formal specifications, thereby making the blueprinting approach computationally actionable and scalable.

In product design, DTs have been utilized to enhance collaboration between design and manufacturing. For instance, [4] developed a set of theories and tools for design-oriented DTs, while [5] proposed a 3D product configuration DT model to bridge design and manufacturing workflows. [6] introduced a DT design framework with potential applications in various domains. Despite these advancements, existing efforts often lack a formal foundation for knowledge integration and concrete IT implementations, limiting their scalability and applicability in complex manufacturing environments.

In production planning, the literature on DTs is notably sparse. [7] proposed a digital-twin-centric control approach, where a DT derived from a product model orchestrates assembly plans and resources. Similarly, [8] and [9] employed DT models to manage geometrical variations in production processes. However, these approaches are limited in scope and do not address the seamless translation of product designs into optimized production plans.

In contrast, the blueprinting digital twin approach proposed in this article provides a formal knowledge model and an expressive meta-programming environment for integrating product design and production planning. This approach not only supports the initial stages of the product lifecycle but can also be extended to subsequent processes, such as monitoring, with rigorous solutions and concrete IT implementations.

2.2 Product Customization

Product customization, defined as the production of goods and services tailored to individual customer needs while maintaining near mass production efficiency [10, 11] has emerged as a critical component of Industry 4.0. Research in this area has focused on knowledge models for representing product family platforms [12, 13]. For example, [12] proposed a module-based integrated design scheme to support product platform establishment, family generation, and customized assessment. [13] introduced a knowledge model for product architecture design, leveraging a design repository to reduce data redundancy and improve accuracy.

At the operational level, product customization has been driven by the need to empower customers and enhance their engagement in the design process. [14] explores the concept of mass customization blending the efficiency of mass production with the personalization of custom-made products. [15] highlighted the importance of customer-centric approaches, while [16] proposed an innovative method to rationalize product variety by linking product variants to customer profiles. A knowledge-based system was developed to capture customer needs, functional constraints, and design parameters, enabling more effective customization. However, existing implementations often focus narrowly on the solution space—i.e., product attributes and structure—while neglecting broader information flows, such as customer preferences, supplier data, and product quality metrics [17, 18]. This limitation hinders the holistic integration of customization processes with other aspects of the product lifecycle.

The product ideation, co-design, and customization DT approach presented in this article addresses these gaps by: (i) using a formal knowledge model based on blueprints, (ii) enhancing usability through a Domain-Specific Language (DSL) and 3D visualization features, and (iii) enabling continuous collaboration between customers, designers, and engineers during the customization process. Furthermore, the proposed approach extends to subsequent lifecycle processes, providing an integrated knowledge-based framework for end-to-end customization.

2.3 Meta-programming Languages

Meta-programming enables programs to generate, analyze, and modify other programs or itself. Lisp and its dialects are prime examples of metaprogramming languages due to their historical significance and the simplicity and power of their metaprogramming capabilities [19]. In software engineering, meta-programming aims to transition from unique software systems to semi-automated production, enabling the creation of customized and optimized software products on demand by modeling software families [20].

Despite the potential of meta-programming, most existing systems rely on ad hoc techniques for program development, limiting their applicability in complex domains such as smart manufacturing. Early efforts, such as MetaML [21], introduced multi-level languages as intermediate representations for partial evaluation and runtime code generation. More recent developments, such as NodeRED (nodered.org) and Converge [22], have focused on visual programming and compile-time meta-programming, respectively. However, these platforms are often platform-dependent and lack the flexibility required for smart manufacturing environments.

To address these limitations, [23] proposed a highly configurable service approach, identifying groups of digital services that can be bundled to perform demanding computing tasks. A Domain-Specific Language (DSL) was used to capture the decision space, incorporating interrelated concepts critical to service delivery workflows. Automated analysis operations were also introduced to streamline the execution of service tasks. While these advancements represent significant progress, they remain limited in their ability to fully digitize physical assets and processes in manufacturing environments.

The blueprint model and its associated meta-programming environment proposed in this article aim to overcome these challenges by enabling the seamless integration of physical and digital worlds. This approach supports the vision of smart factories by digitizing all physical assets and processes, connecting factory sites, plants, and self-regulating machines, and customizing outputs while optimizing resource allocation. By leveraging a formal knowledge model and an expressive meta-programming environment, the proposed approach provides a robust foundation for realizing the full potential of Industry 4.0.

2.4 Actors as Meta-objects: Behavioral Reflection

In Gul Agha's Actor model, formalized in the 1980s [24], one of the most powerful ideas is that actors can modify their own behavior at runtime, effectively reprogramming themselves. This is reflective meta-programming in which code can be changed dynamically. Meta-programming involves reifying, i.e., making parts of the system's semantics explicit and manipulable. Agha's model treats computation and behavior as first-class—they can be passed, changed, replaced, and composed. This opens the door for actor systems where message handling, scheduling, or communication topology can be adapted programmatically at runtime. In advanced implementations, this leads to reflective actor systems, where you can introspect or alter the semantics of actors (schedulers, mailboxes, routing strategies).

Meta-programming enables custom actor behaviors, like timeouts, replication, or supervision trees, using code generation or reflective APIs. In Agha-inspired systems, you can use meta-programming to generate actor classes with specific concurrency patterns or compose new behavior dynamically. For example, the open-source toolkit Akka for building concurrent, distributed, resilient message-driven applications in Java and Scala, although not directly descended from Agha's work, uses reflection and meta-programming (via traits and macros) to build supervision strategies and typed actors.

Some actor systems inspired by Agha (like OpenCom, Rebeca, or DARe) adopt meta-level architectures that separate base-level actors (implementing business logic) from meta-level actors (managing behavior and policies). Here, meta-programming enables dynamic policy injection, monitoring, and adaptation. In such systems, meta-programming allows you to add logging, monitoring, or fault-tolerance strategies dynamically and rewrite or wrap actor behaviors at runtime—much like aspect-oriented programming.

2.5 Summary of Contributions

The related work reviewed in this section highlights significant advancements in digital twins, product customization, and meta-programming languages. However, existing approaches often lack formal knowledge models, holistic integration, and concrete IT implementations, limiting their applicability in complex manufacturing environments.

The proposed blueprinting digital twin approach addresses these gaps by providing a formal knowledge model, an expressive meta-programming environment, and an integrated framework for product design, customization, and production planning. This approach enhances the usability and scalability of existing solutions and extends their applicability to subsequent stages of the product lifecycle, thus paving the way for fully digitized and interconnected smart factories.

3 Manufacturing Meta-programming Environment

Manufacturing facilities generate vast amounts of data from a multitude of sources, including shop-floor equipment, control systems, quality tracking, PLM (Product Lifecycle Management), CAD/CAM (Computer-Aided Design/Manufacturing), maintenance systems, and monitoring systems. However, this data is often fragmented, unstructured, and not fully digitized in a way that enables efficient search, retrieval, and analysis. Hence, this data remains underutilized. The challenge lies in transforming this raw data into actionable insights that can drive efficiency, innovation, and decision-making. To address this, a formalized approach is required to capture, structure, interrelate, and curate manufacturing knowledge through a formal knowledge model that ensures accessibility and usability.

The current state of manufacturing data is characterized by dispersion and a lack of integration. Data is often siloed, making it difficult to access, search, and analyze. This fragmentation hinders the ability to derive meaningful insights and optimize processes. To overcome these gaps, advanced technologies are needed to seamlessly connect diverse data sources, services, sensors, resources, and processes. These technologies must adopt an intuitive, user-friendly "plug & use" approach, enabling interoperability and contextual alignment across the manufacturing ecosystem. This is largely an open research problem, particularly in the context of smart manufacturing applications.

Meta-Programming Languages (MPLs) present a promising solution for addressing challenges such as interoperability, contextual alignment, and end-to-end process computations in manufacturing. By providing pre-defined abstractions that represent domain-specific concepts, MPLs allow developers to write code tailored to specific manufacturing applications. This ensures that the code is both optimized and domain specific.

Additionally, MPL compilers enhance this capability by further optimizing the code for specific domains, ensuring efficient execution and scalability. This combination of abstractions and compiler optimizations makes MPLs a powerful tool for streamlining complex manufacturing processes.

The meta-programming approach proposed in this paper leverages type-oriented programmable abstraction mechanisms designed for manufacturing artifacts. These mechanisms are tailored to manage complexity and facilitate the integration of data, processes, devices, and resources across the entire supply chain, from plant operations to the broader network.

The core of our meta-programming approach comprises the Manufacturing Blueprint Knowledge Model (MBKM) and Programming Language (MBPL). These tools provide a structured framework for representing and managing manufacturing knowledge, enabling seamless interoperability and scalability. The MBKM and MBPL offer a set of extendable abstractions, expressive notations, and a novel programming paradigm tailored for manufacturing applications. This enables developers to create modular, higher-level software solutions that streamline the design-to-production process.

The MBKM and MBPL are built on type-directed programmable abstraction mechanisms, which manage complexity and facilitate the integration of data, processes, devices, and resources across the supply chain and plant operations. This approach ensures that manufacturing knowledge is not only captured but also conserved and reused, fostering a more efficient and agile manufacturing environment.

3.1 Manufacturing Blueprints: Supporting the Essential Characteristics of Self-describing Products and Processes

The Manufacturing Blueprint Knowledge Model (MBKM) serves as a knowledge-modelling framework that represents and programs "bundles" of customer-focused combinations of product components, services, and manufacturing data. Its primary goal is to add value to core product and service offerings while optimizing production processes. The MBKM achieves this through manufacturing blueprint images—programmable abstract knowledge types that transform conventional products into smart self-describing products.

These blueprints store, link, combine, and analyze raw data collected throughout a product's lifecycle, creating smart actionable data. This data forms the foundation for generating knowledge and triggering production processes, enabling the creation of tailor-made, on-demand products and services. By leveraging model-based design techniques, manufacturing blueprints manage and interlink product data, manufacturing assets, and operational requirements, providing a comprehensive basis for actionable intelligence and fact-based decision-making.

The MBKM encapsulates supplier, product, and production knowledge through five interconnected, extendable abstract knowledge types (as illustrated in Fig. 1):

1. **Supplier Blueprint**: Defines a partner firm's business and technical details, including production capabilities, capacity, and stakeholder roles.
2. **Product Blueprint**: Represents details of standard or configurable products, parts, and materials, coupled with machine parameters, customer order data, and personnel skills. It also defines product families and connects them to relevant entities.
3. **Service Blueprint**: Describes services associated with physical products, including service types, metrics, schedules, compliance standards, and cost estimates.
4. **Production Process Blueprint**: Represents standard assembly and production solutions, embedding end-to-end processes into workflows and linking discrete activities on the factory floor.
5. **Quality Assurance Blueprint**: Defines process performance and product quality metrics (KPIs) to monitor operations and resolve issues across supply and production chains. It alerts operators to critical events and enables corrective actions.

These blueprints enable a shared understanding of manufacturing information, facilitate knowledge reuse, and separate manufacturing knowledge from operational knowledge. They also support the implementation of digital twins, which are critical for modern manufacturing:

- **Product Digital Twins**: Support iterative product ideation and co-design processes, enabling highly customizable and reusable product designs. These twins are supported by powerful DSLs (Domain-Specific Languages) and 2D/3D visualization tools.
- **Production Digital Twins**: Translate customized product designs into optimized production processes and schedules, allowing engineers to plan, analyze, validate, and simulate production workflows.
- **Performance Digital Twins**: Monitor and analyze operational data to improve product quality and system efficiency, leveraging machine learning and big data analytics.

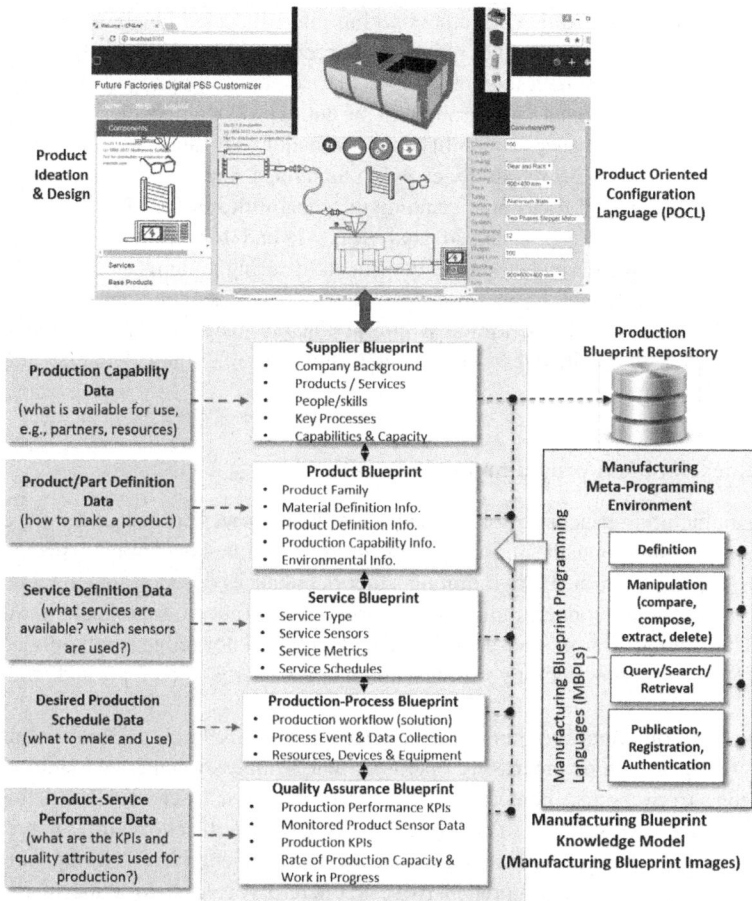

Fig. 1. Manufacturing blueprint types and its programming environment

The blueprints are stored in a *Manufacturing Blueprints Repository*, providing a global view of all aspects of customized products. This repository enhances the serviceability and reliability of products across various industry sectors. To ensure genericity and interoperability, the blueprint model aligns with industry-wide standards such as ISA-88/95 and the Supply Chain Operations Model (SCOR). While generic in nature, the blueprint model can be extended incrementally to suit specific industry structures and production methods, making it a versatile tool for creating effective supply chains and networks.

The blueprinting model is implemented using the Ontology Web Language (OWL), which is formally grounded in Description Logic (DL). This foundation ensures a robust, scalable, and interoperable framework for managing complex manufacturing knowledge across diverse systems and stakeholders. By leveraging OWL's reasoning capabilities, the model can automatically infer implicit relationships, detect inconsistencies, and validate both structural and semantic correctness within interconnected blueprints. As a result, all digital twin instances—whether representing products, production workflows, or performance analytics—remain logically consistent, semantically aligned, and compliant with domain-specific constraints throughout the entire product lifecycle. This automated reasoning not only enhances reliability but also enables dynamic reconfiguration and adaptation of digital twins in rapidly evolving manufacturing environments.

Future research will focus on expanding the capabilities of the MBKM and MBPL, particularly in integrating advanced analytics, AI, and IoT technologies to further enhance the intelligence and adaptability of manufacturing systems.

By adopting this meta-programming approach, manufacturers can unlock the full potential of their data, transforming it into actionable insights that drive innovation, efficiency, and competitiveness in an increasingly complex and dynamic industrial landscape.

3.2 Blueprint Meta-programming Language

The Manufacturing Blueprint Solution substantially improves product and service management by addressing the most labor-intensive and time-consuming aspects of the process. It provides robust programming support, enhances decision-making with data-driven insights, and connects all stakeholders to a centralized, searchable knowledge base. This unified approach ensures that manufacturing knowledge is not only accessible but also actionable, enabling seamless collaboration across the supply and production chain.

The Blueprint Meta-Programming Language (BMPL) is the cornerstone of this solution, offering a suite of processing operators that seamlessly integrate manufacturing knowledge from the five blueprint types (Supplier, Product, Service, Production Process, and Quality Assurance). These operators ensure that all actions are synchronized, timely, and fully integrated, enabling a cohesive and efficient manufacturing workflow.

The BMPL provides a comprehensive set of operators designed to define, manipulate, and query manufacturing blueprints. These operators are categorized as follows:

- **Blueprint Definition Operators**: Definition operators provide the foundational constructs required to define the five knowledge templates (blueprints) described earlier. They enable users to create structured, domain-specific representations of manufacturing elements, ensuring consistency and interoperability across the system.
- **Blueprint Manipulation Operators**: Manipulation operators empower users and stakeholders to retrieve, compare, and compose blueprints from the **Manufacturing Blueprints Repository**. They facilitate the creation of new products by assembling individual parts and subassemblies, along with generating corresponding production schedules.

  - A key feature of these operators is their *closure property*: each operation takes one or more compatible blueprints as input and returns a higher-level blueprint as output. Compatibility is determined by the type of blueprints involved (e.g., product-to-product or production-process-to-production-process).

- The ***compose operation*** is particularly powerful, enabling the end-to-end interconnection of multiple blueprints. This operation captures all characteristics, parts, services, quality metrics, and operational aspects of a customized product, ensuring a holistic representation of the manufacturing process.

- **Simple Query Services**: Query services allow users to query blueprints or drill down into individual blueprints to extract valuable information for decision-making. By identifying and validating recurring query patterns from the perspectives of different stakeholders (e. g., customers, engineers), the system ensures that the most relevant insights are readily available.

3.3 Formal Representation of Manufacturing Blueprints and Programming Languages

To ensure the rigor and precision of the proposed blueprint model and its programming environment, this section formalizes the concept of blueprints and its associated programming language using First Order Logic (FOL). The formal representation of the five core blueprints introduced in Sect. 3.1 is shown in Table 1. For brevity and clarity, the formalization focuses on the essential properties and their relationships.

Given R_c as the minimal set of first-order formulae representing the MBKB, the following definitions apply:

- If c is the name of a class or blueprint definition, then c is a unary predicate (arity one) such that $c \in R_c$. For example, the first expression in each blueprint definition in Table 1 declares the blueprint as a concept, e.g., Supplier$(x) \in R_c$.
- If t is the name of an association relationship, then t is a binary predicate (arity two) such that $t(x,y) \in R_c$.
- The predicate *comp* represents a binary composition relationship, i.e., $comp(x,y) \in R_c$. For instance, the *partOf*(x,y) relationship between the *Product* blueprint and itself indicates that *Product* x is part of *Product* y. This relationship recursively captures assemblies, modules, components, and parts within a product.
- The predicate unary *lex* represents the set of attributes or properties, i.e., $lex(x) \in Rc$. For example, If l is the name of a property of a blueprint c, then l is a binary predicate such that $l(c,a) \in R_c =$. Hence, serviceType(x,y) is a property of the *Service* blueprint, as defined in Table 1.

In Table 1, predicate Properties defines the features of the respective blueprint. These may be instances or types of auxiliary classes, whose definitions are omitted for brevity. Predicate Relationships in the FOL definition specifies the main association, composition, and ISA/inheritance relationships between pairs of blueprints. Table 2 provides the formal specification of the basic blueprint programming operators in First-Order Logic (FOL). The implementation of blueprint operators uses SPARQL query mechanisms to programmatically manipulate OWL-based ontological structures. This approach enables the dynamic retrieval, creation, and modification of individuals and their relationships within the knowledge base, while maintaining semantic consistency across blueprint instances. Additionally, it supports automated reasoning, ensuring that changes remain aligned with the underlying ontology and domain logic.

Table 1. Blueprint Formal Specification in FOL.

Blueprint	FOL Representation
Supplier	$Supplier(x) \in R_c$ Properties: $\forall x \forall y (background(x, y) \rightarrow (Supplier(x) \land lex(y)))$ $\forall x \forall y (skills(x, y) \rightarrow (Supplier(x) \land lex(y)))$ $\forall x \forall y (keyProcesses(x, y) \rightarrow (Supplier(x) \land lex(y)))$ $\forall x \forall y (capability(x, y) \rightarrow (Supplier(x) \land lex(y)))$ $\forall x \forall y (capacity(x, y) \rightarrow (Supplier(x) \land lex(y)))$ Association relationships: $\forall x \forall y (supplies(x, y) \rightarrow (Supplier(x) \land Product(y)))$ ISA (taxonomy) relationships: $\forall x (InhouseSupplier(x) \rightarrow Supplier(x))$ $\forall x (OutsourcedSupplier(x) \rightarrow Supplier(x))$
Product	$Product(x) \in R_c$ Properties: $\forall x \forall y (materialDef(x, y) \rightarrow (Product(x) \land lex(y)))$ $\forall x \forall y (productDef(x, y) \rightarrow (Product(x) \land lex(y)))$ $\forall x \forall y (productCapability(x, y) \rightarrow (Product(x) \land lex(y)))$ $\forall x \forall y (enviroInfo(x, y) \rightarrow (Product(x) \land lex(y)))$ $\forall x \forall y (productFamily(x, y) \rightarrow (Product(x) \land lex(y)))$ Association relationships $\forall x \forall y (hasService(x, y) \rightarrow (Product(x) \land Service(y)))$ Composition relationships $\forall x \forall y (partOf(x, y) \rightarrow (Product(x) \bigwedge Product(y) \bigwedge comp(x, y)))$ ISA (taxonomy) relationships: $\forall x (BaseProduct(x) \rightarrow Product(x))$ $\forall x (ConfiguredProduct(x) \rightarrow BaseProduct(x))$ $\forall x (RequestedProduct(x) \rightarrow BaseProduct(x) \lor ConfiguredProduct)$
Service	$Service(x) \in R_c$ Properties: $\forall x \forall y (serviceType(x, y) \rightarrow (Service(x) \land lex(y)))$ $\forall x \forall y (sensors(x, y) \rightarrow (Service(x) \land lex(y)))$ $\forall x \forall y (serviceMetrics(x, y) \rightarrow (Service(x) \land lex(y)))$ $\forall x \forall y (serviceSchedules(x, y) \rightarrow (Service(x) \land lex(y)))$ $\forall x \forall y (servicePlans(x, y) \rightarrow (Service(x) \land lex(y)))$ $\forall x \forall y (complianceReq(x, y) \rightarrow (Service(x) \land lex(y)))$ Composition relationships $\forall x \forall y (partOfService(x, y) \rightarrow (Service(x) \bigwedge Service(y) \bigwedge comp(x, y)))$
Prod. Process	$ProdProcess(x) \in R_c$ Properties: $\forall x \forall y (prodWorkflow(x, y) \rightarrow (ProdProcess(x) \land lex(y)))$ $\forall x \forall y (processEvent(x, y) \rightarrow (ProdProcess(x) \land lex(y)))$ $\forall x \forall y (resource(x, y) \rightarrow (ProdProcess(x) \land lex(y)))$ Association relationships: $\forall x \forall y (manufacturesProduct(x, y) \rightarrow (ProdProcess(x) \land Product(y)))$

(continued)

Table 1. (*continued*)

Blueprint	FOL Representation
Quality Assur	$QA(x) \in R_c$ Properties: $\forall x \forall y (sensorData(x, y) \rightarrow (QA(x) \wedge lex(y)))$ $\forall x \forall y (performanceKPI(x, y) \rightarrow (QA(x) \wedge lex(y)))$ $\forall x \forall y (rateProdCapacity(x, y) \rightarrow (QA(x) \wedge lex(y)))$ $\forall x \forall y (workInProgress(x, y) \rightarrow (QA(x) \wedge lex(y)))$ Association relationships: $\forall x \forall y (hassupplierKPI(x, y) \rightarrow (QA(x) \wedge Supplier(y)))$ $\forall x \forall y (hasProductKPI(x, y) \rightarrow (QA(x) \wedge Product(y)))$ $\forall x \forall y (hasServiceKPI(x, y) \rightarrow (QA(x) \wedge Service(y)))$ $\forall x \forall y (hasProdProcessKPI(x, y) \rightarrow (QA(x) \wedge ProdProcess(y)))$ ISA (taxonomy) relationships: $\forall x (ServiceQuality(x) \rightarrow QA(x))$ $\forall x (ProductQuality(x) \rightarrow QA(x))$ $\forall x (SupplierQuality(x) \rightarrow QA(x))$ $\forall x (ProductKPI(x) \rightarrow ProductQuality(x))$ $\forall x (Compliance(x) \rightarrow ProductQuality(x))$ $\forall x (Reputation(x) \rightarrow SupplierQuality(x))$ $\forall x (Certification(x) \rightarrow SupplierQuality(x))$

Table 2. Basic Blueprint Operators' Formal Specification

Operation	FOL definition
Define	$insert(P) = \{x : (KB \cup P)\}$, where *insert* is a predicate that takes another predicate P as an argument capturing the blueprint instance to be added to the KB, and returns Boolean x, indicating wether the inseresstion has been successfully done
Compose	$compose(P, Q) = \{PQ : (bType(P) = bType(Q)) \wedge (PQ = union(P, Q)) \wedge (bType(PQ) = bType(P))\}$, where $union(P, Q)$ is a function that merges two blueprints P and Q of the same blueprint type and returns new composed blueprint PQ of the same blueprint type
Compare	$compare(P, Q) = \begin{cases} True, bType(P) = bType(Q) \wedge equals(P, Q) \\ diff(P, Q), bType(P) = BluePrintType(Q) \wedge \neg equals(P, Q) \\ False, otherwise \end{cases}$,where $equals(P, Q)$ is a predicate that computes the similarity between blueprints P and Q of the same type. *equals* Returns *True* if the two blueprints are identical. The difference between the two blueprints are returned otherwise (represented by $diff(P, Q)$ function
Query	$query(P) = \{x : (KB \models P \rightarrow x = True) \wedge (KB \not\models P \rightarrow x = False)\}$, where *query* is a predicate that takes predicate P as an argument capturing the query request. *query* Either returns True or False indicating if P is satisfied in the KB
Retrieve	$retrieve(P) = \{S = \{x_1, \ldots, x_n\} : KB \models P \wedge \forall x \in S(matches(P, x))\}$, where *retrieve* is a function that takes as an argument predicate P capturing the query request; S is the set of returned blueprints instances $x_1, \ldots, x_n$ that satisfies predicate P (represented by the predicate *matches*)

4 Application of the Manufacturing Programming Environment on a Pilot Case

To demonstrate the flexibility and practical application of the manufacturing approach proposed in this paper, we present a comprehensive industrial-strength "make-to-order" pilot provided by PRIMA Industries, a leading manufacturer of laser and sheet metal machinery and a partner in the ICP4Life project consortium. This pilot study focuses on a scenario where a turbine engine manufacturer (customer) orders a multi-axis 3D cutting, drilling, and welding laser system for processing parts of a twin-spool axial flow turbofan engine used in the Airbus A318. The pilot highlights how OEM product designers and production engineers collaborate with the customer to co-design the laser processing system using a novel Product-oriented Configuration Language (PoCL). PoCL is a user-centric language that provides 3D CAD/CAM interactive capabilities, enabling customers to collaborate with designers and engineers in exploring ideas and converting them into digital product and service configurations [25].

The laser processing system in this pilot is designed for high-volume applications requiring precision 3D laser cutting, welding, and drilling, as well as high-power fiber laser capabilities. It must offer flexibility and multiple configurations to meet the demands of the aerospace market, which requires rapid prototyping, manufacturing flexibility, and quick changeovers.

To support this, the OEM engages a network of tier-two suppliers (subcontractors) who provide specialized components such as angle-torches, acetylene valves, plasma cutters, and optical focus control parts within a digital supply network. This collaborative ecosystem ensures that the final product meets the customer's exact specifications.

The customer interacts with the system through the PoCL Graphical User Interface (GUI) (see upper part of Fig. 1). Using standardized 2D or 3D symbols in PoCL, the customer specifies the desired characteristics of the laser processing system, including mechanical, welding, construction, and electrical wiring requirements. This process is iterative and incremental, transforming a potentially vague concept into a concrete digital twin (DT) design for the product.

4.1 Product Design and Customization

The design and customization process begins with the customer and product designer or an engineer searching and querying the Manufacturing Blueprints Repository to identify a base smart product or variant that closely matches the customer's requirements. This is facilitated by the 'retrieve' blueprint operator (defined in Sect. 3.2) and the user-friendly PoCL GUI.

For example, the customer may search for a laser processing system with:

- a new-generation beam director laser positioning capability combined with
- a high-accuracy rotary table motion.

The beam director should provide a rotary axis motion of 900°, a tilt axis motion of 300°, and an axis speed of 90 rpm. Referring to the definitions in Table 2, this search can be formally expressed as:

$S = retrieve(Product(beamDirector, highAccuracy, 900, 300, 90)) = \{p_1, p_2, p_3\}$
where S represents the set of products (or variants) that satisfy the customer's requirements. In this pilot case, the system retrieves three products: p_1, p_2, and p_3. After comparing these products using the 'compare' binary operator, the stakeholders select p_1 as the **base product**.

Customization Scenarios
The system supports three key customization scenarios:

- Parameterized Customization:
  Once p_1 is selected, a new smart product variant p_{11} is created. This variant inherits all characteristics of p_1, such as components, parts, and assemblies. Now, the customer may adjust the working area of p_{11} to X 600 mm – Y 600 mm – Z 600 mm, while p_1 originally has a working area of X 700 mm – Y 500 mm – Z 600 mm. The PoCL interface allows the customer to make these adjustments intuitively, while the underlying blueprint framework validates the changes in real-time. Formally, this can be expressed as:

$$(p_{11} \equiv p_1) \wedge (p_{11} \in Rc) \wedge$$
$$(KB \vDash p_{11}(beamDirector, highAccuracy, 900, 300, 90,$$
$$workingArea(600, 600, 600)))$$

This creates a branching mechanism for generating new variants from existing base products or variants.

- Adaptive Customization:
  The customer may further customize p_{11} by adding a cross-jet element to the laser welding nozzle to prevent molten metal spatter and weld zone fumes from contaminating the protective lens cover. Additionally, the customer may replace the conventional Nd:YAG laser (Yttrium Aluminum Garnet doped with neodymium ions) with a fiber laser to improve beam quality and enable miniaturization. Formally, this is expressed as:

$$partOf(p_{11}, crossJet) \wedge \neg partOf(p_{11}, YAGLaser) \wedge partOf(p_{11}, fiberLaser)$$

- Service Customization:
  The customer may also request an advanced failure prediction maintenance service for p_{11}. This service, say s_1, uses IoT sensors to monitor the machine's state and predict failures, reducing the risk of unplanned downtime. Formally, this is expressed as:

$$hasService(p_{11}, s_1)$$

The service includes temperature sensors attached to the machine:

$$sensors(s_1, Sensors(tempSensor_1, tempSensor_2, tempSensor_3)) \wedge$$
$$partOf(p_{11}, tempSensor_1) \wedge partOf(p_{11}, tempSensor_2) \wedge$$
$$partOf(p_{11}, tempSensor_3)$$

The system then enables the customer to calculate the cost of the customized product variant p_{11} based on the knowledge encapsulated in the blueprints. This feature addresses the challenge of long cost-calculation cycles for customized products [26], allowing the customer to make informed decisions and iterate on the design to meet cost constraints.

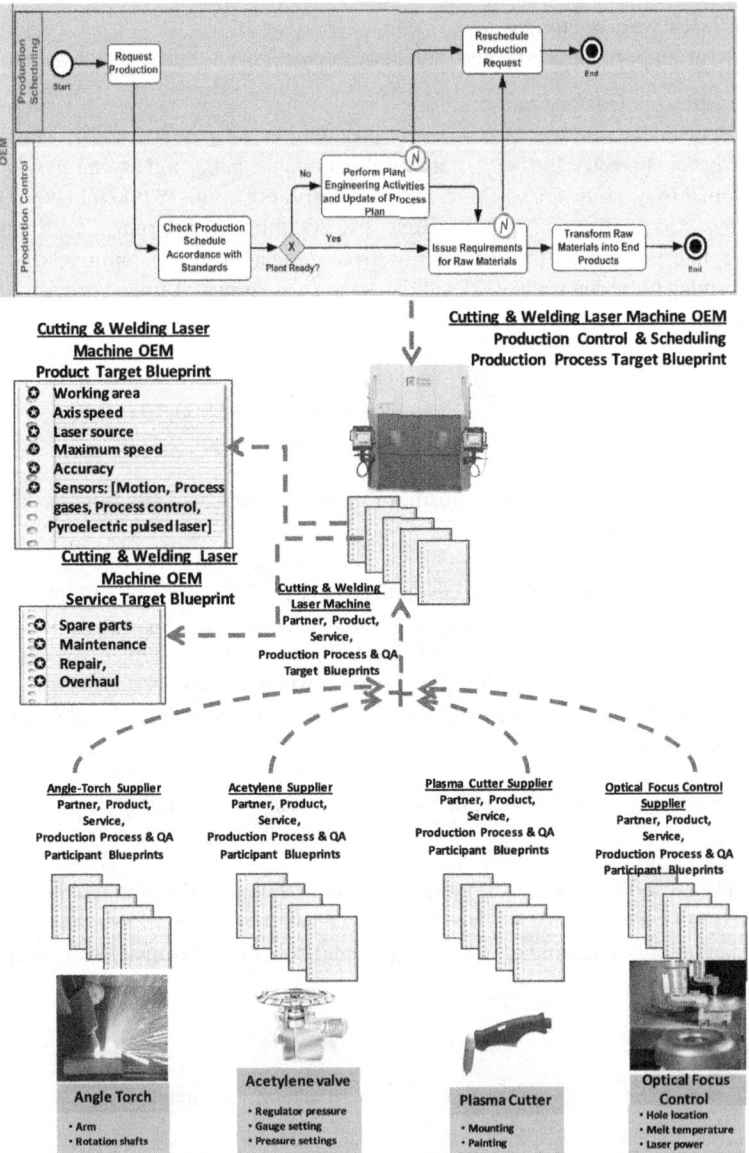

Fig. 2. Merging blueprints into a complete manufacturing solution

In addition to Product DTs, the system uses performance and utilization data from the multi-axis laser processing machine to enable value-added offerings such as: predictive maintenance, quality control, plant-floor efficiency optimization, and enhanced customer engagement. These capabilities address performance DT issues, further enhancing the system's value proposition.

In Fig. 2, the digital production process is represented as a simplified version of two inter-linked SCOR (Supply Chain Operations Reference) Level 4 sub-processes: "Production Scheduling" and "Production Control." These sub-processes are integral components of the "Cutting & Welding Laser Machine" production process. The depiction utilizes BPMN (Business Process Model and Notation) 2.0 notation to illustrate the workflow and interactions between these sub-processes.

Figure 2 illustrates the integration of the "Cutting & Welding Laser Machine" Production Process with other target OEM blueprints, including the Product and Service blueprints. Additionally, the figure demonstrates how supplier blueprints from four key suppliers—Angle-Torch ($Supp_1$), Acetylene Valve ($Supp_2$), Plasma Cutter ($Supp_3$), and Optical Focus Control parts ($Supp_4$)—are combined with the Cutting & Welding Laser Machine OEM blueprint to produce the final product p_{11}.

In Fig. 2, the compose operator is represented by the + symbol) within the manufacturing meta-programming environment (as detailed in Sect. 3.2). This operator merges the blueprint images of tier-two suppliers in a pairwise and compatible manner, resulting in a comprehensive manufacturing solution.

Each supplier contributes specific products or parts, denoted as Ps_x, where x ∈ {1,2,3,4} corresponds to the supplier number. Similarly, the production processes and quality assurance procedures provided by each supplier are denoted as Ps_x and QAs_x, respectively. This structured representation underscores the collaborative nature of the manufacturing process, where inputs from multiple suppliers are seamlessly integrated to achieve the final product.

$$targetSupplier = compose(compose(compose(supp_1, supp_2), supp3), supp4)$$
$$targetProduct = (compose(compose(p_{s1}, p_{s2}), p_{s3}), p_{s4})$$
$$targetService = \\ compose\left(compose\left(compose\left(\frac{compose}{(spareParts, maintenance)}, repair\right), overhaul\right) failurePredictionMaintenance)$$
$$targetProductionProcess = (compose(compose(pP_{s1}, pP_{s2}), pP_{s3}), pP_{s4})$$
$$targetQA = (compose(compose(QA_{s1}, QA_{s2}), QA_{s3}), QA_{s4})$$

The interlinking of the overall target OEM and supplier blueprints, as described above, provides the end-to-end visibility necessary for an OEM to drive effective supply chain performance and enhance operational effectiveness across the entire manufacturing network. This interconnected blueprinting approach serves as a critical tool, enabling manufacturers to make efficient, holistic decisions and plan coordinated responses to both individual and collective manufacturing needs within the supply network, as illustrated in Fig. 2.

This blueprinting production digital twin approach **realizes several** value delivery use cases, as identified in [26]:

- **Optimization of Remote Production Execution:**
  By using formal blueprint models, this approach enables a digital real-time representation of production processes across all sites within a dynamic digital manufacturing network. This facilitates the visualization and monitoring of operating performance through various dashboards, ensuring efficient execution on the factory floor.
- **Digitized Operating Standard Procedures with Integrated Workflow:**
  The production process blueprint, along with its interconnections with other blueprints, provides digitized operating standard procedures. This addresses the business challenge of inconsistent paper-based procedures, which often lead to lost productivity in manual processes such as changeover, start-up, and line cleaning.
- **Automation and Optimization of Manual Material Selection:**
  The approach automates and optimizes manual material selection, tackling the issues associated with manual-based production scheduling and sequencing. These manual processes often result in quality problems (e.g., rework, scrap) and poor traceability of issues, which are effectively mitigated through this digital twin solution.
- **Aggregation of Demand Across the End-to-End Supplier Network:**
  By mapping all parts used across suppliers and sites within the digital manufacturing network, the approach enables the **aggregation of demand** across the entire supplier network. This resolves the problem of supply chain delays caused by poor communication of demand needs, ensuring smoother and more efficient operations.

5 Conclusions and Future Work

This paper presents a novel digital twin approach based on comprehensible blueprinting technology, which integrates a manufacturing knowledge model and a programming environment to support every stage of the customized product lifecycle (encompassing product, production, and performance digital twins). The manufacturing blueprints knowledge model provides a set of high-level abstract knowledge types that can be assembled and programmed using a purpose-built meta-programming language. This enables the formal representation, assembly, cross-correlation, and processing of knowledge related to all aspects of a customized product, including product services, production processes, and quality assurance.

By using digital twins, the manufacturing model, and the programming environment, manufacturers can:

- Gain insights to improve digital models.
- Capture, aggregate, and analyze operational data.
- Enhance product quality and production system efficiency.

The approach employs a user-friendly 2D/3D interactive Domain-Specific Language (DSL), enabling engineers and customers to co-design and customize individualized products and services. Engineers can then efficiently plan production processes across a smart manufacturing network. To ensure genericity and interoperability, the blueprint model is grounded in well-accepted standards such as ISA-88/95 and SCOR.

While digital fabrication is currently used primarily for prototyping, its increasing sophistication—coupled with the integration of software and robotics into new types of assembly lines—will make high levels of specification the norm. To this end, future work will focus on extending the manufacturing meta-programming environment with autonomic features to optimize manufacturing activities at the machine, unit manufacturing facility, and supply network levels. This includes enabling self-adapting manufacturing processes in response to various conditions, such as machine breakdowns, unexpected demand variations, and outsourcing options.

Acknowledgments. This research has received funding from the European Union's Horizon Europe project NARRATE (regeNerAtive Resilient smaRt mAnufacTuring nEtworks) under grant agreement No GA n. 101138094.

References

1. Grieves M. Digital twin: Manufacturing excellence through virtual factory replication (While paper). University of Michigan (2014)
2. Papazoglou, M., Elgammal, A.: The manufacturing blueprint environment: bringing intelligence into manufacturing. In: IEEE International Conference on Engineering, Technology and Innovation (ICE), Portugal (2017)
3. Tao, F., Zhang, H., Liu, A., Nee, A.Y.C.: Digital twin in industry: state-of-the-art. IEEE Trans. Ind. Inf. **15**(4), 2405–2415 (2019). https://doi.org/10.1109/TII.2018.2873186
4. Zhuang, C.B., Liu, J.H., Xiong, H., Ding, X.Y., Liu, S.L., Weng, G.: Connotation, architecture and trends of product digital twin. Comput. Integr. Manuf. Syst. **32**(4) (2017)
5. Yu, Y., Fan, S.T., Peng, G.Y., Dai, S., Zhao, G.: Study on application of digital twin model in product configuration management. Aeron. Manuf. Technol. **526**(77), 41–45 (2017). https://doi.org/10.16080/j.issn1671-833x.2017.07.041
6. Tao, F.: Digital twin and its potential application exploration. Comput. Integr. Manuf. Syst. **23**(1), 1–18 (2018). https://doi.org/10.13196/j.cims.2018.01.001
7. Sierla, S., Kyrki, V., Aarnio, P., Vyatkin, V.: Automatic assembly planning based on digital product descriptions. Comput. Ind. **97**, 34–46 (2018). https://doi.org/10.1016/j.compind.2018.01.013
8. Schleich, B., Anwer, N., Mathieu, L., Wartzack, S.: Shaping the digital twin for design and production engineering. CIRP Ann. **66**(1), 141–144 (2017). https://doi.org/10.1016/j.cirp.2017.04.040
9. Söderberg, R., Wärmefjord, K., Carlson, J.S., Lindkvist, L.: Toward a digital twin for real-time geometry assurance in individualized production. CIRP Ann. **66**(1), 137–140 (2017). https://doi.org/10.1016/j.cirp.2017.04.038
10. Pine, B.J.: Mass Customization: The New Frontier in Business Competition. Harvard Business School Press (1999)
11. Joergensen, S.N., Hvilshøj, M., Madsen, O.: Designing modular manufacturing systems using mass customisation theories and methods. Int. J. Mass Customisation. **4**, 171–194 (2013)
12. Zha, X.F., Sriram, R.D.: Platform-based product design and development: a knowledge-intensive support approach. Knowl.-Based Syst. **19**(7), 524–543 (2006). https://doi.org/10.1016/j.knosys.2006.04.004

13. Nomaguchi, Y.: Proposal of knowledge model for designing product architecture and product family. In: IJCC Workshop 2006 on Digital Engineering (2006)
14. Tseng, M.M., Jiao, J.: Mass Customization. Handbook of Industrial Engineering, Technology and Operation Management. 3rd ed. Wiley, Hoboken (2000)
15. Salvador, F., De Holan, P.M., Piller, F.: Cracking the code of mass customization. MIT Sloan Manag. Rev. **50**, 71–78 (2009)
16. Giovannini, A., Aubry, A., Panetto, H., El Haouzi, H., Pierrel, L., Dassisti, M.: Approach for the rationalisation of product lines variety. IFAC Proc. Vol. **47**(3), 3280–3291 (2014). https://doi.org/10.3182/20140824-6-ZA-1003.02226
17. Papazoglou, M., van den Heuvel, W.J., Mascolo, J.: Reference architecture and knowledge-based structures for smart manufacturing networks. IEEE Softw. **32**, 1–1 (2015). https://doi.org/10.1109/MS.2015.79
18. Jørgensen, K.A.: Product Configuration and Product Family Modelling (2009)
19. Gabriel, R.P., Kiczales, G.: Des Rivières J, DGBobrow, The Art of the Metaobject Protocol. Artif Intell. **61**, 331–342 (1993)
20. Czarnecki, K., Eisenecker, U.W.: Generative Programming: Methods, Tools, and Applications. Addison Wesley, Boston (2000)
21. Taha, W., Sheard, T.: MetaML and multi-stage programming with explicit annotations. Theoret. Comput. Sci. **248**(1), 211–242 (2000). https://doi.org/10.1016/S0304-3975(00)00053-0
22. Tratt, L.: Compile-time meta-programming in converge. King's College London, Department of Computer Science (2004)
23. Oberortner, E., Zdun, U., Dustdar, S.: Domain-specific languages for service-oriented architectures: an explorative study. In: Mähönen, P., Pohl, K., Priol, T. (eds.) ServiceWave 2008. LNCS, vol. 5377, pp. 159–170. Springer, Heidelberg (2008). https://doi.org/10.1007/978-3-540-89897-9_14
24. Agha, G.: Actors: A Model of Concurrent Computation in Distributed Systems. MIT Press, Cambridge (1986)
25. Elgammal, A., Papazoglou, M., Krämer, B., Constantinescu, C.: Design for customization: a new paradigm for product-service system development. In: The 9th CIRP IPSS Conference: Circular Perspectives on Product/Service-Systems. Elsevier, Denmark (2017)
26. Leurent, H. B. (ed.): The Next Economic Growth Engine: Scaling Fourth Industrial Revolution Technologies in Production. Would Economic Forum in collaboration with McKinsey & Company (2018)

Experiences with Composability for Resilient IoT Systems

Nalini Venkatasubramanian[1(✉)], Fangqi Liu[2], and Yusuf Sarwar[3]

[1] University of California Irvine, Irvine, CA 92617, USA
nalini@uci.edu
[2] Vanderbilt University, Nashville, TN, USA
fangqi.liu@vanderbilt.edu
[3] University of Missouri, Kansas City, USA
muddin@umkc.edu

Abstract. IoT deployments in a variety of applications are characterized by the ubiquitous presence of devices for sensing, compute, communication and actuation. Mobile platforms (smartphones, rovers, drones) weave through already deployed (insitu) components adding new opportunities for data collection and processing. When deployed in mission-critical settings, IoT applications must satisfy multiple concurrent requirements (timeliness, dependability, interoperability etc.) - albeit with increasing complexity in terms of control and communication. In this article, we discuss how composability criteria have an influence across the IoT lifecycle - from design time abstractions and planning to on-the-fly adaptation to meet performance goals. Drawing from our experiences in high-stakes applications, we highlight key challenges and discuss building blocks towards the design of flexible, dependable and composable services for an improved IoT ecosystem.

Keywords: Middleware · Internet-of-Things · Composition

1 Community-Scale Distributed Systems with IoT

In recent years, the utilization of the Internet-of-Things (IoT) has experienced a notable surge, enabling new applications in diverse domains such as transportation, healthcare, smart cities, manufacturing, environmental monitoring, and emergency response. Technology advances, including edge accelerators, emerging wireless networks, cloud technologies and AI/ML have played a pivotal role in bridging the gap between the physical space and digital worlds. Emerging IoT ecosystems are characterized by: (a) the proliferation of heterogeneous device platforms for sensing, computing, and actuation that vary in cost and capabilities; (b) new forms of connectivity including multiple access networks and channels over which interaction can occur anytime, anywhere; and (c) concurrent applications that allow users (and devices) to be an active participant in the collection, sharing, and dissemination of context and information.

In this article, we discuss the multiple requirements that arise in scaling next-generation IoT systems to community-scale settings; issues of interoperability, extensibility, dependability, timeliness and cost-effectiveness must be addressed. For instance, device and network heterogeneity points to the need for interoperability at different levels. IoT deployments in communities must be extensible, i.e. function with an evolving set of devices, networks, platforms, protocols, and applications. Trustworthy operation of high-stakes applications implies that the end-to-end system must be robust - dependability techniques must ensure service continuity under a range of failures. Time-sensitive applications must additionally ensure timely capture, delivery, and processing of information. Adapting the underlying systems to accommodate change while meeting the above requirements [28,48] adds further complexity.

In our work, we focus on mission-critical IoT applications where new users (e.g. first responders), platforms and ecosystems (e.g. public safety networks) must be brought in, integrated instantaneously and controlled meaningfully. Likewise, dependability in mission-critical IoT deployments (healthcare, public safety etc.), is essential to provide reliable and timely application requirements (e.g., safety, data accuracy) in the presence of failures and uncertainty. While these multiple requirements raise interesting challenges individually [12,43], techniques to realize these goals interact with each other in subtle ways - making simultaneous support of composite requirements even more challenging.

1.1 Smart Firefighting: A Driving Usecase

We highlight the importance of composability in IoT systems design through a driving application—smart firefighting. In particular, we consider two usage scenarios: high-rise building fires and wildland fires. High-rise fires present unique challenges due to restricted access, complex airflow, water supply limitations, and minimal escape routes. Rapid situational awareness is critical, as conditions can shift drastically. Recent highrise fire events include wind-driven fires [49] (1998 Vandalia Ave., New York) or those involving combustible exteriors [34] (2017 Grenfell Tower, London). Similar challenges are observed with wildland fires, a persistent threat in rural areas and the wildland-urban interface (WUI). From 2012 to 2021, the U.S. experienced an average of 61,289 wildfires annually, affecting 7.4 million acres. Here, geophysical conditions such as vegetation and topography can influence the severity and extent of the fires. In the SPARx project, we focus on using mobile IoT (e.g. drones) to monitor of prescribed (Rx) fires—a critical forest management tool used to reduce hazardous fuels and prevent catastrophic wildfires [1]. Despite their benefits, Rx fires carry risks: under certain conditions, they may escape control and become destructive wildfires. For example, the 2012 Lower North Fork fire in the Schell Creek Range [77] led to civilian deaths, property loss, and over $11 million in damages. These risks underscore the need for fine-grained, real-time monitoring to ensure the safe execution and broader acceptance of Rx fires in WUI communities.

Maintaining situational awareness (SA) in any fire involves the integration and enrichment of static data (building plans, ventilation information and exits,

(a) High-Rise Building Fire Scenario   (b) Prescribed Fire Scenario

Fig. 1. Representative fire monitoring settings

burn site topography, presence of hazardous material) and dynamic data published by devices (in the space and/or brought by firefighters (FFs)). Mobile platforms (UGVs, UAVs), when deployed and used intelligently are extremely useful, capturing the evolving fire scene and delivering fire suppression and retardant resources where needed. With reliable and timely information, the incident commander can assess fire spread and detect emerging hazards such as flashovers or high smoke levels; when combined with analytics, these data can help detect the presence of humans and building occupancy levels to coordinate evacuations. These services reveal that interoperating with emerging components reliably and rapidly are critical in extreme events [31,35]. In this application, we observe that a slew of techniques must compose to meet (a) real-time constraints of fire response (b) extensibility to new and evolving hw/sw components in the systems landscape and (c) Dependability of decisions derived from information gathered (Fig. 1).

The need for composability of services and protocols has been raised in the context of distributed systems [72,73]. The smart firefighting example illustrates interactions between seemingly independent goals. An extensible IoT system that allows diverse devices (e.g., different sensors with overlapping sensing capability) must be dynamically configured and integrated into the system. Mechanisms to discover devices and integrate messaging protocols (e.g., MQTT, CoAP) using appropriate adapters must be instantiated on-the-fly. Such a capability, however, comes at a cost. Device discovery and protocol integration introduce overheads which can increase runtimes and end-to-end latency as compared to a more rigid system which only supports a fixed set of custom devices with custom protocols. In general, support for extensibility will reduce operational timeliness. Highly dependable or secure systems are often constrained – they may build on a specific architecture (or rely on a specific protocol) limiting extensibility. Enabling the interoperation of reliable and unreliable IoT devices may further reduce dependability.

While the examples above highlight competing goals, other techniques for achieving composability may also assist each other. Consider a system supporting devices that provide similar information - knowledge of room occupancy in a smart building can be provided by image analysis from cameras or less expensive Bluetooth beacons. These alternative sensing modes can help increase information reliability when devices fail. Likewise, an extensible system that supports integrated multiple access networks may provide alternate (redundant) paths for data transfer and increase opportunities for reliable communication. The ability to task mobile sensors can extend sensing and communication capabilities to regions where instrumentation is lacking or damaged, albeit with added latency. In the following sections, we aim to structure the composability issue for IoT systems and discuss issues in the creation and operation of IoT systems that address composability-by-design and correctness as a fundamental criteria.

2 Composability and Concurrency for Trustworthy IoT

A few interesting observations arise as we begin to understand the design space of solutions to support composability needs. First, solutions to realize composability in IoT systems must be cross-layer - i.e. implemented across layers in the operational systems stack (end-devices, networks, software services, applications). Aspects such as dependability and timeliness are inherently end-to-end properties; failures at any layer can impact the utility of derived information and time-delays at any layer can cause timing violations at the application layer. Second, the set of tasks to realize composability can be viewed as design time challenges or on-the-fly runtime concerns. This naturally lends itself to two classes of techniques (design and runtime) that can support and inform each other. Third, metrics to assess and validate IoT applications can vary - extensibility is measured qualitatively while timeliness and dependability can be measured using quantitative metrics (e.g. packet loss rates, failures-in-time etc.).

Expressing the combined needs of IoT applications as constraints in a logical framework allows us to apply formal reasoning tools to check satisfiability of constraints under different conditions including tools that leverage the Actor model of concurrency [2,4]. In past work by authors, such a logical framework has been explored to reason about ditributed garbage collection, QoS-enabled multimedia servers, mobile multimedia and heterogeneous network [59,61,70,71,74,75]. Alternatively, the tradeoffs associated with composing multiple criteria can also be expressed as optimization problems with multiple objectives and constraints. Solutions to joint satisfaction of constraints or heuristics to implement tradeoffs can further be used to provide recommendations for adaptations and/or actuate changes. Finally, deploying IoT systems for use in mission-critical settings requires a human-in-the-loop approach. Working with practitioners and domain experts will enable us to understand application needs and develop solutions that are viable in real world situations. In the smart firefighting application, decisions are made by individuals in the field. Incident commanders use situational awareness information to guide and direct first responders in structural and wildland fires. In the prescribed burn usecase, forest management experts and burn managers develop detailed ignition plans and manage the safe execution of prescribed burns. The determination of timing, reliability and interoperability constraints in practice requires human/operator involvement.

Building upon our experience of over two decades on community-scale systems with co-existing needs (reliability, timeliness, security/privacy, data quality), we discuss our insights into the design and operation of resilient IoT systems. Composability criteria have an influence across the IoT lifecycle – from design time plans to on-the-fly adaptations to meet performance goals. Design-time methods help identify and represent system components, plan for their deployment to support composability constraints such as timeliness, extensibility and dependability. Runtime methods trigger the actuation of CPS devices, instantiate and adapt software operators and will support a progressive approach to computation so as to meet timing and accuracy needs. The involvement of humans in the loop (citizens, planners, utility operators) from specification of tasks at design-time to evaluating the effect of runtime decisions is also evident. To realize composability, we adopt a middleware-based approach - we argue that this is the appropriate level at which to address interactions of needs - QoS, interoperability and dependability. In particular, we envision the design of a flexible middleware microservices stack that can adapt sensing, computation and communication across the device-edge-cloud IoT continuum. In the following three sections, we discuss the design of composable IoT middleware systems along three dimensions:

- **Design-time Abstractions and Planning for Composability:** At design-time, a declarative approach will help create flexible/extensible specifications of an IoT environment. Separation of concerns is crucial here - we will develop semantic abstractions at the application layer that can be viewed independently of physical infrastructure elements and the function they provide. Design-time planning techniques will enable robust adaptation at runtime; for this, we must consider the underlying physical world while planning for redundancy across system layers. Tradeoffs include cost, sensor coverage, data quality, energy efficiency, and deployment ability. Human input will help design domain-specific rules that will instantiate runtime tasks so as to meet the necessary tradeoffs for flexible and dependable interactions.
- **Operation-time Composability Techniques:** The goal here is to provide support for adaptations that can help manage the IoT ecosystem at run-time. Techniques for resource provisioning and task execution must ensure that application requirements are realized by the underlying infrastructure as system conditions and needs change. In extreme conditions, where the state of the system is uncertain, rapid reconfigurability is essential for fault tolerance and robust operation. We will discuss methods to actuate devices and workflows to manage reliable communication and task prioritization requirements. Rules formulated at design-time will be used to rapidly generate runtime tasks by capturing evolution of the physical world in logic-based operators for dependable operation.

– **Towards Designing and Validating Composability in Platforms:** A Middleware platform will integrate a priori knowledge and current state (from stream observations) with design-time and runtime mechanisms to operate the CPS environment efficiently under dynamic change. We will discuss the role of design-time and run-time methodologies through diverse mission-critical use cases from the domain of smart firefighting âĂŞ situational awareness for first responders during high-rise fires in an urban campus, execution of controlled burns by forestry experts in wildland areas for wildfire resilience and depleted urban neighborhood inspections for fire hazards by city agencies. We are inspired by our past work in real world testbeds in each case âĂŞ a smart multistory building at UCI, access to prescribed burn sites at the Blodgett Forest Station in Berkeley, CA.

2.1 Related Work

Addressing non-functional requirements of IoT applications such as interoperability, timeliness and dependability has been explored in the context of pervasive computing at different system layers and in diverse application contexts. Interoperability methods focus on designing standards that can absorb high technology diversity at both infrastructure, data and software levels [13,48]. Techniques to enable interoperability have been developed at sensor devices, gateways [7] and cloud platforms. Solutions aim to collect data from IoT devices [11] using diverse data link protocols [28]. Middleware solutions custom protocols and APIs in specific contexts [76] (e.g., smart buildings) [6]. These solutions support interoperability through a one-to-one mapping of data/protocol semantics and are often not extensible in dynamic settings, where new IoT devices, protocols and data models may appear and must coexist with others. Service-oriented [63] or Model-driven [23] approaches support systems extensibility. In recent years, we have seen the emergence of data meta-models such as ontologies [10], that can be used to unambiguously define the meaning of terms for sensor-based sytems, e.g. in the smart building context, such as BASont [58], LinkSmart [26], SENSO [44], and IntelliDomo [30]; one can argue that a single standard is unlikely to emerge [30].

The cross-layer adaptation methods are also relevant in situations where timeliness and dependability must be satisfied. Dependability has also been studied in the context of large-scale systems from the days of the Internet [41] and grid computing systems. Systems can be made dependable by using (a) proactive methods at design time: redundant provision of system components [37], functional requirements [24], relevant specifications, and necessary configurations [5], and by using (b) reactive methods (during operation) – fault-tolerance techniques [64], failure recovery. Cross-layer optimization has been used to manage time-sensitive and reliable data delivery for resource-constrained mobile platforms (e.g., Dynamo [52], xTune [60]). Agent-based approaches for sensor network exploration and health monitoring have been explored – here, a genetic algorithm is used to determine the number of agents and their itineraries, followed by techniques for in-network adaptation to unpredictable component failures. Dependability has also been explored in domain-specific IoT application contexts: such as building automation [19], healthcare [40], critical infrastructure [68], sentient systems [62], and vehicles/cars [33]. Usually, dependability is measured in terms of correct/non-faulty operations of a system [25] under failures. Other examples of resilience techniques have been studied in the context of smart infrastructure – e.g. for water systems robustness [36]) and mobile data collection with transit vehicles [47]).

3 Design-Time Concerns for Composable IoT Systems

To enable system composability at design time, we study declarative specifications to model IoT components, applications and their execution. For this, we develop abstractions of the IoT environment, its execution and use these abstractions to customize IoT deployment planning. Tools to analyze a variety of tradeoffs (cost, reliability, timeliness) and perform what-if analysis allow human experts to refine deployments appropriately.

3.1 Semantic Modeling of IoT Environments and Applications

The goal here is to model the fundamental elements of the IoT space, where physical phenomena are observed by sensors, transformed into higher-level information, using which devices and software components can be adapted and controlled. We will develop abstractions that capture the IoT environment at two levels: (a) Higher-level semantic concepts: Here, we capture and constrain the scope of the IoT system space. It includes spatial entities (e.g. highrise buildings, urban neighborhoods, wildland zones), humans in specific roles (e.g. firefighters,

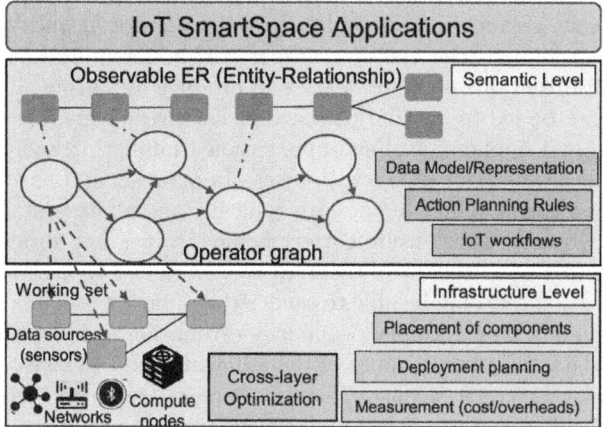

Fig. 2. Semantic Modeling of IoT Environments and Applications

building occupants), and activities (e.g. meetings, evacuation, fire spread). The semantic model will capture applications (e.g. smart firefighting tasks) and application requirements (monitoring frequencies, information priority, spatiotemporal granularities, deadlines) and be able to represent current and predicted future situations. (b) Low-level device/infrastructure elements: such as sensing/actuation devices (insitu and mobile), edge machines, network components, computational servers, and their properties (e.g. flying height of drones, max network bandwidth, and CPU speed).

One can model IoT spaces by leveraging database modeling techniques such as Entity-Relationship (ER) diagrams where application logic can be built around languages such as SQL as shown in Fig. 2. To capture the semantics of the "observable physical world," however, we will need to extend the ER model appropriately to capture the dynamically changing properties of the real-world entities (e.g., location of people, occupancy of rooms, etc.). This will result in an "Observable ER (OER) model". that models physical spaces using semantic concepts and relates these concepts to the underlying sensing and actuation infrastructure to capture the dynamically changing state of the physical world. The decoupled representation in the OER model is a natural mechanism to optimize data acquisition since the model captures data quality needs and application tolerances; Such an OER abstraction captures the extensibility to diverse types of insitu and mobile IoT devices/sensors, allowing their capabilities and state to be specified. Our initial efforts [78] have shown promising results – here, we develop a framework to support the management of smart buildings by modeling its semantics, the low-level characteristics of its devices as well as their bridging. One can further extend domain-specific representations using an ontological approach to annotate smartspace applications and infrastructure components [79] while capturing the multiresolution, hierarchical spatial properties (floors in a building, rooms on a floor).

To model end-to-end application execution, we next introduce the notion of IoT workflows. Here, we consider a graph-based representation where nodes are information sources and compute subtasks (i.e. operators); links represent the flow of information between operators. Operators are computational tasks that assimilate data from one or more devices to produce an output. The output of an operator can be fed to another operator or can be delivered to an individual user or to an end application. Each application running in the system can be represented as an operator graph with a set of operators and a set of interconnections among them. While an operator typically assimilates data from a given set of sources/operators to ensure correct behavior, it is not always possible or required to obtain data from all of them. Instead, a subset of operators, which we refer to as working set, may be able to render the same service, albeit with lower accuracy or quality. For example, occupancy estimation inside a smart building may require data from one or more of the following: Wi-Fi traces, Beacon logs, door lock/unlock records, acoustic sensors, camera feeds, etc. Different working sets incur different costs in network throughput, processing power, etc. For instance, a room occupancy service relying on Bluetooth beacons is lightweight as compared to one based on camera feeds. One can potentially embellish the operator graphs for an IoT workflow with attributes that indicate performance, timing and reliability attributes.

Populating and maintain these working sets for operators at hand is challenging. Measurement studies play an important role in here – given a context, such studies allow us to capture the different costs (overheads) and benefits (accuracy, dependability) of potential working sets for an operator graph. Furthermore, analysis of the operator graphs can help assess whether composability criteria can be satisfied. It also provides us with the necessary abstractions to determine how to reconstruct the graph to meet the composability needs. As new devices and services are added to the systems, the operator graph and working sets must be appropriately extended. A point to note is that these extensions may impact robustness of ongoing operations.

3.2 Rule-Based Systems to Guide End-to-End System Operation

Beyond structural modeling and workflows, effective IoT systems must also respond dynamically to evolving user goals and environmental conditions. To support this, we incorporate a rule-based reasoning framework that bridges semantic knowledge with runtime system operation. This framework integrates high-level user intent and domain-specific knowledge into the IoT operation management loop, enabling runtime guidance. Monitoring goals are specified at design time, often using a formal, logic-based rule language. This declarative approach allows users to define sensing objectives, spatial and temporal constraints (e.g., frequency, location), and task priorities in a structured and adaptable manner.

Below we illustrate sample rules that are used to generate tasks for a drone-based wildland fire monitoring application [45]. The goal is to generate tasks at the start of each time epoch to guide drones in periodically collecting sensing data for four types of monitoring missions: burn site monitoring (BM) to track firefighter and equipment status, fire detection (FD) to identify new ignitions, fire tracking (FT) to monitor fire spread near the front, and fire intensity inspection (FI) to assess temperature and flame length. To express spatial and temporal aspects, we begin by partitioning the monitoring area (the burn site) $\mathbf{G}$ into spatial grids, where each grid $g \in \mathbf{G}$ represents the local fire status. The state of each grid can take one of the following values: Unknown (UK): no data received; Burning (B): fire detected; Not burning (N): no fire present; and Burnt out (O): fire has already burned out. Grid state is updated as fire events are detected using sensing data. We formalize grid states and fire events as logical facts:

- $State(g, st)$: the grid g is in st
- $NoFire(g, t)$: g has no fire in the data captured at time t.
- $Fire(g, t)$: fires are detected in g from data captured at time t.

Based on these facts, we define grid state transition rules:

- $State(g, \mathbf{UK}) \wedge NoFire(g, t) \Rightarrow State(g, \mathbf{N})$

- $State(g, \mathbf{UK}) \wedge Fire(g,t) \Rightarrow State(g, \mathbf{B})$
- $State(g, \mathbf{N}) \wedge Fire(g,t) \Rightarrow State(g, \mathbf{B})$
- $State(g, \mathbf{B}) \wedge NoFire(g,t) \Rightarrow State(g, \mathbf{O})$

The first two rules reflect state changes based on newly received data, while the latter two capture transitions due to fire ignition or burnout.

At runtime, the rule-based platform is integrated with a physics-based fire propagation model that simulates fire spread (e.g. FarSite [29] for wildland fires, CFAST [57] or FDS [50] for structural fires). To predict fire evolution, we input the current fire status (e.g., fire perimeters) into the FARSITE simulator. FARSITE produces a forecast of fire spread, which is mapped onto the grid to estimate each cell's expected fire arrival time (EFA), denoted as $EFA(g)$. We then define a set of rule-based actions to generate monitoring tasks:

- $UpdEFA(t)$: run simulator; obtain expected fire arrival times given fire status at t.
- $STMonitor(t)$: start monitoring phase at time t.
- $Add(mission, g, st, et)$: add task for *mission* at g, $st(et)$ denote start(end) times.
- $Update(mission, g, st, et)$: update start(end) times $st(et)$, at grid g at t for *mission*.
- $Delete(mission, g)$: remove the task for *mission* at g.

We also define a temporal fact $Epoch(t)$ to indicate the start of each planning epoch. We propose task generation rules as shown in Fig. 3. If the initial fire status is unknown, the system enters a fire detection phase, executing the FD mission to scan the entire burn site. Rules **RFD-1** and **RFD-2** govern this process: Rule **RFD-1** generates FD tasks for all grids at the start of the first epoch. Rule **RFD-2** removes FD tasks from grids whose state has changed due to new detections. We use $\sim$ to indicate the end time of the next epoch. Once fire status becomes known, the system transitions into a dynamic monitoring phase. At the beginning of each epoch, if all grid states are known, Rule **RM-1** triggers FARSITE to update $EFA(g)$ values. Based on these predictions: Rule

RFD-1: $Epoch(t) \wedge State(g, \mathbf{UK}) \Rightarrow Add(FD, g, t, \sim)$

RFD-2: $State(g, \mathbf{UK}) \wedge (Fire(g,t) \vee NoFire(g,t)) \Rightarrow Delete(FD, g, t)$

RM-1: $Epoch(t) \wedge \forall g(\neg State(g, \mathbf{UK})) \Rightarrow UpdEFA(t) \wedge STMonitor(t)$

RM-2: $State(g, \mathbf{B}) \wedge Epoch(t) \Rightarrow Add(FI, g, t, \sim)$

RM-3: $State(g, \mathbf{N}) \wedge Epoch(t) \Rightarrow Add(BM, g, t, \max\{t, EFA(g) - \delta_{ft}\}) \wedge Add(FT, g, \max\{t, EFA(g) - \delta_{ft}\}, \sim)$

RM-4: $State(g, \mathbf{N}) \wedge Fire(g,t) \Rightarrow Delete(FT, g) \wedge Add(FI, g, t, \sim)$

RM-5: $State(g, \mathbf{B}) \wedge NoFire(g,t) \Rightarrow Delete(FI, g)$

Fig. 3. Task Generation Rules for Drone-based Fire Monitoring

RM-2 generates FI tasks at grids with active fires. We uss Rule RM-3 generate FT tasks at grids with imminent fires (i.e., where $EFA(g) < \delta_{ft}$) and BM tasks at all other grids. Rules RM-4 and RM-5 manage the addition or removal of FI and FT tasks in response to newly detected or extinguished fires. Together, these rules enable a phased and adaptive fire monitoring strategy, starting with global fire detection and progressing to predictive, task-driven monitoring as the fire evolves.

In this example, we integrate real-time sensor data, predictive modeling, and formalized user intent to help dynamically update system state and prioritize tasks to meet the composability needs of the driving application. One may view this specification as a way to define automated, goal-driven monitoring plans aligned with dynamic change in an IoT system.

3.3 Planning and Deployment of IoT Infrastructure

While the rule-based system enables dynamic decision-making, it must be supported by a carefully planned infrastructure capable of adapting to changing conditions. We now turn to the challenge of planning and deploying IoT components—both static and mobile—to ensure resilient and composable operation.

In mission-critical settings, such as high-rise fire response, it is essential to accommodate rapid, real-time information flow. This requires strategic planning of where static devices are deployed and when mobile devices should be introduced, particularly in dynamic and evolving environments. We frame this as an IoT placement problem: optimizing the locations of pre-deployed components—including distributed edge servers, communication infrastructure, in-situ sensing units, and software operators—to support concurrent applications while meeting cost, dependability, and timing constraints. Prior work on IoT deployment has addressed the placement of high-performance sensors, and accurate learning models on the collected data. Our initial work on SmartParcels [21] and QuiCIoT [20] has shown promising results with using MILP-based offline planning across system layers for smart city IoT applications.

To realize these plans in practice, planner modules are developed to guide the runtime behavior of IoT devices. These planners are responsible for generating executable task plans that coordinate heterogeneous sensing resources to meet evolving monitoring requirements. This includes path planning and scheduling for mobile platforms (e.g., drones) to ensure timely and continuous data collection, as well as strategies for managing and triggering in-situ sensors to complement mobile sensing efforts.

In essence, task planning must be tightly coupled with networking considerations to ensure reliable communication during mobile operations. Planners may employ techniques from operations research (e.g., MILP), metaheuristics, and AI-based methods such as reinforcement learning, predictive modeling, and control-theoretic strategies. Communication-related decisions—such as protocol selection, bandwidth allocation, and routing policies affect both data transmission and the coordination of sensing devices. Thus, effective planning must jointly consider sensing goals, control strategies, and communication constraints to achieve system composability.

Role of Measurement and Profiling in IoT Planning: To perform optimized placement of components, we must study the costs of communication, computation, and sensing choices that result when CPS workflows are deployed through comprehensive measurement studies. In our experience, measurement studies in operational testbeds, like UCI TIPPERS [51], or with detailed (physics-based) emulators, such as CFAST for fire propagation can help derive cost/benefit model parameters. Initial empirical measurement studies can also be used to approximate analytical models using queuing theoretic approaches [17]. The resulting models can be used in dynamic adaptation and deeper theoretical analysis of composability metrics. Measurement studies with mobile units that capture live data are more complex. Sensor configurations today use measures such as field of view to capture data resolution requirements for effective data analysis. Experiments will help determine the impact of observation distance in mobile sensors viz-a-viz quality of data. In the smart FF usecase, preliminary measurements and accuracy evaluation regarding distance and data resolution in an IoT deployment site can support future planning for mobile sensing and optimization of the tradeoff between accuracy and sensing coverage.

Constructing Resource-Aware Data Analysis Components: With the growing availability of advanced AI techniques, data analysis modules in modern IoT systems increasingly support complex perception and decision-making tasks. However, this also introduces new challenges in computational resource allocation—particularly under constrained environments. A key design-time concern is balancing the accuracy and sophistication of AI models with their runtime efficiency, energy usage, and latency. These trade-offs must be addressed across heterogeneous computing layers, including lightweight mobile platforms (e.g., drones), edge devices, and cloud infrastructure. For instance, in an IoT-based wildland fire monitoring system, analytical tasks such as fire detection, fire intensity estimation, human presence detection, and activity recognition span diverse workflows. These must be intelligently mapped onto a distributed infrastructure comprising mobile sensors, edge nodes, and cloud services. Achieving this requires dynamic allocation of data streams and computing containers, informed by current network topology, available bandwidth, and device mobility patterns. To ensure responsiveness, scalability, and robustness, the placement and scheduling of data analysis components must be co-designed with the system architecture.

An interesting observation is that composability at design-time can be addressed by using semantic models of systems and intelligently leveraging traditional constraint-based optimization methods to meet the multiple objectives. For instance, dependability methods may build redundancy in sensing, communication and compute resources; the cost of such redundancy must be quantified and used to configure the edge computing architecture. Support for time-sensitive processing will determine what data must be quickly delivered, e.g. prioritizing the delivery of information from grid cells with fire to the fire incident command post will influence response actions – e.g. dispatch of drones for more detailed data capture at given locations within in the IoT space. Our past work on composing models at each layer through a unified queueing theoretic framework [65] has been used to model data exchange at the middleware level [18].

4 Runtime Challenges for Composability in IoT Systems

At runtime, IoT systems face a wide range of uncertainties and disruptions—ranging from hardware failures and sensor mobility to network congestion and compute overloads. These challenges directly impact the system's ability to deliver mission-critical data and maintain dependable, context-aware behavior. As such, enabling resilient operation requires mechanisms that can adapt to evolving conditions without compromising the core design-time abstractions or the goals of the deployed application. To support such dynamic adaptation, a composable IoT system must begin with **dynamic state capture**, which involves continuously monitoring the operational context of both in-situ and mobile devices. Parameters such as device location, energy availability, latency, and data fidelity—defined during the system's design phase—serve as the basis for runtime introspection. This runtime state information is crucial for estimating overall system health and identifying the need for adaptive measures. Building on this, **adaptive software component** management becomes essential. Components must be flexible and responsive, with the ability to reconfigure or migrate across nodes, degrade gracefully under resource constraints, or even be substituted in response to performance or availability anomalies. These adaptations must honor the initial composability contracts while ensuring that the system remains functional and efficient under duress. Finally, many IoT applications are inherently data-driven, often dealing with streaming or progressive analytics. Thus, **progressive computation** with error and accuracy guarantees provides an additional layer of adaptability. This involves adjusting the granularity or precision of computation based on current system state, resource availability, and the urgency or fidelity requirements of the end-user application—enabling informed trade-offs between computational cost and output quality.

4.1 Dynamic State Capture via Insitu and Mobile IoT Devices

In IoT-based cyber-physical systems, in situ and static sensors constitute the primary mechanism for environmental and situational state capture. These sensors are typically deployed during the system's design phase using domain-specific knowledge and optimization methods, such as Mixed-Integer Linear Programming (MILP), to ensure effective spatial coverage and system observability. Once deployed, they continuously collect and transmit data for real-time analysis and decision-making. However, in dynamic and unpredictable environments—such as those impacted by natural disasters or infrastructural degradation—static infrastructure may prove inadequate. While these sensors serve as persistent sources of information, their fixed nature limits responsiveness, necessitating supplementary mechanisms for adaptive sensing.

To overcome the inherent limitations of static sensors, mobile sensing entities including Unmanned Aerial Vehicles (UAVs)/drones–are dynamically introduced at runtime. These mobile platforms extend system observability by providing agile and on-demand sensing capabilities, particularly in environments where in-situ infrastructure is sparse, damaged, or nonexistent. Integration of such devices requires AI-driven techniques for path planning, resource-aware task allocation, and coordination with existing in-situ devices. The mobility of these units offers significant advantages, such as rapid redeployment, flexible coverage, and expanded functional range. For example, in fire response scenarios, UAVs may be actuated to perform not only data collection but also direct physical interventions. This dynamic augmentation enhances the overall resilience and adaptability of the system architecture.

To ensure effective cooperation among heterogeneous sensing entities, it is essential to develop runtime mechanisms for intelligent role assignment and coordinated action planning. Roles are defined according to device capabilities—for instance, UAVs may be assigned tasks involving aerial inspection or high-mobility sensing, whereas UGVs may perform ground-level transport, delivery, or environmental sampling. Optimization techniques such as Integer Linear Programming, heuristic algorithms, AI-based planning [55], and market- or game-theoretic approaches are employed to solve the role assignment problem under resource and temporal constraints [42,67]. Subsequent action planning addresses challenges including obstacle avoidance, optimal spatial positioning for data quality, and adherence to service deadlines. In application domains such as high-rise fire response, UAVs may sequentially survey specific windows for human presence [46], triggering follow-up actions based on sensor analysis. A mixed deployment strategy that fuses static and mobile sensing modalities—coupled with meta-heuristic optimization techniques such as Local Search, Genetic Algorithms, and Simulated Annealing—and Software-Defined Networking (SDN)-based communication prioritization builds on prior queuing-theoretic approaches in edge-cloud environments to enable scalable and resilient system operation.

4.2 Adapting IoT Software Components at Runtime

Ensuring dependable and timely behavior in dynamic and potentially degraded environments necessitates the continuous adaptation of software components within IoT systems. Runtime adaptation techniques, such as operator migration and working set modification are essential to maintain quality-of-service (QoS) under evolving system conditions. Operator migration enables the redirection of computation from failing or overloaded nodes to alternate compute resources, thereby preserving the flow of critical information and service continuity. The use of semantic-level operator graphs that express quality requirements can help guide placement and dynamically allocate operators to the most appropriate nodes in the available infrastructure. Existing work [38] explores the optimal deployment of operators onto in-network IoT devices to reduce latencies and achieve desired QoS. This implies that the composability aspects must be handled in a joint manner across devices and operators.

Operator placement strategies studied include distributed algorithms [69], greedy heuristics [39] and dynamic programming techniques [27]. While effective under stable configurations, these methods typically assume static infrastructure and fail to accommodate real-time changes such as node failures or fluctuating workloads. A desirable method is to integrate online and reactive placement to adjust mappings dynamically and preserve operator-level QoS in the presence of runtime disturbances. We build upon recent graph-theoretic frameworks for operator placement [22] and extend them to enable low-overhead, real-time migration of operators across device-edge-cloud boundaries. Notably, the cost of migration itself can be significant; one can incorporate log-based checkpointing methods [66] to minimize state transfer overhead while ensuring continuity of service.

Towards an Agile Edge Microservices Architecture: New advances in flexible software stacks, such as containerization techniques offer tools to encapsulate a IoT application and its dependencies [56]. A container is a lightweight, standalone, and executable package that allows an application to run consistently across different host OS environments without worrying about dependencies or conflicts with the underlying system. Using containers, a complex IoT application can be broken down into smaller, independent, and loosely coupled microservices (i.e. operators/operator-graphs in our semantic model). Mapping operators in the IoT workflow into a microservices architecture decouples the service from its internal implementation – making it easier to update, modify, or add new features without impacting the entire application. It also enables the use of different technologies for services and hence inherently accommodates adaptation to diverse task requirements (i.e. working set adaptation) Together, containerization techniques and microservices based application design allows us to provide integrated data processing and analytical services at different points in the architectural device-edge-cloud continuum. The ability to dynamically change or move containers makes deploying and migrating microservices less cumbersome. Such adaptive microservice provisioning capabilities can help manage the dynamically changing needs of IoT applications.

Implementing a containerized microservices architecture introduces several composability challenges. Based on our initial experiences, the task of encapsulating IoT microservices efficiently into containers at different points in the architectural pipeline requires careful engineering and crafting of images, Managing distributed data for microservice execution also poses a significant hurdle, requiring strategies for data consistency, synchronization, and ensuring data integrity across multiple services. Maintaining robust communication channels among microservices becomes complex, necessitating new mechanisms for inter-service communication while handling potential issues like latency, network failures, and service discovery.

Beyond individual operator relocation, significant infrastructure disruptions or substantial shifts in system requirements may necessitate working set adaptation—the modification or replacement of the entire set of active components in the processing pipeline. In such cases, graceful degradation strategies are essential to maintain partial output quality. We propose the design of adaptive working set selection mechanisms that account for cost-quality tradeoffs, enabling the system to dynamically balance redundancy, accuracy, and resource constraints. Higher dependability can be achieved through strategies such as activating redundant components or utilizing multiple concurrent network paths. Furthermore, in crisis scenarios where workloads spike unpredictably, we will develop dynamic task prioritization algorithms to ensure that critical workflows receive preferential treatment. These adaptive methods will be extended to support multi-application environments with concurrent workflows, necessitating allocation strategies that consider multi-tenancy, component dependencies, and the prioritization of emergent services in time-sensitive events such as fires.

Adaptive AI Model Deployment between Edge and Cloud: A particularly demanding class of computational tasks involves the deployment and execution of deep learning models across heterogeneous infrastructure. Traditional cloud-centric model execution often fails to meet the latency and responsiveness constraints of real-time applications. Consequently, emerging strategies for edge intelligence focus on distributing inference workloads between edge devices and cloud or edge servers. These strategies require dynamic adaptation to hardware capabilities, runtime context, and application-specific requirements.

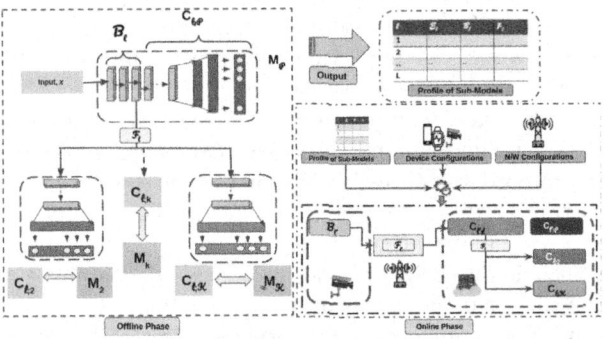

Fig. 4. The schematic of Chimera, excerpted from [54].

Two recent efforts, Chimera [54] and FactionFormer [53], exemplify this runtime adaptability in AI workloads. Chimera presents a framework for the efficient deployment of multitask deep learning models in a collaborative edge-cloud architecture. The schematic diagram of the technique is shown in Fig. 4. The offline phase ("design time") of Chimera involves training lightweight task-specific sub-models using knowledge distillation from pre-trained models. These sub-models are significantly more resource-efficient than the originals, facilitating low-latency inference on constrained devices. In the online phase ("runtime"),

Chimera dynamically determines deployment strategies based on contextual constraints, selecting one or more model layers as split points to distribute inference across the device and cloud. Similarly, FactionFormer addresses the challenge of deploying vision transformer (ViT) models on resource-constrained edge devices. In design time, it leverages the insight that edge devices often operate in contexts involving only a subset of the model's full classification space and prepares a number of classification heads. At runtime, it identifies the subset of relevant classes (termed a "faction") and automatically constructs a bespoke, lightweight ViT variant, called "modelette", and let it execute on the device and perform preliminary inference. When uncertain or incomplete, inference is offloaded to a full ViT model on the cloud. The model split is dynamically constructed by determining the optimal exit layer and classification threshold to minimize latency and classification errors.

4.3 Progressive Computation with Error/accuracy Guarantees

To ensure timely and dependable results in IoT systems, we explore the design of *progressive operators*—computational routines that incrementally improve output quality over time. These operators initially produce coarse but actionable results within tight time constraints and refine them as additional resources or data become available. For example, in building occupancy estimation, waiting for complete, high-fidelity data (e.g., from beacons, Wi-Fi traces, and video feeds) may yield accurate outcomes, but often too late for effective response. Instead, progressively generated partial results (e.g., room-level estimates) allow earlier intervention.

Three modalities of progressive computation can be considered: (i) producing partial results on demand, (ii) streaming increasingly accurate outputs over time, and (iii) returning coarse complete results followed by refined versions. Each output is accompanied by probabilistic accuracy guarantees (e.g., confidence intervals or error bounds), enabling adaptive integration and fusion of partial results within application workflows. This integration consequently supports trade-offs between resource constraints and result quality through adaptive plan-act cycles. At each step, the system allocates remaining resources based on current output quality and time budgets, allowing iterative improvement of result accuracy under bounded execution time. Prior work in progressive data cleaning and entity resolution [8,9] can be extended towards CPS analytics with operator graphs. This raises key challenges, such as estimating costs and benefits of analyzers online, generating execution plans, and balancing computation versus decision-making. Integrating progressive computation with caching and pre-computation is another interesting aspect to enhance both timeliness and resilience.

Another important runtime aspect can arise in IoT application is *progressive sensemaking*—an ability to quickly observe and analyze what is most important through a narrow focus without losing the sight of a wider view of what's going on all around. While the physical world can arguably have an infinite degree of detail that would be very hard, if not impossible, to sense, acquire and process, it is rather important to possess

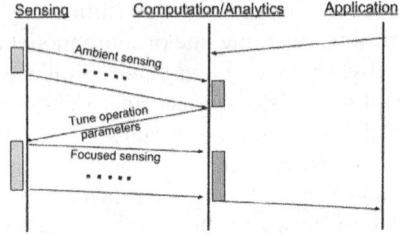

Fig. 5. Progressive sensemaking.

the ability to focus on what is most important when needed. This ability can be achieved by a judicious combination of an ambient always-on sensing with the ability of targeted sensemaking. While an ambient low-resolution sensing operation over the entire space-time gives a coarse situational awareness and also helps to determine where and when to look for details, a more focused and aggressive sensing operation with finer resolution can be initiated anytime as the computation progresses and when the necessity arises (Fig. 5). This ability cannot be obtained from sensing alone, rather the sensing task needs to be guided by the computation module in accordance with the end application goals. This allows for an interleaved sensing and computation where they affect and are affected by each other. The role of progressive sensing and computation is therefore paramount in mission-centric IoT deployment when sensors are heterogeneous and when they have varying space and time resolution requirements.

5 Experimenting with Composability

The goals in terms of validating the correctness and efficacy of composability techniques span two levels. At a higher level, the goal is to determine the extent to which the proposed abstractions can capture the composability needs (timeliness, dependability, extensibility, security) for a variety of IoT applications and settings. At a pragmatic level, one can take a systems-level view to validation – here, prototypes developed using design-time and run-time methods can be instantiated in real-world scenarios under dynamic conditions. This will allow us to empirically evaluate how well design-time and run-time methods address the composability goals. Through our experience with various IoT domains, we highlight a possible set of steps to validate and experiment with composability for real-world application domains including: i) Scenario construction and determination of evaluation metrics, ii) Prototype system design, iii) Validation of the prototype through testbeds and pilot studies, iv) Simulation-based approaches and digital twins, and v) End-to-end system verification using formal methods. Based on the deployment and scenario, one may intersperse these steps to enable agile design and operation of IoT systems. We next illustrate a walkthrough of these steps through our experience with smart firefighting usecases.

Sample Scenario Construction and Requirements Abstraction: This step will allow us to elicit and quantify the composability needs and constraints for a sample scenario. The expectation is that such a requirements analysis will help define rules at design-time and enforce the required constraints at runtime through the adaptation techniques. The smart firefighting use case is informed by the US NIST and National Fire Protection Association (NFPA) Smart Firefighting (SFF) Research Roadmap [35] that establishes the scientific and technical basis of SFF. In this application, we aim to develop an IoT platform designed to manage heterogeneous IoT devices, including fixed sensors and mobile assets such as drones, to support continuous monitoring and situational awareness. These capabilities are critical for assisting first responders, particularly in high-rise building fires where ground-based sensors may be unreachable, and in wildland fire scenarios where in-situ sensors and communication infrastructure are often unavailable.

Prototype System Design: Building upon the requirements and composability constraints identified in Step 1, the next step focuses on the design and implementation of a prototype system. This prototype aims to instantiate the abstractions and adaptation mechanisms proposed at both design-time and runtime. The system architecture should incorporate modular components that can be independently developed, deployed, and dynamically reconfigured in response to changing environmental conditions. For the smart firefighting use case, the prototype may consist of sensing units (e.g., thermal cameras, gas sensors), communication infrastructures (e.g., mobile ad hoc networks), and decision-making modules (e.g., hazard estimation, resource coordination). To meet application requirements such as continuous situational awareness, the design must also consider constructing a CPS (Cyber-Physical System) feedback loop. This loop should enable sensing data and human input to be processed by the decision-making modules and further communicated to the controller modules responsible for operating the sensing IoT devices. Through this closed-loop interaction, the system can dynamically adapt its behavior to evolving conditions while adhering to composability requirements.

Validation of Prototype Through Testbeds and Pilot Studies: Testbeds and pilot studies serve as living labs that can help understand and implement composability by design. The IoT smartspaces created can be used for effective space utilization, energy-efficient HVAC/lighting and fire agency training, including in drills and exercises. In our experience with fire personnel, drills and usecase scenarios are designed based on real-world fire incidents – e.g. apartment and warehouse fires in New York and S. Carolina [32]. The pilot studies generate data for evaluation; techniques such as Situation Awareness Global Assessment Technique (SAGAT) allow us to measure situational awareness at "freeze" points in the drill and can help understand how well composability criteria are met. In past projects, we have used a asmartspace testbed at UCI, TIPPERS, to emulate the dispatch of sensors and drones for urban emergency response. Tasks include detecting ventilation issues that can impact fire flow, monitoring exterior walls for fire progression, and assisting in evacuation [14,46]. Donald Bren Hall

(DBH), a 90,000+ square feet 6-story building is a deeply sensed environment equipped with more than 400 sensors including (a) Surveillance cameras covering all the corridors and doors (for security purposes), (b) instrumented Wi-Fi Access Points for connectivity, Bluetooth beacons, Power outlet meters for monitoring energy usage and multi-sensor platforms with PIR, smoke, explosive gas sensors. Working with local emergency management agencies, we evaluate new technologies in annual drills/exercises. A similar approach was used in the UC-LANL SPARx project on prescribed (Rx) fires [1] – our team participated in controlled burns conducted by experts under admissible weather conditions to reduce the possibility of future wildfires. Fine-grained real-time monitoring of Rx fires is essential for safe execution and public acceptance in WUI communities due to the potential for escaped fires that may cascade into catastrophic events. Working with forestry experts, we have participated in live prescribed burns at the Blodgett Forest Research Station – in addition to in-field testing, this has provided us with insights on composability needs for time-sensitive decision-making [20,45]. At design-time, we use the expert-developed burn plans to generate an in situ IoT deployment plan. This is augmented at run-time with drone-based monitoring for expert-identified tasks such as Burnsite monitoring and Fire intensity inspection.

Simulation Studies, Digital Twins, Logical Explorations: A deeper evaluation uses simulation-based tools. Here, a series of scenarios evaluate the efficacy of systems under situations that exercise the metrics of composability (e.g. timeliness and dependability). One may use historical data to drive the simulations, e.g. building data in our testbed to generate real-time fire status updates and external data for weather, water supply etc. Modeling dynamic changes in the simulation environment may also leverage real data from sensors deployed in buildings (e.g. BMS systems, wireless connectivity data, environmental and camera sensors). Extensibility can be mimicked through sensors carried by fire personnel, drones, and ground vehicles; the dynamic network conditions may result in failures and loss of data. In our work, sample data has been used to meaningfully generate real and synthetic data to create digital twins for different types of buildings, thereby extending pure simulation methods. Recent efforts on developing smartspace digital twins aim to replicate real-world settings and superimpose synthetically generated situations in the instrumented space. Our ongoing work aims to develop "disaster digital twins" that enhance the backend data management and simulations to create situational dashboards, AR/VR and extended reality playback environments. The accurate representation of composability needs and constraint violations in such tools can help better decision support and training. While testbed, simulation studies and digital twins can allow us to empirically evaluate whether composability has been met and whether the tradeoff choices have resulted in violations (e.g. of deadlines), they are not proofs of composability. Such experimental studies pave the way driving end-to-end system verification using formal methods.

5.1 Developing Platforms that Support Service Composability

Service-oriented architectures have for long been employed to create distributed platforms; the art of designing systems which incorporate plug-and-play middleware services to implement robust IoT operation is challenging. Our understanding of safe composability of services and protocols has often developed from one-off use cases. Generalizable principles have emerged – the CAP conjecture and its instantiation for distributed database systems stand as a prime example of composability issues that must be solved in distributed systems. Our early efforts in exploring composability in the context of distributed streaming multimedia systems [71] with QoS constraints pointed to the possibility of a hierarchical design where a small subset of core services, carefully designed and analyzed for composability, can serve as building blocks for a larger set of plug-and-play middleware services.

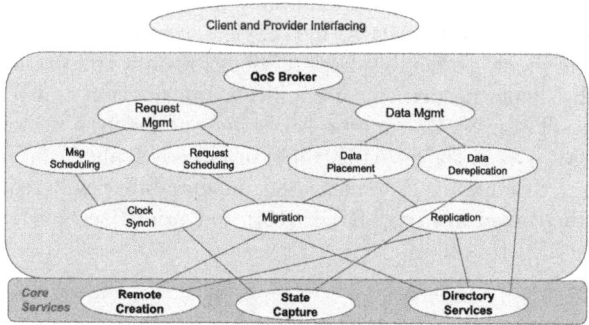

Fig. 6. Composable Services: A QoS broker for Streaming Multimedia [72]

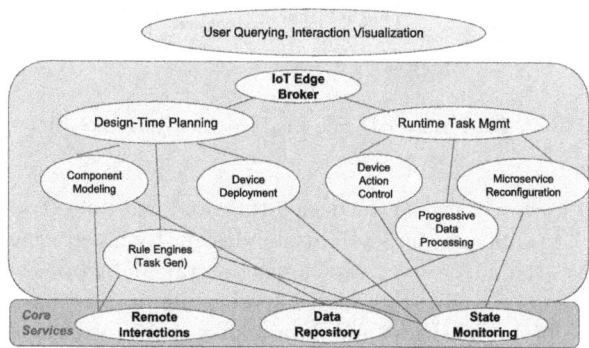

Fig. 7. Composable Services: An IoT Edge Broker Architecture

Figure 6 illustrates how a QoS-enabled brokerage service for streaming multimedia can be modularly composed using a key set of services that include (a) state capture, (b) directories/registries that maintain system/application information and (c) capabilities to trigger remote execution. We conjecture that a similar strategy can be used in the case of IoT deployments whose components operate under varying degrees of change and uncertainty. Our work adapts the popular microservices architecture for instantiation of IoT services to meet composability constraints and tradeoffs. Accordingly, we aim to extract a core set of microservices using which other selected safe services can be deployed – such an adaptive service composition strategy is necessary for IoT systems as their needs and deployment conditions change. In Fig. 7 we illustrate a hierarchical schematic for service composition in an IoT edge broker.

Figure 8 illustrates a system flow schematic of DOME, a smart firefighting prototype [45, 46] that can be adapted for highrise fires, wildland fires and prescribed burns. The need for service composition was evident as we created the initial DOME prototype. We leveraged building blocks from TIPPERS for managing application and system data. IoT devices (in situ, mobile) incorporated container-based clients to flexibly host services for data collection, analysis and device control. Clients needed to communicate information and receive instructions from an edge-server or edge-broker using open-source messaging services (MQTT, ZeroMQ) as in the SCALE [15] affordable IoT platform. Extending the messaging layer to support timeliness and dependability will require the integration of resilient overlays (e.g. RIDE [16]) and prioritized IoT data exchange (e.g. PrioDEX [17]) protocols.

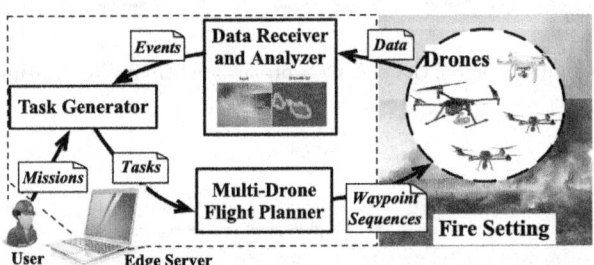

Fig. 8. DOME: A Platform for Drone-Enabled Monitoring of Emergent Events

Our future work will utilize the design-time and run-time strategies as illustrated in Fig. 7 to support composability-by-design. By integrating the semantic data model into the edge-server, we can ingest raw data from stationary and mobile sensors, process and store higher-level semantic information. For seamless interoperability, data ingest and data management modules will utilize the semantic model to gather, store infrastructure data and semantic information generated by analytics operators. State monitoring services implement separate device and service registries that hold information about potential devices, operators and services when integrated into the IoT environment. A discovery engine will implement mechanisms to locate desired functionalities and support dynamic detection of in-network services. The edge server records device/service additions/deletions. Registered devices and services periodically transmit status via local telemetry protocols (e.g.LoRa or WiFi). Planning, Tasking and Reconfiguration components will implement the design-time planning and run-time reconfiguration techniques. The resulting actions and reconfigurations can then be instantiated on the physical infrastructure. Through customized dashboards, end-users may visualize and query information from the underlying deployment.

6 Concluding Remarks and a Personal Note

In this article, we discussed the emerging landscape of IoT-enabled distributed applications and the importance of composability as a design criteria to provide assurances in the underlying behavior of such applications. Based on our past experience, we highlighted how careful design-time and run-time strategies can help systems adapt to changing conditions at run-time while providing assurances of behavior. One of the key aspects that was not addressed in this manuscript is the role of formal methods and verification techniques. This is an interesting direction of future work. Formal methods based reasoning tools and verification techniques are helpful in ensuring that reconfigurable IoT sytems meet composability criteria. With the rapid growth in AI-based analytics in IoT workflows, ensuring composability has become challenging. Our preliminary work has explored the use of the Maude concurrent rewriting logic framework to study dependability aspects of cyberphysical systems. In the coming years, we expect that such lightweight verification methods can work alongside multi-objective optimization techniques and heuristics that are implemented to manage system tradeoffs. Determining how formal methods can help augment IoT implementations to capture composability invariants at design-time and rapidly verify their satisfaction at run-time based on live state is an important direction of future work.

A Personal Note from Nalini Venkatasubramanian

Gul and I arrived at UIUC in the same year, 1989; Gul as faculty and me as a graduate student. Having read the Actors book [2] as an undergrad and given my interest in working on parallel computing and declarative languages, I was delighted to have the opportunity to work with Gul. My PhD dissertation on "Adaptive middleware services for global distributed systems" introduced safe composability as a key challenge in integration of services to manage large-scale global distributed systems and applications and an actor-based meta-architectural approach to execute and reason about composability [72]. The challenge of safe integration in distributed systems, however, began early on – during my M.S. thesis work (1991) with Gul, on developing a garbage collection technique for Actors and reasoning about its correctness. I was intrigued by the ease with which Gul navigated concurrent programming languages, efficiency and parallelism in distributed systems and formal verification methods to ensure correctness in algorithms and protocols. Through my seven years of industry experience at Hewlett-Packard Corp. and HP Labs, and in observing dedicated students of Gul working on Actor runtimes, it became evident to me that for systems to work meaningfully, the distributed algorithms had to work simultaneously. Gul's pioneering ideas on composition for dependability [3] motivated me to further explore composability in distributed systems.

A key milestone in my ability to continue this pursuit with rigor was again created by Gul – he introduced me to Carolyn Talcott, with whose help, over numerous weekend meetings, I started to compose a concurrent GC algorithm with actor migration methods. Gul and Carolyn have patiently developed in me a deep-rooted appreciation for formal semantics and the need for accurate specifications to guide system design – our collaborations have continued to this very day. Gul then helped translate my industry experience in QoS for networked multimedia systems into the composition of real-time needs with techniques for performance and dependability. The software engineer in Gul guided me to address the separation-of-concerns and through a meta-architectural approach [71]. This naturally led to my future work in the use of computational reflection for a variety of real-world systems and applications - most recently in the IoT setting.

I am thankful to Gul for his vision in guiding and encouraging me to pursue this fundamental direction; his push to make me think about composability and computational reflection as a basic approach to handle adaptation is one I found to be relevant as technologies and computing have evolved over the last three decades. For his kindness, humanity, patience, flexibility and confidence in my ability to continue my academic dreams, I am deeply indebted to Gul. A lifelong mentor who has shown me how one can be both deeply intellectual and deeply compassionate – I hope to pass a bit of this along in my academic career.

References

1. SPARxCal: Smart Power-Aware Resilient eXperimental Calibration Platform (2025). https://sparxcal.ics.uci.edu/. Accessed 09 July 2025
2. Agha, G.: Actors: A Model of Concurrent Computation in Distributed Systems. The MIT Press (1986)
3. Agha, G., Frølund, S., Panwar, R., Sturman, D.: A linguistic framework for dynamic composition of dependability protocols. In: Landwehr, C.E., Randell, B., Simoncini, L. (eds.) Dependable Computing for Critical Applications 3. Dependable Computing and Fault-Tolerant Systems, vol. 8, pp. 345–363. Springer, Vienna (1993). https://doi.org/10.1007/978-3-7091-4009-3_15
4. Agha, G.A., Mason, I.A., Smith, S.F., Talcott, C.L.: A foundation for actor computation. J. Funct. Program. **7**(1), 1–72 (1997)
5. Aizpurua, J.I., Papadopoulos, Y., Muxika, E., Chiacchio, F., Manno, G.: On cost-effective reuse of components in the design of complex reconfigurable systems. Qual. Reliab. Eng. Int. **33**(7), 1387–1406 (2017)

6. Al-Fuqaha, A., Guizani, M., Mohammadi, M., Aledhari, M., Ayyash, M.: Internet of things: a survey on enabling technologies, protocols, and applications. IEEE Commun. Surv. Tutor. (2015)
7. Aloi, G., et al.: A mobile multi-technology gateway to enable IoT interoperability. In: IEEE IoTDI (2016)
8. Altowim, Y., Kalashnikov, D.V., Mehrotra, S.: Progressive approach to relational entity resolution. Proc. VLDB Endow. **7**(11), 999–1010 (2016)
9. Altowim, Y., Mehrotra, S.: Parallel progressive approach to entity resolution using MapReduce. In: IEEE International Conference on Data Engineering (ICDE) (2017)
10. Androcec, D., Vrcek, N.: Thing as a service interoperability: Review and framework proposal. In: IEEE International Conference on Future Internet of Things and Cloud (FiCloud), Vienna, Austria (2016)
11. Atzmueller, M., Hilgenberg, K.: Towards capturing social interactions with SDCF: an extensible framework for mobile sensing and ubiquitous data collection. In: 4th International Workshop on Modeling Social Media (2013)
12. Avizienis, A., Laprie, J.C., Randell, B., Landwehr, C.: Basic concepts and taxonomy of dependable and secure computing. IEEE Trans. Dependable Secure Comput. **1**(1), 11–33 (2004)
13. Bandyopadhyay, S., Sengupta, M., Maiti, S., Dutta, S.: Role of middleware for internet of things: a study. Int. J. Comput. Sci. Eng. Surv. (2011)
14. Benson, K., Bouloukakis, G., et al.: FireDeX: a prioritized IoT data exchange middleware for emergency response. In: 19th International Middleware Conference, Rennes, France (2018)
15. Benson, K., Fracchia, C., Wang, G., Zhu, Q.: SCALE: safe community awareness and alerting leveraging the internet of things. IEEE Commun. Mag. (2015)
16. Benson, K., W., G., K., Y.J., Venkatasubramanian, N.: Ride: a resilient IoT data exchange middleware leveraging SDN and edge cloud resources. In: ACM/IEEE International Conference on Internet-of-Things Design and Implementation (IoTDI) (2018)
17. Bouloukakis, G., et al.: PrioDeX: a data exchange middleware for efficient event prioritization in SDN-based IoT systems. ACM Trans. IoT **2**(3) (2021)
18. Bouloukakis, G., Kattepur, A., Georgantas, N., Issarny, I.: Queueing network modeling patterns for reliable and unreliable publish/subscribe protocols. In: 15th EAI International Conference on Mobile and Ubiquitous Systems: Computing, Networking and Services (2018)
19. Burkert, M., Volmer, J., Krumm, H., Fiehe, C.: Rule-based technical management for the dependable operation of networked building automation systems. In: IFIP/IEEE Symposium on Integrated Network and Service Management (IM) (2017)
20. Chang, T.C., et al., T.B.: QuIC-IoT: model-driven short-term IoT deployment for monitoring physical phenomena. In: IOTDI (2023)
21. Chang, T.C., Bouloukakis, G., Hsieh, C.Y., Hsu, C.H., Venkatasubramanian, N.: SmartParcels: a what-if analysis and planning tool for IoT-enabled smart communities: demo abstract. In: Proceedings of the International Conference on Internet-of-Things Design and Implementation, pp. 267–268 (2021)
22. Chio, A., Bouloukakis, G., Hsu, C.H., Mehrotra, S., Venkatasubramanian, N.: Adaptive mediation for data exchange in IoT systems. In: Proceedings of the 18th Workshop on Adaptive and Reflexive Middleware, pp. 1–6 (2019)
23. Ciccozzi, F., Crnkovic, I., Di Ruscio, D., Malavolta, I., Pelliccione, P., Spalazzese, R.: Model-driven engineering for mission-critical IoT systems. IEEE Softw. (2017)

24. Costa, B., Pires, P.F., Delicato, F.C.: Specifying functional requirements and QoS parameters for IoT systems. In: IEEE 15th International Conference on Dependable, Autonomic and Secure Computing, pp. 407–414 (2017)
25. Debieux, V., Pignolet, Y.A., Sivanthi, T.: Faster exact reliability computation. In: DSN-W, pp. 121–124 (2017)
26. Eisenhauer, M., Rosengren, P., Antolin, P.: A development platform for integrating wireless devices and sensors into ambient intelligence systems. In: 6th IEEE Annual Communications Society Conference on Sensor, Mesh and Ad Hoc Communications and Networks Workshops, Rome, pp. 1–3 (2009)
27. Elgamal, T., Sandur, A., Nguyen, P., Nahrstedt, K., Agha, G.: DROPLET: distributed operator placement for IoT applications spanning edge and cloud resources. In: CLOUD (2018)
28. Felfernig, A., Erdeniz, S.P., Azzoni, P., et al.: Towards configuration technologies for IoT gateways. In: 18th International Configuration Workshop (2016)
29. Finney, M.A.: Farsite: Fire area simulator–model development and evaluation. Technical report, USDA Forest Service, Rocky Mountain Research Station (1998)
30. Gao, J., Ploennigs, J., Berges, M.: A data-driven meta-data inference framework for building automation systems. In: Proceedings of the 2nd ACM International Conference on Embedded Systems for Energy-Efficient Built Environments (BuildSys 2015), pp. 23–32. ACM (2015)
31. Georgantas, N.: Service oriented computing in mobile environments: abstractions and mechanisms for interoperability and composition. Ph.D. thesis, Sorbonne Université (2018)
32. Grant, C.C., Jones, A., Hamins, A., Bryner, N.: Realizing the vision of smart fire fighting. IEEE Potentials **34**(1), 35–40 (2015)
33. Großwindhager, B., et al.: Dependable internet of things for networked cars. Int. J. Comput. **16**(4), 226–237 (2017)
34. Hackitt, J.: Building a safer future: independent review of building regulations and fire safety – final report. Technical report, UK Ministry of Housing, Communities & Local Government (2018)
35. Hamins, A., Grant, C., Bryner, N., Jones, A., Koepke, G.: NIST special publication 1191 research roadmap for smart fire fighting. Technical report, NIST (2015)
36. Han, Q., Mehrotra, S., Venkatasubramanian, N.: Aquaeis: middleware support for event identification in community water infrastructures. In: Middleware (2019)
37. Harbi, Y., Aliouat, Z., Hammoudi, S.: Enhancement of IoT applications dependability using bayesian networks. In: Amine, A., Mouhoub, M., Ait Mohamed, O., Djebbar, B. (eds.) CIIA 2018. IAICT, vol. 522, pp. 487–497. Springer, Cham (2018). https://doi.org/10.1007/978-3-319-89743-1_42
38. Hong, H.J., et al., P.H.T.: On optimization of distributed IoT analytics in a fog computing ecosystem. ACM Trans. Internet Things (2018)
39. Hong, H.J., Tsai, P.H., Cheng, A.C., Uddin, M.Y.S., Venkatasubramanian, N., Hsu, C.H.: Supporting internet-of-things analytics in a fog computing platform. In: CloudCom (2017)
40. Jensen, C.B.: The wireless nursing call system: politics of discourse, technology and dependability in a pilot project. Comput. Support. Coop. Work **15**(5–6) (2007)
41. Kempf, J., Arkko, J., Beheshti, N., Yedavalli, K.: Thoughts on reliability in the internet of things (2011)
42. Laporte, G., Semet, F.: Classical heuristics for the capacitated VRP. In: The Vehicle Routing Problem, pp. 109–128. SIAM (2002)

43. Laprie, J.C.: Dependability—its attributes, impairments and means. In: Randell, B., Laprie, JC., Kopetz, H., Littlewood, B. (eds.) Predictably Dependable Computing Systems. ESPRIT Basic Research Series, pp. 3–18. Springer, Heidelberg (1995). https://doi.org/10.1007/978-3-642-79789-7_1
44. Legat, C., Seitz, C., Vogel-Heuser, B.: Unified sensor data provisioning with semantic technologies. In: ETFA, pp. 1–8. IEEE (2011)
45. Liu, F., et al., J.A.: DOME: drone-assisted monitoring of emergent events for wildland fire resilience. In: ICCPS (CPS-IoT Week), pp. 56–67 (2023)
46. Liu, F., Fan, T.Y., et al.: Dragonfly: drone-assisted high-rise monitoring for fire safety. In: SRDS (2021)
47. Liu, F., et al., Q.Z.: Cost-effective sensor data collection from internet-of-things zones using existing transportation fleets. In: SMARTCOMP (2019)
48. Lu, C.H.: Improving system extensibility via an IoT-interoperable platform for dynamic smart homes. In: ICASI (2017)
49. Madrzykowski, D., Walton, W.D.: Wind-driven fire conditions in a structure—vandalia avenue fire, New York. Technical report, NIST IR 6923, National Institute of Standards and Technology (2002)
50. McGrattan, K., Hostikka, S., et al.: Fire dynamics simulator, technical reference guide. Technical report, NIST Special Publication 1018-5, NIST (2013)
51. Mehrotra, S., Kobsa, A., Venkatasubramanian, N., Rajagopalan, S.R.: Tippers: a privacy cognizant IoT environment. In: PerCom Workshops (2016)
52. Mohanty, S., Akyildiz, I.F.: Performance analysis of handoff techniques based on mobile IP, TCP-migrate, and SIP. IEEE Trans. Mob. Comput. **6**(7) (2007)
53. Nimi, S.T., Adnan Arefeen, M., et al.: FactionFormer: context-driven collaborative vision transformer models for edge intelligence. In: SMARTCOMP (2023)
54. Nimi, S.T., Arefeen, M.A., et al.: Chimera: context-aware splittable deep multitasking models for edge intelligence. In: SMARTCOMP (2022)
55. Nägeli, T., et al.: Real-time planning for automated multi-view drone cinematography. ACM Trans. Graph. (TOG) (2017)
56. Pallewatta, S., Kostakos, V., Buyya, R.: Placement of microservices-based IoT applications in fog computing: a taxonomy and future directions. ACM Comput. Surv. (2023)
57. Peacock, R.D., Jones, W.W., Bukowski, R.W., Reneke, P.A.: CFast - consolidated model of fire growth and smoke transport (version 7): Technical reference guide. Technical report, NIST Special Publication 1026, NIST (2013)
58. Ploennigs, J., Hensel, B., Dibowski, H., Kabitzsch, K.: BASont - a modular, adaptive building automation system ontology. In: Proceedings of IECON 2012 - 38th Annual Conference on IEEE Industrial Electronics Society (2012)
59. Qin, Z., Denker, G., Talcott, C., Venkatasubramanian, N.: Achieving resilience of heterogeneous networks through predictive, formal analysis. In: Proceedings of the 2nd ACM International Conference on High Confidence Networked Systems, pp. 85–92. Association for Computing Machinery, New York (2013)
60. Rahimi, M.R., Venkatasubramanian, N., Mehrotra, S., Vasilakos, A.V.: On optimal and fair service allocation in mobile cloud computing. IEEE Trans. Cloud Comput. **6**(3), 815–828 (2018)
61. Ren, S., Venkatasubramanian, N., Agha, G.: Formalizing multimedia QoS constraints using actors. In: Bowman, H., Derrick, J. (eds) Formal Methods for Open Object-based Distributed Systems. IFIP Advances in Information and Communication Technology, pp. 139–153. Springer, Boston (1997). https://doi.org/10.1007/978-0-387-35261-9_10

62. Rice, A.C.: Dependable systems for sentient computing. Technical report, UCAM-CL-TR-686, University of Cambridge, Computer Laboratory (2007)
63. Roth, F.M., Becker, C., et al.: XWARE - a customizable interoperability framework for pervasive computing systems. Pervasive Mob. Comput. (2018)
64. Sanislav, T., Zeadally, S., Mois, G.D., Fouchal, H.: Reliability, failure detection and prevention in cyber-physical systems (CPSs) with agents. Concurr. Comput.: Pract. Exp. e4481 (2018)
65. Schroter, A., Muhl, G., Kounev, S., et al: Stochastic performance analysis and capacity planning of publish/subscribe systems. In: DEBS (2010)
66. Singh, A., Zhou, Y., Mehrotra, S., Sadoghi, M., Sharma, S., Nawab, F.: WedgeBlock: an off-chain secure logging platform for blockchain applications (2023)
67. Torreno, A., et al.: Cooperative multi-agent planning: a survey. ACM Comput. Surv. (CSUR) **50** (2017)
68. Tran, T., Ha, Q.P.: Dependable control systems with internet of things. ISA Trans. **59**, 303–313 (2015)
69. Tziritas, N., Loukopoulos, T., Khan, S.U., Xu, C.Z.: Distributed algorithms for the operator placement problem. IEEE Trans. Comput. Soc. Syst. **2**(4) (2015)
70. Venkatasubramanian, N., Talcott, C.: Meta architectures for resource management in open distributed systems. In: ACM PODC (1995)
71. Venkatasubramanian, N., Talcott, C., Agha, G.: A formal model for reasoning about adaptive QoS-enabled middleware. ACM Trans. Softw. Eng. Methodol. **13**(1) (2004)
72. Venkatasubramanian, N.: An adaptive resource management architecture for global distributed computing. Ph.D. thesis (1998)
73. Venkatasubramanian, N.: Safe 'composability' of middleware services. Commun. ACM **45**(6) (2002)
74. Venkatasubramanian, N., Agha, G.: An actor based framework for managing multimedia QoS. In: Proceedings of the 3rd International Workshops on Multimedia Information Systems (1997)
75. Venkatasubramanian, N., Agha, G., Talcott, C.: Scalable distributed garbage collection for systems of active objects. In: Bekkers, Y., Cohen, J. (eds.) IWMM 1992. LNCS, vol. 637, pp. 134–147. Springer, Heidelberg (1992). https://doi.org/10.1007/BFb0017187
76. Westlin, J., Laine, T.: ManySense: an extensible and accessible middleware for consumer-oriented heterogeneous body sensor networks. Int. J. Distrib. Sens. Netw. (2014)
77. Wildland Fire Lessons: North Schell Escaped RX (2012). https://tinyurl.com/bdddnksc
78. Yus, R., Bouloukakis, G., Mehrotra, S., et al.: Abstracting interactions with IoT devices towards a semantic vision of smart spaces. In: BuildSys (2019)
79. Yus, R., Bouloukakis, G., Mehrotra, S., Venkatasubramanian, N.: The semiotic ecosystem: a semantic bridge between IoT devices and smart spaces. ACM Trans. Internet Technol. (2022)

Hamiltonian Formulation of a Finite-State Automaton

YoungMin Kwon[1](✉) and Gul Agha[2]

[1] Department of Computer Science, The State University of New York, Korea, Incheon, South Korea
youngmin.kwon@sunykorea.ac.kr
[2] Department of Computer Science, University of Illinois at Urbana-Champaign, Urbana, USA
agha@illinois.edu

Abstract. A Finite–state Automaton (FA) is a simple model that has long been used to capture the behaviors of various systems. In our previous work, we have developed a translation technique for a FA to a quantum circuit to utilize efficient quantum algorithms for the problems described in a FA [19]. While we generate a quantum circuit composed of quantum logic gates in our earlier work, in this paper, we develop another translation technique that synthesizes a Hamiltonian from a FA so that accepted strings can be found using quantum optimization techniques such as QAOA. As a first step, we develop a set of Hamiltonian construction rules for a Binary Decision Diagram (BDD), which can represent Boolean functions compactly. Applying the rules, we translate the state transition function of a FA into a Hamiltonian. We further combine those Hamiltonians to generate a Hamiltonian for the acceptance of a string. Finally, a quantum circuit that simulates the evolution of quantum states under the Hamiltonian is synthesized such that quantum optimization techniques such as QAOA can be utilized to find accepted strings efficiently from the superposition of all strings. The technique is experimentally validated by solving a model validation problem. The work has applications to model checking, programming language models based on FAs, DNA sequencing, and so on.

1 Introduction

Quantum computing technologies have been making a rapid progress in recent years. Quantum processors with a large number of qubits are announced, and new quantum algorithms and quantum applications are published faster than ever before [5,6]. Using the quantum phenomena of superposition, entanglement, and interference, quantum algorithms can solve certain problems faster than their classical counterparts. For example, Shor's period finding algorithm showed an exponential speedup [29], and Grover's search algorithm achieved a quadratic speedup [14]. Recently, quantum supremacy, when classical computers can no longer simulate quantum computers, was declared.

Hamiltonian is an operator corresponding to the total energy of a system. Using the Hamiltonian of a system, the time evolution of a quantum state can be described by a Schrödinger equation. Because a quantum system can have energies corresponding only to the eigenvalues of its Hamiltonian, some optimization problems are formulated as a Hamiltonian such that its ground-energy eigenstate is an optimal solution of the problem. For example, *Variational Quantum Eigensolver* (VQE) [26,27] is a hybrid optimization technique that finds a ground eigenstate of a system by generating a quantum state through a parameterized quantum circuit called *ansatz*. VQE has been used in chemistry to simulate molecules [26]. Another example of a quantum optimization technique is a *Quantum Adiabatic Optimization* (QAO), where a ground state of a problem Hamiltonian is searched by slowly changing the Hamiltonian from a Hamiltonian with a known and easy-to-prepare ground state to the problem Hamiltonian [11,31]. Using a gate-based quantum processor *Quantum Approximate Optimization Algorithm* (QAOA) simulates QAO, where a classical optimization algorithm finds a series of quantum simulation durations [10]. Many NP problems are formulated as an Ising problem and solved using QAOA [17,23].

A *Finite-state Automaton* (FA) is a simple computational model that represents many real-world systems such as mechanical systems, electrical circuits, control systems, compilers, etc. [1,16,20]. The set of strings that a FA accepts is called a language. One of the interesting problems about the languages of FAs is a language containment problem, i.e., deciding whether the language of a FA is contained in the language of another FA. For example, checking whether all the behaviors of a system modeled by a FA satisfy the allowed behaviors specified by a FA is a language containment problem. This containment problem between two *Nondeterministic FAs* (NFAs) has exponential time complexity [21].

To make use of the power of quantum computers, there have been approaches to design a *Quantum Finite-state Automaton* (QFA). From a theoretic perspective, properties of QFAs have been theoretically explored by building a state transition matrix for each input symbol and multiplying them for a given string [18,25]. In [32], a specialized QFA that divides a prime number p by the length of an input string with a remainder r, was built to demonstrate its space-efficiency. In our previous work [19], we built a regular language classifier by translating a state transition function of a NFA into a quantum circuit using reversible logic [28,34]. In this paper, we develop a translation technique for a NFA to a Hamiltonian so that quantum optimization techniques such as QAOA can be utilized to find accepted strings efficiently.

Given a Boolean function, a Hamiltonian representing it can be constructed by adding penalties to the parameters that do not satisfy the Boolean function. However, when a Boolean function is given in a Boolean expression, a Hamiltonian representing it can be constructed directly from the expression [15] without enumerating the parameters. Furthermore, Boolean functions are often more compactly represented by a *Binary Decision Diagram* (BDD) [3] than by a Boolean expression because isomorphic subgraphs are merged and redundant nodes are eliminated [3,7,30] in BDDs. In this paper, we develop a set of translation rules to synthesize a Hamiltonian from a BDD.

The key contributions of the paper are: (1) we develop a translation technique for a NFA to a Hamiltonian; (2) a Hamiltonian construction technique for a BDD is developed so that Boolean functions can be translated efficiently; and (3) the technique is experimentally validated by solving a model validation problem using Qiskit tools [9]. Our approach can potentially be extended to solve model checking problems [2,12] on quantum computers.

2 Background

The state of an n qubit system can be represented by a 2^n dimensional complex vector. Using Dirac notation, let $|x\rangle$ be a 2^n dimensional column vector whose x^{th} entry, counting from 0, is 1 and the others are 0, and $\langle x|$ be $|x\rangle^T$. Let $x_{n-1}x_{n-2}\cdots x_0$ be the binary representation of x such that $x = x_{n-1}2^{n-1} + x_{n-2}2^{n-2} + \cdots + x_0 2^0$, then $|x\rangle$ is equal to $|x_{n-1}\rangle \otimes |x_{n-2}\rangle \otimes \cdots \otimes |x_0\rangle$, where $\otimes$ is the Kronecker product, $|0\rangle = [1,0]^T$, and $|1\rangle = [0,1]^T$. For a Boolean function $f : \{0,1\}^n \to \{0,1\}$, we simply write $f(x)$ for $f(x_{n-1},\ldots,x_0)$. The set $\{|0\rangle,\ldots,|2^n-1\rangle\}$ is called the Computational basis and the state of n-qubit system can be written as a linear combination of the basis vectors.

We say that a Hamiltonian $H_f \in \{0,1\}^{2^n \times 2^n}$ *represents* a Boolean function $f : \{0,1\}^n \to \{0,1\}$ if for all 2^n computational basis vectors $|x\rangle$,

$$H_f \cdot |x\rangle = f(x) \cdot |x\rangle \text{ or equivalently } \langle x| \cdot H_f \cdot |x\rangle = f(x).$$

H_f can be constructed as the diagonal matrix of diag($[f(0),\ldots,f(2^n-1)]$) by enumerating $f(x)$ for $x = 0,\ldots,2^n-1$.

Let Z_i be the diagonal matrix of the form $I \otimes \cdots \otimes Z \otimes \cdots \otimes I$ such that $Z = \text{diag}([1,-1])$ is at the ith position, i.e., $Z_i = I^{\otimes i} \otimes Z \otimes I^{\otimes(n-i-1)}$, where $I^{\otimes m}$ is $\bigotimes_{i=1}^{m} \text{diag}([1,1])$ if $m > 0$ and $[1]$ if $m = 0$. Then, H_f can be symbolically expressed in a multinomial of Z_i's as

$$H_f = \sum_{x=0}^{2^n-1} f(x) \cdot term(x), \quad (1)$$

$$term(x) = \prod_{i=0}^{n-1} T_i(x), \text{ where } T_i(x_{n-1}\cdots x_0) = \begin{cases} \frac{1}{2}(I+Z_i) & \text{if } x_i = 0 \\ \frac{1}{2}(I-Z_i) & \text{if } x_i = 1 \end{cases}$$

Observe that $\frac{1}{2}(I+Z_i) \cdot |x\rangle$ is $|x\rangle$ when $x_i = 0$ and $\mathbf{0}$, the vector of zeros, when $x_i = 1$. Similarly $\frac{1}{2}(I-Z_i) \cdot |x\rangle$ is $|x\rangle$ when $x_i = 1$ and $\mathbf{0}$ when $x_i = 0$. Therefore, $term(x') \cdot |x\rangle$ is $\mathbf{0}$ if $x' \neq x$ and $|x\rangle$ when $x' = x$. Moreover, $H_f \cdot |x\rangle = \sum_{x'=0}^{2^n-1} f(x') \cdot term(x') \cdot |x\rangle = f(x) \cdot |x\rangle$. However, computing $f(x) \cdot term(x)$ 2^n times is not practical for a large n. When $f(x)$ is given in a Boolean expression, H_f can also be constructed directly from the formula [15]. In this paper, we construct a Hamiltonian from a BDD. We refer the readers to [3,13] for more details.

Quantum algorithms such as QAOA utilize the time evolution of quantum states which can be described by the Schrödinger equation. Given a Hamiltonian

H_f, the quantum state at time t can be obtained by solving the Schrödinger equation as $|x(t)\rangle = e^{-i \cdot t \cdot H_f} \cdot |x(0)\rangle$. This dynamics equation can be simulated by constructing a quantum circuit composed of CX and RZ gates [4,33].

Example 1. As an example, suppose that $H_f = a \cdot Z_{012} + b \cdot Z_{01}$[1], then a quantum circuit simulating $|x(t)\rangle = e^{-i \cdot t \cdot H_f} \cdot |x(0)\rangle$ from $x(0) = x_2 x_1 x_0$ is as below:

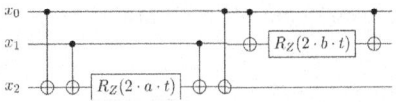

Fig. 1. A quantum circuit for $e^{-i \cdot t \cdot (a \cdot Z_0 \cdot Z_1 \cdot Z_2 + b \cdot Z_0 \cdot Z_1)}$.

Particularly, $e^{-i \cdot t \cdot (a \cdot Z_0 \cdot Z_1 \cdot Z_2 + b \cdot Z_0 \cdot Z_1)}$ can be factored into $e^{-i \cdot a \cdot t \cdot Z_0 \cdot Z_1 \cdot Z_2}$ · $e^{-i \cdot b \cdot t \cdot Z_0 \cdot Z_1}$ because the multiplication of diagonal matrices is commutative. The two exponential terms can be independently implemented as the first 5 gates and the remaining 3 gates of Fig. 1 and put together for the multiplication. In the first term, $e^{-i \cdot a \cdot t \cdot Z_0 \cdot Z_1 \cdot Z_2} = \sum_{k=0}^{\infty} \frac{1}{k!} \cdot (-i \cdot a \cdot t \cdot Z_0 \cdot Z_1 \cdot Z_2)^k$ and because for all computational basis vectors $|x\rangle$, $(Z_0 \cdot Z_1 \cdot Z_2)^k \cdot |x\rangle = |x\rangle$ if there are even number of 1's in x_0, x_1, and x_2 and $(Z_0 \cdot Z_1 \cdot Z_2)^k \cdot |x\rangle = (-1)^k \cdot |x\rangle$ if there are odd number of 1's. Hence, $e^{-i \cdot a \cdot t \cdot Z_0 \cdot Z_1 \cdot Z_2} \cdot |x\rangle = e^{-i \cdot a \cdot t} \cdot |x\rangle$ if there are even number of 1's in x and $e^{-i \cdot a \cdot t \cdot Z_0 \cdot Z_1 \cdot Z_2} \cdot |x\rangle = e^{i \cdot a \cdot t} \cdot |x\rangle$ otherwise. The first 5 gates of the circuit implement $e^{-i \cdot a \cdot t \cdot Z_0 \cdot Z_1 \cdot Z_2}$: if there are even number of 1's in x, the eigenvalue $e^{-i \cdot a \cdot t}$ corresponding to the eigenvector $|0\rangle$ of $R_Z(2 \cdot a \cdot t) = \text{diag}([e^{-i \cdot a \cdot t}, e^{i \cdot a \cdot t}])$ is multiplied to the phase of $|x\rangle$ and if there are odd number of 1's in x, the eigenvalue $e^{i \cdot a \cdot t}$ corresponding to the eigenvector $|1\rangle$ is multiplied to $|x\rangle$. In other words, the first 5 gates of the circuit implement $e^{-i \cdot a \cdot t \cdot Z_0 \cdot Z_1 \cdot Z_2}$. Similarly, the next three gates implement $e^{-i \cdot b \cdot t \cdot Z_0 \cdot Z_1}$. □

3 Constructing a Hamiltonian for a BDD

When a Boolean function is described in a Boolean expression with logical operators such as ∧, ∨, ¬, etc., a Hamiltonian representing the function can be constructed directly from the expression [15]. However, because BDDs often represent a Boolean function more compactly than Boolean expressions, in this section we develop a set of Hamiltonian construction rules from a BDD. For simplicity, we write B to refer to a BDD node or a BDD rooted at the node B when its meaning is clear from the context.

Definition 1. *Let B be a BDD with n Boolean variables $v_{n-1}, \ldots, v_0$. We say that B represents a Boolean function $f : \{0,1\}^n \to \{0,1\}$ if for all $x = x_{n-1} \cdots x_0$, $B|_{v=x}$, the value of B when $v_i = x_i$ for $i = 0, \ldots, n-1$, is equal to $f(x)$. We say that a Hamiltonian H_f represents a BDD B if H_f represents a Boolean function f that B represents.*

---

[1] For simplicity we write Z_{ij} for $Z_i \cdot Z_j$, Z_{ijk} for $Z_i \cdot Z_j \cdot Z_k$, and so on.

(a) $H_f = \frac{1}{2}(I - Z_i)$
(b) $H_f = \frac{1}{2}(I + Z_i)$
(c) $H_f = \frac{1}{2}(I - Z_i) \cdot H_{\text{high}(f)}$
(d) $H_f = \frac{1}{2}(I + Z_i) + \frac{1}{2}(I - Z_i) \cdot H_{\text{high}(f)}$
(e) $H_f = \frac{1}{2}(I + Z_i) \cdot H_{\text{low}(f)}$
(f) $H_f = \frac{1}{2}(I - Z_i) + \frac{1}{2}(I + Z_i) \cdot H_{\text{low}(f)}$
(g) $H_f = \frac{1}{2}(I + Z_i) \cdot H_{\text{low}(f)} + \frac{1}{2}(I - Z_i) \cdot H_{\text{high}(f)}$

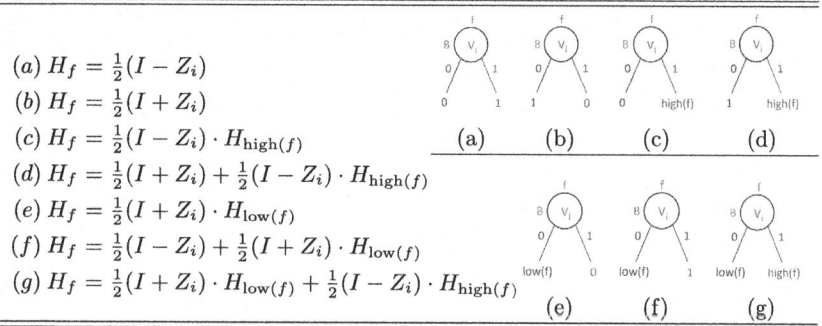

Fig. 2. Hamiltonian construction rules for a BDD.

As an example, the Fig. 3(b) is a BDD that represents the Boolean function k described in a Boolean expression as in the Fig. 3(a).

$$k = \overline{q_0} \cdot q_1 \cdot q_2 + q_0 \cdot q_1 \cdot q_2 +$$
$$q_0 \cdot q_1 \cdot \overline{q_2} + q_0 \cdot \overline{q_1} \cdot q_2 + q_0 \cdot \overline{q_1} \cdot \overline{q_2},$$

where $^-$, $\cdot$, and $+$ operators mean the logical operators $\neg$, $\wedge$, and $\vee$ respectively.

(a)   (b)

Fig. 3. (a) a Boolean function k; (b) a BDD that represents k.

Figure 2 shows Hamiltonian construction rules for a BDD. In the figure, f is the Boolean function represented by the BDD rooted at B with a variable v_i; high(f) and low(f) are the Boolean functions represented by high(B) and low(B), the BDDs rooted at the right child of B and at the left child of B respectively. The value of f is equal to the value of high(f) when $v_i = 1$, and equal to the value of low(f) when $v_i = 0$. Figure 2 shows a Hamiltonian construction rules for the 7 nontrivial configurations of a BDD. A Hamiltonian that represents a BDD can be constructed by recursively applying the construction rules. The two trivial cases are when the value of a BDD is always 0 or always 1: for the former, $H_f = \mathbf{0}$, a matrix of zeros, as $H_f \cdot |x\rangle = 0 \cdot |x\rangle$ for all x and for the latter, $H_f = I$ as $H_f \cdot |x\rangle = |x\rangle$ for all x.

Example 2. As an example, let us construct a Hamiltonian H_k that represents the BDD of Fig. 3. B_0, B_1, and B_2 nodes of Fig. 3 correspond to (f), (c), and (a) cases of Fig. 2 respectively. Hence, the Hamiltonian H_k that represents the BDD is

$$H_2 = \tfrac{1}{2}(I - Z_2) \qquad\qquad\qquad\qquad : H_2 \text{ represents } B_2$$
$$H_1 = \tfrac{1}{2}(I - Z_1) \cdot H_2 = \tfrac{1}{4}(I - Z_1 - Z_2 + Z_{12}) \qquad : H_1 \text{ represents } B_1$$
$$H_k = \tfrac{1}{2}(I - Z_0) + \tfrac{1}{2}(I + Z_0) \cdot H_1 \qquad\qquad : H_k \text{ represents } B_0$$
$$ = \tfrac{1}{8}(5I - 3Z_0 - Z_1 - Z_2 - Z_{01} - Z_{02} + Z_{12} + Z_{012})$$

□

Theorem 1. *Let f be the Boolean function represented by a BDD B, then the Hamiltonian H_f constructed by the rules of Fig. 2 represents B.*

Proof. Let height(B) be the *height* of a BDD node B, the maximum number of edges from the node to the constant nodes. We prove Theorem 1 by the induction on the height of BDD nodes. Let x be a binary number of the form $x_{n-1}x_{n-2}\cdots x_0$; $x^{(i)}$ be its suffix $x_i x_{i-1} \cdots x_0$; $f^{(i)}$ be the Boolean function represented by a BDD rooted at a node with a variable v_i; and $H_f^{(i)}$ be the Hamiltonian computed by the rules of Fig. 2 for $f^{(i)}$. Because there are possibly more than one nodes with the same v_i, $f^{(i)}$ and $H_f^{(i)}$ may not be unique.

The BDDs of Fig. 2(a) and Fig. 2(b) are the induction bases, i.e., the BDD nodes with height 1.

Case (a): The Boolean function represented by B is $f^{(0)}(x^{(0)}) = x_0$. If $H_f^{(0)}$ represents $f^{(0)}$, then $H_f^{(0)} \cdot |x^{(0)}\rangle = x_0 \cdot |x^{(0)}\rangle$ for both $x_0 = 0$ and $x_0 = 1$ cases. Multiplying $\langle x^{(0)}|$ and $|x^{(0)}\rangle$ to both sides of the rule,

$$\langle x^{(0)}| \cdot H_f^{(0)} \cdot |x^{(0)}\rangle = \tfrac{1}{2}\left(1 - \langle x^{(0)}| \cdot Z_0 \cdot |x^{(0)}\rangle\right) = \begin{cases} 0 \text{ if } x_0 = 0 \\ 1 \text{ if } x_0 = 1 \end{cases}$$

Case (b): The Boolean function represented by B is $f^{(0)}(x^{(0)}) = (1 - x_0)$. If $H_f^{(0)}$ represents $f^{(0)}$, then $H_f^{(0)} \cdot |x^{(0)}\rangle = (1 - x_0) \cdot |x^{(0)}\rangle$ for both $x_0 = 0$ and $x_0 = 1$ cases. Multiplying $\langle x^{(0)}|$ and $|x^{(0)}\rangle$ to both sides of the rule,

$$\langle x^{(0)}| \cdot H_f^{(0)} \cdot |x^{(0)}\rangle = \tfrac{1}{2}\left(1 + \langle x^{(0)}| \cdot Z_0 \cdot |x^{(0)}\rangle\right) = \begin{cases} 1 \text{ if } x_0 = 0 \\ 0 \text{ if } x_0 = 1 \end{cases}$$

As an induction step, we show that $\langle x^{(i)}| \cdot H_f^{(i)} \cdot |x^{(i)}\rangle = f^{(i)}(x^{(i)})$ for nodes at height i with the induction hypothesis that $\langle x^{(j)}| \cdot H_f^{(j)} \cdot |x^{(j)}\rangle = f^{(j)}(x^{(j)})$ is true for the nodes at heights less than i. Let H_f^h and H_f^l be the Hamiltonians representing the BDDs high(B) and low(B) respectively. Because of the induction hypothesis, H_f^h and H_f^l represent high(B) and low(B) respectively. Because redundant nodes are removed from a BDD, to match the dimensions, let $\Delta h = \text{height}(B) - \text{height}(\text{high}(B))$, $\Delta l = \text{height}(B) - \text{height}(\text{low}(B))$, $H_{\text{high}(f)} = I^{\otimes \Delta h} \otimes H_f^h$, and $H_{\text{low}(f)} = I^{\otimes \Delta l} \otimes H_f^l$, then $H_{\text{high}(f)} \cdot |x^{(i)}\rangle = \text{high}(f)(x^{(i-\Delta h)}) \cdot |x^{(i)}\rangle$[2] and $H_{\text{low}(f)} \cdot |x^{(i)}\rangle = \text{low}(f)(x^{(i-\Delta l)}) \cdot |x^{(i)}\rangle$ for all $x^{(i)}$.

---

[2] Because high(f) returns a function, high(f)($x^{(i-\Delta h)}$) means applying the function high(f) to the parameter $x^{(i-\Delta h)}$.

Case (c): The Boolean function $f^{(i)}(x^{(i)})$ represented by B is 0 if $x_i = 0$ and $\text{high}(f)(x^{(i-\Delta h)})$ if $x_i = 1$. Multiplying $\langle x^{(i)}|$ and $|x^{(i)}\rangle$ to both sides of the rule,

$$\langle x^{(i)}| \cdot H_f^{(i)} \cdot |x^{(i)}\rangle = \tfrac{1}{2}(1 - \langle x^{(i)}| \cdot Z_i \cdot |x^{(i)}\rangle) \cdot \text{high}(f)(x^{(i-\Delta h)})$$
$$= \begin{cases} 0 & \text{if } x_i = 0 \\ \text{high}(f)(x^{(i-\Delta h)}) & \text{if } x_i = 1 \end{cases}$$

Case (d): The Boolean function $f^{(i)}(x^{(i)})$ represented by B is 1 if $x_i = 0$ and $\text{high}(f)(x^{(i-\Delta h)})$ if $x_i = 1$. Multiplying $\langle x^{(i)}|$ and $|x^{(i)}\rangle$ to both sides of the rule,

$$\langle x^{(i)}| \cdot H_f^{(i)} \cdot |x^{(i)}\rangle = \tfrac{1}{2}(1 + \langle x^{(i)}| \cdot Z_i \cdot |x^{(i)}\rangle)$$
$$+ \tfrac{1}{2}(1 - \langle x^{(i)}| \cdot Z_i \cdot |x^{(i)}\rangle) \cdot \text{high}(f)(x^{(i-\Delta h)})$$
$$= \begin{cases} 1 & \text{if } x_i = 0 \\ \text{high}(f)(x^{(i-\Delta h)}) & \text{if } x_i = 1 \end{cases}$$

Case (e): The Boolean function $f^{(i)}(x^{(i)})$ represented by B is $\text{low}(f)(x^{(i-\Delta l)})$ if $x_i = 0$ and 0 if $x_i = 1$. Multiplying $\langle x^{(i)}|$ and $|x^{(i)}\rangle$ to both sides of rule,

$$\langle x^{(i)}| \cdot H_f^{(i)} \cdot |x^{(i)}\rangle = \tfrac{1}{2}(1 + \langle x^{(i)}| \cdot Z_i \cdot |x^{(i)}\rangle) \cdot \text{low}(f)(x^{(i-\Delta l)})$$
$$= \begin{cases} \text{low}(f)(x^{(i-\Delta l)}) & \text{if } x_i = 0 \\ 0 & \text{if } x_i = 1 \end{cases}$$

Case (f): The Boolean function $f^{(i)}(x^{(i)})$ represented by B is $\text{low}(f)(x^{(i-\Delta l)})$ if $x_i = 0$ and 1 if $x_i = 1$. Multiplying $\langle x^{(i)}|$ and $|x^{(i)}\rangle$ to both sides of the rule,

$$\langle x^{(i)}| \cdot H_f^{(i)} \cdot |x^{(i)}\rangle = \tfrac{1}{2}(1 - \langle x^{(i)}| \cdot Z_i \cdot |x^{(i)}\rangle)$$
$$+ \tfrac{1}{2}(1 + \langle x^{(i)}| \cdot Z_i \cdot |x^{(i)}\rangle) \cdot \text{low}(f)(x^{(i-\Delta l)})$$
$$= \begin{cases} \text{low}(f)(x^{(i-\Delta l)}) & \text{if } x_i = 0 \\ 1 & \text{if } x_i = 1 \end{cases}$$

Case (g): The Boolean function $f^{(i)}(x^{(i)})$ represented by B is $\text{low}(f)(x^{(i-\Delta l)})$ if $x_i = 0$ and $\text{high}(f)(x^{(i-\Delta h)})$ if $x_i = 1$. Multiplying $\langle x^{(i)}|$ and $|x^{(i)}\rangle$ to both sides of the rule,

$$\langle x^{(i)}| \cdot H_f^{(i)} \cdot |x^{(i)}\rangle = \tfrac{1}{2}(1 + \langle x^{(i)}| \cdot Z_i \cdot |x^{(i)}\rangle) \cdot \text{low}(f)(x^{(i-\Delta l)})$$
$$+ \tfrac{1}{2}(1 - \langle x^{(i)}| \cdot Z_i \cdot |x^{(i)}\rangle) \cdot \text{high}(f)(x^{(i-\Delta h)})$$
$$= \begin{cases} \text{low}(f)(x^{(i-\Delta l)}) & \text{if } x_i = 0 \\ \text{high}(f)(x^{(i-\Delta h)}) & \text{if } x_i = 1 \end{cases}$$

□

BDDs may represent Boolean functions more compactly than Boolean expressions, but they do not reduce the number of symbolic terms in the Hamiltonian H_f that represents the function. However, with a compact representation, a Hamiltonian can be built more efficiently from a BDD than from a Boolean expression. In addition, hybrid optimization techniques such as VQE, QAOA, etc., require evaluations of the Boolean function from a classical computer, where a BDD representation can make the evaluation faster.

Now, let us consider the gate complexity to implement $e^{-i \cdot t \cdot H_f}$. Hamiltonians can be constructed symbolically as a multinomial of Z_i's as in Eq. (1). That is,

$$H_f = \sum_{x=0}^{2^n-1} c_x \cdot Z_0^{x_0} \cdot Z_1^{x_1} \cdots Z_{n-1}^{x_{n-1}},$$

where $x_{n-1} x_{n-2} \cdots x_0$ is the binary representation of x, i.e. $x = x_{n-1} 2^{n-1} + \cdots + x_0 2^0$ and $x_i \in \{0, 1\}$. As can be seen in Example 1, when translating $e^{-i \cdot t \cdot H_f}$ into a quantum circuit, the number of the product terms $(Z_0^{x_0} \cdot Z_1^{x_1} \cdots Z_{n-1}^{x_{n-1}})$ as well as the number of Z_i's in each product term ($Z_i^0 = I$) affect the number of gates in the resulting quantum circuit. As in Example 2, the number of product terms can potentially grow exponentially with the height of a BDD. Particularly in Fig. 2, a Hamiltonian for a node is constructed by multiplying either or both of $\frac{1}{2}(I + Z_i)$ and $\frac{1}{2}(I - Z_i)$ to the Hamiltonian obtained from the child nodes. Because Z_i does not occur in $H_{\text{low}(f)}$ and $H_{\text{high}(f)}$, $I \cdot H_{\text{low}(f)}$ and $I \cdot H_{\text{high}(f)}$ make terms without Z_i and $Z_i \cdot H_{\text{low}(f)}$ and $Z_i \cdot H_{\text{high}(f)}$ make terms with Z_i. Because the number of product terms can be doubled for each height of a BDD, the number of product terms in H_f representing a BDD B is $O(2^{\text{height}(B)})$.

Given a product term $Z_0^{x_0} \cdot Z_1^{x_1} \cdots Z_{n-1}^{x_{n-1}}$, let J be the index set such that $J = \{j \mid x_j \neq 0\}$. Then, implementing $e^{-i \cdot t \cdot \prod_{j \in J} Z_j}$ with $|J| = k$ into a quantum circuit requires $2 \cdot k$ CX gates and 1 RZ gate as demonstrated in Fig. 1.[3] Without any cancellation, the number of such product terms with k Z_i's in a Hamiltonian for a BDD with height h is $\binom{h}{k}$ and to implement such a term, $2 \cdot k \cdot \binom{h}{k}$ CX gates and $\binom{h}{k}$ RZ gates will be needed. Hence, in the worst case, the total number of gates is:[4]

$$\text{number of } CX \text{ gates} = O\left(\sum_{k=0}^{h} 2 \cdot k \cdot \binom{h}{k}\right) = O\left(h \cdot 2^h\right), \qquad (2)$$

$$\text{number of } RZ \text{ gates} = O\left(\sum_{k=0}^{h} \binom{h}{k}\right) = O\left(2^h\right). \qquad (3)$$

---

[3] In the actual quantum circuit implementation, due to the limited connectivity, extra SWAP gates may be inserted.

[4] By the binomial theorem, $(x + y)^n = \sum_{k=0}^{n} \binom{n}{k} x^k y^{n-k}$. Setting $x = 1$ and $y = 1$, $\sum_{k=0}^{n} \binom{n}{k} = 2^n$. Taking the derivative with respect to x on both sides of the binomial equation: $n \cdot (x+y)^{n-1} = \sum_{k=0}^{n} k \cdot \binom{n}{k} x^{k-1} y^{n-k}$. Setting $x = 1$ and $y = 1$, $\sum_{k=0}^{n} k \cdot \binom{n}{k} = n \cdot 2^{n-1}$.

4 Constructing a Hamiltonian for a Finite-State Automaton

In this section, we construct a cost Hamiltonian H for a NFA such that $\langle x|\cdot H\cdot|x\rangle$ has a ground energy of 0 when x, composed of a bounded string and a run, is accepting and valid. We reduce the gate complexity by building a Hamiltonian for a weaker relation.

4.1 Encoded Finite-State Automaton

Because quantum operators are reversible, before constructing a Hamiltonian for a NFA, we convert it to an equivalent DFA and binary encode its components. More details of this step can be found in [19]. Formally, a NFA N is a five-tuple $N = \langle \Sigma, K, \Delta, k_{ini}, A\rangle$, where Σ is a set of symbols, K is a set of states, $\Delta : \Sigma \times K \to 2^K$ is a nondeterministic state transition relation, $k_{ini} \in K$ is the initial state, and $A \subseteq K$ is the set of accepting states. A DFA D also is a five-tuple $D = \langle \Sigma, K, \Delta, k_{ini}, A\rangle$, but it does not have nondeterminism in the state transition. Hence, $\Delta : \Sigma \times K \to K$. We write $k \xrightarrow{\sigma} k'$ for $(k, \sigma, k') \in \Delta$.

A NFA can be converted to an equivalent DFA using the subset construction algorithm [22]. However, to avoid an exponential growth in the number of states, we convert a NFA to a DFA by extending the symbols with nondeterministic choices in the state transitions [19]. For example, the state transition diagram in Fig. 4 (a) has a nondeterminism: $\Delta(X, q) = \{X, Y\}$. We remove the nondeterminism by extending the set of symbols $\Sigma = \{p, q\}$ to $\Sigma' = \{p, q\} \times \{0, 1\}$, where the set $\{0, 1\}$ represents the nondeterministic choices. The state transition function is updated accordingly, e.g., $\Delta'(X, q0) = X$, $\Delta'(X, q1) = Y$, etc.

An encoding function enc : $\Sigma \cup K \to \mathbb{N}^+$ is a function that maps a symbol and a state to a natural number, unique in their respective kind. With enc, a DFA $D = \langle \Sigma', K', \Delta', k'_{ini}, A'\rangle$ can be converted to an encoded DFA $Q = \langle \Sigma, K, \Delta, k_{ini}, A\rangle$ such that $\Sigma = \{\text{enc}(\sigma) \mid \sigma \in \Sigma'\}$, $K = \{\text{enc}(k) \mid k \in K'\}$, $\Delta = \{\text{enc}(k) \xrightarrow{\text{enc}(\sigma)} \text{enc}(k') \mid k \xrightarrow{\sigma} k' \in \Delta'\}$, $k_{ini} = \text{enc}(k'_{ini})$, and $A = \{\text{enc}(k) \mid k \in A'\}$. In other words, enc renames the states and symbols of D.

Example 3. As an example, after extending the symbols with nondeterministic choices, the DFA D for the NFA with the state transition diagram of Fig. 4 (a) is $D = \langle \Sigma', K', \Delta', k'_{ini}, A'\rangle$, where $\Sigma' = \{p0, p1, q0, q1\}$, $K' = \{X, Y\}$, $\Delta' = \{X \xrightarrow{p0} X, X \xrightarrow{p1} X, X \xrightarrow{q0} X, X \xrightarrow{q1} Y, Y \xrightarrow{p0} Y, Y \xrightarrow{p1} Y, Y \xrightarrow{q0} Y, Y \xrightarrow{q1} Y\}$, $k'_{ini} = X$, $A' = \{Y\}$. If D accepts a string with the extended symbols, N accepts the string without the nondeterministic choices.

With an encoding function of enc$(p0) = 00$, enc$(p1) = 01$, enc$(q0) = 10$, enc$(q1) = 11$, enc$(X) = 0$, and enc$(Y) = 1$, DFA D can be encoded as $Q = \langle \Sigma, K, \Delta, k_{ini}, A\rangle$, where $\Sigma = \{00, 01, 10, 11\}$, $K = \{0, 1\}$, $\Delta = \{0 \xrightarrow{00} 0, 0 \xrightarrow{01} 0, 0 \xrightarrow{10} 0, 0 \xrightarrow{11} 1, 1 \xrightarrow{00} 1, 1 \xrightarrow{01} 1, 1 \xrightarrow{10} 1, 1 \xrightarrow{11} 1\}$, $k_{ini} = 0$, $A = \{1\}$. We can define a family of state transition functions Δ_i for each bit i of the output states such that Δ_i maps the current state and the symbol to the ith bit of

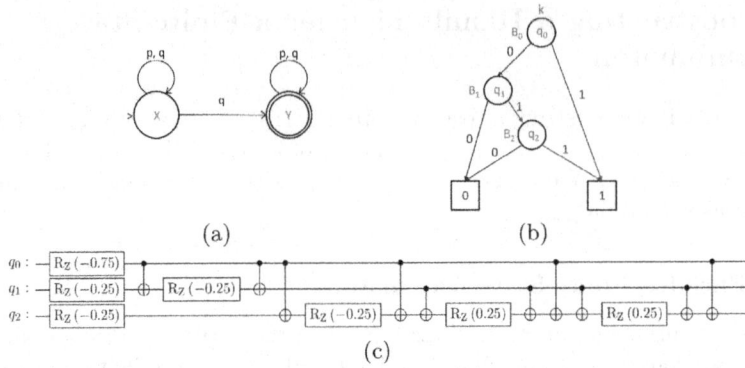

Fig. 4. (a) A state transition diagram of a NFA example, (b) A BDD representation of the state transition function Δ of Q. (c) A quantum circuit for $e^{-i \cdot t \cdot H_{\text{diff}}}$.

the next state. Each Δ_i defines a Binary Decision Tree that can be compactly represented by a BDD as in Fig. 4(b). In the BDD, q_0 is a variable for the current state; q_1 and q_2 are variables for the input symbol; and the leaf nodes are a bit of the next state. For example, from state 0 ($q_0 = 0$), if an input symbol is 10 ($q_1 = 1, q_2 = 0$), the next state is 0, i.e. $\Delta(0, 10) = 0$ and from state 0 ($q_0 = 0$), if an input symbol is 11 ($q_1 = 1, q_2 = 1$), the next state is 1, i.e. $\Delta(0, 11) = 1$. □

4.2 Hamiltonian for the State Transition Function of a FA

In the previous section, we convert a NFA to an encoded DFA and build BDDs for a family of Δ_i corresponding to each bit of the next state. Using this result, let us begin this section with a simple example. Continuing from Example 3, let us define a Hamiltonian that represents the state transition function Δ of the encoded DFA Q and build a quantum circuit for its matrix exponentiation.

Example 4. The BDD of Fig. 4(b) represents the state transition function Δ of the encoded DFA Q. In particular, this BDD is identical to the BDD of Fig. 3, and hence the Boolean expression k of Fig. 3 represents the Boolean function Δ. Copying the result of Example 2, a Hamiltonian H_k that represents the BDD is

$$H_k = \tfrac{1}{8}(5I - 3Z_0 - Z_1 - Z_2 - Z_{01} - Z_{02} + Z_{12} + Z_{012}).$$

To quickly examine whether H_k represents the Boolean function k, let us check whether $\langle q_2 q_1 q_0 | \cdot H_k \cdot | q_2 q_1 q_0 \rangle = \Delta(q_0, q_1 q_2)$ for $q_2 q_1 q_0 = 010$ and $q_2 q_1 q_0 = 110$.

$$\langle 010 | \cdot H_k \cdot | 010 \rangle = \tfrac{1}{8}(5 - 3 + 1 - 1 + 1 - 1 - 1 - 1) = 0 = \Delta(0, 10)$$
$$\langle 110 | \cdot H_k \cdot | 110 \rangle = \tfrac{1}{8}(5 - 3 + 1 + 1 + 1 + 1 + 1 + 1) = 1 = \Delta(0, 11)$$

As we demonstrated in Example 1, we can synthesize a quantum circuit for the matrix exponential of H_k from the symbolic representation of H_k. Figure 4(c) shows $e^{-i \cdot t \cdot H_k}$ when $t = 1$. □

Now, we construct H_Δ, a Hamiltonian for the whole state transition function Δ, using a family of H_i, for the bits of the next state.

Definition 2. *We say that a Hamiltonian H_Δ represents the state transition function Δ of an encoded DFA $Q = \langle \Sigma, K, \Delta, k_{ini}, A \rangle$ if for all $(k, \sigma, k') \in K \times \Sigma \times K$,*

$$H_\Delta \cdot |k'\sigma k\rangle = \begin{cases} 1 \cdot |k'\sigma k\rangle & \text{if } \Delta(k, \sigma) = k' \\ 0 \cdot |k'\sigma k\rangle & \text{if } \Delta(k, \sigma) \neq k' \end{cases} \qquad (4)$$

Theorem 2. *Let an encoded DFA Q be $Q = \langle \Sigma, K, \Delta, k_{ini}, A \rangle$, $n = \lceil \log_2 |K| \rceil$, $\ell = \lceil \log_2 |\Sigma| \rceil$, and H_i be the Hamiltonian representing the Boolean function for the ith output state bit of Δ, i.e., $H_i \cdot |\sigma k\rangle = \Delta(k, \sigma)_i \cdot |\sigma k\rangle$, where $\Delta(k, \sigma)_i$ is the ith bit of the output state. Considering that H_Δ is applied to a vector of the form $|k'\sigma k\rangle$ and H_i is applied to a vector of the form $|\sigma k\rangle$, to align the components, let Z'_i be $Z'_i = Z_i \otimes I^{\otimes(\ell+n)}$. Then, H_Δ defined as below represents Δ:*

$$H_\Delta = \prod_{i=0}^{n-1} \tfrac{1}{2}(I + Z'_i) - Z_i \otimes H_i \qquad (5)$$

Proof. Let us consider each bit of an output state k' in $|k'\sigma k\rangle$. Let x_i be the ith bit of k' at its position, suffixed with σk, i.e., $x_i = k'_i 2^i \cdot 2^{\ell+n} + (\sigma_{\ell-1} 2^{\ell-1} + \cdots + \sigma_0 2^0) \cdot 2^n + (k_{n-1} 2^{n-1} + \cdots + k_0 2^0)$, then

Cases		Results
k'_i	$H_i \cdot \|\sigma k\rangle$	$(\tfrac{1}{2}(I + Z'_i) - Z_i \otimes H_i) \cdot \|x_i\rangle$
0	$0 \cdot \|\sigma k\rangle$	$\tfrac{1}{2}(\|x_i\rangle + \|x_i\rangle) + 0 = \|x_i\rangle$
0	$1 \cdot \|\sigma k\rangle$	$\tfrac{1}{2}(\|x_i\rangle + \|x_i\rangle) - \|x_i\rangle = 0$
1	$0 \cdot \|\sigma k\rangle$	$\tfrac{1}{2}(\|x_i\rangle - \|x_i\rangle) + 0 = 0$
1	$1 \cdot \|\sigma k\rangle$	$\tfrac{1}{2}(\|x_i\rangle - \|x_i\rangle) + \|x_i\rangle = \|x_i\rangle$

The Results column of the table shows that for all $i = 0, \ldots, n-1$,

$$\left(\tfrac{1}{2}(I + Z'_i) - Z_i \otimes H_i\right) \cdot |x_i\rangle = \begin{cases} |x_i\rangle & \text{if } k'_i \cdot |x_i\rangle = Z_i \otimes H_i \cdot |x_i\rangle \\ 0 & \text{otherwise} \end{cases}$$

Because H_Δ is the product of $\tfrac{1}{2}(I + Z'_i) - Z_i \otimes H_i$ for all $i = 0, \ldots n-1$,

$$H_\Delta \cdot |k'\sigma k\rangle = \begin{cases} 1 \cdot |k'\sigma k\rangle & \text{if } \Delta(k, \sigma) = k' \\ 0 \cdot |k'\sigma k\rangle & \text{if } \Delta(k, \sigma) \neq k' \end{cases}$$

□

An issue with H_Δ is that the product in Eq. (5) will double the number of terms for each $i \in [0, n-1]$: the terms with and without Z'_i's. Specifically, the product operation $(\prod_{i=0}^{n-1})$ adds $O(2^n = |K|)$ terms of $Z'^{k_0}_0 \cdot Z'^{k_1}_1 \cdots Z'^{k_{n-1}}_{n-1}$, where $k_i \in \{0, 1\}$ for $i = 0, \ldots, n-1$. To reduce the number of terms, we define *formulates*, a more relaxed relation than *represents*.

Definition 3. We say that a Hamiltonian H_{diff} formulates Δ if for all $(k', \sigma, k) \in K \times \Sigma \times K$,

$$H_{\text{diff}} \cdot |k'\sigma k\rangle = \begin{cases} 0 \cdot |k'\sigma k\rangle & \text{if } \Delta(k,\sigma) = k' \\ p \cdot |k'\sigma k\rangle & \text{if } \Delta(k,\sigma) \neq k', \text{ where } p > 0 \end{cases} \quad (6)$$

Comparing Eq. (4) and Eq. (6), there are changes in the eigenvalues and their conditions: 1 in the former becomes 0 and 0 in the former is *relaxed* to a positive number. The switch in the ground-energy condition is to use H_{diff} as a cost Hamiltonian for a minimization problem.

One can make a cost Hamiltonian using H_Δ as $I - H_\Delta$, the negation of H_Δ. Obviously $I - H_\Delta$ formulates Δ. However, it does not remove the product operation and results in the same gate complexity. We construct a relaxed cost Hamilton H_{diff} by adding n cost Hamiltonians H_{diff}^i conditioned on the equality of each output state bit $\Delta(k,\sigma)_i = k'_i$.

Theorem 3. *Let an encoded DFA Q be $Q = \langle \Sigma, K, \Delta, k_{ini}, A\rangle$, $n = \lceil \log_2 |K| \rceil$, $\ell = \lceil \log_2 |\Sigma| \rceil$, and H_i be the Hamiltonian representing the Boolean function for the ith output state bit of Δ, i.e., $H_i \cdot |\sigma k\rangle = \Delta(k,\sigma)_i \cdot |\sigma k\rangle$. Let $Z'_i = Z_i \otimes I^{\otimes(\ell+n)}$, then H_{diff} defined as below formulates Δ.*

$$H_{\text{diff}} = \sum_{i=0}^{n-1} H_{\text{diff}}^i = \sum_{i=0}^{n-1} \tfrac{1}{2}(I - Z'_i) + Z_i \otimes H_i.$$

Proof. As in the previous proof, let us consider each bit of an output state k' in $|k'\sigma k\rangle$. Let x_i be the ith bit of k' at its position, suffixed with σk, i.e., $x_i = k'_i 2^i \cdot 2^{\ell+n} + (\sigma_{\ell-1}2^{\ell-1} + \cdots + \sigma_0 2^0) \cdot 2^n + (k_{n-1}2^{n-1} + \cdots + k_0 2^0)$, then

Cases		Results
k'_i	$H_i \cdot \|\sigma k\rangle$	$\left(\tfrac{1}{2}(I - Z'_i) + Z_i \otimes H_i\right) \cdot \|x_i\rangle$
0	$0 \cdot \|\sigma k\rangle$	$\tfrac{1}{2}(\|x_i\rangle - \|x_i\rangle) + 0 \quad = \quad 0$
0	$1 \cdot \|\sigma k\rangle$	$\tfrac{1}{2}(\|x_i\rangle - \|x_i\rangle) + \|x_i\rangle \quad = \quad \|x_i\rangle$
1	$0 \cdot \|\sigma k\rangle$	$\tfrac{1}{2}(\|x_i\rangle + \|x_i\rangle) + 0 \quad = \quad \|x_i\rangle$
1	$1 \cdot \|\sigma k\rangle$	$\tfrac{1}{2}(\|x_i\rangle + \|x_i\rangle) - \|x_i\rangle \quad = \quad 0$

The Results column of the table shows that for all $i = 0, \ldots, n-1$,

$$\left(\tfrac{1}{2}(I - Z'_i) + Z_i \otimes H_i\right) \cdot |x_i\rangle = \begin{cases} 0 & \text{if } k'_i \cdot |x_i\rangle = Z_i \otimes H_i \cdot |x_i\rangle \\ |x_i\rangle & \text{otherwise} \end{cases}$$

Because H_{diff} is the sum of $\tfrac{1}{2}(I - Z'_i) + Z_i \otimes H_i$ for all $i = 0, \ldots n - 1$,

$$H_{\text{diff}} \cdot |k'\sigma k\rangle = \begin{cases} 0 \cdot |k'\sigma k\rangle & \text{if } \Delta(k,\sigma) = k' \\ p \cdot |k'\sigma k\rangle & \text{if } \Delta(k,\sigma) \neq k', \end{cases}$$

where p is a positive number. In particular, p is the Hamming distance between k' and $\Delta(k,\sigma)$. □

Example 5. Continuing from Example 4, the Hamiltonian H_{diff} that formulates Δ is

$$H_{\text{diff}} = \tfrac{1}{2}(I - Z_3) + Z_3 \cdot I \otimes H_k$$
$$= \tfrac{1}{8}(4I - 4Z_3 + 5Z_3 - 3Z_{30} - Z_{31} - Z_{32} - Z_{301} - Z_{302} + Z_{312} + Z_{3012})$$

To quickly examine H_{diff}, let us check the expected energy of H_{diff} for $0 \xrightarrow{11} 0$ ($\notin \Delta$) and $0 \xrightarrow{11} 1$ ($\in \Delta$).

$$\langle 0\,11\,0| \cdot H_{\text{diff}} \cdot |0\,11\,0\rangle = \tfrac{1}{8}(4 - 4 + 5 - 3 + 1 + 1 + 1 + 1 + 1 + 1) = 1$$
$$\langle 1\,11\,0| \cdot H_{\text{diff}} \cdot |1\,11\,0\rangle = \tfrac{1}{8}(4 + 4 - 5 + 3 - 1 - 1 - 1 - 1 - 1 - 1) = 0$$

□

Let us compute the gate complexity for H_{diff}. Let an encoded DFA be $Q = \langle \Sigma, K, \Delta, k_{ini}, A \rangle$ with $\ell = \lceil \log_2 |\Sigma| \rceil$ and $n = \lceil \log_2 |K| \rceil$. The time evolution of quantum states by H_{diff} can be simulated as $e^{-i \cdot t \cdot H_{\text{diff}}} = \prod_{i=0}^{n-1} e^{-i \cdot t \cdot H_{\text{diff}}^i}$ because H_{diff}^i is a diagonal matrix. In H_{diff}^i, (1) Z_i is appended to the existing terms of H_i and (2) a single term of Z_i' is added freshly. Hence, to implement $e^{-i \cdot t \cdot H_{\text{diff}}^i}$, two additional CX gates are required for each of the existing terms in H_i for (1), and 1 RZ gate is necessary for (2).

Because H_i represents a BDD with $n + \ell$ variables, the gate complexity to implement $e^{-i \cdot t \cdot H_{\text{diff}}^i}$ is

$$\text{number of } CX \text{ gates} = O\left(\sum_{k=0}^{n+\ell}(2 + 2 \cdot k) \cdot \binom{n+\ell}{k}\right) = O\left((n+\ell) \cdot 2^{n+\ell}\right)$$
$$\text{number of } RZ \text{ gates} = O\left(1 + \sum_{k=0}^{n+\ell} \binom{n+\ell}{k}\right) = O\left(2^{n+\ell}\right)$$

Because n $e^{-i \cdot t \cdot H_{\text{diff}}^i}$'s are sequentially appended to implement $e^{-i \cdot t \cdot H_{\text{diff}}}$, its gate complexity is

$$\text{number of } CX \text{ gates} = O\left(n \cdot (n+\ell) \cdot 2^{n+\ell}\right)$$
$$= O\left((\log_2 |K|^2 + \log_2 |K| \cdot \log_2 |\Sigma|) \cdot |K| \cdot |\Sigma|\right), \quad (7)$$
$$\text{number of } RZ \text{ gates} = O\left(n \cdot 2^{n+\ell}\right) = O\left(\log_2 |K| \cdot |K| \cdot |\Sigma|\right). \quad (8)$$

4.3 Hamiltonian to Validate the Runs of a FA

In the previous section, we construct a Hamiltonian accounting for a single state transition of a FA. In this section, we extend the Hamiltonian to identify the valid runs of a FA for a bounded string of symbols. An immediate way to construct such a Hamiltonian is to extend the BDD to the length of the input string. However, this approach grows the number of gates exponentially with the length of the string. In particular, let b be the length of a string, then the number of CX and RZ gates are the same as Eq. (7) and Eq. (8) with ℓ replaced by $b \cdot \ell$. Hence, both equations have $2^b \cdot |\Sigma|$ terms and the number of gates grows exponentially in terms of the bound b.

Chaining the cost Hamiltonian H_{diff} using ancillary qubits, the exponential gate complexity problem can be solved. To build a cost Hamiltonian H_{run} for a string of symbols, we prepare an H_{diff} for each symbol position of a string and wire them such that the output state of a previous H_{diff} is used as the input state of the next H_{diff}. H_{run} is the sum of the individual H_{diff}'s: if a quantum state $|x\rangle$, composed of the states of an automaton and the input symbols, is the ground-energy state of H_{run}, i.e., $H_{\text{run}} \cdot |x\rangle = \mathbf{0}$, then $|x\rangle$ satisfies all the equality constraints of individual H_{diff}'s.

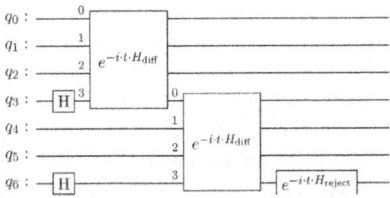

Fig. 5. A block diagram of $e^{-i \cdot t \cdot H_Q}$ that handles a string of symbols.

As an example, Fig. 5 shows a block diagram of this modular design. Each of the blocks labeled as $e^{-i \cdot t \cdot H_{\text{diff}}}$ is an abstracted module of Fig. 4 (c) extended with the equality constraint for the output state: in the diagram q_0 holds the initial state, q_3 and q_6 are ancillary qubits for the next two states, $q_1 q_2$ and $q_4 q_5$ are the first and the second symbols of a string. Each H_{diff} adds a positive cost when $q_3 \neq \Delta(q_0, q_1 q_2)$ and when $q_6 \neq \Delta(q_3, q_4 q_5)$.

Definition 4. *Let $Q = \langle \Sigma, K, \Delta, k_{ini}, A \rangle$ be an encoded DFA, $n = \lceil \log_2 |K| \rceil$, and $\ell = \lceil \log_2 |\Sigma| \rceil$. We say that a Hamiltonian H_{run} formulates* the runs of Q of length b *if for any bit string $x \in \{0,1\}^{b \cdot (n+\ell)+n}$,*

$$H_{\text{run}} \cdot |x\rangle = \begin{cases} \mathbf{0} \cdot |x\rangle & \text{if } x = k_b \sigma_{b-1} k_{b-1} \cdots k_1 \sigma_0 k_0, \text{ such that } \sigma_i \in \Sigma, k_i \in K, \\ & \Delta(k_i, \sigma_i) = k_{i+1}, \text{ and } k_0 = k_{ini} \\ p \cdot |x\rangle & \text{otherwise, where } p > 0 \end{cases}$$

One way to make a cost Hamiltonian that formulates the runs of Q of length b is to wire H_{diff} blocks b times while shifting the input by $n + \ell$ qubits for each state transition as depicted in Fig. 5. That is, H_{run} defined as below is such a cost Hamiltonian

$$H_{\text{run}} = \sum_{i=0}^{b-1} I^{\otimes m \cdot (b-i-1)} \otimes H_{\text{diff}} \otimes I^{\otimes m \cdot i},$$

where $m = n + \ell$.

Theorem 4. *Let $Q = \langle \Sigma, K, \Delta, k_{ini}, A \rangle$ be an encoded DFA, then H_{run} formulates the runs of Q of length b.*

Proof. Let x be $x = k_b\sigma_{b-1}k_{b-1}\cdots\sigma_2 k_1 \sigma_0 k_0$, where $\sigma_i \in \Sigma$ for $i \in [0, b-1]$, $k_i \in K$ for $i \in [0, b]$, and $k_0 = k_{ini}$, then

$$\langle x| \cdot H_{\text{run}} \cdot |x\rangle = \langle k_1 \sigma_0 k_{ini}| \cdot H_{\text{diff}} \cdot |k_1 \sigma_0 k_{ini}\rangle + \langle k_2 \sigma_1 k_1| \cdot H_{\text{diff}} \cdot |k_2 \sigma_1 k_1\rangle + \cdots +$$
$$\langle k_b \sigma_{b-1} k_{b-1}| \cdot H_{\text{diff}} \cdot |k_b \sigma_{b-1} k_{b-1}\rangle.$$

Because of Theorem 3,

$$\langle x| \cdot H_{\text{run}} \cdot |x\rangle = \begin{cases} 0 & \text{if } \Delta(k_i, \sigma_i) = k_{i+1} \text{ for } i = 0, \ldots, b-1 \\ p & \text{otherwise, for some } p > 0 \end{cases}$$

□

Now, let us consider the gate complexity to implement $e^{-i\cdot t\cdot H_{\text{run}}}$. Because of the modular design of H_{diff}, the product terms of Z_i's in one H_{diff} block do not affect the terms in other blocks. In other words, although some qubits are overlapping across two blocks as depicted in Fig. 5, the set of product terms, $\prod_{i \in J} Z_i$, of different blocks are disjoint. Hence, the gate complexity is simply the length of strings times the gate complexity of each $e^{-i\cdot t\cdot H_{\text{diff}}}$ module. That is,

$$\text{number of } CX \text{ gates} = O\left(b \cdot n \cdot (n + \ell) \cdot 2^{n+\ell}\right)$$
$$= O\left(b \cdot (\log_2 |K|^2 + \log_2 |K| \cdot \log_2 |\Sigma|) \cdot |K| \cdot |\Sigma|\right), \quad (9)$$
$$\text{number of } RZ \text{ gates} = O\left(b \cdot n \cdot 2^{n+\ell}\right) = O\left(b \cdot \log_2 |K| \cdot |K| \cdot |\Sigma|\right). \quad (10)$$

4.4 Hamiltonian for the Acceptance Condition of a FA

As a last component, let us consider a Hamiltonian for the acceptance conditions of a FA. Let $Q = \langle \Sigma, K, \Delta, k_{ini}, A \rangle$ be an encoded DFA with $n = \lceil \log_2 |K| \rceil$, then the acceptance condition, whether $k_{n-1}\cdots k_0 \in A$, can be written in a Boolean expression as

$$\text{accept}(k_{n-1}\cdots k_0) = \bigvee_{a \in A} \bigwedge_{i=0}^{n-1} B_{a_i}(k_i),$$

where $a = a_{n-1}\cdots a_0$ and $B_{a_i}(k_i) = \begin{cases} k_i & \text{if } a_i = 1 \\ \neg k_i & \text{if } a_i = 0 \end{cases}$

A Hamiltonian H_{accept} that represents the Boolean function *accept* can be constructed from its BDD. Because we are interested in minimizing a cost function, we construct a Hamiltonian that represents *reject*, i.e., $\text{reject}(k) = \neg \text{accept}(k)$, the negation of *accept*, as: $H_{\text{reject}} = I - H_{\text{accept}}$. H_{reject} formulates *accept* because

$$\langle k| \cdot H_{\text{reject}} \cdot |k\rangle = \begin{cases} 0 & \text{if } k \in A \\ 1 & \text{if } k \notin A \end{cases} \quad (11)$$

Because the BDD for reject is composed of n Boolean variables, based on Eq. (2) and Eq. (3), the gate complexity for $e^{-i \cdot t \cdot H_{\text{reject}}}$ is

$$\text{number of } CX \text{ gates} = O\left(n \cdot 2^n\right) = O\left(\log_2 |K| \cdot |K|\right), \quad (12)$$
$$\text{number of } RZ \text{ gates} = O\left(2^n\right) = O\left(|K|\right) \quad (13)$$

4.5 Hamiltonian for Deciding the the Acceptance of a String

Finally, combining the Hamiltonian H_{run} that identifies the valid runs of a FA and the Hamiltonian H_{reject} that checks whether a state is an accepting state, we build a Hamiltonian for the acceptance of a string. Figure 5 shows a block diagram of a quantum circuit simulating the evolution of quantum states by the combined Hamiltonian: $e^{-i \cdot t \cdot H_{\text{run}}}$ is constructed by cascading $e^{-i \cdot t \cdot H_{\text{diff}}}$'s for each symbol and appending $e^{-i \cdot t \cdot H_{\text{reject}}}$ to the last state of a run.

Definition 5. *Let $Q = \langle \Sigma, K, \Delta, k_{\text{ini}}, A\rangle$ be an encoded DFA, $n = \lceil \log_2 |K| \rceil$, and $\ell = \lceil \log_2 |\Sigma| \rceil$. We say that a Hamiltonian H_Q formulates an encoded DFA Q for strings of length b if for any bit string $x \in \{0,1\}^{b \cdot (n+\ell)+n}$,*

$$H_Q \cdot |x\rangle = \begin{cases} 0 \cdot |x\rangle & \text{if } x = k_b \sigma_{b-1} k_{b-1} \cdots k_1 \sigma_0 k_0, \text{ such that } \sigma_i \in \Sigma, k_i \in K, \\ & \Delta(k_i, \sigma_i) = k_{i+1}, k_0 = k_{\text{ini}}, \text{ and } k_b \in A, \\ p \cdot |x\rangle & \text{otherwise, where } p > 0 \end{cases}$$

We can construct such a Hamiltonian H_Q by multiplying H_{accept} to the resulting state of H_{run} as Fig. 5 shows. Let $m = n + \ell$, then we can build H_Q as:

$$H_Q = H_{\text{run}} + H_{\text{reject}} \otimes I^{\otimes m \cdot (b-1)}$$

Theorem 5. *Let $Q = \langle \Sigma, K, \Delta, k_{\text{ini}}, A\rangle$ be an encoded DFA, then H_Q formulates Q for strings of length b.*

Proof. Let x be $x = k_b \sigma_{b-1} k_{b-1} \cdots \sigma_2 k_1 \sigma_0 k_0$, where $\sigma_i \in \Sigma$ for $i \in [0, b-1]$, $k_i \in K$ for $i \in [0,b]$, and $k_0 = k_{\text{ini}}$. Using Theorem 4 and Eq. (11),

$$\langle x| \cdot H_Q \cdot |x\rangle = \langle x| \cdot H_{\text{run}} \cdot |x\rangle + \langle k_b| \cdot H_{\text{reject}} \cdot |k_b\rangle$$
$$= \begin{cases} 0 & \text{if } k_b \cdots k_0 \text{ is a valid run and } \sigma_{b-1} \cdots \sigma_0 \text{ is accepted by } Q \\ p & \text{otherwise, where } p > 0 \end{cases}$$

□

Example 6. Continuing from Example 5, let us construct H_Q for the strings of length 2. Figure 5 shows us a hint: it implements $e^{-i \cdot t \cdot H_Q}$ by adding $e^{-i \cdot t \cdot H_{\text{reject}}}$ to the last output state q_6. H_{reject} represents the BDD of Fig. 2(b) because the only accepting state of Q is 1. Hence, the Hamiltonian H_Q that formulates Q for the strings of length 2 is

$$H_Q = H_{\text{run}} + \tfrac{1}{2}(I + Z_6) = I^{\otimes 3} \otimes H_{\text{diff}} + H_{\text{diff}} \otimes I^{\otimes 3} + \tfrac{1}{2}(I + Z_6)$$
$$= \tfrac{1}{8}\left(4I - 4Z_3 + 5Z_3 - 3Z_{30} - Z_{31} - Z_{32} - Z_{301} - Z_{302} + Z_{312} + Z_{3012}\right)$$
$$+ \tfrac{1}{8}\left(4I - 4Z_6 + 5Z_6 - 3Z_{63} - Z_{64} - Z_{65} - Z_{634} - Z_{635} + Z_{645} + Z_{6345}\right)$$
$$+ \tfrac{1}{2}(I + Z_6)$$

As an example, let us check the expected energies of H_Q for the runs $0 \xrightarrow{11} 0 \xrightarrow{11} 1$ (invalid run), $0 \xrightarrow{01} 0 \xrightarrow{01} 0$ (valid rejecting run), and $0 \xrightarrow{01} 0 \xrightarrow{11} 1$ (valid accepting run).

$$\langle 1\,11\,0\,11\,0| \cdot H_Q \cdot |1\,11\,0\,11\,0\rangle = \langle 0110| \cdot H_{\text{diff}} \cdot |0110\rangle + \langle 1110| \cdot H_{\text{diff}} \cdot |1110\rangle + 0$$
$$= 1 + 0 + 0$$
$$\langle 0\,01\,0\,01\,0| \cdot H_Q \cdot |0\,01\,0\,01\,0\rangle = \langle 0010| \cdot H_{\text{diff}} \cdot |0010\rangle + \langle 0010| \cdot H_{\text{diff}} \cdot |0010\rangle + 1$$
$$= 0 + 0 + 1$$
$$\langle 1\,11\,0\,01\,0| \cdot H_Q \cdot |1\,11\,0\,01\,0\rangle = \langle 0010| \cdot H_{\text{diff}} \cdot |0010\rangle + \langle 1110| \cdot H_{\text{diff}} \cdot |1110\rangle + 0$$
$$= 0 + 0 + 0$$

$\square$

Let us compute the gate complexity to implement $e^{-i \cdot t \cdot H_Q}$. Because H_Q can be constructed by adding H_{reject} to H_{run} and because they are both diagonal matrices, $e^{-i \cdot t \cdot H_Q}$ can be implemented by multiplying $e^{-i \cdot t \cdot H_{\text{reject}}}$ to $e^{-i \cdot t \cdot H_{\text{run}}}$ as in Fig. 5. Hence, the gate counts for $e^{-i \cdot t \cdot H_Q}$ are Eq. (9) and Eq. (10) for $e^{-i \cdot t \cdot H_{\text{run}}}$ plus Eq. (12) and Eq. (13) for $e^{-i \cdot t \cdot H_{\text{reject}}}$ respectively for CX and RZ gates. However, because $e^{-i \cdot t \cdot H_{\text{reject}}}$ occurs only once at the end of b state transitions, its gate counts can be ignored in the big O notation. Hence, the gate complexity to implement $e^{-i \cdot t \cdot H_Q}$ is the same as Eq. (9) and Eq. (10).

5 Example

The ground states of the cost Hamiltonian H_Q for an encoded FA Q satisfy the state transition conditions as well as the acceptance condition. Hence, the accepted strings of a FA are in the ground states of its cost Hamiltonian H_Q. In this section, we utilize *Quantum Approximate Optimization Algorithm* (QAOA) [10] to find the accepted strings of a FA. QAOA is a hybrid optimization algorithm, where a parameterized quantum circuit simulates the evolution of quantum states and a classical algorithm finds a set of simulation durations such that a ground state can be measured. In particular, given a set of parameters $\gamma = \{\gamma_0, \ldots, \gamma_{s-1}\}$ and $\beta = \{\beta_0, \ldots, \beta_{s-1}\}$, QAOA alternately simulates a *problem* Hamiltonian H_p for γ_i and a *mixer* Hamiltonian H_m for β_i starting from a ground state $|x_{ini}\rangle$ of H_m to a final state $|x_{\gamma,\beta}\rangle$. That is,

$$|x_{\gamma,\beta}\rangle = e^{-i \cdot \beta_{s-1} \cdot H_m} \cdot e^{-i \cdot \gamma_{s-1} \cdot H_p} \ldots e^{-i \cdot \beta_0 \cdot H_m} \cdot e^{-i \cdot \gamma_0 \cdot H_p} \cdot |x_{ini}\rangle.$$

The initial state $|x_{ini}\rangle$ is a known ground state of H_m and based on the *adiabatic theorem* [11], if the system change is slow enough, the final state $|x_{\gamma,\beta}\rangle$ remains at a ground state throughout the changes. A classical optimization algorithm finds the simulation durations γ_i and β_i for $i = 0, \ldots, s - 1$ such that the expected energy $\langle x_{\gamma,\beta}| \cdot H_p \cdot |x_{\gamma,\beta}\rangle$ is minimized.

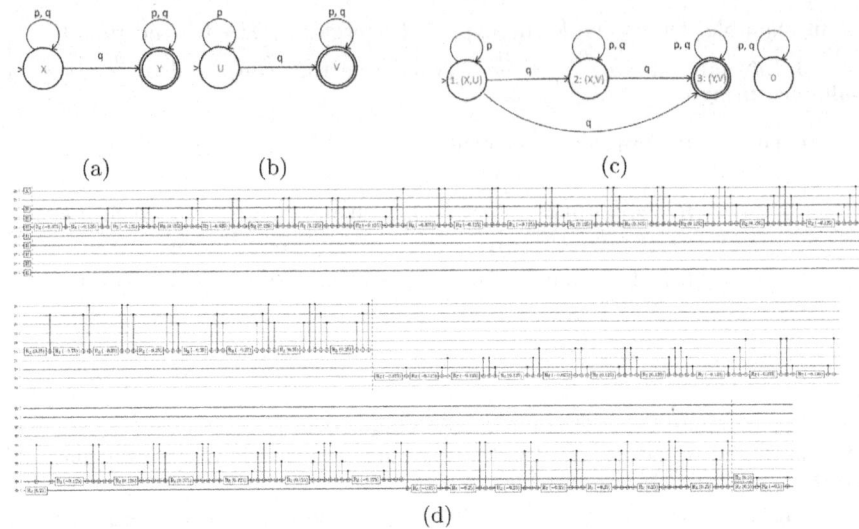

Fig. 6. (a) A state transition diagram for A. (b) A state transition diagram for $\overline{B}$. (c) A state transition diagram for $A \cap \overline{B}$. (d) A quantum circuit for simulating the Hamiltonian of the intersection automaton for the strings of length 2.

5.1 Model Validation Problem

Let $\mathcal{L}(A)$ and $\mathcal{L}(B)$ be the set of strings accepted by NFAs A and B respectively. A regular language containment problem decides whether $\mathcal{L}(A) \subseteq \mathcal{L}(B)$ [24]. Model checking is an example of a language containment problem that checks whether $\mathcal{L}(A)$, the behaviors of a system, are contained in $\mathcal{L}(B)$, the allowed behaviors of a specification [7]. $\mathcal{L}(A) \subseteq \mathcal{L}(B)$ can be checked by examining the emptiness of $\mathcal{L}(A \cap \overline{B})$, the language accepted by the intersection automaton between A and $\overline{B}$, the negation of B.

Figure 6(a), Fig. 6 (b), and Fig. 6(c) are state transition diagrams of A, $\overline{B}$, and $A \cap \overline{B}$ respectively. For an encoded DFA Q of the intersection automaton $A \cap \overline{B}$, we construct a Hamiltonian H_Q that formulates Q for strings of length 2. Figure 6(d) shows a synthesized quantum circuit for $e^{-i \cdot t \cdot H_Q}$. The quantum circuit in between the first and the third barriers implements $e^{-i \cdot t \cdot H_{\text{run}}}$ for the runs of Q of length 2. This circuit is composed of 2×24 RZ gates and 2×88 CX gates. The three RZ gates after the third barrier implement $e^{-i \cdot t \cdot H_{\text{reject}}}$ for the acceptance condition.

Using the quantum circuit of Fig. 6(d), we construct a QAOA circuit composed of 20 layers ($s = 20$) of problem and mixer simulations. The COBYLA optimization algorithm [8] is employed to find the optimal values for the 20 γ_i and 20 β_i parameters, which are initialized to 0.1. We multiplied a weight of 0.5 to H_{reject} and a larger weight of 1.0 to H_{run}, considering that accepted strings from invalid runs are useless. Figure 7(a) shows the measurement histogram of all runs: out of the total 1024 runs, 340 runs are valid accepting runs (33.20%).

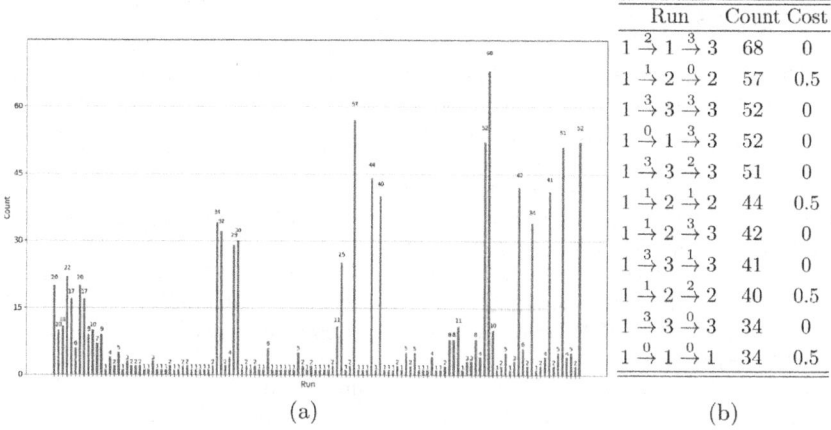

Fig. 7. (a) Histogram of runs. (b) Top occurrences of decoded runs with their counts and costs.

Due to the space limitations, showing the bit strings on the x-axis is not useful and thus, in Fig. 7(b), we listed only the runs with the top counts. In the table, the cost of 0 means that the run is valid and the string is accepted.

Because there are runs with the cost of 0 in Fig. 7 (b), $\mathcal{L}(A \cap \overline{B})$ is not empty and those runs are counterexamples witnessing $\mathcal{L}(A) \nsubseteq \mathcal{L}(B)$.

6 Conclusion

We have developed a translation technique for a FA to a cost Hamiltonian. The technique provides an abstraction mechanism that enables a user to describe problems in a FA and solve them on a quantum computer without knowing the details of the complex quantum mechanism. The gate complexity of a synthesized quantum circuit for a NFA is linear with respect to the length of input strings. The usefulness of the translation technique is experimentally demonstrated by solving a model validation problem using Qiskit.

A set of rules to synthesize a Hamiltonian representing a BDD is developed as well. Because BDDs often represent a Boolean function more compactly than Boolean expressions, this translation technique would be useful especially when translating a large Boolean function into a quantum circuit.

The translation technique for a FA to a Hamiltonian opens a new possibility to bring a wide range of problems expressed in FAs to utilize quantum technologies. Moreover, translation techniques for an abstract description of a problem to a quantum circuit will be more useful as quantum computers with a large number of qubits [5,6] are being developed rapidly.

Acknowledgement. This work was supported by the MSIT, Korea, under the ICTCCP(IITP-2020-2011-1-00783) supervised by the IITP.

References

1. Aho, A., Ullman, J., Sethi, R., Lam, M.: Compilers: Principles, Techniques, and Tools, 2nd edn. Addison Wesley (2006)
2. Biere, A., Cimatti, A., Clarke, E., Zhu, Y.: Symbolic model checking without BDDs. In: Cleaveland, W.R. (eds) TACAS 1999. LNCS, vol. 1579, pp. 193–207. Springer, Heidelberg (1999). https://doi.org/10.1007/3-540-49059-0_14
3. Bryant, R.E.: Graph-based algorithms for Boolean function manipulation. IEEE Trans. Comput. **C-35**(8), 677–691 (1986)
4. Campbell, C., Dahl, E.: QAOA of the highest order. In: IEEE International Conference on Software Architecture Companion, pp. 141–146 (2022)
5. Castelvecchi, D.: IBM releases first-ever 1,000-qubit quantum chip. Nature **624**(238) (2023)
6. Choi, C.Q.: IBM unveils 433-qubit osprey chip > next year entanglement hits the kilo-scale with big blue's 1,121-qubit condor. IEEE Spectrum (2022)
7. Clarke, E.M., Grumberg, O., Peled, D.A.: Model checking. MIT Press (1999)
8. Conn, A.R., Scheinberg, K., Toint, P.L.: On the convergence of derivative-free methods for unconstrained optimization. In: Approximation Theory and Optimization: Tributes to MJD Powell, pp. 83–108 (1997)
9. Aleksandrowicz, G., et. al.: Qiskit: an open-source framework for quantum computing (2021)
10. Farhi, E., Goldstone, J., Gutmann, S.: A quantum approximate optimization algorithm. arXiv preprint arXiv:1411.4028 (2014)
11. Farhi, E., Goldstone, J., Gutmann, S., Lapan, J., Preda, A.L.D.: A quantum adiabatic evolution algorithm applied to random instances of an Np-complete problem. Science **292**, 472–475 (2001)
12. De Giacomo, G., Vardi, M.Y.: Linear temporal logic and linear dynamic logic on finite traces. In: Proceedings of the Twenty-Third International Joint Conference on Artificial Intelligence, IJCAI 2013, pp. 854–860. AAAI Press (2013)
13. Grimaldi, R.P.: Discrete and Combinatorial Mathematics An Applied Introduction, 2nd edn. Addison Wesley (1989)
14. Grover, L.K.: A fast quantum mechanical algorithm for database search. In: Proceedings of the Twenty-Eighth Annual ACM Symposium on Theory of Computing, pp. 212–219. Association for Computing Machinery (1996)
15. Hadfield, S.: On the Representation of Boolean and Real Functions as Hamiltonians for Quantum Computing. ACM Trans. Quantum Comput. **2**, 1–21 (2021)
16. Kaeslin, H.: Digital Integrated Circuit Design: From VLSI Architectures to CMOS Fabrication, 1st edn. Cambridge University Press (2008)
17. Kochenberger, G., et al.: The unconstrained binary quadratic programming problem: a survey. J. Combin. Optim. **28**, 58–81 (2014)
18. Kondacs, A., Watrous, J.: On the power of quantum finite state automata. In: Proceedings 38th Annual Symposium on Foundations of Computer Science, pp. 66–75 (1997)
19. Kwon, Y.M., Agha, G.: Bounded quantum regular language generator. In: IEEE International Conference on Quantum Computing and Engineering, pp. 580–590 (2023)
20. Kwon, Y.M., Kim, E.: Bounded model checking of hybrid systems for control. IEEE Trans. Autom. Control **60**, 2961–2976 (2015)
21. Lewis, H., Papadimitriou, C.H.: Elements of the Theory of Computation, 2nd edn. Prentice-Hall (1998)

22. Lewis, H.R., Papadimitriou, C.H.: Elements of the Theory of Computation, 2nd edn. Prentice-Hall (1998)
23. Lucas, A.: Ising formulations of many Np problems. Front. Phys. **2**, 1–27 (2014)
24. Meyer, A.R., Stockmeyer, L.J.: The equivalence problem for regular expressions with squaring requires exponential space. In: 13th Annual Symposium on Switching and Automata Theory (swat 1972), pp. 125–129 (1972)
25. Moore, C., Crutchfield, J.P.: Quantum automata and quantum grammars. Theoret. Comput. Sci. **237**(1), 275–306 (2000)
26. O'Malley, P.J.J., et al.: Scalable quantum simulation of molecular energies. Phys. Rev. X **6**, 031007 (2016)
27. Peruzzo, A., et al.: A variational eigenvalue solver on a photonic quantum processor. Nat. Commun. **5**, 1–7 (2014)
28. Shende, V.V., Prasad, A.K., Markov, I.L., Hayes, J.P.: Synthesis of reversible logic circuits. IEEE Trans. Comput. Aided Des. Integr. Circuits Syst. **22**(6), 710–722 (2003)
29. Shor, P.W.: Algorithms for quantum computation: discrete logarithms and factoring. In: Proceedings 35th Annual Symposium on Foundations of Computer Science, pp. 124–134 (1994)
30. Somenzi, F.: Cudd: Cu decision diagram package release 2.4.1 (2005)
31. Somma, R.D., Nagaj, D., Kieferová, M.: Quantum speedup by quantum annealing. Phys. Rev. Lett. **109**, 050501 (2012)
32. Tian, Y., Feng, T., Luo, M., Zheng, S., Zhou, X.: Experimental demonstration of quantum finite automaton. NPJ Quantum Inf.**5** (2019)
33. Welch, J., Greenbaum, D., Mostame, S., Aspuru-Guzik, A.: Efficient quantum circuits for diagonal unitaries without ancillas. New J. Phys. **16**, 1–15 (2014)
34. Wille, R., Drechsler, R.: Towards a Design Flow for Reversible Logic. Springer, Dordrecht (2010)

Decentralized Machine Learning with Asynchronous Communication

Tavonput Luangphasy and Xinghui Zhao[✉]

School of Engineering and Computer Science, Washington State University,
Vancouver, WA 98686, USA
{tavonput.luangphasy,x.zhao}@wsu.edu

Abstract. Edge devices, which include a wide range of hardware from smartphones to IoT sensors, wearables, and autonomous vehicles, exhibit considerable heterogeneity in terms of computational power, memory, network capabilities, and data availability. This diversity introduces several challenges for distributed machine learning frameworks, such as federated learning. In this paper, we integrated the actor model of concurrency with federated learning, and supported the distributed learning process using asynchronous communication. Our experimental results show this approach has great potential of achieving better performance when executing on heterogeneous edge devices. Using the actor model as the underlying computational platform, we expect that decentralized machine learning paradigms can become more efficient and widely applicable across diverse and large-scale edge AI applications. This shift toward asynchronous and distributed learning architectures is crucial for the future of personalized AI, industrial automation, healthcare, and autonomous systems, where real-time learning and adaptability are essential.

Keywords: Actor Model · Federated Learning · Asynchronous Communication · Edge Computing

1 Introduction

The rapid expansion of the Internet of Things (IoT) has transformed industries by enabling real-time data collection and intelligent decision-making at an unprecedented scale [3,14,24]. From smart cities and industrial automation to healthcare monitoring and autonomous vehicles, IoT devices continuously generate vast amounts of data. In many IoT scenarios, devices operate in environments where sending raw data to a centralized cloud for processing introduces high latency and bandwidth constraints. For example, in autonomous driving, self-driving cars rely on real-time machine learning models to make split-second decisions. A delay in sending data to a cloud server for inference and receiving a response could lead to accidents. Instead, distributed learning at the edge allows each vehicle to locally process data, train models, and even share insights with other vehicles or infrastructure (such as traffic lights or smart roads) in a decentralized manner. Distributed Machine Learning has become essential to efficiently train and deploy AI models across millions of connected IoT devices.

Besides efficiency, data privacy is another key driving factor for distributed machine learning [22]. Healthcare IoT devices, such as wearable monitors or hospital sensors, generate sensitive patient data. Instead of sending raw patient data to a centralized server, distributed machine learning enables each device to train a local model and share only encrypted model updates. This ensures compliance with data privacy regulations while still benefiting from collaborative learning across multiple devices. Similarly, smart home assistants and industrial IoT systems use distributed learning to improve their AI capabilities without exposing confidential user or operational data to external networks [19].

Furthermore, scalability and fault tolerance make distributed machine learning indispensable for IoT ecosystems. As IoT networks grow, centralized machine learning solutions become bottlenecked by increasing computational demands and network congestion. Distributed machine learning allows dynamic scaling, where additional devices can join the learning process without overwhelming a single central server. Moreover, if an IoT node fails, redundant nodes can take over, ensuring uninterrupted model training and inference. This resilience is particularly critical in critical infrastructure, such as energy grids, industrial automation, and aerospace systems, where system failures can have severe consequences. With billions of IoT devices generating data at the edge, distributed machine learning is no longer optional—it is essential. It ensures low-latency AI processing, privacy-preserving learning, real-time adaptability, and efficient resource utilization, making modern IoT ecosystems smarter, faster, and more autonomous.

Federated Learning [10,12,17] is a widely used distributed machine learning approach, which enables multiple devices or edge nodes to collaboratively train a shared model without sharing raw data. The process begins with a global model initialized by a central server and sent to participating devices. Each device trains the model locally using its own private dataset, computing model updates (such as weight adjustments or gradients) instead of sharing raw data. These local updates are then sent back to the central aggregator, where they are combined using techniques like Federated Averaging (FedAvg) [17] to improve the global model. Once the updates are aggregated, the refined model is redistributed to all devices, and the process repeats iteratively until convergence. This approach requires all devices to complete their local training before aggregating model updates, which can introduce delays, especially in heterogeneous environments where devices have varying computational power, connectivity, and availability [13,15,27]. Therefore, deploying federated learning efficiently in a heterogeneous and dynamic environment is challenging [12].

To address these challenges, we have investigated various ways to support federated learning paradigms with asynchronous communication, leveraging the Actor model of concurrency. Specifically, we have built distributed system architectures in which model updates are performed asynchronously, eliminating the requirement of frequency synchronization. Various communication paradigms are explored and evaluated.

2 Related Work

Federated Learning [17] has emerged as a crucial paradigm for privacy-preserving, distributed AI training across various domains, including healthcare, finance, IoT, and mobile computing. Initially introduced by Google in 2016, FL has evolved into a key enabler of edge AI, allowing devices to collaboratively learn from decentralized data while minimizing privacy risks. Since then, federated learning has been widely used in many real-world applications. However, despite its advancements, federated learning still faces technical and deployment challenges. One of the major challenges is the straggler problem, which arises when some participating clients (devices) take significantly longer to complete local model training and send updates to the central server. This issue is particularly common in heterogeneous environments, where devices vary in processing power, network stability, battery constraints, and workload capacity. In traditional federated learning, the server waits for all selected clients to finish before aggregating model updates. Therefore, the slowest devices, i.e., stragglers, can delay the entire learning process, leading to inefficiencies, slower convergence, and underutilization of resources. This bottleneck is especially problematic in IoT, mobile edge computing, and large-scale federated networks, where client capabilities are highly diverse.

Various approaches have been proposed to address these challenges introduced by the heterogeneity of edge devices. For example, instead of using all clients in every training round, the server selects a subset of faster, more reliable clients to participate [5,25]. This approach, through client selection and sampling, improves efficiency while still ensuring diverse data contributions over multiple rounds. Deadline-based aggregation [11,23] is another widely adopted approach. The server sets a time limit for each round. Clients that fail to submit updates within the deadline are excluded or their updates are given lower weight in aggregation. In addition, there are approaches for creating efficient model compression and communication [26], e.g., gradient sparsification, quantization, and model pruning. These approaches reduce the size of model updates, allowing slow devices to send updates faster.

In this paper, we take a different approach by allowing model updates through asynchronous communication. This approach is built upon the Actor model of concurrency. The Actor model [1] provides a convenient way to program parallel applications. In the Actor model, autonomous concurrently executing objects called actors, communicate with each other using buffered, asynchronous, point-to-point messages. An actor encapsulates a state, a number of methods, which can change the state of the actor, and a thread of control. Actors are distributed over time and space. Each actor has a globally unique mail address, and it maintains a queue of unprocessed messages it has received. Figure 1 shows the structure of an actor. The Actor model has become the *de facto* model of concurrency underlying a number of languages [4,20,21], and it has also been widely used in large-scale cloud-based applications, such as Facebook and Twitter, among others [2].

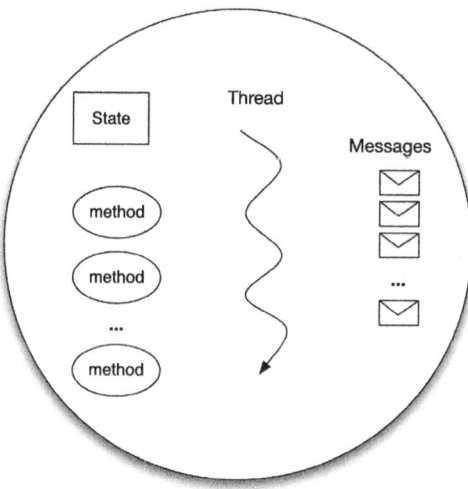

Fig. 1. Structure of an Actor.

The Actor model is especially beneficial for distributed machine learning, as its architecture ensures fault tolerance, i.e., failed actors can be restarted without affecting the overall system. Additionally, the dynamic scalability of the Actor Model allows for automatic allocation and deallocation of resources, optimizing workload distribution across cloud or edge computing environments. In the context of federated learning, where decentralized devices train local models before aggregating updates, actors provide a natural way to manage individual nodes without strict global synchronization requirements.

3 System Design for Asynchronous Federated Learning

To fully exploit the potential of using the Actor model to support asynchronous federated learning, we have investigated various system architectures and communication patterns. In this section, we introduce four different federated learning paradigms, Traditional Server-Client, Asynchronous Server-Client, Asynchronous Peer-to-Peer, and Asynchronous Hybrid, as shown in Fig. 2. For each approach, we discuss an overview of the system, the system structured in the context of the actor model if applicable, and an analysis on the potential benefits and challenges of the model.

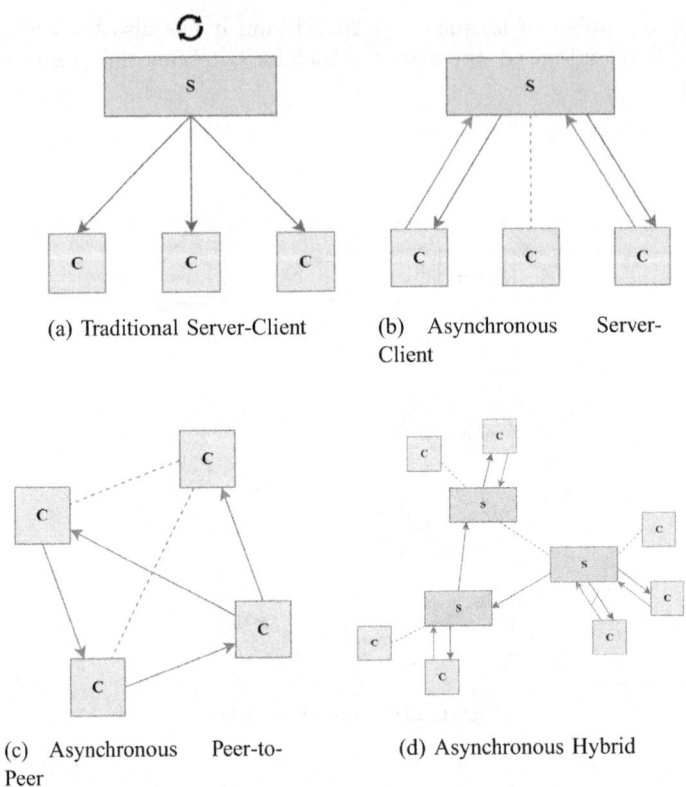

Fig. 2. Traditional and Asynchronous System Architectures.

3.1 Traditional Server-Client

The Traditional Server-Client architecture, shown in Fig. 2(a), follows the synchronous training structure proposed in the original federated learning work. The system consists of one central server and a number of clients, all working in parallel. The server is responsible for aggregating parameter updates from the clients and orchestrating the federated learning process by sending training tasks to the clients. The clients are responsible for processing training tasks using their own local datasets and send parameter updates back to the server. Thus, the typical pipeline for a federated learning round is as follows: First, the server sends training tasks to the clients along with an updated model to train. Second, each client will train the given model with their local data in parallel. Once a client finishes, it will send its updates back to the server; Finally, once all clients have finished, the server will aggregate all the updates and issue the next federated learning round.

In the traditional setup, this federated learning pipeline requires synchronization between the server and clients. For example, when the server sends the training requests to the clients, the server will block until all clients have responded with their updates. Although, with a minor change to how the server waits for client responses, we can modify the server's behavior to be asynchronous, thus allowing the usage of the actor model.

In this architecture, two types of actors are implemented, namely ServerActor and ClientActor. The ServerActor will allocate training tasks to clients by maintaining an internal counter and will additionally handle update aggregation. The ServerActor can receive the following message:

- **ClientUpdate:** Contains the training results of a client. Upon receiving, the ServerActor will increment its internal counter and store the context of the ClientUpdate. Once the internal counter reaches a threshold, the ServerActor will perform update aggregation, send out new training messages, and reset the internal counter.

For example, as shown in Fig. 2(a), the ServerActor sends out training requests to three clients. The ServerActor will then expect three ClientUpdate messages and will use the internal counter to keep track of this. Once three ClientUpdate messages have been received, the ServerActor can proceed to aggregation and can follow up by sending out the next round of training requests.

The ClientActor in this architecture will process training tasks on local data and send the updated parameters back to the server. The ClientActor can receive the following message:

- **Train:** Contains a model to train and the training context (i.e. round, epochs, ...). Upon receiving, the ClientActor will proceed with the training process with its local data. On completion, the ClientActor will send a ClientUpdate message to the ServerActor.

With these two types of actors, the traditional server-client model can be expressed with asynchronous message passing and thus be structured with the actor model.

The traditional server-client approach allows the machine learning model to be learned in a synchronous fashion, even when using asynchronous communication. Every training round, the participating clients will all be sent the same model. Additionally, the actor implementation allows the server to process tasks while the clients are training. Though, the traditional server-client approach does pose some challenges related to efficiency and scalability. Despite the use of asynchronous communication, the server still needs to wait for all clients to finish training before the next round can proceed. Thus, straggler clients, those that exhibit longer responses, will still slow down the system from proceeding. Additionally, clients that fail to respond, possibly due to a crash, will halt the training system entirely unless a timeout is in place.

3.2 Asynchronous Server-Client

The Asynchronous Server-Client model follows a similar structure to the actor-based Traditional Server-Client model, where the server sends clients train tasks and the clients respond with model updates. The difference is in the server aggregation stage and when the training tasks are sent out. Instead of waiting for all clients to respond, the asynchronous server will process client updates immediately as they come in. Once a client update is processed, a new training task is again immediately sent back to the client. This removes the requirement for all participating clients to finish training before the next round can start. Note that the ClientActor for the Asynchronous Server-Client model will be the same as in the Traditional model.

The new immediate aggregation and train allocation process requires a different implementation of the ServerActor upon receiving a ClientUpdate. The new ClientUpdate message will be processed as follows:

- **ClientUpdate:** Contains the training results of a ClientActor. Upon receiving, the ServerActor will perform an update aggregation and send out a new training message back to the ClientActor.

Again, the Asynchronous Server-Client approach removes the need for a client to wait for all other clients to finish. When a client completes its training task and sends its update to the server, the client will receive the next training task once the server processes the update. Unlike the Traditional model, the server will handle ClientUpdates immediately as they come in instead of waiting for the arrival of all ClientUpdates. This allows for greater computational efficiency as we are able to minimize the training downtime. Additionally, the system is more robust to client failures. In the Traditional model, if a client goes down, it will potential halt the entire system as it is unable to provide its response. The removal of cross-client dependency in the Asynchronous Server-Client model eliminates this issue entirely. This approach also provides greater scalability as a growing number of clients can become a bottleneck with a synchronous structure.

Despite the before mentioned advantages of the Asynchronous Server-Client model, this structure will impose new challenges. Due to the introduction of asynchronous updating, the problem of information staleness becomes apparent in heterogeneous device settings. Updates from slower clients represent older versions of the global model, potentially degrading convergence. To combat the staleness problem, we can introduce techniques such as staleness weighting or incorporating delay-awareness into the aggregation function. Additionally, challenges in communication efficiency and scalability can still be an issue due to the decrease in client downtime. The increased communication traffic, caused by more frequent updates, consumes more bandwidth and can potentially overwhelm the server at a large scale. Techniques such as sparse updates and quantization have been developed to help mitigate this issue [8,9,16]. For example, topâĂŠk sparsification methods selectively transmit only the largest gradient components, often combined with quantization to reduce bit-width per value. Quantized update schemes (e.g., one-bit or multi-bit global update quantization) compress both server-to-client and client-to-server communications with minimal impact on convergence.

3.3 Asynchronous Peer-to-Peer

To address the robustness and scalability limitation of the server-client model, we can introduce the Asynchronous Peer-to-Peer model. This approach eliminates the reliance on a central server by removing it entirely, distributing the responsibility for update aggregation and training coordination among a decentralized client network. By adopting a decentralized topology we enable clients to directly communicate and exchange model updates with one another, improving scalability and fault tolerance concerns.

A typical asynchronous decentralized workflow will consist of a network of clients. Each client will have the following computation pipeline: First, the client will train their model on local data. Once training is complete, the updated model will be sent out to other clients. Then, the client will process any incoming updates that it had received while training, aggregating them into its local model. Finally, the client will begin the next training round and repeat this process.

To formalize the Asynchronous Peer-to-Peer system into the actor model, we only need the ClientActor. The ClientActor will now be responsible for the following tasks: local training, sending model updates to other ClientActors, and aggregating updates from other ClientActors. The ClientActor messages are defined as follows:

- **Train:** Upon receiving, the ClientActor will proceed with the training process with its local data. On completion, the ClientActor will send a ReceiveUpdate message to other ClientActors. Additionally, the ClientActor will send the next Train message to itself.
- **ReceiveUpdate:** Contains the training results of an external ClientActor. Upon receiving, the local ClientActor will perform an aggregation to incorporate the incoming update in into the local learning model.

Notice here that the ClientActor Train message does not contain a model to train or a training context as done in the Asynchronous Server-Client model. Since there is no server, the ClientActor acts independently, thus maintains the state of its own learning model and training context. Additionally, we assume the actors are able to send themselves messages. Although, if self-messaging is not allowed, this functionality can still be reproduced by an actor spawning a child actor to send the message back to themselves.

The Asynchronous Peer-to-Peer model offers several advantages over the Server-Client approaches, particularly in terms of fault tolerance, scalability, and compute efficiency. By removing the reliance on a central server, we eliminate the single point of failure, ensuring that the system can continue to operate during the event of a failure to any part of the system. The decentralized architecture also enhances scalability and compute efficiency, as the computation load is distributed across the network, allowing for optimal handling of large scale systems with many clients. Additionally, with this approach being asynchronous, it also inherits the core benefits of the Asynchronous Server-Client model.

Despite its advantages, the Asynchronous Peer-to-Peer model still faces a fair number of challenges. One major issue is the complexity of convergence by operating in an asynchronous and decentralized setting. It shares the same information staleness problem as in the Asynchronous Server-Client model, causing potentially unstable convergence and learning model divergence. Additionally communication overhead can become a bottleneck in dense or unoptimized networks, as frequent peer-to-peer exchanges may require higher bandwidth. Finally, managing the network topology efficiently is nontrivial, as poorly connected or unbalanced topologies can hinder overall performance.

Potential solutions to these challenges focus on improving the efficiency and robustness of the learning process. To address the staleness and communication efficient issues, the same solutions for the Asynchronous Server-Client model can be used, in particular, staleness-aware aggregation, sparse updates, and quantization. For structuring efficient network topologies, a dynamic approach can be used to improve connectivity and information flow.

3.4 Asynchronous Hyrbid

The asynchronous hybrid model integrates both server-client and peer-to-peer communication, effectively functioning as a cluster-based system. Each cluster operates an asynchronous server-client system, where clients train models and communicate updates asynchronously with a designated server. Meanwhile, inter-cluster communication occurs in a peer-to-peer fashion, allowing clusters to exchange model updates. This structure enables a two-level workflow:

- **Intra-cluster level:** Within a cluster, the system follows the asynchronous server-client workflow. Clients train locally and send updates to their respective server, which aggregates and maintains the cluster-wide model.
- **Inter-cluster level:** Servers from different clusters exchange model updates, allowing information to be shared across the system. Each server periodically communicates its cluster's model state to other servers.

To structure this hybrid system with actors, we first note that the ClientActor will be the same as in the asynchronous server-client approach. Then we can define the ServerActor messages as the following:

- **ClientUpdate:** Contains training results from a client. Upon receiving this request, the server aggregates the update into its cluster-wide model and sends a new training request back to the client. Additionally, it triggers an inter-cluster update, broadcasting the current state of the model to other servers.
- **ServerUpdate:** Contains the model parameters from an external training cluster. Upon receiving this request, the server integrates the external update with its cluster-wide model through aggregation.

This hybrid model offers a balance between the fully centralized and fully decentralized approaches. It inherits the robustness seen in the peer-to-peer system while also allowing the clients to focus their computational resources on training, as model aggregation and inter-cluster communication is done by the server. As noted in the peer-to-peer architecture, the server-client models suffer from a single point of failure, that being the central server. The hybrid approach allows the system to continue learning in the event of a server failure since there will still be other servers running. Additionally, the clients attached to the failed server could temperately migrate to functioning servers.

Special Case of Asynchronous Hybrid. Notice, when we configure the asynchronous hybrid system such that the number of servers equals the number of clients and each server is assigned a single client, the system closely resembles the asynchronous peer-to-peer approach. In this special case, each node consists of a server-client pair, where the client is responsible for training, while the server handles external communication by sending out training results and aggregating incoming updates. However, despite their structural similarity, this setup is not algorithmically equivalent to the fully asynchronous peer-to-peer system, specifically in the internal handling of model aggregation. Our motivation for exploring this special case comes from empirical observations showing that this seemingly identical setup to the peer-to-peer system performs differently. Additionally, since server and client actors exist as distinct entities, a server-client pair incurs increased resource allocation when compared to the fully peer-to-peer approach, where only clients participate. Though, this resource allocation problem can be potentially mitigated by combining the server-client pair into a single entity, effectively merging their roles. This could reduce resource consumption while preserving the system's behavior in decentralized update sharing.

4 Experimental Results

4.1 Evaluation Actors

The proposed actor-based federated learning system introduces differences in communication and computational patterns, such as synchronous versus asynchronous execution. These differences can lead to unfair comparisons when evaluating accuracy over time. Model evaluation requires computing predictions on a test set, and in an ideal federated learning setup, we aim to assess model accuracy after each federated round. However, frequent evaluations impose significant computational demands on clients, as the time required for testing is non-trivial. Since we measure training performance over time, allocating compute resources for evaluation may lead to misleading results. This issue is further heightened in asynchronous settings, where additional evaluation benchmarks can negatively impact performance. In heterogeneous environments with devices of varying computational power and network speeds, faster clients may spend disproportionate time on evaluations compared to slower clients, further skewing fairness. An illustration of this issue is shown in Fig. 3

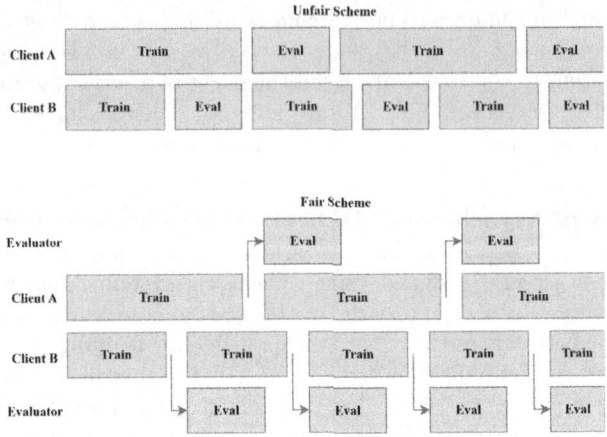

Fig. 3. Illustration of an unfair and a fair evaluation scheme. In the unfair scheme, Client B spends more resources computing benchmarks than Client A. In the fair scheme, both clients offload their evaluation to separate evaluator nodes.

To address this unfair evaluation problem, we leverage the actor model by introducing evaluation actors, or evaluators, into the system. Evaluators are dedicated nodes responsible for offloading evaluation computations from clients. When a client completes a training round, instead of performing a local evaluation, it sends a copy of its model to an evaluator, which handles the evaluation asynchronously. The client can then proceed immediately to the next training round. This process is illustrated in Fig. 3.

We define the evaluation actor with the following message type:

- **Evaluate:** Contains a model to evaluate along with relevant context (e.g., client id, time stamp). Upon receiving this request, the evaluator tests the model on the designated test set and stores the results.

By offloading evaluation to dedicated evaluators, clients avoid additional computational overhead, eliminating benchmarking-related delays. Furthermore, since clients no longer need to store or fetch test data, they benefit from reduced memory usage and improved efficiency.

4.2 Experiment Design

To demonstrate the benefits of asynchronous communication and computation patterns in federated learning, we design an experiment in a heterogeneous device setting. We simulate varying compute capabilities by assigning an efficiency level to each client, where lower efficiencies are modeled by inserting delays after each local epoch. This approach mimics real-world federated learning scenarios where clients have different hardware capabilities, network considerations, or workloads, leading to varying processing speeds. We define a system with 8 clients: 4 operate at 100% efficiency, 2 at 75%, and 2 at 50%. Each client performs 5 local epochs, and training runs for 30 min. For the Asynchronous Hybrid model, we deploy three servers with the following client and efficiency assignments:

- Server 1: 3 clients (2 at 100%, 1 at 75%)
- Server 2: 3 clients (1 at 100%, 1 at 75%, 1 at 50%)
- Server 3: 2 clients (1 at 100%, 1 at 50%)

The learning framework is implemented in PyTorch, starting from a pretrained MobileNetV3 Small model. Every client optimizes using SGD with a learning rate of 0.001 and a batch size of 512. We use CIFAR-10 as the training dataset, partitioning it into 8 independent and identical distributed (IID) subsets each assigned to a client. This method of partitioning means that all client datasets will effectively have the same class distribution across their samples. Model aggregation is performed using simple parameters averaging (i.e. arithmetic mean). More in depth reasoning on why we choose to experiment with IID data partitions and simple arithmetic mean model aggregation is described in the discussions sections of this work.

Communication and task distribution is implemented using Ray, an actor-based distributed systems library. We define clients, servers, and evaluators as Ray actors that exchange messages asynchronously. The experiment runs on an Intel Core i9-10900X CPU with two NVIDIA RTX 3080 GPUs. Resource allocation is as follows:

- Servers: 1 CPU core each
- Clients: 1 CPU core + 0.2 GPUs each
- Evaluators: 1 CPU core + 0.2 GPUs each

We empirically verify that these resource allocations are sufficient for efficient training and communication given our hardware and implementation.

4.3 Results and Discussion

To evaluate the computational efficiency of the proposed actor-based federated learning systems, we measure the federated round throughput by computing the number of rounds processed by the system per second. A round is defined to be one client training iteration. For example, if our system contains 8 clients that all completed 10 local training iterations, the total number of rounds completed across the system would be 80. The throughput measurements are displayed in Table 1. We see that the fully asynchronous systems output $1.60\times$ to $1.65\times$ round throughput relative to the traditional server-client approach. This is because the clients in the asynchronous system are working at near maximum compute efficiency as they are designed to minimize idle time, while the traditional clients need to wait for all other clients to finish before the entire system can proceed.

In addition to round throughput, we measure the running loss and accuracy over time in Figs. 4 and 5. Loss (in this case cross-entropy loss) and accuracy

Table 1. Round throughput (rounds per second)

	Traditional SC	Async SC	Async P2P	Async P2P Sp	Async Hybrid
Total Rounds	1080	1786	1728	1745	1765
Throughput	0.60	0.99	0.96	0.97	0.98
Difference	–	1.65×	1.60×	1.61×	1.63×

are the typical metrics used to measure the learning performance of a model. For loss, clients compute the average loss per training sample for each federated round. For accuracy, clients send an evaluation request to an evaluator after every round, offloading the benchmark computation to a separate compute node. This system for taking loss and accuracy metrics during runtime by utilizing the evaluator actors proposed previously allows the benchmark collection to be fair across the different federated learning systems. Additionally, to handle the server-client and peer-to-peer structural differences, we choose to compare the systems at the client level, meaning we examine the behavior of each client to get a good understanding of the entire system as a whole. This is necessary as the peer-to-peer and hybrid systems do not have a single central server that can provide a global performance estimation. Additionally, since the experiment setting ran 8 clients with 3 levels of efficiency, 100%, 75%, and 50%, we aggregate the loss and accuracy measurement into their respective efficiency groups. So for example, there are 4 clients running at 100% efficiency, thus their loss and accuracy measurements are combined together. We argue that this evaluation setup for loss and accuracy convergence provides a fair comparison between the different federated learning system.

Examining the accuracy plots, we see the asynchronous server-client, hybrid, and special peer-to-peer systems achieve a better convergence than the traditional server-client system across all efficiency levels. Similarly, the same behavior is observed in the loss convergence plots, with the addition that the 50% efficient clients for the traditional server-client system eventually catches up with the three mentioned asynchronous systems.

One interesting observation is that the asynchronous peer-to-peer system surprisingly performs poorly in comparison to all the others. According to the loss and accuracy plots, the asynchronous peer-to-peer system starts off matching the convergence efficiency of the other asynchronous systems, but begins to fall behind, converging even slower than the traditional server-client system despite having 1.6× greater round throughput. We hypothesize that this behavior could be due to model divergence and potential overfitting. Note that the implementation of the asynchronous peer-to-peer system seems to weigh the contribution of the local dataset more than the external client updates. Specifically, in the asynchronous peer-to-peer workflow, the local model is updated directly using the gradients computed during training with the local dataset while the external client parameter updates are only averaged into the local model. Comparing this to the server-client approach, the latter treats the contributions of all clients the same as all parameter updates are averaged in rather than being directly applied. Additionally, we see that the special peer-to-peer case, despite having a similar structure to the fully peer-to-peer system, performs on par with the other asynchronous server-client structures. This potentially further supports our reasoning as the special peer-to-peer case internally treats all clients equally, hence it is more in line with the server-client structure. Admittedly, this hypothesis for the poor peer-to-peer performance is still based on initial intuition and will require more in-depth exploration to fully understand its behavior.

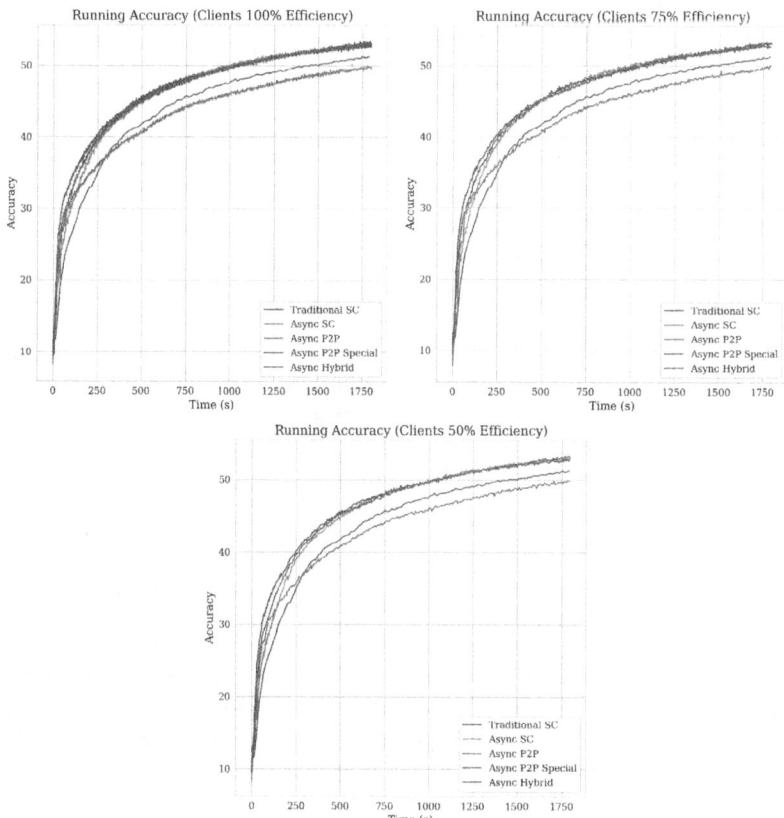

Fig. 4. Running accuracy over time of the different federated learning structures.

Most federated learning research focuses on non-IID (Independent and Identical Distributed) settings, where data distributions vary across clients [6,17]. However, in our experimentation and implementation, we use an IID settings for several reasons. First, IID setting are commonly used as a baseline [7,17,18]. Second, our primary focus is on communication patterns and system design in heterogeneous device environments. Introducing non-IID data would impose

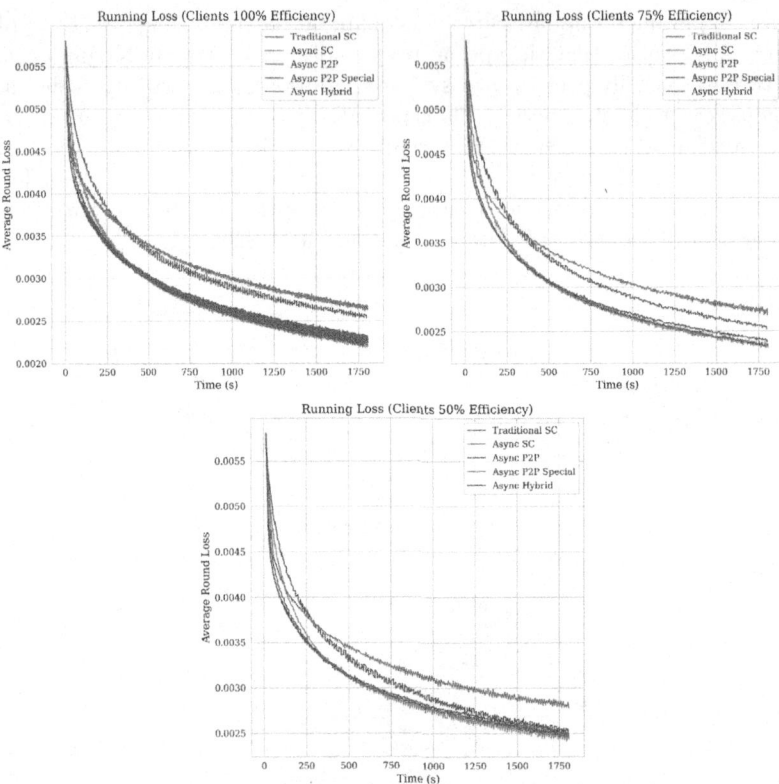

Fig. 5. Running loss over time of the different federated learning structures.

additional complexity by altering gradient distributions across clients, potentially obscuring the effects of communication and compute capacity. Third, federated learning applications with IID data do exist, particularly in controlled data collection environments. Additionally, our parameter aggregation strategy is a simple arithmetic mean. While, other federated learning approaches employ more sophisticated aggregation strategies that may incorporate staleness weighting or momentum, we opt for simplicity since aggregation strategy design is not our focus. Further, all four described systems treat aggregation differently due to the fundamental differences in structure, thus we try to keep each aggregation strategy as simple and similar as possible. Moreover, with IID data, all clients work with identical distributions, thus eliminating the need for aggregation strategies that account for data heterogeneity, such as FedAvg.

5 Conclusion

Federated learning has gained significant popularity as a privacy-preserving, decentralized machine learning approach that enables edge devices to collaboratively train models without sharing raw data. With the increasing adoption of smartphones, IoT devices, autonomous vehicles, and wearable technologies, federated learning has become crucial for applications that require personalized AI models, such as healthcare, smart assistants, predictive maintenance, and cybersecurity. However, despite its advantages, federated learning faces many deployment challenges, particularly with synchronous training methods, which can hinder efficiency and scalability, especially in a highly dynamic and heterogeneous environment involving edge devices. In a synchronous federated learning method, a central server coordinates training by selecting a group of edge devices, distributing a global model, and waiting for all participating clients to complete their local updates before aggregating the results. This approach ensures model consistency, but it often suffers from the straggler problem. Additionally, connectivity issues, device dropouts, and limited battery life further exacerbate the problem, causing inefficiencies, slower convergence, and wasted computational resources.

To address these challenges, we have investigated an approach to integrate the Actor Model of Concurrency into federated learning for enhanced performance. The actor model structures computation as a collection of independent, message-passing entities (actors) that can process information concurrently without shared state. In the context of federated learning, each participating device (or edge node) can act as an autonomous actor, asynchronously exchanging model updates with a central server or with each other in a peer-to-peer manner. We have implemented this approach with various architectures and communication paradigms, and used a benchmark deep learning application to evaluate the performance. Our experimental results on asynchronous communication in federated learning show great potential in achieving better performance than the traditional approach in a heterogeneous environment.

Integrating the actor model with federated learning enables scalable and distributed training, allowing IoT devices to participate in learning at their own pace, without blocking the system. Additionally, by leveraging localized decision-making and hierarchical actor-based aggregation, the federated learning framework can be more resilient to network delays, device dropouts, and energy constraints, making it highly suitable for smart cities, industrial IoT, healthcare monitoring, and autonomous systems where devices continuously generate data in real-time. For future work, we will investigate advanced aggregation techniques for the asynchronous actor based federated learning framework, and further validate the system by deploying it on real-world IoT applications, such as smart health and autonomous driving applications.

Acknowledgment. This research is supported in part by the National Science Foundation through awards CNS #2216108 and OAC #2243980.

References

1. Agha, G.: Actors: A Model of Concurrent Computation in Distributed Systems. MIT Press, Cambridge, MA, USA (1986)
2. Agha, G.: Actors programming for the mobile cloud. In: 2014 IEEE 13th International Symposium on Parallel and Distributed Computing, pp. 3–9. IEEE (2014)
3. Al-Sarawi, S., Anbar, M., Abdullah, R., Al Hawari, A.B.: Internet of things market analysis forecasts, 2020–2030. In: 2020 Fourth World Conference on Smart Trends in Systems, Security and Sustainability (WorldS4), pp. 449–453 (2020)
4. Armstrong, J.: Programming Erlang: Software for a Concurrent World. Pragmatic Bookshelf (2007)
5. Fu, L., Zhang, H., Gao, G., Zhang, M., Liu, X.: Client selection in federated learning: principles, challenges, and opportunities. IEEE Internet of Things J. (2023)
6. Hsu, T.M.H., Qi, H., Brown, M.: Measuring the effects of non-identical data distribution for federated visual classification. arXiv preprint arXiv:1909.06335 (2019)
7. Huang, L., Yin, Y., Fu, Z., Zhang, S., Deng, H., Liu, D.: Loadaboost: Loss-based adaboost federated machine learning with reduced computational complexity on iid and non-iid intensive care data. PLoS ONE **15**(4), e0230706 (2020)
8. Ji, Y., Chen, L.: Fedqnn: A computation–communication-efficient federated learning framework for iot with low-bitwidth neural network quantization. IEEE Internet Things J. **10**(3), 2494–2507 (2023). https://doi.org/10.1109/JIOT.2022.3213650
9. Jia, N., Qu, Z., Ye, B., Wang, Y., Hu, S., Guo, S.: A comprehensive survey on communication-efficient federated learning in mobile edge environments. IEEE Commun. Surv. Tutorials (2025). https://doi.org/10.1109/COMST.2025.3535957
10. Kairouz, P., et al.: Advances and open problems in federated learning. CoRR abs/arXiv: 1912.04977 (2019)
11. Lee, J., Ko, H., Pack, S.: Adaptive deadline determination for mobile device selection in federated learning. IEEE Trans. Veh. Technol. **71**(3), 3367–3371 (2021)
12. Li, T., Sahu, A.K., Talwalkar, A., Smith, V.: Federated learning: challenges, methods, and future directions. IEEE Signal Process. Mag. **37**(3), 50–60 (2020)
13. Li, T., Sanjabi, M., Beirami, A., Smith, V.: Fair resource allocation in federated learning (2020)
14. Lueth, K.: State of the iot 2018: Number of iot devices now at 7b – market accelerating (May 2022). https://iot-analytics.com/state-of-the-iot-update-q1-q2-2018-number-of-iot-devices-now-7b/
15. Mach, P., Becvar, Z.: Mobile edge computing: a survey on architecture and computation offloading. IEEE Commun. Surv. Tutorials **19**(3), 1628–1656 (2017). https://doi.org/10.1109/COMST.2017.2682318
16. Malekijoo, A., et al.: Fedzip: A compression framework for communication-efficient federated learning. arXiv preprint arXiv:2102.01593 (2021)
17. McMahan, B., Moore, E., Ramage, D., Hampson, S., y Arcas, B.A.: Communication-efficient learning of deep networks from decentralized data. Artifi. Intell. Statist., 1273–1282. (2017)
18. Sattler, F., Korjakow, T., Rischke, R., Samek, W.: Fedaux: leveraging unlabeled auxiliary data in federated learning. IEEE Trans. Neural Netw. Learn. Syst. **34**(9), 5531–5543 (2021)
19. Teo, Z.L., et al.: Federated machine learning in healthcare: a systematic review on clinical applications and technical architecture. Cell Rep. Med. **5**(2) (2024)
20. The E Language (2000). http://www.erights.org/elang

21. Varela, C., Agha, G.: Programming dynamically reconfigurable open systems with SALSA. ACM SIGPLAN Notices **36**, 20–34 (2001)
22. Wei, K., et al.: Federated learning with differential privacy: algorithms and performance analysis. IEEE Trans. Inf. Forensics Secur. **15**, 3454–3469 (2020)
23. Yang, C., et al.: Flash: heterogeneity-aware federated learning at scale. IEEE Trans. Mob. Comput. **23**(1), 483–500 (2022)
24. Yazici, M.T., Basurra, S., Gaber, M.M.: Edge machine learning: enabling smart internet of things applications. Big Data Cognitive Comput. **2**(3) (2018)
25. Zhang, D., Sun, W., Zheng, Z.A., Chen, W., He, S.: Adaptive device sampling and deadline determination for cloud-based heterogeneous federated learning. J. Cloud Comput. **12**(1), 153 (2023)
26. Zhang, M., et al.: Joint compression and deadline optimization for wireless federated learning. IEEE Trans. Mobile Comput. (2023)
27. Zhou, L., Pan, S., Wang, J., Vasilakos, A.V.: Machine learning on big data: opportunities and challenges. Neurocomputing **237**, 350–361 (2017)

Learning with Hypothesis Formation and Curiosity: An Actors Approach

Nadeem Jamali[1](✉), Aditya Phadke[2], and Zhe Chen[1]

[1] Department of Computer Science, University of Saskatchewan, 110 Science Place, Saskatoon, SK S7N 5C9, Canada
jamali@cs.usask.ca, zhe.chen@usask.ca

[2] Deloitte, Toronto, Canada
adphadke@deloitte.ca

http://agents.usask.ca

Abstract. This paper presents an efficient symbolic approach to learning which leads to better hypothesis formation than LLMs. An agent starting without prior knowledge learns by receiving new natural language statements from a teacher. Each sentence is understood only in the context of previously received statements. Hypothesis formation happens naturally through a process we call *coduction*, which is ultimately grounded in a primitive instinct to compress textual knowledge. As a side-effect of the attempt to form hypotheses, the agent becomes *curious* about related facts, and asks the teacher questions, potentially requiring exploration/experimentation in her world.

A highly concurrent Actor-based implementation is presented, where a dedicated actor actively manages the relationships of each concept with other concepts, forming a sort of *symbolic connectionist* network. The arrival of a new statement leads to a multitude of messages flowing concurrently through the network of connected actors, exploring new hypotheses and pursuing new questions.

Results of both quantitative and qualitative evaluations are presented.

Of the two quantitative evaluations, the first uses a social media connections dataset with only one type of symmetric relationships, and the second uses a synthetic database of familial ralations with varied relationships. In the two evaluations, given only 20% of the statements in the ground truth, the agent discovered additional 68.4% and 44.9% (respectively) of the ground truth through fact checks and hypothesis testing. In the family network case, some *types* of relationships not introduced in the training were discovered. Finally, given identical training data, coduction – using fact-checking and hypothesis generation – was found to outperform a fine-tuned LLM. Most notably, for the family relations

---

Conception, algorithm design, and initial prototyping of coduction was done by Jamali. The prototype used for the evaluation presented in this paper was developed as part of Phadke's MSc research. The experimental evaluation presented here was carried out by Phadke and Chen as parts of their respective MSc thesis projects.

© The Author(s), under exclusive license to Springer Nature Switzerland AG 2026
J. Meseguer et al. (Eds.): Gul Agha Festschrift, LNCS 16120, pp. 346–368, 2026.
https://doi.org/10.1007/978-3-032-05291-9_15

dataset, the LLM consistently failed to generalize to identify 7.15% of the facts that coduction learned.

The qualitative evaluation learned using statements adapted from a wildlife website for children. Given 51 statements, the agent learned 63 more.

1 Introduction

People learn by making observations and receiving knowledge from other people across time and space, both the personal interactions such as parental guidance and formal education, as well as the text, the art and the artifacts that others have left behind. Being that the text available today contains both knowledge and conversations (e.g., on social media platforms), a lot can be learned from text alone. This is what allows Transformer-based Generative AI [16] to essentially bypass direct observations and communications, and to be able to act the way the creators of past artifacts would in similar circumstances.

The question that arises then is whether this is sufficient. If the objective is to be able to do things which human beings can do using acquired knowledge, we need to consider what it is that human being do with their knowledge.

Let's limit ourselves to natural language conversations. Given that Generative AI chatbots have learned from more knowledge than any human beings ever have, they should – in principle – be able to surpass any human being's ability to use the knowledge for engaging in illuminating conversations which are limited to existing knowledge. But what about scientific discovery? Unbounded curiosity, such as what is exhibited by some human beings in scientific discovery, leads to enhancement of knowledge and capability, sometimes even without immediate application. Beyond immediate requirements for survival, this is a very deliberate exercise predicated on the belief that creating new knowledge is ultimately worthwhile. Does learning from large amounts of existing knowledge bypass the scientific method [14]?

To an extent, yes, because if the results of past reasoning and consequent discoveries are already available in existing knowledge, the reasoning is possibly no longer needed. To someone not as knowledgeable as a Generative AI chatbot, which is essentially all human beings today, a conversation with the chatbot can create the *illusion of discovery* happening in real time, even though it is simply a presentation of learned knowledge. But what happens when the knowledge required simply does not yet exist? In that situation, new discovery is required: hypotheses have to be made, and evidence has to be collected. Let us consider these in turn.

One source for hypotheses can be the type of generalization that neural networks-based machine learning [8] systems do. For example, if a chatbot cannot say something with high confidence, what it can still say is something that it "thinks" is likely to be true. Sometimes it gets lucky; other times, the guesses get counted as "hallucinations" (or "confabulations" according to Hinton). Important discoveries – such as the Nobel-winning protein structures generated using

AlphaFold2 [6] – have been attributed to such generalizations being taken as hypotheses. We contend that this generalization is not always a good source of hypotheses.

Evidence collection can sometimes be automated; however, in physical sciences, it can require exploration and experimentation in the real-world, which require physical resources, which are typically bounded. Not to mention that carrying out real-world experiments requires real-time grounding in the world, even if it is indirectly through an external physical agent (e.g., a physical robot, a human being). Plus, with the passage of time, new events take place, and the world changes, creating new spatiotemporal knowledge yet to be captured.

In summary, many types of scientific discovery require grounding, and a scalable scientific discovery enterprise requires good narrowly-focused hypotheses rather than randomly spread ones.

In this paper, we present an alternative way of learning called *coduction*, which can generate hypotheses, and can ask for evidence collection on its behalf. Coduction is similar in spirit to Transformer-based systems in that it works directly with natural language, and teases out patterns from NL sentences; however, it does it using a highly-efficient symbolic *protological* mechanism. Plus, in our preliminary experiments, it outperforms deep learning-based LLMs in forming hypotheses.

2 Related Work

Hypothesis formation has long been a topic of interest to philosophers of science like the 19th century pragmatist Charles Sanders Peirce. Peirce [14] offered important insights into the fundamental nature of reasoning, which have inspired work by cognitive scientists like John Holland [5]. Among other contributions, Peirce organized reasoning into three orders of *induction*: first, rudimentary induction; second, abduction; and third, statistical induction. Rudimentary induction is simply about making conclusions based on what you observe; if you have not seen an instance of something, you imagine it to be false. Abduction is the process by which one comes up with and refines hypotheses. The third and final order, statistical induction, is where, given a hypothesis, statistical evidence is examined for and against the hypothesis. Among these, statistical induction most closely resembles machine learning approaches such as deep learning [8]. Foundational works in statistical induction include Tom Mitchell's [12] characterization of a variety of generalization techniques used in learning as search problems, and Leslie Valiant's PAC learning [15], which offers a rigorous approach to managing the error in generalizations.

We believe our approach most closely fits Peirce's second order of induction, abduction. Abduction has attracted relatively little attention, partly because it is not as well understood. It is something thought of as not being as accessible as induction is to precise and close examination and subsequent automation. The process of coming up with hypotheses is arguably different from generalization, and does not require the large amount of data that generalization does.

Unlike Allen Newell's Soar [7] and related approaches, our work does not focus on goal-oriented problem solving. Instead, it is broadly in the tradition of projects like Douglas Lenat's Cyc [9], John McCarthy's Elephant 2000 [11], and most notably Tom Mitchell's Never Ending Language Learner (NELL) [3], except with much less structure, and more primitive mechanisms. While NELL's implicit (albeit unstated) object is to become knowledgable about everything, our presentation of coduction here is more narrowly focused on illustrating a very particular type of a primitive learning mechanism using a small amount of data. Unlike NELL's differentiation between predicates/classes (e.g., "Cities") and objects (e.g., "Paris"), coduction keeps them at the same level as *bits* of text, and the *contexts* in which they appear. NELL only learns relationships between coduction's equivalent of bits; coduction additionally learns relationships between contexts as first class statements. In coduction, the learner also actively *pulls* very specific knowledge from the world. NELL uses variables and forms probabilistic horn clauses; coduction uses finite – and overlapping – bit and context classes, dealing only with instances rather than generalizations.

3 Coduction

In the broader spirit of methodological solipsism [4], consider a *learner* – an artificial learning agent – that operates entirely in the space of strings. It has no grounding in the world from which any knowledge is drawn, except through its *teacher* who provides natural language statements containing the knowledge. Each statement is assumed to independently contain a piece of knowledge.

What can this learner do with received statements containing knowledge? It can record them, thereby gaining the primitive ability to check for existence of received statements (by simply searching for them), or finding them through substring search.

The first statement the learner receives has no meaning to it except for the statement's existence and implicitly the teacher's belief in it. If we imagine the *tabula rasa* state of the learner as a blank space, then the statement appears simply as a dot in it, because there is no basis for parsing it. Subsequent statements too can appear as dots; however, with the emergence of similarities between statements – such as in the words they are composed of – opportunities arise for matching words in one statement with those in another.

Now consider the possibility that some similarities have been found which can be the basis for compressing the knowledge base of received statements out of a purely resource conservation concern. For example, consider the case where two statements have a substring s_1 in common, which appears in contexts c_1 and c_2; and another two statements have a different substring s_2 in common, but appearing in the same contexts c_1 and c_2 that s_1 had appeared in. This leads to the *loss free* opportunity to represent all four statements – and only them – using only three: the first two, and then an additional one recording a relation between s_1 and s_2. Alternatively, the two statements with context c_1 can be recorded alongside a third relation between c_1 and c_2. We call this protological process for changing representations *coduction*.

The implications of this – beyond the obvious data compression – are noteworthy. We argue that statements with shared substrings – or contexts made up of multiple substrings – exist because of a kind of order in the world; David Hume implied it when he talked about the "uniformity of nature." One reason for this order is that, even though the world is highly complex, many of the rules governing its progress from one state to another are simple. It is the transitions governed by these rules – from one state to another – which lead to the evolving facts in the world. When facts in one state lead to multiple facts in the following state, the consequent facts are related. Natural language descriptions of such related facts can end up sharing substrings of text.

Notably, when a relationship between substrings s_1 and s_2 is recorded in a statement as described above, it could well be representing an actual relationship in the world. In other words, hidden relationships can potentially be discovered by examining similarities – such as shared substrings – in statements about observable facts; as can other related facts.

Example: Populating a Family Relations Graph

Consider the family tree in Fig. 1. Let us say the learner knows only the following four facts:

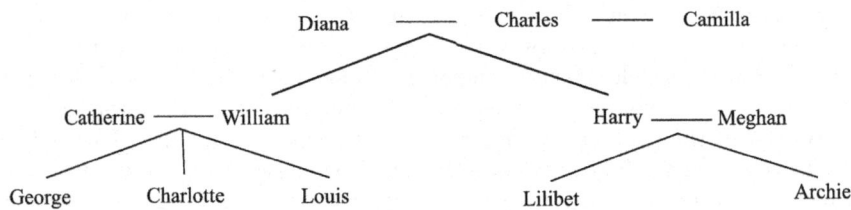

Fig. 1. Parent-Child and Couple Relationships.

Charles is a parent of William; Charles is a parent of Harry
Diana is a parent of William; Diana is a parent of Harry

The first two statements have William and Harry appearing in the context *Charles-is-a-parent-of*;[1] and the next two statements have William and Harry appearing in the context *Diana-is-a-parent-of*. Alternatively, we can also say that *is-a-parent-of-William* and *is-a-parent-of-Harry* are the substrings appearing in the context of both Charles and Diana. Applying coduction in different ways leads to the learner hypothesizing about relations respectively tying Charles to Diana (as co-parents) and William to Harry (as siblings). In this way, the learner can begin constructing unseen parts of the graph, and begin tracking classes of related concepts.

Similarly, consider that typically one does not learn about a particular family's relationships by looking at a family tree. Particularly, one can learn about

---

[1] Hyphens added to aid readability.

family relationships in any order: an uncle-nephew relationship might be learned before any parent-child relationships are learned. Let us say that the learner first learns of only the following four relationships:

George is a nephew of Harry; George is a child of Catherine
Louis is a nephew of Harry; Louis is a child of Catherine

In this case, coduction leads to hypothesizing the sibling relationship between George and Louis, and a more general type of relationship – covering both siblings and siblings-in-law – between Harry and Catherine.

The newly discovered relations, if confirmed and provided culturally relevant names (e.g., sibling-in-law) by the teacher, can be added as new first class statements in the knowledge space, themselves open to being analyzed in a similar fashion. Even if not confirmed (or even confirmable) by the teacher, they are still recorded and used in the learner's internal organization of its knowledge. On subsequently discovering William's parentage of George and Louis, the learner would first hypothesize that William too is Harry's sibling-in-law, but on being told otherwise by the teacher, will learn to separate the sibling-in-law and sibling relationships. Given enough instances, subsequently, it will also learn that the sibling-in-law and sibling relationships themselves are in a relationship. Similarly, the relationships hypothesized could be between being a child of Catherine ("— is a child of Catherine") and being a nephew of Harry ("— is a nephew of Harry").

Curiosity: Now let's say that having learned all of that, the learner next encounters the fact about Charlotte being Catherine's child. This creates the opportunity to place Charlotte in the same set as George and Louis of those who are both Catherine's and William's children and Harry's nephews. To confirm this, the learner pursues a curiosity about whether Charlotte is also Harry's nephew, and asks the teacher if it is so. If the teacher says yes, Charlotte is placed in the same class as George and Louis; otherwise (as is the case here, the child is female and a niece, not a nephew), a case is recorded of someone being Catherine's child but being Harry's niece (and not a nephew). Similarly, the learner asks if the new child is also William's child. If the teacher does not readily know the answer, she could conceivably research it or carry out an experiment (such as a DNA test) to obtain the answer. Exposure to a sentence saying that Charlotte is a daughter of Catherine (not just a child) will lead to more questions, and learning of even finer-grained distinctions △

3.1 Knowledge Representation and Evolution

Knowledge representation for supporting coduction has two goals:

- To record the base knowledge provided to the agent by the teacher. This can be achieved by recording the received statements verbatim, where each statement contributes a piece of knowledge, which may or may not reference elements of what is already known. This base knowledge could then be recalled in response to questions asking whether they are known.

– To enable hypothesis formation, which also manifests itself in an *agent-initiated inquiry* into the world, and addition of new statements to the knowledge base.

Coduction treats statements as sequences of words, and partitions them into subsequences. For instance, sentences can be broken up into (*bit, context*) pairs, where a bit is any contiguous sequence of words in the statement being considered, and the context is made up of the sequences of words appearing before and / or after the bit. For example, the statement "William is a parent of Louis" can be partitioned to create bit-context pairs like ("is a parent of", "William—Louis"), ("a parent of", "William is—Louis"), and so on.

For each bit-context pair, then, the fact that the bit and the context appear together can be recorded. However, if multiple bits appear with the same multiple contexts, those bits are potentially related; they are placed in a *bit class*, and the corresponding contexts are placed in a *context class*, with the *appears-with* relationship between the context class and the bit class being recorded. This means that each bit in the bit class is known to appear with every context in the context class.

When the teacher confirms a relationship between a pair of bits or contexts – conceivably, after carrying out experiments in her world – a *new statement* is constructed to represent the relationship using a name from the teacher's world, and fed to the agent.

The bit classes and context classes emerge naturally as more statements containing already known bits and contexts are received.

Additionally, when some new statement is received containing a known bit and a new context, it leads to *curiosity* about whether the context might belong in the context classes which some of the bit's bit classes may be linked to. This is handled by asking the teacher questions about potential truths. If the teacher confirms a truth, the new context is placed in those context classes. Similarly for newly learned bits.

4 Implementation

A prototype of the learner has been implemented as a highly concurrent Actor system. An Actor system is made up of concurrently executing primitive agents called actors, based on the Actor model of concurrency [2]. Each actor has a globally unique name, and actors communicate by sending asynchronous messages to each other, and can create new actors on the fly. Actors are supported in several modern languages and libraries [1]. Large distributed systems, such as Twitter, have been implemented using Actors. Our prototype has been implemented in Scala [13] with the Akka Actors library [10].

Actors were chosen to realize coduction because of their support of massive concurrency. Coduction involves maintaining of active relationships between a large number of concepts represented as bits or contexts, and their classes. There is a highly distributed state of this knowledge, with opportunities for some explorations to continue while new ones are initiated. For example, a fact check that cannot be immediately performed for lack of teacher knowledge or absence of knowledge (pending novel experiments), can persist as a questions in a local space; an eventual answer to the question can lead to continuation of the exploration once suspended for lack of an answer.

Despite dealing with symbolic data, this system is essentially *connectionist* in the sense that it is made up of a large number of highly connected actors – autonomous processes – each concerned with a single concept: a bit or a context.

The learner receives and processes statements containing knowledge, one at a time. These statements are broken up into bits and contexts. Each new bit and context has a dedicated actor created for it, as do the bit and context classes. For every new statement received, for every bit-context pair, every bit's actor is sent the correspondent context actor, and every context is sent the correspondent bit actor. Each actor concurrently processes the message and pursues its implications. Consequently, a bit actor knows its own text, and maintains the set of contexts with which it has appeared in statements, as well as classes of contexts shared with other bits. Similarly for context actors. The bit and context classes emerge and evolve over time as new relationships between bits (and equivalently, contexts) are recognized and confirmed by the teacher.

Figure 2 shows a snapshot of the knowledge base at any time. It shows bit and context actors, with one each of a bit actor and a context actor blown up to show their internal details. Also shown are bit and context classes to which the bits and contexts which are shared by (respectively) multiple contexts and multiple bits can belong. Inside the blown-up bit actor, there are two sets: one, the set of all contexts which this bit has appeared in statements with, and the other, the set of all context classes which it shares with other bit actors. Similarly for the blown-up context actor. The bit and context classes emerge and evolve over time as new relationships between bits (and equivalently, contexts) are recognized and confirmed by the teacher.

Note that the existence of a bit or context class means that there are *potentially verifiable* relations between the bits / contexts in the class, and these potential relations are flagged to the teacher for verification. If verified, these relations lead to new statement which are then given to the learning agent to process. The relationships between bits are verified straightforwardly by asking if there is a meaningful relationship between a pair of bits, and what phrase would connect them to represent the relationship in a statement. The relationships between contexts can be between noun phrases representing the entire contexts (e.g., context "William—Louis" drawn from the statement "William is a parent of Louis" would become "The way William relates to Louis"). In the absence of a teacher, the process can be automated to the extent that it is meaningful, inventing "internal" relationship names which stand in for more culturally relevant names whenever they are eventually learned.

4.1 Algorithm

Algorithm 1 presents the key algorithm for the context actor – one for each context – which receives a new bit every time a new sentence is received which

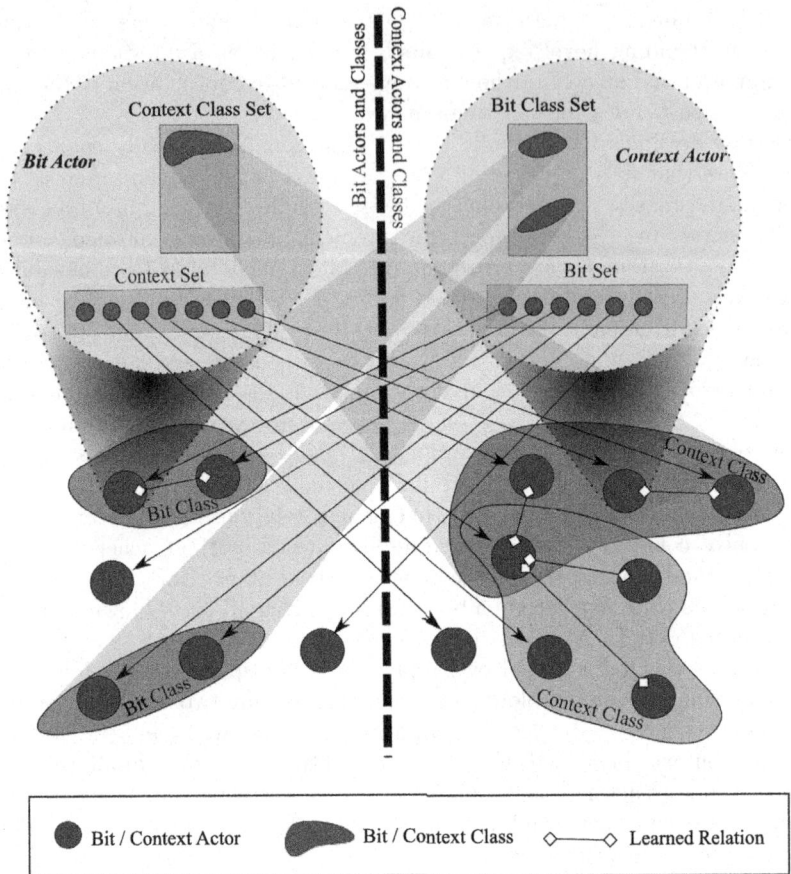

Fig. 2. Snapshot of Bit and Context Actors.

contains a new bit in that context. When a bit is received by a context actor, first the bit is recorded in the context's bit set containing bits which have appeared in the context. Next, the learner checks whether the new bit should belong in some of the context's existing bit classes, and whether creation of a new class (for the context) is warranted.

Note that even though the bit is new to this context, it may already exist in other contexts' bit classes.

The determination of whether the bit in the new context-bit pair belongs in a bit class for the context is made in two ways: first, by checking if it belongs in one of the context's existing bit classes (lines 5 through 34), and second, if a new bit class needs to be created (lines 35 through 72).

To check whether the bit belongs in one of the context's existing bit classes, the bit is checked for appearance with other contexts sharing those classes. For a

Algorithm 1 Context Actor

```
 1: actor ContextActor c
 2: receive new bit b       ▷ Must be new because otherwise,
    sentence would have been previously known
 3:   add b to c's bit set
 4:   SS ← ∅
 5:   for every bit class bc of c do
 6:     SC ← set of contexts sharing bc with c    ▷ From
        bc's actor
 7:     for every context ci ∈ SC do
 8:       check if b previously appeared with ci    ▷ Ask
          ci's actor
 9:       if yes then
10:         SS ← SS ∪ {ci}
11:       else if no then
12:         ask teacher if b should appear with ci
13:         if teacher says "yes" then
14:           SS ← SS ∪ {ci}
15:           feed in true statement made with b and
              context
16:         else if teacher says "no" then
17:           feed in false statement made with b and
              context
18:         end if
19:       end if
20:     end for
21:     if SS = SC then
22:       add b to bit class bc
23:       for every pair (b, ob) where ob ∈ bc do
24:         obtain name of relationship between b and
            ob from teacher and feed in new sentence
25:       end for
26:     else if existing bit class ebc has exactly b and bits
          in bc then
27:       have c and SS share ebc    ▷ Do necessary
          book-keeping
28:     else
29:       create new bit class nbc with b and bits from
          bc to be shared between SS and c    ▷ Do necessary
          book-keeping
30:       for every pair (b, ob) where ob ∈ bc do
31:         obtain name of relationship between b and
            ob from teacher and feed in new sentence
32:       end for
33:     end if
34:   end for
35:   C ← contexts which b has appeared with (from b's
      actor)
36:   for every context bc ∈ C do
37:     obtain bc's set of bits from its context actor
38:   end for
39:   select contexts OC ⊆ C with which c has >1 overlap-
        ping bits    ▷ Threshold for curiosity about
        relation
40:   OS ← ∅    ▷ Set of overlapping bit sets
41:   for each oc ∈ OC do
42:     if oc's set of bits is not equal to c's set of bits
        then
43:       OB ← set of overlapping bits between oc and
          c
44:       ns ← statements with non-overlapping bits of
          oc and c in other context
45:       ask teacher if statements in ns are true or false
46:       feed in responses from teacher as new true or
          false statements    ▷ False statements ignored for now
47:       OB ← OB ∪ new overlapping bits between oc
          and c just learned from teacher
48:       OS ← OS ∪ (oc, {OB})
49:     end if
50:   end for
51:   for each (oc, ob) ∈ OS do
52:     create a bit class bc with ob
53:     create bit class actor for bc; give it names of c and
          oc
54:     for every pair (b_1, b_2) where b_1 ∈ ob and b_2 ∈ ob
          and b_1 ≠ b_2 do
55:       obtain name of relationship between b_1 and b_2
          from teacher and feed in new sentence
56:     end for
57:     ask teacher for a linguistic name for bit class bc
          and record it    ▷ (e.g., "edibles")
58:     if OC ≠ ∅ then
59:       NPC ← noun phrase for c obtained from
          teacher ▷ (e.g., "that John likes something" for "John
          likes _")
60:       for each oc ∈ OC do
61:         NPOC ← noun phrase for oc obtained
            from teacher
62:         for each pair (npc, npoc) where npc ∈
              NPC and npoc ∈ NPOC and npc ≠ npoc do
63:           ask teacher if npc and npoc are related
64:           if teacher says "yes" then
65:             r1 ← name from teacher for how npc
                relates to npoc    ▷ (e.g., "causes")
66:             r2 ← name from teacher for how
                npoc relates to npc    ▷ (e.g., "is caused by")
67:             feed in "c r1 oc" and "oc r2 c" as
                new statements
68:           end if
69:         end for
70:       end for
71:     end if
72:   end for
```

bit class, if the other contexts sharing it have already appeared with the bit, the bit it added to the shared bit class. If the appearance of the bit with one of the other contexts is known to be false, then the bit is not added to the existing bit class. If neither of these cases is true, the teacher is asked whether the resulting statements for the other contexts are true or false. For each question, if the teacher responds in "yes" for all other contexts, the bit is added to the bit class; if she responds in a "no" for any of the other contexts, the bit is not added to the bit class. If she responds in "don't know," or simply does not reply, the process for deciding whether or not the bit belongs in the bit class keeps waiting for the message.

In addition to this scenario, there is always the potential of new bit classes being created for the context in the context-bit pair. The determination for this is made by searching for other contexts in which the new bit (new with this context, not necessarily with other contexts) is known to have appeared. For each of these other contexts in which the bit has previously appeared, a test is done to determine if addition of this new bit to the context has led to enough commonality between the context and the other context to warrant creation of a new bit class. If that turns out to be the case, a new bit class is created, which is then shared with that other context. If multiple other contexts share the same bits with the context in the new context-bit pair, they all come to share the new bit class.

At the time of creation of a new bit class, the teacher is asked if for the contexts which share the bit class, whether each pair of contexts has a relation, and if so, for bit-equivalent names for the two contexts, and for a names for the forward and backward relations between them. If the teacher says "yes," then a new statement is constructed for each relation using the relation name and the new bit-equivalent names, which is fed back to the learner.

Bit actors handle new contexts in a similar manner, updating or creating context classes as necessary.

Time Complexity. The cumulative processing time complexity of handling a statement is $O(l^2 c_b b_c \log(b_c c_b))$ where l is the number of words in the statement, b_c is the number of bits that appear in a context, and c_b is the number of contexts per bit. This can be further simplified by making assumptions about statement structure, particularly that meaningful bits would often be relations, and contexts would contain related things, and consequently, there would often be a small number of bits per context, and likely large number of contexts per bits. If b_c is bounded by a small constant, the complexity could be written as $O(l^2 c_b \log c_b)$. An important thing to note is that this creates an incentive for reducing the number of contexts per bit, as well as a basis for judging whether some word sequence is a good bit. In other words, less substantial bits with very few words appearing with exceedingly large numbers of contexts could be naturally garbage collected over time for statements with more meaningful larger bits.

5 Experimental Evaluation

Multiple sets of experiments were carried out to do both quantitative and evaluations of a prototype Actor implementation of coduction. These utilized real and synthetic data.

5.1 Quantitative Evaluation 1: Facebook Connections

For our first quantitative evaluation, we extracted a cluster of 1,983 symmetric Facebook connections involving 206^2 unique individuals from a larger dataset.[3] The dataset contains a sorted list of connections, each connection simply represented as a pair of integers, one connection per line.

---

[2] With the potential of 42,230 connections.
[3] Available at: https://snap.stanford.edu/data/ego-Facebook.html.

We used these pairs to construct sentences stating the connections; for example, for the pair (1, 2), the statement "1 is related to 2" is created. Given the complete set of these sentences, we randomly selected a number of them to feed to coduction. We were attracted to this dataset because it contained all actual connections – the *ground truth* – meaning that to know anything more about these connections, all we had to do was to search the set of sentences, eliminating the need for a subjective human teacher's involvement.

Hypothesis Generation. Figure 3 shows the results obtained using the dataset when different percentages of the ground truth were used for learning. The y-axis shows the number of fruitful fact checks and the number of hypotheses verified to be correct, along with the percentage of the entire ground truth that they represent. Note that because there is only one type of relationship involved in this dataset, the checked facts and the hypotheses all have the "x is related to y" format; in other words, the creation of the hypotheses involves identification of potentially related individuals, followed by determining the relationship between then, but the relationship (if there) has to be "is related to." The checking and verification is done automatically against the ground truth.

Note that the amount of learning drops as more of the dataset is used to learn from; this is simply because there is less of the ground truth that remains to be learned. Also note that the sets of facts checked and the hypotheses verified are not necessarily disjoint. The fact checks are done to see if there's a pattern warranting creation of a hypothesis, and if so, the hypothesis is checked against the ground truth.

Figure 4 shows the proportion of the entire ground truth known at the completion of the learning. For each of the cases, this number is slightly smaller than the sum of the size of the training dataset and what is learned. This is because the serial nature of the delivery of training statements to the learner leads to some statements contained in the training dataset to be learned by the learner ahead of the statements being first provided to it. In other words, some of the statements in the training datasets do not get to be used for training, because the learner has already predicted and verified them to be true.

Comparison with LLMs. We compared the learning capability of coduction with that of Meta LLaMA-3.2-3B using the 1,983 relations cluster of Facebook connections.

We first trained coduction using 396 randomly picked facts (20%) from the ground truth. The training was done 5 times with different randomly picked sets of statements. The training led to 1,357.2 (on average) successful fact checks and verified hypotheses combined (68.4% of the ground truth).

Next, we carried out experiments with LLaMA.

The training dataset we developed for LLaMA is made up of 792 statements, created by combining randomly drawn 396 statements (20%) from the ground truth, and another 396 statements randomly drawn from a set of 1,983 false relationships (again, randomly) drawn from the false hypotheses proposed by coduction. Providing both known true and known false statements to LLaMA helps it better learn to differentiate between true and false statements than

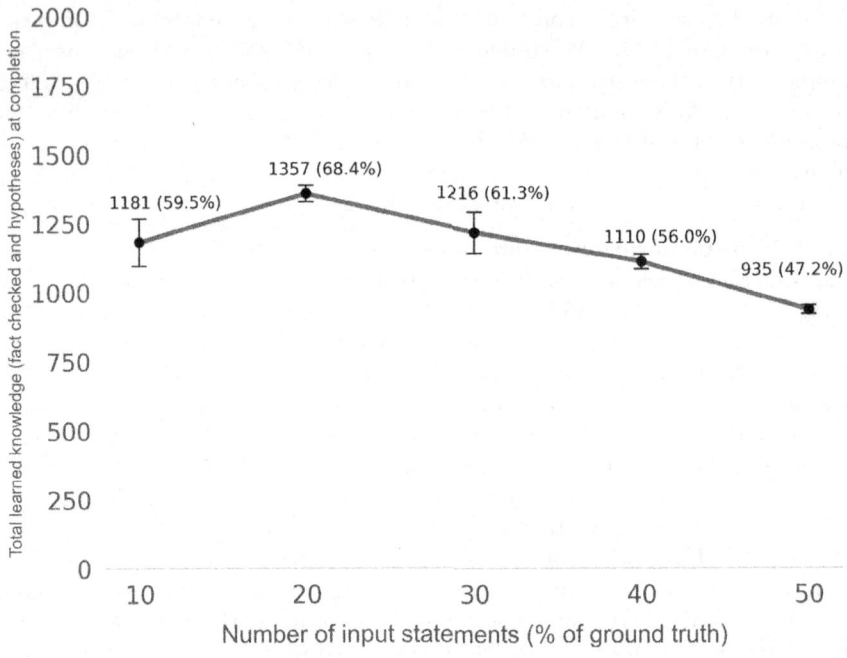

Fig. 3. Fruitful fact checks and verified hypotheses generated for different %ages of ground truth fed to learner. Avg. of 5.

just providing it with only true statements would. The set of false hypotheses generated by coduction was used because coduction implicitly learned that those hypotheses were false while still in the process of learning; we thought it would be most helpful for LLaMA to know these possibly more likely facts to be false.

The test dataset was a set of 3,174 statements, created by combining all the 1,587 remaining facts in the ground truth which were not used in training, with the 1,587 false hypotheses that were also not used in training.

The fine-tuning using the training dataset was done using LoRA (Low-Rank Adaptation) which is an efficient method for fine-tuning large pre-trained models, which limits the learning to selected layers, while keeping the rest of the network unchanged.

The testing was done 5 times, with a new random selection of the right number of facts each time, and the results were averaged. Here are the findings averaged over 5 tests:

– LLaMA correctly identified 993.6 true facts (62.61% of the 1,587 size test data for true relations; 50.11% of the ground truth for true relations)
– LLaMA correctly identified 606.8 false facts (38.23% of the 1,587 size test data for true relations; 30.6% of the ground truth for false relations). It incorrectly identified the remaining 61.77% of the false relation test set as true.

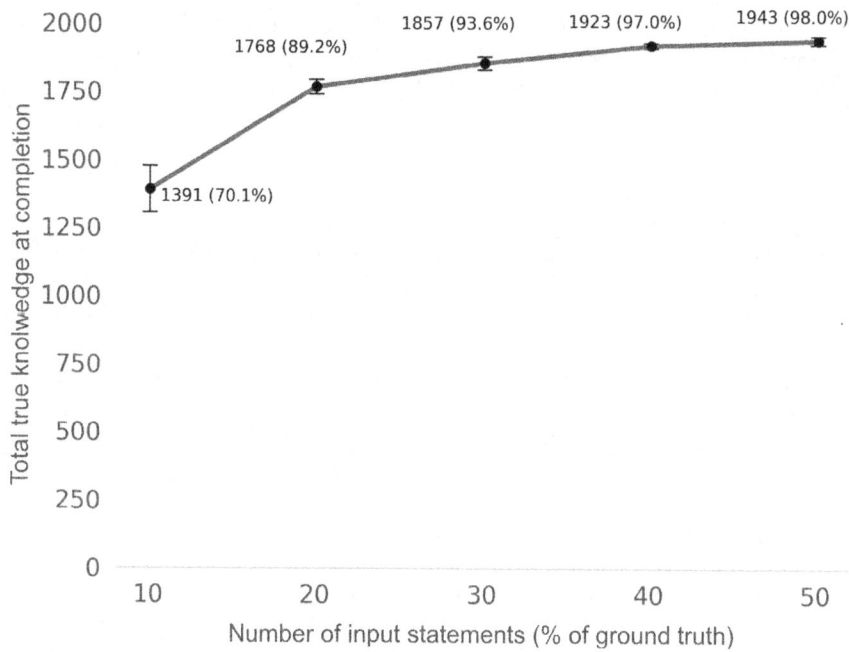

Fig. 4. Learner's knowledge at the completion of learning for different %ages of ground truth fed to learner. Avg. of 5.

In other words, about 62% of the statements in the test set were identified by LLaMA as true regardless of whether they were true or false.

In comparison, coduction learned 1,357.2 additional true facts (up to 85.5%[4] of the 1,587 remaining in the ground truth after removing the training set; 68.4% of the entire ground truth) through fact checks and hypothesis verification.

Finally, note that coduction began with no past knowledge, and LLaMA is a 3B parameter model trained using 3 trillion tokens. Training coduction took a small fraction of the time taken to fine-tune LLaMA.

5.2 Quantitative Evaluation 2: Synthetic Family Network

This second quantitative evaluation used another modestly sized but highly relationship-dense – synthetic – dataset which attempted to capture the family relations in a community. This dataset was different in that it involved a variety of relationships between individuals, with meta-relationships between

---

[4] Some facts from the training set are typically learned by coduction before encountering them. This is positive in the sense that the training actually required fewer statements than planned, but it also means that a slightly smaller percentage (smaller by about 1% of the 1,587 remaining facts) of facts would be learned relative to the remaining facts in the ground truth.

the relationships. As in Sect. 5.1, the teacher's role was played by a search into the pre-known ground truth of relationships. As part of this evaluation, we also collected processing time data for datasets of different sizes.

Hypothesis Generation. Our experiments used a dataset of 1108 statements encoding 8 types of relationships among a group of 20 individuals and their offsprings over 5 generations. The relationships were: parent (142), child (142), sibling (92) coparent (68), grandparent (196), grandchild (196), pibling (136), nibling (136).[5] Statements randomly selected from the dataset were provided to the learner, specifically *excluding pibling and nibling relationships*. This exclusion was to test for the learner's ability to discover unknown relation types. Consequently, the randomly selected statements given to the learner were drawn from the 836 statements encoding information about the remaining 6 types of relationships.

When a hypothesized relationship is not already of a type encoded in the ground truth, the corresponding hypothesis is still created, along with the revision of bit and context classes; however, no new statement is created for the learner's consideration. A closer examination of such hypotheses revealed that the hypothesized relationships still make sense when viewed from a wider lens. For example, a frequently hypothesized relationship was parent-in-law/child-in-law, neither used in the ground truth. In fact, about 10% of the parent-in-law relationships which could be indirectly drawn from the ground truth are hypothesized by the learner.

Figures 5 and 6 show the number of fruitful fact checks and verified hypotheses, respectively, for a series of experiments carried out using various percentages of statements from the ground truth as input. Given 20% of the ground truth as input, an average of 348.1+149.8 = 497.9 (44.9%) additional truths are discovered. Notably, in addition to the discovered statements about unfamiliar pibling / nibling relationships (which are included above), hypotheses are also generated about relationships not encoded in the ground truth, such as parent-in-law relationships; these could not be automatically verified, and are not included in the 44.9%.

Although the graphs appear to peak at 30%, note that as the input size increases in terms of %age of ground truth, fewer facts remain to be found. Percentage of ground truth known in the end is 26.2%, 59.4%, 72.7%, 77.5% and 83.2%, respectively. Several statements meant to be input were actually discovered before being input, which too reduces these percentages.

Computational Performance. Experiments were also carried out to establish the learner's computational performance using family relations datasets of progressively larger sizes. These experiments were carried out using a 6-core Intel Core i7-9750H CPU with 2.6GHz, and 16GB RAM and 12MB cache.

Datasets with increasing numbers of ground truths were constructed by varying the number of initial members of the community. Inputs to the learner were

---

[5] Pibling and nibling are gender-neutral terms for uncle/aunt and nephew/niece, respectively.

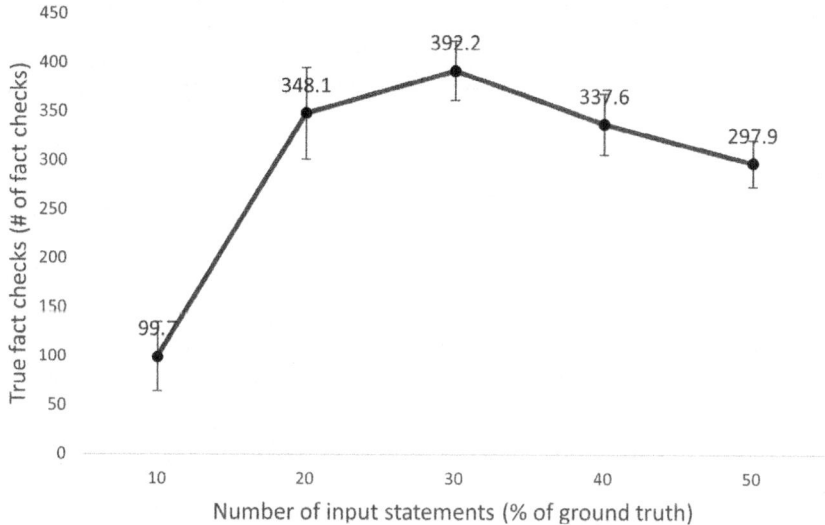

Fig. 5. Fruitful fact checks generated for different %ages of ground truth fed to learner. Avg. of 10.

kept at 20% of the ground truth. Figure 7 shows the processor times for the various experiments. Each experiment was carried out 5 times. The time taken for processing the given statements increases roughly linearly with the increase in the size of the dataset (note that both axes are exponential): from 60.04 s for a ground truth of 500 statements to 1066.75 s for the ground truth of 4000 statements. Standard deviation becomes significant for larger datasets, in part because for every experiment, statements were randomly picked from the ground truth. The opportunity and timing of the application of coduction depends on the particular statements presented to the learner, and the order in which they are presented. Early creation of large numbers of context and bit classes – which can happen here because of the highly dense nature of the family relations dataset – can lead to a wide variance in processing time for the same number of statements.

The roughly linear increase in time broadly conforms to our complexity analysis which expects time complexity of processing a sentence to be $O(l^2 c_b \log c_b)$, where l is the number of words in the sentence, and c_b is the number of known contexts for the bits in the sentence, which grows relatively slowly except in knowledge bases densely focused on a few concepts. It can be argue that our family relations example does have that high-density characteristic.

Comparison with LLMs. For this comparison, we used a ground truth of 556 family relations involving 48 individuals and 8 possible relationship types. We first ran coduction on 222 (40%) randomly picked facts (excluding the nibling and pibling relationships) from the ground truth. Next, we carried out experiments with LLaMA using the same set of training facts, but in 5 different orders.

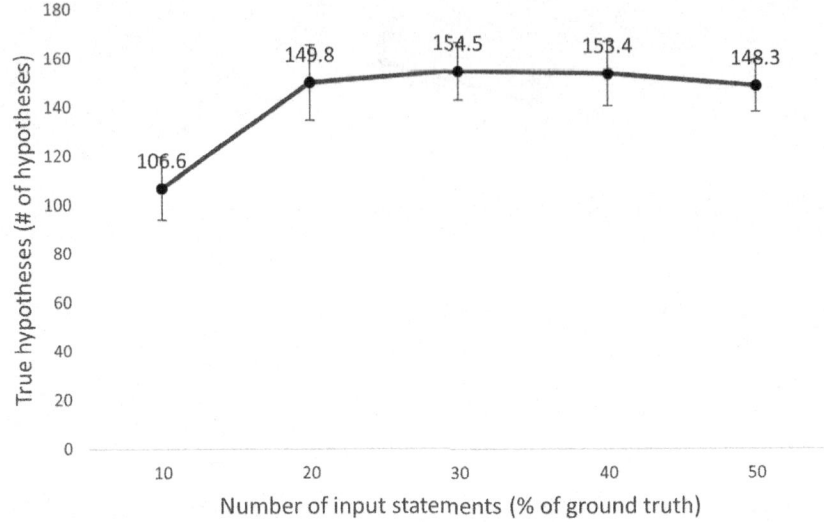

Fig. 6. Verified hypotheses generated for different %ages of ground truth fed to learner. Avg. of 10.

The LLaMA training dataset was a set of 444 statements, created by combining the same 222 statements (40%) from the ground truth which were previously used for coduction-based training, and another 222 statements randomly drawn from a set of 400 synthetically created false relationships involving the original 48 individuals. Providing both known true and known false statements to LLaMA helps it better learn to differentiate between true and false statements than just providing it with only true statements would. The fine-tuning of LLaMA with the data was done using the training dataset was done using LoRA (Low-Rank Adaptation).

The testing dataset for LLaMA was a set of 1130 statements, created by combining all the 334 remaining facts in the ground truth which were not used in training, with all the 796 false hypotheses made by coduction. The testing was done 5 times, and the results were averaged. Here are the findings averaged over 5 tests:

- LLaMA correctly identified 123.4 true facts (36.95%) out of the 334
- LLaMA correctly identified 457.6 false facts (57.49%) out of the 796; it incorrectly identified the remaining 42.51% of the false statements as true

In comparison, by means of fact checks and hypothesis verifications, coduction learned 210 additional true facts (62.87%) out of the 334 facts in the ground truth which remained after removing the training set. Also, notably:

- 15 of these facts which coduction consistently learned were not learned by LLaMA in any of the 5 tests.

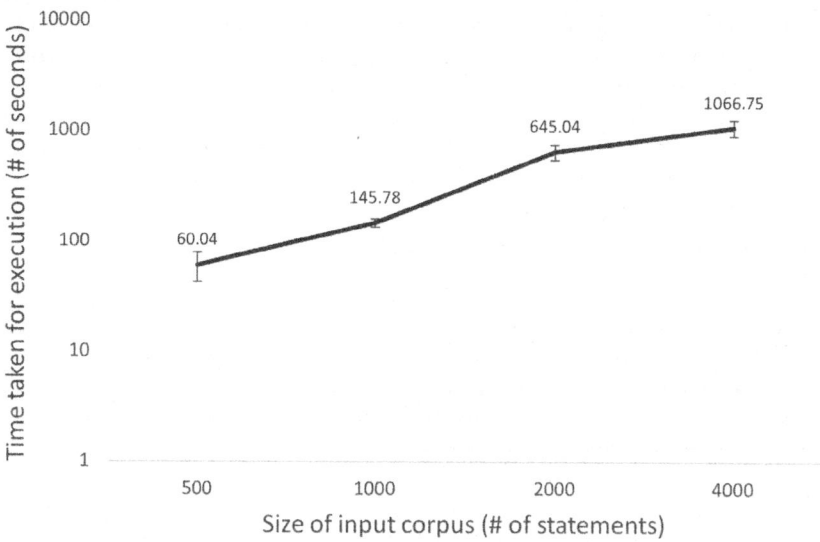

Fig. 7. Processor time taken. Avg. of 5. Exponential axes.

– There were 0 (zero) facts which LLaMA could consistently identify as being true, which coduction had not learned.

Recall that where coduction began with no past knowledge, LLaMA is a 3B parameter model trained using 3 trillion tokens. Training coduction from scratch took a small fraction of the time taken to fine-tune LLaMA.

5.3 Qualitative Evaluation: Arthropod Dataset

We used the set of statements about arthropods in Fig. 8, which are adapted from a website for children, to carry out a qualitative evaluation.[6] A human teacher provided the statements to the learning agent one at a time, answering questions as they were asked by the agent. On receiving the input statements, the agent explored several hypotheses, and proposed several potential facts to the teacher as questions to test the hypotheses. For the 51 sentences input to the agent, it posed 6 questions to the teacher, of which the teacher agreed to 3 (50% of posed questions) and rejected 3 (i.e., said "no" or "don't know" to).[7] Figure 9 shows the accepted and rejected proposed facts. Figure 10 shows the hypotheses generated. 70 potential hypotheses were suggested to the teacher,

---

[6] Wildlife website: https://nhpbs.org/wild/Arthropoda.asp.
[7] "nos" and "don't knows" both lead to rejection of the posed questions in these experiments.

of which the teacher accepted 60 (30 if symmetric relations counted once[8]) and rejected 10 (i.e., said "no" or "don't know" to; each of the 5 rejections corresponds to 2 potential hypotheses).

To summarize, for the 51 original sentences, 5.9% additional base facts were learned, and 117.7%[9] additional facts were learned as (meta) hypotheses, making a total of 63 (113.6%) new facts.[10] Both base facts and hypotheses accepted by the teacher got fed back to the learner as new base statements, becoming immediately available for processing of subsequent statements.

1: the thorax is the part of the body between the head and the abdomen
2: arthropods have an open circulatory system
3: arthropods that live in the water have gills
4: arthropods are bilaterally symmetrical
5: if you sliced arthropods from top to bottom each half would be exactly the same
6: there are four subphylums in the arthropoda phylum
7: insects do not have spines
8: insects are invertebrates
9: insects have segmented bodies
10: insects have three sections the head the thorax and the abdomen
11: insects have an exoskeleton
12: the head has antennae and a pair of compound eyes
13: insects have six legs one pair on each of its three segments
14: some insects also have wings
15: the exoskeleton is an outside covering that protects the insects internal organs
16: there are over 800000 species of insects more than all the other animal groups combined
17: insects can be found in a wide variety of environments all over the world
18: crustaceans do not have spines
19: crustaceans are invertebrates and breathe through gills
20: crustaceans have segmented bodies
21: crustaceans have three sections the head the thorax and the abdomen
22: crustaceans have pairs of branched appendages on each segment of their bodies
23: crustaceans may or may not have appendages on their abdomens
24: crustaceans have an exoskeleton or hard shell that protects their internal organs
25: as crustaceans grow they shed their exoskeleton and grow a new one
26: there are over 31500 living species of crustaceans
27: most crustaceans are found in the ocean
28: some crustaceans are found in fresh water
29: some crustaceans are even found on land
30: species in the crustacean subphylum include crabs lobsters shrimp wood lice and crayfish
31: there are 13000 species in the myriapoda subphylum
32: myriapoda means many legged
33: myriapoda have long wormlike bodies
34: myriapoda range in size from microscopic to almost a foot in length
35: myriapoda live on the land
36: myriapoda are usually found under leaf litter in the soil or under rocks
37: myriapoda are found all over the world in temperate and tropical areas
38: there are four classes in the myriapoda subphylum
39: symphyla and pauropoda are microscopic
40: diplopoda are the millipedes
41: chilopoda are the centipedes
42: the chelicerata subphylum includes a diverse group of species including ticks spiders and horseshoe crabs
43: chelicerata have bodies divided into two segments the prosoma and the opisthosoma
44: the prosoma is the front part of the body
45: in some species like the scorpions the pedipalps are claws
46: the opisthosoma is the rear segment
47: the opisthosoma lacks appendages
48: most chelicarata are found on land
49: some chelicarata like the horseshoe crab are found in the ocean
50: some chelicarata like ticks and mites are parasites
51: chelicerata unlike most arthropods do not have antennae

Fig. 8. Input Dataset: Statements given to the learner. Capitalizations and punctuations were removed.

1: insects have an exoskeleton or hard shell that protects their internal organs
2: crustaceans have pairs of branched appendages on each segment of their bodies
3: crustaceans have an exoskeleton
4: ~~insects have pairs of branched appendages on each segment of their bodies~~
5: ~~insects are invertebrates and breathe through gills~~
6: ~~crustaceans have six legs one pair on each of its three segments~~

Fig. 9. Fact checks (those rejected by teacher struck out) leading to new base-level knowledge being learned.

---

[8] When accepted, the teacher provided the verb phrases needed to connect the pairs of bits / contexts in both orders to create two natural language statements for each pair.
[9] 58.85% if symmetric hypotheses counted only once.
[10] 33 (64.7%) if symmetric hypotheses counted only once.

1: some crustaceans are found on land just like most chelicarata
2: most chelicarata are found on land just like some crustaceans
3: being the rear segment is a feature of the opisthosoma just like lacking appendages
4: lacking appendages is a feature of the opisthosoma just like being the rear segment
5: 13000 species in the myriapoda are classified into four classes in the myriapoda
6: four classes in the myriapoda include 13000 species in the myriapoda
7: 13000 species in the myriapoda subphylum are classified into four classes
8: four classes in the myriapoda subphylum include 13000 species
9: subphylums in the arthropoda phylum include classes in the myriapoda subphylum
10: classes in the myriapoda subphylum belong to subphylums in the arthropoda phylum
11: organisms usually found under leaf litter in the soil or under rocks belong to myriapoda that also include organisms found all over the world in temperate and tropical areas
12: organisms found all over the world in temperate and tropical areas belong to myriapoda that also include organisms usually found under leaf litter in the soil or under rocks
13: organisms found in fresh water belong to crustaceans that also include organisms found on land
14: organisms found on land belong to crustaceans that also include organisms found in fresh water
15: 800000 species of insects are a subphylum of arthropods just like 31500 living species of crustaceans
16: 31500 living species of crustaceans are a subphylum of arthropods just like 800000 species of insects
17: insect bodies may have similarities to crustaceans bodies
18: crustaceans bodies may have similarities to insect bodies
19: crustaceans with an exoskeleton or hard shell are a subphylum of arthropods just like insects with an exoskeleton or hard shell
20: insects with an exoskeleton or hard shell are a subphylum of arthropods just like crustaceans with an exoskeleton or hard shell
21: crustaceans with an exoskeleton are a subphylum of arthropods just like insects with an exoskeleton
22: insects with an exoskeleton are a subphylum of arthropods just like crustaceans with an exoskeleton
23: the fact that crustaceans have x may have similarities to the fact that insects have x
24: the fact that insects have x may have similarities to the fact that crustaceans have x
25: exoskeleton includes exoskeleton or hard shell that protects internal organs
26: exoskeleton or hard shell that protects internal organs is an example of an exoskeleton
27: the exoskeleton that protects the insects illustrates the same arthropod trait as the fact that crustaceans have an exoskeleton or hard shell
28: the fact that crustaceans have an exoskeleton or hard shell reflects the same arthropod feature as the exoskeleton that protects the insects
29: segmented bodies sometimes have pairs of branched appendages on each segment
30: pairs of branched appendages on each segment can be found in some segmented bodies
31: organisms with segmented bodies sometimes include organisms with pairs of branched appendages on each segment of their bodies
32: organisms with pairs of branched appendages on each segment of their bodies are examples of organisms with segmented bodies
33: the fact that insects have three sections is similar the fact that crustaceans have three sections
34: the fact that crustaceans have three sections is similar to the fact that insects have three sections
35: the fact that insects have three of x may have similarities to the fact that crustaceans have three x
36: the fact that crustaceans have three x may have similarities to the fact that insects have three of x
37: segmented bodies sometimes include three sections the head the thorax and the abdomen
38: three sections the head the thorax and the abdomen are examples of segmented bodies
39: the fact that insects have x may have similarities to the fact that crustaceans have x
40: the fact that crustaceans have x may have similarities to the fact that insects have x
41: invertebrates means spinelessness
42: spinelessness means invertebrates
43: having segmented bodies is a feature of arthropods just like spinelessness
44: spinelessness is a feature of arthropods just like having segmented bodies
45: having three sections the head the thorax and the abdomen is a feature of some insects like spinelessness
46: spinelessness is a feature of some insects like having three sections the head the thorax and the abdomen
47: the feature that organisms have an exoskeleton is a feature of arthropods just like spinelessness
48: spinelessness is a feature of arthropods just like the feature that organisms have an exoskeleton
49: the feature that organisms have six legs one pair on each of its three segments is a feature of insects just like spinelessness
50: spinelessness is a feature of insects just like the feature that organisms have six legs one pair on each of its three segments
51: the exoskeleton is a feature of arthropods just like spinelessness
52: spinelessness is a feature of arthropods just like the exoskeleton
53: insects are a subphylum of arthropods just like crustaceans
54: crustaceans are a subphylum of arthropods just like insects
55: four subphylums in the arthropoda phylum include one with over 800000 species of insects
56: over 800000 species of insects constitute one of four subphylums in the arthropoda phylum
57: thorax is a part of insects
58: insects have thorax
59: segmented bodies sometimes have three sections the head the thorax and the abdomen
60: three sections the head the thorax and the abdomen are examples of segmented bodies
61: ~~Does 'spinelessness' relate to 'being found all over the world'? (y/n)~~
62: ~~Does 'spinelessness' relate to 'having over 800000 species'? (y/n)~~
63: ~~Does 'spinelessness' relate to 'the fact that some species also have wings'? (y/n)~~
64: ~~Does 'some chelicarata like the horseshoe crab' relate to 'most crustaceans'? (y/n)~~
65: ~~Does 'the fact that ticks and mites are parasites' relate to 'the fact that animals like the horseshoe crab are found in the ocean'? (y/n)~~

Fig. 10. Generated hypotheses (those rejected by teacher struck out), leading to new higher-level knowledge being learned, and new first-class statements being available to learner for applying coduction.

Figure 11 shows a transcript of the very beginning of the interaction between the learner and the teacher, and the creation of the first two hypotheses and addition of the corresponding facts to the knowledge base.

```
> Statement: the thorax is the part of the body between the head and the abdomen
Added to true knowledge
> Statement: arthropods have an open circulatory system
Added to true knowledge
> Statement: arthropods that live in the water have gills
Added to true knowledge
> Statement: arthropods are bilaterally symmetrical
Added to true knowledge
> Statement: if you sliced arthropods from top to bottom each half would be exactly the same
Added to true knowledge
> Statement: there are four subphylums in the arthropoda phylum
Added to true knowledge
> Statement: insects do not have spines
Added to true knowledge
> Statement: insects are invertebrates
Added to true knowledge
> Statement: insects have segmented bodies
Added to true knowledge
> Statement: insects have three sections the head the thorax and the abdomen
Added to true knowledge
What is the noun phrase for three sections the head the thorax and the abdomen ?
> three sections the head the thorax and the abdomen
What is the noun phrase for segmented bodies ?
> segmented bodies
Does 'three sections the head the thorax and the abdomen' relate to 'segmented bodies'? (y/n)
> y
What is the relation between three sections the head the thorax and the abdomen and segmented bodies?
> are examples of
TRUE HYPOTHESIS> three sections the head the thorax and the abdomen are examples of segmented bodies |
queued for processing by the learner.
Does 'segmented bodies' relate to 'three sections the head the thorax and the abdomen'? (y/n)
> y
What is the relation between segmented bodies and three sections the head the thorax and the abdomen?
> sometimes have
TRUE HYPOTHESIS> segmented bodies sometimes have three sections the head the thorax and the abdomen |
queued for processing by the learner.
What is the noun phrase for insects have three sections the head the thorax ?
> insects
What is the noun phrase for the thorax is the part of the body between the head ?
> thorax
Does 'insects' relate to 'thorax'? (y/n)
> y
What is the relation between insects and thorax?
> have
TRUE HYPOTHESIS> insects have thorax | queued for processing by the learner.
Does 'thorax' relate to 'insects'? (y/n)
> y
What is the relation between thorax and insects?
> is a part of
TRUE HYPOTHESIS> thorax is a part of insects | queued for processing by the learner.
```

Fig. 11. Transcript showing formation of the first two hypotheses.

```
> Statement: crustaceans have pairs of branched appendages on each segment of their bodies
Added to true knowledge
> Statement: crustaceans may or may not have appendages on their abdomens
Added to true knowledge
> Statement: crustaceans have an exoskeleton or hard shell that protects their internal organs
Added to true knowledge
Does 'insects have pairs of branched appendages on each segment of their bodies' make sense? (y/n/don't
know(dk))
> n
FALSE FACT CHECK: insects have pairs of branched appendages on each segment of their bodies
Does 'insects have an exoskeleton or hard shell that protects their internal organs' make sense? (y/n/don't
know(dk))
> y
TRUE FACT CHECK: insects have an exoskeleton or hard shell that protects their internal organs | queued for
processing by the learner.
```

Fig. 12. Transcript showing first instance of a fact check requested by learner.

Figure 12 shows a transcript of the first instance of the interaction between the learner and the teacher where the learner asks the teacher to confirm a possible fact.

6 Discussion

Because this approach abstracts over linguistic differences, it can be used for learning in different languages. The meaning of the learner's knowledge comes from the teacher's and eventual queriers' grounding in the world with that language.

Although processing of any individual statement is highly concurrent internally, the learner's processing of only one statement at a time could still limit the opportunity to parallelize. However, available parallelism can be fully utilized by having an ensemble of independent learners taking turns pulling out statements from a high-velocity stream to learn independently from different subsets of the available statements and periodically sharing their hypotheses with each other. In other words, the learners could learn from subsets of statements and subsequently teach each other the higher-level relational knowledge they have learned.

Finally, the approach is notable in its focus on knowledge maintenance, and in that the hypothesis formation mechanism is primitive and relies on little more than the ability to match substrings. This incidental relationship between space conservation and learning could possibly offer insights into evolution of reasoning. Just storing of knowledge statements independently has to be a precursor to the ability of finding similarities between them and somehow organizing and analyzing them. If the ability to identify relations can be shown to follow from a need to compress the knowledge bases, that could serve as a clue about the evolutionary path that relation-identification might have taken.[11]

7 Conclusion and Future Work

This paper presented coduction, a symbolic approach to maintaining knowledge, forming hypotheses and enabling a type of curiosity. A learning agent employing coduction learns by using textual similarity between statements to form hypotheses about related things. We argued that this works because many rules governing the complex world that we live in are relatively simple, affording opportunities for hypothesizing based on what can be observed. A highly concurrent Actor-based implementation was described. Quantitative results show a high degree of learning and a learning time that has a linear relationship with the size of the dataset. The qualitative evaluation shows that coduction can be used for learning from even small amounts of unstructured data, and demonstrates the nature of this learning.

Early experiments comparing coduction with a particular LLM showed superior learning in coduction as a result of fact checks and hypothesis creations. Particularly, for the synthetic family relations dataset, coduction was able to learn new facts which LLaMA could not generalize to in several tests; there were no consistent LLaMA generalizations which coduction could not learn.

---

[11] That said, given the usefulness of relationship discovery, there would be even better reasons for evolution to keep and build on the mechanism for just that purpose.

Work is continuing to obtain more authoritative results showing the advantage of coduction in hypothesis generation over the latest LLMs.

Finally, we are working on a capability to interface with both traditional algorithms (such as for carrying out mathematical computations) as well as with LLM technology to enhance LLMs' scientific discovery capability.

Dedication. This paper is dedicated to Gul Agha in celebration of his contributions to concurrent programming.

References

1. Agha, G.: Actors programming for the mobile cloud. In: Proceedings of the IEEE International Symposium on Parallel and Distributed Computing, pp. 3–9 (2014)
2. Agha, G.A.: Actors: A Model of Concurrent Computation in Distributed Systems. MIT Press (1986)
3. Carlson, A., Betteridge, J., Kisiel, B., Settles, B., Hruschka, E.R., Mitchell, T.M.: Toward an architecture for never-ending language learning. In: Proceedings of the AAAI Conference on Artificial Intelligence (2010)
4. Fodor, J.: Methodological solipsism considered as a research strategy in cognitive psychology. Behav. Brain Sci. **3**(1), 63–73 (1980)
5. Holland, J.H., Holyoak, K.J., Nisbett, R.E., Thagard, P.R.: Induction: Processes of inference, learning, and discovery. MIT press (1989)
6. Jumper, J., et al.: Highly accurate protein structure prediction with alphafold. Nature **596**(7873), 583–589 (2021)
7. Laird, J., Rosenbloom, P., Newell, A.: Chunking in soar: The anatomy of a general learning mechanism. Mach. Learn. **1**, 11–46 (1986)
8. LeCun, Y., Bengio, Y., Hinton, G.: Deep learning. Nature **521**(7553), 436–444 (2015)
9. Lenat, D.B.: Cyc: a large-scale investment in knowledge infrastructure. Commun. ACM **38**(11), 33–88 (1995)
10. Lightbend: Akka Framework (2020). http://www.akka.io
11. McCarthy, J.: Elephant 2000: A programming language based on speech acts (1989), unpublished Draft
12. Mitchell, T.M.: Generalization as search. Artifi. intell. **18**(2), 203–226 (1982)
13. Odersky, M., et al.: An Overview of the Scala Programming Language. Tech. rep, EPFL (2004)
14. Peirce, C.S.: Collected papers of Charles Sanders Peirce. Harvard University Press (1931)
15. Valiant, L.: Probably Approximately Correct: Nature's Algorithms for Learning and Prospering in a Complex World. Basic Books (2013)
16. Vaswani, A., et al.: Attention is all you need. In: Proceedings of the Conference on Neural Information Processing Systems, pp. 1–11. Longbeach, CA, USA (2017)

Formal Methods

Logical Time in Actor Systems

Edward A. Lee

UC Berkeley, Berkeley 94720, CA, USA
eal@berkeley.edu

Abstract. The nondeterministic ordering of message handling in the original actor model makes it difficult to achieve the consistency across a distributed system that some applications require. This paper explores a number of mitigations, focusing primarily on the use of logical time to define a semantic ordering for messages. A variety of coordination mechanisms can ensure that messages are handled in logical time order, but they all come with costs. A fundamental tradeoff (the CAL theorem) makes it impossible to achieve consistency without paying a price in availability, where the price depends on the latencies introduced by network communication, computation overhead, and clock synchronization error. This paper shows how to use the Lingua Franca coordination language to navigate this tradeoff, and particularly how to ensure eventual consistency while bounding unavailability with manageable risk.

Keywords: actors · distributed systems · consistency vs. availability

Prologue

This paper is dedicated to my friend, colleague, and mentor, Gul Agha, and offered as a contribution to his Festschrift. Gul's work on concurrent and distributed programming models has been and continues to be an inspiration.

1 Introduction

Gul Agha's actor model of computation [1–6] provides an elegant way to express concurrent and distributed programs. It has had enormous influence through realizations in Erlang [8], Akka [38], Rebeca [40], CAF [13], and many other software frameworks. The original model has inspired many variants, including several that strive for more deterministic computation. Several of these are realized in the Ptolemy II system [37], for example.

In the actor model, components (called actors) maintain local state and communicate via asynchronous message passing. When messages arrive, procedures (message handlers) are invoked in a mutually exclusive fashion. The principal source of nondeterminism in the model is that when messages arrive from a multiplicity of other actors, the order in which they are handled is not defined. While there are many applications for which such nondeterminism is not problematic (and may even be a feature), some applications require more control over the possible behaviors. In particular, many applications require some form of *consistency*, which we can think of broadly as some form of agreement on shared knowledge across a distributed system.

Although it has proved difficult for the community to agree on the meaning of consistency [21], there is general agreement that inconsistencies often arise because distributed nodes see events in a different order. Consider two physically separated nodes that are each attempting to maintain state machines that track each other, as in, for example, a digital twin application, a replicated database, or redundant controllers for fault tolerance. Events that cause state changes can result in persistent inconsistent states if they are not handled in the same order. I develop here a very simple application that illustrates this problem and several of the many solutions that have been proposed and implemented.

The key problem addressed in this paper is that of maintaining consistency across a distributed system. Even when assuming reliable, in-order delivery of messages on a point-to-point connection, as realized for example by TCP, the widely used internet protocol, distributed components may see messages in different order when the arrive from diverse sources. This can result in inconsistent states across the system. Ensuring consistency unavoidably implies a timing penalty, a fundamental result known as the CAL theorem [29,30]. This paper shows how to augment the actor model with timestamps to ensure consistency, how to manage the resulting timing penalties, and how to keep timing penalties bounded in the presence of faults.

2 Motivating Example

Consider a brutally simplified example application that replicates data: a distributed banking system with just one account. I distill it down to the barest minimum, where there are two nodes at physically different locations. Each node manages an ATM machine that can dispense cash, and each node maintains a copy of the bank balance.

This application is perhaps the world's smallest distributed database. It maintains exactly one integer-valued record, the bank balance. It allows this record to be modified at either node, through deposits or withdrawals at the ATM machines. It requires at least *eventual consistency*, which means that if all transactions stop, then eventually the two nodes should agree on what the balance is. And it requires *availability*, in the sense that customers will not be happy if the ATM refuses to dispense cash because the network is down. But it also has some features that make it more interesting than a simple distributed database. In particular, overdrafts may be hard to prevent without sacrificing availability.

This application is typical of many distributed applications, where distributed nodes all monitor the same input data and evolve their state according to that data. The challenge is to maintain some form of consistency in their states. We assume they will all eventually see the same input data, but not necessarily in the same order and possibly with considerable delays.

I will give a series of implementations, beginning with an actor implementation. In the actor implementation, the intrinsic nondeterminism in the model of computation is not problematic if overdrafts are not a problem. But if they are, the nondeterministic order in which messages are handled becomes a problem. Subsequent implementations offer a variety of ways to deal with the problems. I conclude by outlining the fundamental limits that this series of examples faces, arguing that there is no perfect solution. Every solution requires compromises, and which compromises to select depends very much on the application.

Each implementation is realized using the federated version [10] of the Lingua Franca (LF) coordination language [34]. I describe the features of LF as we go.

2.1 An Actor Solution

Figure 1 shows a Lingua Franca program together with its automatically-generated diagram.[1] This program uses features of LF to make the semantics of the program conformant with the actor model.

First, LF is a coordination language, not a programming language. It coordinates programs written in conventional languages. In this case, the language chosen is C, as indicated by the `target` directive on the first line. Line 19 declares the main program to be `federated`, which means that each component (called a reactor) that is instantiated within this federated reactor will become a standalone program. The programs can be run all on one machine or on several machines or cloud instances. The network communication and any required coordination are automatically generated.

In this program, there are four federate instances, instantiated on lines 20 through 23. Instances `w1` and `w2` are instances of an imported reactor class called `IntWebSocketServer`, which is not shown. That class realizes a simple web server that connects to the LF program via a web socket that sends a stream of integers to and from a browser. The browser stands in for an ATM machine, providing a simple HTML interface enabling a user to deposit and withdraw cash (see Fig. 2). The details of the implementation of these reactors are not important. All we need to know is that `w1` outputs a positive integer when a user deposits cash and a negative integer when a user withdraws cash.

When the user deposits or withdraws cash (via the web interface), an integer output appears on the `received` output port of the web server reactor (see the diagram in Fig. 1). This integer is forwarded to both account managers, and one of those account managers (presumably the local one) responds over the feedback connection with the balance in the account after the deposit or withdrawal is completed. The web server receives this input on its `response` input port. The web server reactor then sends this balance over a web socket to the browser, which will display it to the user as the reported balance.

The account manager instances `a1` and `a2` are instances of the reactor class called `ACIDAccountManager` defined starting on line 4. This class defines a single `reaction`, which is triggered by a message on either of its input ports, `in1` or `in2`. The code in the reaction body, surrounded by the delimiters {= ... =}, is C code. It uses LF C target API to check whether each input port has a message to process, and, if it does, to

---

[1] Some details are omitted for brevity; full programs (and more) and all supporting files can be found at https://github.com/lf-lang/lf-demos/tree/main/federated-decentralized.

```
1  target C {coordination: decentralized}
2  import IntWebSocketServer from "lib/IntWebSocketServer.lf"
3
4  reactor ACIDAccountManager(STA: time = 0) {
5    input in1: int
6    input in2: int
7    output out: int
8    state balance: int = 0
9    reaction(in1, in2) -> out {=
10     if (in1->is_present) {
11       self->balance += in1->value;
12     }
13     if (in2->is_present) {
14       self->balance += in2->value;
15     }
16     lf_set(out, self->balance);
17   =}
18 }
19 federated reactor {
20   w1 = new IntWebSocketServer(...)
21   w2 = new IntWebSocketServer(...)
22   a1 = new ACIDAccountManager()
23   a2 = new ACIDAccountManager()
24
25   w1.received ~> a1.in1
26   w2.received ~> a2.in2
27   w1.received ~> a2.in1
28   w2.received ~> a1.in2
29   a1.out ~> w1.response
30   a2.out ~> w2.response
31 }
```

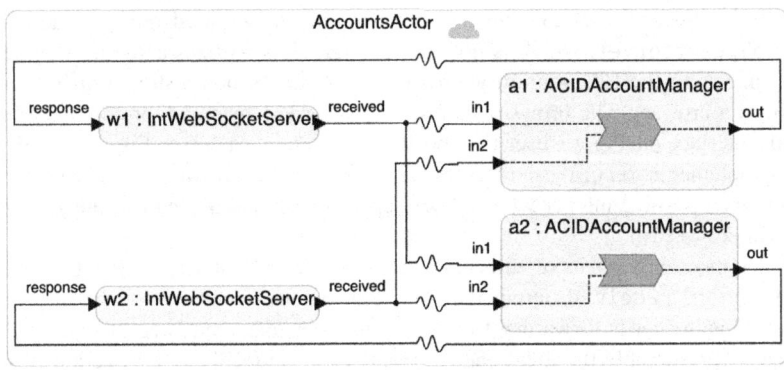

Fig. 1. A simple distributed banking system in the actor style realized in Lingua Franca.

add the value of that message to its state variable named balance. It then produces the resulting balance on its output.

The connection statements on lines 25 through 30 establish connections between the reactor instances, as shown in the diagram. These connections are of a particular type in LF called a *physical connection*, created with the syntax ~> and depicted in the diagram with a squiggly line. A physical connection in LF uses TCP to reliably deliver messages in order, but otherwise there is no coordination between messages. Each account manager here has two inputs, one coming from a local web server (its ATM machine) and the other coming from a remote web server (a remote ATM machine). Because of the

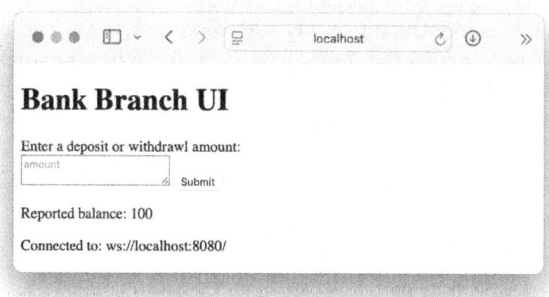

Fig. 2. Our crude browser-based user interface standing in for an ATM machine.

physical connections, there is no ordering semantics to these messages, and they will be handled in whatever order they happen to be received. Hence, the reaction starting on line 9 has similar semantics to a message handler in an actor language. It handles incoming messages in the order in which they are received.

Now, suppose these federates are deployed so that one web server and account manager are in Singapore and the other pair is in London. Each account manager maintains its own copy of the bank balance. It is reasonable to demand that these balances be consistent, but what exactly do we mean by that? A naive approach would be to insist that the two balances agree at an instant in time. But there is no such thing as an "instant in time" for a distributed system, even in theory [36], but much less in practice. And even if we could perfectly synchronize a clock in Singapore with one in London, which we cannot [19], communication delays would have to be accounted for.

The particular algorithm realized in the program, however, has some rather nice properties. Ignoring the possibility of integer overflow in C, the operations performed by the reaction starting on line 9 are associative and commutative. Because the network communication is realized with a TCP socket, the operation is effectively also idempotent. In distributed systems, idempotence means that if a message is delivered more than once, it has the same effect as if it had been delivered exactly once. The TCP connection guarantees exactly once delivery. Hence, handling of messages satisfies the properties that Helland and Campbell call "ACID 2.0" [22], a revision of the classic ACID database properties (atomicity, consistency, isolation, and durability) to stand for associative, commutative, idempotent, and distributed. This means that regardless of network latencies and nondeterministic message ordering, as long as both account managers eventually see the same messages, they will eventually agree on the balance.

These ACID 2.0 properties have been identified by Shapiro et al. as realizing what they call a "conflict free replicated datatype" (CRDT) [39]. The `ACIDAccountManager` with its state variable `balance` and its operation defined by its reaction is, perhaps, the world's simplest CRDT.

A slightly tortured interpretation also allows us to see the operation of the account manager is being monotonic in a partial order, which by the CALM theorem [7,28] then guarantees eventual consistency. Under this interpretation, each account manager's balance is simply a compact representation of a multiset of all deposits and withdrawals that it has seen, and each operation simply adds a number to the multiset. Set union is a monotonic operation in a partial order defined by the subset relation, and hence the CALM theorem applies, albeit in a rather tortured way.

All of this gives us beautiful theory, but it does not give us something any bank would actually use. This design would permit customers to withdraw any amount of money irrespective of their balance. Unfortunately, fixing this flaw also loses most of these nice properties, as I explore next.

2.2 An Inconsistent Solution

Suppose that we replace the reaction in the account manager with the one shown in Fig. 3. This reaction implements a particular (arbitrary) business logic that denies withdrawals greater than the balance and applies a $30 penalty for any attempt to overdraw the account. This operation is no longer commutative, so, when put in the structure shown in Fig. 1, leads to nondeterministic disagreements about the balance in the account. Suppose that a deposit of $200 takes place in London nearly simultaneously with a withdrawal of $200 in Singapore. It is possible that one account manager will deem an overdraft to have occurred while the other did not. The two will now permanently disagree on the balance.

Fixing this inconsistency requires considerable sophistication in distributed computing. One relatively simple solution is to maintain the balance at exactly one node rather than in a distributed fashion. This has a cost of creating a single point of failure, and communication latencies or network outages can result in unavailability. Even this solution, however, requires paying careful attention to atomicity, for example using transactions [20,26]. The designer has to be careful that a withdrawal at another site cannot occur between querying for the balance and granting a local withdrawal, for example.

Distributed transactions offer a more sophisticated solution, but the algorithms are tricky and getting good performance is challenging [17]. Here, I offer an alternative approach, which is to enhance the semantics of actors with timestamps that define an order for messages. I then explore infrastructure-level middleware techniques that enforce the ordering. These are not intrinsically simpler than other distributed computing techniques, but they make application development simpler by absorbing many of the complexities into the infrastructure. The application designer can focus on realizing the business logic rather than on the intricacies of distributed computing.

2.3 Using Timestamps

If a deposit occurs in London nearly simultaneously with a withdrawal in Singapore, how should we determine whether an overdraft has occurred? Fundamentally, it is not possible to unambiguously determine the order in which two closely-timed events occur at two distinct physical locations. The theory of relativity tells us that the ground-truth order may depend on the observer. Fortunately, we do not need to find a ground-truth order. We just need for the components of the distributed system to *agree* on the order and for the resulting order to appear reasonable to human observers.

For this purpose, let us assume that the computers in London and Singapore each have local clocks that are reasonably well synchronized with one another, using for example the network time protocol (NTP) [35], the precision time protocol (PTP) [19], or GPS, for example. We can use these physical clocks to assign logical timestamps to the deposits and withdrawals. A Lingua Franca program that does this is shown in Fig. 4. This is identical to the program in Fig. 1 except that the connections between components now carry timestamps, and the non-commutative account manager of Fig. 3 is used. The use of timestamps is specified in the program using the connection syntax -> instead of ~> on lines 7 through 12, which results in the diagram shown in Fig. 4. The diagram shows straight line connections instead of squiggly lines.

The Lingua Franca semantics now defines a correct execution of the program to be one where every reactor handles messages in timestamp order. Hence, a correct execution of the program in Fig. 4 results in the two account managers agreeing on the value of the balance at any *timestamp*. The timestamp becomes a *logical time*, distinct from physical time [33] in that when Singapore learns about a deposit that occurred in London, that deposit will carry a timestamp that was assigned in London. The machine in Singapore will process that deposit in timestamp order relative to any other events, even local events that are assigned timestamps using its local physical clock.

The use of timestamps gives a semantics to message ordering. Timestamps are numbers, so one slight complication is that now there is a notion of two messages being *simultaneous*. They have the same timestamp. No such notion exists in the classical actor model, where messages are queued and handled one-at-a-time.

The `AccountManager` reactor defined in Fig. 3 specifies a particular behavior when two inputs arrive with the same timestamp. In this case, there will be just one invocation of the reaction starting on line 7, and both in1->is_present and in2->is_present

```
1  reactor AccountManager(STA: time = 0) {
2    input in1: int
3    input in2: int
4    output out: int
5    state balance: int = 0
6
7    reaction(in1, in2) -> out {=
8      int in1_val = 0;
9      int in2_val = 0;
10     if (in1->is_present) {
11       if (self->balance >= -in1->value) {
12         self->balance += in1->value;
13       } else {
14         self->balance -= 30; // Apply penalty
15       }
16     }
17     if (in2->is_present) {
18       if (self->balance >= -in2->value) {
19         self->balance += in2->value;
20       } else {
21         self->balance -= 30; // Apply penalty
22       }
23     }
24     lf_set(out, self->balance);
25   =}
26 }
```

Fig. 3. An inconsistent account manager.

```
 1  federated reactor {
 2      w1 = new IntWebSocketServer(...)
 3      w2 = new IntWebSocketServer(...)
 4      a1 = new AccountManager()
 5      a2 = new AccountManager()
 6
 7      w1.received -> a1.in1
 8      w2.received -> a2.in2
 9      w1.received -> a2.in1
10      w2.received -> a1.in2
11      a1.out -> w1.response
12      a2.out -> w2.response
13  }
```

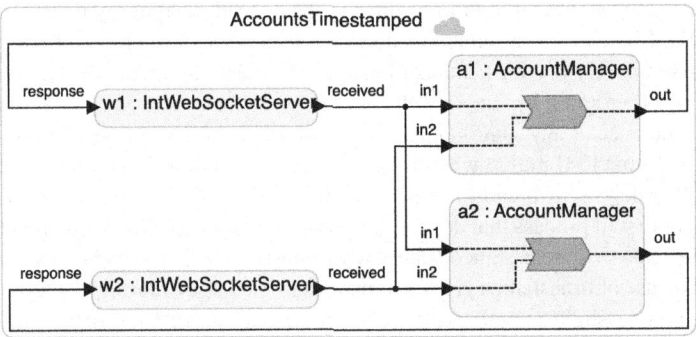

Fig. 4. Our distributed banking system with timestamped communication.

will be true. The logic given in this program, therefore, will give preference to a deposit or withdrawal on in1, honoring it first if there is sufficient balance. A withdrawal on in2 will be honored only if the balance is sufficient after handling in1. Because of the way the connections are made in Fig. 4, both account managers will give preference to the upper instance of the web server, and, hence, if one honors a withdrawal, so will the other, thereby maintaining consistency.

The use of timestamps here provides a stronger form of consistency than eventual consistency. This form of consistency asserts that two components agree on the value of a shared quantity *at a logical time*. As shown by Lee et al. [29,30], this consistency comes with an intrinsic cost in availability that is a function of the latency in communication (the CAL theorem). In this case, "availability" refers to the physical time one must wait before one can access the value of a shared quantity at a particular logical time. The longer one has to wait, the less available the shared quantity is. The waiting time is the price paid for ensuring a "correct" behavior, where all messages are handled in timestamp order. I now address the mechanisms provided by Lingua Franca for achieving a correct behavior and for relaxing consistency to improve availability.

3 Achieving Correct Behavior

Now that we have defined "correct behavior," how do we achieve it? In Lingua Franca, by default, when you create a federated program, the distributed execution relies on a single, centralized coordinator called the RTI, for runtime infrastructure [10]. When a node wishes to process a timestamped event, it queries the RTI for permission, and the RTI grants permission only when it can assure that the node has already received all messages with lesser timestamps. This coordination strategy ensures our strong form of consistency. However, it has considerable disadvantages. The RTI is a single point of failure, a potential bottleneck for communication, and a source of additional latency because of the required two-way communication. Consequently, I focus here on an experimental decentralized coordinator for federated Lingua Franca programs. I will show how this coordinator can be used to achieve a variety of strategies with different tradeoffs.

3.1 Decentralized Coordination in Lingua Franca

Lingua Franca offers an alternative coordination strategy that is decentralized [10]. A programmer declares to use the decentralized coordinator as shown on line 1 in Fig. 1. Coordination is based on PTIDES [18,43], a technique that was developed in my group and independently reinvented at Google to become the backbone of Google Spanner, a globally distributed database system [14,15].

Like the (default) centralized coordinator, a runtime infrastructure (RTI) node orchestrates the startup (and shutdown) of the federation, but unlike the centralized coordinator, the RTI plays little role during the execution of the program. Its function is limited to handling requests to shut down the federation, and to performing runtime clock synchronization, if this is enabled. Many applications will disable this clock synchronization and rely instead on built-in mechanisms such as NTP, PTP, or GPS.

When using the decentralized coordinator, each federate makes its own decisions about when to advance to a timestamp and invoke reactions to events with that timestamp. To govern these decisions, there are two key parameters that a programmer can specify:

1. **STA**: The **safe to advance** offset is a physical time quantity that asserts that the federate can advance to a timestamp t when its local physical clock time T satisfies $T \geq t + \text{STA}$.
2. **STAA**: The **safe to assume absent** offset is a physical time quantity that asserts that the federate, if it has not received a message with timestamp t or larger, can assume an input to be absent at timestamp t when its local physical clock time T satisfies $T \geq t + \text{STA} + \text{STAA}$.

If we choose finite value for STA and STAA, these two thresholds are guaranteed to be satisfied eventually under only the assumption that physical time continues to advance. This can be used to ensure liveness in a distributed system. As we will see, however, sometimes it is useful to choose infinite values for STA or STAA, thereby ensuring consistency at the expense of liveness.

```
reactor A(STA:time = <time value>) { ... }
```

The STA is a property of a federate and is defined as a parameter for the reactor class:

```
reactor A {
  input in:<type>
  reaction(in) {=
    <normal operation>
  =} STAA(<time value>) {=
    <fault handler>
  =}
}
```

Any network input port will have that STAA applied to it if it is a trigger for or is used by a reaction that declares an STAA handler. If more than one STAA is declared for the same input port, the minimum time value will be the one in effect.

If, for example, our account manager reactor has an STA of 100 ms, then, when it receives a deposit or withdrawal message from its local web server with timestamp t, it waits until its local clock hits $t + 100$ ms and then processes the message. In our application, this will ensure that messages are processed in a timely fashion (unavailability is limited to 100 ms), but messages will be processed "correctly" (in timestamp order) only under specific assumptions. In particular, we would have to ensure that any message with timestamp less than t from Singapore is received in London before London's physical clock hits $t+100$ ms. Assuming the timestamp in Singapore was assigned using Singapore's local physical clock, this implies that the sum of the clock synchronization error and the network latency (plus any processing overhead) cannot exceed 100 ms. This is quite a stringent requirement that may be difficult to achieve without dedicated networks and sophisticated clock synchronization (both used by Google Spanner).

What happens if this requirement is violated? In our particular application, it is quite possible that nothing bad will happen. Correctness is assured as long as messages are handled in timestamp order. If the deposits and withdrawals are sufficiently sparse, then it becomes extremely unlikely that two of them will be close enough in time time to trigger a fault. Nevertheless, if a message with timestamp t arrives after messages with timestamp t or larger have been processed, then the <fault handler> in the above code will be executed instead of the <normal operation> code in the reaction. If no <fault handler> is given for an input port that receives such an out-of-order message, then Lingua Franca issues a warning and proceeds to process the message at the wrong timestamp. For applications using CRDTs, this may not be a problem, although then it would be better to use the style of connections in Fig. 1, which discard timestamps, so that no warnings are generated. But for our banking application, this strategy is not acceptable.

Choosing suitable STAs, STAAs, and fault handlers for a program is challenging and depends on many factors. I will continue to develop our running application to illustrate the reasoning that a system designer must perform. Our overarching goal is to enable business strategies that weigh the risks of failure and the quality of service while ensuring eventual consistency.

3.2 Optimistic Techniques

There is a long history, dating back at least to Jefferson's TimeWarp [23], of "optimistic" distributed computing. In such techniques, messages are processed when they are available, and, if an out-of-order message later arrives, the execution is rolled back in (logical) time and redone with messages processed in order. This requires that a snapshot state of the component be periodically saved and that inputs that arrive with timestamps greater than that of the snapshot also be saved. This strategy would be easy to implement with relatively small changes to our Lingua Franca program.

However, rolling back is not always possible. Cyber-physical systems, for example, perform actuation in the physical world that may be difficult or impossible to undo. It's hard to unlaunch a missile or claw back the dollars that have been dispensed by the ATM. Also, if the reactions use any legacy code or third-party libraries, creating snapshots of the state may be difficult, expensive, or impossible. As a consequence, optimistic techniques have mostly been used only for distributed *simulation*, not for actual system implementation, except in the much more limited form of transactions.

3.3 Transactions

Database-style transactions provide a more limited form of optimistic computation [20,26]. In our banking application, each node could tentatively make a decision to dispense cash, but only actually dispense cash (i.e. commit the transaction) after receiving confirmation from a quorum of other nodes. This is perhaps a reasonable approach for this application, and it can be implemented in Lingua Franca, but the logic is complex and it's easy to get the program wrong. Moreover, there will be considerable overhead, like with centralized coordination, that will increase latencies and network congestion. There are more attractive alternatives.

3.4 Conservative Techniques

There is a long history, dating back at least to Chandy and Misra [12] of conservative techniques that guarantee distributed processing of events in timestamp order. These have mostly been used for distributed simulation, but the same principles can be used in online applications like our banking system. The centralized coordinator in Lingua Franca provides such conservative coordination loosely based on the High-Level Architecture (HLA) [27,42]. But the decentralized coordinator is also capable of conservative coordination based on Chandy and Misra [12], as I will show now.

Suppose we set STA to `forever`, which is done in Lingua Franca as follows:

```
reactor A(STA:time = forever) { ... }
```

This tells any instance of this reactor that, in order to advance its logical time to some t and handle a message with that timestamp, it must know the status of *all* inputs up to and including timestamp t. If the input status is unknown, the federate must wait until it is known, with no upper bound on the wait time.

```
1  target C { coordination: decentralized }
2  import IntWebSocketServer from "lib/IntWebSocketServer.lf"
3  import AccountManager from "lib/AccountManager.lf"
4
5  reactor Server(hostport: int = 8080, initial_file: string = {= NULL =},
         null_message_period: time = 1 s) {
6    input in: int
7    output received: int
8    timer t(0, null_message_period)
9    w = new IntWebSocketServer(hostport = hostport, initial_file = initial_file)
10   in -> w.response
11   reaction (w.received, t) -> received {=
12     if (w.received->is_present) {
13       lf_set(received, w.received->value);
14     } else {
15       // Send a null message.
16       lf_set(received, 0);
17     }
18   =}
19 }
20 federated reactor {
21   w1 = new Server( ... )
22   w2 = new Server( ... )
23   a1 = new AccountManager(STA = forever)
24   a2 = new AccountManager(STA = forever)
25   w1.received -> a1.in1
26   w2.received -> a2.in2
27   w1.received -> a2.in1
28   w2.received -> a1.in2
29   a1.out -> w1.in
30   a2.out -> w2.in
31 }
```

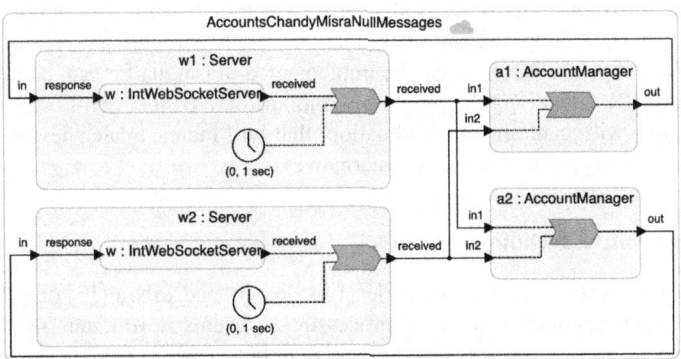

Fig. 5. Our distributed banking system with Chandy and Misra style coordination.

How does the status of an input port become known up to and including logical time t? First, recall that TCP underlies all communication between federated programs in LF. TCP provides a semantics of reliable, in-order delivery. Moreover, LF assures that messages sent along any connection between federates are sent in timestamp order, and that at most one message bears a particular timestamp t. Hence, when a federate receives a message with timestamp t, it is assured that it has seen all messages up to and including timestamp t for this connection.

In this application, messages are sent only when a deposit or withdrawal is made. This means that if a1 receives a withdrawal request on in1 with timestamp t, it must wait until it receives a deposit or withdrawal on in2 with timestamp at least t. This wait time is not bounded and will not be acceptable in this application. The Chandy and Misra technique, therefore, adds the notion of a "null message" that is sent periodically.

Figure 5 shows an implementation using the Chandy and Misra technique with null messages. The IntWebSocketServer reactors are wrapped in another reactor that, in addition to deposit and withdrawal messages, sends periodic null messages (which in this case are just the integer zero, indicating no deposit or withdrawal). On lines 23 and 24, the STA is set to forever for the two account managers, which tells them that they must wait, with no upper bound on the wait time, until all inputs are known up to and including logical time t before processing any message with timestamp t.

The null messages are triggered by a Lingua Franca timer, declared on line 8, which has an offset of zero (the timer starts when the program starts) and a period of one second. The reaction that starts on line 11 is triggered by *either* a deposit or withdrawal from the web server or the timer (or both). If there is a real deposit or withdrawal, it simply forwards it to the output, and otherwise it sends a null message.

With this strategy, the wait time in the account managers is bounded. However, this strategy creates a tight coupling between the components. If one of the Server federates fails, for example, then the null messages will stop and the account managers will both be blocked. Hence, although this strategy guarantees strong consistency, it does so at a potentially unbounded cost in availability.

The CAL theorem tells us that there is no strategy that guarantees strong consistency without a potentially unbounded cost in availability [29, 30]. To bound unavailability, we have to relax consistency. I explore how to do that next.

3.5 Trading Off Consistency and Availability

It is impossible to achieve strong consistency and bounded unavailability under all network behaviors. For this application, eventual consistency is a requirement for at least the balance state variable. All copies of the bank balance must eventually agree. But we can design a system that provides bounded unavailability for at least some transactions.

Figure 6 shows a design that responds in bounded time to deposits, but not necessarily to withdrawals. The Account reactors in this design are the same as the AccountManager reactors in Fig. 5. They have STA set to forever, and hence will maintain strongly consistent balances. The Server reactors, like those in Fig. 5, send null messages periodically.

The QuickDeposit reactors, which are defined by the code shown in the figure, have STA set to 30 ms. These reactors receive inputs from the local web server, and, if the input is positive, immediately process the deposit and send an acknowledgement back to the web server. Line 11 checks whether the transaction is a deposit, and it it is not, then the reactor ignores the input. This results in a quick response to a deposit regardless of network conditions.

The QuickDeposit reactors also have a true_balance input, which gets a message each time the Account reactors update their copy of the true balance. As shown on line 8, it simply updates its copy of the balance upon receiving this input. However, because the STA is only 30 ms for the QuickDeposit reactors and is forever for the Account reactors, it is possible for the true_balance input to receive a message late. Specifically, true_balance may receive an input with timestamp t after the QuickDeposit federate has processed deposit inputs with larger timestamps. Hence, the QuickDeposit reactor is being asked to process messages out of timestamp order.

Line 16 specifies an STAA of zero. Together with the STA of 30 ms, as explained above, this means that if QuickDeposit receives a deposit input with timestamp t, and it has not received a true_balance input with timestamp t or greater, then when its physical clock reading T exceeds t + STA + STAA = t + 30 ms, it will assume that the true_balance input is absent and proceed to process the deposit input. If it later receives a true_balance input with timestamp less than or equal to t, then the requirement to handle inputs in timestamp order has been violated, and the exception code starting on line 17 will be invoked instead of the regular reaction.

The exception handling code starting on line 17 handles true_balance inputs just the same as if there were no error. The business logic here is that the balance is used

```
1   reactor QuickDeposit(STA: time = 30 ms) {
2     input deposit: int
3     input true_balance: int
4     output ack: int
5     state balance: int = 0
6     reaction(true_balance, deposit) -> ack {=
7       if (true_balance->is_present) {
8         self->balance = true_balance->value;
9       }
10      if (deposit->is_present) {
11        if (deposit->value >= 0) {
12          self->balance += deposit->value;
13          lf_set(ack, self->balance);
14        }
15      }
16    =} STAA(0) {=
17      if (true_balance->is_present) {
18        self->balance = true_balance->value;
19      }
20      if (deposit->is_present) {
21        // ERROR. Take ATM offline for service?
22      }
23    =}
24  }
```

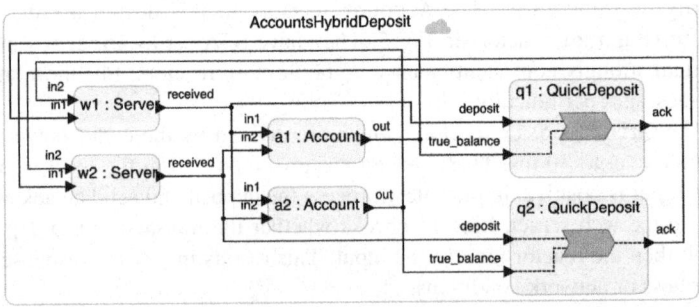

Fig. 6. Distributed banking system with strong consistency and guaranteed availability for deposits.

only to report back to the user what the balance is after the deposit, and if this balance is inaccurate because of delayed messages from the remote server, this will only result in transient errors. This code handles late `deposit` inputs as errors, however. The logic here is that the system is designed to give low delays between the server and the `QuickDeposit` reactors, and if the delays get large, something is wrong with the local system.

Note now that the design of `QuickDeposit` is governed more by *business* decisions than by the intricacies of distributed computing. An alternative design, for example, would also handle small withdrawals quickly and only delay the handling of large withdrawals. This is a business decision to accept some risk in exchange for better, more reliable customer service. Many other designs now become possible (and easy in Lingua Franca).

3.6 Fault Tolerance

Any federate with an STA of `forever` is vulnerable to blocking indefinitely if its upstream federate fails. For the example in Fig. 6, this will only block withdrawals (or large withdrawals, if that option is chosen), which may be acceptable business logic. A better design, however, would use a smaller STA and use the exception handler to handle fault conditions. For example, the "true balance" could be defined by a quorum of nodes rather than by unanimous consent, as done here. (A quorum makes little sense with just two nodes, but a real application will have many more.) The exception handling code could make corrections late to the "true balance," but also alert human maintainers to instability in the system. As long as all nodes agree on which deposits and withdrawals have been actually executed, none of these strategies will compromise eventual consistency.

4 Zero-Delay Cycles

In the above examples, we have not had any particular need for the STAA parameter. Such a need arises only for programs that have zero-delay cycles, where a federate sends an output at tag t and expects a response from other federates at the same tag t. It is extremely tricky to support such cycles. The centralized coordinator in Lingua Franca does support them [16], but when using the decentralized coordinator, some programs become impossible to support without compromises.

The banking application above appears to have such a zero-delay cycle, in that the web server reactors produce a `received` output when a user begins a deposit or withdrawal, and they expect a response with the same timestamp t. However, the web server application has no particular need to process these responses in timestamp order relative the outputs. If another output is sent with timestamp $t' > t$ before the response with timestamp t has been received, no logic errors will result as long as the responses are processed in the same order as the `received` outputs. Hence, the STA and STAA for the web server federates can be set to zero, and the exception handler can simply process late responses identically to responses that are received on time. The pattern looks like this:

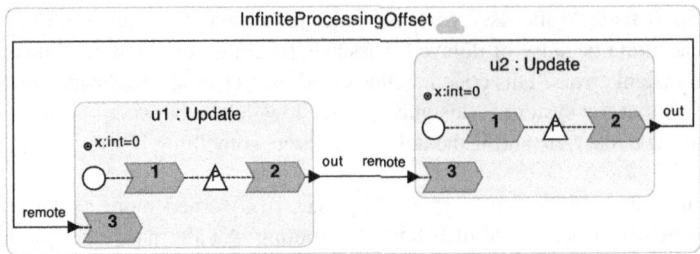

Fig. 7. A feedback system with infinite processing offsets.

```
reaction(in) {=
  // Do something.
=} STAA(0) {=
  // Do the same something.
=}
```

Note that this pattern can also be implemented by just providing no STAA clause at all. But in such an implementation, LF will issue warnings stating that tag-order violations occurred and warning that there is no handler.

4.1 Impossible Consistency

However, not all applications are so forgiving. Consider a program with the pattern shown in Fig. 7. Suppose that the two Update reactors maintain a replica of an integer quantity x. Each reactor can spontaneously update x at an arbitrary time using a Lingua Franca construct called a **physical action**, depicted in the diagram as a triangle with a "P" inside. The physical action asynchronously injects timestamped events when some external input is received, such as a message arrival. Suppose that reactions 2 and 3 in the Update reactors perform non-commutative updates to the value of x. Then, in order to maintain consistency, it becomes imperative to process the physical action events and remote input events in timestamp order in both federates. Only then can we assure that at any logical time t, the two Update reactors have the same value for x.

It is easy to see that there are no values for STA and STAA that make this program executable without timestamp-order violations. Suppose that the physical clocks have negligible clock synchronization error, and that communication between reactors takes 4 ms, at most. Then it might be tempting use an STA of, say, 5 ms in each reactor. But this will not work.

Suppose that the physical action in u1 triggers at (elapsed) physical time 10 ms, according to the local physical clock. It assigns a logical time of 10 ms to the event. If the STA is 5 ms, then, in the absence of any signaling from u2, u1 will wait 5 ms (physical time) and then invoke reaction 2 at physical time 15 ms. Suppose now that u2's physical action had triggered at 9 ms. It too waits 5 ms, invoking its reaction 2 at physical time 14 ms. The message sent from u2 to u1 will arrive by physical time 18 ms. This will trigger a safe-to-process violation because the arriving message has timestamp 9 ms, but u1 has already advanced to logical time 10 ms and sent an output message with that timestamp.

It might be tempting to use an STA of zero and an STAA of 5 ms. But this too will not work. The same scenario as above will again trigger a timestamp-order violation.

This scenario is identified by Lee et al. [29] as one where communication network has a positive cycle mean, which results in the processing offsets diverging to infinity. In effect, each reactor seems to have to wait forever before advancing logical time.

4.2 A Solution

The centralized coordinator in LF is able to execute the program in Fig. 7 without safe-to-process violations using the sophisticated techniques described by Donovan et al. [16]. We can use insights from that coordinator to augment the decentralized coordinator so that it too can execute this program. The key is that we can exploit some knowledge of the semantics of the physical action in Lingua Franca.

A physical action, when triggered, creates an event with a timestamp taken from the local physical clock. Suppose that we augment the decentralized coordination mechanism with a new kind of signal that is similar to the null messages used above, but with a critical difference. Each federate in Fig. 7 could periodically send a null message *without advancing its logical time*. Now, each federate can use an STA of `forever` and the program will execute correctly with no safe to process violations, giving us a conservative strategy similar to that provided by the centralized coordinator, but without any centralized coordinator.

Consider three scenarios. First, assume that u1 has nothing to send for a long time. Suppose that every 5 ms, it sends a null message with logical times spaced by 5 ms, for example at (elapsed) logical times 0, 5 ms, 10 ms, etc. These messages are shown in blue in Fig. 8. These null messages will flow in both directions, but to reduce clutter, we show only one direction until the symmetric case in Fig. 8(c).

Suppose now that at physical time 12 ms, the physical action in u2 triggers, ① in Fig. 8(a). Assume u2 has an STA of forever. Assume again perfectly synchronized clocks and a communication latency bound of 4 ms. By physical time 14 ms, u2 will receive a null message with timestamp 10 ms, ② in Fig. 8(a), which is not sufficient to allow it to advance. By physical time 19 ms, however, u2 will receive a null message with timestamp 15 ms, ③ in Fig. 8(a), which is sufficient. It can now commit and invoke reaction 2 at logical time 12 ms and physical time 19 ms. That reaction will send a message to u1, which will arrive at by physical time 23 ms and will have a lag of 11 ms, ④ in Fig. 8(a), It is easy to see that in this case, the lag is bounded by 14 ms (twice the null message period plus the latency bound). Hence, with bounded latency, we achieve perfect consistency and bounded unavailability.

The second scenario we need to consider is where the two reactors' physical actions trigger close together in time. For example, as above, assume that at physical time 12 ms, the physical action in u2 triggers, ⑤ in Fig. 8(b), and at physical time 11 ms, the physical action in u1 triggers, ⑥ in Fig. 8(b). As above, u1 will send a null message at 10 ms, but it cannot send one at 15 ms until it has processed the physical action. Similarly, u2 will have sent a null message at 10 ms, but it too is blocked until it can process its event at 12 ms. How do we break the deadlock?

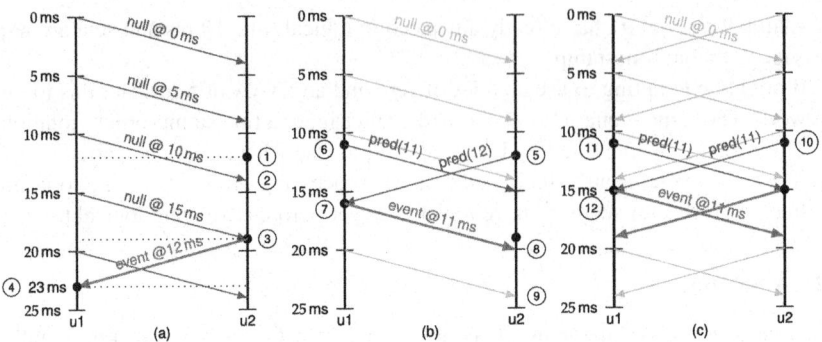

Fig. 8. Three scenarios where federates may send spontaneous messages to one another.

Simple! When a physical action triggers, at 11 ms in u1 and 12 ms in u2, u1 should send a null message with timestamp pred(11 ms) and u2 with timestamp pred(12 ms), where pred(t) is the largest timestamp less than t. This will break the deadlock. By physical time 16 ms, u1 will receive u2's null message with timestamp pred(12 ms), ⑦ in Fig. 8(b). This timestamp is larger than its pending event timestamp of 11 ms, so it can safely advance its logical time to 11 ms and send a real message, shown in red in Fig. 8(b). Federate u2 will receive this message by physical time 20 ms, ⑧ in Fig. 8(b), and it can immediately process the message because its own earliest pending message has timestamp 12 ms, which is greater than 11. To process its own pending event with timestamp 12, it will have to wait for another null message from u1, ⑨ in Fig. 8(b), but the same mechanisms will work, and the lag will again be bounded.

The third scenario is where the two reactors' physical actions coincidentally trigger at exactly the same time, resulting in events with identical timestamps, say, 11 ms, ⑩ and ⑪ in Fig. 8(c), Now, when u1 receives u2's null message with timestamp pred(11 ms), ⑫ in Fig. 8(c), what should it do? It has a pending event with timestamp 11 ms, which is greater than pred(11 ms), so it seems it cannot safely advance. Here, fortunately, the semantics of Lingua Franca helps tremendously. First, note that u1 *can* safely commit to advancing its logical time to 11 ms. It knows there will be no future input with timestamp *less than* 11 ms. It *cannot*, however, safely assume anything about whether the input is present or absent *at* 11 ms.

First, once each federate has advanced its logical time to 11 ms, it can execute any reactions that do not depend on inputs to the federate and precede all reactions that do depend on an input. They can both, therefore, safely execute reaction 2 and send out their messages with timestamps 11 ms, red in Fig. 8(c). But they must block before executing reaction 3 because they do not know the status of the input port at logical time 11 ms. They will become unblocked when they receive each others' messages.

In the decentralized coordinator, a federate with an STA of t_1 and an input port with an STAA of t_2 must wait until physical time $t + t_1 + t_2$ before it can assume that the input port is absent at logical time t. Because of this, we can set the STAA of the input port to 0. The STA is `forever`, so the federate will block indefinitely before executing reaction 3. Specifically, it will block until it receives the message with timestamp 11 ms from the other reactor, exactly the behavior we want!

The above strategy generalizes easily. It does not require perfectly synchronized clocks. Because the STA is `forever`, it delivers strong consistency. However, if latencies get large, this will come at a price in availability. As with the previous examples, we can compromise and choose a smaller STA and then provide fault handlers to deal with safe-to-process violations. How and whether to do that is entirely application dependent.

4.3 Using After Delays

A connection in Lingua Franca can have an `after` delay, as follows:

```
a.out -> b.in after 10 ms
```

This means that the timestamp at the receiving end will be 10 ms larger than the timestamp at the sending end. This feature can be used to realize a generalization of the logical execution time (LET) principle, as explained by Lee and Lohstroh [31]. This feature also relaxes consistency by a measured amount, allowing the source and destination to disagree on the value of a shared quantity for a bounded amount of logical time. As explained in Lee et al. [29], this can be used to improve availability.

It is tempting to assume that the subtleties we have dealt with occur only when a program demands strong consistency and features zero-delay cycles. However, the same problems arise in all programs whenever physical time latencies around a cycle exceed the logical time of the `after` delays. If we cannot enforce a strict bound on network latencies, then we inevitably have to deal with the possibility that this can occur. As I have shown, we can always choose either an approach emphasizing consistency, using STA of forever, or an approach emphasizing availability, using a finite STA and providing fault handlers. If we choose the approach emphasizing consistency, we can still provide fault handlers to deal with violations of our availability requirements using either Lingua Franca deadlines or watchdogs [9].

5 Related Work

Among the widely deployed variants that yield more deterministic behaviors are Kahn process networks [24], usually realized using the Kahn-MacQueen policy of blocking reads [25], and closely related dataflow models [32]. In the Kahn-MacQueen variant, for example, communication channels are assumed to have reliable in-order delivery of messages, and sequential processes block on channel reads until a message is available. Kahn and MacQueen showed that such processes realize prefix-monotonic functions on sequences of messages, and that a network of such processes defines a deterministic computation that is the least fixed point of a monotonic function constructed from the process functions.

Another family of widely deployed variants is based on discrete-event (DE) systems, which have historically been used for simulation [11,41], but can also be used as a deterministic execution model for actors [34]. In DE models, every message sent between actors has a tag, which is a value drawn from a totally-ordered set, and all messages are processed by actors in tag order. The model realized in Lingua Franca is closely related to these classic DE systems.

6 Conclusions

The nondeterministic ordering of message handling in the original actor model makes it difficult to achieve the consistency across a distributed system that some applications require. I have explored a number of mitigations, focusing primarily on the use of timestamps to define a semantic ordering and coordination mechanisms to ensure that messages are handled in timestamp order. A fundamental tradeoff (the CAL theorem) makes it impossible to achieve consistency without paying a price in availability, where the price depends on the latencies introduced by network communication, computation overhead, and clock synchronization error. Using the Lingua Franca coordination language, I have shown how to navigate this tradeoff, and particularly how to ensure eventual consistency while bounding unavailability with manageable risk.

Acknowledgments. The work in this paper was supported in part by the National Science Foundation (NSF), award #CNS-2233769 (Consistency vs. Availability in Cyber-Physical Systems), and the iCyPhy Research Center (Industrial Cyber-Physical Systems) at UC Berkeley.

Disclosure of Interests. The author has no competing interests to declare that are relevant to the content of this article.

References

1. Agha, G., Frolund, S., Kim, W., Panwar, R., Patterson, A., Sturman, D.: Abstraction and modularity mechanisms for concurrent computing. IEEE Parallel Distributed Technol. Syst. Appl. **1**(2), 3–14 (1993)
2. Agha, G.: ACTORS: A Model of Concurrent Computation in Distributed Systems. The MIT Press Series in Artificial Intelligence, MIT Press, Cambridge, MA (1986)
3. Agha, G.: Concurrent object-oriented programming. Commun. ACM **33**(9), 125–140 (1990)
4. Agha, G.: Computing in pervasive cyberspace. Commun. ACM **51**(1), 68–70 (2008). https://doi.org/10.1145/1327452.1327484
5. Agha, G.A.: Abstracting Interaction Patterns: A Programming Paradigm for Open Distributed Systems. In: Najm, E., Stefani, J.-B. (eds.) Formal Methods for Open Object-based Distributed Systems. IAICT, pp. 135–153. Springer, Boston, MA (1997). https://doi.org/10.1007/978-0-387-35082-0_10
6. Agha, G.A., Mason, I.A., Smith, S.F., Talcott, C.L.: A foundation for actor computation. J. Funct. Program. **7**(1), 1–72 (1997)
7. Alvaro, P., Conway, N., Hellerstein, J.M., Marczak, W.R.: Consistency analysis in bloom: a CALM and collected approach. In: 5th Biennial Conference on Innovative Data Systems Research (CIDR) (2011)
8. Armstrong, J., Virding, R., Wikström, C., Williams, M.: Concurrent programming in Erlang. Prentice Hall, second edn. (1996)

9. Asch, B., Jellum, E., Lohstroh, M., Lee, E.A.: Software-defined watchdog timers for cyber-physical systems. Embedded Syst. Lett. (2024). https://doi.org/10.1109/LES.2024.3467332
10. Bateni, S., et al.: Risk and mitigation of nondeterminism in distributed cyber-physical systems. In: ACM-IEEE International Conference on Formal Methods and Models for System Design (MEMOCODE) (2023). https://doi.org/10.1145/3610579.3613219
11. Cassandras, C.G.: Discrete Event Systems. Irwin, Modeling and Performance Analysis (1993)
12. Chandy, K.M., Misra, J.: Distributed simulation: a case study in design and verification of distributed programs. IEEE Trans. Softw. Eng. **5**(5), 440–452 (1979)
13. Charousset, D., Hiesgen, R., Schmidt, T.C.: CAF - the C++ actor framework for scalable and resource-efficient applications. In: International Workshop on Programming based on Actors Agents and Decentralized Control (AGERE), pp. 15–28. ACM (2014). https://doi.org/10.1145/2687357.2687363
14. Corbett, J.C., et al.: Spanner: Google's globally-distributed database. In: OSDI (2012). https://doi.org/10.1145/2491245
15. Corbett, J.C., et al.: Spanner: Google's globally-distributed database. ACM Trans. Comput. Syst. (TOCS) **31**(8) (2013). https://doi.org/10.1145/2491245
16. Donovan, P., et al.: Strongly-consistent distributed discrete-event systems. arXiv 2405.12117v1 [cs.DC] (2024)
17. Dragojević, A., et al.: No compromises: distributed transactions with consistency, availability, and performance. In: Symposium on Operating Systems Principles (SOSP), pp. 54–70 (2015). https://doi.org/10.1145/2815400.2815425
18. Eidson, J., Lee, E.A., Matic, S., Seshia, S.A., Zou, J.: Distributed real-time software for cyber-physical systems. Proc. IEEE (special issue on CPS) **100**(1), 45–59 (2012). https://doi.org/10.1109/JPROC.2011.2161237
19. Eidson, J.C.: Measurement, Control, and Communication Using IEEE 1588. Springer (2006)
20. Gray, J., Reuter, A.: Transaction Processing: Concepts and Techniques. Morgan Kaufmann, San Mateo, CA (1993)
21. Helland, P.: Don't get stuck in the "con" game: consistency, convergence and confluence are not the same! Queue **19**(330), 16–35 (2021). https://doi.org/10.1145/3475965.3480470
22. Helland, P., Campbell, D.: Building on quicksand. In: Conference on Innovative Data Systems Research (CIDR). ACM (2009). https://arxiv.org/abs/0909.1788
23. Jefferson, D.: Virtual time. ACM Trans. Program. Languages Syst. **7**(3), 404–425 (1985)
24. Kahn, G.: The semantics of a simple language for parallel programming. In: Proc. of the IFIP Congress 74, pp. 471–475. North-Holland Publishing Co. (1974)
25. Kahn, G., MacQueen, D.B.: Coroutines and networks of parallel processes. In: Gilchrist, B. (ed.) Information Processing, pp. 993–998. North-Holland Publishing Co., Amsterdam (1977)
26. Kossmann, D.: The state of the art in distributed query processing. ACM Comput. Surv. (CSUR) **32**(4), 422–469 (2000). https://doi.org/10.1145/371578.371598
27. Kuhl, F., Weatherly, R., Dahmann, J.: Creating Computer Simulation Systems: an Introduction to the High Level Architecture. Prentice Hall PTR (1999)
28. Laddad, S., Power, C., Milano, M., Cheung, A., Crooks, N., Hellerstein, J.M.: Keep CALM and CRDT on. arXiv **2210.12605v1 [cs.DB]** (2022). https://doi.org/10.48550/arXiv.2210.12605
29. Lee, E.A., Akella, R., Bateni, S., Lin, S., Lohstroh, M., Menard, C.: Consistency vs. availability in distributed cyber-physical systems. ACM Trans. Embedded Comput. Syst. (TECS) **22**(5s), 1–24 (2023). https://doi.org/10.1145/360919, presented at EMSOFT, September 17-22, 2023, Hamburg, Germany

30. Lee, E.A., Bateni, S., Lin, S., Lohstroh, M., Menard, C.: Trading off consistency and availability in tiered heterogeneous distributed systems. Intell. Comput. **2**(Article 0013), 1–23 (2023). https://doi.org/10.34133/icomputing.0013
31. Lee, E.A., Lohstroh, M.: Generalizing logical execution time. In: Raskin, J.F., Chatterjee, K. (eds.) Principles of Systems Design: Essays Dedicated to Thomas A. Henzinger on the Occasion of His 60th Birthday. vol. LNCS 13660, pp. 1–22. Springer Nature (2022). https://doi.org/10.1007/978-3-031-22337-2_8
32. Lee, E.A., Matsikoudis, E.: The Semantics of Dataflow with Firing. Cambridge University Press (2009). http://ptolemy.eecs.berkeley.edu/publications/papers/08/DataflowWithFiring/
33. Lohstroh, M., Lee, E.A., Edwards, S., Broman, D.: Logical time for reactive software. In: Workshop on Timing-Centric Reactive Software (TCRS), in Cyber-Physical Systems and Internet of Things Week (CPSIoT). ACM (2023). https://doi.org/10.1145/3576914.3587494
34. Lohstroh, M., Menard, C., Bateni, S., Lee, E.A.: Toward a lingua franca for deterministic concurrent systems. ACM Trans. Embedded Comput. Syst. (TECS) **20**(4), Article 36 (2021). https://doi.org/10.1145/3448128
35. Mills, D.L.: Computer Network Time Synchronization – The Network Time Protocol. CRC Press, Boca Raton, FL (2006)
36. Muller, R.A.: Now – The Physics of Time. W. W, Norton and Company (2016)
37. Ptolemaeus, C.: System Design, Modeling, and Simulation using Ptolemy II. Ptolemy.org, Berkeley, CA (2014). http://ptolemy.org/books/Systems
38. Roestenburg, R., Bakker, R., Williams, R.: Akka in Action. Manning Publications, 2nd edn. (2023)
39. Shapiro, M., Preguiça, N., Baquero, C., Zawirski, M.: Conflict-free replicated data types. Report, INRIA (2011). https://pages.lip6.fr/Marc.Shapiro/papers/RR-7687.pdf
40. Sirjani, M., Movaghar, A., Shali, A., de Boer, F.S.: Modeling and verification of reactive systems using Rebeca. Fund. Inform. **63**(4), 385–410 (2004). https://doi.org/10.3233/FUN-2004-63405
41. Zeigler, B.: Theory of Modeling and Simulation. Wiley Interscience, New York (1976)
42. Zeigler, B.P., Lee, J.S.: Theory of quantized systems: formal basis for DEVS/HLA distributed simulation environment. In: SPIE Conference on Enabling Technology for Simulation Science. vol. SPIE Vol. 3369, pp. 49–58 (1998). https://doi.org/10.1117/12.319354
43. Zhao, Y., Lee, E.A., Liu, J.: A programming model for time-synchronized distributed real-time systems. In: Real-Time and Embedded Technology and Applications Symposium (RTAS), pp. 259 – 268. IEEE (2007). https://doi.org/10.1109/RTAS.2007.5

Open CPS: A Symbolic Model

Farhad Arbab[1,2] and Carolyn Talcott[3(✉)]

[1] Centrum Wiskunde and Informatica, Science Park 123, 1098 XG Amsterdam, The Netherlands
farhad@cwi.nl
[2] Leiden University, Leiden, Netherlands
[3] SRI, Menlo Park, USA
carolyn.talcott@gmail.com

Abstract. Modeling of the environment presents a challenge in all open systems, particularly in open cyber-physical systems where the environment is nature. In some cases the environment can be considered and modeled as yet another actor or component in the system. However, in cases of complex systems with intricate interactions with nature as their environment, the unpredictability of this environment and the complexity of the physics involved in its modeling make "environment as a component" an untenable approach.

Concurrent Rules Machines (CRMs) constitute a model for formal specification and analysis of open, distributed cyber-physical systems [3]. The CRM model makes interaction with the environment explicit and offers an algebra of composition and decomposition for construction and analysis of systems through their constituent components. Systematic and automatic verification of properties of systems modeled as CRMs remains a significant challenge. Symbolic representations have been used to model the inherently continuous properties of physics. In this paper we introduce symbolic execution as a means of reasoning about behaviors of CRM models. A symbolic execution represents possibly infinitely many executions and can focus on environments meeting requirements such as physically reasonable actions. We show that symbolic execution is sound, and is complete for a natural class of CRMs. We illustrate our ideas with a simple cyber-physical system example.

1 Introduction

Cyber-physical systems interact with, affect, and are affected by their environment, which is often unpredictable. Not every aspect of an environment directly affects the behavior of a given CPS that runs in that environment. For instance, the thermostat component of a CPS functions correctly so long as the temperature and humidity in an environment each remains within some prescribed range, allowing the CPS to behave properly in any environment that satisfies those temperature and humidity constraints. Analogously, a concrete environment with specific ranges for its temperature and humidity may be a suitable host for a family of systems whose temperature and humidity requirements fall within those ranges.

Replacing concrete values in the model of the behavior of a CPS with symbols subject to additional constraints allows one to compactly model parameterized families of systems, reason about their behavior starting from potentially infinitely many initial states, and to represent effects of actions by the external environment subject to constraints.

Concurrent Rules Machines (CRM) constitute a model for formal specification and analysis of open, distributed cyber-physical systems [3]. The CRM model makes interaction with the environment explicit and offers an algebra of composition and decomposition for construction and analysis of systems through their constituent components. CRM semantics recognizes the environment as a distinct entity and explicitly represents its interactions with the CRM system.

The CRM model addresses the challenge of making interaction with an external environment explicit. The CRM model supports representation of systems that have both discrete and continuous behavior, which introduces another challenge: how to analyze and verify properties of systems using such models. Differential Dynamic Logic and variants support reasoning about hybrid systems and their composition, but mechanisms for representing and reasoning about unknown external environments are not considered [18,26]. Actors are another model of open systems [1]. In [2] a notion of observational equivalence was introduced to characterize actor system behavior in the context of larger systems. However the set of contexts consists of other actors. Rewriting modulo SMT has been proposed to reason about parameterized families of systems [22,27]. This allows verifying properties of possibly infinite sets of initial system configurations, where some variables may represent aspects of the environment.

Inspired by the work on symbolic rewriting, we define symbolic execution of a CRM, generalizing the CRM operational semantics. Symbolic execution provides the basis for automating analysis of properties of CRM execution in an arbitrary or possibly constrained, possibly hostile environment.

Contributions. The main contributions of this paper are

- Definition of symbolic execution of a CRM parameterized by (possibly trivial) constraints on the behavior of the environment.
- A proof of soundness of symbolic execution: every instance of a symbolic execution of a CRM is a valid execution according to the operational semantics.
- Characterization of a class CRMs for which symbolic execution is complete: every execution of the operational semantics is an instance of some symbolic execution.
- The power of symbolic execution is demonstrated: using a simple example, several properties of interaction with the environment are verified using symbolic execution.

Plan. In the rest of this introduction we describe our running example. In Sect. 2 we discuss some related work. The definition of CRM is recapped in Sect. 3.

Symbolic execution of a CRM is defined in Sect. 4. In Sect. 5 we use our running example to illustrate how symbolic execution works, and to verify some illustrative properties. Soundness and (restricted) completeness of symbolic execution for CRMs are defined and proved in Sect. 6. We conclude with a summary and future work in Sect. 7.

1.1 Motivating Examples

To illustrate CRM symbolic execution we use the water tank example introduced in [17,18] and used in [3]. A water tank has an input valve, an output valve, a water level sensor and a controller that operates the input valve. The output valve is either set to a fixed value or left to control by the environment. The water tank is characterized by global constants WL.mx, the maximum water level and WL.mn, the minimum water level. Units are chosen so that the water level dynamics obeys a simple equation

$$wl(t) = wl(t0) + (fin - fout) * (t - t0)$$

where fin (fout) is the rate of flow through the input (output) valve and ranges between 0 and 1.

The water tank model has two components, the water level sensor, and a flow controller. We consider a scenario in which the output valve is controlled by the environment. Using symbolic execution we can model the behavior of an input controller in an arbitrary environment using different control parameters.

2 Related Work

Origins of Symbolic Execution. Symbolic execution was proposed in [9] as a software testing technique. In this use of symbolic execution, programs are executed on symbolic inputs (variables) which get propagated by symbolic application of operators. The idea has been incorporated in a number of tools for testing, static analysis, and debugging. Two examples are Symbolic Java PathFinder [25] and KLEE [6,28]. Programs that interact with the external world such as through reading/writing files or reading sensors present a challenge. KLEE addresses this challenge by providing an explicit model of the external resources.

The work in this paper concerns symbolic execution of executable models of cyberphysical systems rather than code. Here the focus is on dynamic execution in unknown or unpredictable environments. An important aspect of modeling CPS is representing change over time. Treating time symbolically allows one to explore a range of sampling rates to trade efficiency of lazy sampling with greater safety obtained by frequent sampling. Another benefit of symbolic execution of CPS is identifying (ideally, the strictest set of) constraints on the environment under which an executable specification can meet its requirements, including both safety and sufficient satisfaction of task requirements. The results can be used to prevent operation in unsuitable environments, or to adapt the design to be more resilient.

Symbolic Execution in Rewriting Logic. Rewriting Logic (RWL) [19,20] is a logic for specifying and reasoning about concurrent and distributed systems. A system is specified by a rewrite theory (Σ, E, R) where Σ is an order sorted signature, E is a set of equations used to define functions and relations, and R is a set of rewrite rules. RWL and CRM share the feature that in both formalisms behavior is specified by rewrite rules that can be applied concurrently subject to non-conflict constraints.

The rewrite relation has been generalized for large classes of rewrite theories to symbolic rewriting either as rewriting modulo SMT [27] or symbolic reachability (using unification rather than matching for rule application) [7,22]. In [22] generalized rewrite theories are defined and used to develop the semantic foundations for several forms of symbolic execution. Symbolic execution supports representation and reasoning about open systems and system interaction with the environment by rewriting terms with variables. Using symbolic reachability analysis one can often reduce an infinite state space to a finite set of state patterns.

Example uses of rewriting modulo SMT include: automating verification of safe controllers for autonomous vehicles [24], semantics, verification and parameter synthesis for Parametric Timed Petri Nets [4] and Parametric Timed Automata [5]. Rewriting modulo SMT has been used to formally analyze a variety of real-time systems including PLC ST programs [14], virtually synchronous cyber-physical systems [12,13,15], and soft agents [23]. In [8] a method for combining narrowing and SMT is proposed and used to analyze parametric timed automata with additional features. This approach allows reasoning about symbolic states that have logical variables of sorts not handled by SMT.

Modeling Challenges for Engineering of Open CPS. Lee discusses challenges to developing models for engineering cyber-physical systems in [10,11]. He identifies three classes of modeling challenges: chaotic behavior, continuous behavior, and tension between simplicity and incompleteness of deterministic models. Traditional cyber models do not deal well with continuous aspects of the physical world and continuous modeling techniques do not deal well with discreteness. Traditional abstractions do not treat concurrency or time inherently.

CRMs are a step toward addressing these modeling challenges. To model effects of the environment it is important to represent the environment explicitly. The environment has charge of time in the physical world, while CRMs can also have internal clocks. Variables of a CRM state can be discrete or continuous. The challenge is to find the right rate of sampling to not miss anything important, while being as simple as possible. Symbolic execution has potential to model chaos and to address the tension between non-determinism and simplicity.

3 CRM Background

In this section we summarize the concepts and definitions of a Concurrent Rules Machine introduced in [3]. In this summary, we slightly change some notation and refine certain concepts used in [3] to establish the necessary background to support definition of symbolic execution in Sect. 4.

3.1 Notation

We use $\mathbb{B}$ to denote the set of Boolean values $\{\bot, \top\}$, $\mathbb{N}_0$ to denote the set of natural numbers including zero, $\mathbb{R}_0^+$ the set of real numbers greater than or equal to zero, and $\mathbf{D} \supseteq \mathbb{B} \cup \mathbb{N}_0 \cup \mathbb{R}_0^+$ to denote a data domain. By **Name** we denote the set of all variable names.[1] We use *fresh*(**Name**) to obtain a fresh new variable name in **Name**.

To support symbolic execution of a CRM we assume the data domain, $\mathbf{D}$, is partitioned into constants ($\mathbf{D}_{Const}$) and symbols ($\mathbf{D}_{Sym}$). As for names, we assume a mechanism to generate fresh symbols, *fresh*($\mathbf{D}_{Sym}$).

For a set X, we use $\mathcal{P}(X)$ to denote the set of all finite subsets of X, and X^k, X^*, and X^ω to denote, respectively, the set of all sequences of length $k \in \mathbb{N}_0$, all finite-length sequences, and all infinite-length sequences of elements of X. We use angular brackets to denote concrete sequences, with $\langle\rangle$ denoting the null sequence. We also treat a sequence σ of length $0 \le k \le \infty$ over X as a (partial) function $\sigma \in \mathbb{N}_0 \to X$, in order to refer to its $i + 1^{st}$ element as $\sigma(i)$.

We use $f : D \rightsquigarrow R$ to denote f as a *pseudo function* that maps every element of the (domain) set D into a nondeterministically selected element of the (range) set R, where for a $d \in D$, two evaluations of $f(d)$ may or may not map into the same $r \in R$.

We use $Dom(f)$ and $Range(f)$ to refer to the domain and the range of a (pseudo) function f, respectively, and use $\vec{\emptyset}$ to denote the special function whose domain and range are both empty, i.e., $\vec{\emptyset} : \emptyset \to \emptyset$.

We do not specify a syntax for defining functions that appear in a CRM; we allow any well-defined mathematical notation that is convenient.

3.2 Utility Functions

A *valuation function* $v : N \mapsto \mathbf{D}$ maps a subset $N \in \mathcal{P}(\mathbf{Name})$ of variable names to values $d \in \mathbf{D}$.[2] We use $\mathbf{V}$ to denote the set of all valuation functions.

The function *revise* : $\mathbf{V} \times \mathbf{V} \times \mathcal{P}(\mathbf{Name}) \to \mathbf{V}$, below, updates an old valuation function W with a new one, Z, excluding the latter's value bindings for the names in $N \in \mathcal{P}(\mathbf{Name})$, such that:

$$revise(W, Z, N)(x) = \begin{cases} Z(x) & \text{if } x \in Dom(Z) \setminus N \\ W(x) & \text{otherwise} \end{cases} \quad (1)$$

---

[1] The CRM model supports arrays and allows $\mathbf{D} \supset \mathbf{Name}$ in order to support *indirection* (i.e., the value of a variable may be the name of another variable) and *dereferencing*. To simplify our presentation, we ignore such "dynamically computed variable names" in this paper.

[2] We assume the existence of a type system that associates a data type with each variable name in **Name** and ensures that the $\mathbf{D}$ value image of every $n \in \mathbf{Name}$ under every $v \in \mathbf{V}$ is compatible with the data type of n.

For convenience, by $W \triangleleft Z$ we denote the result of updating W by Z defined as:

$$(W \triangleleft Z)(x) = \mathit{revise}(W, Z, \emptyset)(x) \qquad (2)$$

Given sets X and Y, we use the pseudo function $\mathit{fold} : (X \times Y \to X) \times X \times \mathcal{P}(Y) \rightsquigarrow X$ to accumulate the images of the elements of a set $S \in \mathcal{P}(Y)$ under an accumulator function $f : X \times Y \to X$ with an initial accumulator value $x \in X$.

$$\mathit{fold}(f, x, S) = \begin{cases} x & \text{if } S = \emptyset \\ \mathit{fold}(f, f(x, s), S') & \text{otherwise, where } s \in S \text{ and } S' = S \setminus \{s\} \end{cases} \qquad (3)$$

Intuitively, $\mathit{fold}(f, x, S)$ takes an accumulator function, f, an initial accumulator value, x, and a set, S, and accumulates the images of all elements of S under f to return an element of the same type as x. The accumulator function f itself takes two parameters (the first of the same type as that of x, and the second of the same type as that of the elements of S), and maps them to an image of the same type as x.

Observe that the choice of $s \in S$ to split $S = \{s\} \cup S'$ in each round of recursion of fold is nondeterministic. Therefore, every recursive path that $\mathit{fold}(f, x, S)$ takes to exhaustively visit all elements of S reflects a nondeterministic choice out of the $n!$ possible paths, $n = |S|$, in the set of all permutations of the elements of S, mapping each permutation, $s_1, s_2, ..., s_n$ to its image $f(...(f(f(x, s_1), s_2), ...), s_n)$. We call the images of these permutations *alleles*. Thus, generally, $\mathit{fold}(f, x, S)$ is a pseudo function that maps its arguments to one nondeterministically selected allele in its set of all possible image alleles of S under f. However, in the special case where $f(x, s)$ is associative and commutative within the domain of its second argument (or at least over S), the set of image alleles of $\mathit{fold}(f, x, S)$ becomes a singleton and we can treat fold as a function: regardless of the nondeterministic splittings of S, the image of $\mathit{fold}(f, x, S)$ is the same unique $y \in X$.

3.3 Guards

A *guard* $g = p(n_1, n_2, ..., n_k)$ is a function of $k \in \mathbb{N}_0$ arguments that given a valuation function $v \in \mathbf{V}$, maps a sequence of values $d_i = v(n_i), 0 \leq i \leq k$ to a Boolean. We denote the set of all guards as $\mathbf{G}$. For $g = p(n_1, n_2, ..., n_k)$, we use g^N to denote the arguments (read variables) of p. We use $v \models g$ to denote the evaluation of a guard g in the context of a valuation function v, which produces a Boolean value.

3.4 Actions

An *action* $a \in \mathbf{Name}^k \times (\mathbf{D}^k \to \mathbf{V})$ is a pair of a finite sequence $\langle n_1, n_2, ..., n_k \rangle$ of $k \geq 0$ argument variable names $n_i \in \mathbf{Name}, 1 \leq i \leq k$, and an *update function* u. We denote the set of all actions as $\mathbf{A}$.

For $a = (\langle n_1, n_2, ..., n_k \rangle, u)$, we use a^R to denote the set $\{n_1, n_2, ..., n_k\}$ of its *arguments* or *read* variables $n_i \in \mathbf{Name}, \forall 1 \leq i \leq k$ of a; a^U to denote the instance of u, the update function of a. We use a^W to denote the set of *write variables* of a, and refer to $a^N = a^R \cup a^W$ as the set of *variables* of a. Moreover, we use $A^W = \bigcup_{a \in A} a^W$ to denote the set of write variables of a set of actions $A \subseteq \mathbf{A}$.

Example 1. Consider action $a_1 = (\langle\rangle, \lambda()(\mathtt{fin} := 1))$ where $\mathtt{fin} \in \mathbf{Name}$. Then we have $a_1^R = \emptyset$ and $a_1^W = \{\mathtt{fin}\}$.

Example 2. Consider action $a_2 = (\langle \mathtt{wl}, \mathtt{fin0}, \mathtt{fout0}, \mathtt{wl0}, \mathtt{t0}, \mathtt{t}\rangle, \lambda(wl, fin_0, fout_0, wl_0, t_0, t)(wl := wl_0 + (fin_0 - fout_0) \times (t - t_0)))$ where $\mathtt{fin0}, \mathtt{fout0}, \mathtt{wl0}, \mathtt{t0}, \mathtt{t} \in \mathbf{Name}$. Then we have $a_2^R = \{\mathtt{fin0}, \mathtt{fout0}, \mathtt{wl0}, \mathtt{t0}, \mathtt{t}\}$ and $a_2^W = \{\mathtt{wl}\}$.

Performing an action $a = (\langle n_1, n_2, ..., n_k \rangle, u) \in \mathbf{A}$ in the context of a valuation function $v \in \mathbf{V}$ such that $a^N \subseteq Dom(v)$, applies the update function u on n_i's to yield a new valuation function, v', where generally $Dom(v') \neq Dom(v)$ and the intersection $Dom(v') \cap Dom(v)$ may or may not be empty. We use the function *perform* : $\mathbf{V} \times \mathbf{A} \to \mathbf{V}$ to obtain v' by performing an action $(\langle n_1, n_2, ..., n_k \rangle, u) \in \mathbf{A}$ in the context of $v \in \mathbf{V}$:

$$v' = perform(v, (\langle n_1, n_2, ..., n_k \rangle, u)) \equiv u(v(n_1), v(n_2), ..., v(n_k))) \qquad (4)$$

Observe that v', the image of *perform*(), represents merely the "change" that results from performing the action $(\langle n_1, n_2, ..., n_k \rangle, u)$ in the context of v. Intuitively, v' is *not* an "updated version" of v, but rather the "change delta" to v. We use the function *revise*() or ◂ (Eqs. 1 and 2) to incorporate the image of a *perform*() into another valuation function. See the CRM semantics defined in Table 1 in Sect. 3.10.

Example 3. Consider action $a = (\langle d, b \rangle, u)$ where $u = \lambda(y, z)(c := y * z)$, and the valuation function v such that $\{b, d\} \subseteq Dom(v)$, where $v(b) = 6$, and $v(d) = 3$. Since $(\langle d, b \rangle, \lambda(y, z)(c := y * z))^W = \{c\}$, we have:

$$\begin{aligned} v' &= perform(v, (\langle d, b \rangle, u)) \equiv \\ &\lambda(y, z)(c := y * z)(v(d), v(b)) = \\ &\lambda(y, z)(c := y * z)(3, 6) = \\ &(c := 3 * 6) = [c \mapsto 18] \end{aligned}$$

Note that $Dom(v) \cap Dom(v') \subseteq \{c\}$, i.e., v' does not contain value bindings for all names in $Dom(v)$; it contains only the name-value bindings that performing the update function of the action changes.

We use the left-associative operator ";" to denote the sequential composition of actions, where for $a_1, a_2, a_3 \in \mathbf{A}$: $perform(v, a_1; a_2) = perform(perform(v, a_1), a_2)$, and $perform(v, a_1; a_2; a_3) = perform(perform(v, a_1; a_2), a_3)$.

3.5 Non-conflicting Actions

Consider two actions $a_1, a_2 \in \mathbf{A}$ and update valuation functions $v_i = \textit{perform}(v, a_i), i \in \{1, 2\}$ that result from performing them in the context of a pre valuation function $v \in \mathcal{V}$. Recall that v_i contains only those name-value bindings that performing a_i changes in the context of v (see *perform* in Sect. 3.4 and Example 3). In order to obtain a valuation function that reflects how performing both a_1 and a_2 changes v, we need to "update" v with v_1 and v_2 in some order using *revise* (Eq. 1). In the special case where the result of updating v with v_1 and v_2 is order independent, we can perform the actions a_1 and a_2 concurrently in the context of v.

We say actions a_1 and a_2 conflict in the context of a valuation function v if $(v \triangleleft v_1) \triangleleft v_2 \neq (v \triangleleft v_2) \triangleleft v_1$, and say they are non-conflicting in the context of v, otherwise. We use *nonconflicting* : $\mathbf{A} \times \mathbf{A} \times \mathbf{V} \to \mathbb{B}$ to denote whether or not two actions conflict in the context of a specific valuation function.

Intuitively, a_1 and a_2 are non-conflicting in the context of a valuation function v if performing a_1 and a_2 concurrently in v either involves no race condition, or cannot produce different results due to a race condition. For instance, consider the two actions $a_1 \equiv y := 2 \times x$ and $a_2 \equiv y := 2 + x$ and the valuation function $v = [x \mapsto 2, y \mapsto 6]$. In this case because $2 \times x = 2 + x = 4$, we have $v_1 = \textit{perform}(v, a_1) = [y \mapsto 4]$ and $v_2 = \textit{perform}(v, a_2) = [y \mapsto 4]$. Therefore $(v \triangleleft v_1) \triangleleft v_2 = (v \triangleleft v_2) \triangleleft v_1 = [x \mapsto 2, y \mapsto 4]$, which means performing a_1 and a_2 concurrently in the context of v produces the same end result regardless of (the existence of) a race condition. On the other hand, if we perform a_1 and a_2 concurrently in the context of the valuation function $v' = [x \mapsto 3, y \mapsto 6]$, we get $v_1 = \textit{perform}(v', a_1) = [y \mapsto 6]$ and $v_2 = \textit{perform}(v', a_2) = [y \mapsto 5]$. In this case, we have $(v' \triangleleft v_1) \triangleleft v_2 = [x \mapsto 2, y \mapsto 5]$ whereas $(v' \triangleleft v_2) \triangleleft v_1 = [x \mapsto 2, y \mapsto 6]$: the race condition between a_1 and a_2 in the context of v' does not produce a unique result.

We use *neverconflicting* : $\mathbf{A} \times \mathbf{A} \to \mathbb{B}$ to denote whether or not two actions have absolutely no conflict in the context of any valuation function.

$$\textit{neverconflicting}(a_1, a_2) \iff (v \in \mathbf{V} \implies \textit{nonconflicting}(a_1, a_2, v)) \tag{5}$$

For instance *neverconflicting*(a_1, a_2) holds for the actions $a_1 \equiv y := 2 \times x$ and $a_2 \equiv z := 2 + x$ because there is no valuation function in the context of which performing these two actions concurrently can lead to a race condition.[3]

We use *nonconflicting*(A, v) to extend the notion of non-conflicting pairs of actions to sets of actions $A \in \mathcal{P}(\mathbf{A})$. Intuitively, a set of actions $A \in \mathcal{P}(\mathbf{A})$ is non-conflicting in the context of a valuation function $v \in \mathbf{V}$ if for $a_k \in A, 1 \leq k \leq |A|$, cumulatively revising v with all $v_k = \textit{perform}(v, a_k)$ in any sequential order yields the same final valuation function.

---

[3] The concepts of non-conflicting and never-conflicting actions become more significant and less trivial with "computed names" such as array elements and indirection incorporated in the model (see footnote 4). For instance, *nonconflicting*(a_1, a_2, v) may or may not hold for $a_1 \equiv y[i] := 2 \times x$ and $a_2 \equiv y[j] := 2 + x$ depending on the value-bindings for i and j in v.

Formally, let $A^!$ be the set of all permutations of all elements of $A \in \mathcal{P}(\mathbf{A})$, with $n = |A|$. For $1 \le k \le n!$, denote ordered sequences in $A^!$ as $A^k = [a_1^k, a_2^k, ..., a_n^k] \in A^!$. The set of actions in A are non-conflicting in the context of a valuation function $v \in \mathbf{V}$ if we have:

$$nonconflicting(A, v) \iff \begin{pmatrix} \forall 1 \le i, j \le n!, n = |A|, \\ (((v \triangleleft perform(v, a_1^i)) \triangleleft perform(v, a_2^i)) \triangleleft ...) \triangleleft perform(v, a_n^i) = \\ (((v \triangleleft perform(v, a_1^j)) \triangleleft perform(v, a_2^j)) \triangleleft ...) \triangleleft perform(v, a_n^j) \end{pmatrix} \quad (6)$$

We use $neverconflicting : \mathcal{P}(\mathbf{A}) \to \mathbb{B}$ to denote whether or not a set of actions have absolutely no conflict with each other in the context of any valuation function.

$$neverconflicting(A) \iff (v \in \mathcal{V} \implies nonconflicting(A, v)) \quad (7)$$

3.6 Concurrent Actions

To define the valuation function that results from performing a set of actions $A \subseteq \mathbf{A}$ concurrently in the context of a valuation function v, we first define an auxiliary function. The auxiliary function $corevise : \mathbf{V} \to (\mathbf{V} \times \mathbf{A} \to \mathbf{V})$ maps a valuation function $z \in \mathbf{V}$ to another function $corevise(z) \in \mathbf{V} \times \mathbf{A} \to \mathbf{V}$ where:

$$(corevise(z))(v, a) = v \triangleleft perform(z, a) \quad (8)$$

See Eq. 2 for $\triangleleft$.

Using $corevise$, we extend the definition of $perform$ from performing a single action $a \in \mathbf{A}$ (Eq. 4) to performing a set of actions $A \subseteq \mathbf{A}$ concurrently in the context of a valuation function v as follows:

$$perform(v, A) = fold(corevise(v), v, A) \quad (9)$$

Strictly speaking, the image of $perform(v, A)$ in Eq. 9 is one nondeterministically selected alternative out of a set of the image alleles of the pseudo function $fold$ (Eq. 3). However, in the special case where $nonconflicting(A, v)$ holds (Eq. 6), $perform(v, A)$ maps to a unique image, in which case we can treat the pseudo function $perform(v, A)$ as if it were a true function analogous to $perform(v, a)$ [3]. Note that the meaning of $perform$ when applied to a set of actions in the context of a valuation function, actaully performs the update, while in the context of a single action it simply computes the update!

3.7 Sequential Composition of Concurrent Actions

We have assumed that the syntax of actions supports sequential composition of actions $a_1, a_2 \in \mathbf{A}$, which we denote here as $a_1; a_2$ (see the text that follows Eq. 4). We now extend the sequential composition of actions to sequential composition of sets of actions $A_1, A_2 \in \mathcal{P}(\mathbf{A})$, which we denote as $A_1; A_2$. Intuitively, $A_1; A_2$ is a single (composite) action that first performs all actions $a \in A_1$ in some arbitrary order, and then performs all actions $a \in A_2$ in some arbitrary order.

In Sect. 3.5 we showed the valuation function that results from performing the composite action $a_1; a_2$ in the context of a valuation function $v \in \mathcal{V}$. We now use Eq. 9 to define the valuation function that results from performing the action $A_1; A_2$ in the context of a valuation function v as:

$$perform(v, A_1; A_2) = perform(perform(v, A_1), A_2) \qquad (10)$$

Recall that the image of $perform(v, a_1)$ is an "update" valuation function for revising v, i.e., this image does not include the name-value bindings that are not changed by the action a_1 (see the paragraph after Eq. 4 and Example 3). On the other hand, Eqs. 9 and 8 mean that the image of $perform(v, A_1)$ is a "replacement" valuation function for v (i.e., this image already includes name-value bindings that are not changed by actions in A_1, as well as those that are). For convenience, for $a \in \mathbf{A}$ and $A \in \mathcal{P}(\mathbf{A})$ we also define $perform(v, A; a) = perform(perform(v, A), \{a\})$ and $perform(v, a; A) = perform(perform(v, \{a\}), A)$.

3.8 Rules

A *rule* $r \in \mathbf{G} \times \mathcal{P}(\mathbf{A})$ is a pair of a guard and a set of concurrent actions. We denote the set of all rules as $\mathbf{R}$.

For $r = (g, A) \in \mathbf{R}$, we use r^G and r^A to denote the guard and the set of actions of r. We call $r^N = (r^A)^N$, $r^R = (r^A)^R$, and $r^W = (r^A)^W$ the *variables*, the *read-only variables*, and the *write variables* of r, respectively. Moreover, we extend our r^G, r^A, r^N, r^R, r^W notation to sets of rules in the obvious way.

A rule $r \in \mathbf{R}$ is *enabled* in the context of a valuation function $v \in \mathbf{V}$ only if $v \models r^G$ and $nonconflicting(r^A, v)$.

3.9 Concurrent Rules Machines

A Concurrent Rules Machine (CRM) is a concurrent transition system that interacts with its environment. A CRM consists of an interface, a set of initialization actions, a set of rules, and a set of termination actions [3].

Definition 1 (Concurrent Rules Machine). *A Concurrent Rules Machine (CRM) consists of a tuple* $(I, A_0, R, T) \in (\mathcal{P}(\mathbf{Name}) \times \mathcal{P}(\mathbf{Name}) \times \mathcal{P}(\mathbf{Name})) \times \mathcal{P}(\mathbf{A}) \times \mathcal{P}(\mathbf{R}) \times \mathcal{P}(\mathbf{A})$ *where:*

- $I = (Exp, Imp, Sh) \in \mathcal{P}(\mathbf{Name}) \times \mathcal{P}(\mathbf{Name}) \times \mathcal{P}(\mathbf{Name})$ *is its interface where:*
  - *Exp, Imp, and Sh are mutually disjoint,*
  - $\{envstep\} \subseteq Sh$,
- $A_0 \subseteq \mathbf{A}$ *is the finite set of its initialization actions such that* $neverconflicting(A_0)$.
- $R \subseteq \mathbf{R}$ *is its finite set of rules,*
- $T \subseteq \mathbf{A}$ *is a finite set of termination actions such that* $neverconflicting(T)$.

*The sets of variable names **Exp**, **Imp**, and **Sh** in the interface I constitute the sets of exported, imported, and shared variable names of the CRM, respectively.*

The distinguished shared Boolean variable *envstep* $\in$ *Sh* coordinates the interaction between a CRM and its environment; see Sect. 3.10.

We denote the set of all concurrent rules machines by **CRM**. We use C^I, C^{A_0}, C^R, and C^T to refer to the interface, the set of initialization actions, the set of rules, and the set of termination actions of a CRM $C \in$ **CRM**, respectively. We use C^{Exp}, C^{Imp}, and C^{Sh} to refer to their respective elements in C^I.

Intuitively, the exported variables in C^{Exp} are the interface variables that C *offers as read-only* variables to its environment: C, another CRM, or the environment can read the values of the variables in C^{Exp}, but only C has the right to change the values of variables in C^{Exp}. The imported variables in C^{Imp} are the interface variables that C *uses as read-only* variables: another CRM or the environment has the right to read or change the values of variables in C^{Imp}, but C may use them only as read-only variables. The shared variables in C^{Sh} are the interface variables that C *shares with* its environment for both read and write: C, another CRM, or the environment may atomically read and/or change the values of variables in C^{Sh}.

The initialization actions in C^{A_0} must be never-conflicting and they must initialize the exported interface variables in C^{Exp}. Neither initialization actions in C^{A_0} nor rules in C^R may modify the values of the read-only interface variables in C^{Imp}.

3.10 CRM Operational Semantics

Informally, a CRM C iterates indefinitely, performing the actions of some of its rules, in mutual interaction with the environment. In each round, it interacts with the environment to obtain new observation values for its imported and shared interface variables, then nondeterministically picks a subset of its enabled rules whose action sets are non-conflicting, and atomically performs those actions to revise its current valuation function for its next round (see Table 1). Meanwhile, the environment independently, perhaps continuously, changes the values of some of the interface variables of C. We use the distinguished Boolean variable *envstep* to coordinate the interaction between a CRM and its environment (see multi-steps, below)[4].

Formally, we define the dynamic behavior of $C = (I, A_0, R, T) \in$ **CRM** as an iterative revision of its valuation function, $\mathcal{V}$, where for $i \in \mathbb{N}_0$, its revised version, $\mathcal{V}^i$, for the ith iteration is derived from its $i-1^{st}$ iteration version, $\mathcal{V}^{i-1}$, as defined in Table 1. The iteration starts by the environment providing a valuation function $\mathcal{V}^{-1} \in \mathbf{V}$ to initialize those interface variables of C that are not initialized by its initialization actions A_0, i.e., by picking a $\mathcal{V}^{-1}$ such that $Dom(\mathcal{V}^{-1}) \subseteq$ *RequiredVars* where:

$$RequiredVars = C^{Imp} \cup C^{Sh} \setminus (A_0^W \cup T^W) \tag{11}$$

---

[4] Observe that by Definition 1, *envstep* $\in C^{Sh}$ for every CRM C.

Table 1. Semantics of a CRM $C = (I, A_0, R, T)$

Pick $\mathcal{V}^{-1} \in \mathbf{V}$ such that $\textit{RequiredVars} \subseteq \textit{Dom}(\mathcal{V}^{-1})$; see Equation 11 for $\textit{RequiredVars}$.

$$\mathcal{V}^i = \textit{perform}(\mathcal{E}^i, S^i; T)$$

$$\mathcal{E}^i = \begin{cases} \mathcal{V}^{-1} \triangleleft [\textit{envstep} \rightarrow \top] & \text{if } i = 0 \\ \textit{interact}(\mathcal{V}^{i-1}, C^{\textit{Exp}} \cup C^{\textit{Priv}} \cup \{\textit{envstep}\}) & \text{otherwise} \end{cases}$$

$$\textit{interact}(V, P) = \begin{cases} \textit{revise}(V, \textit{xchange}(V), P) & \text{if } V(\textit{envstep}) \\ V & \text{otherwise} \end{cases}$$

$$S^i = \textit{pickedacts}(E_R^i, \emptyset, \mathcal{E}^i, i > 0)$$

$$\textit{pickedacts}(F, S, V, I) = \begin{cases} S & \text{if } F = \emptyset \vee (I \wedge \textit{Toss}()) \\ \textit{annex}(A, F \setminus \{A\}, S, V) & \text{otherwise, where } A \in F \end{cases}$$

$$\textit{annex}(A, F, S, V) = \begin{cases} \textit{pickedacts}(F, S \cup A, V, \top) & \text{if } \textit{nonconflicting}(S \cup A, V) \\ \textit{pickedacts}(F, S, V, \top) & \text{otherwise} \end{cases}$$

$$E_R^i = \begin{cases} \{A_0\} & \text{if } i = 0 \\ \{A \mid (g, A) \in R, \mathcal{E}^i \models g \wedge \textit{nonconflicting}(A, \mathcal{E}^i)\} & \text{otherwise} \end{cases}$$

The pseudo function $\textit{Toss} : \emptyset \rightsquigarrow \mathbb{B}$ in the definition of *pickedacts* nondeterministically maps to $\top$ or $\bot$. See [3] for details.

Conceptually, in every round the equations in Table 1 specify two sequential steps through which first the environment of C and then C take turns to change the values of the variables in C^I, the interface of C. For $i \in \mathbb{N}_0$, $\mathcal{E}^i$ represents the valuation function that reflects the incremental modifications that the environment makes to the values of the variables in C^I as round i begins (i.e., before C acts).

4 Symbolic Execution

Symbolic execution is a mechanism for reasoning about CRM behavior. It allows one to reason about reachability from possibly infinitely many initial states and to represent effects of action by the external environment as symbols subject to constraints.

Recall that $\mathbf{D}_{\textit{Const}}$ and $\mathbf{D}_{\textit{Sym}}$ represent partitions of the data domain $\mathbf{D}$. In a purely concrete execution the set $\mathbf{D}_{\textit{Sym}}$ is empty, and application of functions and predicates is assumed to return a concrete value (i.e., a constant in $\mathbf{D} = \mathbf{D}_{\textit{Const}}$). Thus update actions produce (concrete) update valuations. In the case of symbolic execution, applications of functions/predicates generally produce symbolic expressions (i.e., expressions involving operations applied to both constants and symbols). Actions produce updates that are valuations whose range may include symbols together with constraints on the allowed values of the symbols. Symbolic execution of a CRM transforms symbolic valuation–pairs consisting of a valuation function and a constraint on the variables in the range of the valuation via the symbolic interpretation of actions.

We use the notation of Sect. 3 with some added notation below to handle symbolic aspects. We use $\bar{n}, \bar{m}$ to denote lists of names, $m, n \in$ **Name**, and $\bar{s}$ to denote a list of symbols, $s \in \mathbf{D}_{Sym}$.

Symbolic Valuations. A symbolic valuation is a pair (W, b) where $W \in \mathbf{V}$ and b is a boolean expression (over $\mathbf{D}$) constraining symbols in the range of W.

Substitutions, σ, are finite maps from symbols, $\mathbf{D}_{Sym}$, to $\mathbf{D}$. By $e[\sigma]$ we denote the usual application of a substitution σ to an expression e replacing each symbol, s, in its domain by its image, $\sigma(s)$. Applying a substitution to a valuation map $W[\sigma]$ is effectively the composition of σ and W

$$(W[\sigma])(n) = W(n)[\sigma]$$

A substitution, σ, is an instance of a symbolic valuation (W, b) if $b[\sigma]$ is true, in which case its corresponding instance valuation is $W[\sigma]$. The meaning of a symbolic valuation is the set of its instance valuations.

For a CRM to be symbolically executable automatically, we require an algorithm, such as an SMT solver, that can (partially) decide if there exists a substitution σ such that $b[\sigma]$ is true for b appearing in execution constraints ($isSat(b)$).

Symbolic Guards. Let $g = (\bar{n}, P)$ be a CRM guard, where P is a boolean function. The meaning of g in the context of a symbolic valuation (W, b), written $g[[(W, b)]]$ is the symbolic (boolean) expression $P(W(\bar{n}))$. We say that (W, b) *is consistent with* g if there is an instance σ of (W,b) such that $g[[(W, b)]][\sigma]$ is true. (W, b) *uniformly* satisfies (or just satisfies) g if $g[[(W, b)]][\sigma]$ is true for all instances σ of (W, b).

Symbolic Actions. Let $a = (\bar{n}, u)$ be a CRM action where u is an update function whose range is a valuation interpreted as a valuation update. The interpretation of an action, a, in the context of a symbolic valuation, (W,b) is a symbolic valuation

$$a[[(W, b)]] = u(W(\bar{n}))$$

We require that the set of write variables of an action is independent of the valuation context. Thus we can rewrite $u(W(\bar{n}))$ as (Z^a, b^a) where $Dom(Z^a)$ is the set of write variables of a, the range, $\bar{s}$, consists of fresh symbols and b^a is equivalent to the conjunction of $s_i = u(W(\bar{n}))(n_i)$ for $s_i \in \bar{s}$.

In a CRM execution step, sets of actions are performed, not just single actions. These sets are required to be non-conflicting in the context of the valuation they are acting on (see Sect. 3). To apply an action set A in the context of a symbolic valuation, we require A to be non-conflicting in the context of each valuation instance. In this case, we can form the joint symbolic update of A, as follows. Let $\bar{n}_a$ be the write names of $a \in A$, and let $\bar{s}_a$ be its corresponding list of fresh symbols. Pick an order on A and let $\bar{n}$ be the concatenation of the $\bar{n}_a$ for all $a \in A$ in the chosen order, omitting names from $\bar{n}_a$ that are in $\bar{n}_{a'}$ for earlier a'. Let $\bar{s}$ be the corresponding concatenation of the $\bar{s}_a$ (omitting symbols whose names have been omitted). Then $A[[W]] = (Z^A, b^A)$ where $Z^A(\bar{n}) = \bar{s}$ and b^A is the conjunction of the constraints b^a for $a \in A$ together with equations $s_{a,i} = s_{a',j}$ if $\bar{n}_a(i) = \bar{n}'_a(j)$.

Symbolic Execution. Recall that a CRM, C, has the form (I, A_0, Rs, T) where A_0 is the set of initialization actions, T is the set of termination actions, and Rs is the set of rules. Symbolic Execution of C generalizes the step relation on valuation functions of a CRM to a relation on symbolic valuation functions:

$$(W, b) \Rightarrow (W', b')$$

As for concrete CRM execution, every symbolic step consists of two substeps: the environment and the CRM (sub)steps. The CRM step has two substeps: application of the actions of a candidate rule set, R, followed by application of the set of terminal actions, T.

$$(W, b) \to_E (W^E, b \wedge b^E)$$
$$\to_R (W^R, b \wedge b^E \wedge b^R)$$
$$\to_T (W^T, b \wedge b^E \wedge b^R \wedge b^T)$$

These symbolic substeps are explained below. We use the convention that $W^E, W^E_j, \ldots$ each represents a valuation variable denoting a valuation resulting from an environment action, and $b^E, b^E_j, \ldots$ each represents the constraint for that environment action. Similarly the superscript R or A indicates the result of actions of a rule, and the superscript T indicates the result of the set of terminal actions.

The initial step starts with an empty valuation ($W_{-1} = \emptyset$) and true constraint ($b_{-1} = \top$). We let $\bar{e}$ denote the set of names the environment is required to write. In the case of timed systems this includes the special name **time**. The environment is constrained uniformly by a constraint specification *envB* which has the form $(\bar{n}, cs)$ where cs is a set of assignments and boolean expressions over $\bar{n}$. *envB* constrains the action of an environment, thus the meaning depends on the starting valuation and the updated valuation: $envB[[W(\bar{n}), W^E(\bar{n})]]$ Where W^E is W updated by fresh symbols for $\bar{e}$.

A sequence $[(W_j, b_j), R_j \mid -1 \le j]$ is a symbolic execution of CRM , C, (with respect to the partition of **D** and an environment constraint *envB*) if $isSat(b_{j+1})$ holds and:

$(W_j, b_j) \rightarrow_E (W_j^E, b_j \wedge b_j^E)$

$\rightarrow_{R_j} (W_j^A, b_j \wedge b_j^E \wedge b_j^A)$

$\rightarrow_T (W_j^T, b_j \wedge b_j^E \wedge b_j^A \wedge b_j^T) = (W_{j+1}, b_{j+1})$

where

$\overline{s}_j$ is the jth fresh symbols for $\overline{e}$

$W_{-1}(\overline{e}) = \overline{s}_{-1}$

$b_{-1}^E = envB[\overline{s}_{-1}, \overline{s}_{-1}]$

$b_j^E = envB[W_j(\overline{e}), \overline{s}_j]$

$A = if \ j < 0 \ then \ A_0 \ else \ acts(R_j) \ fi$

$(Z_j^A, b_j^A) = A[[W_j^E]]$

$W_j^A = W_j^E \triangleleft Z_j^A$

$(Z_j^T, b_j^T) = T[[W_j^A]]$

$W_j^T = W_j^A \triangleleft Z_j^T = W_{j+1}$

$b_j^E = envB[[W_j(\overline{n}), W_j^E(\overline{n})]]$

and R_j is a candidate rule set for $(W_j^E, b_j \wedge b_j^E)$, that is $A = acts(R_j)$ is non-conflicting and the guard of each $r \in R_j$ is true in every instance of (W_j, b_j).

We note that to simplify our presentation we have tacitly assumed the shared name *envstep* is true in all reachable valuations, thus the environment acts at every step. It is straight-forward to remove that assumption in practice.

5 Water Tank Input Controller CRM: Symbolic Execution

In the following we use the water tank input controller CRM, iCtl, to illustrate symbolic reasoning enabled by symbolic execution. After defining the CRM, we work out some steps of symbolic execution, and then consider some properties of the controller in an environment that obeys the physical water-level law (Sect. 1.1), but can change the outflow valve arbitrarily (between 0 and 1).

In the definition we use the convention that unquoted names (such as t, fin0 or WL.R), represent (global or local) *mathematical* variables or constants, whereas quoted names (such as 'fin, 'time, or 'wl), represent *CRM variable names* which will be replaced by their respective values that the CRM semantics (see Sect. 3.10) finds through look-up in its valuation function at run time.

Definition 2 (iCtl CRM.).

```
iCtl = (iCtl.I, iCtl.A0, iCtl.R, iCtl.T)
where
  iCtl.I = ({'wl,'time}, {'fin}, {})
      --- the interface with imports ('wl 'time),
      --- exports ('fin)
```

```
            --- no shared variables ({}).
  iCtl.A0 = {(< >, \lambda (). 'fin := finInit)}
            --- the initialization action parameterized by finInit
  iCtl.R = { (true, {ic.fin})}
            --- the rule updating the input flow
  iCtl.T = (< 'fin >, \lambda f. 'fin0 := f)
            --- the termination action that caches value of 'fin
where
  ic.fin= (< 'fin0, 'wl >,
           \lambda (f0,   wl).
                 'fin := (if wl > WL.smx
                          then 0
                          else (if wl < WL.smn
                                then 1
                                else 1/2 fi) fi) )
```

For illustration, we fix the values of the water tank constants as follows (to keep examples small).

```
    wlInit = 3     finInit = 1
    WL.mx = 5      WL.mn = 3
    WL.smx = 9/2   WL.smn   = 7/2
```

A valuation is represented as a set of bindings (NAME := VALUE). mt denotes the empty valuation. The initialization and first concrete execution step of the iCtl CRM are shown below. We use => to represent the full step relation, while -e>, -r>, and -t> indicate the environment, rule, and terminal action substeps, respectively.

```
mt
  -e> ('time := 0) ('fout := 0) ('wl := 3)
  -r> ('time := 0) ('fout := 0) ('wl := 3) ('fin := 1)
  -t> ('time := 0) ('fout := 0) ('wl := 3) ('fin := 1) ('fin0 := 1)
=>
  -e> ('time := 1) ('fout := 1/2) ('wl := 4)
  -r> ('time := 1) ('fout := 1/2) ('wl := 4) ('fin := 1/2)
  -t> ('time := 1) ('fout := 1/2) ('wl := 4) ('fin := 1/2) ('fin0 := 1)
```

For symbolic execution of iCtl, we add a set of symbols, $\mathbf{D}_{Sym}$, to the constants of the concrete execution, and define the environment constraint $envB = (\overline{n}, cs)$. $\mathbf{D}_{Sym}$ has elements $v(n, j)$ for $n \in$ **Name** and $j \in \mathbb{N}_0$. Intuitively $v(n, j)$ is the jth value assigned to the name n (i.e., at the jth step). The environment constraint is

```
envB =
(<'wl 'fin 'fout 'time 't0 >,
  WL.mn <= 'wl and 'wl <= WL.mx and
 'wl := 'wl + ('fin - 'fout) * ('time - 't0)
)
```

Recall that *envB* is interpreted in a pair of valuation maps (W_j, W_{j+1}). The Boolean constraints are interpreted in W_{j+1} while assignment right-hand-sides are interpreted in W_j and equated to the value of the name in the left-hand-side interpreted in W_{j+1} Valuation functions are represented as in the concrete case where the range now includes symbols in addition to constants (here, real numbers).

The first two steps of symbolic execution follow.

Symbolic initialization step

```
(mtVMap , true) ==>
  -e>
  (('wl := v('wl,0)) ('time := 0) ('t0 := 0),Cstr0e)
  -r>
  (('fin := v('fim,0)) ('wl := v('wl,0)) ('time := 0) ('t0 := 0),
   Cstr0e and Cstr0r)
  -t>
  (('fin0 := v('fin,0) ('fin := v('fim,0))
   ('wl := v('wl,0)) ('time := 0) ('t0 := 0),
    Cstr0e and Cstr0r
   =  (W_0,Cstr0) )
where
Cstr0e = (v('wl,0) >= 3) and (v('wl,0) <= 5) and (v('wl,0) === initWL)
Cstr0r =   (0 <= v('fin,0)  and (v('fin,0) <= 1)
```

Symbolic step 1

```
(W_0,Cstr0)
  -e>
  (('wl := v('wl,1) ('time := 1) ('t0 := 0)
 ('fin0 := v('fin,0)) ('fin := v('fim,0)),
    Cstr0 and Cstr1e )
  -r>
  (('fin0 := v('fin,0) ('fin := v('fim,1))
   ('wl := v('wl,1) ('time := 1) ('t0 := 0),
    Cstr0 and Cstr1e and Cstr1r )
  -t>
  (('fin0 := v('fin,1) ('fin := v('fim,1))
   ('wl := v('wl,1) ('time := 1) ('t0 := 0),
    Cstr0e and Cstr0r and Cstr1e and Cstr1r )
where
Cstr1e ~~
   ( v('wl,1) >= 3 and v('wl,1) <= 5 and
     v('wl,1) === v('wl,0) + (v('fin,0) - v('fout,0)) * 1 )
Cstr1r =
   (vvWLCi.fin#1:Real === (0/1).Real
   or
     vvWLCi.wl#1:Real <= (7/2).Real) and
```

```
    vvWLCi.fin#1:Real === (1/1).Real
or
    vvWLCi.wl#1:Real < (9/2).Real and
    (7/2).Real < vvWLCi.wl#1:Real and
      vvWLCi.fin#1:Real === (1/2).Real)
```

Symbolic Reasoning. Two simple examples of the questions one can ask of iCtrl using symbolic execution are: Starting with water level 3 (minimum):

(1) Can the water level go above `WL.smx`?
(2) Can the water level reach `WL.mx`?

The answer to the first question is yes. Here is one concrete solution:

```
(v('fin,0) := 31/32) (v('fout,0) := 1/32) (v('wl,0) := 3)
(v('fin,1) := 1/2)   (v('fout,1) := 1/16) (v('wl,1) := 63/16)
(v('fin,2) := 1/2) (v('fout,2) := 1/8) (v('wl,2) := 35/8)
(v('fin,3) := 0)     (v('fout,3) := 1/2) (v('wl,3) := 19/4)
```

The answer to the second question is up to time 12, no. However if we change the time step to be increments of 2, then the answer is yes. Here is a witness

```
(v('fin,0) := 1)   (v('fout,0) := 0 (v('wl,0) := 3)
(v('fin,1) := 0)   (v('fout,1) := 1/2) (v('wl,1) := 5
```

This emphasizes that the choice of time interval matters. To investigate effects of the choice of time interval we can turn that interval into a symbol, 'dt. If we constrain 'dt to be in the interval [1/2, 2/1] and ask question 2 again, there are several solutions depending on the upper-bound on number of steps. Here is one witness where the step upper-bound is 6.

```
v('dt,0)  := 7/4
v('fin,0) := 1/2   v('fout,0) := 1/4    v('wl,0) := 3
v('fin,)1 := 1     v('fout,1) := 3/28   v('wl,1) := 55/16
v('fin,2) := 0     v('fout,2) := 1/2    v('wl,2)   := 5
```

If we ask question 2 with 'dt constrained to be in the interval [1/2, 1/1] there is no solution up to 12 steps. An interesting question for future work is: can we find k such that no solution up to k steps implies there is no solution. The idea is to find a constraint on states such that after k steps that constraint holds again, yielding an induction condition. See [24] for an example of such reasoning.

6 Soundness and Partial Completeness

For symbolic execution to be useful as a reasoning method, it is important that it gives accurate information about CRM behavior. For example, is an instance of a symbolic trace a trace of the CRM according to the operational semantics (soundness)? Conversely, if there is no symbolic trace instance violating a given property, might there be a trace of the operational semantics that violates that property (completeness)?

In the following we prove soundness for all CRMs that admit symbolic execution. We also prove completeness for CRMs that satisfy a simple additional condition.

6.1 Soundness

Soundness says that given a symbolic trace of a CRM with environment constrained by *envB* any instance of (a finite prefix of) this trace is a concrete trace of that CRM.

An instance of a symbolic trace

$$[(W_j, b_j) \to_{E_j, R_j} (W_{j+1}, b_{j+1}) \mid -1 <= j < m]$$

is a sequence

$$[V_j \to_{F_j, R_j} V_{j+1} \mid -1 <= j < m]$$

given by an instance σ of b_m where

$$[V_j = W_j[\sigma] \mid -1 <= j < m]$$

and F_j given by the equations of b_j^E and and σ.[5]

Note that by the definition of instance and the monotonic nature of the constraints b_j, if σ is an instance of b_m then σ is an instance of b_j for $j <= m$.

Theorem 1. *Each instance of a symbolic trace of a CRM is a (concrete) trace of that CRM.*

Proof. Fix a symbolic trace as above and instance substitution σ. Consider step j

$$(W_j, b_j) \to_{E_j, R_j} (W_{j+1}, b_{j+1})$$

of the symbolic trace for some $j < m$. Note that σ is an instance of b_j and of b_{j+1}. We show that the corresponding instance step is a valid (concrete) CRM step.

By definition, the rule set of the jth step, R_j, is a valid choice of concurrent rule set for a CRM step. We show that the instance of each substep of step j is a valid substep.

Finally, as noted above $isSat(b_{j+1})$ holds with witness σ.

Environment Substep.

$$(W_j, b_j) \to_{E_j} (W_j^E, b_j \wedge b_j^E)$$

where $Z_j^E(\overline{e}) = \overline{s}_j$(fresh symbols), $W_j^E = W_j \triangleleft Z_j^E$, and $b_j^E = envB[[W_j^E]]$.

The instance substep is

$$V_j \to_{F_j} V_j^E$$

where F_j is given by the equations of b_j^E (corresponding to the assignments of *envB*) and σ; $V_j = W_j[\sigma]$ and $V_j^E = W_j \triangleleft Z_j^E[\sigma] = V_j \triangleleft F_j$. A valid environment step.

---

[5] The expression $(W_j, b_j) \to_{E_j, R_j} (W_{j+1}, b_{j+1})$ represents the result of the three parts of a CRM step, parameterized by the environment update E_j, a rule set R_j, and the terminal actions T, left implicit as it is the same actions for each step.

Rule action substep

$$(W_j^E, b_j \wedge b_j^E) \to_{R_j} (W_j^R, b_j \wedge b_j^E \wedge b_j^R)$$

where $W_j^R = W_j^E \triangleleft Z_j^R$, A_j is the union of action sets of R_j $(Z_{j}^R, b_j^R) = A_j[[W_j^E]]$

At the concrete level, $V_j = W_j[\sigma]$ and by definition of symbolic trace step, the guards of rules in R_j are true in V_j and the joint action set is non-conflicting in the context of V_j. Also letting $V_j^R = V_j^E \triangleleft Z_{A_j}$, we have $V_j^R = W_j^R[\sigma] = W_j^E \triangleleft Z_j^R$.

Termination Action Substep. The termination step is

$$(W_j^R, b_j \wedge b_j^E \wedge b_j^R) \to_T (W_j^T, b_j \wedge b_j^E \wedge b_j^R \wedge b_j^T) = (W_{j+1}, b_{j+1})$$

The argument for termination action set case is the same as for rule action set case.

6.2 Restricted Completeness

Completeness of symbolic execution holds under under some conditions on the rules of a CRM. For example CRMs where rule guards depend only on names that are always bound to constants, the write variables of a rule is independent of valuation context, and no two rules write the same variable. These conditions hold for many classes of CRM.

Definition 3 (Symbolically complete CRM).
A CRM is symbolically complete if given any (reachable) symbolic valuation (W, b), and substitution, σ, that satisfies b; if rule set R is a candidate for execution in the context of $W[\sigma]$ (all guards are true and the union of their action sets is non-conflicting) then R is a candidate for execution in the context of $W[\sigma']$ for any σ' satisfying b.

A CRM in which rule guards depend on variables whose values are always constants (not symbolic) and the write variables of actions in action sets within or across rules are independent of valuation and disjoint, is symbolically complete. This is true for a large class of CRMs modeling CPSs.

Lemma 1 (One (sub)step completeness).
If CRM, C, is symbolically complete, (W, b) a reachable symbolic valuation, σ an instance of (W, b) (σ satisfies b), $V = W[\sigma]$ the corresponding valuation instance, and A a nonconflicting action set.[6] then

$$V \to_R V' \text{ implies } (W, b) \to_A (W', b')$$

where V' is an instance of (W', b').

---

[6] A could be an environment action set, the initialization actions A_0, the actions of a rule set R of rules enabled in V, or the set of termination actions T.

Proof. The idea is the following. Let $\overline{m} = A^W$ (the write variables of A), $U = A[V]$ the joint update function of actions of A in V, and $Z, b^a = A[[W]]$, the joint symbolic update function of A in W. Let σ' be defined by

$$\sigma'(W'(\overline{m})) = V'(\overline{m}) = U(\overline{m})$$

then $b' = b \wedge b^a$,

$$b^a = \wedge_{m_i \in \overline{m}}(W'(m_i) = U(m_i))$$

and $\sigma + \sigma'$ satisfies b' is the desired instance mapping (W', b') to V'.

Theorem 2 (Restricted Completeness).

If CRM, C, is symbolically complete, and

$$Tr = V_j \to_{F_j, R_j} V_{j+1} \mid -1 \leq j < m$$

is a concrete trace of C such that F_j satisfies envB for $-1 \leq j < m$, then there is a symbolic trace, Tr^*, of C with environment constraint envB such that Tr is an instance of Tr^*.

Proof. Given Tr, we show that there is a symbolic trace Tr^* firing the same sequence of rule sets as Tr, and Tr is an instance of Tr^*.

We first show that the initialization step ($j = -1$) of Tr is an instance of the initialization step of C, which is the same for any symbolic trace (constrained by *envB*). Then we show that for any $j > 0$, assuming by induction that we have Tr_j^* with Tr up to j an instance, then Tr_j^* can be extended using R_j, so that Tr is an instance up to $j + 1$.

Initialization Step. We show that the initialization step of Tr is an instance of the initialization step of Tr^*. Tr initialization has 3 substeps.

$$\to_{F_0} V^E = F_0$$
$$\to_{A_0} V^A = V^E \triangleleft U^A$$
$$\to_T V^T = V^A \triangleleft U^T = V_1$$

where F_0 is an update valuation with domain the environment required variables $U^A = A_0[[V^E]]$, and $U^T = T[[V^A]]$.

The symbolic initialization has three symbolic substeps

$$\to_{E_0} (W^E, b^E)$$
$$\to_{A_0} (W^E \triangleleft Z^A, b^E \wedge b^A) = (W^A, b^{EA})$$
$$\to_T (W^A \triangleleft Z^T, b^{EA} \wedge b^T) = (W_0, b_0)$$

where $(Z^A, b^A) = A_0[[W^E]]$, and] $(Z^T, b^T) = T[[W^A]]$.

Define the substitution, σ_0, making Tr initialization an instance of Tr^* initialization as follows.

For $n \in dom(E_0) = Dom(F_0)$, $\sigma_0(E_0[n]) = F_0[n]$. For $n \in dom(Z^A)$, $\sigma_0(Z^A[n]) = V^A[n]$. For $n \in dom(Z^T)$, $\sigma_0(Z^T[n]) = V^T[n]$. Note that the sets $dom(E_0)$, $dom(Z^a)$, $dom(Z^T)$ are disjoint due to freshness of symbols at each substep.

By definition, $V_0 = W_0[\sigma_0]$. It remains to show that σ_0 satisfies b_0. σ_0 satisfies b^E due to the requirement that environment actions satisfy $envB$. σ_0 satisfies b^A and σ_0 satisfies b^T by Lemma 1.

Step $j \geq 0$. Assume the jth stop of Tr is

$$V_j \rightarrow_{F_j} V_j \triangleleft F_j = V_j^E$$
$$\rightarrow_{R_j} V_j^E \triangleleft Y_A = V^A$$
$$\rightarrow_T V_j^A \triangleleft Y_T = V_j^T = V_{j+1}$$

where the F_j substep satisfies $envB$.

Assume by induction that (W_j, b_j) is the corresponding symbolic state and σ_j the substitution instance such that σ_j satisfies b_j and $W_j[\sigma_j] = V_j$.

Then by symbolic completeness R_j is enabled in (W_j, b_j) so

$$(W_j, b_j) \rightarrow_{E_j} (W_j \triangleleft E_j, b_j \wedge b_j^E) = (W_j^E, b_j \wedge b_j^E)$$
$$\rightarrow_{R_j} (W_j^E \triangleleft Z^A, b_j \wedge b_j^E \wedge b_j^A) = (W_j^A, b_j^{EA})$$
$$\rightarrow_T (W_j^A \triangleleft Z^T, b_j^{EA} \wedge b_j^T) = (W_{j+1}, b_{j+1})$$

where $dom(E_j) = dom(F_j)$, $rng(E_j)$ is a set of fresh symbols, $b_j^E = envB[W_j, W_j^E]$, A_j is the joint actions of R_j, $(Z_j^A, b^A) = A_j[[W_j^E]]$, and $(Z_j^T j, b^T) = T[[W_j^A]]$.

By Lemma 1 V_{j+1} is an instance of $(W_{j+1} bi_{j+1})$ using an extension of σ_j to new symbols.

7 Conclusion

In this paper we defined symbolic execution of Concurrent Rules Machines, a model of open distributed systems with explicit interaction with the environment. We show that symbolic execution is sound and it is complete for a large class of CRMs. We illustrated the utility of symbolic execution by verification of properties of interaction of a simple water level controller with the environment.

This is just the beginning. There are several directions for future work.

Compositionality of CRMs and their view of the environment suggest that symbolic execution of CRM models is also a promising approach to compositionally reason about the properties of larger systems through property-preserving symbolic composition of their constituent subsystems.

The reasoning examples in this paper were worked out using a first version of an implementation of symbolically executable CRMs using Rewriting modulo SMT. Once a robust implementation is available, we intend to carry out substantial case studies.

An alternative to reasoning symbolically about interactions with the environment, is to assign probability distributions to effects of actions (exported variables) and to observations by a CRM (import variables), and use mechanisms such a probablistic or statistical model checking to reason about system behavior and effects on the environment. This is also an important approach to investigate. To the best of our knowledge there is no theory supporting a sound and computable combination of symbolic and probabilistic/statistical reasoning. However, the formal patterns/theory transformation approach used for analyzing Maude executable models allows one to understand analysis results in the context of a common base model [16,21].

Dedication. This paper is dedicated to Gul Agha in celebration of his many contributions to the understanding and development of open distributed systems.

References

1. Agha, G.: Actors: A Model of Concurrent Computation in Distributed Systems. MIT Press, Cambridge, MA (1986)
2. Agha, G., Mason, I.A., Smith, S.F., Talcott, C.L.: A foundation for actor computation. J. Funct. Program. **7**, 1–72 (1997)
3. Arbab, F., Talcott, C.: Concurrent rules machines. In: Rebeca for actor analysis in action: essays in the honour of Marjan Sirjani LNCS Festschrift, vol. 15560. Springer (2025). https://doi.org/10.1007/978-3-031-85134-6_12
4. Arias, J., Bae, K., Olarte, C., Ölveczky, P.C., Petrucci, L., Rømming, F.: Symbolic analysis and parameter synthesis for time petri nets using Maude and SMT solving. arXiv:2303.08929 (2023)
5. Arias, J., Bae, K., Olarte, C., Ölveczky, P.C., Petrucci, L., Rømming, F.: Symbolic analysis and parameter synthesis for networks of parametric timed automata with global variables using Maude and SMT solving. Sci. Comput. Programm. **233**, 103074 (2024)
6. Cadar, C., Dunbar, D., Engler, D.R.: KLEE: Unassisted and automatic generation of high-coverage tests for complex systems programs. In: 8th USENIX Symposium on Operating Systems Design and Implementation, pp. 209–224. USENIX Association (2008)
7. Durán, F., et al.: Equational unification and matching, and symbolic reachability analysis in Maude 3.2 (system description). In: Blanchette, J., Kovács, L., Pattinson, D. (eds.) Automated Reasoning - 11th International Joint Conference, IJCAR 2022, Haifa, Israel, 8-10 August 2022, Proceedings. LNCS, vol. 13385, pp. 529–540. Springer, Cham (2022). https://doi.org/10.1007/978-3-031-10769-6_31
8. Escobar, S., López-Rueda, R., Sapiña, J.: Symbolic analysis by using folding narrowing with irreducibility and SMT constraints. In: 9th ACM SIGPLAN International Workshop on Formal Techniques for Safety- Critical Systems (FTSCS 2023), pp. 14–25. ACM (2023)
9. King, J.C.: Symbolic execution and program testing. Commun. ACM **19**(7), 385–394 (1976)
10. Lee, E.A.: Cyber physical systems: Design challenges. In: 11th IEEE International Symposium on Object and Component-Oriented Real-Time Distributed Computing. IEEE (2008)

11. Lee, E.A.: Fundamental limits of cyber-physical systems modeling. In: ACM Transactions on Cyber-Physical Systems (2016)
12. Lee, J., Bae, K., Kim, S., Kang, M., Ölveczky, P.C.: Modeling and formal analysis of virtually synchronous cyber-physical systems in AADL. Int. J. Softw. Tools Technol. Transfer **24**(6), 911–948 (2022)
13. Lee, J., Kim, S. and Bae, K.: An extension of HybridSynchAADL and its application to collaborating autonomous UAVs. In: Leveraging Applications of Formal Methods, Verification and Validation. Adaptation and Learning (ISoLA 2022), LNCS, pp. 47–64. Springer (2022). https://doi.org/10.1007/978-3-031-19759-8_4
14. Lee, J., Kim, S., Bae, K.: Bounded model checking of plc ST programs using rewriting modulo SMT. In: 8th ACM SIGPLAN International Workshop on Formal Techniques for Safety-Critical Systems (FTSCS 2022), pp. 56–67. ACM (2022)
15. Lee, J., Kim, S., Bae, K., Ölveczky, P.C.: HYBRID SYNCHAADL: modeling and formal analysis of virtually synchronous CPSs in AADL. In: Silva, A., Leino, K.R.M. (eds.) CAV 2021. LNCS, vol. 12759, pp. 491–504. Springer, Cham (2021). https://doi.org/10.1007/978-3-030-81685-8_23
16. Liu, S., Meseguer, J., Ölveczky, P.C., Zhang, M., Basin, D.: Bridging the semantic gap between qualitative and quantitative models of distributed systems. Proc. ACM Program. Lang. **6**(OOPSLA2), 315–344 (2022)
17. Lunel, S., Boyer, B., Talpin, J.P.: Compositional proofs in differential dynamic logic DL. In: 2017 17th International Conference on Application of Concurrency to System Design (ACSD), pp. 19–28 (2017)
18. Lunel, S., Mitsch, S., Boyer, B., Talpin, J.-P.: Parallel composition and modular verification of computer controlled systems in differential dynamic logic. In: ter Beek, M.H., McIver, A., Oliveira, J.N. (eds.) FM 2019. LNCS, vol. 11800, pp. 354–370. Springer, Cham (2019). https://doi.org/10.1007/978-3-030-30942-8_22
19. Meseguer, J.: Conditional rewriting logic as a unified model of concurrency. Theoret. Comput. Sci. **96**(1), 73–155 (1992)
20. Meseguer, J.: Twenty years of rewriting logic. J. Log. Algebraic Methods Program. **81**(7–8), 721–781 (2012)
21. Meseguer, J.: Taming distributed system complexity through formal patterns. Sci. Comput. Program. **83**, 3–34 (2014)
22. Meseguer, J.: Generalized rewrite theories, coherence completion, and symbolic methods. J. Log. Algebraic Methods Program **110**, 100483 (2020)
23. Nigam, V., Talcott, C.: Automating safety proofs about cyber-physical systems using rewriting modulo SMT. In: Bae, K. (eds.) Rewriting Logic and its Applications, LNCS, pp. 212–229. Springer, Cham (2022). https://doi.org/10.1007/978-3-031-12441-9_11
24. Nigam, V., Talcott, C.: Automating recoverability proofs for cyber-physical systems with runtime assurance architectures. In: David, C., Sun, M. (eds.) (eds.) Theoretical Aspects of Software Engineering - 17th International Symposium, Proceedings. LNCS, vol. 13931, pp. 1–19. Springer, Cham (2023). https://doi.org/10.1007/978-3-031-35257-7_1
25. Păsăreanu, C.S., Visser, W., Bushnell, D., Geldenhuys, J., Mehlitz, P., Rungta, N.: Symbolic pathfinder: integrating symbolic execution with model checking for java bytecode analysis. Automated Softw. Eng. **20**, 391–425 (2013). https://doi.org/10.1007/s10515-013-0122-2
26. Quesel, J.-D., Mitsch, S., Loos, S., Aréchiga, N., Platzer, A.: How to model and prove hybrid systems with KeYmaera: a tutorial on safety. Int. J. Softw. Tools Technol. Transfer **18**, 67–91 (2016)

27. Rocha, C., Meseguer, J., Muñoz, C.A.: Rewriting modulo SMT and open system analysis. J. Log. Algebraic Methods Program. **86**(1), 269–297 (2017)
28. Zhang, Y., Li, P., Ding, Y., Wang, L., Williams, D., Meng, N.: Broadly enabling KLEE to effortlessly find unrecoverable errors in rust. In: ACM/IEEE International Conference on Software Engineering: Software Engineering in Practice. ACM/IEEE (2024)

Type Congruence, Duality and Iso-Recursive Binary Session Types

Marco Giunti and Nobuko Yoshida

University of Oxford, Oxford, UK
{marco.giunti,nobuko.yoshida}@cs.ox.ac.uk

Abstract. Session types express a *protocol* which specifies the order and type of messages exchanged by concurrently executing processes. Prior work has been adapted to many frameworks including Agha's work [10], which has successfully extended session types to model distributed asynchronous multi-actors. Most works on session types, including Agha's work, take an equi-recursive approach and do not distinguish among a recursive type and its unfolding. One main problem of an equi-recursive type system is that its mechanisation in proof assistants is utterly complex and eventually requires co-induction. To overcome this problem, this paper presents an *iso-recursive* type system for *binary* sessions based on a novel *congruence on types* which relates recursive types and their unfolding. Our system based on type congruence enables to use a simple syntactic-directed *duality* without complicating the typability of processes. We mechanise the type congruence relation in Rocq without resorting to coinductive types, and use the proof assistant to show that our iso-recursive typing system satisfies subject reduction.

1 Introduction

Session types [28,30,50] are an effective framework to govern the behaviour of distributed processes that interact with message-passing. Their process algebraic properties based on the calculi of mobile processes (the π-calculus) [39,40] have been studied and used for about 30 years. As Robin Milner stated [38], mobile processes act as a *canonical encapsulation* of the concurrent object paradigm [53] represented by *actors* by Agha and Hewitt [2]. Actors are independent agents (processes) which perform computations by purely exchanging asynchronous messages. The actors' model plays a key role for developing the syntactically "minimum", expressive and implementable π-calculus (the asynchronous

---

This work is partially supported by EPSRC EP/T006544/2, EP/N027833/2, EP/T014709/2, EP/Y005244/1, EP/V000462/1, EP/X015955/1, Horizon EU TaRDIS 101093006 and Advanced Research and Invention Agency (ARIA) Safeguarded AI.

π-calculus) [29] and its semantic theories [31], for measuring the expressiveness of a family of process algebras, and for designing distributed implementations [5]. To cope with asynchronous actor semantics, Agha, with Charalambides and Dinges, has extended multiparty session types for specifying parameterised, multi-actor protocols with inherent asynchrony [10]. This powerful framework enables us to express a large class of asynchronous communication protocols, including the sliding window protocol, and is successfully integrated into an actor programming language.

This paper attempts to propose a tractable but expressive typing system for session processes which are based on a simple type duality relation. In most works on session types, including Agha's work, recursive types follow an *equi-recursive* view [44] and represent infinite trees that are manipulated *co-inductively*. This representation does not have a direct counterpart in eager programming languages, as modelled by an object calculus [1], which typically resort to *iso-recursive* types [44] that are manipulated *inductively*. Moreover, lazy evaluation of predicates on equi-recursive trees might not terminate, and is thus not effective for static program analysis. In practice, session types are embedded in non-lazy languages by encoding equi-recursive types; for instance, [33] defines infinite sequence of types as polymorphic lenses [16] by using OCaml generalised algebraic data types.

Our proposal to overcome this problem consists in introducing a theory of *iso-recursive session types* relying on a type system that uses a novel notion of *type congruence* to relate the types of dual sessions. This contribution complements recent results [25] presenting a theory of iso-recursive multiparty session types. The theory in [25] relies on the bottom-up approach known as *generalised multiparty session types*, e.g. [6,8,19,27,34,43,48,49], and decides deadlock-freedom without using global types. Differently from previous work, it considers iso-recursive types and computes the properties of session environments in the type system, instead of assessing these properties with model checkers (cf. [48]).

In this paper, we account for type checking the parallel composition of sessions typed with *folded* and *unfolded* dual iso-recursive session types by introducing a *type congruence* that is closed under simple *syntax-directed session type duality*, and under *labelled transitions* of types. The following example illustrates these ideas.

Equi-recursive vs iso-recursive types: OAuth2 example. Consider a simplified version of the OAuth 2.0 protocol [48] relying on *two dual participants*. Let us indicate *send to* and *receive from* participant p as the *types* $p!l(S).T$ and $p?l(S).T$, respectively, where l is a *label* indicating the nature of the communication, S is the *sort* of the payload, and T is the type of the continuation. Selection among (branching on) different output (input) types is done by means of the binary operator $+$. Recursion is provided by the construct $\mu X.T$, which binds the type variable X in T. Termination is represented by type end. Sorts describe the types of string and unit values. The protocol says that the client (c) sends the password (pwd, carrying a string) to the authorisation server (a) and the session restarts, or c sends quit to a, and the session ends.

$$T_\mathsf{c} \stackrel{\text{def}}{=} \mu X.(\mathsf{a!pwd(str)}.X + \mathsf{a!quit(unit).end})$$

$$T_\mathsf{a} \stackrel{\text{def}}{=} \mu X.R_\mathsf{a} \qquad R_\mathsf{a} \stackrel{\text{def}}{=} \mathsf{c?pwd(str)}.X + \mathsf{c?quit(unit).end}$$

Most type disciplines for binary sessions rely on *equi-recursion* and *type duality*, e.g. [17,23,30]. Equi-recursion establishes that a recursive type and its unfolding are *equal*. Consider the types $T_\mathsf{a}^{*'} \stackrel{\text{def}}{=} R_\mathsf{a}\{T_\mathsf{a}/X\}$, $T_\mathsf{a}^{**} \stackrel{\text{def}}{=} R_\mathsf{a}\{T_\mathsf{a}^*/X\}$, and so on. Following the equi-recursive approach, we have $T_\mathsf{a} = T_\mathsf{a}^* = T_\mathsf{a}^{**} = \cdots$. We note that mechanising equi-recursive session types in proof assistants is quite complex, and eventually relies on co-induction [14]. Duality swaps participants, and ?/! with !/?, in a type T, noted $\overline{T}$: it verifies the compatibility of the two participants of a session. The composition of two end-points of the communication is allowed only if their types are dual: this is mandatory for subject reduction [22,24,51].

To show an example of *equi-recursive session typing*, consider the processes implementing the client (P_c) and the server (P_a), which mirror their types T_c and T_a, respectively, but that the payload of input and output are (bound) variables and expressions, respectively, and that there is a process variable χ:

$$P_\mathsf{c} \stackrel{\text{def}}{=} \mu\chi.(\mathsf{a!pwd}\langle\text{"fido"}\rangle.\chi + \mathsf{a!quit}\langle\rangle)$$

$$P_\mathsf{a} \stackrel{\text{def}}{=} \mu\chi.Q_\mathsf{a} \qquad Q_\mathsf{a} \stackrel{\text{def}}{=} \mathsf{c?pwd}(x).\chi + \mathsf{c?quit}(x)$$

The composition of processes P_c and $P_\mathsf{a}^* \stackrel{\text{def}}{=} Q_\mathsf{a}\{P_\mathsf{a}/\chi\}$ is typed by the rule for parallel composition, where the type $\bot$ indicates that no further interactions are possible [30]. The equality $\overline{T_\mathsf{c}} = T_\mathsf{a}^*$ is interpreted on regular infinite trees [12]: "to check whether a given end point type T_1 is dual of another type T_2, we first build the dual of T_1 and then check that the thus obtained type is equivalent to T_2" [24, p. 213].

$$\text{Equi-T-Sess} \frac{\Gamma \vdash P_\mathsf{c} : T_\mathsf{c} \qquad \Gamma \vdash P_\mathsf{a}^* : T_\mathsf{a}^* \qquad \overline{T_\mathsf{c}} = T_\mathsf{a}^*}{\Gamma \Vdash \mathsf{c} \triangleleft P_\mathsf{c} \parallel \mathsf{a} \triangleleft P_\mathsf{a}^* : \bot}$$

The approach proposed in this paper relies on *iso-recursive session types* and is mechanised in Rocq without resorting to coinductive types (cf. command `CoInductive` [46]). First, we define a *congruence* on types relating folded and unfolded types, noted $\equiv$. Then, to type check the parallel composition of the client $\mathsf{c} \triangleleft P_\mathsf{c}$ and of the server $\mathsf{a} \triangleleft P_\mathsf{a}^*$, we *provide a proof that* $\overline{T_\mathsf{c}} \equiv T_\mathsf{a}^*$.

$$\text{Iso-T-Sess} \frac{\Gamma \vdash P_\mathsf{c} : T_\mathsf{c} \qquad \Gamma \vdash P_\mathsf{a}^* : T_\mathsf{a}^* \qquad \overline{T_\mathsf{c}} \equiv T_\mathsf{a}^*}{\Gamma \Vdash \mathsf{c} \triangleleft P_\mathsf{c} \parallel \mathsf{a} \triangleleft P_\mathsf{a}^* : \bot}$$

We show that the typing system based on rule Iso-T-Sess is sound by relying on the "types as processes" approach (cf. [37]) and by introducing labelled transition semantics of types.

Outline. § 2 introduces the syntax and the labelled transition semantics of iso-recursive session processes. § 3 presents a type congruence relating folded and unfolded types. The iso-recursive type system is developed in § 4, along with the type duality involution. § 5 is devoted to the proof of subject reduction. We conclude in § 6 by briefly discussing related work.

All the *results* of the paper are *mechanised in Rocq* and are publicly available in an *online repository* [21]. Along the paper, we map definitions and lemmas to their Rocq counterpart by means of *hyperlinks* denoted by the *Roc bird symbol* 🐦.

2 Iso-Recursive Sessions

In this section, we present the syntax and the semantics of binary sessions. The syntax of types and processes is in Definition 1. We consider *iso-recursive* types of the form $\mu X.T$ where $\mu X.T$ and its unfolding are not equal, but isomorphic. We stress that types have a *finite representation* rather than abstract infinite trees (cf. equi-recursive types). We require all terms to be contractive, i.e. $\mu X_1.\mu X_2.\ldots\mu X_n.X_1$ is not allowed as a subterm for any $n \geq 1$ [44, p. 300], which can be alternatively stated as type variables must occur guarded [13].

Definition 1 (Syntax of types and processes).

$S := \mathsf{nat} \mid \mathsf{int} \mid \mathsf{str} \mid \mathsf{bool} \mid \mathsf{unit}$ — Sorts

$T := \mathbf{r}!l(S).T \mid \mathbf{r}?l(S).T \mid T + T \mid \mathsf{end} \mid \mu X.T \mid X \mid \bot$ — Types

$v := n \mid z \mid s \mid () \mid \mathsf{true} \mid \mathsf{false}$ — Values

$e := v \mid e_1 \wedge e_2 \mid e_1 \vee e_2 \mid \neg e \mid e_1 == e_2 \mid e_1 < e_2$ — Expressions

$P := \mathbf{r}!l\langle e\rangle.P \mid \mathbf{r}?l(x).P \mid P + P \mid \mu\chi.P \mid \chi \mid \mathsf{if}\ e\ \mathsf{then}\ P\ \mathsf{else}\ Q \mid \mathbf{0}$ — Processes

$\mathcal{M} := \mathbf{r} \triangleleft P \mid (\mathbf{p} \triangleleft P \parallel \overline{\mathbf{p}} \triangleleft Q)$ — Sessions

We use $\mathsf{p, q, r}$ to range over the set $\mathcal{P}$ of *participants*, and let $dual: \mathcal{P} \to \mathcal{P}$ be an involution, noted $\overline{\mathsf{r}}$. We use n to range over *natural values*, z to range over *integer values*, and s to range over *string values*; () indicates the *empty value*. We use l to range over *labels*, i, j to range over *indexes* (natural numbers), X to range over *type variables*, x to range over *variables*, and χ to range over *process variables*.

A *thread* is the decoration of a process P with a participant p, noted $\mathsf{p} \triangleleft P$. Sessions $\mathcal{M}$ belong to the set $\mathbb{M}$; types T belong to the set $\mathcal{T}$. To ease the presentation, $\mathcal{M}$ contains at most two threads having dual participants: having multiple pairs of threads with dual participants does not affect our results. Type $\bot$ is reserved for closing the composition of two threads (cf. § 4).

The constructor μ is a *binder* in types and processes: we let X be bound in $\mu X.T$ and *free* in T; similarly, χ is bound in $\mu\chi.P$ and free in P. The remaining binder for processes is input: variable x is bound in $\mathbf{r}?l(x).P$. *Closed* terms are those without free variables. We assume the *substitution* of free occurrences of a type variable X in a type T_1 with a closed type T_2, written $T_1\{T_2/X\}$. We assume substitution of free occurrences of a process variable χ in process P_1 with a closed process P_2, written $P_1\{P_2/\chi\}$, and substitution of free occurrences of variable x in process P with a value v, written $P\{v/x\}$.

The symbol $=$ is reserved for Leibniz equality.

Definition 2 (Session notation).

$\oplus_{i \in I} \mathtt{r}!l_i(S_i).T_i \stackrel{def}{=} \mathtt{r}!l_1(S_1).T_1 + \cdots + \mathtt{r}!l_n(S_n).T_n \quad I = (1, \ldots, n), n \geq 1$

$\&_{i \in I} \mathtt{r}?l_i(S_i).T_i \stackrel{def}{=} \mathtt{r}?l_1(S_1).T_1 + \cdots + \mathtt{r}?l_n(S_n).T_n \quad I = (1, \ldots, n), n \geq 1$

2.1 Well-Formed Types

We only consider *well-formed* types implementing the session notation in Definition 2. Well-formedness is decided by collecting the labels of types in multi-sets; the inference system $\mathsf{wf}(T)$ is in Fig. 1.

Intuitively, a sum type T_1+T_2 is *well-formed* when it has no duplicated labels, T_1 and T_2 have the same polarity, and T_i does not contain type $\bot$, $i \in \{1,2\}$.

Let $\{\!|l_1,\ldots,l_n|\!\}$ denote *multisets* of labels, and let $\mathsf{nodup}(\{\!|l_1, \ldots, l_n|\!\})$ hold whenever l_i is unique, for all $i \in \{1,\ldots,n\}$.

Let labels be a function mapping types to multisets of labels, and assume $\mathsf{labels}(\mathtt{r}?l(S).T) \stackrel{def}{=} \{\!|l|\!\}$, $\mathsf{labels}(\mathtt{r}!l(S).T) \stackrel{def}{=} \{\!|l|\!\}$, and $\mathsf{labels}(T_1 + T_2) \stackrel{def}{=} \mathsf{labels}(T_1) \uplus \mathsf{labels}(T_2)$, and $\mathsf{labels}(T) \stackrel{def}{=} \emptyset$ otherwise.

Let $\mathsf{polarity}$ be a partial function mapping types to polarities $p \in \{!, ?\}$, and let $\mathsf{polarity}(T) \downarrow$ whenever $\mathsf{polarity}$ is defined on type T. Let $\mathsf{polarity}(\mathtt{r}?l(S).T) \stackrel{def}{=} ?$, $\mathsf{polarity}(\mathtt{r}!l(S).T) \stackrel{def}{=} !$, and $\mathsf{polarity}(T_1 + T_2) \stackrel{def}{=} p$ whenever $\mathsf{polarity}(T_1) = p$ and $\mathsf{polarity}(T_2) = p$, and $\mathsf{polarity}(T)$ be undefined otherwise.

Well-formed types contain sums having the same polarity and without duplicated labels, and do not contain the type $\bot$, which is reserved for the typing system (cf. § 4). The formal definition is in Fig. 1.

$$\text{WF-INP} \frac{\mathsf{wf}(T)}{\mathsf{wf}(\mathtt{r}?l(S).T)} \qquad \text{WF-OUT} \frac{\mathsf{wf}(T)}{\mathsf{wf}(\mathtt{r}!l(S).T)}$$

$$\text{WF-SUM} \frac{\mathsf{nodup}(\mathsf{labels}(T_1 + T_2)) \quad \mathsf{polarity}(T_1 + T_2) \downarrow \quad \mathsf{wf}(T_1) \quad \mathsf{wf}(T_2)}{\mathsf{wf}(T_1 + T_2)}$$

$$\text{WF-END} \frac{}{\mathsf{wf}(\mathsf{end})} \qquad \text{WF-REC} \frac{\mathsf{wf}(T)}{\mathsf{wf}(\mu X.T)} \qquad \text{WF-VAR} \frac{}{\mathsf{wf}(X)}$$

Fig. 1. Well-formed types

Example 1. Examples of well-formed types include $\mathtt{p}?l(\mathsf{nat}).\mathtt{p}!l(\mathsf{bool}).T_1$, and $\mathtt{p}?l_1(\mathsf{str}).T_1 + \mathtt{p}?l_2(\mathsf{int}).T_2 + \mathtt{p}?l_3(\mathsf{unit}).T_3$, and $\mathtt{p}!l_1(\mathsf{str}).T_1 + \mathtt{p}!l_2(\mathsf{int}).T_2 + \mathtt{p}!l_3(\mathsf{unit}).T_3$, and $\mu X.(\mathtt{p}?l_1(\mathsf{str}).X + \mathtt{p}?l_2(\mathsf{int}).T_2)$, whenever l_1, l_2 and l_3 are distinct, and T_1, T_2 and T_3 are well-formed.

A first example of ill-formed type is $p?l(\text{str}).T_1 + p?l(\text{int}).T_2$, because the label l is used twice.

The type $T \stackrel{\text{def}}{=} \mu X.(p?l_1(\text{str}).X) + p?l_2(\text{int}).T_1$ is ill-formed, because polarity(T) is undefined: this follows from polarity$(\mu X.(p?l_1(\text{str}).X))$ undefined. To recover well-formedness, whenever $p?l_2(\text{int}).T_1$ is well-formed and does not contain free occurrences of X (which can be enforced by alpha-renaming $\mu X.(p?l_1(\text{str}).X)$), we can lift recursion up: wf$(\mu X.(p?l_1(\text{str}).X + p?l_2(\text{int}).T_1))$.

The type $p!l(\text{int}).(p?l(\text{bool}).\text{end} + \text{end})$ is ill-formed, because polarity$(p?l(\text{bool}).\text{end} + \text{end})$ is undefined: this follows from polarity(end) undefined.

2.2 Labelled Transition Semantics

Transition rules for sessions: $\boxed{\mathcal{M} \stackrel{\alpha}{\to} \mathcal{M}}$

$$\text{R-Inp} \frac{}{p \triangleleft \overline{p}?l(x).P \stackrel{\overline{p}?l(v)}{\longrightarrow} p \triangleleft P\{v/x\}} \qquad \text{R-Out} \frac{e \downarrow v}{p \triangleleft \overline{p}!l\langle e\rangle.P \stackrel{\overline{p}!l\langle v\rangle}{\longrightarrow} p \triangleleft P}$$

$$\text{R-Sum-L} \frac{r \triangleleft P \stackrel{\alpha}{\to} r \triangleleft P'}{r \triangleleft P + Q \stackrel{\alpha}{\to} r \triangleleft P'}$$

$$\text{R-Com} \frac{p \triangleleft P \stackrel{\overline{p}?l(v)}{\longrightarrow} p \triangleleft P' \quad \overline{p} \triangleleft Q \stackrel{p!l\langle v\rangle}{\longrightarrow} \overline{p} \triangleleft Q'}{p \triangleleft P \parallel \overline{p} \triangleleft Q \stackrel{\tau}{\to} p \triangleleft P' \parallel \overline{p} \triangleleft Q'}$$

$$\text{R-Rec} \frac{}{p \triangleleft \mu\chi.P \parallel \overline{p} \triangleleft Q \stackrel{\tau}{\to} p \triangleleft P\{\mu\chi.P/\chi\} \parallel \overline{p} \triangleleft Q}$$

$$\text{R-IfT} \frac{e \downarrow \text{true}}{p \triangleleft \text{if } e \text{ then } P \text{ else } Q \parallel \overline{p} \triangleleft R \stackrel{\tau}{\to} p \triangleleft P \parallel \overline{p} \triangleleft R}$$

$$\text{R-Str} \frac{\mathcal{M}'_1 \equiv \mathcal{M}_1 \quad \mathcal{M}_1 \stackrel{\alpha}{\to} \mathcal{M}_2 \quad \mathcal{M}_2 \equiv \mathcal{M}'_2}{\mathcal{M}'_1 \stackrel{\alpha}{\to} \mathcal{M}'_2}$$

Fig. 2. Labelled transition rules for sessions (we omit R-IfF)

We assume an *evaluation* (partial) function $\downarrow$ transforming expressions e into values v, written $e \downarrow v$.

The operational semantics of sessions are defined modulo a *structural congruence* relation over sessions $\mathcal{M}$, noted $\equiv\, \subseteq \mathbb{M} \times \mathbb{M}$.

$$p \triangleleft P \parallel \overline{p} \triangleleft Q \equiv \overline{p} \triangleleft Q \parallel p \triangleleft P$$

The *labelled transition rules* are defined in Fig. 2; we just present the left rules. The rule have the form $\mathcal{M} \xrightarrow{\alpha} \mathcal{M}$, where $\alpha \in \mathcal{A}$ is an *action*.

$$\alpha := \mathbf{r}?l(v) \mid \mathbf{r}!l\langle v \rangle \mid \tau$$

A *computation* is a sequence of τ-transitions or *reductions* $\mathcal{M}_1 \xrightarrow{\tau} \mathcal{M}_2 \xrightarrow{\tau} \cdots$. We are mainly interested in analysing computations of well-typed sessions (cf. § 4).

Rule R-INP says that a participant p waiting for a value from its dual $\bar{\mathrm{p}}$ on the label l can do a transition labelled by $\bar{\mathrm{p}}?l(v)$ and instantiate the formal parameter x with the value v in the continuation P, noted as $P\{v/x\}$.

Rule R-OUT allows a participant p sending to $\bar{\mathrm{p}}$ on label l an expression e that can be evaluated as v to do a transition labelled by $\bar{\mathrm{p}}!l\langle v \rangle$ and continue as P.

Non-deterministic reductions are allowed by means of rule R-SUM-L, which says that a participant r non-deterministically choosing among process P and Q, denoted $P + Q$, can do a transition labelled by α and reach $\mathbf{r} \triangleleft P'$ whenever $\mathbf{r} \triangleleft P$ can fire the same transition and reach the same redex.

Communication among two dual participants p and $\bar{\mathrm{p}}$ is performed by means of rule R-COM. Whenever $\mathrm{p} \triangleleft P$ can do a transition labelled by the input action $\bar{\mathrm{p}}?l(v)$ and reach the redex $\mathrm{p} \triangleleft P'$, and $\bar{\mathrm{p}} \triangleleft Q$ can do a transition labelled by the output action $\mathrm{p}!l\langle v \rangle$ and reach the redex $\bar{\mathrm{p}} \triangleleft Q'$, we can infer a τ transition from the composition of $\mathrm{p} \triangleleft P$ and $\bar{\mathrm{p}} \triangleleft Q$ to the composition of $\mathrm{p} \triangleleft P'$ and $\bar{\mathrm{p}} \triangleleft Q'$.

Rule R-REC allows a participant p recursively defined as $\mu\chi.P$ and running in parallel with its dual $\bar{\mathrm{p}} \triangleleft Q$, to do an internal transition τ and unfold the body P while instantiating the occurrences of χ in P with $\mu\chi.P$, thus reaching the redex $\mathrm{p} \triangleleft P\{\mu\chi.P/\chi\} \parallel \bar{\mathrm{p}} \triangleleft Q$.

Rule R-IFT says that a participant p with the body if e then P else Q and running in parallel with the dual thread $\bar{\mathrm{p}} \triangleleft R$, can do a τ-transition and reach the redex $\mathrm{p} \triangleleft P \parallel \bar{\mathrm{p}} \triangleleft R$ whenever the expression e evaluates to true.

Rule R-STR rearranges processes with structural congruence.

Example 2. Consider the authorisation protocol in § 1 and let

$$\mathcal{M} \stackrel{\mathrm{def}}{=} \mathrm{c} \triangleleft P_\mathrm{c} \parallel \mathrm{a} \triangleleft P_\mathrm{a}^*$$

where process P_c implements the client c, and process $P_\mathrm{a}^* \stackrel{\mathrm{def}}{=} Q_\mathrm{a}\{P_\mathrm{a}/\chi\}$ implements the (unfolding of the) authorisation server a. Assume that $\bar{\mathrm{c}} = \mathrm{a}$: that is, the server and the client are dual participants.

We want to analyse a communication of the server a with the client c depicting a *password* transaction, that is a reduction inferred from the label pwd. A first application of rule R-REC unfolds the server c:

$$\mathcal{M} \xrightarrow{\tau} \mathrm{c} \triangleleft P_\mathrm{c}^* \parallel \mathrm{a} \triangleleft P_\mathrm{a}^* \stackrel{\mathrm{def}}{=} \mathcal{M}^*$$

where $P_\mathrm{c}^* \stackrel{\mathrm{def}}{=} \mathrm{a}!\mathrm{pwd}\langle\text{"fido"}\rangle.P_\mathrm{c} + \mathrm{a}!\mathrm{quit}\langle\rangle$.

Now we apply rule R-COM to infer a communication among the server a and the client c on the label pwd, followed by R-STR:

$$\text{R-STR} \frac{\text{R-COM} \dfrac{(A) \quad (B)}{\mathsf{a} \triangleleft P_\mathsf{a}^* \,\|\, \mathsf{c} \triangleleft P_\mathsf{c}^* \xrightarrow{\tau} \mathsf{a} \triangleleft P_\mathsf{a} \,\|\, \mathsf{c} \triangleleft P_\mathsf{c}}}{\mathcal{M}^* \xrightarrow{\tau} \mathsf{c} \triangleleft P_\mathsf{c} \,\|\, \mathsf{a} \triangleleft P_\mathsf{a}}$$

where

$$\text{R-SUM-L} \frac{\text{R-INP} \dfrac{}{\mathsf{a} \triangleleft \mathsf{c}?\mathsf{pwd}(x).P_\mathsf{a} \xrightarrow{\mathsf{c}?\mathsf{pwd}(\text{``fido''})} \mathsf{a} \triangleleft P_\mathsf{a}}}{(A)\ \mathsf{a} \triangleleft P_\mathsf{a}^* \xrightarrow{\mathsf{c}?\mathsf{pwd}(\text{``fido''})} \mathsf{a} \triangleleft P_\mathsf{a}}$$

and

$$\text{R-SUM-L} \frac{\text{R-OUT} \dfrac{}{\mathsf{c} \triangleleft \mathsf{a}!\mathsf{pwd}\langle\text{``fido''}\rangle.P_\mathsf{c} \xrightarrow{\mathsf{a}!\mathsf{pwd}\langle\text{``fido''}\rangle} \mathsf{c} \triangleleft P_\mathsf{c}}}{(B)\ \mathsf{c} \triangleleft P_\mathsf{c}^* \xrightarrow{\mathsf{a}!\mathsf{pwd}\langle\text{``fido''}\rangle} \mathsf{c} \triangleleft P_\mathsf{c}}$$

2.3 Mechanisation and Implementation of Types and Processes

The mechanisation of types and processes in Rocq [46] relies on the command Inductive. As an example, we show the mechanisation 🐾 of iso-recursive session types (cf. types T of Definition 1). In the code below, var is notation for nat, participant and label are types built using seeds of type nat, and styp implements sorts S of Definition 1.

```
Inductive typ : Set :=
 | typ_var : var → typ
 | typ_mu : var → typ → typ
 | typ_sum : typ → typ → typ
 | typ_input : participant → label → styp → typ → typ
 | typ_output : participant → label → styp → typ → typ
 | typ_end : typ
 | typ_bot : typ.
```

The mechanisation of the syntax of processes is similar. The semantics of sessions of Fig. 2 are instrumented 🐾 with two technical devices to simplify the proof of subject reduction:

(i) We distinguish among τ-actions originating from unfolding (cf. R-REC) and from if-then-else (e.g. R-IFT);
(ii) We shift the bound identifiers of the recursive processes $\mu\chi.P$ that substitutes process variable χ in the continuation of R-REC.

Item (ii) allows to maintain a *freshness invariant*: to avoid using the same identifier twice in binders. That is, we require that all variables x and process variables χ occurring in processes $\mathtt{r?}l(x).P$ and $\mu X.P$, respectively, are syntactically distinct (cf. § 4.3).

The implementation of rule R-REC below relies on a natural number M bigger than the maximum seed (cf. `max_seed`) used in the (bound) identifiers of the process, and on function `shiftP` shifting all identifiers used in bound variables and bound process variables of M positions. Action `aunfold` implementes the τ-action for unfolding (cf. (i)).

```
Check r_rec: ∀ (p : participant ) (X : process_var ) (P Q RP : process ) (M : nat),
    max_seed (proc_mu X P) < M → RP = shiftP M (proc_mu X P) →
    lts (parallel_session  (p, proc_mu X P) (pdual p, Q)) aunfold
       (parallel_session  (p, substP P RP X) (pdual p, Q)).
```

Implementation. Types and processes can be exported to functional languages as *algebraic data types* by using the command `Extraction` . We note that the labelled transition semantics of Fig. 2 are mechanised by using the command `Inductive` , and in turn cannot be executed. However, we could easily define `Fixpoint` -based semantics by identifying a termination measure (cf. [25,26]) to provide for a certified interpreter that can be extracted e.g. to OCaml and ran. Alternatively, we could compile processes into Go programs [20] and run them.

3 Type Congruence

In this section, we introduce type congruence and explain its Rocq mechanisation.

3.1 Type Congruence

To recover the flexibility of type systems based on equi-recursive types, e.g. [17,23,30], we define a notion of *type congruence* (noted $\equiv$) relating folded and unfolded types, and use it at top level when composing two sessions (cf. § 4). Following the approach pioneered by [37, Chapter 4], we let type congruence be the union of all symmetric equivalences.

We devise a notion of type equivalence that is tailored at equating folded and unfolded *well-formed* types (cf. Definition 2 and § 2.1).

Definition 3 (Type Equivalence). *A relation* $\mathcal{R} \subseteq \mathcal{T} \times \mathcal{T}$ *is a type equivalence whenever* $T_1 \mathcal{R} T_2$ *and*

- $T_1 = \mu X.U_1$ and $T_2 = \mu X.U_2$ imply $U_1 \mathcal{R} U_2$ and $U_1\{\mu X.U_1/X\} \mathcal{R} T_2$ and $T_1 \mathcal{R} U_2\{\mu X.U_2/X\}$
- $T_1 = \mu X.U_1$ and $T_2 \neq \mu X.U_2$ imply $U_1\{\mu X.U_1/X\} \mathcal{R} T_2$
- $T_1 \neq \mu X.U_1$ and $T_2 = \mu X.U_2$ imply $T_1 \mathcal{R} U_2\{\mu X.U_2/X\}$
- $T_1 = X_1$ and $T_2 = X_2$
- $T_1 = \mathsf{end}$ and $T_2 = \mathsf{end}$
- $T_1 = \mathtt{p?}l(S).U_1 + R_1$ and $T_2 = \mathtt{p?}l(S).U_2 + R_2$ imply $U_1 \mathcal{R} U_2$ and $R_1 \mathcal{R} R_2$
- $T_1 = \mathtt{p!}l(S).U_1 + R_1$ and $T_2 = \mathtt{p!}l(S).U_2 + R_2$ imply $U_1 \mathcal{R} U_2$ and $R_1 \mathcal{R} R_2$

- $T_1 = \mathsf{p}?l(S).U_1$ and $T_2 = \mathsf{p}?l(S).U_2$ imply $U_1 \mathcal{R} U_2$
- $T_1 = \mathsf{p}!l(S).U_1$ and $T_2 = \mathsf{p}!l(S).U_2$ imply $U_1 \mathcal{R} U_2$
- T_1 and T_2 do not match the cases above imply False.

Definition 4 (Structural Equivalence). *A relation $\mathcal{R} \subseteq \mathcal{T} \times \mathcal{T}$ is a structural equivalence whenever it is (i) a type equivalence and (ii) symmetric.*

Definition 5 (Type Congruence). Type congruence, noted $\equiv \subseteq \mathcal{T} \times \mathcal{T}$, is the union of all structural equivalences.

3.2 Mechanisation of Type Congruence

In this section, we mechanise type congruence (cf. Definition 5) in Rocq. The objective is to obtain a computer aided proof of two results (cf. Lemma 5 and Lemma 6) used to close subject reduction. We also showcase a method to prove that two types are congruent (cf. Example 3).

```
1   Notation X £ T := (substT T X (typ_mu X T)) (at level 40).
2   Definition equiv R := ∀ (t1 t2 : typ), R t1 t2 →
3       match t1, t2 with
4       | typ_mu X1 U1, typ_mu X2 U2 ⇒ R U1 U2 ∧ R (X1 £ U1) t2 ∧ R t1 (X2 £ U2)
5       | typ_mu X U, _ ⇒ R (X £ U) t2
6       | _, typ_mu X U ⇒ R t1 (X £ U)
7       | typ_var X1, typ_var X2 ⇒ True
8       | typ_end , typ_end ⇒ True
9       | typ_sum (typ_input p1 l1 s1 u1) r1, typ_sum (typ_input p2 l2 s2 u2) r2 ⇒
10          p1 = p2 ∧ l1 = l2 ∧ s1 = s2 ∧ R u1 u2 ∧ R r1 r2
11      | typ_sum (typ_output p1 l1 s1 u1) r1, typ_sum (typ_output p2 l2 s2 u2) r2 ⇒
12          p1 = p2 ∧ l1 = l2 ∧ s1 = s2 ∧ R u1 u2 ∧ R r1 r2
13      | typ_input p1 l1 s1 u1, typ_input p2 l2 s2 u2 ⇒
14          p1 = p2 ∧ l1 = l2 ∧ s1 = s2 ∧ R u1 u2
15      | typ_output p1 l1 s1 u1, typ_output p2 l2 s2 u2 ⇒
16          p1 = p2 ∧ l1 = l2 ∧ s1 = s2 ∧ R u1 u2
17      | _, _ ⇒ False
18      end.
19  Definition struct_equiv R := equiv R ∧ symmetric typ R.
20  Definition relation2 (X Y: Type) := X → Y → Prop.
21  Definition set(X: Type) := X → Prop.
22  Section 0.
23      Variables X Y: Type.
24      Definition union_st (P: set (relation2 X Y)) := fun x y ⇒ exists2 R, P R & R x y.
25  End 0.
26  Definition typ_scongr := union_st typ typ struct_equiv .
27  Notation "T1 == T2" := (typ_scongr T1 T2) (at level 40).
28  Lemma equiv_scongr : equiv typ_scongr .
```

Fig. 3. Mechanisation of type congruence in Rocq

The mechanisation is in Fig. 3. The predicate `equiv` on binary relations over `typ` implements Definition 3. The key cases for iso-recursion are lines 4–6: in order for a relation $\mathcal{R}$ to satisfy `equiv`, it must be that whenever a folded type $\mu X.T$ is related to U, then its unfolding $T\{\mu X.T/X\}$ is also related to U. The remaining cases are homomorphic.

The predicate `struct_equiv` implements Definition 4 and holds for relations $\mathcal{R}$ that satisfy `equiv` and are symmetric. The relation `typ_scongr` mechanises $\equiv$ and is defined as the union of all relations $\mathcal{R}$ that satisfy `struct_equiv` . The operator union_st implementing this abstraction is defined in lines 20–25, which are taken from the formalisation of [45]. The notation `exists2 R, P x & Q x` expresses the existence of R which satisfies both predicates P and Q.[1]

The lemma in line 28 mechanises the following result.

Lemma 1. *Type congruence is a type equivalence.*

$$\text{S-Nat}\frac{n \in \mathbb{N}}{\Gamma \vdash n : \text{nat}} \qquad \text{S-Int}\frac{z \in \mathbb{Z}}{\Gamma \vdash z : \text{int}} \qquad \text{S-Str-E}\frac{}{\Gamma \vdash \text{""} : \text{str}}$$

$$\text{S-Str}\frac{c \in \text{Char} \quad \Gamma \vdash s : \text{str}}{\Gamma \vdash c\hat{\ }s : \text{str}} \qquad \text{S-Bl}\frac{b \in \{\text{true}, \text{false}\}}{\Gamma \vdash b : \text{bool}} \qquad \text{S-Uni}\frac{}{\Gamma \vdash () : \text{unit}}$$

$$\text{S-Var}\frac{}{\Gamma, x : S \vdash x : S} \qquad \text{S-Lt}\frac{\Gamma \vdash e_1 : S \quad \Gamma \vdash e_2 : S \quad S \in \{\text{nat}, \text{int}\}}{\Gamma \vdash e_1 < e_2 : \text{bool}}$$

$$\text{S-Eq}\frac{\Gamma \vdash e_1 : S \quad \Gamma \vdash e_2 : S}{\Gamma \vdash e_1 = e_2 : \text{bool}} \qquad \text{S-Neg}\frac{\Gamma \vdash e : \text{bool}}{\Gamma \vdash \neg e : \text{bool}}$$

$$\text{S-And}\frac{\Gamma \vdash e_1 : \text{bool} \quad \Gamma \vdash e_2 : \text{bool}}{\Gamma \vdash e_1 \wedge e_2 : \text{bool}} \qquad \text{S-Or}\frac{\Gamma \vdash e_1 : \text{bool} \quad \Gamma \vdash e_2 : \text{bool}}{\Gamma \vdash e_1 \vee e_2 : \text{bool}}$$

Fig. 4. Sorting rules

Example 3. Take a participant q and labels l_1, l_2, and consider the types T_1 and T_2 defined below. Let i and b be short for int and bool, respectively. We have that $T_1 \equiv T_2$.

$$T_1 \stackrel{\text{def}}{=} \mu X.(\mathsf{q}?l_1(\mathsf{b}).\mathsf{q}!l_1(\mathsf{i}).X + U_1) \qquad U_1 \stackrel{\text{def}}{=} \mathsf{q}?l_2(\mathsf{i}).\mathsf{q}!l_2(\mathsf{i}).\mathsf{q}!l_2(\mathsf{i}).\mu Y.\mathsf{q}!l_2(\mathsf{i}).Y$$

$$T_2 \stackrel{\text{def}}{=} \mathsf{q}?l_1(\mathsf{b}).\mathsf{q}!l_1(\mathsf{i}).T_1 + U_2 \qquad U_2 \stackrel{\text{def}}{=} \mathsf{q}?l_2(\mathsf{i}).\mu Y.\mathsf{q}!l_2(\mathsf{i}).Y$$

To prove this claim we provide a relation $\mathcal{R}$ that satisfies `struct_equiv` and s.t. $T_1 \mathcal{R} T_2$. In order to systematically use this methodology, we deploy a proof technique in the tactic language Ltac.

```
Lemma exist_struct_equiv : ∀ (R : typ → typ → Prop) (t1 t2 : typ),
    struct_equiv R → R t1 t2 → t1 == t2.
Ltac prove_scongr R := match goal with | ⊢ ?W1 == ?W2 ⇒
    eapply (exist_struct_equiv R); eauto end.
```

4 Type System

The sorting rules used in the typing system are presented in Fig. 4.

---

[1] https://rocq-prover.org/doc/v8.20/stdlib/Coq.Init.Logic.html

Typing rules for processes: $\boxed{\Gamma \vdash P : T}$

$$\text{T-End}\frac{}{\Gamma \vdash 0 : \text{end}} \qquad \text{T-Rec}\frac{\Gamma, \chi : \mu X.T \vdash P : T\{\mu X.T/X\}}{\Gamma \vdash \mu\chi.P : \mu X.T}$$

$$\text{T-Var}\frac{\Gamma(\chi) = \mu X.T}{\Gamma \vdash \chi : \mu X.T} \qquad \text{T-Inp}\frac{\Gamma, x : S \vdash P : T}{\Gamma \vdash r?l(x).P : r?l(S).T}$$

$$\text{T-Out}\frac{\Gamma \vdash e : S \quad \Gamma \vdash P : T}{\Gamma \vdash r!l\langle e \rangle.P : r!l(S).T} \qquad \text{T-Sum}\frac{\Gamma \vdash P : T_1 \quad \Gamma \vdash Q : T_2}{\Gamma \vdash P + Q : T_1 + T_2}$$

$$\text{T-Sum-L}\frac{\Gamma \vdash P : T_1}{\Gamma \vdash P : T_1 + T_2} \qquad \text{T-Sum-R}\frac{\Gamma \vdash P : T_2}{\Gamma \vdash P : T_1 + T_2}$$

$$\text{T-If}\frac{\Gamma \vdash e : \text{bool} \quad \Gamma \vdash P : T \quad \Gamma \vdash Q : T}{\Gamma \vdash \text{if } e \text{ then } P \text{ else } Q : T}$$

Typing rules for sessions: $\boxed{\Gamma \Vdash \mathcal{M} : T}$

$$\text{T-Thr}\frac{\Gamma \vdash P : T \quad \text{wf}(T)}{\Gamma \Vdash p \triangleleft P : T}$$

$$\text{T-Sess}\frac{\Gamma \Vdash p \triangleleft P : T_1 \quad \Gamma \Vdash \bar{p} \triangleleft Q : T_2 \quad \overline{T_1} \equiv T_2}{\Gamma \Vdash p \triangleleft P \parallel \bar{p} \triangleleft Q : \bot}$$

Fig. 5. Type system

Type environments Γ map variables to sorts and process variables to types:

$$\Gamma ::= \emptyset \mid \Gamma, x : S \mid \Gamma, \chi : T$$

We first present the rules for values v. Rule S-Nat allows for typing a number n in the set of naturals $\mathbb{N}$ with type nat. Rule S-Int is used to type a number z in the set of integers $\mathbb{Z}$ with type int. Rule S-Str-E type-checks the empty string. Non-empty strings are typed by concatenating characters c with strings s, written $c\,\widehat{}\,s$, by means of rule S-Str. Boolean constants are typed with rule S-Bl. The only value of type unit is the empty value, noted (), and is typed by using rule S-Uni.

Variables x are typed with rule S-Var.

Expressions e are typed with the remaining rules. Rule S-Lt accepts a "less than" test among expressions e_1 and e_2 whenever e_1 and e_2 have the same numerical sort. Rule S-Eq does an equality test among expressions e_1 and e_2 of the same sort. Rule S-Neg is used to negate a boolean expression e. Rule S-And type-checks a conjunction of two boolean expressions e_1 and e_2. Rule S-Or accepts a disjunction of two boolean expressions e_1 and e_2.

4.1 Typing Processes

The type system is defined in Fig. 5; in this section we analyse the rules for processes, while § 4.2 is devoted to the rules for sessions.

Typing judgements for processes have the form $\Gamma \vdash P : T$, while typing judgements for sessions have the form $\Gamma \Vdash \mathcal{M} : T$ and invoke the type system $\vdash$. The type system for sessions $\Vdash$ only invokes the type system for processes $\vdash$ with *well-formed types* (cf. § 2.1): for this reason, the typing rules for processes involving type sums can be simplified (cf. rules T-SUM,T-SUM-L,T-SUM-R).

The rule depicting the essence of iso-recursive session types is T-REC. In order to allow Γ to type a recursion process $\mu\chi.P$ with a type $\mu X.T$, we require that $\Gamma, \chi : \mu X.T$ types the continuation P with the unfolded type $T\{\mu X.T/X\}$. That is, in our iso-recursive setting the continuation must be typed by explicitly unfolding the recursive type. This is different from the equi-recursive approach, e.g. [18], where the type of $\mu\chi.P$ and the type of the continuation P can be equal, because types $\mu X.T$ and $T\{\mu X.T/X\}$ are equal. For the same reason, in rule T-VAR an environment $\Gamma, \chi : \mu X.T$ assigns the type $\mu X.T$ to the process variable χ: note that it is not possible to assign a non-recursive type to process variables.

Rule T-INP allows Γ to type a input process $\mathtt{r}?l(x).P$ with type $\mathtt{r}?l(S).T$ whenever $\Gamma, x : S$ assigns the type T to the continuation P. Dually, rule T-OUT allows Γ to type an output process $\mathtt{r}!l\langle e\rangle.P$ with type $\mathtt{r}?l(S).T$ whenever the expression has sort S and Γ assigns the type T to the continuation P.

Rule T-SUM is used for branching and selection, that are sums containing only input types without duplicated labels, or output types without duplicated labels, respectively (cf. § 2.1). Note indeed that well-formed types do not contain types of the form e.g. $T_1 + \mu X.T_2$, or $\mathtt{end} + T$. The rule says that if Γ can be used to type a process P_1 with type T_1, and a process P_2 with type T_2, then Γ types $P_1 + P_2$ with type $T_1 + T_2$.

While rule T-SUM types exactly each input and output with their corresponding input and output type singletons, rule T-SUM-L allows for typing a process P having type T_1 with the type $T_1 + T_2$. For instance, if P is the branching process $\mathtt{r}?l_1(x).P_1 + \cdots + \mathtt{r}?l_n(x).P_n$ then we can use T-SUM-L to assign to P the type $\&_{i \in 1,\ldots,n+1}\mathtt{r}?l_i(S).T_i$ (cf. Definition 2). Rule T-SUM-R does the same thing, on the right: if P has type T_2 then we can use the rule to assign to P the type $T_1 + T_2$.

The increased flexibility offered by rules T-SUM-L, T-SUM-R is used in the rule for if-then-else, that is T-IF. In order to type process $\mathtt{if}\ e\ \mathtt{then}\ P\ \mathtt{else}\ Q$ with type T we require that e has a boolean sort, and that both P and Q have type T. To allow P and Q to use different labels to communicate in input/output with a participant, we use rules T-SUM-L and T-SUM-R in the premises of T-IF, thus mimicking a simple form of subtyping. The next example illustrates this idea.

Example 4. Consider the variant of the authentication protocol of Fig. 6, where $U_\mathsf{c}, U_\mathsf{a}$ are the types of the client c and of the authorisation server a, respectively, and $Q_\mathsf{c}, Q_\mathsf{a}$ are process implementations of the client c and of the authorisation

$U_c \stackrel{def}{=} \mu X.(\text{a!pwd(str)}.(\text{a?ok(bool)}.\chi + \text{a?fail(unit)}.\text{end}) + \text{a!quit(unit)}.\text{end})$

$U_a \stackrel{def}{=} \mu X.(\text{c?pwd(str)}.(\text{c!ok(bool)}.\chi + \text{c!fail(unit)}.\text{end}) + \text{c?quit(unit)}.\text{end})$

$Q_c \stackrel{def}{=} \mu\chi.(\text{a!pwd}\langle\text{"fido"}\rangle.(\text{a?ok}(x).\chi + \text{a?fail}(x)) + \text{a!quit}\langle\rangle)$

$Q_a \stackrel{def}{=} \mu\chi.(\text{c?pwd}(x).Check_a + \text{c?quit}(x))$

$Check_a \stackrel{def}{=} \text{if } x = \text{"miau" then c!ok}\langle\text{true}\rangle.\chi \text{ else c!fail}\langle\rangle$

Fig. 6. Variant of authorisation protocol in § 1

server a, respectively. The semantics of the protocol are better described by the types U_c and U_a. Type U_c prescribes that, as in the protocol of § 1, the client c sends a password to the server a, or it quits. Differently from § 1, the client c after sending the password waits for an ack from the server a: the server can send *ok* and the protocol reinitiates, or it can send *fail* and the protocol ends. The behaviour of the server a described by its type U_a is *dual* to the one of the client c (cf. Definition 6).

Consider now the implementations Q_c and Q_a of the client c and of the server a, respectively. Process Q_c mirrors the behaviour of its type U_c. Process Q_a presents an interesting behaviour based on the *check* of the password received by the client c: if the password is correct, then Q_a sends an *ok* ack and the protocol restarts, else it sends a *fail* ack and the protocol ends.

Based on the rules for processes of Fig. 5, we have the following typings:

(i) $\emptyset \vdash Q_c : U_c$;
(ii) $\emptyset \vdash Q_a : U_a$.

We discuss the typing of (ii), which is relevant to show that process $Check_a$ is well-typed.

The type inference (ii) is obtained by applying T-REC to the hypothesis

$$\chi : U_a \vdash \text{c?pwd}(x).Check_a + \text{c?quit}(x) : \text{c?pwd(str)}.C_a + \text{c?quit(unit)}.\text{end} \quad (1)$$

$C_a \stackrel{def}{=} \text{c!ok(bool)}.U_a + \text{c!fail(unit)}.\text{end}$

To type check (1), we apply T-SUM to the hypotheses

$$\chi : U_a \vdash \text{c?pwd}(x).Check_a : \text{c?pwd(str)}.C_a \quad (2)$$

$$\chi : U_a \vdash \text{c?quit}(x) : \text{c?quit(unit)}.\text{end} \quad (3)$$

The item (3) is discharged by using T-INP, followed by T-END. To tackle (2), we apply T-INP to the hypothesis below, where $\Gamma \stackrel{def}{=} \chi : U_a, x : \text{str}$:

$$\Gamma \vdash Check_a : C_a \quad (4)$$

Item (4) is obtained by an application of T-IF to the hypotheses

$$\Gamma \vdash \text{c!ok}\langle\text{true}\rangle.\chi : C_a \quad (5)$$

$$\Gamma \vdash \text{c!fail}\langle\rangle : C_a \quad (6)$$

To type check (5) we apply T-Sum-L to the hypothesis

$$\Gamma \vdash \text{c!ok}\langle\text{true}\rangle.\chi : \text{c!ok(bool)}.U_a \tag{7}$$

while to type check (6) we apply T-Sum-R to the hypothesis

$$\Gamma \vdash \text{c!fail}\langle\rangle : \text{c!fail(unit).end} \tag{8}$$

Item 7 is proved by applying T-Out, followed by T-Var. Item 8 is a consequence of applying T-Out, followed by T-End.

4.2 Type Checking Sessions

The typing rules for sessions of Fig. 5 have the form $\Gamma \Vdash \mathcal{M} : T$ and use the rules for processes $\Gamma \vdash P : T$. Rule T-Thr is used for *single threads* and says that if the type system for processes $\vdash$ can be used to type a process P with a well-formed type T (cf. Fig. 1), then the type system $\Vdash$ assigns the type T to the thread $p \triangleleft P$.

Rule T-Sess is used to type *a pair of threads*, and it relies on *type congruence* (cf. § 3) and on *type duality*. Since we consider iso-recursive types, we define duality as a terminating function rather than as a coinductive relation (cf. [17]).

Definition 6 (Type Duality). *Function* $\overline{\cdot} : \mathcal{T} \to \mathcal{T}$ *is defined by the following patterns:*

$$\overline{r!l(S).T} \stackrel{def}{=} \overline{r}?l(S).\overline{T} \qquad \overline{r?l(S).T} \stackrel{def}{=} \overline{r}!l(S).\overline{T} \qquad \overline{\mu X.T} \stackrel{def}{=} \mu X.\overline{T}$$

$$\overline{T_1 + T_2} \stackrel{def}{=} \overline{T_1} + \overline{T_2} \qquad \overline{T} \stackrel{def}{=} T \ (else)$$

Lemma 2 (Termination 🐓). *Type duality is a terminating function.*

The recursive definition is accepted by Rocq because it is "guarded on 1st argument". The involution `pdual` implements duality of participants.

```
Function typ_dual (t : typ) : typ :=
  match t with
  | typ_mu x t0 ⇒ typ_mu x (typ_dual t0)
  | typ_sum t1 t2 ⇒ typ_sum (typ_dual t1) (typ_dual t2)
  | typ_input p l s t0 ⇒ typ_output (pdual p) l s (typ_dual t0)
  | typ_output p l s t0 ⇒ typ_input (pdual p) l s (typ_dual t0)
  | _ ⇒ t
  end.
```

Lemma 3 (Involution 🐓). *Type duality is an involution.*

Lemma 4 (Injectivity 🐓). *Type duality is injective.*

These results are mechanised by structural induction on the parameters.

```
Lemma typ_dual_involution : ∀ t : typ, typ_dual (typ_dual t) = t.
Lemma dual_injective    : ∀ t1 t2 : typ, typ_dual t1 = typ_dual t2 → t1 = t2.
```

Example 5. Consider types U_c and U_a of Fig. 6. By applying the definition, we have $\overline{U_c} = U_a$. The result can be obtained by using the function introduced in the proof of Lemma 2 and by applying the tactic `repeat simpl`.

The rule for composing threads says that if a session is composed with a participant and its dual, and those are typed respectively with T_1 and T_2, and there is a *proof* that $\overline{T_1} \equiv T_2$ (cf. Example 3), then the session is typed with type $\bot$. As outlined in § 2, the rule can be extended to multiple pairs of dual participants.

Example 6. We show an example of application of rule T-SESS. Consider the OAuth2 protocol of § 1, which we recap here for convenience by letting $s \stackrel{def}{=}$ "fido", s be short for str, and u be short for unit. Remember that $\overline{c} = a$.

$$T_c \stackrel{def}{=} \mu X.(\text{a!pwd}(s).X + \text{a!quit}(u).\text{end}) \qquad T_a \stackrel{def}{=} \mu X.R_a$$

$$R_a \stackrel{def}{=} \text{c?pwd}(s).X + \text{c?quit}(u).\text{end} \qquad T_a^* \stackrel{def}{=} R_a\{T_a/X\}$$

$$P_c \stackrel{def}{=} \mu\chi.(\text{a!pwd}\langle s\rangle.\chi + \text{a!quit}\langle\rangle) \qquad P_a \stackrel{def}{=} \mu\chi.Q_a$$

$$Q_a \stackrel{def}{=} \text{c?pwd}(x).\chi + \text{c?quit}(x) \qquad P_a^* \stackrel{def}{=} Q_a\{P_a/\chi\}$$

To illustrate the folding/unfolding mechanism while typing sessions, we show that the composition of $c \triangleleft P_c$ and $a \triangleleft P_a^*$ is well-typed.

In the following, we prove that the folded process P_c type-checks with the folded type T_c, while the unfolded process P_a^* type checks with the unfolded type T_a^*. We note that these choices of folding and unfolding types are indeed mandatory. That is, iso-recursive session types do not allow to type-check e.g. P_a^* with T_a, or P_a with T_a^*: this is in contrast with equi-recursive session types, e.g. [18], where T_a and T_a^* are equal, and can thus be exchanged at any time.

We start by assigning the type T_c to the client process P_c.

$$\text{T-REC} \frac{\text{T-SUM} \frac{(A) \quad (B)}{\chi: T_c \vdash \text{a!pwd}\langle s\rangle.\chi + \text{a!quit}\langle\rangle : \text{a!pwd}(s).T_c + \text{a!quit}(u).\text{end}}}{\emptyset \vdash P_c : T_c}$$

$$\text{T-OUT} \frac{\text{T-VAR} \frac{}{\chi: T_c \vdash \chi: T_c}}{(A) \ \chi: T_c \vdash \text{a!pwd}\langle s\rangle.\chi : \text{a!pwd}(s).T_c}$$

$$\text{T-OUT} \frac{\text{T-END} \frac{}{\chi: T_c \vdash \mathbf{0}: \text{end}}}{(B) \ \chi: T_c \vdash \text{a!quit}\langle\rangle : \text{a!quit}(u).\text{end}}$$

Next we assign the type T_a^* to the unfolded server P_a^*. Let $\Gamma \stackrel{def}{=} x: s, \chi: T_a$.

$$\text{T-SUM} \frac{(C) \quad (D)}{\emptyset \vdash P_a^* : \text{c?pwd}(s).T_a + \text{c?quit}(u).\text{end}}$$

$$\text{T-Inp} \frac{\text{T-End} \frac{}{x:\, \mathsf{u} \vdash \mathbf{0}:\, \mathsf{end}}}{(D)\; \emptyset \vdash \mathsf{c?quit}(x):\, \mathsf{c?quit}(\mathsf{u}).\mathsf{end}}$$

$$\text{T-Inp} \frac{\text{T-Rec} \frac{\text{T-Sum} \frac{(E) \quad (F)}{\Gamma \vdash Q_\mathsf{a}:\, T_\mathsf{a}^*}}{x:\, \mathsf{s} \vdash P_\mathsf{a}:\, T_\mathsf{a}}}{(C)\; \emptyset \vdash \mathsf{c?pwd}(x).P_\mathsf{a}:\, \mathsf{c?pwd}(\mathsf{s}).T_\mathsf{a}}$$

$$\text{T-Inp} \frac{\text{T-Var} \frac{}{\Gamma, x':\, \mathsf{s} \vdash \chi:\, T_\mathsf{a}}}{(E)\; \Gamma \vdash \mathsf{c?pwd}(x).\chi:\, \mathsf{c?pwd}(\mathsf{s}).T_\mathsf{a}}$$

$$\text{T-Inp} \frac{\text{T-End} \frac{}{\Gamma, x':\, \mathsf{u} \vdash \mathbf{0}:\, \mathsf{end}}}{(F)\; \Gamma \vdash \mathsf{c?quit}(x):\, \mathsf{c?quit}(\mathsf{u}).\mathsf{end}}$$

We note that both T_c and T_a^* are well-formed (cf. § 2). An application of T-Thr to both $\emptyset \vdash P_\mathsf{c}:\, T_\mathsf{c}$ and $\emptyset \vdash P_\mathsf{a}^*:\, T_\mathsf{a}^*$ let us infer:

$$\emptyset \Vdash \mathsf{c} \triangleleft P_\mathsf{c}:\, T_\mathsf{c} \qquad (9)$$

$$\emptyset \Vdash \mathsf{a} \triangleleft P_\mathsf{a}^*:\, T_\mathsf{a}^* \qquad (10)$$

To apply T-Sess and type the composition $\mathsf{c} \triangleleft P_\mathsf{c} \parallel \mathsf{a} \triangleleft P_\mathsf{a}^*$ we need to prove that $\overline{T_\mathsf{c}} \equiv T_\mathsf{a}^*$. Note that $\overline{T_\mathsf{c}} = T_\mathsf{a}$. We proceed as in Example 3 and find a relation $\mathcal{R}$ s.t. $T_\mathsf{a} \mathcal{R} T_\mathsf{a}^*$, and $\mathcal{R}$ is a structural equivalence. We can then conclude:

$$\text{T-Sess} \frac{(9) \quad (10) \quad \overline{T_\mathsf{c}} \equiv T_\mathsf{a}^*}{\emptyset \Vdash \mathsf{c} \triangleleft P_\mathsf{c} \parallel \mathsf{a} \triangleleft P_\mathsf{a}^*:\, \bot}$$

Example 7. To see an example of an untyped session, remember the type and process definitions in Example 6 and consider the type

$$T_\mathsf{a}^{\#} \stackrel{\text{def}}{=} \mathsf{c?pwd}(\mathsf{s}).\mu X.\mathsf{c?pwd}(\mathsf{s}).X + \mathsf{c?quit}(\mathsf{u}).\mathsf{end}$$

and a server implementation $P_\mathsf{a}^{\#}$ typed with $T_\mathsf{a}^{\#}$. We cannot type $\mathsf{c} \triangleleft P_\mathsf{c} \parallel \mathsf{a} \triangleleft P_\mathsf{a}^{\#}$ because we cannot relate the dual of the type T_c of the client c with the type $T_\mathsf{a}^{\#}$ of the server a by means of type congruence.

To see that, we show that the hypothesis (ABS) leads to a contradiction.

$$(\text{ABS}) \qquad \overline{T_\mathsf{c}} \equiv T_\mathsf{a}^{\#}$$

We use the following mechanised results.

```
Lemma scongr_symmetric  : symmetric typ typ_scongr .
Lemma scongr_comp  : ∀ (X : var) (T U : typ), (@ X T) == U → (X ℒT) == U.
Lemma scongr_sum   : ∀ (t1 t2 t3 t4 : typ),
   typ_sum t1 t2 == typ_sum t3 t4 → t1 == t3 ∧ t2 == t4.
Lemma scongr_input : ∀ (p : participant ) (l : label ) (s : styp) (t1 t2 : typ),
   (p ? l s . t1) == (p ? l s . t2) → t1 == t2.
Lemma scongr_input_sum_false  : ∀ (p : participant ) (l : label ) (s : styp) (t t1 t2 : typ),
   (p ? l s . t) == typ_sum t1 t2 → False.
```

First, note that $\overline{T_c} = \mu X.(\text{c?pwd}(s).X + \text{c?quit}(u).\text{end}) = T_a$. We apply `scongr_comp` to (ABS) and obtain

$$\text{c?pwd}(s).T_a + \text{c?quit}(u).\text{end} \equiv T_a^{\#} \qquad (11)$$

We apply `scongr_sum` to (11) and infer

$$\text{c?pwd}(s).T_a \equiv \text{c?pwd}(s).\mu X.\text{c?pwd}(s).X \qquad (12)$$

We apply `scongr_input` to (12) and obtain

$$T_a \equiv \mu X.\text{c?pwd}(s).X \qquad (13)$$

We apply `scongr_symmetric` , `scongr_comp` , `scongr_symmetric` to (13) and infer

$$T_a \equiv \text{c?pwd}(s).\mu X.\text{c?pwd}(s).X \qquad (14)$$

An application of `scongr_comp` to (14) let us infer

$$\text{c?pwd}(s).T_a + \text{c?quit}(u).\text{end} \equiv \text{c?pwd}(s).\mu X.\text{c?pwd}(s).X \qquad (15)$$

We apply lemma `scongr_symmetric` , `scongr_input_sum_false` to (15) and obtain `False`, contradiction.

4.3 Mechanisation and Implementation of the Type System

The main purpose of the formalisation of the typing system in Rocq is to set the basis for the mechanisation of the Theorem of subject reduction (cf. Theorem 1). The mechanisation 🐟 of the type system of Fig. 5 relies on an `Inductive` predicate that follows the structure of the rules in the Figure, with one technical variation. To avoid issues related to the reuse of the same identifier in bound variables and bound process variables, we require that each *extension operation* $\Gamma, x: S$ (resp. $\Gamma, X : T$) carries a proof that $x \notin \text{dom}(\Gamma)$ (resp. $X \notin \text{dom}(\Gamma)$).

Specifically, we equip the rules in Fig. 5 that make use of extension with an extra parameter carrying a proof that the extended variable is *fresh*. In the code below, `evar_beq` and `process_var_beq` are boolean equalities over variables and process variables, respectively.

```
Function extend  {A B}  (eqb : A → A → bool) (g : partial_fun A B) (x : A) (s : B)
    (pf : fresh g x) := fun y ⇒ if eqb x y then Some s else g y.
(** Extension  of  type  environments  *)
Notation "g ',,'   x '-:' t @ pf" := (extend evar_beq g x t pf) (at level 40).
(** Extension  of  process  environments  *)
Notation "h ',,'   x '=:' t @ pf" := (extend process_var_beq h x t pf) (at level 40).
```

Note that the freshness assumption does not affect the expressiveness of the typing system, because we can always alpha-rename variables and process variables of processes before type checking.

Implementation of the Type Checker. Besides the `Inductive`-based implementation of the type system of Fig. 5 in Rocq, in related work [25,26] we implemented the typing rules for multiparty sessions in OCaml and automatically verified their soundness in Why3 (cf. [11,15,42]), thus making available a *certified type checker* for multiparty sessions. [26, App. I] contains all the details. Intuitively, the key idea is to rely on a fixed-point technique that allows *unfolding* iso-recursive session types *up-to a length* n: the parameter is given in input to the type checking function. This allows the termination of rule T-REC of Fig. 5. Specifically, in [25,26] we achieved decidable type checking by using in the rule for session composition (cf. T-SESS) a *terminating function* to assess the *compliance* of the multiparty session participants.

In order to deploy a decidable type checker for the system in Fig. 5, we need to implement the proof-based formulation of T-SESS as a function, and in turn to devise a suitable notion of *duality up-to type congruence*. We envision that this concept can be deployed following the guideline of the implementation of function *cstep* in [26, App. I]: the code should be simpler, because of the presence of exactly two participants.

We plan to add to the repository [21] a folder containing the source code of a fully executable type checker implementing the system in Fig. 5.

5 Proof of Subject Reduction

Transition rules for types: $\boxed{T \xrightarrow{\alpha} T}$

$$\text{E-OUT} \frac{\emptyset \vdash v : S}{r!l(S).T \xrightarrow{r!l\langle v \rangle} T} \qquad \text{E-IN} \frac{\emptyset \vdash v : S}{r?l(S).T \xrightarrow{r?l\langle v \rangle} T}$$

$$\text{E-SEL-L} \frac{T_1 \xrightarrow{r!l\langle v \rangle} T'}{T_1 + T_2 \xrightarrow{r!l\langle v \rangle} T'} \qquad \text{E-BRA-L} \frac{T_1 \xrightarrow{r?l\langle v \rangle} T'}{T_1 + T_2 \xrightarrow{r?l\langle v \rangle} T'}$$

$$\text{E-REC} \frac{}{\mu X.T \xrightarrow{\tau} T\{\mu X.T/X\}} \qquad \text{E-BOT} \frac{}{\bot \xrightarrow{\tau} \bot}$$

Fig. 7. Labelled transition system of types

To attack the proof of subject reduction, we define a LTS of types. We will use the transition system to match the actions of processes, so it is practical to use the same actions α of the LTS of Fig. 2.

The left rules for types are in Fig. 7. The rules are designed for well-formed types (cf. § 2.1), as we discuss below (cf. rules E-SEL-L, E-BRA-L).

Rule E-OUT says that a type doing an output to the participant r on label l with payload S and continuing as T can fire the action $r!l\langle v \rangle$ and reach the redex T whenever v is a value of sort S.

Dually, rule E-IN allows an input type from r on label l with payload S and continuing as T to do an action $\mathtt{r}?l(v)$ and reach the redex T, if v has sort S.

Rule E-SEL-L allows a sum type $T_1 + T_2$ to do an output action $\mathtt{r}!l\langle v\rangle$ and reach the redex T' whenever T_1 can fire this action and reach T'.

Dually, rule E-BRA-L allows a sum type $T_1 + T_2$ to do an input action $\mathtt{r}?l(v)$ and reach the redex T' if T_1 can fire this action and reach T'. Note that input and output are the only actions that a sum type can fire. This is because types as e.g. $T_1 + \mu X.T$ or $T_1 + (\mu X.T + T_2)$ are not well-formed.

Rule E-REC allows a recursive type to execute a τ action and to unfold itself.
Rule E-BOT allows type $\bot$ to execute a τ action and reach itself.

5.1 Preliminary Lemmas

We now analyse the properties of type congruence (cf. Definition 5), and use these results in the proof of Theorem 1 (Subject Reduction). Some preliminary results on type congruence have been already introduced along the paper (cf. Lemma 1, Example 3, and Example 7).

A first result establishes that type congruence is preserved by duality.

Lemma 5. *If $T_1 \equiv T_2$ then $\overline{T_1} \equiv \overline{T_2}$.*

Remember that the notation == is short for typ_scongr (cf. Fig. 3). The lemma is mechanised 🐾 by using the Ltac tactic prove_scongr (cf. Example 3).

```
Lemma scongr_dual  :  ∀ (T1 T2 : typ), T1 == T2 → typ_dual T1 == typ_dual T2.
```

In order to introduce the next step towards subject reduction, we define the *duality predicate* between actions.

Definition 7 (Action duality). *The action duality predicate $\mathcal{D} \subseteq \mathcal{A} \times \mathcal{A}$ is defined by the following axioms:*

$$\overline{\mathtt{p}?l(v) \; \mathcal{D} \; \overline{\mathtt{p}}!l\langle v\rangle} \qquad \overline{\mathtt{p}!l\langle v\rangle \; \mathcal{D} \; \overline{\mathtt{p}}?l(v)}$$

Remind the notation $\mathsf{wf}(T)$ to indicate that T is well-formed (cf. § 2.1 and rule T-THR of Fig. 5). A key result is that type congruence is preserved by the LTS of Fig. 7, in the following sense.

Lemma 6. *Assume that $\mathsf{wf}(T_1)$ and $\mathsf{wf}(T_2)$, and let $T_1 \equiv \overline{T_2}$. Let $\alpha_1 \mathcal{D} \alpha_2$, $T_1 \xrightarrow{\alpha_1} U_1$, and $T_2 \xrightarrow{\alpha_2} U_2$. We have that $U_1 \equiv \overline{U_2}$.*

The lemma is mechanised 🐾 by using dependent induction [36] on $T_1 \xrightarrow{\alpha_1} U_1$ and $T_2 \xrightarrow{\alpha_2} U_2$. In the following code, typ_lts corresponds to the transition system $T \xrightarrow{\alpha} T$ of Fig. 7, while action_dual mechanises Definition 7.

```
Lemma elts_dual_scongr  :  ∀ (T1 T2 : typ) (a : proc_action ) (U1 U2 : typ) (b : proc_action ),
    wf T1 → wf T2 → T1 == typ_dual T2 → typ_lts T1 a U1 →  typ_lts T2 b U2 →
    action_dual  a b  → U1 == typ_dual U2.
```

Next, we establish further results used in the proof of Theorem 1, that are type preservation of structural congruence, and of value and process substitution.

Lemma 7. *If $\Gamma \Vdash \mathcal{M}_1 : T$ and $\mathcal{M}_1 \equiv \mathcal{M}_2$ then $\Gamma \Vdash \mathcal{M}_2 : T$.*

The mechanisation 🔖 of Lemma 7 simply follows by inversion of $\Gamma \Vdash \mathcal{M}_1 : T$. The predicate `types_session G K M U` corresponds to the judgement $\Gamma, \mathcal{K} \Vdash \mathcal{M} : U$ of Fig. 5, where Γ is used for variables and $\mathcal{K}$ is used for process variables. The relation `proc_equiv` implements $\equiv$.

```
Lemma types_struct    : ∀ (G : typ_env ) (H : proc_env ) (M1 M2 : session ) (U : typ),
    types_session  G H M1 U → proc_equiv M1 M2 → types_session G H M2 U.
```

Lemma 8 (Value Substitution). *Assume that the following hold:*

1. $\Gamma, x : S \vdash P : U;$
2. $\Gamma \vdash v : S.$

We have that $\Gamma \vdash P\{v/x\} : U$.

The proof 🔖 proceeds by induction on the judgement for processes. The predicate `stypes G e s` implements the judgement $\Gamma \vdash e : S$ (cf. Fig. 4). Process `substV P v x` deploys $P\{v/x\}$.

```
Lemma substitution : ∀ (G : typ_env ) (H : proc_env ) (x : var) (s : styp) (P : process )
    (t : typ) (v : value ) (pf : fresh G x):
    types (G,, x -: s @ pf) H P t → stypes G (expr_val v) s →
    types G H (substV P v x) t.
```

Lemma 9 (Process Substitution). *Assume that the following hold:*

1. $\Gamma, \chi : T \vdash P : U;$
2. $\Gamma \vdash Q : T.$

We have that $\Gamma \vdash P\{Q/\chi\} : U$.

Process substitution is mechanised 🔖 by applying structural induction to P. The predicate `types G K P U` corresponds to the judgement $\Gamma, \mathcal{K} \vdash P : U$ of Figure 5. Predicate `closedP` corresponds to notion of closed processes, function `bv` (resp. `bvP`) returns the bound variables (resp. bound process variables) of process P, and predicate `disjoint` holds when the lists received as parameters do not share any element. Process `substP P Q X` is $P\{Q/\chi\}$.

```
Lemma types_substP : ∀ (P Q : process ) (T U : typ) (G : typ_env ) (K : proc_env )
    (X : proc_var ) (pf : fresh K x),
    closedP Q → disjoint (bv P) (bv Q) → disjoint (bvP P) (bvP Q) →
    types G (K,, X =: T @ pf) P U → types G K Q T → types G K (substP P Q X) U.
```

5.2 Subject Reduction Theorem

Subject reduction ensures that if a closed well-typed session fires a step then the redex is well-typed.

Theorem 1 (Subject Reduction). *Let $\mathcal{M}$ be a closed session. If $\emptyset \Vdash \mathcal{M} : T$ and $\mathcal{M} \xrightarrow{\alpha} \mathcal{M}'$ then there is T' s.t. $T \xrightarrow{\alpha} T'$ and $\emptyset \Vdash \mathcal{M}' : T'$.*

The theorem is a by-product 🐾 of two core results.

Lemma 10 (Action Preservation). *If $\Gamma \Vdash M : T$ and $M \xrightarrow{\alpha} M'$ then there is T' s.t. $T \xrightarrow{\alpha} T'$.*

The mechanisation 🐾 of Lemma 10 proceeds by induction on the session transition. The type lts deploys the LTS of sessions of Fig. 2.

```
Lemma lts_typ_ltsM : ∀ (M1 M2 : session ) (a : proc_action ) (G : typ_env ) (H : proc_env )
    (T : typ),
    lts M1 a M2 → types_session G H M1 T → ∃ U, typ_lts T a U.
```

Lemma 11 (Type Preservation). *Let $\mathcal{M}$ be a closed session and assume that there are types T, T' and action α s.t.:*

(i) $\emptyset \Vdash \mathcal{M} : T$;
(ii) $\mathcal{M} \xrightarrow{\alpha} \mathcal{M}'$;
(iii) $T \xrightarrow{\alpha} T'$.

We have $\emptyset \Vdash \mathcal{M}' : T'$.

The mechanisation 🐾 of Lemma 11 proceeds by induction on the session transition, and relies on the lemmas introduced in the paper and on additional results dealing with the mechanism of shifting bound identifiers 🐾 in the LTS of sessions (cf. § 2.3).

The predicate closedS holds when all processes in the session parameter are closed, while the predicate wfm holds when all processes in the session parameter do not reuse bound identifiers.

```
Lemma subject_reduction   (M M' : session ) (a : proc_action ) (U U' : typ):
    closedS M → wfm M → types_session empty_env empty_penv M U → lts M a M' →
    typ_lts U a U' → types_session empty_env empty_penv M' U'.
```

6 Related and Future Work

To the best of our knowledge, only few works follow an iso-recursive approach to session types.

Our Work. In recent papers [25,26] we present iso-recursive multiparty sessions relying on a terminating function that decides the soundness of the environments inferred from the processes' types, and we mechanise both the function and the typing system in tools of the OCaml ecosystem relying on Why3 [11,15,42].

The approach presented in this paper complements the results of [25]:

This paper A type system for iso-recursive binary session types mechanised in Rocq. To type check a process composition, it is required to provide a proof that the dual types assigned to the processes are included in *type congruence*. This proof technique is reminiscent of that used for bisimilarity [37], while type congruence is more syntactical.

[25] A type system for iso-recursive multiparty session types mechanised in Why3. To type check a process composition, it is required to execute a terminating function that decides if the environment assigned to the process composition satisfies *compliance*. We showcase the implementation and verification of the function in OCaml by decorating the code with GOSPEL annotations [11,42].

Related Work. The paper [32] studies iso-recursive and equi-recursive subtyping for binary sessions. Session types are interpreted as propositions of multiplicative/additive linear logic extended with least and greatest fixed points (cf. [9,52]). The typing rules correspond to the proof rules in [4], and include the unfolding of least and greatest fixed points. The authors compare the two subtyping relations, and note that the relations preserve not only the usual safety properties, but also termination.

Many recent papers [35,41,47,54–57] rely on iso-recursive types for variants of the λ-calculus, following the seminal work on Amber rules [1]. While the setting is different from ours, these papers provide several insights on the advantage of iso-recursive types and on their algorithmic implementation and mechanised verification. Previous papers [3,7] studied iso-recursive types for a concurrent λ-calculus that can be seen as the foundational theory of core $F^{\sharp}$.

As mentioned above, iso-recursive types have been first studied formally in the setting of Amber rules for modelling objects [1]. Pierce [44] further discusses the differences between iso-recursive and equi-recursive types.

Future Work. Concurrent actors and object programming are inherently *eager*: computations proceed by delegating and dividing a task to distributed actors which are running in parallel independently [2]. Our future work includes incorporating iso-recursive multiparty session types [25] into parameterised concurrent multiparty session types by Agha [10] to model and specify asynchronous multi-actor interactions.

References

1. Abadi, M., Cardelli, L.: A Theory of Objects. Monographs in Computer Science, Springer (1996). https://doi.org/10.1007/978-1-4419-8598-9
2. Agha, G.: Actors: A Model of Concurrent Computation in Distributed Systems. The MIT Press (1986). https://doi.org/10.7551/mitpress/1086.001.0001
3. Backes, M., Hritcu, C., Maffei, M.: Union, intersection and refinement types and reasoning about type disjointness for secure protocol implementations. J. Comput. Secur. **22**(2), 301–353 (2014). https://doi.org/10.3233/JCS-130493
4. Baelde, D., Doumane, A., Kuperberg, D., Saurin, A.: Bouncing threads for circular and non-wellfounded proofs: towards compositionality with circular proofs. In: Baier, C., Fisman, D. (eds.) LICS '22: 37th Annual ACM/IEEE Symposium on Logic in Computer Science, Haifa, Israel, August 2 - 5, 2022, pp. 63:1–63:13. ACM (2022). https://doi.org/10.1145/3531130.3533375
5. Barwell, A.D., Ferreira, F., Yoshida, N.: CONCUR test-of-time award for the period 1994–97 interview with Uwe Nestmann and Benjamin C. Pierce. J. Log. Algebraic Methods Program. **125**, 100744 (2022). https://doi.org/10.1016/J.JLAMP.2021.100744
6. Barwell, A.D., Scalas, A., Yoshida, N., Zhou, F.: Generalised multiparty session types with crash-stop failures. In: Klin, B., Lasota, S., Muscholl, A. (eds.) 33rd International Conference on Concurrency Theory, CONCUR 2022, September 12-16, 2022, Warsaw, Poland. LIPIcs, vol. 243, pp. 35:1–35:25. Schloss Dagstuhl - Leibniz-Zentrum für Informatik (2022). https://doi.org/10.4230/LIPICS.CONCUR.2022.35
7. Bengtson, J., Bhargavan, K., Fournet, C., Gordon, A.D., Maffeis, S.: Refinement types for secure implementations. ACM Trans. Program. Lang. Syst. **33**(2), 8:1–8:45 (2011). https://doi.org/10.1145/1890028.1890031
8. Brun, M.A.L., Dardha, O.: Magπ: types for failure-prone communication. In: Wies, T. (ed.) Programming Languages and Systems - 32nd European Symposium on Programming, ESOP 2023, Held as Part of the European Joint Conferences on Theory and Practice of Software, ETAPS 2023, Paris, France, April 22-27, 2023, Proceedings. Lecture Notes in Computer Science, vol. 13990, pp. 363–391. Springer (2023). https://doi.org/10.1007/978-3-031-30044-8_14
9. Caires, L., Pfenning, F.: Session types as intuitionistic linear propositions. In: Gastin, P., Laroussinie, F. (eds.) CONCUR 2010 - Concurrency Theory, 21th International Conference, CONCUR 2010, Paris, France, August 31-September 3, 2010. Proceedings. Lecture Notes in Computer Science, vol. 6269, pp. 222–236. Springer (2010). https://doi.org/10.1007/978-3-642-15375-4_16
10. Charalambides, M., Dinges, P., Agha, G.A.: Parameterized, concurrent session types for asynchronous multi-actor interactions. Sci. Comput. Program. **115–116**, 100–126 (2016). https://doi.org/10.1016/J.SCICO.2015.10.006
11. Charguéraud, A., Filliâtre, J., Lourenço, C., Pereira, M.: GOSPEL - providing OCaml with a formal specification language. In: ter Beek, M.H., McIver, A., Oliveira, J.N. (eds.) Formal Methods - The Next 30 Years - Third World Congress, FM 2019, Porto, Portugal, October 7-11, 2019, Proceedings. Lecture Notes in Computer Science, vol. 11800, pp. 484–501. Springer (2019). https://doi.org/10.1007/978-3-030-30942-8_29
12. Courcelle, B.: Fundamental properties of infinite trees. Theor. Comput. Sci. **25**, 95–169 (1983). https://doi.org/10.1016/0304-3975(83)90059-2

13. Demangeon, R., Honda, K.: Full abstraction in a subtyped pi-calculus with linear types. In: Katoen, J., König, B. (eds.) CONCUR 2011 - Concurrency Theory - 22nd International Conference, CONCUR 2011, Aachen, Germany, September 6-9, 2011. Proceedings. Lecture Notes in Computer Science, vol. 6901, pp. 280–296. Springer (2011). https://doi.org/10.1007/978-3-642-23217-6_19
14. Ekici, B., Yoshida, N.: Completeness of asynchronous session tree subtyping in coq. In: Bertot, Y., Kutsia, T., Norrish, M. (eds.) 15th International Conference on Interactive Theorem Proving, ITP 2024, September 9-14, 2024, Tbilisi, Georgia. LIPIcs, vol. 309, pp. 13:1–13:20. Schloss Dagstuhl - Leibniz-Zentrum für Informatik (2024). https://doi.org/10.4230/LIPICS.ITP.2024.13
15. Filliâtre, J., Paskevich, A.: Why3 - where programs meet provers. In: Felleisen, M., Gardner, P. (eds.) Programming Languages and Systems - 22nd European Symposium on Programming, ESOP 2013, Held as Part of the European Joint Conferences on Theory and Practice of Software, ETAPS 2013, Rome, Italy, March 16-24, 2013. Proceedings. Lecture Notes in Computer Science, vol. 7792, pp. 125–128. Springer (2013). https://doi.org/10.1007/978-3-642-37036-6_8
16. Foster, J.N., Greenwald, M.B., Moore, J.T., Pierce, B.C., Schmitt, A.: Combinators for bidirectional tree transformations: a linguistic approach to the view-update problem. ACM Trans. Program. Lang. Syst. **29**(3), 17 (2007). https://doi.org/10.1145/1232420.1232424
17. Gay, S.J., Hole, M.: Subtyping for session types in the Pi calculus. Acta Informatica **42**(2–3), 191–225 (2005). https://doi.org/10.1007/S00236-005-0177-Z
18. Ghilezan, S., Jaksic, S., Pantovic, J., Scalas, A., Yoshida, N.: Precise subtyping for synchronous multiparty sessions. J. Log. Algebraic Methods Program. **104**, 127–173 (2019). https://doi.org/10.1016/J.JLAMP.2018.12.002
19. Ghilezan, S., Pantović, J., Prokić, I., Scalas, A., Yoshida, N.: Precise subtyping for asynchronous multiparty sessions. ACM Trans. Comput. Logic **24**(2) (2023). https://doi.org/10.1145/3568422
20. Giunti, M.: GoPi: Compiling linear and static channels in Go. In: Bliudze, S., Bocchi, L. (eds.) Coordination Models and Languages - 22nd IFIP WG 6.1 International Conference, COORDINATION 2020, Held as Part of the 15th International Federated Conference on Distributed Computing Techniques, DisCoTec 2020, Valletta, Malta, June 15-19, 2020, Proceedings. Lecture Notes in Computer Science, vol. 12134, pp. 137–152. Springer (2020). https://doi.org/10.1007/978-3-030-50029-0_9
21. Giunti, M.: Iso-Recursive Session Types: a mechanisation in Rocq (2025). https://github.com/marcogiunti/Iso-Recursive-Session-Types
22. Giunti, M., Honda, K., Vasconcelos, V.T., Yoshida, N.: Session-based type discipline for pi calculus with matching. In: Programming Language Approaches to Concurrency and Communication (PLACES 2009) (2009). http://ctp.di.fct.unl.pt/~mgiunti/places09.pdf
23. Giunti, M., Vasconcelos, V.T.: A linear account of session types in the Pi calculus. In: Gastin, P., Laroussinie, F. (eds.) CONCUR 2010 - Concurrency Theory, 21th International Conference, CONCUR 2010, Paris, France, August 31-September 3, 2010. Proceedings. Lecture Notes in Computer Science, vol. 6269, pp. 432–446. Springer (2010). https://doi.org/10.1007/978-3-642-15375-4_30
24. Giunti, M., Vasconcelos, V.T.: Linearity, session types and the pi calculus. Math. Struct. Comput. Sci. **26**(2), 206–237 (2016). https://doi.org/10.1017/S0960129514000176

25. Giunti, M., Yoshida, N.: Iso-recursive multiparty sessions and their automated verification. In: Vafeiadis, V. (ed.) Programming Languages and Systems - 34th European Symposium on Programming, ESOP 2025, Held as Part of the International Joint Conferences on Theory and Practice of Software, ETAPS 2025, Hamilton, ON, Canada, May 3-8, 2025, Proceedings, Part I. Lecture Notes in Computer Science, vol. 15694, pp. 349–378. Springer (2025). https://doi.org/10.1007/978-3-031-91118-7_14
26. Giunti, M., Yoshida, N.: Iso-Recursive Multiparty Sessions and their Automated Verification – Technical Report. CoRR abs/2501.17778 (2025). https://doi.org/10.48550/ARXIV.2501.17778
27. Harvey, P., Fowler, S., Dardha, O., Gay, S.J.: Multiparty session types for safe runtime adaptation in an actor language. In: Møller, A., Sridharan, M. (eds.) 35th European Conference on Object-Oriented Programming, ECOOP 2021, July 11-17, 2021, Aarhus, Denmark (Virtual Conference). LIPIcs, vol. 194, pp. 10:1–10:30. Schloss Dagstuhl - Leibniz-Zentrum für Informatik (2021). https://doi.org/10.4230/LIPIcs.ECOOP.2021.10
28. Honda, K.: Types for dyadic interaction. In: Best, E. (ed.) CONCUR '93, 4th International Conference on Concurrency Theory, Hildesheim, Germany, August 23-26, 1993, Proceedings. Lecture Notes in Computer Science, vol. 715, pp. 509–523. Springer (1993). https://doi.org/10.1007/3-540-57208-2_35
29. Honda, K., Tokoro, M.: An object calculus for asynchronous communication. In: America, P. (ed.) ECOOP'91 European Conference on Object-Oriented Programming, Geneva, Switzerland, July 15-19, 1991, Proceedings. Lecture Notes in Computer Science, vol. 512, pp. 133–147. Springer (1991). https://doi.org/10.1007/BFB0057019
30. Honda, K., Vasconcelos, V.T., Kubo, M.: Language primitives and type discipline for structured communication-based programming. In: Hankin, C. (ed.) Programming Languages and Systems - ESOP'98, 7th European Symposium on Programming, Held as Part of the European Joint Conferences on the Theory and Practice of Software, ETAPS'98, Lisbon, Portugal, March 28 - April 4, 1998, Proceedings. Lecture Notes in Computer Science, vol. 1381, pp. 122–138. Springer (1998). https://doi.org/10.1007/BFB0053567
31. Honda, K., Yoshida, N.: On reduction-based process semantics. Theor. Comput. Sci. **151**(2), 437–486 (1995). https://doi.org/10.1016/0304-3975(95)00074-7
32. Horne, R., Padovani, L.: A logical account of subtyping for session types. J. Log. Algebraic Methods Program. **141**, 100986 (2024). https://doi.org/10.1016/J.JLAMP.2024.100986
33. Imai, K., Neykova, R., Yoshida, N., Yuen, S.: Multiparty session programming with global protocol combinators. In: Hirschfeld, R., Pape, T. (eds.) 34th European Conference on Object-Oriented Programming, ECOOP 2020, November 15-17, 2020, Berlin, Germany (Virtual Conference). LIPIcs, vol. 166, pp. 9:1–9:30. Schloss Dagstuhl - Leibniz-Zentrum für Informatik (2020). https://doi.org/10.4230/LIPICS.ECOOP.2020.9
34. Lange, J., Ng, N., Toninho, B., Yoshida, N.: A static verification framework for message passing in Go using behavioural types. In: Chaudron, M., Crnkovic, I., Chechik, M., Harman, M. (eds.) Proceedings of the 40th International Conference on Software Engineering, ICSE 2018, Gothenburg, Sweden, May 27 - June 03, 2018, pp. 1137–1148. ACM (2018). https://doi.org/10.1145/3180155.3180157

35. Ligatti, J., Blackburn, J., Nachtigal, M.: On subtyping-relation completeness, with an application to Iso-recursive types. ACM Trans. Program. Lang. Syst. **39**(1), 4:1–4:36 (2017). https://doi.org/10.1145/2994596
36. McBride, C.: Elimination with a motive. In: Callaghan, P., Luo, Z., McKinna, J., Pollack, R. (eds.) Types for Proofs and Programs, International Workshop, TYPES 2000, Durham, UK, December 8-12, 2000, Selected Papers. Lecture Notes in Computer Science, vol. 2277, pp. 197–216. Springer (2000). https://doi.org/10.1007/3-540-45842-5_13
37. Milner, R.: Communication and concurrency. PHI Series in computer science, Prentice Hall (1989)
38. Milner, R.: Functions as processes. Math. Struct. Comput. Sci. **2**(2), 119–141 (1992). https://doi.org/10.1017/S0960129500001407
39. Milner, R.: Communicating and Mobile Systems: the π-Calculus. Cambridge University Press (1999)
40. Milner, R., Parrow, J., Walker, D.: A Calculus of Mobile Processes, Parts I and II. Info.& Comp. **100**(1) (1992)
41. Patrignani, M., Martin, E.M., Devriese, D.: On the semantic expressiveness of recursive types. Proc. ACM Program. Lang. **5**(POPL), 1–29 (2021). https://doi.org/10.1145/3434302
42. Pereira, M., Ravara, A.: Cameleer: a deductive verification tool for OCaml. In: Silva, A., Leino, K.R.M. (eds.) Computer Aided Verification - 33rd International Conference, CAV 2021, Virtual Event, July 20-23, 2021, Proceedings, Part II. Lecture Notes in Computer Science, vol. 12760, pp. 677–689. Springer (2021). https://doi.org/10.1007/978-3-030-81688-9_31
43. Peters, K., Yoshida, N.: Separation and encodability in mixed choice multiparty sessions. In: Sobocinski, P., Lago, U.D., Esparza, J. (eds.) Proceedings of the 39th Annual ACM/IEEE Symposium on Logic in Computer Science, LICS 2024, Tallinn, Estonia, July 8-11, 2024, pp. 62:1–62:15. ACM (2024). https://doi.org/10.1145/3661814.3662085
44. Pierce, B.C.: Types and programming languages. MIT Press (2002)
45. Pous, D.: Up-to techniques for weak bisimulation. In: Caires, L., Italiano, G.F., Monteiro, L., Palamidessi, C., Yung, M. (eds.) Automata, Languages and Programming, 32nd International Colloquium, ICALP 2005, Lisbon, Portugal, July 11-15, 2005, Proceedings. Lecture Notes in Computer Science, vol. 3580, pp. 730–741. Springer (2005). https://doi.org/10.1007/11523468_59, https://github.com/rocq-archive/weak-up-to
46. Rocq Team: Reference manual. https://coq.inria.fr/doc/V8.20.0/refman/
47. Rossberg, A.: Mutually Iso-recursive subtyping. Proc. ACM Program. Lang. **7**(OOPSLA2), 347–373 (2023). https://doi.org/10.1145/3622809
48. Scalas, A., Yoshida, N.: Less is more: multiparty session types revisited. Proc. ACM Program. Lang. **3**(POPL), 30:1–30:29 (2019). https://doi.org/10.1145/3290343
49. Scalas, A., Yoshida, N., Benussi, E.: Verifying message-passing programs with dependent behavioural types. In: McKinley, K.S., Fisher, K. (eds.) Proceedings of the 40th ACM SIGPLAN Conference on Programming Language Design and Implementation, PLDI 2019, Phoenix, AZ, USA, June 22-26, 2019, pp. 502–516. ACM (2019). https://doi.org/10.1145/3314221.3322484
50. Takeuchi, K., Honda, K., Kubo, M.: An interaction-based language and its typing system. In: Halatsis, C., Maritsas, D.G., Philokyprou, G., Theodoridis, S. (eds.) PARLE '94: Parallel Architectures and Languages Europe, 6th International PARLE Conference, Athens, Greece, July 4-8, 1994, Proceedings. Lecture Notes

in Computer Science, vol. 817, pp. 398–413. Springer (1994). https://doi.org/10.1007/3-540-58184-7_118
51. Vasconcelos, V.T., Giunti, M., Yoshida, N., Honda, K.: Type safety without subject reduction for session types (2010). http://ctp.di.fct.unl.pt/~mgiunti/vgyh_ts_without_sr.pdf
52. Wadler, P.: Propositions as sessions. J. Funct. Program. **24**(2–3), 384–418 (2014). https://doi.org/10.1017/S095679681400001X
53. Yonezawa, A., Tokoro, M.: Object-Oriented Concurrent Programming. MIT Press, Cambridge, MA, USA (1986)
54. Zhou, L., Oliveira, B.C.d.S.: QuickSub: Efficient Iso-recursive subtyping. Proc. ACM Program. Lang. **9**(POPL), 954–985 (2025). https://doi.org/10.1145/3704860
55. Zhou, L., Wan, Q., d. S. Oliveira, B.C.: Full Iso-recursive types. Proc. ACM Program. Lang. **8**(OOPSLA2), 192–221 (2024). https://doi.org/10.1145/3689718
56. Zhou, L., Zhou, Y., d. S. Oliveira, B.C.: Recursive subtyping for all. Proc. ACM Program. Lang. **7**(POPL), 1396–1425 (2023). https://doi.org/10.1145/3571241
57. Zhou, Y., Zhao, J., d. S. Oliveira, B.C.: Revisiting Iso-recursive subtyping. ACM Trans. Program. Lang. Syst. **44**(4), 24:1–24:54 (2022). https://doi.org/10.1145/3549537

Programming and Verifying Actor Systems in Rewriting Logic

José Meseguer[✉]

University of Illinois at Urbana-Champaign, Urbana, IL 61801, USA
meseguer@illinois.edu

Abstract. Actors and rewriting logic were made for each other. This work explains the semantic relationship between both and describes research since 1990 at the intersection of both areas in topics such as: (i) software composition methods for distributed systems; (ii) formal verification of Actor systems; (iii) formal specification of probabilistic Actor systems and statistical model checking analysis of their qualitative properties; and (iv) automatic generation of correct-by-construction implementations of Actor system designs formally specified in the Maude rewriting logic language and verified in its formal tool environment.

Keywords: Actors · Rewriting Logic · Maude · Reflection · Qualitative and Quantitative Property Verification · Open Distributed Systems

1 Introduction

Gul Agha and I met for the first time in the 1980s in Tokyo at an international conference organized by the Japanese Fifth Generation Project. This was the beginning of a life-long friendship and of a very fruitful scientific collaboration between us and our students. I find no better way of honoring Gul in this joyous occasion than to dedicate to him a *tour d'horizon* describing the mutual enrichment and the many advances between the theory of Actors led by Gul and rewriting logic and Maude that have taken place since 1990 to the present. Besides my deeply personal reasons for doing so there is also a strictly scientific one. A Festschrift offers a unique opportunity for what I would call *scientific reflection*: taking stock of scientific developments in a certain area or, as in this case, at the intersection of two areas, not during a few years, or a decade, but, as in this paper, over 35 years. I consider such efforts for scientific reflection much needed, because there is a relentless pressure for over-specialization that can easily lead to an almost total amnesia and can cripple many scientists, particularly young ones for whom such a pressure may require a struggle for survival.

I begin by explaining in §2 how the Actor model and rewriting logic and Maude have been intimately related since 1990 and the various ways in which, as I further explain later in the paper, that mutual relationship has flourished over the years yielding many fruitful results and ideas developed in joint collaborations between researchers in both fields, including Gul and myself.

I then describe in §3 a remarkable 25-year-long conceptual evolution that has taken place in the area of *software composition methods for distributed systems* stimulated by Gul's seminal 1993 paper with his students Svend Frølund, Rajendra Panwar and Daniel Sturman on the *onion skin model* of Actor reflection [3]. Grit Denker, Carolyn Talcott and I formalized the onion skin model in rewriting logic in 2000 [22]. In 2002 Carolyn Talcott and I generalized the onion skin model to what we called the *Russian dolls* model [50], which supports nested configurations of meta-actors, each encapsulating entire subconfigurations of other meta-actors, and provides a novel combination of object-oriented Actor reflection with the mechanism for *logical reflection* offered by rewriting logic [21] and Maude [19]. In 2014 I extended both the onion skin and the Russian dolls composition methods for distributed systems into the more general method of *formal patterns*. This area is constantly growing with new applications. I consider it of key importance for scalability, modularity and reusability of software design and verification. Gul's paper with his students on the onion skin model was the proverbial stone cast into the pond that has generated wider and wider waves.

The relationship between Actors and rewriting logic and Maude offers a useful advantage: Actor systems programmed in Maude are rewrite theories; and it is much easier to formally verify a rewrite theory $\mathcal{R}$ which has an associated initial model $\mathbb{T}_\mathcal{R}$ (a mathematical model of the concurrent system defined by $\mathcal{R}$) than it is to verify an imperative program written in a language that may even lack a formal semantics. For this reason I summarize in §4 how formal requirements of Actor systems written in Maude can be formally verified using various tools in Maude's Formal Environment.

In §5 I consider two other closely related stones cast into the pond, both of them seminal papers that have generated waves that expand up to the present: a 2002 paper by Nirman Kumar, Koushik Sen, Gul and myself [42], and a 2006 paper by Gul, Koushik Sen and myself [4]. The first expanded the scope of rewriting logic and its applications by allowing it to model *probabilistic concurrent systems* by means of *probabilistic rewrite theories* [42]. The second paper built on the first and drew important benefits from it for Actor systems by identifying the class of probabilistic Actor systems whose probabilities model the delays in the system's message passing communication in a given underlying network as those systems definable in the PMaude language proposed in [4]. PMaude—in conjunction with seminal contributions by Koushik Sen, Mahesh Viswanathan and Gul to the then nascent field of *statistical model checking* [74–76]—opened up the possibility of analyzing performance properties of Actor systems by statistical model checking. In [4] this was achieved by: (i) observing that if the probability distributions of the PMaude system were *continuous*, the PMaude system was *purely probabilistic* (had no non-determinism) and therefore amenable to statistical model checking analysis; (ii) introducing the QuaTEx probabilistic temporal logic to specify qualitative properties of a PMaude specification; and (iii) implementing a statistical model checking algorithm for QuaTEx expressions in the VeStA tool. This has enabled a wide range of applications. I also explain in §5.2 how the method of formal patterns discussed in

§3.3 has recently made it possible to automate the statistical model checking of QuaTEx properties for PMaude specifications by means of the formal patterns provided in [44].

One can see §6 as the answer to two questions. The first is: In which way does Maude contain an *Actor programming language* as a sublanguage? Maude supports formal specification of Actor system *designs* that are executable in the Maude interpreter and analyzable w.r.t. their qualitative and quantitative properties in the Maude Formal Environment. Furthermore, using Maude's support for *external objects* [20,24] Actor system designs can be *implemented* in Maude itself as distributed systems. But this raises a second question: How can the *formality gap* between an already verified Actor system design and its Maude distributed implementation be bridged? I explain how this is answered by the D formal pattern [48], and how this formal pattern has been recently extended in [24] to a methodology to design, verify and implement *open* distributed systems.

I present some concluding remarks and discuss some future directions in §7.

2 Actor Systems in Rewriting Logic and Maude

After giving a brief introduction to rewriting logic I explain how Actor systems can be specified as rewrite theories and programmed in the Maude rewriting logic language.

2.1 Rewriting Logic

Rewriting logic [53,57] is a computational logic ideally suited to program a wide variety of concurrent systems [56,57]. A rewrite theory is a triple $\mathcal{R} = (\Sigma, E, R)$ with (Σ, E) an equational theory with function symbols Σ and equations E, and R a collection of (possibly conditional) rewrite rules of the form $u \rightarrow v\ \textit{if cond}$, where u, v are Σ-terms, and *cond* is the rule's condition, which must be met for the rule to be applied. What $\mathcal{R} = (\Sigma, E, R)$ specifies is a concurrent system whose *concurrent states* are the elements of the initial algebra $\mathbb{T}_{\Sigma/E}$, and whose *local concurrent transitions* are specified by the rules in R. In rewriting logic concurrent computation *coincides* with logical deduction, in the sense that a concurrent computation $\alpha : [w] \rightarrow [w']$ between concurrent states $[w], [w'] \in \mathbb{T}_{\Sigma/E}$ is *possible* in the concurrent system specified by $\mathcal{R}$ if and only if it can be *proved* in the theory $\mathcal{R}$, i.e., if and only if α is a *proof term* proving in rewriting logic the existence of a concurrent computation $\alpha : [w] \rightarrow [w']$ [16,53].

Rewriting logic is a *computational logic* in the sense that, under reasonable assumptions on the rewrite theory $\mathcal{R} = (\Sigma, E, R)$ [57], deduction in $\mathcal{R}$ can be efficiently implemented, so that $\mathcal{R}$ becomes a *declarative program* in a declarative programming language to program concurrent systems. The Maude language [19,23] is a high-performance implementation of rewriting logic as a declarative programming language.

2.2 Actor Systems as Concurrent Object Systems in Maude

The *Actor* model [1,2] is one of the most widely used models of concurrency. From the earliest rewriting logic publications [51,52] the Actor model was seen and formalized in rewriting logic as the model of concurrency describing those *concurrent object systems* that communicate through *asynchronous message passing*. Furthermore, the importance of the Actor model was reflected in Maude's language design, where special syntax for concurrent object systems, and in particular for Actor systems, was introduced [19,51,54].

Let me explain how concurrent object systems are modeled as rewrite theories. An *object* of a given object class C has a *unique identity* or *name*, say, o, and its own *local state*. The local state of an object o can be abstractly characterized by the current *values* of each of its *attributes*. For example, a bank account object o of class *Accnt* may have attributes such as the owner's street *address*, the current *balance*, and the interest *rate* that accrues to the account. An object o of class C can be represented in somewhat different ways. A natural representation of o in a given state is as a record-like structure of the form:

$$\langle o : C \mid a_1 : v_1, \ldots, a_k : v_k \rangle$$

where the $a_1, \ldots, a_k$ are the object's *attributes*, and the $v_1, \ldots, v_k$ are the corresponding *current values* of those attributes. We can abstractly model the concurrent state (called a *configuration*) of a given concurrent object system as a *multiset* of objects (possibly of different classes) and *messages* addressed to some of those objects. Even though object names are required to be unique, a configuration is in general a multiset rather than a set of objects and messages, because several copies of a message may be present in a given configuration.

The rewrite theories $\mathcal{R} = (\Sigma, E, R)$ specifying any concurrent object systems of this kind have some key common features that are easy to explain assuming that (as supported by Maude) the signature Σ of typed function symbols is *order-sorted* [34], i.e., it supports *subtype inclusions* such as, for example, the subtype inclusions $Nat < Int < Rat$ between natural, integer and rational numbers. We can then easily specify configurations, i.e., the concurrent states, as having type (in Maude called *sort*) *Conf*, with subtype inclusions *Object Msg* $<$ *Conf*, where *Object* is the type of objects, *Msg* is the type of messages, and multiset union is specified (with empty syntax, i.e., as juxtaposition) as:

$$\_\_ : Conf\ Conf \rightarrow Conf$$

where underbars '_' indicate argument places, and the equations E include the associativity $(X\,Y)\,Z = X\,(Y\,Z)$, commutativity $X\,Y = Y\,X$, and identity $X\,null = X$ axioms for multiset union of configurations, where *null* denotes the empty multiset. Of course, additional state constructors are needed, such as constructors building objects of the general form, $\langle o : C \mid a_1 : v_1, \ldots, a_k : v_k \rangle$, and messages, which we may assume have the form, *to o from o' : m*, with o the receiver, o' the sender, and m the message's payload.

What about the rewrite rules R? They are rules of the form $u \rightarrow v$ *if cond* where u and v are terms of sort *Conf*; that is, both u and v may include object and message subexpressions. For example, in a concurrent object system of bank accounts we may have rewrite rules such as:

1. $to\ B\ from\ A\ :\ credit(M)\ \langle B\ :\ Accnt\ |\ balance\ :\ N, ATTS\rangle \rightarrow \langle B\ :\ Accnt\ |\ balance\ :\ N + M, ATTS\rangle$
2. $to\ B\ from\ A\ :\ debit(M)\ \langle B\ :\ Accnt\ |\ balance\ :\ N, ATTS\rangle \rightarrow \langle B\ :\ Accnt\ |\ balance\ :\ N - M, ATTS\rangle\ if\ N \geq M$

where A, B are variables of type Oid (object identifiers), N, M are variables of type Rat, and $ATTS$ is a variable of type $Atts$ (attribute sets), whose elements are sets $a_1 : v_1, \ldots, a_k : v_k$ of attribute-value pairs. In this way, the object attributes that do not change in a given rewrite rule, such as the *address* and *rate* attributes of an account in the above two rules, need not be mentioned. As we shall see shortly, the above two rules, which describe *asynchronous message passing* communication, are typical of Actor systems.

In general, of course, several object terms could appear in the lefthand side of a rule $u \rightarrow v\ if\ cond$. For example, a rule in which a network node object having a *cell* attribute (whose value is either empty (denoted mt) or a natural number) that is currently empty reads the first number from a non-empty buffer object holding a queue of numbers in its q attribute may have the form:

$$\langle A : Node\ |\ cell : mt, ATTS\rangle\ \langle B : Buffer\ |\ q : N; L, ATTS'\rangle \rightarrow$$
$$\langle A : Node\ |\ cell : N, ATTS\rangle\ \langle B : Buffer\ |\ q : L, ATTS'\rangle$$

where $N; L$ denotes a list with first element N and remaining list L. The above rule can rightly be called *synchronous*,[1] since in the transfer of number N from the buffer to the node's cell attribute both objects must be synchronized.

The Actor model can be characterized as the class of concurrent object system rewrite theories $\mathcal{R} = (\Sigma, E, R)$ whose rules R have the general form:

$$to\ B\ from\ A : P\ \langle B : C\ |\ atts\rangle \rightarrow \langle B : C\ |\ atts'\rangle\ msgs\ objs$$

where: (i) $atts$ and $atts'$ are terms of sort $Atts$ describing the pre- and post-state of object B, (ii) $msgs$ is a term evaluating to a (possibly empty) multiset of messages sent by B to various objects as a result of receiving the message; and (iii) $objs$ is a term evaluating to a (possibly empty) set of new objects created by B as a result of receiving the message.

As described in [19, 54], Maude supports a special syntax that makes it easier to specify concurrent object systems, and in particular Actor systems, because: (i) the fact that configurations are multisets of objects and messages is taken for granted and need not be mentioned; (ii) object classes and multiple class inheritance are directly supported; and (iii) the attribute-value pairs of an object that do not change in a rewrite transition need not be mentioned. This special syntax is just useful *syntactic sugar*, so that the actual rewrite theory $\mathcal{R} = (\Sigma, E, R)$ defining the given concurrent object system is obtained by an automatic desugaring process.

---

[1] More generally, any concurrent object system's rewrite rule having two or more object expressions in its lefthand side is called a *synchronous* rule.

The rewriting logic approach to concurrent object systems and Actors has advanced the theory of Actors in several ways:

1. It has made explicit the relationship between Actor systems and the broader class of concurrent object systems and class inheritance for such systems.
2. It has solved the so-called *inheritance anomaly* [54,55]; that is, the lack of modularity encountered in various Actor languages, which required redefining the code of an actor of a given class when a subclass of it was introduced.
3. It has stimulated declarative rewriting logic languages like Maude and CafeOBJ [32] to program concurrent object systems and Actor systems.
4. It has led to the notion of *generalized Actor rewrite theories*, whose rules have the general form,

$$[to\ B\ from\ A : P]\ \langle B : C \mid atts \rangle \rightarrow \langle B : C \mid atts' \rangle\ msgs\ objs$$

where the notation $[to\ B\ from\ A : P]$ means that a message need not be present in the rule's lefthand side. This supports *active objects*, which can perform transitions on their own without having to receive a message. In practice this leads to simpler specifications. The rules of generalized Actor systems provide a fully general notion of *asynchronous object-oriented rule*.
5. As explained in §3, it has substantially advanced the concepts and methods of *Actor reflection*.
6. As explained in §5, in joint work with Gul Agha and Koushik Sen [4] it has opened up the area of modeling in the PMaude language, and analyzing by statistical model checking the quantitative properties of Actor systems.

As explained in the rest of the paper, the above-mentioned conceptual advances have stimulated and supported many applications in various areas, including: distributed algorithms, network protocols, distributed databases; real-time and cyber-physical systems; reflective and adaptive Actor systems; and security.

3 From the Onion Skin Model to Formal Patterns

Actors are not plants inside a greenhouse or animals inside a zoo. They interact with various other actors in *open systems* and must meet safety and reliability requirements in diverse, changing, and potentially hostile or unreliable communication environments. Programming Actor systems so as to anticipate the different problems that they may encounter in various hostile or unreliable environments would lead to bloated, monolithic and highly complex systems. It would also lead to inefficient systems, because of the extra computational cost of preventing various potential problems that may not arise in a given environment.

Reflection mechanisms provide a modular way of enabling Actor systems to *adapt* to new, possibly hostile environments and meet the associated challenges posed by such environments, which may include, for example, safety, security, fault tolerance, and Quality of Service (QoS) challenges. The key idea of *distributed object-oriented reflection* is to delegate the different communication challenges that actor systems may encounter to different classes of *meta-objects*, each mediating actor communication so as to meet a specific challenge. Genericity and modularity are achieved because, since a given meta-object class meets a challenge common to many systems, such a class can be highly *generic*, and this makes meta-objects *modular and composable* so that: (i) the actors of the original system need not be changed in any way; and (ii) several meta-objects may be composed with the same original actor to meet different challenges.

3.1 The Onion-Skin Model

In their seminal paper [3], Agha, Frølund, Panwar and Sturman proposed a very useful reflective model of meta-objects called the *onion skin model*. In the authors' own words:

> Thus, a model of objects resembling the layers of an onion is created; each addition of a protocol adds a new layer in the same way regardless of how many layers currently exist. With the above rules [regulating the object-meta-object communication], protocols can be composed without any previous knowledge that the composition was going to occur and protocols can now be added and removed without regard not just to the actor itself, but also without regard to existing protocols.

Let me comment on the above description: (i) meta-actors can be viewed as generic *protocols*; for example, meta-actors providing fault-tolerant communication to their underlying actors can be viewed as a generic fault-tolerant communication protocol; (ii) a meta-actor is viewed as a "wrapper" encapsulating and mediating the communication of its underlying actor, thus providing an additional layer of the "onion;" (iii) the code, and therefore the behavior, of the underlying actor is not changed at all, thus achieving modularity and reusability; (iv) the actor-meta-actor composition is itself a *new actor*; and therefore, (v) such a new, layered actor can be endowed with arbitrarily many additional "outer" layers by composing it with new meta-actors, thus the onion metaphor.

The figure below shows actors A and B wrapped by corresponding meta-actors that mediate their communication in a hostile environment. The messages pictured as envelopes are not those sent by A and B, but those sent by their meta-actors. Actors A and B send and receive their original messages oblivious to how their communication is mediated by their meta-actors.

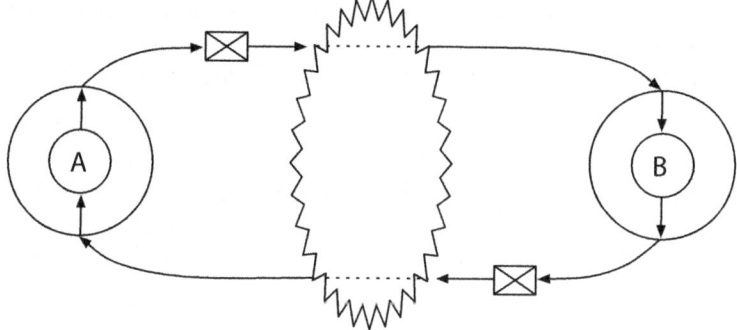

The onion-skin model was formalized in rewriting logic by Denker, Meseguer and Talcott in [22] and, as I explain below, has been widely used in many Maude applications. I refer to [22] for details and summarize here the main ideas. How is the wrapping of an actor o of class C by a corresponding meta-actor of class MC formalized? By endowing (meta-)actors of class MC with, among others, three attributes: (i) $conf$, an actor configuration containing a single object (namely, actor o) and possibly messages sent by or addressed to o; (ii) $in.buff$, a buffer containing incoming messages (from other meta-actors) received by the meta-actor, whose name is the *same* as that of the actor it wraps; and (iii) $out.buff$, a buffer containing outgoing messages sent to other actors by the actor o it wraps. Therefore, the state of a meta-actor o wrapping an actor o has the general form:

$$\langle o : MC \mid conf : (\langle o : C \mid atts \rangle\ msgs), in.buff : L, out.buff : L', atts' \rangle$$

where $msgs$ are messages from or to actor o, and L, resp. L', are lists of incoming, resp. outgoing, messages. The behavior of meta-actors of class MC are specified by rewrite rules describing how: (i) messages sent to, say, actor o', by a wrapped actor o are transformed into corresponding messages from meta-actor o to meta-actor o'; and (ii) messages received by meta-actor o from another meta-actor o' are transformed back into the original messages sent by its wrapped actor o' to actor o. Such meta-actor rewrite rules are *generic*, in the sense that they do not depend on the specific details[2] of the class C of the wrapped actor. For example, meta-actors of class MC may provide a *cryptographic protocol* for secure actor communication. In that case, their rewrite rules will specify how messages sent by actor o to actor o' will be encrypted by o's meta-actor and decrypted by o''s meta-actor. Actors o and o' will remain oblivious to any such encryption/decryption: they will behave according to the rewrite rules of their original classes, which will be applied inside the "bubbles" encapsulating them in the $conf$ attribute of their encrypting/decrypting meta-actors o and o'.

---

[2] However, meta-actors of class MC may not apply to just any actor class C, but to a general set of Actor classes. For example, the meta-actors of some class MC, though generic, may only apply to client-server Actor systems.

The onion skin model has been used in various application areas of Maude. Besides the fault tolerance and cryptographic protocol applications described in [22], applications in the following areas can be mentioned:

1. **Cyber-physical systems**: Safe Operation of Medical Devices [78–80].
2. **Security**:
   - Cookies [17] (for Distributed Denial of Service (DDoS) protection).
   - Adaptive Selective Verification (ASV) [8] (for DDoS protection).
   - Protocol Dialects [33,81].

3.2 The Russian Dolls Model

The onion skin model was later generalized by Carolyn Talcott and I to the so-called "Russian dolls" model in [50]. The Russian dolls model was also formalized in rewriting logic. Its main features are:

1. a meta-object can mediate/coordinate/control not just a single object but a sub-configuration containing several objects;
2. generalizing the onion layers, the objects inside a meta-object's subconfiguration can themselves be meta-objects encapsulating subconfigurations of other (meta-)objects; in this way we arrive at a model of nested wrapped subconfigurations of objects, thus the "Russian dolls" metaphor;[3]
3. object-based reflection can be combined with logical reflection for greater adaptability and generality (more on this below).

The Russians dolls model contains the onion-skin model [3], the TLAM model [82] of Venkatasubramanian, Talcott and Agha, and the Mobile Maude language [25] of Durán, Eker, Lincoln, and Meseguer as special cases.

I will focus on the Mobile Maude language because it illustrates the usefulness of logical reflection (feature (3)). The point is that, besides supporting concurrent object reflection, which is achieved by meta-objects controlling and/or mediating the behavior of other objects, rewriting logic has another important reflection mechanism, namely, *logical reflection*. What this means is that rewriting logic is *reflective* [21]; that is, it can represent crucial aspects of its own meta-theory because it has a *universal theory* $\mathcal{U}$ such that: (i) can meta-represent any (finitely presented) rewrite theory $\mathcal{R}$, including $\mathcal{U}$ itself, as a term $\overline{\mathcal{R}}$ in $\mathcal{U}$; (ii) can likewise meta-represent any term u in any rewrite theory $\mathcal{R}$ as a term $\overline{u}$ in $\mathcal{U}$; and (iii) any rewriting logic computation in any rewrite theory $\mathcal{R}$ can be faithfully *simulated* by a corresponding rewriting logic computation in $\mathcal{U}$ in a way analogous to how a universal Turing machine can faithfully simulate any Turing machine, including itself. Maude efficiently supports logical reflection by means of its `META-LEVEL` module.

---

[3] The famous Russian folk art dolls, which contain smaller dolls inside, and so on; but, unlike the usual Russian dolls, a meta-object may contain not one but *several* immediate subobjects inside, each possibly containing several others in a nested way.

Let me sketch the main ideas about Mobile Maude, a language supporting *mobile objects*, which can migrate in the Internet and execute at different locations. Additional details can be found in [25], and for its reflective distributed implementation in [19]. Mobile Maude has two kinds of entities, both of them meta-objects, called *mobile objects* and *environments*. Mobile objects are wrapped actors; but of what class? Of *any Actor class*. This is achieved by logical reflection; because, unlike a standard onion skin meta-actor o encapsulating an actor o of class C in a configuration attribute $conf : (\langle o : C \mid atts \rangle\ msgs)$, what the mobile meta-actor o now encapsulates are two terms in META-LEVEL, namely: (i) the term $\overline{\mathcal{R}}$ meta-representing the actor rewrite theory $\mathcal{R}$, i.e., the code of the inner actor o, and (ii) the term $\overline{\langle o : C \mid atts \rangle\ msgs}$ meta-representing the current state of the inner actor o and messages to or from o.

Environments are located computational environments in which mobile objects execute, communicate with other objects, and can move in or out. Therefore, Mobile Maude provides a Russian dolls architecture where environments encapsulate mobile objects, and mobile objects encapsulate actors. The figure below describes nested configurations in Mobile Maude, where mobile meta-objects can reside and execute inside environments depicted as rectangular meta-objects, can communicate with other mobile meta-objects in the same or in different environments, and can move from one environment to another.

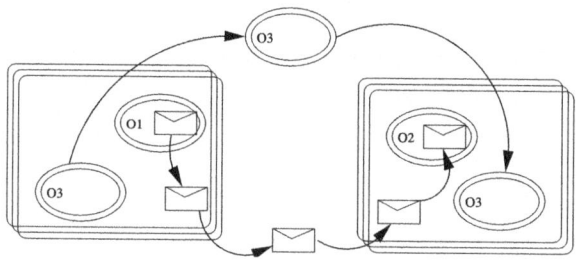

What is common to Russian doll meta-objects and to the simpler onion-skin meta-objects is that their semantics is characterized at the rewriting logic level by so-called *boundary-crossing* rewrite rules. For example, in the above figure the fact that messages and objects can go into an environment or out of it is governed by meta-object rewrite rules at the environment level. Likewise, since in Mobile Maude individual objects are also wrapped by an onion skin wrapper, messages addressed to the inner object have to go inside the wrapper, and messages addressed to other objects have to go outside the wrapper, which is again accomplished by the boundary-crossing wrapper's rewrite rules.

Besides the work on Mobile Maude [19, 25], other applications of the Russian dolls model include work of Gutierrez-Nolasco, Venkatasubramanian and Talcott on a reflective model of safe protocol interaction [37], and work of Eckhardt, Mühlbauer, AlTurki, Meseguer and Wirsing on the composition of the onion skin ASV DDoS protection meta-objects in [8] with a Russian dolls server replication meta-object to achieve a DDoS protection mechanism that can maintain a roughly constant level of availability in spite of a growing number of DDoS attackers [31].

3.3 Formal Patterns

The onion skin model and its Russian dolls generalization provide modular and generic *system composition mechanisms* that can extend an Actor system with new capabilities and endow it with new properties not available in the original system. They are both instances of the more general notion of a *formal pattern* [58,60]. Formal patterns are formally-specified *generic solutions to commonly occurring computational problems*. Being generic, a formal pattern applies, not just to a single system, but to a typically infinite class of systems that satisfy specified *semantic requirements*. Application of a formal pattern to a system satisfying the formal pattern's input requirements results in a new system with new functionality that is *correct by construction*. Such correctness takes the form of an *assume-guarantee formal assurance*: assuming that the original system meets the formal pattern's semantic requirements, then the application of the formal pattern to such a system is guaranteed to enjoy specific properties. Formal patterns are very useful for formal system design because, as already illustrated by the onion skin and Russian dolls models, they support a high degree of genericity, modularity and reusability of system designs. Furthermore, they can drastically reduce formal verification efforts.

Mathematically, a formal pattern is a *theory transformation* P that maps a declarative program in rewriting logic,[4] that is, a rewrite theory $\mathcal{R}$ in a class $\mathcal{C}$ of rewrite theories satisfying the pattern's input requirements, perhaps with some *additional parameters* $\boldsymbol{p}$, into a new theory $P(\mathcal{R}, \boldsymbol{p})$ specifying the new correct-by-construction system generated by P, i.e., we can describe P as a (possibly partial) function,

$$P : \mathcal{C} \times \mathit{Params} \ni (\mathcal{R}, \boldsymbol{p}) \mapsto P(\mathcal{R}, \boldsymbol{p}) \in \mathit{Th}_{RewritingLogic}$$

where $\mathit{Th}_{RewritingLogic}$ denotes the class of finitary rewrite theories. Thanks to the fact that rewriting logic enjoys logical reflection we can view P as a *meta-program*, that is, as a Maude program that transforms a given Maude program $\mathcal{R}$ in the class of programs $\mathcal{C}$ into another Maude program $P(\mathcal{R}, \boldsymbol{p})$.

Typically, the system defined by $P(\mathcal{R}, \boldsymbol{p})$ is a *substantial extension*, enjoying new features and properties, of that defined by $\mathcal{R}$. Quite often, and this is indeed the case when $P(\mathcal{R}, \boldsymbol{p})$ is obtained using the onion skin or the Russian dolls models, the semantics of $P(\mathcal{R}, \boldsymbol{p})$ *extends* that of $\mathcal{R}$ while respecting $\mathcal{R}$ itself, which remains intact as a *subcomponent* of $P(T, \boldsymbol{p})$. That is, the code of $\mathcal{R}$ is not changed at all.

However, in other examples of formal pattern (e.g., [12,44,47,48,63]), the input theory $\mathcal{R}$ may not be kept as a subcomponent of $P(\mathcal{R}, \boldsymbol{p})$. Instead, the

---

[4] More generally formal patterns can be defined in a computational logic enjoying good properties [60]. For the sake of concreteness, in what follows I will assume the the computational logic in question is rewriting logic.

assume-guarantee properties relating $\mathcal{R}$ and $P(\mathcal{R}, \boldsymbol{p})$ may include considerably more general properties, such as the existence of a *simulation* or *bisimulation* (including the case of a *stuttering* simulation or bisimulation) between $\mathcal{R}$ and $P(\mathcal{R}, \boldsymbol{p})$.

Besides the already mentioned applications of formal patterns based on the onion skin or Russian dolls models, formal patterns specified as Maude *metaprograms* have been defined and proved correct in various application areas, including:

1. **Cyber-physical systems**: Physically Asynchronous/Logically Synchronous (PALS) pattern for real-time distributed systems [63,64], Multi-Rate PALS [10,12,14], and Hybrid PALS [13].
2. **Distributed systems' implementation and model checking**:
   – The D Transformation [48] for correct-by-construction distributed system implementation (more on this in §6.1).
   – The P, Sim and M transformations for statistical model checking (SMC) analysis of generalized Actor systems [44] (more on this in §5).
   – The M Transformation for automatically verifying consistency properties of distributed transaction systems [47].
3. **Theorem proving and executability transformations**:
   – The $\mathcal{E} \mapsto \mathcal{E}^{\equiv}$ [36] and $\mathcal{E} \mapsto \mathcal{E}$: [61] Transformations.
   – The $\mathcal{R} \mapsto \overline{\mathcal{R}}_l$ and $\mathcal{R} \mapsto \overline{\mathcal{R}}_{\Sigma_1,l,r}^{\Omega}$ Transformations [59].
   – The $\mathcal{R} \mapsto \mathcal{R}_U$ Transformation [27].
   – Partial Evaluation Transformations [6].

The transformations in (1) and (2) involve Actor systems. Instead, the transformations in (3) apply to more general classes of rewrite theories. Detailed discussion of the above formal patterns is beyond the scope of this paper. I refer to [58,60] for overviews of many of them, and to the references for the various formal patterns given above and in §3.1–3.2 for full details.

4 Verifying Qualitative Properties of Actor Systems

A (generalized) Actor system is formalized in Maude as a rewrite theory $\mathcal{R} = (\Sigma, E, R)$, where (Σ, E) is an equational theory (in fact an equational program) specifying the system's data types and auxiliary functions, and R is the collection of rewrite rules specifying the behavior of actors in the Actor classes defined in $\mathcal{R}$. The initial model $\mathbb{T}_{\mathcal{R}}$ is a mathematical model of the Actor system $\mathcal{R}$, but its states are elements of the initial algebra $\mathbb{T}_{\Sigma/E}$ of its equational theory (Σ, E). The *properties* of the Actor system $\mathcal{R}$ may involve just the states in $\mathbb{T}_{\Sigma/E}$ or, more generally, the actual concurrent system $\mathbb{T}_{\mathcal{R}}$. Furthermore, these properties may be either: (i) *qualitative* properties, which receive a yes/no, i.e., a true/false, answer to the question of whether the formalization of such a property as a formula φ in a suitable logic is true in the initial model $\mathbb{T}_{\mathcal{R}}$ (or for state properties in the initial algebra $\mathbb{T}_{\Sigma/E}$); or (ii) *quantitative* properties of the Actor system $\mathcal{R}$, such as latency, throughput, or other performance and QoS properties, based on some assumptions about the environment and infrastructure where the Actor system $\mathcal{R}$ operates. I discuss the specification and verification of qualitative properties here, and that of quantitative ones in §5.2.

Some of the qualitative formal requirements of $\mathcal{R}$ may be purely functional, because they only involve $\mathbb{T}_{\Sigma/E}$. For such requirements the following Maude tools can verify various functional properties: (i) the Church-Rosser Checker [28]; (ii) the Maude Termination Tool (MTT) [26]; (iii) the Sufficient Completeness Checker (SCC) [38]; and (iv) the New Inductive Theorem Prover (NuITP) [30].

Many other qualitative formal requirements of $\mathcal{R}$ will involve $\mathbb{T}_{\mathcal{R}}$, i.e., the Actor system's behavior. Some of these requirements, expressible in modal logic as reachability requirements (e.g. invariants) or as LTL (resp. LTLR) properties, can be verified in Maude itself (resp. in the LTLR model checker [11]) either by:

1. **Explicit-state** model checking features such as: (i) Maude's `search` command, (ii) Maude's LTL model checker (resp. the LTLR model checker in [11]); or (iii) the extension of the LTL model checker to verify properties under user-specified strategies reported in [70]. Furthermore, the tool described in §6 of [69] makes it possible to model check CLT* and μ-calculus temporal logic properties of Actor systems through an interface to the LTSim model checker [40].
2. **Infinite-state, narrowing-based** model checking of either: (i) invariants and other reachability properties with Maude's `fvu-narrow` search command; or (ii) infinite-state model checking of LTL properties supported by the Maude Logical Model Checker tool [9].

In addition, qualitative properties of Actor systems with *real time* features, expressed in either LTL or in timed CTL (TCTL), can be verified in the Real-Time Maude tool [65].

5 PMaude and Analysis of Quantitative Actor Properties

My move from SRI International's Computer Science Laboratory to the Computer Science Department at the University of Illinois at Urbana-Champaign in 2001 made possible a very fruitful long-term collaboration with Gul Agha and his students. An important problem that we investigated together was how to extend rewriting logic so as to be able to specify concurrent systems that have *probabilistic* features. We investigated that problem in full generality, arriving at the notion of a *probabilistic rewrite theory* [42]; but of course we always kept in mind the specific case of probabilistic Actor systems.

5.1 Probabilistic Rewrite Theories

Let me first explain what a probabilistic rewrite theory is and then discuss probabilistic Actor systems. Usually, a rewrite rule $u \to v$ *if cond* is such that the variables in the pattern v and the condition *cond* are a *subset* of the set of variables x in the lefthand side pattern u. However, it is perfectly possible to model system transitions that exhibit *non-deterministic choice* by means of rewrite rules of the form:

$$u(x) \to v(x, y) \; if \; cond(x)$$

That is, for each matching substitution ρ of the variables x in $u(x)$ that satisfies the condition $cond(x)\rho$, the resulting state is not a single state $v(x)\rho$, but a possibly infinite family of states of the form $\{v(x,y)\rho \uplus \tau\}_\tau$, indexed by the choice of a substitution τ instantiating the extra variables y. For example, the rewrite rule:

$$\langle n, m \rangle \to \langle n, k \rangle$$

transforms a state consisting of a pair $\langle n, m \rangle$ of natural numbers into a new state $\langle n, k \rangle$ where we have changed the second component m by *any choice* of a natural number k. Of course, in such a rule there is no rhyme or reason about the choice of k. But there may be a reason. For example, we might choose k according to a *probability distribution* on the natural numbers. This leads to the notion of a *probabilistic rewrite rule*, which is a rewrite rule of the form:

$$u(x) \to v(x, y) \; if \; cond(x) \; with \; probability \; y := \pi(x)$$

That is, for each matching substitution ρ of the variables x in $u(x)$ that satisfies the condition $cond(x)\rho$, the substitution τ instantiatiating the extra variables y and resulting in the new state $v(x, y)\rho \uplus \tau$ is chosen according to a probability distribution $\pi(x)\rho$ on the product of data types of the variables y, where the probability distribution $\pi(x)\rho$ need not be a fixed one, but may instead be parametric on the choice of values ρ instantiating the variables x. For example, y may be a single Boolean variable b, and $\pi(x)$ may be the Bernoulli distribution, parametric on the bias $x \in (0, 1)$ of the tossed coin, with x itself a variable in x (or the value of an expression $w(x)$), i.e., the probability distribution $\pi(x)\rho$ may depend on the matching substitution ρ instantiating $u(x)$.

A *probabilistic rewrite theory* is then a rewrite theory where *some* of its rewrite rules are probabilistic in the sense just described.

5.2 PMaude and Quantitative Analysis of Actor Systems

Once the notion of a probabilistic rewrite theory was available to us and, furthermore, Koushik Sen, Mahesh Viswanathan and Gul had made seminal contributions to the then novel field of *statistical model checking* [74–76], Gul, Koushik and I investigated the following two questions:

1. How can we model with probabilistic rewrite theories the communication of Actor systems where messages are sent using an underlying network whose communication delays are random, yet are empirically describable by some probability distribution?

2. Using probabilistic rewrite theories that model the communication delays of an Actor system, how can we: (i) specify various performance properties of such a system in a *probabilistic temporal logic*; and (ii) automatically analyze those performance properties through *statistical model checking*?

We answered both questions in [4]. We proposed the PMaude language as the answer to question (1), and the probabilistic temporal logic of *Quantitative Temporal Expressions* (QuaTEx) and a statistical model checking algorithm for it implemented in the VeStA statistical model checker as the respective answers to questions (2).(i) and (2).(ii). I refer to [4] for details and give here a brief summary. First of all, what is PMaude? It is an Actor language generalizing Actor Maude programs by allowing some of their rules to be probabilistic. For example, in Maude one of the rules of a client-server Actor system, where a server replies to a client's request, may have the general form:

$$to\ B\ from\ A : req\ \langle B : Server \mid atts \rangle \rightarrow$$

$$\langle B : Server \mid atts' \rangle\ to\ A\ from\ B : repl(req, atts)$$

where the details about the request expression *req* and the reply *repl(req, atts)* may vary depending on the specific client-server system. Instead, in PMaude the same rule becomes probabilistic. We may, for example, have good empirical grounds to assume that the random time it takes for a message from B to A to travel through the given network infrastructure follows the $Lognormal(\mu_0, \sigma_0^2)$ distribution, where μ_0 and σ_0 are concrete real numbers instantiating the corresponding parameters μ and σ of the distribution. Then, the corresponding rule in PMaude will have the form,

$$to\ B\ from\ A : req\ \langle B : Server \mid atts \rangle \rightarrow$$

$$\langle B : Server \mid atts' \rangle\ [to\ A\ from\ B : repl(req, atts), d]$$

$$with\ probability\ d := Lognormal(\mu_0, \sigma_0^2)$$

where $[to\ A\ from\ B : repl(req, atts), d]$ is a *delayed message* with delay d, where the choice of d is governed by the $Lognormal(\mu_0, \sigma_0^2)$ distribution. A delayed message cannot be received by its addressee until d becomes 0, i.e., until the message has reached its destination. Message arrival is modeled by the equation $[m, 0] = m$, where m is a variable of type *Msg*. The point is that in PMaude the global state is now a pair $(conf, t)$, with *conf* a configuration of actors, delayed messages, and (undelayed) messages that have already arrived at their destination and t is the current *global time*. A delayed message $[m, d]$ in such a configuration *conf* acts as a *timer*, i.e., it will become the arrived message m at global time $t+d$. As in Real-Time Maude [65], in a PMaude module there are two kinds of rules: (i) 0-*time* rules, like the above PMaude rule for a server to answer a client's request (meaning that a message is received by its addressee *as soon as it arrives*); and (ii) a discrete-event-simulation-like *time-advancing* rule, which advances the global time t by the smallest delay d_{min} in the subconfiguration of delayed messages and decreases by d_{min} the delays in all delayed messages.

A crucial property in many statistical model checking algorithms (see [5] for a survey) is the *absence of non-determinism* (AND) assumption. That is, the assumption that the system is *purely probabilistic*. In a probabilistic rewrite theory this means that in any reachable state (i) it will never be the case that more than one rewrite rule can ever be applied, and (ii) if one such rule can be applied, it will not be applicable in more than one way. For PMaude specifications, under reasonable assumptions on the Actor system (see [44]), this exactly means that at any given global time t either (i) all the messages in *conf* are delayed messages with non-zero delays; or (ii) there is *at most one* undelayed message in the configuration. How can this be ensured? If the probability distributions used in the PMaude rewrite rules are *continuous* distributions, reachable configurations in the PMaude system will always have either no undelayed message or at most one such message with probability 1, and this will ensure the AND property. Intuitively, this is so because the probability that two delayed messages in a reachable configuration *conf* have the same delay d is 0 if the probability distribution those delays are chosen from is continuous.

PMaude Actor system specifications therefore assume that the probability distributions in their rules are always continuous. Thanks to the AND property thus ensured, this makes possible the formal analysis of the quantitive properties of such probabilistic Actor systems by statistical model checking. As mentioned above, such properties can be specified in the QuaTEx quantitative probabilistic temporal logic [4]. I refer to [4] for details about QuaTEx and its statistical model checking algorithm and summarize here the basic ideas. In a standard temporal logic a formula evaluates to a true/false value. This is because the basic *state predicates* mentioned in the formula are Boolean-valued predicates. By contrast, in QuaTEx the analog of state predicates are so-called *state expressions*, whose values can be of various types but are often *real-valued*, so as to measure some *quantitative property* of the current state. In standard model checking a temporal logic formula φ evaluates to a true/false value in any given computation path from an initial state. Instead, for a PMaude Actor system a QuaTEx formula φ evaluates to a real number value in any given computation path from an initial state. Such formulas may, for example, express properties such as latency, throughput, various QoS properties, and also probabilities.

How is a QuaTEx formula φ evaluated from an initial state of a PMaude Actor system by statistical model checking? The PMaude specification itself is *not* executable. However, its path computations from an initial state can be *simulated* by well-known *sampling* methods that sample the values of a given probability distribution, i.e., make choices about their random values that simulate the given distribution. Let me introduce some notation. Originally we may begin (as in our client-server example) with a standard, executable Actor rewrite theory $\mathcal{R}$. By providing a specification Π of how message delays in the arrival of messages sent by actors executing various rewrite rules in $\mathcal{R}$ are governed by probability distributions (as we did for our client-server rule example) we arrive at a corresponding, non-executable PMaude specification $P(\mathcal{R})_\Pi$. Using sampling methods we can then transform $P(\mathcal{R})_\Pi$ into an *executable* rewrite theory $Sim(P(\mathcal{R})_\Pi)$, where the value of the delay d governed by the probability distribution $\pi(\boldsymbol{x})$ which appeared in a PMaude probabilistic rewrite rule as the clause *where* $d := \pi(\boldsymbol{x})$ is now computed by sampling $\pi(\boldsymbol{x})$. This, however, is not yet enough to quantitatively analyze our probabilistic Actor system. Why not? Because the QuaTEx formula φ will often use state expressions that have not been defined anywhere, just as some standard temporal logic formula φ expressing some qualitative property of the Actor system $\mathcal{R}$ may use state predicates that have not been defined in $\mathcal{R}$. Furthermore, we need to define not only the desired state expressions, but also the *events* (associated with the application of specific Actor rewrite rules by means of a map m) which we want to *observe* in the configuration. This can be done by enriching a configuration *conf* with a *monitor object* that, when a rule is applied, logs the event associated with it and the current global time. The result of adding such a monitor object can itself be described as a further executable rewrite theory $M(Sim(P(\mathcal{R})_\Pi), m)$, which is the one in which a QuaTEx formula φ can be evaluated. In summary, as described in detail by Liu, Meseguer, Ölveczky, Zhang and Basin in [44], we have a sequence of theory transformations:

$$\mathcal{R} \mapsto P(\mathcal{R})_\Pi \mapsto Sim(P(\mathcal{R})_\Pi) \mapsto M(Sim(P(\mathcal{R})_\Pi), m)$$

As mentioned in §3.3 and proved in [44], the theory transformations P, Sim and M are *formal patterns* that enjoy associated assume-guarantee properties such as the following: (i) if $\mathcal{R}$ is a generalized Actor rewrite theory satisfying the requirements in [44], then $P(\mathcal{R})_\Pi$ enjoys the AND property; (ii) the theory $Sim(P(\mathcal{R})_\Pi)$ *faithfully simulates* $P(\mathcal{R})_\Pi$ by sampling using the *inverse transform method* [35,67]; and (iii) $Sim(P(\mathcal{R})_\Pi)$ and $M(Sim(P(\mathcal{R})_\Pi), m)$ are *bisimilar*. Until the publication of [44], the passage from $\mathcal{R}$ to $M(Sim(P(\mathcal{R})_\Pi), m)$ needed to be *programmed by hand* for each Actor rewrite theory $\mathcal{R}$, a labor-intensive and error-prone process. Thanks to the P, Sim and M transformations, such a passage has now been *automated*, making the quantitative analysis of Actor systems much easier to carry out correctly by users not familiar with the inner details and techniques involved in those transformations.

Let me finish this section by briefly summarizing how the value of a QuaTEx formula φ from an initial state in a PMaude specification $P(\mathcal{R})_\Pi$ is estimated by statistical model checking, the tools currently available for this, and some of the applications in which they have been used. As mentioned above, the rewrite theory used is $M(Sim(P(\mathcal{R})_\Pi), m)$. The QuaTEx formula φ may require defining some state expressions over the state of $M(Sim(P(\mathcal{R})_\Pi), m)$; φ can then be evaluated from the given initial state by Monte Carlo simulation, that is, by generating as many computation paths in $M(Sim(P(\mathcal{R})_\Pi), m)$ from the initial state as needed (which of course involves sampling the given probability distribution each time a probabilistic rewrite rule in the path is applied) and computing the real number to which φ evaluates to in each such path. The number of paths that have to be generated to compute the expected value of φ from the given initial state up to a given statistical confidence level $(1 - \alpha)$ depends on two user-specified parameters α and δ, so that the expected value of φ is iteratively evaluated w.r.t. those parameters until a value v is obtained which lies in the confidence interval $[v-\frac{\delta}{2}, v+\frac{\delta}{2}]$ of size δ with confidence $(1-\alpha)$.

The statistical model checking tools available to compute the expected value of a QuaTEx formula φ from an initial state of a PMaude specification w.r.t. parameters α and δ are those in the VeStA family of tools [4,7,73], as well as the more recent QMaude tool [71].

Quantitative analysis of Actor systems in Maude by means of statistical model checking has been performed for a wide range of applications, including: (i) *sensor networks protocols* [41]; (ii) *security applications* such as: DDoS protection, using the onion skin and Russian dolls formal patterns [8,31] already mentioned in §3; a secure bandwidth reservation algorithm [83]; and the DNS protocol [43]; (iii) various industrial and academic distributed data bases, including those described in the survey [15] as well as the more recent work in [48]; and (iv) the *P* domain-specific language for specifying asynchronous, event-driven systems [29].

6 Designing, Verifying and Implementing Open Systems

Designing and implementing open distributed systems of high quality that meet needed qualitative and quantitative formal requirements is challenging. To begin with, distributed systems are notoriously hard to debug and get right and their performance is often only known after they are implemented. Furthermore, the heterogeneity of open systems makes the challenge even greater. As I have argued in [62], there is overwhelming evidence that one way *not* to meet this challenge is the usual **post facto** approach, where formal verification is performed, if at all, after the system has been implemented. I have also argued in [62] and illustrated with substantial case studies there that a much more promising approach is an **ab origine** one, where distributed system designs are captured early on by *formal executable specifications* and their qualitative and quantitative properties are formally analyzed *as early as possible* in the system design process.

Maude is well positioned to naturally span the entire spectrum from early design and verification to implementation. This is because Maude is *simultaneously* an executable formal specification language based on rewriting logic which is ideally suited for capturing concurrent system designs *and* a very high level, efficient declarative programming language to program distributed systems. Furthermore, as explained in §3, formal patterns can greatly increase the modularity and reusability of designs and can drastically reduce verification efforts. And, as detailed in §4–5, both the qualitative and quantitative properties of distributed system designs captured in Maude can be formally analyzed by various tools in Maude's formal environment.

I first explain in §6.1 how distributed system designs captured as Actor systems in Maude and verified w.r.t. their qualitative and quantitative properties can be automatically transformed into correct-by-construction distributed implementations by means of the *D-transformation* formal pattern [48]. Then, in §6.2 I broaden the picture to explain how open heterogeneous systems—many of whose components need not be programmed in Maude or can even be physical devices or humans interacting with the system—can be designed, verified and implemented following the same methodology.

6.1 From Maude Actor System Designs to Correct Implementations

The D transformation automatically transforms a Maude actor program (i.e., an actor-based rewrite theory $\mathcal{R}$) which captures an Actor system design into a distributed Maude implementation of it by: (i) mapping the various actors into specified machines; and (ii) providing the required *middleware* (also written in Maude as so-called *mediator* objects) for communication between objects across different machines. The actual communication across machines is supported by Maude's TCP/IP *socket objects* [19], which provide message-passing communication between Maude objects located in different machines. Pictorially, if we represent actors by circles and messages by envelopes traveling between actors, we can visualize the D transformation by means of the following figure in [48]:

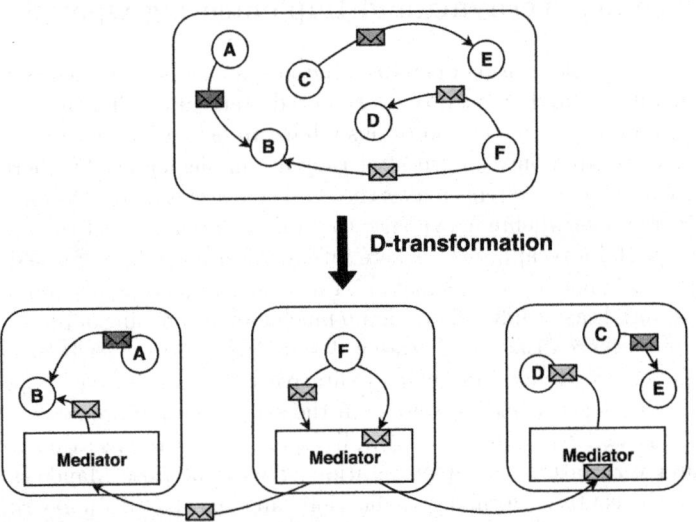

The D transformation has the form:

$$D : (\mathcal{R}, init, di) \mapsto D(\mathcal{R}, init, di)$$

where:

- $\mathcal{R}$ is a *Maude generalized actor system module*
- *init* is an *initial state* in $\mathcal{R}$
- di is a *distribution information function* $di : id_{obj} \mapsto (ip, session\#)$, and
- $D(\mathcal{R}, init, di)$ is the Maude program deployment that distributes $\mathcal{R}$ according to di with initial state $init_{D_{di}}(ip, i)$.

The main formal guarantee provided by the D-transformation is the following (see [48]):

Theorem 1. $\mathcal{R}$ and $D(\mathcal{R}, init, di)$ *are stuttering bisimilar.*

Therefore, for any formula $\varphi \in CTL^* \setminus \bigcirc$ we have:

$$(\mathcal{R}, init) \models \varphi \Leftrightarrow (D(\mathcal{R}, init, di), init_{D_{di}}(ip, i)) \models \varphi.$$

That is, all $CTL^* \setminus \bigcirc$ properties already verified about the mathematical model $\mathcal{R}$ from the initial state $init$ are also satisfied by the distributed implementation $D(\mathcal{R}, init, di)$ [49]. The trusted code base includes the Maude implementation itself and the correct implementation of the TCP/IP protocol used by Maude's TCP/IP socket objects.

The D transformation has been automated and prototyped in Maude and has been experimentally validated through case studies [48]. The D prototype is a proof of concept that should be optimized in a mature tool. The experience gained so far suggests two encouraging advantages: (1) Although the efficiency of the automatically generated distributed Maude implementation is currently not as high as that of high-quality implementations in conventional languages, its code size is much smaller. (2) Another attractive advantage of the D transformation is that it is possible to develop and thoroughly analyze both the logical and the quantitative properties of a *new* distributed system design before it is implemented, and then automatically generate a correct-by-construction distributed implementation of that system design in Maude using D. This has been demonstrated for ROLA [46], a new distributed transaction system occupying a previously unexplored point in the spectrum of tradeoffs between performance and database consistency, whose design was captured in Maude and was formally analyzed w.r.t. its qualitative and quantitative properties before it was implemented using the D transformation. The experimental evaluation of ROLA's D implementation confirmed the good performance properties that had been formerly predicted by statistical model checking using its Maude design [48].

6.2 From Open System Designs to Correct Implementations

The D transformation can automatically generate a Maude distributed implementation of an Actor system from its previously verified Maude design, but it does not support the design, verification and distributed implementation of *open systems* [39], which are heterogeneous, have components programmed in different languages, and may also involve physical devices or humans interacting with the system. However, in [24] the design, verification and distributed implementation methodology supported by the D transformation has been recently extended to open systems. The main reason why this has been possible is that in the last two decades Maude has been extended to support message-passing interaction with a wide variety of *external objects* (see [20, 24] for detailed descriptions), including: (i) the already mentioned TCP/IP *socket objects*; (ii) *file* I/O objects; (iii) *directory* objects; (iv) Unix *process* objects; (v) *timer* objects; (vi) external objects definable using the Maude as a library infrastructure [68]; and (vii) Maude metainterpreters, which, while not being properly "external" to Maude, provide a way for different Maude interpreters to concurrently interact with each other.

Besides the flexibility of asynchronous message passing communication, another great advantage offered by the Actor model for designing and implementing open systems is that it *abstracts away* the inner details of an actor's local state and implementation. This of course means that different actors in an open system may be implemented in different programming languages, provided that they agree on the shared *message signature* specifying the messages by which they communicate with each other. Using this insight, the D transformation methodology for designing, verifying and implementing Actor systems in Maude has been extended in [24] to a more general Maude-based methodology for designing, verifying and implementing heterogeneous open systems based on the following three steps:

1. **Maude Design**. The open system is specified in Maude as an actor rewrite theory $\mathcal{R} = (\Sigma, E, R)$ without any distinctions about its actual *heterogeneity*, that is, disregarding the choices about which actors will be implemented in Maude or in other programming languages, or may be actual physical devices or humans interacting with the system. The typed signature Σ of function symbols of such an open system design includes of course the *message subsignature*, Σ_{Msg} which provides an *abstract API* for (eventually heterogeneous) actors to communicate with each other. A key point about the methodology is that Σ_{Msg} *never changes*: it will be the same for the open system's design and for its implementation.

    Regarding the equations E and the actor rules R, the design $\mathcal{R}$ *fully specifies* the Maude actors, that is, those actors that will remain Maude actors in the implementation, and may *partially specify* those actors that, from Maude's point of view, will be *external objects*. From the behavioral point of view what this partial specification amounts to is an *over-approximation* of behaviors: the observable behaviors in a correct open system implementation will be a *subset* of those in their design $\mathcal{R}$.

2. **Verification of the Design**. Before the open system is implemented it can, and should, be formally analyzed with respect to both its qualitative and quantitative properties. For example, its safety properties may be verified by explicit-state or symbolic model checking techniques. Such safety properties will then hold of an implementation that is over-approximated by its design $\mathcal{R}$. Likewise, using the P, Sim and M transformations, the design's qualitative properties can be estimated by statistical model checking.

3. **Open System Implementation**. The open system's heterogeneous distributed implementation is achieved by keeping the same message signature Σ_{Msg} which specified the abstract API between actors of different classes in the design $\mathcal{R}$, but providing a corresponding *concrete API* for it, precisely by associating to each non-Maude actor a corresponding *external object interface* in Maude that will support the two-way communication between

Maude actors and other actors.[5] Once external object interfaces are defined in Maude by their corresponding *external object definitions*, the open system can then be deployed on a given infrastructure, which may include both networked machines and physical devices or humans interacting with the system, by a method analogous to the one used in the D transformation; that is, by mapping the various actors to their underlying implementations running on specific machines and devices. The implementation process can thus be decomposed into two steps: (i) replace each non-Maude actor class in the design $\mathcal{R}$ by a corresponding external object definition, always preserving the same message signature Σ_{Msg}; and (ii) deploy the heterogeneous system thus implemented on specific machines and devices.

The just-mentioned methodology to design and implement heterogeneous open systems in Maude was proposed in [24] and was illustrated by a Patient Controlled Analgesia (PCA) system case study, depicted in [24] by means of the picture below, which describes the different actors involved: patients, doctors and nurses, medical devices and sensors, GUIs, a database, and Maude objects.

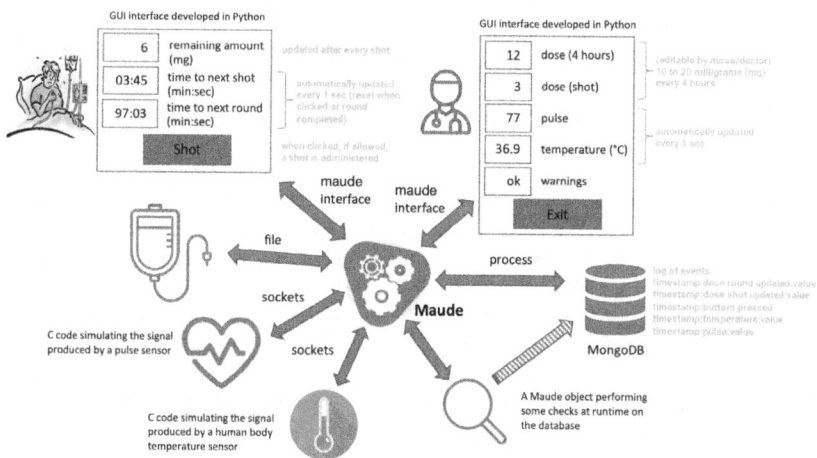

The entire code implementing this open system is available in the GitHub repository referenced in [24]. All the steps (1)–(3) of the above-described methodology as well as the Maude external objects used in the above case study are described in detail in [24]. The methodology itself is clearly automatable as a formal pattern that generalizes the D transformation. However, the detailed definition of such a formal pattern as well as its automation was outside the scope of [24] and has been left for future work.

---

[5] At present the methodology does not support *direct* communication between two heterogeneous non-Maude actors having different implementations, although *indirect* communication through Maude actors used as proxies is currently possible.

7 Conclusion and Future Directions

I have explained some of the ways in which Actors and rewriting logic and Maude have enriched each other for 35 years as the result of very fruitful long-term collaborations between researchers in both fields, including Gul Agha and myself. I have focused on topics such as software composition methods for distributed systems, formal verification of Maude Actor systems, PMaude specification of probabilistic Actor systems and statistical model checking verification of their qualitative properties, and automatic generation of correct-by-construction implementations of Maude Actor system designs. I have covered many application areas along the way, but certainly not all of them. A flagrant omission is the area of *real-time* Actor systems, but fear not: you can consult the excellent survey on this topic by Kyungmin Bae, Carlos Olarte and Peter Ölveczky in this Festschrift volume. I have also omitted applications to: (i) distributed algorithms, for which I refer to Ölveczky's book [66]; (ii) browser security, for which I refer to the papers [18,72,77]; and (iii) network algorithms for which, besides the few references here, I refer to the references in [57] and the paper [45].

The future looks bright. I expect new developments in several areas, including: (i) software composition methods for distributed systems; (ii) formal verification methods and tools for Actor systems; (iii) PMaude and statistical model checking of its specifications; and (iv) Maude as a programming language for developing correct-by-construction implementations of open Actor systems.

Acknowledgments. I have borrowed and adapted some material from several previous papers of mine, including [58,60,62]. The work I have described is joint work at the intersection of two areas. I have tried to mention and cite many of the researchers involved and have pointed out some omissions I am aware of. I apologize in advance for any other work that I may have inadvertently omitted to cite. I thank Francisco Durán, Peter Ölveczky, Carolyn Talcott and the reviewers for their very helpful comments that have allowed me to improve the paper.

Disclosure of Interests. The author has no competing interests to declare that are relevant to the content of this article.

References

1. Agha, G.: Actors. MIT Press (1986)
2. Agha, G., Hewitt, C.: Concurrent programming using actors. In: Yonezawa, A., Tokoro, M. (eds.) Object-Oriented Concurrent Programming, pp. 37–53. MIT Press (1988)
3. Agha, G., Frølund, S., Panwar, R., Sturman, D.: A linguistic framework for dynamic composition of dependability protocols. In: Landwehr, C.E., Randell, B., Simoncini, L. (eds.) Dependable Computing for Critical Applications 3, pp. 345–363. Springer Vienna (1993)
4. Agha, G., Meseguer, J., Sen, K.: PMaude: rewrite-based specification language for probabilistic object systems. Electr. Notes Theor. Comput. Sci. **153**(2), 213–239 (2006)

5. Agha, G., Palmskog, K.: A survey of statistical model checking. ACM Trans. Model. Comput. Simul. **28**(1), 6:1–6:39 (2018)
6. Alpuente, M., Cuenca-Ortega, A., Escobar, S., Meseguer, J.: A partial evaluation framework for order-sorted equational programs modulo axioms. J. Log. Algebraic Methods Program. **110**, 100501 (2020)
7. AlTurki, M., Meseguer, J.: PVESTA: a parallel statistical model checking and quantitative analysis tool. In: Corradini, A., Klin, B., Cîrstea, C. (eds.) CALCO 2011. LNCS, vol. 6859, pp. 386–392. Springer, Heidelberg (2011). https://doi.org/10.1007/978-3-642-22944-2_28
8. AlTurki, M., Meseguer, J., Gunter, C.: Probabilistic modeling and analysis of DoS protection for the ASV protocol. Electr. Notes Theor. Comput. Sci. **234**, 3–18 (2009)
9. Bae, K., Escobar, S., Meseguer, J.: Abstract logical model checking of infinite-state systems using narrowing. In: Rewriting Techniques and Applications (RTA 2013). LIPIcs, vol. 21, pp. 81–96. Schloss Dagstuhl–Leibniz-Zentrum fuer Informatik (2013)
10. Bae, K., Krisiloff, J., Meseguer, J., Ölveczky, P.C.: Designing and verifying distributed cyber-physical systems using Multirate PALS: an airplane turning control system case study. Sci. Comput. Program. **103**, 13–50 (2015)
11. Bae, K., Meseguer, J.: Model checking linear temporal logic of rewriting formulas under localized fairness. Sci. Comput. Program. **99**, 193–234 (2015)
12. Bae, K., Meseguer, J., Ölveczky, P.C.: Formal patterns for multirate distributed real-time systems. Sci. Comput. Program. **91**, 3–44 (2014)
13. Bae, K., Ölveczky, P.C., Kong, S., Gao, S., Clarke, E.M.: SMT-based analysis of virtually synchronous distributed hybrid systems. In: Proceedings 19th International Conference on Hybrid Systems: Computation and Control, HSCC 2016, pp. 145–154 (2016)
14. Bae, K., Ölveczky, P.C., Meseguer, J.: Definition, semantics, and analysis of multirate synchronous AADL. In: Jones, C., Pihlajasaari, P., Sun, J. (eds.) FM 2014. LNCS, vol. 8442, pp. 94–109. Springer, Cham (2014). https://doi.org/10.1007/978-3-319-06410-9_7
15. Bobba, R., Grov, J., Gupta, I., Liu, S., Meseguer, J., Ölveczky, P.C., Skeirik, S.: Survivability: design, formal modeling, and validation of cloud storage systems using Maude. In: Campbell, R.H., Kamhoua, C.A., Kwiat, K.A. (eds.) Assured Cloud Computing, chap. 2, pp. 10–48. Wiley-IEEE Computer Society Press (2018)
16. Bruni, R., Meseguer, J.: Semantic foundations for generalized rewrite theories. Theor. Comput. Sci. **360**(1–3), 386–414 (2006)
17. Chadha, R., Gunter, C.A., Meseguer, J., Shankesi, R., Viswanathan, M.: Modular preservation of safety properties by cookie-based DoS-protection wrappers. In: Barthe, G., de Boer, F.S. (eds.) FMOODS 2008. LNCS, vol. 5051, pp. 39–58. Springer, Heidelberg (2008). https://doi.org/10.1007/978-3-540-68863-1_4
18. Chen, S., Meseguer, J., Sasse, R., Wang, H.J., Wang, Y.M.: A systematic approach to uncover security flaws in GUI logic. In: IEEE Symposium on Security and Privacy, pp. 71–85. IEEE (2007)
19. All About Maude - A High-Performance Logical Framework. LNCS, vol. 4350. Springer, Heidelberg (2007). https://doi.org/10.1007/978-3-540-71999-1
20. Clavel, M., et al.: Maude manual (version 3.5) (2024). https://maude.cs.illinois.edu/manual.pdf
21. Clavel, M., Meseguer, J., Palomino, M.: Reflection in membership equational logic, many-sorted equational logic, Horn logic with equality, and rewriting logic. Theoret. Comput. Sci. **373**, 70–91 (2007)

22. Denker, G., Meseguer, J., Talcott, C.: Rewriting semantics of meta-objects and composable distributed services. In: ENTCS 36, Proceedings of the 3rd. International Workshop on Rewriting Logic and its Applications. Elsevier (2000)
23. Durán, F., Eker, S., Escobar, S., Martí-Oliet, N., Meseguer, J., Rubio, R., Talcott, C.L.: Programming and symbolic computation in Maude. J. Log. Algebraic Methods Program. **110**, 100497 (2020)
24. Durán, F., Eker, S., Escobar, S., Martí-Oliet, N., Meseguer, J., Rubio, R., Talcott, C.L.: Programming open distributed systems in Maude. In: Bruni, A., Momigliano, A., Pradella, M., Rossi, M., Cheney, J. (eds.) Proceedings of the 26th International Symposium on Principles and Practice of Declarative Programming, PPDP 2024, Milano, Italy, 9-11 September 2024, pp. 7:1–7:12. ACM (2024). https://doi.org/10.1145/3678232.3678237
25. Durán, F., Eker, S., Lincoln, P., Meseguer, J.: Principles of Mobile Maude. In: Kotz, D., Mattern, F. (eds.) ASA/MA -2000. LNCS, vol. 1882, pp. 73–85. Springer, Heidelberg (2000). https://doi.org/10.1007/978-3-540-45347-5_7
26. Durán, F., Lucas, S., Meseguer, J.: MTT: The Maude Termination Tool (System Description). In: Armando, A., Baumgartner, P., Dowek, G. (eds.) IJCAR 2008. LNCS (LNAI), vol. 5195, pp. 313–319. Springer, Heidelberg (2008). https://doi.org/10.1007/978-3-540-71070-7_27
27. Durán, F., Lucas, S., Meseguer, J.: Termination Modulo Combinations of Equational Theories. In: Ghilardi, S., Sebastiani, R. (eds.) FroCoS 2009. LNCS (LNAI), vol. 5749, pp. 246–262. Springer, Heidelberg (2009). https://doi.org/10.1007/978-3-642-04222-5_15
28. Durán, F., Meseguer, J.: On the Church-Rosser and coherence properties of conditional order-sorted rewrite theories. J. Algebraic and Logic Programming **81**, 816–850 (2012)
29. Durán, F., Ramírez, C., Rocha, C., Pozas, N.: A rewriting logic semantics for the analysis of P programs. J. Log. Algebraic Methods Program. **144**, 101048 (2025)
30. Durán, F.J., Escobar, S., Meseguer, J., Sapiña, J.: NuITP: An inductive theorem prover for equational program verification. In: Bruni, A., Momigliano, A., Pradella, M., Rossi, M., Cheney, J. (eds.) Proceedings of the 26th International Symposium on Principles and Practice of Declarative Programming, PPDP 2024, Milano, Italy, 9-11 September 2024, pp. 6:1–6:11. ACM (2024), https://doi.org/10.1145/3678232.3678236
31. Eckhardt, J., Mühlbauer, T., AlTurki, M., Meseguer, J., Wirsing, M.: Stable availability under denial of service attacks through formal patterns. In: de Lara, J., Zisman, A. (eds.) FASE 2012. LNCS, vol. 7212, pp. 78–93. Springer, Heidelberg (2012). https://doi.org/10.1007/978-3-642-28872-2_6
32. Futatsugi, K., Diaconescu, R.: CafeOBJ Report. World Scientific (1998)
33. Galán, D., García, V., Escobar, S., Meadows, C.A., Meseguer, J.: Protocol dialects as formal patterns. In: Tsudik, G., Conti, M., Liang, K., Smaragdakis, G. (eds.) Computer Security - ESORICS 2023 - 28th European Symposium on Research in Computer Security, The Hague, The Netherlands, 25-29 September 2023, Proceedings, Part II. LNCS, vol. 14345, pp. 42–61. Springer (2023). https://doi.org/10.1007/978-3-031-51476-0_
34. Goguen, J., Meseguer, J.: Order-sorted algebra I: equational deduction for multiple inheritance, overloading, exceptions and partial operations. Theoret. Comput. Sci. **105**, 217–273 (1992)
35. Grimmett, G., Stirzaker, D.: Probability and Random Processes (3rd edn.). Oxford University Press (2001)

36. Gutiérrez, R., Meseguer, J., Rocha, C.: Order-sorted equality enrichments modulo axioms. Sci. Comput. Program. **99**, 235–261 (2015)
37. Gutierrez-Nolasco, S., Venkatasubramanian, N., Talcott, C.: A semantic model for safe protocol interaction. In: Proceedings of the 2006 ACM Symposium on Applied Computing, pp. 1599–1600. SAC 2006, Association for Computing Machinery (2006)
38. Hendrix, J., Meseguer, J., Ohsaki, H.: A Sufficient Completeness Checker for Linear Order-Sorted Specifications Modulo Axioms. In: Furbach, U., Shankar, N. (eds.) IJCAR 2006. LNCS (LNAI), vol. 4130, pp. 151–155. Springer, Heidelberg (2006). https://doi.org/10.1007/11814771_14
39. Hewitt, C., de Jong, P.: Open systems. In: Brodie, M.L., Mylopoulos, J., Schmidt, J.W. (eds.) Perspectives from Artificial Intelligence, Databases, and Programming Languages, pp. 147–164. Springer (1982)
40. Kant, G., Laarman, A., Meijer, J., van de Pol, J., Blom, S., van Dijk, T.: LTSmin: high-performance language-independent model checking. In: Baier, C., Tinelli, C. (eds.) TACAS 2015. LNCS, vol. 9035, pp. 692–707. Springer, Heidelberg (2015). https://doi.org/10.1007/978-3-662-46681-0_61
41. Katelman, M., Meseguer, J., Hou, J.: Redesign of the LMST wireless sensor protocol through formal modeling and statistical model checking. In: Barthe, G., de Boer, F.S. (eds.) FMOODS 2008. LNCS, vol. 5051, pp. 150–169. Springer, Heidelberg (2008). https://doi.org/10.1007/978-3-540-68863-1_10
42. Kumar, N., Sen, K., Meseguer, J., Agha, G.: Probabilistic rewrite theories: Unifying models, logics and tools. Tech. Rep. UIUCDCS-R-2003-2347, CS Dept., University of Illinois at Urbana-Champaign (2003). http://formalmethods.web.engr.illinois.edu/papers/SKMAfme.pdf
43. Liu, S., Duan, H., Heimes, L., Bearzi, M., Vieli, J., Basin, D.A., Perrig, A.: A formal framework for end-to-end DNS resolution. In: Schulzrinne, H., Misra, V., Kohler, E., Maltz, D.A. (eds.) Proceedings of the ACM SIGCOMM 2023 Conference, ACM SIGCOMM 2023, New York, NY, USA, 10-14 September 2023, pp. 932–949. ACM (2023)
44. Liu, S., Meseguer, J., Ölveczky, P.C., Zhang, M., Basin, D.A.: Bridging the semantic gap between qualitative and quantitative models of distributed systems. Proc. ACM Program. Lang. **6**(OOPSLA2), 315–344 (2022)
45. Liu, S., Ölveczky, P.C., Meseguer, J.: Modeling and analyzing mobile ad hoc networks in Real-Time Maude. J. Log. Algebr. Meth. Program. **85**, 34–66 (2016)
46. Liu, S., Ölveczky, P.C., Wang, Q., Gupta, I., Meseguer, J.: Read atomic transactions with prevention of lost updates: ROLA and its formal analysis. Formal Aspects Comput. **31**(5), 503–540 (2019). https://doi.org/10.1007/s00165-019-00489-w
47. Liu, S., Ölveczky, P.C., Zhang, M., Wang, Q., Meseguer, J.: Automatic Analysis of Consistency Properties of Distributed Transaction Systems in Maude. In: Vojnar, T., Zhang, L. (eds.) TACAS 2019. LNCS, vol. 11428, pp. 40–57. Springer, Cham (2019). https://doi.org/10.1007/978-3-030-17465-1_3
48. Liu, S., Sandur, A., Meseguer, J., Ölveczky, P.C., Wang, Q.: Generating correct-by-construction distributed implementations from formal Maude designs. In: Lee, R., Jha, S., Mavridou, A., Giannakopoulou, D. (eds.) NFM 2020. LNCS, vol. 12229, pp. 22–40. Springer, Cham (2020). https://doi.org/10.1007/978-3-030-55754-6_2
49. Meseguer, J., Palomino, M., Martí-Oliet, N.: Algebraic simulations. J. Log. Algebr. Program. **79**(2), 103–143 (2010)

50. Meseguer, J., Talcott, C.: Semantic models for distributed object reflection. In: Magnusson, B. (ed.) ECOOP 2002. LNCS, vol. 2374, pp. 1–36. Springer, Heidelberg (2002). https://doi.org/10.1007/3-540-47993-7_1
51. Meseguer, J.: A logical theory of concurrent objects. In: ECOOP-OOPSLA 1990 Conference on Object-Oriented Programming, Ottawa, Canada, October 1990, pp. 101–115. ACM (1990)
52. Meseguer, J.: Rewriting as a unified model of concurrency. Tech. Rep. SRI-CSL-90-02, SRI International, Computer Science Laboratory (1990), revised June 1990
53. Meseguer, J.: Conditional rewriting logic as a unified model of concurrency. Theoret. Comput. Sci. **96**(1), 73–155 (1992)
54. Meseguer, J.: A logical theory of concurrent objects and its realization in the Maude language. In: Agha, G., Wegner, P., Yonezawa, A. (eds.) Research Directions in Concurrent Object-Oriented Programming, pp. 314–390. MIT Press (1993)
55. Meseguer, J.: Solving the inheritance anomaly in concurrent object-oriented programming. In: Nierstrasz, O.M. (ed.) ECOOP 1993. LNCS, vol. 707, pp. 220–246. Springer, Heidelberg (1993). https://doi.org/10.1007/3-540-47910-4_13
56. Meseguer, J.: Rewriting logic as a semantic framework for concurrency: a progress report. In: Montanari, U., Sassone, V. (eds.) CONCUR 1996. LNCS, vol. 1119, pp. 331–372. Springer, Heidelberg (1996). https://doi.org/10.1007/3-540-61604-7_64
57. Meseguer, J.: Twenty years of rewriting logic. J. Algebraic Logic Programm. **81**, 721–781 (2012)
58. Meseguer, J.: Taming distributed system complexity through formal patterns. Sci. Comput. Program. **83**, 3–34 (2014)
59. Meseguer, J.: Generalized rewrite theories, coherence completion, and symbolic methods. J. Log. Algebraic Methods Program. **110**, 100483 (2020)
60. Meseguer, J.: Building correct-by-construction systems with formal patterns. In: Madeira, A., Martins, M.A. (eds.) Recent Trends in Algebraic Development Techniques - 26th IFIP WG 1.3 International Workshop, WADT 2022, Aveiro, Portugal, 28-30 June 2022, Revised Selected Papers. LNCS, vol. 13710, pp. 3–24. Springer, Cham (2022). https://doi.org/10.1007/978-3-031-43345-0_1
61. Meseguer, J.: Checking sufficient completeness by inductive theorem proving. In: Bae, K. (ed.) Rewriting Logic and Its Applications - 14th International Workshop, WRLA@ETAPS 2022, Munich, Germany, 2-3 April 2022, Revised Selected Papers. LNCS, vol. 13252, pp. 171–190. Springer (2022). https://doi.org/10.1007/978-3-031-12441-9_9
62. Meseguer, J.: Capturing system designs with formal executable specifications. In: Boronat, A., Fraser, G. (eds.) Fundamental Approaches to Software Engineering - 28th International Conference, FASE 2025. LNCS, vol. 15693, pp. 1–32. Springer (2025). https://doi.org/10.1007/978-3-031-90900-9_1
63. Meseguer, J., Ölveczky, P.C.: Formalization and correctness of the PALS architectural pattern for distributed real-time systems. Theor. Comput. Sci. **451**, 1–37 (2012)
64. Miller, S., Cofer, D., Sha, L., Meseguer, J., Al-Nayeem, A.: Implementing logical synchrony in integrated modular avionics. In: Proceedings of the 28th Digital Avionics Systems Conference. IEEE (2009)
65. Ölveczky, P.C., Meseguer, J.: Semantics and pragmatics of Real-Time Maude. Higher-Order Symbolic Comput. **20**(1–2), 161–196 (2007)
66. Ölveczky, P.C.: Designing Reliable Distributed Systems. UTCS, Springer, London (2017). https://doi.org/10.1007/978-1-4471-6687-0
67. Rubinstein, R., Kroese, D.: Simulation and the Monte Carlo Method, 3rd edn. Wiley (2017)

68. Rubio, R.: Maude as a library: An efficient all-purpose programming interface. In: Bae, K. (ed.) Rewriting Logic and Its Applications - 14th International Workshop, WRLA@ETAPS 2022. LNCS, vol. 13252, pp. 274–294. Springer (2022). https://doi.org/10.1007/978-3-031-12441-9_14
69. Rubio, R., Martí-Oliet, N., Pita, I., Verdejo, A.: Strategies, model checking and branching-time properties in Maude. J. Log. Algebraic Methods Program. **123**, 100700 (2021)
70. Rubio, R., Martí-Oliet, N., Pita, I., Verdejo, A.: Model checking strategy-controlled systems in rewriting logic. Autom. Softw. Eng. **29**(1), 7 (2022)
71. Rubio, R., Martí-Oliet, N., Pita, I., Verdejo, A.: QMaude: quantitative specification and verification in rewriting logic. In: Chechik, M., Katoen, J., Leucker, M. (eds.) Formal Methods - 25th International Symposium, FM 2023, Lübeck, Germany, 6-10 March 2023, Proceedings. LNCS, vol. 14000, pp. 240–259. Springer (2023). https://doi.org/10.1007/978-3-031-27481-7_15
72. Sasse, R., King, S.T., Meseguer, J., Tang, S.: IBOS: a correct-by-construction modular browser. In: Păsăreanu, C.S., Salaün, G. (eds.) FACS 2012. LNCS, vol. 7684, pp. 224–241. Springer, Heidelberg (2013). https://doi.org/10.1007/978-3-642-35861-6_14
73. Sebastio, S., Vandin, A.: MultiVeStA: statistical model checking for discrete event simulators. In: Horváth, A., Buchholz, P., Cortellessa, V., Muscariello, L., Squillante, M.S. (eds.) 7th International Conference on Performance Evaluation Methodologies and Tools, ValueTools '13, Torino, Italy, 10-12 December 2013, pp. 310–315. ICST/ACM (2013)
74. Sen, K., Viswanathan, M., Agha, G.: Statistical model checking of black-box probabilistic systems. In: Alur, R., Peled, D.A. (eds.) CAV 2004. LNCS, vol. 3114, pp. 202–215. Springer, Heidelberg (2004). https://doi.org/10.1007/978-3-540-27813-9_16
75. Sen, K., Viswanathan, M., Agha, G.: On statistical model checking of stochastic systems. In: Etessami, K., Rajamani, S.K. (eds.) CAV 2005. LNCS, vol. 3576, pp. 266–280. Springer, Heidelberg (2005). https://doi.org/10.1007/11513988_26
76. Sen, K., Viswanathan, M., Agha, G.A.: VESTA: a statistical model-checker and analyzer for probabilistic systems. In: QEST 2005, pp. 251–252 (2005)
77. Skeirik, S., Meseguer, J., Rocha, C.: Verification of the IBOS browser security properties in reachability logic. In: Escobar, S., Martí-Oliet, N. (eds.) WRLA 2020. LNCS, vol. 12328, pp. 176–196. Springer, Cham (2020). https://doi.org/10.1007/978-3-030-63595-4_10
78. Sun, M., Meseguer, J.: Distributed real-time emulation of formally-defined patterns for safe medical device control. In: Proceedings of the RTRTS 2010. Electronic Proceedings in Theoretical Computer Science, vol. 36, pp. 158–177 (2010)
79. Sun, M., Meseguer, J.: Formal specification of button-related fault-tolerance micropatterns. In: Escobar, S. (ed.) WRLA 2014. LNCS, vol. 8663, pp. 263–279. Springer, Cham (2014). https://doi.org/10.1007/978-3-319-12904-4_15
80. Sun, M., Meseguer, J., Sha, L.: A formal pattern architecture for safe medical systems. In: Ölveczky, P.C. (ed.) WRLA 2010. LNCS, vol. 6381, pp. 157–173. Springer, Heidelberg (2010). https://doi.org/10.1007/978-3-642-16310-4_11
81. Talcott, C.: Dialects for the CoAP IoT messaging protocol. In: Giusto, C.D., Ravara, A. (eds.) COORDINATION 2025. LNCS, vol. 15731. Springer (2025). https://doi.org/10.1007/978-3-031-95589-1_9
82. Venkatasubramanian, N., Talcott, C.L., Agha, G.: A formal model for reasoning about adaptive QoS-enabled middleware. ACM Trans. Softw. Eng. Methodol. **13**(1), 86–147 (2004)

83. Weghorn, T., Liu, S., Sprenger, C., Perrig, A., Basin, D.: N-tube: formally verified secure bandwidth reservation in path-aware internet architectures. In: 2022 IEEE 35th Computer Security Foundations Symposium (CSF), pp. 147–162 (2022)

PMaude Revisited Through Probabilistic Strategies

Rubén Rubio[✉][iD], Adrián Riesco[iD], and Narciso Martí-Oliet[iD]

Facultad de Informática, Universidad Complutense de Madrid, Madrid, Spain
{rubenrub,ariesco,narciso}@ucm.es

Abstract. We introduce an automated translation from PMaude [2] and Actor PMaude specifications of probabilistic rewrite theories into ordinary strategy modules using the probabilistic extension of the Maude strategy language. QMaude [23] tools can then be used to perform probabilistic and statistical model checking on the transformed models out of the box. We also provide a small script to simulate and obtain rich traces about Actor PMaude specifications.

Keywords: PMaude · Probabilistic rewrite theories · Statistical model checking

To Gul Agha,

With gratitude and admiration. Your work has inspired colleagues, students, and friends, leaving a lasting impact on the field and on all who have had the privilege of meeting you.

1 Introduction

In modelling large-scale concurrent systems, such as communication protocols, distributed databases, or cyberphysical devices, probabilities are very helpful and almost unavoidable to obtain meaningful information about the likely behavior of those systems. Other quantitative aspects like time and energy consumption come naturally into play as relevant subjects of study. Well-known techniques for analyzing them are probabilistic [14] and statistical model checking [1], respectively based on discrete probabilistic models and Monte Carlo simulations.

Quantitative aspects can also be specified and analyzed in the context of rewriting logic [17] and its canonical implementation, Maude [6], since the release of Real-Time Maude [19] in 2000. On a different basis, Gul A. Agha, José Meseguer, and Koushik Sen published *PMaude: Rewriting-based Specification Language for Probabilistic Object Systems* [2] in 2006, which has strongly influenced later works in this field. That paper introduced

1. *probabilistic rewrite theories*, i.e. rewrite theories where the right-hand side of rules may contain variables sampled from probabilistic distributions;

2. a syntactic extension of Maude to specify them called PMaude, as well as a procedure to simulate them using built-in Maude features;
3. the Actor PMaude framework for specifying actor-based probabilistic systems with message delays;
4. the *Quantitative Temporal Expressions* language (QuaTEx) for specifying quantitative properties of executions;
5. a statistical model-checking tool called Vesta, which has been later extended to PVeSta [3], MultiVeSta [25], and the scheck command of the umaudemc tool [23].

These formalisms and tools have been used in some of the most notable applications of Maude to the analysis of real systems, like the Cassandra database [15], Google's Megastore [11], wireless sensor networks [13], hybrid systems [18], Business Process Model and Notation processes [9], P programs, which are a domain-specific language designed for specifying asynchronous, event-driven systems [8], among others [16].

However, as far as we know, the syntactic extension for specifying probabilistic rules in a declarative way, like

```
rl l => r with probability y := π(t₁, ..., tₙ) .
```

was never implemented. Instead, PMaude specifications have been traditionally written by programming the sampling of probabilistic distributions within the Maude terms as explained in [2], with the help of some auxiliary modules and the random and counter special operators. The clear advantage of this less declarative approach is that specifications are standard Maude modules, but debugging them is harder because terms become more complex and the counter symbol does not work in the useful search command.

More recently, QMaude [23] was presented as a collection of several tools to analyze quantitative aspects of Maude specifications extended with probabilistic and other quantitative information. Emphasis was put on the separation of concerns principle, so that qualitative and quantitative aspects can be checked on the same specifications with little change. Several methods for specifying probabilities are offered, including a PMaude-compatible one, and models can be checked with probabilistic and statistical methods via the pcheck and scheck commands of the umaudemc tool [22]. One of those methods is a probabilistic extension of the Maude strategy language [10] with three new operators. Strategies have been traditionally used to restrict nondeterminism in different contexts, but they can also be used to quantify it [4], hence allowing for statistical analyses.

In this work, we present an executable translation from Maude modules with probabilistic rules à la PMaude to strategy modules with ordinary rules relying on the probabilistic extension of the Maude strategy language. These specifications can then be analyzed out of the box by the probabilistic and statistical model-checking capabilities of the umaudemc tool. Moreover, they can be simulated from Maude itself using the srewrite command with predefined or custom strategies (for example, to explicitly quantify the nondeterministic choice of rules). We also translate the infrastructure for writing Actor PMaude specifications, which are naturally modelled as strategy-controlled object-oriented systems, taking advantage of the recent additions to the official distribution of Maude. A simulation tool for Actor PMaude specifications using the Maude Python library [20] is also introduced to illustrate the greater traceability of this encoding.

The rest of the paper is structured as follows: Sect. 2 introduces the fundamental concepts about Maude, PMaude, and QMaude required in the rest of the paper. Section 3 presents the translation from PMaude modules into probabilistic strategies, while Sect. 4 describes the examples used to test the transformation and how to execute them. Finally, Sect. 5 concludes and outlines some lines of future work.

2 Preliminaries

We present in this section the basic notions about Maude, PMaude, and QMaude.

2.1 Rewriting Logic

Maude [7] is a logical framework and high-performance rewriting engine. Maude modules correspond to specifications in *rewriting logic* [17], a logic of change that represents state transitions by means of *rewrite rules*. This logic is an extension of *membership equational logic* [5], an equational logic that, in addition to equations, allows the statement of *membership axioms* characterizing the elements of a sort.

Maude modules are executable rewriting logic specifications. Maude functional modules [6, Chap. 4] are executable membership equational specifications that allow the definition of sorts, subsort relations between sorts; operators for building values of these sorts, giving the sorts of their arguments and result, and which may have attributes such as being associative or commutative, for example; memberships asserting that a term has a sort; and equations asserting that terms are equal. Both memberships and equations can be conditional. The behavior of the system is defined on top of this with rewrite rules, which, unlike equations, are not necessarily confluent or terminating; this is done in system modules [7, Chap. 5]. In order to control rule application, Maude also provides a strategy language and strategy modules [10]. Two commands srewrite and dsrewrite allow rewriting terms using strategies, which are expressed by the combination of several operators. The cornerstone of the language is the rule application strategy that allows applying a rule by citing its name, with an optional substitution to be applied to the rule before matching and strategies to control rewriting in its rewriting conditions (if any). More complex strategies can be built with a concatenation operator (α ; β), nondeterministic choice (α | β), iteration (α *), conditionals (α ? β : γ), and also recursive strategies with arguments.

Maude also provides a powerful meta-level, which allows specifiers to use Maude modules and terms as standard data. This feature makes it possible to parse, manipulate, and execute user-defined modules in a simple and efficient way.

2.2 PMaude and Actor PMaude

As mentioned in the introduction, PMaude and Actor PMaude [2] are frameworks to specify general and agent-based probabilistic systems. The latter focus on removing unquantified nondeterminism by construction, and so allows estimating quantitative properties by statistical model checking. The underlying formalism is a *probabilistic rewrite theory*, a 4-tuple $\mathcal{R} = (\Sigma, E \cup A, R, \pi)$ with $(\Sigma, E \cup A, R)$ a rewrite theory with rules $r \in R$ of the form

$$r : l(\boldsymbol{x}) \to r(\boldsymbol{x}, \boldsymbol{y}) \text{ if } C(\boldsymbol{x})$$

where $\boldsymbol{x}$ is the set of variables in l, $\boldsymbol{y}$ is the set of variables in r that are not in l, C is the condition, and π is a function assigning each rule r to a function mapping each matching substitution on $\boldsymbol{x}$ to a probability distribution on the canonical substitutions on $\boldsymbol{y}$.

Actor PMaude allows specifying systems without unquantified nondeterminism using an object-oriented agent-based framework. Configurations consist of a multiset of objects, messages, scheduled objects and messages, and a global time. A `tick` rule is provided to advance the clock to the timestamp of the scheduled object to be executed next. The system evolves by exhaustively applying the probabilistic and ordinary rules in the module, and then executing `tick` to advance the clock.

$$[u]_A \xrightarrow{\neg \texttt{tick}}{}^* [v]_A \xrightarrow{\texttt{tick}} [w]_A$$

PMaude and Actor PMaude have not been used as a syntactic extension of Maude, but as a methodology and a set of helper modules to implement probabilistic rewrite theories using built-in Maude resources. The mechanism for random sampling within a declarative language relies on two special operators: `random(n)`, which gives the n-th element of a pseudorandom sequence fixed when the Maude interpreter starts, and a `counter` symbol that the Maude interpreter rewrites to n when encountered for the n-th time. This latter symbol only works with the `rewrite` commands, but not with the `search` command, hence making debugging very hard. In summary, tools like PVeSta and MultiVeSta follow the Actor PMaude mechanics and expect an ordinary Maude module with a predicate `getTime` from object-oriented configurations to `Float`, a `tick` function acting on configurations to advance the clock, and a `val : Int Config -> Float` function or similar to evaluate observations. Then, in each step, the tools exhaustively rewrite `tick(t)` with the `rewrite` command for the term t of the previous step. Whenever some sufficient conditions on the initial term and the rules are satisfied (see Sect. 3.1 of [2]), the model is free of unquantified nondeterminism and the statistical analyses are sound.

2.3 QMaude and Probabilistic Strategies

QMaude [23] comprises different resources for specifying and verifying quantitative systems in Maude. Standard Maude modules can be assigned probabilities in an orthogonal way by one of several assignment methods: by considering uniform probabilities on the possible rewrites, specifying different weights by label or with expressions depending on the matching substitution written in the metadata attribute of rules, using probabilistic strategies, etc. Such a specification can then be applied probabilistic and statistical model-checking methods through the pcheck and scheck subcommands of the umaudemc tool [22]. The pcheck command derives discrete probabilistic structures like discrete-time Markov chains, Markov decision process, or continuous-time Markov chains, and transparently delegates the verification tasks to model checkers like PRISM [14] or Storm [12]. Transient and steady-state probabilities, the probability of LTL and PCTL properties, and expected rewards can be computed. On the other hand, the scheck command implements discrete-event simulators and a statistical model-checking engine that computes confidence intervals for a given generalized QuaTEx expression, confidence level, and maximum radius.

The most expressive probability assignment method is the probabilistic extension of the Maude strategy language [10], which has been extended with three new operators

- choice $(w_1: \alpha_1, \ldots, w_n: \alpha_n)$ is a quantification of the nondeterministic choice $\alpha_1 \mid \cdots \mid \alpha_n$ with weights $w_1, \ldots, w_n$. These are terms of Nat or Float sort that may depend on the variables in scope. The strategy α_k is executed with probability $\theta(w_k)/\sum_{i=1}^{n} \theta(w_k)$ where θ is the current variable environment.
- matchrew P s.t. C with weight w by x_1 using $\alpha_1, \ldots, x_n$ using α_n is an extension of a standard matchrew operator without the with weight w part. This operator matches the term being rewritten with P and, if the condition C is satisfied, rewrites the subterm matched by x_k in the pattern with the results of evaluating α_k on it. Its probabilistic extension also specifies a weight term w for each match. matchrew can be replaced by amatchrew to match anywhere within the term.
- sample $x := \pi(t_1, \ldots, t_n)$ in α samples a value to the variable x from a probabilistic distribution π with arguments $t_1, \ldots, t_n$ that may depend on the variables in scope. The variable x can then be used in α. The supported distributions are bernouilli(ρ), uniform(a, b), exp(λ), norm(μ, σ), and gamma(α, β).

This extended strategy language is not currently available in the official distribution of Maude, but in a separate build that can be downloaded from maude.ucm.es/strategies. It is also available in the Maude Python library [20], and so it can be used through umaudemc.

3 From PMaude to Probabilistic Strategies

In this section, we describe how to transform a PMaude specification, i.e. a Maude module with probabilistic rules, into an ordinary module controlled by probabilistic strategies. Let us consider a probabilistic rule of the form

```
crl [lbl] l(x) => r(x,y) if C(x) with probability
```
$$y_1 := \pi_1(t_{1,1}, \ldots, t_{1,a_1}), \ldots, y_n := \pi_n(t_{n,1}, \ldots, t_{n,a_n}).$$

where x and y are sets of variables that may occur in the terms, and $t_{k,l}$ may also depend on x. Unconditional rules can be seen as a particular case where C is empty. We derive a nonexecutable rule by stripping the probabilistic information

```
rl [lbl] l(x) => r(x,y) if C(x) [nonexec] .
```

a named strategy pmr-lbl without arguments, and a strategy definition

```
sd pmr-lbl := amatchrew V s.t. l := V by V using
    sample y₁ := π₁(t_{1,1}, ..., t_{1,a₁}) in
    ... in
         sample yₙ := πₙ(t_{n,1}, ..., t_{n,aₙ}) in
              top(lbl[x <- x, y₁ <- y₁, ..., yₙ <- yₙ]) .
```

In other words, each sampling condition $y_k := \pi_k(t_{k,1}, \ldots, t_{k,a_k})$ is translated into a strategy sample y_k := $\pi_k(t_{k,1}, \ldots, t_{k,a_k})$ in α, and the process continues recursively on α. First, the matching position of the rule is found with an amatchrew and its l := V condition, which binds the variables of l to be used in $t_{k,l}$. Finally, the rule is applied on top of the matched position by invoking its label with an initial substitution that maps every matching and sampling variable. We are assuming for readability that each probabilistic rule has a distinct label. This is without loss of generality, since unlabeled rules can be labeled with an arbitrary name, and repeated labels can be disambiguated.[1]

Executing the strategy expression in the right-hand side of the definition is the same as running the probabilistic rule. Indeed, amathrew will find the position and matching substitution of every possible application of the original rule, top and the substitution between brackets will ensure that this same application is executed, and the variables $y_1, \ldots, y_n$ of the right-hand side will be filled with the sampled values as specified in the with probability clause.

The translation is implemented as a metalevel function

```
op transform : Module -> Module .
```

that extends the input module (rules can also be renamed for disambiguation) with several strategies:

1. pmr-*lbl* for each rule label *lbl* as described above,

---

[1] In the Maude implementation of the translation, labels used in multiple rules are disambiguated by appending indices to them. However, a single prm-*lbl* named strategy with the original name and multiple definitions is declared for them.

2. pm-step for a single application of any probabilistic rule, which could be defined as

   sd pm-step := pmr-lbl_1 | $\cdots$ | pmr-lbl_n .

3. pm-all for a single application of any rule, probabilistic or not. It can be simply defined as

   sd pm-all := pm-step | all .

   where all is a predefined strategy operator that applies an (executable) rule once with the standard semantics, and

4. pm-run for exhaustively applying pm-all until no more rewrites are possible. This is specified with the recursive definition

   sd pm-run := pm-all ? pm-run : idle .

   Notice that the behavior of pm-run will be the analog of the rewrite command for the probabilistic model.

3.1 Actor PMaude

The above translation works for any module, even object-oriented ones as explained in [7, Chap. 6]. Hence, the probabilistic actor-based specifications of Actor PMaude can also be translated. Moreover, thanks to the strategy-controlled specification, we can now represent the time-passing logic in Maude itself, as we will see in the following paragraphs. First, we have updated the ACTORS module in [2] with small changes and by extending the predefined CONFIGURATION module. While messages can take any form, we declare the traditional PMaude symbol (_<-_) for convenience, where the first argument is the addressee and the second one the contents of the message. A predefined empty content is also provided:

```
op (_<-_) : Oid Content -> Msg [ctor msg] .
op empty : -> Content [ctor] .
```

The current time is stored in the configuration with the time operator:

```
op time : Float -> Configuration [ctor] .
```

We keep using [_,_] for scheduled entities, that is, both objects and messages paired with the global time in which they will become available:

```
op [_,_] : Float Object -> ScheduledObject [ctor] .
op [_,_] : Float Msg -> ScheduledObject [ctor] .
```

Finally, the rule tick shows how configurations progress as time moves forward:

```
crl [tick] : S => advance(S, NT)
  if NT := smallest(S) [nonexec] .
```

where `advance(S, NT)` advances the `time` value to `NT` and unlocks every scheduled entity whose time is lower than `NT`, and `smallest` calculates the smallest time of a scheduled entity. Note that, for the system to be well defined, `NT` must be greater than 0.

In addition to the `ACTORS` module, the `apmaude.maude` file provides a module `APMAUDE-TRANSLATE` with an operator

```
op atransform : Module -> Module .
```

that applies `transform` to the input module and adds some more strategies to the result. The single-tick step $[u]_A \xrightarrow{\neg \text{tick}}{}^* [v]_A \xrightarrow{\text{tick}} [w]_A$, which has traditionally been implemented out of Maude, can be specified with the following `ap-step` strategy:

```
strats ap-step ap-run @ Configuration .
sd ap-step := pm-all ! ; top(tick) .
sd ap-run := ap-step ? ap-run : idle .
```

The normalization operator (`!`) applies `pm-all`, i.e. a single application of any probabilistic or ordinary rule, until no more applications are possible. Then, it applies the `tick` rule on top with the `top` operator. The left-hand side of the `tick` rule is a `Configuration` variable, so it could match any subset of the configuration multiset, but `top` prevents that. Like `pm-run`, an exhaustive or potentially nonterminating application of `ap-step` steps is defined as the recursive `ap-run` strategy.

Another advantage of describing the semantics of Actor PMaude as a strategy that repeats a step `ap-step`, which in turn repeats a smaller step `pm-all`, is that we can analyze executions more easily in Maude. Using the Maude Python library, we have written a script, `apmsim.py`, that allows obtaining random traces of Actor PMaude executions at the rule application level, where differences between configurations are highlighted. Section 4.3 shows a usage example.

4 Examples

In this section, we illustrate the translation and the verification tools it makes available through several PMaude examples. We revisit all examples in [2], although we start with a simple new one.

4.1 A Fair Die

Our first example models a fair die, where all faces have the same probability of being obtained. Hence, we just import the natural numbers from `NAT`, declare a sort `Dice`, and its constructor `[_]` that wraps a number. Every time the die is thrown, the only rule chooses a face `M`, i.e. a number between 1 and 6, uniformly at random.

```
mod DICE is
  protecting NAT .
  sort Dice .
  op [_] : Nat -> Dice [ctor] .
  vars N M : Nat .
  rl [N] => [M] [nonexec
    metadata "with probability M := uniform(1, 6)"] .
endm
```

Notice that DICE is a standard Maude module with a metadata attribute on the rule. The original syntax

```
rl [N] => [M] with probability M := uniform(1, 6) .
```

could be supported with some parsing or preprocessing, but this is not currently implemented.

We can check that the die is actually fair using the probabilistic model checker command pcheck ⟨*file*⟩ ⟨*initial term*⟩ ⟨*formula*⟩ [⟨*strategy*⟩] of the umaudemc tool:

```
$ umaudemc pcheck dice.maude -M "transform(upModule('DICE, true))"
   '[0]' @steady pm-step --assign strategy --fraction
1/6                     [1]
1/6                     [2]
1/6                     [3]
1/6                     [4]
1/6                     [5]
1/6                     [6]
```

The argument -M selects the transformed DICE metamodule as the model to be analyzed, [0] is the initial state, @steady tells the tool to find steady-state probabilities, --assign strategy chooses to assign probabilities by means of a strategy, and pm-step is that strategy. Thus, the output shows all the possible states and their probabilities after one step (as a fraction because of the --fraction flag).

Temporal properties in LTL and PCTL can also be checked. For example, the probability to obtain two sixes in a row is

```
$ umaudemc pcheck dice.maude -M "transform(upModule('DICE-MC, true))"
   '[0]' 'O (get(6) /\ O get(6))'
   pm-run --assign strategy --fraction
Result: 1/36
```

where get(k) has been defined as an atomic proposition in DICE-MC.

```
op get : Nat -> Prop [ctor] .
vars N M : Nat .
eq [N] |= get(N) = true .
eq [N] |= get(M) = false [owise] .
```

We are using the pm-run strategy to control rewriting and assign probabilities. This strategy repeatedly applies pm-all (in this case, the die-throwing rule) and does not stop unless no more rewrites are possible. Throwing a die is always possible, so pm-run is a nonterminating strategy describing a set of infinite executions, which can be expressed however as a finite discrete-time Markov chain. This is passed to either PRISM [14] or Storm [12] to be checked. More details on this topic can be found in [21,23].

Moreover, systems with unquantified nondeterminism can also be analyzed as Markov decision processes.

```
$ umaudemc pcheck dice.maude
   -M "transform(upModule('DICE-MC, true))"
   '[0]' 'O (get(6) /\ O get(6))' 'pm-step | pm-step ; pm-step'
   --assign strategy --fraction
Result: 1/36 to 1/6
```

If we may nondeterministically choose between throwing a die once or twice, the probability is between $1/36$ and $1/6$. The probability $1/6$ is achieved by throwing a die once due to the standard stuttering extension of finite traces, which stays in the last state forever.

4.2 Exponential Clock

The following example is an updated version of the EXPONENTIAL-CLOCK module in Sect. 2.1 of [2]. A working clock is specified by means of the clock constructor, while a broken one uses broken. In both cases, the first argument stands for the current time and the second one for the remaining battery charge:

```
op clock  : Float Float -> Clock [ctor] .
op broken : Float Float -> Clock [ctor] .
```

Their behavior is described by two rules: advance to advance the current time of the clock, while losing battery charge and perhaps breaking it, and reset to reset the time back to zero. On the one hand, the advance rule samples from a Bernoulli distribution (into a Boolean variable B) whether the clock breaks with probability a thousand of its battery charge C. The current time advances according to an exponential distribution of rate 1 (the delay is sampled to a Float variable D).

```
vars T C D : Float .
var  B     : Bool .

rl [advance] : clock(T, C) =>
   if B then
     clock(T + D, C - C / 1000.0)
   else
     broken(T, C  - C / 1000.0)
   fi
[metadata "with probability B := bernoulli(C / 1000.0),
           D := exponential(1.0)" nonexec] .
```

On the other hand, **reset** sets the current time of a working clock to 0.0:

```
rl [reset] : clock(T, C) => clock(0.0, C) .
```

This specification does not produce a finite model and cannot be analyzed by probabilistic model checking, because it makes use of the continuous exponential distribution. Moreover, since both **advance** and **reset** can be applied to any working clock, the system contains unquantified nondeterminism in the choice of the rule. Thus, it is neither amenable for statistical model checking as is. Fortunately, we can use the probabilistic strategy language to quantify the nondeterminism. For example, we can write a strategy

```
choice(9 : advance, 1 : reset)
```

to indicate that the **advance** should be 9 times more likely than **reset** to occur. These probabilities can take into account term attributes, like the current time or battery charge, by means of a **matchrew** operator like the one used in the translation.

In the following, we will remove the unquantified nondeterminism by not applying the **reset** rule at all. We are interested in knowing what is the mean charge level when the clock breaks. Assuming we have defined a predicate **isBroken** and a **Float**-valued function **charge** in Maude, the charge when the clock breaks can be expressed in the QuaTEx language of [2] as

```
BreakCharge() = if (s.rval("isBroken(Clk:Clock)"))
   then
      s.rval("charge(Clk:Clock)")
   else
      #BreakCharge()
   fi;

eval E[BreakCharge()];
```

In each step, **BreakCharge** checks whether the clock is broken. The argument of **s.rval** (unlike in PVeSta and MultiVeSta) can be any term of **Bool**, **Nat**, or **Float** type with a single variable that will be replaced by the current term. If the clock is broken, the expression returns the value of the battery charge. Otherwise, it continues evaluating the same query recursively in the next step (#). The statement **eval E[BreakCharge()]** computes the expected value of the **BreakCharge** function.

The **scheck** command of the **umaudemc** tool can be used to evaluate the QuaTEx expression by statistical methods. Its general form is

scheck ⟨file⟩ ⟨initial term⟩ ⟨QuaTEx file⟩ [⟨strategy⟩]

with some optional parameters that are explained below for the example.

```
$ umaudemc scheck exponential-clock.maude
   -M "transform(upModule('EXPONENTIAL-CLOCK-PREDS, true))"
   'clock(0.0, 1000.0)' exponential-clock.quatex
```

```
pmr-advance --assign step -d 0.1 -j 6
Number of simulations = 149970
μ = 960.3228432437255    σ = 19.757344850390144
r = 0.0999949299749619
```

The initial state is clock(0.0, 1000.0), exponential-clock.quatex is the previous QuaTEx expression, and pmr-advance --assign step tells that pmradvance (i.e. the application of the probabilistic advance rule) must be the atomic step of the executions in the simulation. This is different from the strategy method used before, which exposes the intermediate steps in the execution of the strategy as steps of the model. Moreover, -d 0.1 indicates that the confidence interval around the estimated value should have a radius of at most 0.1, and -j 6 activates 6 parallel processes for the simulations.

4.3 Simple Client-Server

Actor PMaude support is illustrated by using a simple client-server specification where a client sends messages to the server forever. We use an object-oriented module that imports our predefined ACTORS module [24] and defines two classes: Client, which stores a counter and the server identifier, and Server, which keeps an accumulated sum of the numbers received from the clients. The contents of messages are just natural numbers obtained from the counter in the client:

```
omod SIMPLE-CLIENT-SERVER is
   extending ACTORS .
   protecting NAT .

   vars t t1 t2 T : Float .
   vars C S       : Oid .
   vars N M       : Nat .

   class Client | counter : Nat, server : Oid .
   class Server | total : Nat .

   op ctnt : Nat -> Content [ctor] .
```

Some rules describe the model behavior. The send rule stands for the gratuitous submission of messages from the client to the server.

```
rl [send] : < C : Client | counter : N, server : S >
            (C <- empty) time(T)
         => < C : Client | counter : s N > time(T)
            [T + t1, (C <- empty)]
            [T + t2, (S <- ctnt(N))]
  [metadata "with probability t1 := exponential(2.0),
             t2 := exponential(10.0)" nonexec] .
```

Since we are using object-oriented modules, unused or unchanged class attributes can be omitted. In this rule, C <- empty messages play the role of a self-alarm to schedule when to send the next message. When an empty message is received, a message for the server is prepared to be sent at T + t2, where t2 comes from an exponential distribution of rate 10. The self message is instead distributed with delay t1 from an exponential distribution of rate 2.

The message from the client may get lost if the server is busy when it arrives.

```
rl [busy-drop] :
    [t, < S : Server | total : M >] (S <- ctnt(N))
 => [t, < S : Server | total : M >] .
```

```
├── ⏱ 0.0
│   c <- empty
│   < c : Client | counter : 0, server : s >
│   < s : Server | total : 0 >
├──
│   [0.0288, s <- ctnt(0)]
│   [0.773, c <- empty]
│   < c : Client | counter : 1, server : s >
│   < s : Server | total : 0 >
├── ⏱ 0.0288
│   s <- ctnt(0)
│   [0.773, c <- empty]
│   < c : Client | counter : 1, server : s >
│   < s : Server | total : 0 >
├──
│   [0.773, c <- empty]
│   [1.27, < s : Server | total : 0 >]
│   < c : Client | counter : 1, server : s >
├── ⏱ 0.773
│   c <- empty
│   [1.27, < s : Server | total : 0 >]
│   < c : Client | counter : 1, server : s >
├──
│   [0.775, s <- ctnt(1)]
│   [1.27, < s : Server | total : 0 >]
│   [2.24, c <- empty]
│   < c : Client | counter : 2, server : s >
```

Fig. 1. Simulated execution of 3 steps of the simple server with apmsim.py.

Otherwise, the compute rule processes the message by adding the current message contents to the total attribute. The computation time is exponentially distributed with rate 1:

```
rl [compute] :
    < S : Server | total : M > (S <- ctnt(N)) time(T)
 => [T + t, < S : Server | total : M + N >] time(T)
    [metadata "with probability t := exponential(1.0)"
    nonexec] .
```

Finally, we define an init configuration with one server and one client for testing.

```
    op init :    -> Configuration .
    ops c s :    -> Oid [ctor] .

    eq init = < c : Client | counter : 0, server : s >
              < s : Server | total : 0 > (c <- empty)
              time(0.0) .
endom
```

Some steps of the actor system execution can be observed in Fig. 1, which has been generated with the

```
python apmsim.py simple-client-server.maude init
```

command, which highlights changes between steps and time passing in the trace. The first step applies the `send` rule and introduces two new scheduled messages; then, time passes until the wake time of the first message `s <- ctnt(0)`; then, the server executes `compute` rule, and so on.

Figure 2 graphically shows the value computed by the server in its `total` attribute with respect to time. This is the result of the following query

```
TotalAfter(t) =
  if (s.rval("getTime(C:Configuration)") >= t) then
    s.rval("getTotal(s, C:Configuration)")
  else
    #TotalAfter(t)
  fi;

eval parametric(E[TotalAfter(x)], x, 1, 1, 10)
```

Like in MultiVeSta [25], parametric queries are supported using the syntax shown above. The last four arguments are the variable to be assigned, its initial value, the step size, and the end of the range. This shows that functions like `TotalAfter` can be parametric, but we can further play with their arguments.

```
HowManyLost(n, 1) = if (n == 0) then 1 else
  if (s.rval("hasMessageFor(s, C:Configuration)"))
  then #HowManyLost(n - 1,
    if (s.rval("willBeLost(s, C:Configuration)"))
    then 1 + 1 else 1 fi
  )
  else #HowManyLost(n, 1)
  fi
fi;
```

The expression `HowManyLost(`n`, 0)` computes how many messages are lost out of the n first messages, using some auxiliary predicates `hasMessageFor` (whether there is a message in the configuration) and `willBeLost` (whether the message is about to be rejected by the busy server). The parameter `1` is used as the counter of lost packages (since QuaTEx expressions can only be tail recursive). Using `ap-step` (see Sect. 3) as the atomic step of the simulation, we obtain that almost 2/3 of the packages are lost.

4.4 Symmetric Polling

Finally, we revisit the symmetric polling example from [2]. The object-oriented system is composed of several stations and a server that communicates to them in order. Each station has a buffer that gets refilled periodically. When the buffer is ready, the station answers the server and the latter continues asking the next station. The polling time, the service time, and the arrival time for a message at each station are exponentially distributed.

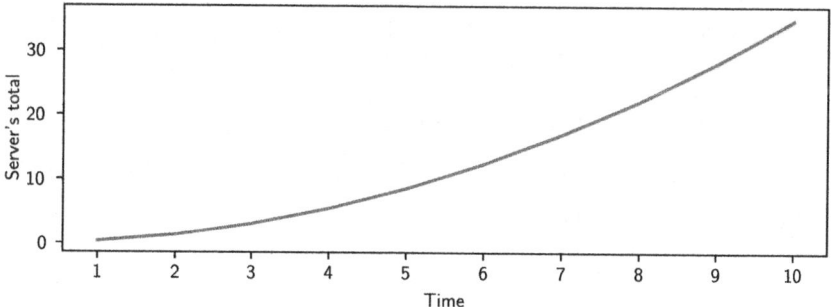

Fig. 2. Total computed by the server with respect to time.

Again, we declare an object-oriented module omod SYMMETRIC-POLLING and the relevant entities as classes in it:

```
class Station | buf : Nat, server : Oid .
class Server  | client : Nat .

ops poll next serve done : -> Content [ctor] .
```

The message types are declared as constants of sort Content. Then, the behavior is defined by means of rules. For brevity, here we only show two of them, while the full commented code is available at [24]. For instance, the produce rule fills the buffer of a station after a period governed by an exponential distribution of rate 0.2. It uses the artifice of sending a message to itself with that delay.

```
rl [produce] : < C : Station | buf : M >
     (C <- empty) time(T)
  => < C : Station | buf : 1 > [T + t, (C <- empty)]
     time(T)
     [metadata "with probability t := exponential(0.2)"
      nonexec] .
```

Another relevant rule is next, which polls the station N and increments its client attribute modulo 5 to continue with the next station.

```
rl [next] : < S : Server | client : N > (S <- next)
   => < S : Server | client : increment(N) >
      (station(N) <- poll) .

op increment : Nat -> Nat .
eq increment(N) = if N >= 5 then 1 else N + 1 fi .
```

This is an ordinary rule that coexists with the other probabilistic ones.

Finally, an initial setting with a server and n polling stations is built as follows:

```
op init : Nat -> Configuration .
eq init(0) = < s : Server | client : 1 >
             (s <- next) time(0.0) .
eq init(s N) = init(N)
     < station(s N) : Station | buf : 1, server : s > .

op init : -> Configuration .
eq init = init(5) .
endom
```

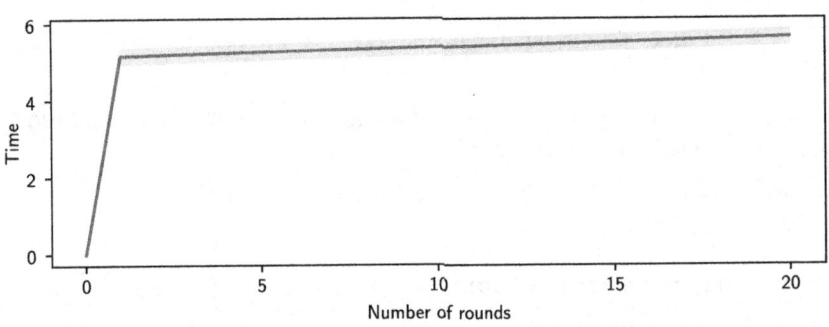

Fig. 3. Time to complete that many polling rounds.

Figure 3 depicts the time needed to complete 1 to 20 polling rounds, i.e. the time until the n-th message is received by the first station for $1 \leq n \leq 20$:

```
TimeNRounds(n) =
  if (s.rval("aboutToServe(1, C:Configuration)"))
  then
     if (n == 0) then    // rounds completed
        s.rval("getTime(C:Configuration)")
     else
```

```
        #TimeNRounds(n - 1)  // next round
    fi
  else
    #TimeNRounds(n)  // stay in the same round
  fi ;

eval parametric(E[TimeNRounds(n)], n, 0, 1, 20);
```

This is a parametric query that can be estimated and plotted by the umaudemc scheck command.

5 Conclusions

We have shown how probabilistic models in the PMaude and Actor PMaude frameworks can be implemented using the probabilistic extension of the Maude strategy language. Moreover, the time-passing logic of Actor PMaude can be naturally expressed as a strategy. This translation makes the specification of probabilities cleaner and more declarative, while providing simulation, probabilistic and statistical model checking for free through the umaudemc tool. We have also developed a script that allows inspecting the intermediate steps of PMaude simulations, which was a very difficult task in the traditional encoding.

Our translation does not directly support the original syntax of [2]. Instead, the with probability clause must be introduced in the metadata attribute of the rule. As future work, this small syntactic gap can be fixed, and the resources for analyzing PMaude specification can be further extended.

Acknowledgments.
This work is partially supported by MCIU/AEI/10.13039/50110-0011033/FEDER,UE through project ProCode 10 (PID2023-149943OB-I00). We would also like to thank the reviewers for their useful suggestions that have improved this paper.

Disclosure of Interests. The authors have no competing interests to declare that are relevant to the contents of this article.

References

1. Agha, G., Palmskog, K.: A survey of statistical model checking. ACM Trans. Model. Comput. Simul. **28**(1), 6:1–6:39 (2018). https://doi.org/10.1145/3158668
2. Agha, G.A., Meseguer, J., Sen, K.: PMaude: rewrite-based specification language for probabilistic object systems. In: Cerone, A., Wiklicky, H. (eds.) QAPL 2005. Electronic Notes in Theoretical Computer Science, vol. 153, no. 2, pp. 213–239. Elsevier (2005). https://doi.org/10.1016/J.ENTCS.2005.10.040
3. AlTurki, M., Meseguer, J.: PVeStA: a parallel statistical model checking and quantitative analysis tool. In: Corradini, A., Klin, B., Cîrstea, C. (eds.) CALCO 2011. LNCS, vol. 6859, pp. 386–392. Springer, Heidelberg (2011). https://doi.org/10.1007/978-3-642-22944-2_28

4. Bentea, L., Ölveczky, P.C.: A probabilistic strategy language for probabilistic rewrite theories and its application to cloud computing. In: Martí-Oliet, N., Palomino, M. (eds.) WADT 2012. LNCS, vol. 7841, pp. 77–94. Springer (2012). https://doi.org/10.1007/978-3-642-37635-1_5
5. Bouhoula, A., Jouannaud, J.P., Meseguer, J.: Specification and proof in membership equational logic. Theor. Comput. Sci. **236**, 35–132 (2000). https://doi.org/10.1016/S0304-3975(99)00206-6
6. Clavel, M., et al.: All About Maude - A High-Performance Logical Framework. LNCS, vol. 4350. Springer, Heidelberg (2007). https://doi.org/10.1007/978-3-540-71999-1
7. Clavel, M., et al.: Maude Manual (version 3.5) (2024), https://maude.lcc.uma.es/maude-manual/
8. Durán, F., Ramírez, C., Rocha, C., Pozas, N.: A rewriting logic semantics for the analysis of P programs. J. Logical Algebraic Methods Program. **144**, 101048 (2025). https://doi.org/10.1016/j.jlamp.2025.101048
9. Durán, F., Rocha, C., Salaün, G.: Stochastic analysis of BPMN with time in rewriting logic. Sci. Comput. Program. **168**, 1–17 (2018). https://doi.org/10.1016/j.scico.2018.08.007
10. Eker, S., Martí-Oliet, N., Meseguer, J., Rubio, R., Verdejo, A.: The Maude strategy language. J. Log. Algebraic Methods Program. **134**, 100887 (2023). https://doi.org/10.1016/J.JLAMP.2023.100887
11. Grov, J., Ölveczky, P.C.: Increasing consistency in multi-site data stores: megastore-CGC and its formal analysis. In: Giannakopoulou, D., Salaün, G. (eds.) SEFM 2014. LNCS, vol. 8702, pp. 159–174. Springer, Cham (2014). https://doi.org/10.1007/978-3-319-10431-7_12
12. Hensel, C., Junges, S., Katoen, J., Quatmann, T., Volk, M.: The probabilistic model checker Storm. Int. J. Softw. Tools Technol. Transf. **24**(4), 589–610 (2022). https://doi.org/10.1007/S10009-021-00633-Z
13. Katelman, M., Meseguer, J., Hou, J.: Redesign of the LMST wireless sensor protocol through formal modeling and statistical model checking. In: Barthe, G., de Boer, F.S. (eds.) FMOODS 2008. LNCS, vol. 5051, pp. 150–169. Springer, Heidelberg (2008). https://doi.org/10.1007/978-3-540-68863-1_10
14. Kwiatkowska, M., Norman, G., Parker, D.: PRISM 4.0: verification of probabilistic real-time systems. In: Gopalakrishnan, G., Qadeer, S. (eds.) CAV 2011. LNCS, vol. 6806, pp. 585–591. Springer, Heidelberg (2011). https://doi.org/10.1007/978-3-642-22110-1_47
15. Liu, S., Ganhotra, J., Rahman, M.R., Nguyen, S., Gupta, I., Meseguer, J.: Quantitative analysis of consistency in NoSQL key-value stores. Leibniz Trans. Embed. Syst. **4**(1), 03:1–03:26 (2017). https://doi.org/10.4230/LITES-V004-I001-A003
16. Liu, S., Meseguer, J., Ölveczky, P.C., Zhang, M., Basin, D.: Bridging the semantic gap between qualitative and quantitative models of distributed systems. Proc. ACM Program. Lang. **6**(OOPSLA2) (2022). https://doi.org/10.1145/3563299
17. Meseguer, J.: Conditional rewriting logic as a unified model of concurrency. Theoret. Comput. Sci. **96**(1), 73–155 (1992). https://doi.org/10.1016/0304-3975(92)90182-F
18. Meseguer, J., Sharykin, R.: Specification and analysis of distributed object-based stochastic hybrid systems. In: Hespanha, J.P., Tiwari, A. (eds.) HSCC 2006. LNCS, vol. 3927, pp. 460–475. Springer, Heidelberg (2006). https://doi.org/10.1007/11730637_35

19. Ölveczky, P.C., Meseguer, J.: The real-time maude tool. In: Ramakrishnan, C.R., Rehof, J. (eds.) TACAS 2008. LNCS, vol. 4963, pp. 332–336. Springer, Heidelberg (2008). https://doi.org/10.1007/978-3-540-78800-3_23
20. Rubio, R.: Maude as a library: an efficient all-purpose programming interface. In: Bae, K. (ed.) WRLA@ETAPS 2022. LNCS, vol. 13252, pp. 274–294. Springer (2022). https://doi.org/10.1007/978-3-031-12441-9_14
21. Rubio, R., Martí-Oliet, N., Pita, I., Verdejo, A.: Strategies, model checking and branching-time properties in Maude. J. Log. Algebraic Methods Program. **123**, 100700 (2021). https://doi.org/10.1016/J.JLAMP.2021.100700
22. Rubio, R.: Unified Maude model-checking tool (umaudemc) (2020–2025), https://github.com/fadoss/umaudemc
23. Rubio, R., Martí-Oliet, N., Pita, I., Verdejo, A.: QMaude: quantitative specification and verification in rewriting logic. In: Chechik, M., Katoen, J., Leucker, M. (eds.) FM 2023. LNCS, vol. 14000, pp. 240–259. Springer (2023). https://doi.org/10.1007/978-3-031-27481-7_15
24. Rubio, R., et al.: Repository of examples of the Maude strategy language (2021–2025), https://github.com/fadoss/strat-examples
25. Sebastio, S., Vandin, A.: MultiVeStA: statistical model checking for discrete event simulators. In: Horváth, A., Buchholz, P., Cortellessa, V., Muscariello, L., Squillante, M.S. (eds.) ValueTools 2013, pp. 310–315. ICST/ACM (2013). https://doi.org/10.4108/ICST.VALUETOOLS.2013.254377

Modeling and Analyzing Real-Time Systems in Rewriting Logic

Kyungmin Bae[1], Carlos Olarte[2], and Peter Csaba Ölveczky[3]

[1] POSTECH, Pohang, South Korea
[2] LIPN, CNRS UMR 7030, Université Sorbonne Paris Nord, France
[3] Department of Informatics, University of Oslo, Oslo, Norway
peterol@uio.no

Abstract. Many sophisticated distributed real-time systems and modeling languages can be formalized in rewriting logic as real-time rewrite theories, which can be analyzed using the Maude and Real-Time Maude tools. In this paper we show how real-time rewrite theories, possibly with user-defined timed strategies, can be specified and analyzed directly in Maude, using both explicit-state and symbolic executions. We then give an overview of applications of Maude and Real-Time Maude to real-time and cyber-physical systems and modeling languages, showing that such analysis can provide useful insights about advanced systems that cannot be easily (or at all) formalized using decidable formalisms such as timed automata. This work also shows the predictive power of model-based performance estimation using statistical model checking.

1 Introduction

It is a privilege to honor the great scientist and gentleman Gul Agha, with whom Bae and Ölveczky were fortunate to interact during our times at the University of Illinois at Urbana-Champaign (UIUC). To celebrate Gul, this paper gives an overview of how *rewriting logic* [68] and the tools Maude [28,27] and Real-Time Maude [88,89,82] have been applied to real-time and cyber-physical systems (CPSs), which exemplify the impact of the following of Gul's many seminal contributions to computer science:

- His work on the *actor* model for distributed computation [1,3].
- Gul was one of the inventors of *statistical model checking* (SMC) [103,109,2,104], and of using SMC to predict the expected value of a measure on behaviors with desired statistical confidence. He is also a developer of the VeStA [105] SMC tool and the QuaTEx logic for defining probabilistic temporal properties and, more generally, measures on behaviors.

The work summarized in this paper shows the impact of Gul's above-mentioned contributions in the following ways:

- Most of the (then-)state-of-the-art applications mentioned in this paper have been modeled in an actor-based style, illustrating the usefulness of the actor model for large real-time systems.

- A number of these applications use SMC, the parallel version PVeStA [7] of Gul's VeStA tool, and the QuaTEx property specification language for model-based predictions of the performance of different design options of distributed real-time systems. This work shows: (i) that such PVeStA/QuaTEx-based statistical model checking scales to large and sophisticated systems; (ii) that such model-based performance comparison of different design options quite accurately reflects their performance differences in actual implementations; and (iii) that the performance estimates obtained by SMC faithfully reflect the performance of the actual implementations when the system parameters are chosen carefully.

Rewriting logic [68] is a logic developed by Gul's longtime friend and colleague José Meseguer. Rewriting logic is an intuitive, general, and expressive logic in which a wide range of distributed systems, models of computation, logics, and modeling and programming languages can be formalized [70]. The Maude tool [28,27] supports various forms of analysis of rewriting logic specifications.

Ölveczky and Meseguer proposed to model real-time systems in rewriting logic as *real-time rewrite theories* [86], and developed the Real-Time Maude tool to support the specification, simulation, and analysis of such theories. Real-Time Maude complements the most popular formal tools for real-time systems—such as those based on timed automata [8,21] and time(d) Petri nets—by supporting actor-based models, object-oriented modeling with subclasses and dynamic object and message creation and deletion, user-defined data types, unbounded data structures, hierarchical models, and the ability to easily model a wide range of communication models at various levels of abstraction. The flip side of this expressiveness and generality is that most properties are undecidable in general. Real-Time Maude analysis is based on "sampling" certain moments in time; however, this may not cover all possible behaviors for dense time [87].

The question is whether the above features are needed to conveniently model real-time systems, and, if so, whether we can obtain useful analysis results for systems that need the above features and that cannot easily (or at all) be modeled as timed automata. In this paper we give a non-exhaustive overview of such real-time systems applications in rewriting logic. These applications are typically either (i) "concrete" applications, such as complex network protocols, or (ii) [Real-Time] Maude semantics and analysis for real-time and CPS modeling languages, which typically combine expressive languages for control programs with real-time (or even continuous) behaviors (Section 6).

Many researchers have used real-time rewrite theories and the methods of Real-Time Maude, but have modeled and analyzed their systems in Maude. Since we are currently redesigning Real-Time Maude, Section 3 introduces real-time rewrite theories and explains how they can be specified and analyzed directly in Maude. We also briefly introduce Real-Time Maude, since it provides analysis methods, such as timed CTL model checking, that are not supported by Maude.

Explicit-state Maude and Real-Time Maude analyses are based on "sampling time," either by advancing time by a fixed amount (e.g., one time unit) or as much as possible ("discrete-event simulation") when time advances. However, other time sampling strategies might be more efficient and/or cover more behaviors. We may also want to analyze a system under different "discrete" execution strategies. Section 4 therefore introduces a recent timed strategy language for real-time rewrite theories in Maude proposed by Olarte and Ölveczky [79]. This language supports the intuitive and modular definition of both discrete and time sampling strategies, and model checking w.r.t. such strategies.

Time sampling makes possible explicit-state model checking of complex real-time systems, but at the cost of possibly not covering all behaviors in dense-time systems. Exploiting the recent integration of SMT solving into Maude, Section 5 explains how we can execute real-time rewrite theories symbolically: the amount of time elapsed in each "idling" step is represented by a new SMT variable. Using "folding" of symbolic states and "eliminating" SMT variables, we have recently showed that such Maude-with-SMT analyses of parametric timed automata and parametric time Petri nets are sound and complete and terminate whenever the corresponding symbolic state spaces are finite [10,9].

Partial overviews of the use of rewriting logic for real-time systems have appeared in 2011 [81] and 2014 [82]. This paper differs from those papers by:

- giving an overview also of many significant applications since 2014;
- explaining how real-time systems can be modeled and analyzed directly in Maude, whereas [81,82] focus on Real-Time Maude; and
- summarizing our recent work on timed strategies and Maude-with-SMT-based symbolic analysis of real-time rewrite theories.

2 Preliminaries: Rewriting Logic and Maude

Rewriting logic [68,70] is a logic of concurrent change developed by José Meseguer. In rewriting logic, data types are defined by algebraic equational specifications and local state changes are modeled by (possibly conditional) labeled rewrite rules. Rewriting logic is a general and flexible executable computation logic, and is suitable for modeling distributed systems in an object-oriented style.

Maude [28,27] is a specification language and high-performance simulation, reachability analysis, and linear temporal logic (LTL) model checking tool for rewriting logic. Maude supports *meta-programming*, where Maude functions can manipulate (meta-represented) Maude specifications (called modules). Maude can also be connected to statistical model checkers [100], which can be used to estimate the expected value of a measure on behaviors (e.g., the average latency of a transaction) up to a desired statistical confidence. Maude has recently been combined with SMT solving [96,20] and with a strategy language that allows users to specify desired execution strategies [35].

A Maude module $M = (\Sigma, E \cup A, L, R)$ specifies a *rewrite theory*, with:

- Σ an algebraic *signature*; i.e., a set of *sorts*, *subsorts*, and *function symbols*.
- $(\Sigma, E \cup A)$ a *membership equational logic* [69] theory, with E a set of possibly conditional equations and membership axioms, and A a set of equational axioms such as associativity, commutativity, and identity, so that equational deduction is performed *modulo* the axioms A.

- L a set (of rule labels).
- R a collection of *labeled conditional rewrite rules* $[l] : t \longrightarrow t'$ **if** *cond*, for $l \in L$ and terms t and t', specifying the system's local transitions.

We briefly summarize the syntax of Maude and refer to [28] for more details. A function f is declared op f : $s_1 \ldots s_n$ -> s, where $s_1 \ldots s_n$ denotes the sorts of its arguments, and s its (value) sort. We can in addition declare that the function is a constructor (ctor) of elements of sort s; and binary function symbols can be declared to be associative (assoc), commutative (comm), and/or have an identity element t (id: t, or right id: t for a right identity element t), so that computation is performed *modulo* such properties. Underbars ('_') in function names denote argument positions in "mix-fix" notation.

Equations and rewrite rules are introduced with, respectively, keywords eq, or ceq for conditional equations, and rl and crl. The equations and rewrite rules are implicitly universally quantified by the mathematical variables appearing in them; such variables are declared with the keywords var and vars, or can have the form *var:sort* and be introduced on the fly. '---' precedes a comment.

A module *imports* another module M using including M or protecting M. In a *parameterized module* $M\{X_1 :: T_1, \ldots, X_n :: T_n\}$ the ("types" of the) *formal parameters* T_i are "modules" called *theories*. A *view* view V_i from T_i to M_i is ... endv declares how the sorts and operations of the formal parameter T_i are mapped to elements in the *actual parameter* module M_i.

In *object-oriented modules* (syntax omod M is ... endom), a declaration

class C | att_1 : s_1, ..., att_n : s_n

declares a *class* C of objects with attributes att_1 to att_n of sorts s_1 to s_n. An *object instance* of class C is represented as a term of the form

< O : C | att_1 : val_1, $\cdots$, att_n : val_n >

where O, of sort Oid, is the object's *identifier*, and val_1 to val_n are the values of the attributes att_1 to att_n. A *message* is a term of sort Msg. A state is modeled as a term of the sort Configuration, and is a *multiset* of objects and messages.

The dynamic behavior of a system is axiomatized by specifying each of its transition patterns by a rewrite rule. For example, the rule (with label 1)

```
rl [1] :   m(O, O'', X)
           < O : C | a1 : Y,      a2 : O',  a3 : Z >
       =>
           < O : C | a1 : Y + X,  a2 : O',  a3 : Z >
           m2(O', O, Y) .
```

defines a family of transitions in which an object O of class C reads a message m(O, O'', X), changes the value of its attribute a1 from Y to Y + X, and generates a new message m2(O', O, Y). Attributes whose values do not change and do not affect the next state need not be mentioned.

Formal Analysis. The command `red` *expr* reduces the expression *expr* to its normal form using the equations E. The rewrite command `rew` *init* simulates one behavior from the initial state *init* by applying rewrite rules, and the bounded rewrite command `rew [n]` *init* performs at most n rewrite steps from *init*.

Given a state pattern *pattern* and an (optional) condition *cond*, Maude's `search` command searches the reachable state space from *init* for all (or optionally a given number of) states that match *pattern* such that *cond* holds:

```
search init =>* pattern [such that cond] .
```

The search command can have optional arguments denoting the maximal number of desired solutions and/or the maximal depth of the search tree.

The command `red modelCheck(`*init*`,` ϕ`)` checks whether the LTL formula ϕ is satisfied by the initial state specified by the term *init*. Atomic propositions in the formula ϕ are user-defined terms of sort `Prop`, and the function op `_|=_ : State Prop -> Bool` specifies which states satisfy a given proposition. LTL formulas are built from state formulas, Boolean connectives, such as `True`, `~` (negation), `/\` (conjunction), `\/` (disjunction), and `->` (implication), and temporal logic operators, such as `[]` ("always"), `<>` ("eventually"), and `U` ("until").

Strategies. Maude provides a language for defining strategies to control and restrict rewriting [27,35]. A strategy may not make rewriting deterministic, and hence multiple behaviors allowed by the strategy may have to be explored.

The command `srew [n]` t `using` *str* returns at most n terms resulting from rewriting the term t according to the strategy *str*. `srew` explores multiple paths in parallel, and ensures that solutions will eventually be found, if they exist. The command `dsrew` t `using` *str* explores the behaviors allowed by *str* in a depth-first way. The extension of Maude in [98,99] supports model checking systems controlled by strategies using the command `red modelCheck(`*init*`,` ϕ`,` *str*`)`.

Basic rewrite strategies *str* include $l[\sigma]$ (apply the rule labeled l once with the optional substitution σ), `all` (perform a single rewrite step with one of the rules, except those marked `nonexec`), `idle` (identity; i.e., do nothing and return the current term), `fail` (return the empty set), and `match` P `s.t.` C, which returns the current term if it matches the pattern P subject to the condition C, and which does not return a solution otherwise. Compound strategies can be defined using concatenation ($\alpha \,;\, \beta$), disjunction ($\alpha \mid \beta$, whose result is the union of the results of α and β), iteration ($\alpha *$), the conditional strategy $\alpha \,?\, \beta : \gamma$ (if α fails, apply strategy γ, otherwise apply strategy $\alpha \,;\, \beta$), α `or-else` β (execute α, and β if α fails), `try(`α`)` (applies α if it does not fail), normalization $\alpha\,!$ (execute α until it cannot be further applied), and so on [27].

Maude-with-SMT. Maude is integrated with SMT solving to enable symbolic reachability analysis of concurrent systems. A (possibly infinite) set of system states is symbolically represented as constrained terms [96,20] of the form $\phi \parallel t$, where t is a state pattern containing variables, and ϕ is an SMT constraint restricting the possible values of those variables. More precisely, $\phi \parallel t$ represents the set of all instances of t such that ϕ holds.

A *symbolic rewrite* on constrained terms represents a (possibly infinite) set of system transitions [96]. Such symbolic rewrites can be "implemented" using ordinary rewrite rules on constrained terms. Specifically, a rewrite rule $l : q \longrightarrow r$ **if** ψ is transformed into a constrained-term rule

$$l : \text{PHI} \parallel q \longrightarrow (\text{PHI and } \psi) \parallel r \text{ if smtCheck}(\text{PHI and } \psi)$$

where PHI is a Boolean variable, and smtCheck invokes the underlying SMT solver to check the satisfiability of the given SMT condition.

Maude provides built-in sorts Boolean, Integer, and Real, which correspond to the SMT theories of Booleans, integers, and reals. Rational constants of sort Real are written n/m (e.g., 0/1). Maude-SE [110] extends Maude with additional functionality for rewriting modulo SMT, such as uninterpreted functions and witness generation. In particular, the Maude-SE command

smt-search $[n,d]$ in M : t => t' such that Φ using $\mathcal{T}$.

symbolically searches for n states, reachable from t (containing variables) within d rewrite steps, that match the pattern t' and satisfy the constraint Φ, using the SMT theory $\mathcal{T}$ (e.g., QF_LRA for quantifier-free linear real arithmetic).

3 Specifying and Analyzing Real-Time Systems in Maude

Real-time systems can be naturally modeled in rewriting logic as *real-time rewrite theories* [86], which are parametric in the (discrete or dense) time domain. The idea is that ordinary rewrite rules model *instantaneous* change/transitions, and that "tick" rewrite rules of the form $[l] : \{t\} \longrightarrow \{t'\}$ **in time** τ **if** *cond* model time elapse in the system. This rule models time advancing by amount τ, which results in a state change from state t to state t'. The term τ may contain variables. The (E-normal form of) the *whole* state should always have the form $\{u\}$, for some term u that does not contain the "global-state" operator $\{\_\}$. This ensures that time advances uniformly in all parts of the state.

Example 1. Let $clock(r)$ model a clock showing time r, and assume a discrete time domain; e.g., the natural numbers. The two rules

$$[reset] : clock(12) \longrightarrow clock(0)$$
$$[tick] : \{clock(X)\} \longrightarrow \{clock(X+1)\} \text{ in time } 1 \text{ if } X < 12,$$

where X is a variable, model a clock which increases its value by 1 when time advances by one time unit, until the clock shows 12. At that time, the clock is *immediately* reset to $clock(0)$ using the instantaneous rule *reset*. This happens without delay, since time cannot advance when the clock shows 12. □

In a discrete time domain, we can cover all moments in time by increasing time by one time unit in each *tick step* (tick rule application). However, for dense time, this is not possible. Then tick rules often have the form

$$[tick] : \{t\} \longrightarrow \{t'\} \text{ in time } T \text{ if } T \leq f(t) \land cond, \qquad (1)$$

where T is a variable that does not appear in t and is not initialized in *cond*.

Example 2. A clock that uses and displays dense time can be modeled as follows:

$$[reset] : clock(12) \longrightarrow clock(0)$$
$$[tick] : \{clock(X)\} \longrightarrow \{clock(X+T)\} \text{ in time } T \text{ if } T \leq 12 - X,$$

where X and T are variables. □

Although discrete time is sufficient for most typical (Real-Time) Maude applications, it is nevertheless important to study such *time-nondeterministic* tick rules also for discrete-time systems. The reason is that in many systems it is not feasible to perform exhaustive analysis if each point in time is explored; e.g., if only a few actions are possible in, say, a 20.000 time unit round of the system. The round trip time system described in Section 3.1 is a discrete-time system where it is unnecessary to stop time advance at each time point.

Since the new variable T does not appear in the left-hand side of the tick rules of form (1), its value is not given by the matching substitution. Given the expressiveness and generality of real-time rewrite theories, analysis has typically been based on *explicit-state* executions, where such time-nondeterministic tick rules have been executed using certain strategies, called *time sampling strategies*, for how to instantiate the variable T. The Real-Time Maude tool (see Section 3.3) supports analysis w.r.t. the following time sampling strategies:

– advance time by a user-defined time value in each tick rule application; and
– advance time as much as possible (i.e., by $f(t)$) in each tick rule application.

Since only a subset of all possible behaviors are analyzed in this way (at least for dense time), analysis with time sampling is in general not sound and complete.

Example 3. If we execute the dense-time clock in Example 2 by advancing time by one time unit in each tick step, reachability analysis will claim that the state $\{clock(\frac{1}{2})\}$ is *not* reachable, which is not correct for the model in Example 2. □

Nevertheless, for the useful class of *time-robust* real-time rewrite theories, which includes many systems that cannot be modeled as timed automata, such time-sampling-based analysis is sound and complete [87].

A recent sound and complete way of analyzing time-nondeterministic real-time rewrite theories exploits the fact that Maude has been combined with SMT solving [96,20], and encodes the amount of time elapsed in each tick rule application as a *new* SMT variable, as explained in Section 5. In this way, we have implemented sound and complete analysis methods for parametric timed automata and parametric time Petri nets that terminate whenever the "symbolic state spaces" of the corresponding automata/nets are finite [10,9].

Real-time rewrite theories are suitable for modeling distributed real-time systems in an object-oriented style. The tick rules then usually have the form

$$[tick] : \{conf\} \longrightarrow \{timeEffect(conf, T)\} \text{ in time } T \text{ if } T \leq mte(conf) \wedge cond,$$

where *timeEffect* is a function defining how the advance of time changes the state, and $mte(conf)$ (for *maximal time elapse*) defines how much time can advance from state *conf* before something *must* happen. These functions usually distribute over the objects and messages in the state, as defined by the following equations, where the variables C_1 and C_2 range over configurations (multisets of objects and (delayed) messages) and the variable T ranges over the time domain:

$$timeEffect(C_1\ C_2, T) = timeEffect(C_1, T)\ timeEffect(C_2, T)$$
$$\text{if } C_1 \neq none \wedge C_2 \neq none$$
$$timeEffect(none, T) = none$$
$$mte(C_1\ C_2) = min(mte(C_1), mte(C_2)) \text{ if } C_1 \neq none \wedge C_2 \neq none$$
$$mte(none) = \infty$$

The user must then define these functions on single objects and messages.

Section 3.1 explains how object-oriented real-time rewrite theories, that are parametric in the time domain, can be specified directly in Maude. We illustrate these techniques with a running example: a simple round trip protocol that features local clocks, timers, and nondeterministic but bounded message delays. Section 3.2 shows how time-nondeterministic real-time rewrite theories can be analyzed in Maude using the time sampling strategies mentioned above. Section 3.3 discusses how real-time rewrite theories can be modeled and analyzed using the Real-Time Maude tool. All the executable Maude and Real-Time Maude specifications, with analysis commands, are available at https://depot.lipn.univ-paris13.fr/real-time-maude/agha-rtm.

3.1 Specifying Real-Time Systems in Maude

We can specify time domains abstractly in Maude as a theory TIME with a value 0, some common operations on time domains, and a sort TimeInf that adds an infinity value INF to the time domain:[4]

```
fth TIME is including BOOL .
  sorts Time NzTime TimeInf .   subsort NzTime < Time < TimeInf .
  op INF : -> TimeInf .
  op 0 : -> Time .
  op _+_ : TimeInf TimeInf -> TimeInf [assoc comm prec 33 gather (E e)] .
  op _monus_ : TimeInf Time -> TimeInf [prec 33 gather (E e)] .
  ops _<=_ _<_ _>=_ _>_ : TimeInf TimeInf -> Bool [prec 37] .
  ops max min : TimeInf TimeInf -> TimeInf [comm] .
  ...
endfth
```

To represent real-time rewrite theories directly in Maude we add the in time construct as a Maude operator. The following module also defines a generic global-state operator {_}, which assumes that the sort of the states is System:

```
fmod TIMED-PRELUDE{X :: TIME} is
  sorts System GlobalSystem ClockedSystem .
```

---

[4] Parts of Maude specifications, terms, and output will be replaced by '...'.

```
  subsort GlobalSystem < ClockedSystem .

  op {_} : System -> GlobalSystem .
  op _in time_ : GlobalSystem X$Time -> ClockedSystem .

  vars T T' : X$Time .   var STATE : ClockedSystem
  eq (STATE in time T) in time T' = STATE in time (T + T') .
endfm
```

The user then defines the sort of her states to be a subsort of System. For example, in object-oriented real-time systems, we declare that configurations are our states: subsort Configuration < System .

The theory TIME can be seen as a *formal parameter* in our modules. We define the following concrete time domains that can be used as actual time domains. We start by defining time as the non-negative natural numbers:

```
fmod NAT-TIME-DOMAIN is including NAT .
  sort TimeInf .                  subsort Nat < TimeInf .
  op INF : -> TimeInf [ctor] .
  op _monus_ : TimeInf Nat -> TimeInf [prec 33 gather (E e)] .
  op _+_ : TimeInf TimeInf -> TimeInf [ditto] .
  op _<=_ : TimeInf TimeInf -> Bool [ditto] .
  ...
  op min : TimeInf TimeInf -> TimeInf [ditto] .
  op max : TimeInf TimeInf -> TimeInf [ditto] .

  vars TI TI' : TimeInf .         var N M : Nat .

  eq INF + TI = INF .             eq INF monus N = INF .
  eq N monus M = if N < M then 0 else sd(N,M) fi .
  eq TI <= INF = true .           eq INF <= N = false .
  eq min(INF, TI) = TI .          eq max(INF, TI) = INF .
  ...
  sorts NzTime Time .             subsort NzTime < Time .
  subsort NzNat < NzTime .        subsort Nat < Time .
endfm
```

The last four declarations allow us to use the sort Time for the natural numbers. We can define a concrete time domain as the non-negative rational numbers:

```
fmod POSITIVE-RAT is protecting RAT .
  sort NNegRat .                  --- non-negative rationals
  subsorts Zero PosRat Nat < NNegRat < Rat .
endfm

fmod POSRAT-TIME-DOMAIN is protecting POSITIVE-RAT .
  sort TimeInf .    subsort NNegRat < TimeInf .
  op INF : -> TimeInf [ctor] .
  op _<_ : TimeInf TimeInf -> Bool [ditto] .
  op _+_ : TimeInf TimeInf -> TimeInf [ditto] .
```

```
   ...
endfm
```

The following *views* define how the "actual" parameters NAT-TIME-DOMAIN and POSRAT-TIME-DOMAIN instantiate the formal parameter TIME:

```
view NatTimeDomain from TIME to NAT-TIME-DOMAIN is
  sort Time to Nat .            sort NzTime to NzNat .
endv

view PosRatTimeDomain from TIME to POSRAT-TIME-DOMAIN is
  sort Time to NNegRat .        sort NzTime to PosRat .
endv
```

Example: A Simple Round Trip Time Protocol. We model a simple protocol for *periodically* computing the *round trip time* between pairs of nodes. This system includes (local) clocks, timers, and nondeterministic message delays.

For each sender/receiver pair, the sender sends an rttReq message to its receiver at the beginning of each period (say, every 5 seconds), with the current value of its local clock. When the receiver receives this message, it responds with an rttResp message with the same clock value ("time stamp") that it received. When the original sender receives this rttResp message, with its original time stamp, it records the round trip time as the difference between the current value of its local clock and the time stamp in the rttResp message. We assume that the "delay" of messages sent from object o is in the time interval $[l_o, u_o]$.

This system can be specified as the following object-oriented real-time theory in Maude, that is parametric in the time domain:

```
omod RTT{X :: TIME} is including TIMED-PRELUDE{X} .
    vars T T1 T2 T3 T4 : X$Time .    vars TI TI' : X$TimeInf .
    var M : Msg .    vars R S : Oid .    vars C1 C2 STATE : Configuration .

    sort DlyMsg .  subsorts Msg < DlyMsg < Configuration < System .
    op dly : Msg X$Time X$Time -> DlyMsg [ctor] . --- upper and lower bounds

    rl [deliver] : dly(M, 0, T) => M . --- can deliver ripe message any time

    msgs rttReq_from_to_ rttResp_from_to_ : X$Time Oid Oid -> Msg .

    class Sender | clock : X$Time,     timer : X$TimeInf,
                   lowerDly : X$Time, upperDly : X$TimeInf,
                   rtt : X$TimeInf,   receiver : Oid,    period : X$Time .

    class Receiver | lowerDly : X$Time, upperDly : X$TimeInf .

    rl [send] :
       < S : Sender | clock : T, timer : 0, period : T2,
                      lowerDly : T3, upperDly : T4, receiver : R >
```

```
        => < S : Sender | timer : T2 >    dly(rttReq T from S to R, T3, T4) .

    rl [respond] :
        (rttReq T from S to R)    < R : Receiver | lowerDly : T3, upperDly : T4 >
        => < R : Receiver | >        dly(rttResp T from R to S, T3, T4) .

    rl [recordRTT] :
        (rttResp T from R to S)    < S : Sender | clock : T2 >
        => < S : Sender | rtt : T2 monus T > .

    crl [tick] :
        {STATE} => {timeEffect(STATE, T)} in time T if T <= mte(STATE) [nonexec] .

    op mte : Configuration -> X$TimeInf [frozen] .
    eq mte(none) = 0 .
    ceq mte(C1 C2) = min(mte(C1), mte(C2)) if C1 =/= none and C2 =/= none .
    eq mte(< S : Sender | timer : TI >) = TI .
    eq mte(< R : Receiver | >) = INF .
    eq mte(dly(M, T, TI)) = TI .
    eq mte(M) = 0 .        --- ripe message must be read immediately

    op timeEffect : Configuration X$Time -> Configuration [frozen] .
    eq timeEffect(none, T) = none .
    ceq timeEffect(C1 C2, T) = timeEffect(C1, T) timeEffect(C2, T)
            if C1 =/= none and C2 =/= none .
    eq timeEffect(< S : Sender | clock : T, timer : TI >, T2)
        = < S : Sender | clock : T + T2, timer : TI monus T2 > .
    eq timeEffect(< R : Receiver | >, T) = < R : Receiver | > .
    eq timeEffect(dly(M, T, TI), T2) = dly(M, T monus T2, TI monus T2) .
    eq timeEffect(M, T) = M .
endom
```

The class sender has the following attributes: clock denotes its local clock; timer denotes the time remaining until the start of the next round; lowerDly and upperDly denote the lower and upper delay bounds of messages traveling *from* this sender; rtt denotes the sender's last recorded RTT value; receiver is the node to which the sender wants to find the round trip time; and period denotes the time between each round of the protocol. The Receiver only has attributes defining the delay interval of messages sent by the receiver.

A message *msg* in transit has the form dly(*msg*, *minRemDly*, *maxRemDly*), where *minRemDly* and *maxRemDly* denote, respectively, the minimal and maximal time remaining until the message arrives and must be read. The rule deliver says that the message *may* be "ripe/delivered" when *minRemDly* is 0.

The rule send starts a round of the protocol when the sender's timer expires (i.e., becomes 0). The sender S then sends a message rttReq T from S to R, where T denotes the current value of its local clock, to its receiver R, *with* the delay interval. The sender also resets its timer. When the receiver receives the rttReq message, it sends back an rttResp with the same time stamp that it received, with a suitable delay interval (rule respond). When the original sender receives the `rttResp` message, with its time stamp, it computes the round trip of this latest session, and stores it in the attribute `rtt` (rule `recordRTT`).

The system is time-nondeterministic: The delay of a message can be any value in an interval. Since the time domain *may* be dense, time advance is modeled by the tick rule which advances time by any amount less than or equal to the maximum time (`mte(STATE)`) that may advance in the system before some action *must* take place. Our tick rule is therefore non-executable (`nonexec`).

The function `mte` is defined for single objects and messages as follows. For sender objects, time cannot advance beyond the time when its timer expires (becomes 0). Receiver objects do not impose restrictions on time advance. Time cannot advance beyond the maximal remaining delay of a (delayed) message, and time cannot advance at all when an "undelayed" message (one without the `dly` operator) is in the state; this forces undelayed messages to be read immediately.

The function `timeEffect` decreases the `timer` value of the sender and increases its local `clock` according to the elapsed time, and decreases the remaining lower and upper delays of a delayed message[5].

3.2 Analyzing Real-Time Systems in Maude

When the `in time` construct in real-time rewrite theories is represented by a Maude operator, a real-time rewrite theory can be executed directly in Maude if the tick rules are executable. If they are non-executable, we must add executable tick rules. "Deterministic time sampling" can be achieved by replacing (or adding to) tick rules of the form (1) with rules of the form

$$[tick] : \{t\} \longrightarrow \{t'\} \text{ in time } T \text{ if } T := \Delta \wedge T \leq f(t) \wedge cond, \qquad (2)$$

which advance time by $\Delta > 0$ in each tick rule application. Executing the system with "maximal time sampling" can be achieved by using tick rules

$$[tick] : \{t\} \longrightarrow \{t'\} \text{ in time } T \text{ if } T := f(t) \wedge T > 0 \wedge cond, \qquad (3)$$

When 'in time' is seen as a Maude operator, the states have the form $\{t\}$ in time r, where r denotes the total time that has elapsed in the behavior (and can be called the "system clock"). The disadvantage of this approach is that the reachable "clocked" state space will be infinite (since the clock value r can grow beyond any bound), so that some analyses may not terminate even when the reachable "unclocked" state space is finite.

One way to obtain a finite reachable state space, *and* to enable *time-bounded* analysis, is to not advance time beyond a user-defined time bound β, using tick rules of the form

$$[tick] : \{t\} \text{ in time } r \longrightarrow \{t'\} \text{ in time } r + T \\ \text{if } T := \Delta \wedge T \leq f(t) \wedge r + T \leq \beta \wedge cond \qquad (4)$$

(and similar for maximal time sampling).

---
[5] x `monus` $y = \max(x - y, 0)$

For *unbounded* analysis, we can maintain finite state spaces by not keeping the "system clock" in the states, by using tick rules of the form

$$[tick] : \{t\} \longrightarrow \{t'\} \text{ if } T := \Delta \wedge T \leq f(t) \wedge cond \tag{5}$$

Analyzing the Round Trip Protocol. The following modules support *time-bounded* analysis with, respectively, deterministic time sampling with time advance `tickAmount` and maximal time sampling, up to time bound `timeBound`:

```
omod RTT-TIMEBOUNDED-DET-TICK{X :: TIME} is including RTT{X} .
  ops tickAmount timeBound : -> X$Time .
  var STATE : Configuration .   var T : X$NzTime .   var T2 : X$Time .
  crl [tick] :
      {STATE} in time T2 => {timeEffect(STATE, T)} in time (T + T2)
          if T := tickAmount /\ T <= mte(STATE) /\ (T + T2) <= timeBound .
endom

omod RTT-TIMEBOUNDED-MAX-TICK{X :: TIME} is including RTT{X} .
  op timeBound : -> X$Time .
  var STATE : Configuration .   var T : X$NzTime .   var T2 : X$Time .
  crl [tick] :
      {STATE} in time T2 => {timeEffect(STATE, T)} in time (T + T2)
          if T := mte(STATE) /\ (T + T2) <= timeBound .
endom
```

For unbounded analyses with deterministic time sampling we can use

```
omod RTT-DET-TICK-NO-CLOCK{X :: TIME} is including RTT{X} .
  op tickAmount : -> X$Time .
  var T : X$NzTime .   var STATE : Configuration .
  crl [tick] :   {STATE} => {timeEffect(STATE, T)}
                if T := tickAmount /\ T <= mte(STATE) .
endom
```

We next choose the time domain and define an initial state `init` with one sender and one receiver:

```
omod RTT-NAT is protecting RTT{NatTimeDomain} .
  ops snd rcv : -> Oid [ctor] .
  op init : -> GlobalSystem .
  eq init
    = {< snd : Sender | clock : 0, timer : 0, period : 5000, lowerDly : 5,
                        upperDly : 20, rtt : INF, receiver : rcv >
       < rcv : Receiver | lowerDly : 8, upperDly : 30 >} .
endom
```

If we replace `NatTimeDomain` with `PosRatTimeDomain` the time values become the nonnegative rational numbers.

We can then analyze the system with deterministic time sampling with time increment 3 in each step, up to time bound 63:

```
omod RTT-DET-TIMEBOUNDED is including RTT-NAT .
  including RTT-TIMEBOUNDED-DET-TICK{NatTimeDomain} .
  eq tickAmount = 3 .
  eq timeBound = 63 .
endom
```

We can then simulate the system up to time 63 with such time sampling:

```
Maude> rew init in time 0 .

result ClockedSystem:
 {< snd : Sender | clock : 63, timer : 4937, lowerDly : 5,
                   upperDly : 20, rtt : 48, receiver : rcv, period : 5000 >
  < rcv : Receiver | lowerDly : 8, upperDly : 30 >} in time 63
```

Next we check whether it is possible to reach in the time interval [50, 63] a state where the recorded rtt value is less than 30:

```
Maude> search [1] init in time 0 =>* {C:Configuration
           < snd : Sender | rtt : T:Time, ATTS:AttributeSet >} in time T2:Time
           such that T:Time < 30 /\ T2:Time >= 50 .

Solution 1 (state 165)
T:Time --> 27        T2:Time --> 51      ...
```

If we instead use time-bounded *maximal* time sampling, then recorded rtt values smaller than 50 cannot be found:

```
omod RTT-MAX-TIMEBOUNDED is including RTT-NAT .
  including RTT-TIMEBOUNDED-MAX-TICK{NatTimeDomain} .
  eq timeBound = 10000 .
endom

Maude> search [1] init in time 0 =>* {C:Configuration
           < snd : Sender | rtt : T2:Time, ATTS:AttributeSet >} in time T:Time
           such that T2:Time < 50 .

No solution.
```

Finally, we perform *unbounded* search, with time sampling with increment 1, to check whether it is possible to record the rtt value 17:

```
omod RTT-DET-UNBOUNDED is including RTT-NAT .
  including RTT-DET-TICK-NO-CLOCK{NatTimeDomain} .
  eq tickAmount = 1 .
endom

Maude> search [1] init =>*
           {C:Configuration < snd : Sender | rtt : 17, ATTS:AttributeSet >} .

Solution 1   ...
```

We can also perform Maude LTL model checking, including time-bounded model checking. The following state proposition `okRttValue` holds in states where the recorded `rtt` value is in the desired interval [13, 50]:

```
omod MODEL-CHECK-RTT is including MODEL-CHECKER .  including RTT-NAT .
  subsort ClockedSystem < State .
  op okRttValue : -> Prop [ctor] .
  vars T T2 : Time .   var REST : Configuration .
  eq {REST < snd : Sender | rtt : T >} |= okRttValue = 13 <= T and T <= 50 .
  eq {REST} in time T2 |= okRttValue = {REST} |= okRttValue .
endom
```

The first equation defines `okRttValue` to hold in all (unclocked) states where the recorded `rtt` value is in the desired interval, and the second equation extends `okRttValue` to clocked states.

We can then perform time-bounded model checking with time increase 1 and time bound 10.000:

```
omod MODEL-CHECK-RTT-TIMEBOUNDED-DET-SAMPLING is including MODEL-CHECK-RTT .
  including RTT-TIMEBOUNDED-DET-TICK{NatTimeDomain} .
  eq tickAmount = 1 .
  eq timeBound = 10000 .
endom
```

```
Maude> red modelCheck(init in time 0, [] okRttValue) .
result ModelCheckResult: counterexample(...)
Maude> red modelCheck(init in time 0, <> okRttValue) .
result Bool: true
Maude> red modelCheck(init in time 0, [] (okRttValue -> [] okRttValue)) .
result Bool: true
```

3.3 The Real-Time Maude Tool

The Real-Time Maude tool [89,88,82] supports more directly the specification and analysis of real-time rewrite theories. The tool automates more sophisticated versions of the "theory transformations" in Section 3.2, and supports various kinds of analyses w.r.t. *deterministic* and *maximal* time sampling applications of time-nondeterministic tick rules, including time-bounded simulation, and time-bounded and unbounded ("clockless") reachability analysis and LTL model checking, as well as finding the shortest and longest time needed to reach a desired state. Although we have seen that many of these analysis methods can be encoded directly in Maude, Real-Time Maude is also equipped with a full (i.e., supporting nested temporal logic formulas) *timed* CTL model checker [52].

Most applications of rewriting logic to real-time systems have used the Real-Time Maude tool, in particular because it supported object-oriented specifications, which are now also supported in Maude. We are currently redesigning and reimplementing Real-Time Maude. Nevertheless, if timed CTL model checking is needed, Real-Time Maude (as of March 2025) can run on version 2 of Maude.

Timed object-oriented modules (`tomod...endtom`) support the specification of object-oriented real-time rewrite theories, and predefine suitable time domains. Our RTT example can be defined in Real-Time Maude as follows:

```
(tomod RTT is protecting NAT-TIME-DOMAIN-WITH-INF .
  ... --- same as before, except that X$Time is replaced with Time
endtom)
```

Instead of adding different tick rules for different analyses and different time sampling strategies, we can just declare that we use maximal time sampling (`set tick max .`), or that we increase time by 3 in each application of a tick rule:

```
Maude> (set tick def 3 .)
```

Real-Time Maude analyses are more sophisticated than those we implement in Section 3.2: the time increment is adjusted when time bounds are reached.

We can then simulate our system, from the above initial state `init`, with the above time sampling strategy up to time 10.000:

```
Maude> (trew init in time <= 10000 .)

Result ClockedSystem :
  {... < snd : Sender | rtt : 50, ... > dly(... , 5, 20)} in time 10000
```

The system is simulated up to time 10.000, even though 10.000 is not a multiple of 3. The corresponding Maude rewrite with time increase 3 stops at time 9999.

We can then use timed search (`tsearch`) to search for states reachable in certain intervals: e.g., can an rtt value different from the initial value INF be recorded within the interval $[2, 12]$?

```
Maude> (tsearch [1] init =>*
          {REST:Configuration < snd : Sender | rtt : T:Time >}
            in time-interval between >= 2 and <= 12 .)

No solution
```

Untimed search (`utsearch`) performs "clockless" search and hence terminates when the reachable state space is finite (which is not the case in our example):

```
Maude> (utsearch [1] init =>* {C:Configuration < snd : Sender | rtt : 21 >} .)

Solution 1   ...
```

Finally, we use the TCTL model checker and define the atomic propositions on "clockless" states:

```
(tomod TCTL-CHECK-RTT is including RTT-INIT-RESET .
  including TCTL-MODEL-CHECKER .
  op okRttValue : -> Prop [ctor] .
  vars TI : TimeInf .   var REST : Configuration .
  eq {REST < snd : Sender | rtt : TI >} |= okRttValue = 13 <= TI and TI <= 50 .
endtom)
```

Since the model checker only terminates when the reachable state space is finite, the module `RTT-INIT-RESET` modifies our RTT example by resetting the sender's local clock whenever its timer expires (rule `send`). We can then analyze the property $AF_{\leq 50}$ okRttValue:

```
Maude> (mc-tctl init |=  AF[<= than 50] okRttValue .)

Property satisfied
```

Although this is a simple formula, our TCTL model checker supports full TCTL. It is implemented using Maude's meta-programming features, and should be seen as a prototype for a future faster and more mature implementation.

4 Analyzing Real-Time Systems with User-Defined Strategies

Section 3 explains how we can analyze real-time systems by selecting a single time sampling strategy to execute all applications of time-nondeterministic tick rules. However, sometimes other time samplings would be desirable:

Example 4. In our RTT example, a time sampling strategy that advances time by one time unit in each tick rule application would cover all possible behaviors for discrete time. However, it would be hopelessly inefficient, since it visits each time value even after the `rtt` value for this "round" has been recorded, and the system is just idling for almost 5000 time units until the next round begins.

On the other hand, advancing time as much as possible in each tick step only gives us those behaviors where the message delays are as long as possible, so that all recorded `rtt` values would be 50. We need "mixed" time sampling that advances time by one time unit when there is a (delayed) message in the state, and that "fast forwards" to the end of the round when there is no message in the state. This would be quite efficient *and* would cover all interesting behaviors. □

One may also want to analyze the system with various execution strategies also on the "discrete" parts of the system, such as prioritizing certain actions or enforcing *eagerness* of some or all actions.

We show in [79] that one can perform Real-Time Maude-style time sampling execution of tick rules using Maude strategies. For example, the Maude command `srew s using (all | tick [T <- 1])` returns all successor states of *s*, obtained by applying either an instantaneous rule (`all`) or (`|`) the `tick` rule with the variable T instantiated to 1 (`tick [T <- 1]`). However, we also show in [79] that those strategies quickly become somewhat complicated for the non-expert.

Therefore, in [79] we define our own strategy language for real-time rewrite theories which provides an intuitive and modular way of defining:

- time sampling strategies, defining *how* a tick rule is applied; and
- "discrete" strategies, defining strategies on how to execute the instantaneous rules, and also *when* (but not *how*) to execute tick rules.

A timed strategy is therefore a pair < δ , τ >, where δ is a "discrete" strategy which specifies "one round" of the system (i.e., with one application of a tick rule), and τ is a time sampling strategy. We have also implemented all Real-Time Maude analysis methods, including time-bounded and unbounded reachability analysis and LTL model checking, except for timed CTL model checking, but where the executions are governed by the user-defined timed strategy < δ , τ >.

4.1 A Strategy Language for Real-Time Rewrite Theories

The basic discrete strategies available to users are:

- apply ℓ applies the instantaneous rule with label ℓ *once*;
- apply [$\mathcal{L}$] applies *once* the first rule in the list of labels $\mathcal{L}$ that succeeds in the current state (i.e., $\mathcal{L}$ defines a *priority* on the next rule to be applied);
- apply {$\mathcal{L}$} applies *once* any of the rules in the set of labels $\mathcal{L}$;
- action applies *any* instantaneous rule once;
- delay applies a tick rule once; and
- eager applies the instantaneous rules as much as possible, followed by *one* "delay" when it is possible.

Conditional and compound discrete strategies can be defined as follows:

- δ ; δ' is the sequential composition of two strategies;
- δ or δ' returns the union of the results obtained from the execution of the strategies δ and δ';
- δ or-else δ' applies δ, but applies the strategy δ' if δ fails;
- if ϕ then δ else δ' fi applies strategy δ if the condition ϕ holds and δ' otherwise. In the condition ϕ, it is possible to: test the value t of the global clock as in $t \in [a,b]$ (gclock in [a, b]), $t > t'$ (gclock > t'), etc; or to check whether the current state matches a given pattern. Larger conditions can be constructed using conjunction, disjunction, and negation. We also support defining *history-dependent* strategies (see [79]).
- stop is the strategy that always fails; and
- skip leaves the current state unchanged.

Time sampling strategies available for the user include:

- fixed-time Δ advances time by the (constant) time value Δ in each application of a tick rule (where advancing time by that amount is possible).
- max-time with default Δ advances time in a tick rule application by the *maximum time* γ possible *for that tick rule*, and advances time by Δ if γ is INF. If γ is 0, the tick rule is not applied.
- The *state-dependent* time sampling strategy switch *cases* otherwise τ, where *cases* is a list of choices of the form when ϕ_j do τ_j. This strategy applies the first time sampling strategy τ_i whose guard ϕ_i holds in the current state; the time sampling strategy τ is applied if none of the guards hold.

Example 5. For a time sampling strategy τ, `< delay or action , `τ` >` applies once any enabled (instantaneous or tick) rule, `< eager , `τ` >` gives higher priority to instantaneous rules, and `< apply ['send 'respond] or-else action or-else delay , `τ` >` gives higher priority to the rules `send` and `respond`, then to the other actions, and finally to the tick rule.

The desired time sampling strategy for the RTT protocol advances time by 1 if there is a *delayed* message in the state, and advances time maximally otherwise:

```
< δ , switch
          when matches ({C1 dly(M, T2, T3)} in time T) do fixed-time 1
          otherwise max-time with default 3 >.
```
□

4.2 Analysis Methods Using Strategies

User-defined timed strategies of the form $< \delta , \tau >$ are given a formal semantics by translating them into Maude strategies. Since such strategies define only "one round" of system execution, we extend them to allow for "repeated" executions, potentially until a state satisfying a desired property is reached. This extension allows for the implementation of a number of analysis methods for analyzing systems that follow user-defined strategies, simply by rewriting the initial state with a suitable *extended strategy* (see [80] for details).

For example, the time-bounded reachability analysis command

`tsearch [`n`] `*init*` => `*pattern*` s.t. `ϕ` using `δ` with sampling `τ` in time [`a,b`]` .

returns the first n states reachable from *init*, w.r.t. to execution with the timed strategy $< \delta , \tau >$, in the time interval $[a, b]$ which match the *pattern* such that ϕ holds. Variations of this command allow us to bound the number of rewrites in the behaviors, to perform depth-first search analysis, and to do unbounded analysis, in which case the system clock is reset to 0 after each tick step.

The time-bounded LTL model checking command

`bmodel-check [`r`] `*init*` |= `φ` using `δ` with sampling `τ` .`

checks whether the LTL formula φ is satisfied by all behaviors up to time r from the initial state *init* that are allowed by the user-defined strategy $\langle\delta,\tau\rangle$. We also provide an unbounded model checking command.

Example 6. We analyze our RTT example from the state `init`, to find the first two reachable states where the recorded `rtt` value is 20, with the time sampling strategy τ in Example 4, formalized at the end of Example 5 (`switch ...`):

```
Real-Time Maude> tsearch [2] init => {< snd : Sender | rtt : 20, ... >} ...
                 using (all | delay) with sampling τ .

Solution 1.
{< snd : Sender | clock : 20, timer : 4980, ... > ...} in time 20

Solution 2.
{< snd : Sender | clock : 5000, timer : 0, ... > ...} in time 5000
```

With this time sampling, we can find any legal rtt value, and then "jump" over all other times until the next round starts (at time 5000). □

5 Symbolic Analysis of Real-Time Systems

We can leverage rewriting modulo SMT [96,20] to achieve sound and complete analysis for dense-time systems. The idea is to represent the (nondeterministic) time advance in each application of a tick rule using a fresh SMT variable, and to encode *mte* as SMT constraints. Each rule must also be transformed into a *topmost* rule to ensure that all rewrites occur at the top of terms [96].

Maude-with-SMT analysis has been applied to various domains, including parametric timed automata (PTAs) and parametric interval time Petri nets (PITPNs) [10,9]. Since each application of a tick rule introduces a new SMT variable, standard Maude search does not terminate. Arias et al. [10,9] therefore propose a new *folding* technique to ensure termination whenever the symbolic state space is finite, which is applicable to a wide range of real-time rewrite theories. Maude-with-SMT can also be used to synthesize system parameter values that make the system satisfy desired properties [10,9].

This section explains how to symbolically analyze real-time rewrite theories using the Maude-SE tool [110]. We begin by transforming a real-time rewrite theory into one admissible for symbolic analysis. Then we describe how Maude-SE can be used to perform symbolic reachability analysis. We use the RTT protocol in Section 3 as a running example, and do not use folding for simplicity.

5.1 Symbolic Specification

We define a *symbolic* time domain for symbolic analysis. Maude provides built-in sorts Boolean, Integer, and Real for the corresponding SMT theories. Time values are declared as values of sort Real, and the sort of relational operators such as _<_ is now Boolean:

```
fmod SYM-TIME-DOMAIN is protecting REAL .
  sort TimeInf .       subsort Real < TimeInf .      vars R R' : Real .
  op INF : -> TimeInf [ctor] .
  op _<_ : TimeInf TimeInf -> Boolean [ditto] .
  op _+_ : TimeInf TimeInf -> TimeInf [ditto] .
  ...
  eq INF monus R = INF .
  eq R monus R' = R < R' ? 0/1 : R - R' .
  ...
endfm
```

The sort Real does not have a designated subsort for non-negative real numbers, since the non-negativity of symbolic expressions cannot be determined syntactically. Instead, non-negativity constraints are explicitly declared as SMT constraints: Whenever an SMT variable X of sort Real is used for time values, we add a constraint X >= 0/1 (unless it is subsumed by other constraints). The monus function is declared using an SMT conditional expression.

Maude-SE requires that for each rule $l : q \longrightarrow r$ **if** ψ, (i) any variable not appearing in q has a built-in sort; (ii) ψ is decomposed into pure SMT formulas and non-SMT conditions; and (iii) q has a top sort, with no operator using it or its subsorts as an argument sort [110]. Thus, each rewrite rule must be transformed into an equivalent rule that meets these conditions.

For example, the `respond` rule in the RTT specification is transformed into the following equivalent topmost rule:

```
vars T T' T1 T2 T3 T4 TT : Real .

rl [respond] :
   {(rttReq T from S to R)
    < R : Receiver | lowerDly : T3, upperDly : T4 > STATE} in time T
=> {< R : Receiver | >
    dly(rttResp T from R to S, T3, T4) STATE} in time T .
```

Any rewrite rule that imposes constraints on SMT variables must use SMT constraints. For example, consider the `deliver` rule: `dly(M, 0, T) => M`, with remaining minimum delay 0. In symbolic analysis, the delay value can be a symbolic expression, which requires SMT solving to determine equality. Therefore, this rule is transformed into:

```
crl [deliver] :
   {dly(M, T', T) STATE} in time TT  =>  {M STATE} in time TT
if (T' === 0/1) = true .
```

The `send` and `recordRTT` rules are transformed into top-most rules:

```
crl [send] :
   {< S : Sender | clock : T, timer : T1, period : T2, lowerDly : T3,
                   upperDly : T4, receiver : R > STATE} in time TT
=> {< S : Sender | timer : T2 >
    dly(rttReq T from S to R, T3, T4) STATE} in time TT
if (T1 === 0/1) = true .

rl [recordRTT] :
   {(rttResp T from R to S)
    < S : Sender | clock : T2 > STATE} in time TT
=> {< S : Sender | rtt : T2 monus T > STATE} in time TT .
```

The `tick` rule is transformed into the following rule, which advances time by T, a fresh SMT variable. The non-negativity of T is given as a constraint, and the condition `T <= mte(STATE)` is replaced by the constraint `mte<=(STATE, T)`:

```
crl [tick] :
   {STATE} in time TT
=> {timeEffect(STATE, T)} in time TT + T
if (T >= 0/1 and mte<=(STATE, T)) = true [nonexec] .
```

The function $\mathtt{mte<=}(\mathit{conf}, \mathit{time})$ gives the SMT constraint that is equivalent to the condition $\mathit{time} \leq \mathtt{mte}(\mathit{conf})$:

```
op mte<= : Configuration Time -> Boolean .
eq mte<=(none, T) = true .
```

```
ceq mte<=(C1 C2, T)
  = mte<=(C1, T) and mte<=(C2, T) if C1 =/= none /\ C2 =/= none .
eq mte<=(< S : Sender | timer : TI >, T) = T <= TI .
eq mte<=(< R : Receiver | >, T) = true .
eq mte<=(dly(M, T', TI), T) = T <= TI .
eq mte<=(M, T) = false .
```

5.2 Symbolic Reachability Analysis using Maude-SE

Maude-SE's symbolic reachability analysis command `smt-search` extends Maude's `smt-search` command by supporting witness generation, folding, uninterpreted functions, and so on [110]. Maude-SE also automates the theory transformations for rewriting modulo SMT mentioned in Section 2. Maude-SE's `show smt-path` command (not available in Maude) returns a path for the last `smt-search` result. Its arguments are a path type (`symbolic` or `concrete`) and a solution number. A symbolic path consists of a sequence of constrained terms and rewrite rules, and a concrete path is an instance of the symbolic path with a satisfying assignment.

For the RTT example, we define an initial state *pattern* init, where the period and the bounds on message delays are given as SMT variables:

```
op init : Time Time Time Time Time -> GlobalSystem .
eq init(T1, T2, T3, T4, T)
 = {< snd : Sender | clock : 0/1, timer : 0/1, period : T, receiver : rcv,
                     lowerDly : T1, upperDly : T2, rtt : INF >
    < rcv : Receiver | lowerDly : T3, upperDly : T4 >} .
```

The following command checks whether it is possible to reach a state where the recorded `rtt` value is less than 30 after a duration of 50, provided that the conditions $T = 5000$, $0 < T1 < T2 < 5000$, and $0 < T3 < T4 < 5000$ hold:

```
MaudeSE> smt-search [1,10] in RTT-SYM :
    init(T1:Real, T2:Real, T3:Real, T4:Real, 5000/1) in time 0/1
 => {C:Configuration
    < snd : Sender | rtt : T:Real, ATTS:AttributeSet >} in time T':Real
  such that 0/1 < T1:Real and T1:Real < T2:Real and T2:Real < 5000/1 and
            0/1 < T3:Real and T3:Real < T4:Real and T4:Real < 5000/1 and
            T:Real < 30/1 and T':Real >= 50/1
  using QF_LRA .
```

The output consists of five parts: a symbolic term (`Symbolic state`) and an SMT constraint (`Constraint`) represent a constrained term for a solution, where the matching substitution of the solution with the goal is given in `Substitution`; and a concrete term (`Concrete state`) represents a concrete witness of the constrained term, where the corresponding satisfying assignment obtained by the underlying SMT solver is given in `Assignment`:

```
Solution 1 (state 142)
Symbolic state:
  {< rcv : Receiver | lowerDly : T3, upperDly : T4 >
   < snd : Sender | clock : %V13 + %V14, lowerDly : %V2, period : %V1,
```

```
                        receiver : rcv, rtt : T, upperDly : %V3,
                        timer : ((%V1 - %V5) - %V9) - %V14 >} in time T'
Constraint:
  (%V1 === 5000/1) and (%V2 === 0/1) and (not(T1 <= 0/1)) and
  (not(T2 <= T1)) and (not(5000/1 <= T2)) and (not(T3 <= 0/1)) and
  (not(T4 <= T3)) and (not(5000/1 <= T4)) and (not(30/1 <= T)) and
  ...
Substitution:
  ATTS <-- clock : %V13 + %V14, lowerDly : %V2, period : %V1,
          receiver : rcv, timer : (((%V1 - %V5) - %V9) - %V14),
          upperDly : %V3
  C <-- < rcv : Receiver | lowerDly : T3, upperDly : T4 >
Assignment:
  T' <--(50/1) .Real
  T1 <--(1/4) .Real
  T2 <--(1/2) .Real
  ...
Concrete state:
  {< rcv : Receiver | lowerDly : 1/4, upperDly : 1/2 >
   < snd : Sender | clock : 50/1, lowerDly : 1/4, period : 5000/1,
                    receiver : rcv, rtt : 1/2, upperDly : 1/2,
                    timer : 4950 >} in time 50/1
```

The following `smt-path` command displays a concrete path that witnesses the reachability result of the above `smt-search` command:

```
MaudeSE> show smt-path concrete 1 .
{< rcv : Receiver | lowerDly : 1/4, upperDly : 1/2 >
 < snd : Sender | clock : 0/1, timer : 0/1, ... >} in time 0/1
=====[ send ]=====>
{dly(rttReq 0/1 from snd to rcv, 1/4, 1/2) < rcv : Receiver | ... >
 < snd : Sender | clock : 0/1, timer : 5000/1, ... >} in time 0/1
=====[ tick ]=====>
...
=====[ tick ]=====>
{< rcv : Receiver | lowerDly : 1/4, upperDly : 1/2 >
 < snd : Sender | clock : 50, timer : 4950, ... >} in time 50/1
```

The following command verifies that a bad state, where the recorded rtt value (T) is greater than the sum of the upper bounds (T2 + T4) or less than the sum of the lower bounds (T1 + T3), is not reachable in 20 rewrite steps:

```
MaudeSE> smt-search [1,20] in RTT-SYM :
            init(T1:Real,T2:Real,T3:Real,T4:Real,5000/1) in time 0/1
     => {C:Configuration
            < snd : Sender | rtt : T:Real, ATTS:AttributeSet >} in time T':Real
     such that 0/1 < T1:Real and T1:Real < T2:Real and T2:Real < 5000/1 and
               0/1 < T3:Real and T3:Real < T4:Real and T4:Real < 5000/1 and
               (T:Real > T2:Real + T4:Real or T:Real < T1:Real + T3:Real)
     using QF_LRA .

No more solutions.
```

6 Applications

The expressive real-time rewrite theory formalism supports the definition of any computable data type, object-oriented modeling with subclasses and dynamic object (and message) creation and deletion, hierarchical models, flexibility to easily define many kinds of communication models, and so on. The price to pay is that analysis until recently has been based on time-sampling-based explicit-state executions, which may make model checking both unfeasible and incomplete [87].

The main question is whether there are systems where these features are needed—and which cannot be conveniently (or at all) be modeled as, e.g., timed automata—and where (Real-Time) Maude analysis provides significant value. This section presents a sample of applications of Maude and Real-Time Maude to real-time systems that answer this question positively.

6.1 Network Protocols

The first significant application of Real-Time Maude was the AER/NCA protocol suite proposed by Kurose and others [43]. AER/NCA aims at achieving efficient multicast in active networks. Its informal description was 50 pages long, and included large functions and a detailed model of communication, which took into account packet sizes, buffer sizes, etc. Real-Time Maude analysis of AER/NCA found all errors known by the protocol developers, as well as some significant errors not known by them [90]. Key enabling features were the ability of defining complex functions (and rewrite rules), the use of subclasses to analyze both single protocol components in isolation as well as various compositions of subprotocols, and the ability to easily model communication at the desired (low, in this case) level of abstraction. Similar techniques were used in [54] to model and analyze the NORM multicast protocol developed by the IETF.

OGDC is a sophisticated density control algorithm for wireless sensor networks. Modeling all relevant features, such as coverage areas and their overlaps, communication delays, energy consumption, transmission radius, and so on, Ölveczky and Thorvaldsen [92] used Real-Time Maude simulations of networks with up to 600 nodes to estimate the performance of OGDC. Analyzing the difference between the performance estimates obtained by Real-Time Maude simulations and published performance figures led to the discovery of a previously unknown significant flaw in OGDC when network delays are taken into account. This work also showed that Real-Time Maude simulations can provide quite accurate performance estimates of advanced wireless sensor networks. Features of Real-Time Maude that made this work possible are the ability to model advanced data types, such as areas and functions on them, of easily being able to model a then-new form of communication presented by wireless sensor networks, and of being to able to simulate complex networks with many nodes.

This work led Katelman et al. [44] to model and analyze another then-state-of-the-art wireless sensor network protocol, the LMST topology control protocol, in Maude (using PVeStA to obtain performance estimates from Maude simulations). Their analysis showed that LMST fails when imprecise local clocks and network contention are taken into account. The authors then redesigned LMST and showed that the new design satisfies all desired properties.

Liu et al. [59] used Real-Time Maude to model and analyze mobile ad hoc networks (MANETs). Their work uncovered a spurious behavior in a well-known MANET leader election algorithm that is due to the subtle interplay between communication delays, node movement, and neighbor discovery. This spurious behavior therefore cannot be found by analyses that abstract from node movement and communication delays.

6.2 Cloud-based Transaction Systems

Large applications, such as Gmail, Facebook, eBay, etc., rely on widely distributed and (partially) replicated data. Transactions over such data must satisfy given consistency properties *and* have good performance. Maude and Real-Time Maude have been used to model, model check consistency properties (e.g., [63]), and estimate the performance of both "industrial" and state-of-the-art academic distributed transaction systems. In many cases, a key goal was to predict the performance of different design choices.

Examples of such applications include Apache Cassandra [64,56] (where statistical model checking of the Maude model indicated that a proposed optimization would not outperform the original Cassandra design), Google's Megastore system (which powers Gmail and Google AppEngine) [40] and an extension of the Megastore design which should provide consistency to more transactions without affecting performance [41], Apache ZooKeeper [106], many versions of UC Berkeley's RAMP transactions [60,58], the P-Store design [83] (where Maude analysis found a number of errors in the supposedly verified design), the Walter design [62], and a new design, ROLA, that provides consistency guarantees that should be sufficient for, e.g., "becoming friends" transactions on social media [61].

In most of these applications, PVeStA statistical model checking was used to estimate the performance of a design. The underlying model was usually an untimed nondeterministic model, which is suitable for analyzing correctness properties. A fully probabilistic "performance model" was then obtained from such a "verification model" by adding communication delays sampled from continuous distributions. This method was generalized to "generalized actor systems" in [57], so that a fully probabilistic "performance model" can be automatically generated from an untimed "verification model" and communication delay distributions.

The authors of the above applications compared the performance estimates obtained by PVeStA statistical model checking of Maude models with the actual performance obtained by running the distributed implementations on cloud infrastructures. These experiments showed that model-based performance comparison between different designs accurately reflects the performance differences between the actual implementations of the different designs [56,65,57,58,61]. For example, Fig. 1, taken from [57], shows the Maude/PVeStA model-based performance estimates of the RAMP-S and RAMP-F designs as a function of transaction sizes for different message delay distributions (plots (a), (b), (d), and (e)), while plots (c) and (f) show system performance in real cloud deployments. These plots indicate that the "curves" correspond quite well, even if the actual values differ. Figure 2, also from [57], shows that the actual performance values obtained by SMC are very similar to those in real implementations when parameters are chosen carefully; see [57] for further discussions.

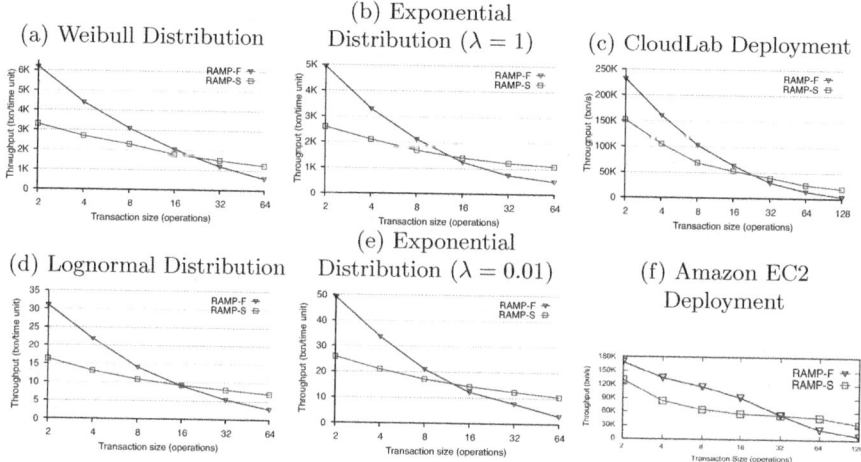

Fig. 1. Throughput comparison in [57] of the RAMP-F and RAMP-S algorithms as the size of transactions grow: SMC-based performance estimates (plots (a), (b), (d), and (e)) and implementation-based performance evaluations (plots (c) and (f)).

6.3 Transportation Systems

AUTOSAR (AUTomotive Open System ARchitecture) is a standard designed to unify and standardize automotive software development methodologies. Its core members include BMW, Bosch, Daimler, Toyota, General Motors, and Volkswagen. Zhu et al. [111] used Real-Time Maude to formalize and analyze several timing properties within a portion of the AUTOSAR operating system. Specifically, they modeled and analyzed various aspects of the scheduling process, including schedulability, fault propagation, and consistent component configuration.

The European Rail Traffic Management System (ERTMS) is a train control standard developed to enhance the performance and capacity of rail traffic across Europe. Berger et al. [22] formalized the ERTMS system using Real-Time Maude, incorporating all subsystems involved in its control cycle. Their work included model checking safety properties, particularly for bi-directional rail yards. This was the first formalization that could handle different components, such as interlockings, radio block centers (RBCs), controllers, and trains in one model, allowing the authors to analyze also the interplay of these components. Up to that point verification was done separately for interlockings and for RBCs. A key

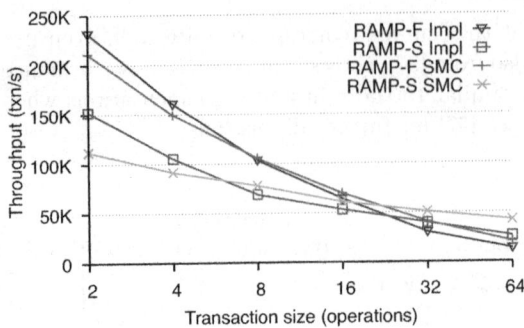

Fig. 2. Comparison in [57] between SMC predictions (yellow for RAMP-S, and red for RAMP-F) and CloudLab evaluations (green for RAMP-S, and blue for RAMP-F).

Real-Time Maude feature that made this effort feasible was support for object-oriented modeling of hybrid systems. While Real-Time Maude analysis did not uncover unknown errors, it demonstrated that the entire system was not fault-tolerant: the overall system fails to be safe if some component fails while the others work correctly.

In integrated modular avionics (IMA), a *cabinet* is a chassis with a power supply, general purpose computing, I/O, etc. Aircrafts use multiple physically separated cabinets to prevent system failure from physical damage. The active standby system, developed by Steve Miller and Darren Cofer at Rockwell-Collins, determines which of two cabinets is *active*. In [72], Meseguer and Ölveczky modeled and analyzed this system using Real-Time Maude. Their analysis showed that the desired properties were not satisfied. They therefore came up with weakened versions of the requirements, which could be verified. These weakened requirements turned out to be the same requirements independently discovered by Cofer and Miller during their NuSMV analysis.

To execute a smooth turn, an airplane's *ailerons* and its *rudder* must move in a synchronized way. A turning algorithm issues commands to the aileron and rudder controllers to achieve a smooth turn of the aircraft. Bae et al. [11] formalized and analyzed a textbook turning algorithm for small aircrafts using Real-Time Maude. Their analysis revealed that the textbook algorithm failed to ensure a smooth turn when the pilot issued a sharp turn command, leading to the development of a revised version. Real-Time Maude model checking showed that the revised algorithm allows the plane to reach the desired direction quickly while keeping the adverse yaw angle small throughout the turn.

Nigam et al. [77] proposed a formal framework, called *Soft Agents*, for specifying and analyzing distributed cyber-physical systems based on real-time rewrite theories. In this framework, agents and environments are represented by collections of logical assertions known as knowledge bases. An agent's local knowledge base reflects its perception of the environment, while the environment knowledge base represents the ground truth. In [78], the Soft Agent framework is combined with rewriting modulo SMT to perform symbolic reachability analysis and is applied to the formal analysis of a vehicle platooning application.

Real-Time Maude has been used by a Japanese research institute to identify time-dependent bugs in embedded car software used by major automakers. The time sampling approach of Real-Time Maude was supposedly crucial in detecting these bugs, that were not found using the usual model-checking tools in industry. However, the findings were not published due to proprietary restrictions.

6.4 Scheduling Algorithms

The idea of the CASH ("capacity sharing") scheduling algorithm is that allocated, but unused, execution times are put in a queue, so that other jobs can use such unused cycles to improve system performance. Real-Time Maude reachability analysis found a missed deadline in a proposed optimization of CASH, invalidating the proposed design, whereas extensive Monte-Carlo simulations failed to discover the missed deadline [85]. Real-Time Maude simulations showed that the queue could grow beyond any bound, implying that CASH cannot be modeled as timed automata or other formalisms requiring bounded data structures.

Real-Time Maude has also been applied to rate-monotonic scheduling [55] and resource-sharing algorithms such as the priority inheritance protocol [91].

6.5 Formal Patterns

Formal patterns [71] are formally specified and verified design patterns. The key advantage is that the effort spent on verifying a formal pattern is amortized over all instances of the pattern. Rewriting logic has been used to formalize a number of formal patterns involving time, including the following.

The *Command-Shaper pattern* [108] aims at ensuring the safe operation of medical devices connected to patients. The idea is to intercept commands from external devices (including the patient) to make sure that the patient is never in a dangerous state. Instances of this pattern include mechanisms to enforce that a sophisticated pacemaker, which adapts to changes in the patient's activity, will never place the patient's heart in stressful situations, and that a patient-operated infusion pump for morphine will not administer too many bolus doses.

In [107], Sun and Meseguer proposed a collection of formal patterns to achieve fault tolerance for commonly occurring faults—such as button bounce, phantom button presses, and stuck buttons—in button interfaces of manually operated devices. These formal patterns ensure specific levels of safety for medical device interfaces in the presence of faults and can also be applied to devices in other domains. They instantiate these patterns with a simple button-press counter.

Many distributed cyber-physical systems, such as avionics and automotive systems, are *virtually synchronous*: in each iteration, components read inputs and perform transitions which generate outputs for the next iteration. Designing and verifying such distributed systems is challenging due to race conditions, clock skews, network delays, and the state space explosion caused by asynchrony. The

PALS formal pattern [72,4] reduces the modeling and verification of virtually synchronous distributed real-time systems to modeling and verifying their much simpler synchronous counterparts, provided that bounds on network delays, clock skews, and execution times are guaranteed. For the active standby system [72], the synchronous design could be model checked in less than a second, while model checking even a very simplified asynchronous system was infeasible.

PALS and other synchronizers for cyber-physical systems, such as TTA [45,101], assume that all components have the same period. However, different controllers may operate at different rates. For example, the aileron controllers and the rudder controller of an airplane typically operate with different periods, yet must synchronize to turn an airplane. PALS was therefore extended to the Multirate PALS pattern [12] for virtually synchronous multirate systems. The MSYNC pattern [13] generalizes, and combines the advantages of, both TTA and PALS, and includes a definition of a multirate extension of TTA as a special case.

PALS abstracts from the time when an event takes place, as long as it happens in a certain time interval. However, many virtually synchronous cyber-physical systems are networks of hybrid components with continuous behaviors combined with sophisticated controllers. In such CPSs with continuous dynamics, it is not possible to abstract from the time when a controller reads a continuous value or sends an actuator command. The Hybrid PALS pattern [17] extends Multirate PALS to such virtually synchronous distributed hybrid systems, taking into account sensing and actuating times that depend on imprecise local clocks.

6.6 Semantics and Formal Analysis for Programming and Modeling Languages

One of the most promising ways to integrate formal analysis into the system development process is to let designers work with their preferred modeling and programming languages, and equip these languages with a formal semantics and intuitive *automatic* formal analyses. However, most formal real-time tools that provide automatic verification are based on formalisms that cannot capture industrial modeling languages. Because of Maude's and Real-Time Maude's expressiveness and generality, they have been used to define the formal semantics of (significant subsets of) a number of programming and modeling languages for real-time and hybrid systems. In some cases, the generation of a (Real-Time) Maude model and the formal analysis have been integrated into the programming/modeling environment of the language, so that the designer gets formal analysis for free, without having to be acquainted with (Real-Time) Maude.

A key to many of the formalization efforts is that (Real-Time) Maude supports both rewrite rules and equations, which allows us to define transitions at the desired level of granularity, and also makes the analysis much more efficient than one based, e.g., on "small-step semantics." Another feature of (Real-Time) Maude that makes it feasible to formalize the semantics of large and complex languages is its support for *object-based* modeling. Finally, Maude's support for *parametric* atomic propositions makes it possible to define generic propositions which allow the developer to write analysis queries without having to understand Maude or her model's formal representation.

The *Architecture Analysis & Description Language* (AADL) [39] is an industrial modeling standard for avionics and other safety-critical applications. A formal semantics for a "behavioral" subset of AADL has been defined in Real-Time Maude [84], and Real-Time Maude code generation and formal analysis have been integrated into the OSATE tool environment for AADL.

AADL models specify asynchronous systems, whose model checking analysis easily can lead to state space explosion. Bae and others have therefore defined the *Synchronous AADL* modeling language for specifying synchronous designs of embedded systems in AADL [15]. They formalized the semantics of Synchronous AADL in Maude, integrated the Real-Time Maude code generation and formal analysis into OSATE as the *SynchAADL2Maude* plug-in [19], and applied Synchronous AADL and SynchAADL2Maude to the active standby avionics system mentioned above. Synchronous AADL is useful to specify synchronous designs in general, and can also be used to specify the underlying synchronous designs of virtually synchronous cyber-physical systems; by the PALS formal pattern, verifying the synchronous design also verifies the corresponding asynchronous "implementation." Bae and others have extended Synchronous AADL, including the integration into OSATE, to multirate systems [18], hybrid systems [49,46], and multirate hybrid systems [14,47]. In the hybrid systems cases, the semantics is formalized using rewriting modulo SMT, and the main forms of analysis supported are randomized simulation, (bounded) symbolic reachability analysis, and their combination. Somewhat surprisingly, the performance of such Maude-with-SMT reachability analysis is, in many cases, comparable to that of state-of-the-art hybrid automata reachability analysis tools.

Ptolemy II [94] is a graphical modeling language and simulation tool for embedded systems used in industry. In Ptolemy II, real-time systems are specified as discrete-event (DE) models. Real-Time Maude has formalized the semantics of such models, which involve finite state machines with unbounded variables, unbounded queues, and requires computing fixed points in hierarchical systems [16]. The synthesis of Real-Time Maude models and Real-Time Maude model checking have been integrated into Ptolemy II, and Real-Time Maude analysis found a previously unknown bug in a Ptolemy II model of a traffic light system [16,52]. Maude has also formalized the semantics of Edward A. Lee's Lingua Franca [66] coordination language for CPSs [67]. This Maude semantics is the first formal semantics of Lingua Franca that captures its desired "synchronous" big-step semantics; other actor-based and SMT-based encodings provide only much less efficient "small-step" semantics.

Programmable logic controllers (PLCs) are computer systems specialized for industrial control applications, such as assembly lines, machinery, and robotic devices. Structured Text (ST) is an imperative programming language for PLCs, defined in the IEC 61131-3 standard. Lee et al. [51] defined a rewriting-based formal executable semantics of PLC ST that takes into account time-related functions over multiple iterations of execution cycles, and proposed a bounded

LTL model checking technique, based on rewriting modulo SMT, for PLC ST programs. Lee and Bae [50] extended the formal semantics of PLC ST to support preemptive multitasking with hard real-time constraints, and proposed state-space reduction techniques for model checking multitask PLC ST programs.

Orc [74] is a language for orchestrating web services. In [6], AlTurki and Meseguer showed: (i) how one can go from an Orc specification to a *distributed Maude implementation* of the Orc specification, using their Maude semantics of Orc and Maude sockets; and (ii) how such distributed implementations can be model checked using Real-Time Maude. AlTurki and Meseguer integrated physical time into their distributed implementations by each distributed node having a local clock object implemented in Java.

BPMN is an ISO/IEC standard graphical notation for specifying business processes. Durán and Salaün [34] formalized timed business processes in Maude and used Maude to analyze, e.g., maximum/minimum/average execution time. In [32], this setting was extended with stochastic durations and delays of tasks and flows, and with probabilities on branching in gateways, to support statistical model checking using PVeStA for this timed and probabilistic extension of BPMN. Maude-based analysis of such timed and probabilistic BPMN models has been used to optimize the allocation of resources in business processes [33,31].

Real-Time Maude has formalized the semantics not only of single modeling languages, but also of timed (model transformation) *frameworks* in which a range of timed domain-specific visual languages and their behaviors can be specified. In particular, Real-Time Maude has provided a formal semantics to a timed extension of the MOF-based MOMENT2 model transformation framework [24] and to the e-Motions model transformation framework [95]. e-Motions facilitates graphically defining the behavior of domain-specific modeling languages (DSMLs) by modeling change as local transformations, with support for defining and analyzing real-time systems [97,30].

Maude and Real-Time Maude have also provided formal semantics, simulation, and model checking for the actor-like modeling languages Real-Time ABS [23], Timed Rebeca [102], and Actors and RTSynchronizers [29], as well as to the $\mathcal{L}$ language for handsets developed at DOCOMO USA Labs [5] and to the CPS modeling language CPSL^{sc} [53].

Example: HybridSynchAADL. We use the HybridSynchAADL tool [49,46,47] to illustrate how Maude analysis can be integrated into an industrial modeling environment, so that the user can specify her system in her favorite modeling standard, define her correctness properties in a fairly intuitive way, and then automatically check these desired properties from within her modeling tool.

The HybridSynchAADL modeling language is a subset of AADL in which synchronous designs of distributed controllers with continuous environments can be specified. A controller is an ordinary software component, where thread behavior is defined using AADL's behavior annex. It also declares the maximal clock skew, and sampling and actuating times as properties. An environment compo-

```
system RoomEnv
    features
        temp: out data port Base_Types::Float;
        power: in data port Base_Types::Float;
        on_ctrl: in event port;
        off_ctrl: in event port;
    properties
        Hybrid_SynchAADL::isEnvironment => true;
end RoomEnv;

system implementation RoomEnv.impl
    subcomponents
        x: data Base_Types::Float;
        p: data Base_Types::Float;
    connections
        C: port x -> temp;           R: port power -> p;
    modes
        hOff: initial mode;          hOn: mode;
        hOff -[on_ctrl]-> hOn;       hOn -[off_ctrl]-> hOff;
    properties
        Hybrid_SynchAADL::ContinuousDynamics =>
            "x(t)= x(0)- 0.1*(x(0)- p/0.1)* t;"  in modes (hOn),
            "x(t)= x(0)*(1 - 0.1 * t);"  in modes (hOff);
end RoomEnv.impl;
```

Fig. 3. An environment component in HybridSynchAADL.

nent specifies continuous dynamics as a property, and can have different modes to specify different trajectories (for example, see Figure 3).

The tool's property specification language allows users to specify invariant and reachability properties as propositional formulas, where atomic propositions are AADL Boolean expressions. For example, reachability properties have the form **reachability** [*id*] φ_{init} ==> φ_{goal} **in time** τ, meaning that a state satisfying φ_{goal} is reachable from a state satisfying φ_{init} within time τ.

The HybridSynchAADL tool provides three analysis methods: (i) symbolic reachability analysis, which verifies all possible behaviors using Maude-SMT; (ii) randomized simulation, which repeatedly runs the model while randomly choosing concrete data values, sampling and actuating times, and so on; and (iii) portfolio analysis, which executes symbolic reachability analysis and randomized simulation in parallel using multithreading.

Figure 4 shows the tool interface, which is fully integrated into OSATE. The left editor shows an AADL model, the bottom right editor shows its graphical representation, and the top right editor displays two properties in the property specification language. The **Portfolio Analysis** item has already been selected, and the **Result** view at the bottom displays the analysis results. The witness of the analysis, if any, is displayed in a readable format if the user clicks the link in the **Location** column.

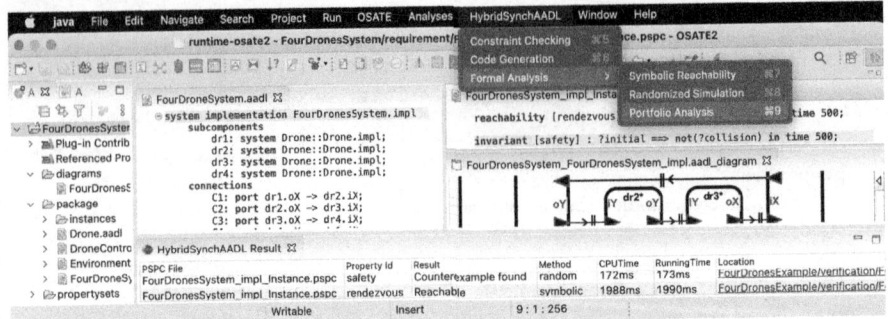

Fig. 4. HybridSynchAADL window in OSATE.

The effectiveness of HybridSynchAADL and MR-HybridSynchAADL has been demonstrated on systems of collaborating drones performing rendezvous, formation control, and packet delivery [48,46,47]. Somewhat surprisingly, the performance of Maude-with-SMT reachability analysis often surpasses that of dedicated hybrid automata reachability tools such as HyComp, SpaceEx, Flow∗, and dReach [49]. Randomized simulation is useful for finding "obvious" bugs and analyzing complex systems that symbolic analysis cannot handle.

6.7 Object-oriented Hybrid Systems

Many cyber-physical systems feature continuous behaviors. In object-based stochastic hybrid systems (OBSHSs) [73], the continuous dynamics of each object is given by stochastic differential equations. This model is aimed at distributed hybrid systems, and the objects communicate by asynchronous message passing. An OBSHS can be specified in the SHYMaude language, which can be translated to Maude by approximating the continuous dynamics using the Euler-Maruyama method. In this way, OBSHSs can be simulated using Maude and therefore also be subjected to statistical model checking using PVeStA.

Many large hybrid systems consist of multiple continuous components whose continuous behaviors influence each other. Consider, e.g., a room with heaters. The continuous behavior (e.g., the temperature) of the entire system depends on how many heaters are in the room. One solution is to define the continuous dynamics of the entire system with one heater, redefine the continuous dynamics of the entire system in case there are two heaters in the room, and so on. This approach is not object-oriented, since the continuous dynamics is not defined at the class level, and makes it an absolute nightmare to define the continuous dynamics of a system with many such components. Is it possible to define such *interacting hybrid systems* in a truly object-oriented way, namely, so that the dynamics of the entire system can be defined at the *class* level? In [37], Fadlisyah and others defined such a way of specifying also the continuous dynamics of large classes of object-oriented hybrid systems at the class level by using the effort/flow approach. The HI-Maude tool [36] supports the specification of such interacting hybrid systems. The continuous dynamics is defined by differential equations, and are approximated using adaptations of the Euler, the Runge-Kutta 2nd order, and the Runge-Kutta 4th order numerical approximation methods, allowing the system to be simulated in Maude. Such decomposition of the definition of the continuous behaviors of very complex hybrid systems made it possible for Fadlisyah et al. to provide a fairly detailed model of the human thermoregulatory system, which they used to simulate how long a person can stay in a hot sauna in different settings [38].

We have previously described that cyber-physical systems with continuous components, whose continuous behaviors do not influence each other, also can be specified and analyzed using HybridSynchAADL [49,48,46,47]. Like in the above approaches, a model can be simulated in Maude by randomly choosing concrete sampling and actuating times, transitions, etc., but unlike them, Maude combined with SMT solving can be used to perform *symbolic* reachability analysis, as long as the continuous dynamics is supported by an SMT solver.

6.8 Some Other Applications

Pita and Riesco [93] used the Kademlia peer-to-peer distributed hash table and Maude sockets to create a peer-to-peer network in Maude. They use Real-Time Maude to analyze an abstract "verification model" of their distributed system.

Nakajima [76,75] used Real-Time Maude to formalize the energy consumption of Android application programs for smartphones, and to search for hidden energy bugs in the program code.

Inspired by work by Cerone [26], Broccia et al. [25] defined an executable formal model of human attention and multitasking in Real-Time Maude. They applied their framework to study under what circumstances: (i) a person can safely interact with a GPS navigation system while driving; (ii) an air traffic controller can avoid making crucial mistakes; and (iii) a nurse can safely set multiple infusion pumps simultaneously.

Co-simulation is the simulation of an entire system by combining the simulators of its subcomponents. Hansen and Ölveczky [42] have formalized co-simulation in Maude, and used Maude to synthesize co-simulation algorithms, parameter values, and instrumentations so that the resulting system satisfies desired properties.

7 Concluding Remarks

We have shown how a wide range of sophisticated real-time and cyber-physical systems can be modeled in rewriting logic as real-time rewrite theories, which can be specified and analyzed using Real-Time Maude, or, as we explain in this paper, directly in Maude. Given the expressiveness and generality of real-time rewrite theories, formal analysis is typically based on explicit-state analysis using a few basic strategies for "sampling" certain moments in time. For dense time, such analysis is in general incomplete since all possible behaviors are not covered.

Nevertheless, we have in this paper given a brief overview of a significant number of advanced applications where this expressiveness was needed and where (Real-Time) Maude still provided useful analysis results. Such applications include both "concrete" distributed real-time systems/protocols/algorithms as well as formalizing the semantics and providing "under-the-hood" automatic model checking analyses for modeling languages for cyber-physical systems.

We have also shown that Maude/PVeStA statistical model checking of purely probabilistic real-time systems gives model-based performance estimates that correlate well with distributed implementations.

Finally, we have summarized two recent developments:

- A timed strategy language that supports defining "discrete" and "time sampling" strategies in an intuitive and modular way, with an implementation of (almost) all Real-Time Maude analysis methods executed according to user-defined strategies. This also allows us to use more effective time sampling strategies than provided by Real-Time Maude, as shown in the paper.
- *Symbolic* analysis, where the amount of time advancing in each "idling" step is represented by a new SMT variable. Symbolic Maude-SE reachability analysis then captures all possible behaviors also for dense time. However, because a new SMT variable is introduced in each idling step, symbolic reachability analysis will typically not terminate when the desired states are unreachable, even with standard "folding" of symbolic states. For parametric timed automata and parametric time Petri nets we have implemented symbolic reachability analysis which terminates whenever the corresponding reachable symbolic state spaces are finite.

Future work includes developing symbolic analysis methods for larger classes of real-time rewrite theories, as well as symbolic temporal logic model checking, and combining symbolic methods with user-defined strategies. These features should be integrated into a new and user-friendly Real-Time Maude tool.

Acknowledgments. Real-time rewrite theories and the Real-Time Maude tool were developed together with our dear friend José Meseguer. We are grateful to the editors of this festschrift for inviting us to submit a paper honoring Gul Agha, and to the anonymous reviewers for very useful comments. This work was supported by the NATO Science for Peace and Security program through grant number G6133 (project SymSafe) and by the PHC project Aurora AESIR. Bae has been partially supported by the National Research Foundation of Korea (NRF) grant (No. RS-2021-NR060080), and Institute of Information & Communications Technology Planning & Evaluation (IITP) grant (No. RS-2024-00439856), both funded by the Korea government (MSIT).

References

1. Agha, G.: Actors: a model of concurrent computation in distributed systems. MIT Press, Cambridge, MA, USA (1986)

2. Agha, G., Palmskog, K.: A survey of statistical model checking. ACM Transactions on Modeling and Computer Simulation **28**(1), 6:1–6:39 (2018)
3. Agha, G.A., Kim, W.: Actors: A unifying model for parallel and distributed computing. Journal of Systems Architecture **45**(15), 1263–1277 (1999)
4. Al-Nayeem, A., Sun, M., Qiu, X., Sha, L., Miller, S.P., Cofer, D.D.: A formal architecture pattern for real-time distributed systems. In: RTSS'09. pp. 161–170. IEEE Computer Society, USA (2009)
5. AlTurki, M., Dhurjati, D., Yu, D., Chander, A., Inamura, H.: Formal specification and analysis of timing properties in software systems. In: FASE'09. Lecture Notes in Computer Science, vol. 5503, pp. 262–277. Springer (2009)
6. AlTurki, M., Meseguer, J.: Dist-Orc: A rewriting-based distributed implementation of Orc with formal analysis. In: RTRTS'10. EPTCS, vol. 36, pp. 26–45 (2010)
7. AlTurki, M , Meseguer, J.: PVeStA: A parallel statistical model checking and quantitative analysis tool. In: Algebra and Coalgebra in Computer Science (CALCO 2011). Lecture Notes in Computer Science, vol. 6859. Springer (2011)
8. Alur, R., Dill, D.L.: A theory of timed automata. Theoretical Computer Science **126**(2), 183–235 (1994)
9. Arias, J., Bae, K., Olarte, C., Ölveczky, P.C., Petrucci, L.: A rewriting-logic-with-SMT-based formal analysis and parameter synthesis framework for parametric time Petri nets. Fundamenta Informaticae **192**(3-4), 261–312 (2024)
10. Arias, J., Bae, K., Olarte, C., Ölveczky, P.C., Petrucci, L., Rømming, F.: Symbolic analysis and parameter synthesis for networks of parametric timed automata with global variables using Maude and SMT solving. Science of Computer Programming **233**, 103074 (2024)
11. Bae, K., Krisiloff, J., Meseguer, J., Ölveczky, P.C.: Designing and verifying distributed cyber-physical systems using Multirate PALS: An airplane turning control system case study. Science of Computer Programming **103**, 13–50 (2015)
12. Bae, K., Meseguer, J., Ölveczky, P.C.: Formal patterns for multirate distributed real-time systems. Science of Computer Programming **91**, 3–44 (2014)
13. Bae, K., Ölveczky, P.C.: MSYNC: A generalized formal design pattern for virtually synchronous multirate cyber-physical systems. ACM Transactions on Embedded Computing Systems **20**(5s), 105:1–105:26 (2021)
14. Bae, K., Ölveczky, P.C.: Formal model engineering of distributed CPSs using AADL: From behavioral AADL models to Multirate Hybrid Synchronous AADL. In: FACS'23. Lecture Notes in Computer Science, vol. 14485, pp. 127–152. Springer (2023)
15. Bae, K., Ölveczky, P.C., Al-Nayeem, A., Meseguer, J.: Synchronous AADL and its formal analysis in Real-Time Maude. In: ICFEM'11. Lecture Notes in Computer Science, vol. 6991, pp. 651–667. Springer (2011)
16. Bae, K., Ölveczky, P.C., Feng, T.H., Lee, E.A., Tripakis, S.: Verifying hierarchical Ptolemy II discrete-event models using Real-Time Maude. Science of Computer Programming **77**(12), 1235–1271 (2012)
17. Bae, K., Ölveczky, P.C., Kong, S., Gao, S., Clarke, E.M.: SMT-based analysis of virtually synchronous distributed hybrid systems. In: HSCC'16. pp. 145–154. ACM (2016)
18. Bae, K., Ölveczky, P.C., Meseguer, J.: Definition, semantics, and analysis of Multirate Synchronous AADL. In: FM'14. Lecture Notes in Computer Science, vol. 8442, pp. 94–109. Springer (2014)

19. Bae, K., Ölveczky, P.C., Meseguer, J., Al-Nayeem, A.: The SynchAADL2Maude tool. In: FASE'12. Lecture Notes in Computer Science, vol. 7212, pp. 59–62. Springer (2012)
20. Bae, K., Rocha, C.: Symbolic state space reduction with guarded terms for rewriting modulo SMT. Science of Computer Programming **178**, 20–42 (2019)
21. Behrmann, G., David, A., Larsen, K.G.: A tutorial on Uppaal. In: Formal Methods for the Design of Real-Time Systems (SFM-RT 2004). LNCS, vol. 3185, pp. 200–236. Springer (2004)
22. Berger, U., James, P., Lawrence, A., Roggenbach, M., Seisenberger, M.: Verification of the European Rail Traffic Management System in Real-Time Maude. Science of Computer Programming **154**, 61–88 (2018)
23. Bjørk, J., de Boer, F.S., Johnsen, E.B., Schlatte, R., Tarifa, S.L.T.: User-defined schedulers for real-time concurrent objects. Innovations in Systems and Software Engineering **9**(1), 29–43 (2013)
24. Boronat, A., Ölveczky, P.C.: Formal real-time model transformations in MOMENT2. In: FASE'10. Lecture Notes in Computer Science, vol. 6013, pp. 29–43. Springer (2010)
25. Broccia, G., Milazzo, P., Ölveczky, P.C.: Formal modeling and analysis of safety-critical human multitasking. Innovations in Systems and Software Engineering **15**(3-4), 169–190 (2019)
26. Cerone, A.: A cognitive framework based on rewriting logic for the analysis of interactive systems. In: SEFM'16. Lecture Notes in Computer Science, vol. 9763, pp. 287–303. Springer (2016)
27. Clavel, M., Durán, F., Eker, S., Escobar, S., Lincoln, P., Martí-Oliet, N., Meseguer, J., Rubio, R., Talcott, C.: Maude Manual (Version 3.5). SRI International (2024), available at http://maude.cs.illinois.edu
28. Clavel, M., Durán, F., Eker, S., Lincoln, P., Martí-Oliet, N., Meseguer, J., Talcott, C.L.: All About Maude – A High-Performance Logical Framework, LNCS, vol. 4350. Springer (2007)
29. Ding, H., Zheng, C., Agha, G., Sha, L.: Automated verification of the dependability of object-oriented real-time systems. In: WORDS'03. pp. 171–178. IEEE Computer Society (2003)
30. Durán, F.: Rewriting logic and Maude for the formalization and analysis of DSMLs, and the prototyping of MDSE tools. J. Object Technol. **21**(4), 4:1–12 (2022)
31. Durán, F., Pozas, N., Rocha, C.: Business processes resource management using rewriting logic and deep-learning-based predictive monitoring. J. Log. Algebraic Methods Program. **136**, 100928 (2024)
32. Durán, F., Rocha, C., Salaün, G.: Stochastic analysis of BPMN with time in rewriting logic. Sci. Comput. Program. **168**, 1–17 (2018)
33. Durán, F., Rocha, C., Salaün, G.: Resource provisioning strategies for BPMN processes: Specification and analysis using Maude. J. Log. Algebraic Methods Program. **123**, 100711 (2021)
34. Durán, F., Salaün, G.: Verifying timed BPMN processes using Maude. In: Proc. of COORDINATION. LNCS, vol. 10319, pp. 219–236. Springer (2017)
35. Eker, S., Martí-Oliet, N., Meseguer, J., Rubio, R., Verdejo, A.: The Maude strategy language. Journal of Logical and Algebraic Methods in Programming **134**, 100887 (2023)
36. Fadlisyah, M., Ölveczky, P.C.: The HI-Maude tool. In: CALCO'13. Lecture Notes in Computer Science, vol. 8089, pp. 322–327. Springer (2013)

37. Fadlisyah, M., Ölveczky, P.C., Ábrahám, E.: Object-oriented formal modeling and analysis of interacting hybrid systems in HI-Maude. In: SEFM'11. Lecture Notes in Computer Science, vol. 7041, pp. 415–430. Springer (2011)
38. Fadlisyah, M., Ölveczky, P.C., Ábrahám, E.: Formal modeling and analysis of interacting hybrid systems in HI-Maude: What happened at the 2010 sauna world championships? Science of Computer Programming **99**, 95–127 (2015)
39. Feiler, P.H., Gluch, D.P.: Model-Based Engineering with AADL: An Introduction to the SAE Architecture Analysis and Design Language. Addison-Wesley, USA (2012)
40. Grov, J., Ölveczky, P.C.: Formal modeling and analysis of Google's Megastore in Real-Time Maude. In: Specification, Algebra, and Software - Essays Dedicated to Kokichi Futatsugi. Lecture Notes in Computer Science, vol 8373, pp. 494–519. Springer (2014)
41. Grov, J., Ölveczky, P.C.: Increasing consistency in multi-site data stores: Megastore-CGC and its formal analysis. In: SEFM'14. Lecture Notes in Computer Science, vol. 8702, pp. 159–174. Springer (2014)
42. Hansen, S.T., Ölveczky, P.C.: Modeling, algorithm synthesis, and instrumentation for co-simulation in Maude. In: WRLA'22. Lecture Notes in Computer Science, vol. 13252, pp. 130–150. Springer (2022)
43. Kasera, S.K., Bhattacharyya, S., Keaton, M., Kiwior, D., Zabele, S., Kurose, J.F., Towsley, D.: Scalable fair reliable multicast using active services. IEEE Network **14**(1), 48–57 (2000)
44. Katelman, M., Meseguer, J., Hou, J.C.: Redesign of the LMST wireless sensor protocol through formal modeling and statistical model checking. In: FMOODS'08. Lecture Notes in Computer Science, vol. 5051, pp. 150–169. Springer (2008)
45. Kopetz, H., Bauer, G.: The time-triggered architecture. Proceedings of the IEEE **91**(1), 112–126 (2003)
46. Lee, J., Bae, K., Ölveczky, P.C.: An extension of HybridSynchAADL and its application to collaborating autonomous UAVs. In: ISoLA'22. Lecture Notes in Computer Science, vol. 13703, pp. 47–64. Springer (2022)
47. Lee, J., Bae, K., Ölveczky, P.C.: Rigorous model engineering of hierarchical multirate CPSs in MR-HybridSynchAADL. In: ISoLA'24. Lecture Notes in Computer Science, vol. 15220, pp. 243–262. Springer (2024)
48. Lee, J., Bae, K., Ölveczky, P.C., Kim, S., Kang, M.: Modeling and formal analysis of virtually synchronous cyber-physical systems in AADL. International Journal on Software Tools for Technology Transfer **24**(6), 911–948 (2022)
49. Lee, J., Kim, S., Bae, K., Ölveczky, P.C.: HybridSynchAADL: Modeling and formal analysis of virtually synchronous CPSs in AADL. In: CAV'21. Lecture Notes in Computer Science, vol. 12759, pp. 491–504. Springer (2021)
50. Lee, J., Bae, K.: Formal semantics and analysis of multitask PLC ST programs with preemption. In: FM'24. Lecture Notes in Computer Science, vol. 14933, pp. 425–442. Springer (2024)
51. Lee, J., Kim, S., Bae, K.: Bounded model checking of PLC ST programs using rewriting modulo SMT. In: FTSCS'22. pp. 56–67. ACM (2022)
52. Lepri, D., Ábrahám, E., Ölveczky, P.C.: Sound and complete timed CTL model checking of timed Kripke structures and real-time rewrite theories. Science of Computer Programming **99**, 128–192 (2015)
53. Li, R., Zhu, H., Banach, R.: An algebraic approach to simulation and verification for cyber-physical systems with shared-variable concurrency. The Journal of Logic and Algebraic Programming **139**, 100973 (2024)

54. Lien, E., Ölveczky, P.C.: Formal modeling and analysis of an IETF multicast protocol. In: Seventh IEEE International Conference on Software Engineering and Formal Methods (SEFM 2009). pp. 273–282. IEEE Computer Society (2009)
55. Liu, J., Zhou, M., Song, X., Gu, M., Sun, J.: Formal modeling and verification of a rate-monotonic scheduling implementation with Real-Time Maude. IEEE Transactions on Industrial Electronics **64**(4), 3239–3249 (2017)
56. Liu, S., Ganhotra, J., Rahman, M.R., Nguyen, S., Gupta, I., Meseguer, J.: Quantitative analysis of consistency in NoSQL key-value stores. Leibniz Transactions on Embedded Systems **4**(1), 03:1–03:26 (2017)
57. Liu, S., Meseguer, J., Ölveczky, P.C., Zhang, M., Basin, D.A.: Bridging the semantic gap between qualitative and quantitative models of distributed systems. Proc. ACM Program. Lang. **6**(OOPSLA2), 315–344 (2022)
58. Liu, S., Ölveczky, P.C., Ganhotra, J., Gupta, I., Meseguer, J.: Exploring design alternatives for RAMP transactions through statistical model checking. In: ICFEM'17. Lecture Notes in Computer Science, vol. 10610, pp. 298–314. Springer (2017)
59. Liu, S., Ölveczky, P.C., Meseguer, J.: Modeling and analyzing mobile ad hoc networks in Real-Time Maude. Journal of Logical and Algebraic Methods in Programming **85**(1), 34–66 (2016)
60. Liu, S., Ölveczky, P.C., Rahman, M.R., Ganhotra, J., Gupta, I., Meseguer, J.: Formal modeling and analysis of RAMP transaction systems. In: SAC'16. pp. 1700–1707. ACM (2016)
61. Liu, S., Ölveczky, P.C., Wang, Q., Gupta, I., Meseguer, J.: Read atomic transactions with prevention of lost updates: ROLA and its formal analysis. Formal Aspects of Computing **31**(5), 503–540 (2019)
62. Liu, S., Ölveczky, P.C., Wang, Q., Meseguer, J.: Formal modeling and analysis of the Walter transactional data store. In: WRLA'18. Lecture Notes in Computer Science, vol. 11152, pp. 136–152. Springer (2018)
63. Liu, S., Ölveczky, P.C., Zhang, M., Wang, Q., Meseguer, J.: Automatic analysis of consistency properties of distributed transaction systems in Maude. In: TACAS'19. Lecture Notes in Computer Science, vol. 11428, pp. 40–57. Springer (2019)
64. Liu, S., Rahman, M.R., Skeirik, S., Gupta, I., Meseguer, J.: Formal modeling and analysis of Cassandra in Maude. In: ICFEM'14. Lecture Notes in Computer Science, vol. 8829, pp. 332–347. Springer (2014)
65. Liu, S., Sandur, A., Meseguer, J., Ölveczky, P.C., Wang, Q.: Generating correct-by-construction distributed implementations from formal Maude designs. In: NFM'20. Lecture Notes in Computer Science, vol. 12229. Springer (2020)
66. Lohstroh, M., Menard, C., Bateni, S., Lee, E.A.: Toward a lingua franca for deterministic concurrent systems. ACM Transactions on Embedded Computing Systems **20**(4), 36:1–36:27 (2021)
67. Marin, M., Ölveczky, P.C., Reja, M., Rukhaia, M., Bae, K.: Semantics and formal analysis of Lingua Franca CPS specifications in rewriting logic. In: Rebeca for Actor Analysis in Action. Lecture Notes in Computer Science, vol. 15560. Springer (2025)
68. Meseguer, J.: Conditional rewriting logic as a unified model of concurrency. Theoretical Computer Science **96**(1), 73–155 (1992)
69. Meseguer, J.: Membership algebra as a logical framework for equational specification. In: Recent Trends in Algebraic Development Techniques (WADT'97). LNCS, vol. 1376, pp. 18–61. Springer (1997)

70. Meseguer, J.: Twenty years of rewriting logic. J. Log. Algebraic Methods Program. **81**(7-8), 721–781 (2012)
71. Meseguer, J.: Taming distributed system complexity through formal patterns. Science of Computer Programming **83**, 3–34 (2014)
72. Meseguer, J., Ölveczky, P.C.: Formalization and correctness of the PALS architectural pattern for distributed real-time systems. Theoretical Computer Science **451**, 1–37 (2012)
73. Meseguer, J., Sharykin, R.: Specification and analysis of distributed object-based stochastic hybrid systems. In: HSCC'06. Lecture Notes in Computer Science, vol. 3927, pp. 460–475. Springer (2006)
74. Misra, J., Cook, W.R.: Computation orchestration. Software and Systems Modeling **6**(1), 83–110 (2007)
75. Nakajima, S.: Formal analysis of android application behavior with Real-Time Maude. In: CPSNA'15. pp. 7–12. IEEE Computer Society (2015)
76. Nakajima, S.: Using Real-Time Maude to model check energy consumption behavior. In: FM'15. Lecture Notes in Computer Science, vol. 9109, pp. 378–394. Springer (2015)
77. Nigam, V., Kim, M., Mason, I.A., Talcott, C.L.: Detection and diagnosis of deviations in distributed systems of autonomous agents. Mathematical Structures in Computer Science **32**(9), 1254–1282 (2022)
78. Nigam, V., Talcott, C.L.: Automating safety proofs about cyber-physical systems using rewriting modulo SMT. In: WRLA'22. Lecture Notes in Computer Science, vol. 13252, pp. 212–229. Springer (2022)
79. Olarte, C., Ölveczky, P.C.: Timed strategies for real-time rewrite theories. In: WRLA'24. Lecture Notes in Computer Science, vol. 14953. Springer, Cham (2024)
80. Olarte, C., Ölveczky, P.C.: RT-strategies (2025), https://depot.lipn.univ-paris13.fr/real-time-maude/rtm-strategies
81. Ölveczky, P.C.: Semantics, simulation, and formal analysis of modeling languages for embedded systems in Real-Time Maude. In: Formal Modeling: Actors, Open Systems, Biological Systems – Essays Dedicated to Carolyn Talcott on the Occasion of Her 70th Birthday, LNCS, vol. 7000, pp. 368–402. Springer (2011)
82. Ölveczky, P.C.: Real-Time Maude and its applications. In: Rewriting Logic and Its Applications (WRLA 2014). Lecture Notes in Computer science, vol. 8663, pp. 42–79. Springer (2014)
83. Ölveczky, P.C.: Formalizing and validating the P-Store replicated data store in Maude. In: WADT'16. Lecture Notes in Computer Science, vol. 10644, pp. 189–207. Springer (2016)
84. Ölveczky, P.C., Boronat, A., Meseguer, J.: Formal semantics and analysis of behavioral AADL models in Real-Time Maude. In: FMOODS/FORTE'10. Lecture Notes in Computer Science, vol. 6117, pp. 47–62. Springer (2010)
85. Ölveczky, P.C., Caccamo, M.: Formal simulation and analysis of the CASH scheduling algorithm in Real-Time Maude. In: FASE'06. Lecture Notes in Computer Science, vol. 3922, pp. 357–372. Springer (2006)
86. Ölveczky, P.C., Meseguer, J.: Specification of real-time and hybrid systems in rewriting logic. Theoretical Computer Science **285**(2), 359–405 (2002)
87. Ölveczky, P.C., Meseguer, J.: Abstraction and completeness for Real-Time Maude. In: WRLA'06. Electronic Notes in Theoretical Computer Science, vol. 176, pp. 5–27. Elsevier (2006)
88. Ölveczky, P.C., Meseguer, J.: Semantics and pragmatics of Real-Time Maude. Higher-Order and Symbolic Computation **20**(1-2), 161–196 (2007)

89. Ölveczky, P.C., Meseguer, J.: The Real-Time Maude tool. In: Tools and Algorithms for the Construction and Analysis of Systems (TACAS 2008). Lecture Notes in Computer Science, vol. 4963, pp. 332–336. Springer (2008)
90. Ölveczky, P.C., Meseguer, J., Talcott, C.L.: Specification and analysis of the AER/NCA active network protocol suite in Real-Time Maude. Formal Methods in System Design **29**(3), 253–293 (2006)
91. Ölveczky, P.C., Prabhakar, P., Liu, X.: Formal modeling and analysis of real-time resource-sharing protocols in Real-Time Maude. In: IPDPS'08. pp. 1–8. IEEE (2008)
92. Ölveczky, P.C., Thorvaldsen, S.: Formal modeling, performance estimation, and model checking of wireless sensor network algorithms in Real-Time Maude. Theoretical Computer Science **410**(2-3), 254–280 (2009)
93. Pita, I., Riesco, A.: Specifying and analyzing the Kademlia protocol in Maude. In: ICTAC'15. Lecture Notes in Computer Science, vol. 9399, pp. 524–541. Springer (2015)
94. Ptolemaeus, C. (ed.): System Design, Modeling, and Simulation using Ptolemy II. Ptolemy.org (2014), http://ptolemy.org/books/Systems
95. Rivera, J.E., Durán, F., Vallecillo, A.: A graphical approach for modeling time-dependent behavior of DSLs. In: IEEE Symposium on Visual Languages and Human-Centric Computing, VL/HCC 2009. pp. 51–55. IEEE Computer Society (2009)
96. Rocha, C., Meseguer, J., Muñoz, C.A.: Rewriting modulo SMT and open system analysis. Journal of Logical and Algebraic Methods in Programming **86**(1), 269–297 (2017)
97. Romero, J.R., Rivera, J.E., Durán, F., Vallecillo, A.: Formal and tool support for model driven engineering with Maude. J. Object Technol. **6**(9), 187–207 (2007)
98. Rubio, R., Martí-Oliet, N., Pita, I., Verdejo, A.: Strategies, model checking and branching-time properties in Maude. Journal of Logical and Algebraic Methods in Programming **123**, 100700 (2021)
99. Rubio, R., Martí-Oliet, N., Pita, I., Verdejo, A.: Model checking strategy-controlled systems in rewriting logic. Autom. Softw. Eng. **29**(1), 7 (2022)
100. Rubio, R., Martí-Oliet, N., Pita, I., Verdejo, A.: QMaude: Quantitative specification and verification in rewriting logic. In: Formal Methods (FM 2023). Lecture Notes in Computer Science, vol. 14000. Springer (2023)
101. Rushby, J.: Systematic formal verification for fault-tolerant time-triggered algorithms. IEEE Transactions on Software Engineering **25**(5), 651–660 (1999)
102. Sabahi-Kaviani, Z., Khosravi, R., Ölveczky, P.C., Khamespanah, E., Sirjani, M.: Formal semantics and efficient analysis of Timed Rebeca in Real-Time Maude. Science of Computer Programming **113**, 85–118 (2015)
103. Sen, K., Viswanathan, M., Agha, G.: Statistical model checking of black-box probabilistic systems. In: Computer Aided Verification (CAV 2004). Lecture Notes in Computer Science, vol. 3114. Springer (2004)
104. Sen, K., Viswanathan, M., Agha, G.: On statistical model checking of stochastic systems. In: Computer Aided Verification (CAV 2005). Lecture Notes in Computer Science, vol. 3576. Springer (2005)
105. Sen, K., Viswanathan, M., Agha, G.A.: VESTA: A statistical model-checker and analyzer for probabilistic systems. In: Second International Conference on the Quantitative Evaluation of Systems (QEST 2005). IEEE Computer Society (2005)
106. Skeirik, S., Bobba, R.B., Meseguer, J.: Formal analysis of fault-tolerant group key management using ZooKeeper. In: CCGrid'13. pp. 636–641. IEEE Computer Society (2013)

107. Sun, M., Meseguer, J.: Formal specification of button-related fault-tolerance micropatterns. In: WRLA'14. Lecture Notes in Computer Science, vol. 8663, pp. 263–279. Springer (2014)
108. Sun, M., Meseguer, J., Sha, L.: A formal pattern architecture for safe medical systems. In: WRLA'10. Lecture Notes in Computer Science, vol. 6381, pp. 157–173. Springer (2010)
109. Younes, H.L.S., Simmons, R.G.: Probabilistic verification of discrete event systems using acceptance sampling. In: Computer Aided Verification (CAV 2002). Lecture Notes in Computer Science, vol. 2404. Springer (2002)
110. Yu, G., Bae, K.: A flexible framework for integrating Maude and SMT solvers using Python. In: WRLA'24. Lecture Notes in Computer Science, vol. 14953, pp. 179–192. Springer (2024)
111. Zhu, L., Liu, P., Shi, J., Wang, Z., Zhu, H.: A timing verification framework for AUTOSAR OS component development based on Real-Time Maude. In: TASE'13. pp. 29–36. IEEE Computer Society (2013)

Author Index

A
Agha, Gul   307
Arbab, Farhad   393

B
Bae, Kyungmin   494

C
Carbone, Paris   81
Castegren, Elias   165
Charousset, Dominik   144
Cheeseman, Luke   165
Chen, Xiaohong   215
Chen, Zhe   346
Clebsch, Sylvan   165

D
De Koster, Joeri   3
De Meuter, Wolfgang   3
Drossopoulou, Sophia   165

E
Elgammal, Amal   259

G
Giunti, Marco   418
Gordon, Colin S.   60

H
Haller, Philipp   81
Hiesgen, Raphael   144

J
Jamali, Nadeem   346
Johansson, Bjarne   189

K
Krämer, Bernd J.   259
Kuehn, Eva Maria   237
Kwon, YoungMin   307

L
Lee, Edward A.   189, 371
Liu, Fangqi   279
Luangphasy, Tavonput   328

M
Marksteiner, Stefan   189
Martí-Oliet, Narciso   475
Meseguer, José   446
Moezkarimi, Zahra   189

O
Olarte, Carlos   494
Ölveczky, Peter Csaba   494
Owe, Olaf   114

P
Papadopoulos, Alessandro V.   189
Papazoglou, Michael   259
Parkinson, Matthew   165
Phadke, Aditya   346
Pourvatan, Bahman   189

R
Riesco, Adrián   475
Rosu, Grigore   215
Rubio, Rubén   475

S
Sarwar, Yusuf   279
Schmidt, Thomas C.   144

Sirjani, Marjan 189
Spenger, Jonas 81

T
Talcott, Carolyn 393

V
Varela, Carlos A. 36
Venkatasubramanian, Nalini 279

W
Wrigstad, Tobias 165

Y
Yoshida, Nobuko 418

Z
Zhao, Xinghui 328

Made in the USA
Monee, IL
03 May 2026